Leadership with Impact

Leadership with Impact

Preparing Health and Human Service Practitioners in the Age of Innovation and Diversity

JUAN CARLOS ARAQUE

AND

EUGENIA L. WEISS

OXFORD
UNIVERSITY PRESS

Oxford University Press is a department of the University of Oxford. It furthers
the University's objective of excellence in research, scholarship, and education
by publishing worldwide. Oxford is a registered trade mark of Oxford University
Press in the UK and certain other countries.

Published in the United States of America by Oxford University Press
198 Madison Avenue, New York, NY 10016, United States of America.

Library of Congress Cataloging-in-Publication Data
Names: Araque, Juan C. (Juan Carlos), author. | Weiss, Eugenia L., author.
Title: Leadership with impact : preparing health and human service practitioners in the age of
innovation and diversity / Juan C. Araque and Eugenia L. Weiss.
Description: New York, NY : Oxford University Press, [2019] |
Includes bibliographical references and index.
Identifiers: LCCN 2018037357 (print) | LCCN 2018050865 (ebook) |
ISBN 9780190932435 (updf) | ISBN 9780190932442 (epub) |
ISBN 9780190932428 (jacketed : alk. paper)
Subjects: LCSH: Human services personnel—Supervision of. | Social work administration. |
Public health personnel—Supervision of. | Health services administration. | Leadership.
Classification: LCC HV40.54 (ebook) | LCC HV40.54.A73 2019 (print) | DDC 361.0068/4—dc23
LC record available at https://lccn.loc.gov/2018037357

9 8 7 6 5 4 3 2 1

Printed by Sheridan Books, Inc., United States of America

This book is dedicated to my beloved parents, Lt. Colonel Luis Rodrigo Araque and Maria de Lourdes Araque, who opened the door to a larger world and gave me the strength to succeed in a new land away from home.

JCA

This book is dedicated to my beloved parents, Hugo and Nelly Liberman, who paved a path of leadership with courage and unconditional love through a woven ancestry of Latin American and Eastern European immigrants who overcame extreme hardships to make my life what it is today.

ELW

CONTENTS

List of Figures ix
List of Tables xi
Foreword xiii
Preface xvii
Acknowledgments xxi
About the Authors xxiii
About the Contributors xxv

1. Introduction to Leadership with Impact: Preparing Health and Human Service Practitioners in the Age of Innovation and Diversity 1

SECTION I Innovation

2. The Power of Innovation in Organizational and Social Change 17

3. Key Leadership Styles for Social Change and Innovation 46

Section I. Appendices: Leader Assessment Instruments 70

SECTION II Design

4. Teamwork, Collaboration, and Motivation 79

5. Leadership and Communication Strategies 111

6. Networking, Community Partnerships, and Social Media—contributed by *Lakeya Cherry* 138

Section II. Appendices: Leader Assessment Instruments 159

SECTION III Diversity

7. Race and Ethnicity: Past and Present 181

8. Cultural Proficiency, Equity, and Diversity 202

9. Women in Leadership 221

Section III. Appendices: Leader Assessment Instruments 243

SECTION IV Execution

10. Organizational Strategic Planning 251

11. Leadership and Effective Supervision 277

12. Conflict Resolution and Negotiation Strategies 309

13. Leadership and Crisis Response 334

Section IV. Appendices: Leader Assessment Instruments 364

SECTION V Assessment

14. Avoiding Burnout and Promoting Job Engagement—contributed by *Fred P. Stone* 373

15. The Mindful Leader—contributed by *Golnaz Agahi* 400

16. Assessing Interventions and Evaluating Programs 417

Section V. Appendices: Leader Assessment Instruments 451

SECTION VI Epilogue

17. Putting It All Together: Application of the I.D.D.E.A. Leadership Framework to Achieve Social Change 459

Index 477

LIST OF FIGURES

0.1 The Plan-Do-Check-Art Cycle xiv

1.1 The I.D.D.E.A. Leadership Framework 7

5.1 Communication Process Effectiveness 112

8.1 The Cultural Proficiency Continuum 205

11.1 Developing Communities of Practice Supervisory Model 293

13.1 Incident Command System Structure 345

16.1 Single-Case Design (ABAB) Graph 423

16.2 Hierarchy of Research Designs 425

16.3 Logic Model Example 431

16.4 Maslow's Hierarchy of Human Needs 433

16.5 S.M.A.R.T. Goals 435

LIST OF TABLES

3.1 Leadership Styles for Social Change and Innovation Chief Descriptors 59

13.1 Goals and Objectives for Individuals, Children, and Families Affected by Disasters 353

17.1 School Year 2012–2013 Demographic Information 466

17.2 The Latino Educational Attainment Initiative Engagement and Skills Parent Survey Pretest and Posttest Results 468

17.3 Student Academic Achievement—2012–2014 473

Leadership with Impact: Preparing Health and Human Service Practitioners in the Age of Innovation and Diversity is a wonderful contribution to the leadership literature. There are several reasons that I am enthusiastic about this book.

One is that it fuses the fields of health and human services together nicely. In many venues, health is the elephant in the living room, and human services is at best the sidecar or even on the sidelines, a sort of attendant to "Doctor."

Second, it clearly talks about *professionals.* The positive professional posture concept sets aside the acidic self-doubt that was unleashed in the 1915 Flexner Report.[1]

Third, the concept of "professional" nicely straddles the main emphasis on senior managers (CEOs, COOs, and top team managers), workaday service deliverers, leaders . . . everyone is a professional.

Fourth, the concept of leadership offered here is "every day every way" leadership. While more is expected, perhaps, from senior managers (I know I do), every professional can be a leader—certainly in a professional capacity but also as a mother, father, and citizen. So let's not wait until we become the boss. Let's lead so we can become a great boss, should that occur.

Fifth, we can implicitly draw from these discussions the importance of accomplishment over achievement. Adam Gonik phrases this distinction well in his *New Yorker* article on "The Parenting Paradox."[2] It's about kids, but we are all kids:

> What typically emerges from looking at kids, gifted and ordinary, is that, from the kids' point of view, accomplishment, that is, the private sense of mastery, the hard thing suddenly made easy, counts for far more in their inner lives than does the achievement—the competition won, the reward secured. The mystery of mastery, felt in the child's mind or muscles, is more compelling than the concreteness of achievement, the trophy pressed in her hands. What sustains us in any competition are the

moments of interiority when the competition vanishes; what sustains us in any struggle are the moments when we forget the struggle.

Sixth, the book organizes its material according to a taxonomic framework that helps the reader both collect the dots and connect the dots. That framework, I.D.D.E.A., stands for **Innovation, Design, Diversity, Execution,** and **Assessment.** Is it the only one? No. Is it effective and transformative? Yes.

It is like **TED** (which stands for **Technology, Entertainment, Design**). I can imagine I.D.D.E.A. talks all over the country like TED talks are.

Other thinkers have had frameworks that have proved useful. For example, Talcott Parsons had the AGIL table (**A**daption, **G**oal Achievement, and **I**ntegration Latency).[3]

	Instrumental Functions	**Consummatory Functions**
External problems	*Adaptation*	*Goal attainment*
	• Natural resources	• Political offices
	• Commodity production	• Common goals
Internal problems	*Latency (or pattern maintenance)*	*Integration*
	• Family	• Religious systems
	• Schools	• Media

And Edwards Deming had the PDCA process (see Figure 0.1)[4] :

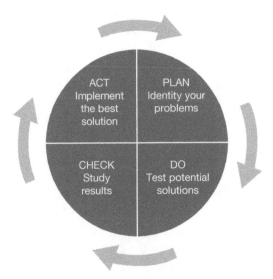

Figure 0.1 The Plan-Do-Check-Art Cycle.

And there is the work of Lynn Wooten and myself—Executive Leadership—A Seven C's Perspective that puts the leadership/management into seven distinct and distinctive buckets.[5] These are:

1. Characteristics
2. Crucibles
3. Collaborations
4. Competencies
5. Conditions (of the agency)
6. Context
7. Change

These, and others, are simply organizational frameworks to help curate material from the vast array of literature out there.

Finally, this book provides one that we all can use, and it stresses some important points—such as innovation and diversity—that tend to be ignored elsewhere.

Read and learn.

John Tropman

NOTES

1. https://socialwelfare.library.vcu.edu/social-work/is-social-work-a-profession-1915/
2. https://www.newyorker.com/magazine/2018/01/29/how-to-raise-a-prodigy
3. https://en.wikipedia.org/wiki/AGIL_paradigm
4. https://www.mindtools.com/pages/article/newPPM_89.htm
5. http://webuser.bus.umich.edu/lpwooten/PDF/pmi%20article%20tropman%20wooten.pdf

The writing of this book was inspired by five converging forces. First, we were teaching a class on leadership for our Master of Social Work students and were not entirely satisfied with the textbook that we were using. While the text was comprehensive and well written, it was built for a survey-type of course on leadership styles. We felt that it was missing practical elements and not specific to health and human services. And like most of the other books that were in fact focused on health and human services leadership, these were not addressing innovation and diversity in one textbook. Second, we were undergoing a dramatic organizational shift with respect to our program in our institution of higher learning, in terms of structure and curricula.

These demands precipitated changing the way we went about our business as usual in educating our students and questioning how the organization could be more effective in meeting student needs while going through internal growing pains given the popularity of our virtual campus offerings. With regard to this organizational change, we, the faculty, had the opportunity to engage in-residence innovators (consultants) who taught us new ways of thinking and innovating. Third, our school was embarking on the *Grand Challenges Initiative* from the American Academy of Social Work and Social Welfare ("Grand Challenges," n.d.) to addressing wicked social problems (such as social isolation, homelessness, family violence, health gaps, economic inequalities, and others). This drove us further in having to innovative and collaborate within and outside of our discipline in ways we had never done before to derive real solutions to significant social issues. Fourth, the community was looking to us as practitioners and researchers to inform health and human services providers in becoming innovative leaders or social architects, through evidence-driven solutions to pervasive societal problems. Fifth, like almost everything else in life, timing and opportunity presented itself, and thus we embraced the honor of the journey that would challenge our imaginations in shaping the way we think about and approach leadership in health and human services fields.

With all of this being said, we feel the need to make some comments and clarifications as to what this book does not offer. For instance, it is not a textbook on managing finances, seeking grant funding, contracting, or fundraising through philanthropy or any other methods. There are plenty of other publications that are specific to these topics, and although these areas are important for an organization's survival and ability to thrive, these are not broached in this book in any specific way. We also do not address risk management in organizations in terms of legalities associated with operating nonprofit organizations or public agencies. What this book does offer are new ways of thinking and approaching complex problems through a conceptual and practical leadership approach founded on innovation and diversity. We named it the I.D.D.E.A. Leadership Framework, which is an acronym for **I**nnovation, **D**esign, **D**iversity, **E**xecution, and **A**ssessment. Through the application of this leadership framework and its various components, health and human services practitioners can easily design, implement, and evaluate innovative programs to help vulnerable populations and promote the social good. By way of an innovative lens, the use of technology and collaborative practices are topics that are emphasized in several chapters of the book, as well as the voices of leaders with perspectives that are true to life. Health and human services leaders were interviewed by us in order to enlighten the reader of their leadership characteristics and their insights and to provide real-world scenarios of their challenges and their innovative (and risk-taking) approaches to solving problems that often led to successful outcomes and other times less so (again, true to life and learning from mistakes).

We also attempted to be responsive in terms of social justice with our use of language in that we have avoided terms such as "subordinate" that could be interpreted as positioning someone in an inferior way, and have used terms such as "employees" (which is often utilized in the business literature), "followers," and "team members" interchangeably. Additionally, although the terms "equality" and "equity" are used interchangeably, in more recent times the word equity has signified more than equal access to resources (equality); rather, it has stood for different resources that will result in more equal outcomes. While this is a subtle use of language, it is worth noting that the differences for those who are affected are very real. Also, the writing style fluctuates between first-person, second-person, and third-person points of view, and this is our deliberate attempt to make the reading more accessible and engaging. Finally, we suggest that what might be helpful to better orient the reader to the proposed I.D.D.E.A. Leadership Framework is to read the chapters and sections of the book in order. We also recommend that the reader take the assessment instruments or scales that are located at the end of each of the five sections to help with leadership development. Finally, we appreciate you for taking the leap of faith into the world of leadership because there is much to be done to make a better world for everyone. We need you, dear reader!

Juan Carlos Araque and Eugenia L. Weiss

REFERENCE

"Grand Challenges." (n.d.). Twelve grand challenges initiative. *American Academy of Social Work and Social Welfare*. Retrieved from: http://aaswsw.org/grand-challenges-initiative/12-challenges/

ACKNOWLEDGMENTS

We are thankful to many individuals who assisted us throughout the development and advancement of writing this book. We are thankful to our three Master of Social Work student research assistants: Stephanie Navarro, who helped us with completing the literature reviews, drafting the annotated bibliography, transcribing leadership profile interviews, and searching leader quotes; Terri Scott, who assisted us with transcribing the majority of the leadership profile interviews and collecting the leader's biographies and pictures; and Gina Jackson for assisting with the literature review and the initial drafting of the *Women in Leadership* chapter. We certainly appreciated the assistance of Carrie Araque, who completed the first draft edits for the majority of the book chapters.

We would like to thank all the health and human services leaders who took time to participate in the leadership profile interviews and shared with us their expertise and insights, including Golnaz Agahi, Alfredo Aguirre, Thenera Bailey, Kristi Batiste, Lakeya Cherry, Dave Coplan, Maricela Rios-Faust, Anthony Hassan, Nahla Kayali, Steven Kim, Nick Macchione, Linda Rosenberg, Patricia Sinay, Fred P. Stone, and Marvin Southard.

We are indebted to our guest contributing authors: Lakeya Cherry, Chapter 6—*Networking, Community Partnerships, and Social Media Messaging*; Fred P. Stone, Chapter 14—*Avoiding Burnout and Promoting Job Engagement*; and Golnaz Agahi, Chapter 15—*The Mindful Leader*.

A special thanks to David Follmer of Lyceum Books, who provided the impetus to write the book and believed in the vision of innovation. To our colleague, Jose E. Coll, at Texas State University, who contributed to the conceptual framework of the book and his conversations with David Follmer to make the project a reality. Lastly, all of the Oxford University Press staff members who helped make this volume possible, namely, Dana Bliss and Andrew Dominello, who have been a source of support in the writing process. Thanks for the production editor, Shanmuga Priya.

Finally, we would like to acknowledge our esteemed colleagues at the University of Southern California Suzanne Dworak-Peck School of Social Work who have shared their leadership wisdom with us throughout the years and our master's and doctoral students who, through their leadership and advocacy for social justice, inspire us to be better innovative leaders every day.

Juan Carlos Araque, PhD, has more than 20 years of experience working in the fields of leadership, community development, diversity, violence prevention, education, and positive youth development. He is interested in the research and design of public, private, and nonprofit system structures to support positive child and adolescent development and robust child-adult-community relationship building. Dr. Araque is currently a full-time faculty member in the University of Southern California (USC) Suzanne Dworak-Peck School of Social Work and teaches graduate courses for the Master of Social Work (MSW) and Doctor of Social Work (DSW) Programs. He provides academic leadership as principal investigator for community research projects primarily in Southern California; he has authored and presented in academic conferences a number of peer-reviewed research studies. Additionally, Dr. Araque provides leadership as the Academic Faculty Lead for Leadership and Research Courses, the Graduate Latino Student Association, and the School of Social Work Latino/a Social Work Caucus. Before entering academia, Dr. Araque was the Executive Director for the USC TRiO Programs, providing educational opportunities for more than 2,500 students in partnership with 20 middle and high schools in South, Central, and East Los Angeles. He also served as the Senior Vice President for Community Investments at the Orange County United Way, where he oversaw the distribution of $30 million in funding going to more than 300 nonprofit agencies. He earned his doctoral degree in Public Administration from the USC Sol Price School of Public Policy. Dr. Araque lives in Southern California with his wife Carrie and children Sean and Rebecca.

Eugenia L. Weiss, PsyD, LCSW, is an educator and a California-licensed clinical social worker and licensed psychologist. She is Clinical Associate Professor at the University of Southern California (USC) Suzanne Dworak-Peck School of Social Work and serves as a Senior Associate Dean of Faculty Affairs.

She maintained a psychotherapy practice serving the Latino/a population and military and veteran families. Her practice included organizational consulting and work with employee assistance programs for more than 18 years. She also worked in private, public, and nonprofit behavioral health services. She is the author and coauthor of multiple peer-reviewed journal publications and co-author/coeditor of several books, including *A Civilian Counselor's Primer to Counseling Veterans* (2nd ed., Linus Books, 2011); *Handbook of Military Social Work* (Wiley & Sons, 2013); *Supporting Veterans in Higher Education: A Primer for Administrators, Faculty and Academic Advisors* (Oxford University Press, 2015); *Transformative Social Work Practice* (Sage, 2015); and *The Civilian Lives of U.S. Veterans: Issues and Identities* (ABC-CLIO, 2017). She was the recipient of the *Hutto Patterson Foundation Award for Distinguished USC School of Social Work Faculty*, representing excellence in teaching; service to the university, school, and community; and accessibility to students. She teaches courses on research methods, program evaluation, and leadership. Her research interests include military/veteran behavioral health, diversity, higher education, and leadership. Dr. Weiss is an Academy Fellow in Higher Education Leadership from the University of California, Berkeley. Serves as Board Member of the Council of Social Work Education (CSWE)—Council on the Role and Status of Women in Social Work Education and is Chair of the Higher Education Working Group and Steering Committee Member—Orange County Veterans and Military Families Collaborative. Lastly, but most important, a proud Army mom.

ABOUT THE CONTRIBUTORS

Golnaz Agahi, DSW, LCSW, MPH
Golnaz Agahi received her dual master's degrees in Public Health and Social Work from San Diego State University. She has more than 20 years of experience working in both public health and social service settings. Presently, she is the Assistant Director at Kaiser Permanente Behavioral Health Department in Orange County and co-chairs the Orange County Kaiser Permanente Family Violence Prevention Program. Also, she teaches part-time at the Suzanne Dworak-Peck School of Social Work at the University of Southern California and earned her doctorate in social work from here.

Golnaz's area of expertise is in program planning, implementation, and evaluation. Her past clinical work, research, and publications (including curriculum development) have addressed the following areas: alcohol and drug prevention and treatment, high-risk and homeless youth services, gang prevention and intervention, crisis intervention, intimate partner violence, and stress management.

Lakeya Cherry, MSSW
Lakeya Cherry is the President and CEO of the Network for Social Work Management, an international membership organization dedicated to strengthening social work leadership in health and human services. Under her leadership, the Network has grown globally and introduced new, innovative programming that meets the needs of social work and human services leaders everywhere. At her previous position with 2U, Inc., a technology company partnering with prestigious universities to place degree programs online, Lakeya was a Senior Regional Field Manager for the University of Southern California Suzanne Dworak-Peck School of Social Work's online Master of Social Work program. Cherry was in charge of spearheading national partnerships and managing field education agency development initiatives. She has also held a

variety of direct service positions in the nonprofit sector and volunteers during her free time. She earned her Master of Science in Social Work from Columbia University and her Bachelor of Arts in Psychology and Legal Studies from the University of California at Santa Cruz. Lakeya also holds a Certificate in Nonprofit Executive Leadership from the National Human Services Assembly in collaboration with The Fund Raising School at the Lilly Family School of Philanthropy at Indiana University, the Executive Education Program at the School of Public and Environmental Affairs at Indiana University, and Arizona State University Lodestar Center for Philanthropy and Nonprofit Innovation.

Fred P. Stone, PhD
Fred P. Stone is a retired US Air Force Colonel, a licensed clinical social worker, and Clinical Associate Professor at the University of Southern California Suzanne Dworak-Peck School of Social Work. He holds a doctoral degree in Social Work and a master's degree in Public Administration from the University of Utah. He also has a master's degree in in Social Work from the University of Texas at Arlington. Dr. Stone spent 29 years in the US Air Force and held a number of leadership positions, including Director of Social Work Services, Director of Behavioral Health, Air Force Medical Doctrine Development section chief, Medical Operations Squadron Commander, Director of Research at Air Command and Staff College, Chief of Air Force Family Advocacy, and Deputy Medical Group Commander. He has lectured extensively on leadership and has taught leadership courses for the Air Force since 2007.

Introduction to Leadership with Impact

Preparing Health and Human Service Practitioners in the Age of Innovation and Diversity

Leadership must first and foremost meet the needs of others.

—Robert Greenleaf

CHAPTER OBJECTIVES

1. Explore the purpose and essence of innovative leadership and how successful leaders become social architects to design and implement organizational and social change;
2. Learn the key elements of the I.D.D.E.A. (**I**nnovation, **D**esign, **D**iversity, **E**xecution, and **A**ssessment) Leadership Framework; and
3. Become acquainted with the book's content and key features.

INTRODUCTION

We live in exciting and uncertain times indeed! Although the world has become a smaller place because of mainly technological advances, the immense problems individuals, organizations, and communities endure are as difficult as ever. Rapid changes in our society call for the need to cope and deal with grand challenges and overcome these. Poverty, discrimination, physical and mental health access inequality, and social injustice and education gaps remain constant problems to be solved. Societal issues are complex and demand innovative and creative thinking to begin solving them. We simply cannot afford to continue doing business as usual and expect different results (such as Albert Einstein's definition of insanity). Isolated and positive strategies in the health and human services fields have proved to be limited, and for the most part, missing sustainable social change. A new leadership approach is required—a leadership that is visualized with a clear purpose, driven with passion, and executed with the necessary skills to inspire individuals and achieve the intended goals. Innovation is designed by identifying and securing resources needed to improve human conditions and finding common ground to ameliorate social problems.

This vision for leadership with impact is based on the idea that the well-being of humanity is our first and foremost priority. We cannot compromise this ethical principle under any circumstance. This is no different than an airline pilot's most important concern being the safety of the crew and the passengers—the well-being of people comes first. Helping vulnerable, stigmatized, and marginalized populations is what health and human services professionals do, and how we provide this support will determine the quality of people's lives. Leaders who innovate have the vision of what is to become and carefully plan how to get there. A significant amount of thinking is given to both the desired place and the roadmap. These leaders acknowledge that one of the first steps is to understand how individuals, organizations, and communities operate. Starting with themselves and then moving outward with team members, partners, and communities, innovative leaders identify and connect with the world around them, having a greater understanding of needs and resources, and skillfully set a plan to follow.

A rigorous and engaged way of thinking, planning, executing, and assessing is needed to overcome the grand social challenges the United States faces today. Unfortunately, we still live in a society of inequalities, resulting in some groups being less privileged and having access to fewer resources than others. Examples of social injustice, immigration manipulation, health care access, socioeconomic inequities, and educational differences seem to be widening gaps. For example, there are disproportionate numbers of African American and Hispanic/Latinos males in the US prison system. In 2011, out of the total 1.6 million prisoners, 93% were male and 75% were people of color; sadly, 63% of the African American and 69% of the Hispanic/Latino incarcerated population were younger than 40 years (Carson & Sabol, 2017). Additionally, US tax payers spend approximately $10 billion annually housing these prisoners compared with $2.8 billion invested in college education for minority students (Carson & Sabol, 2017).

The situation with health care is also troubling, particularly for a developed nation such as the United States. Although the Patient Protection and Affordable Care Act of 2010 (known as Obamacare) had good intentions, it has unfortunately fallen short of initial expectations. In 2013, there were about 42 million Americans without appropriate health care coverage. Vulnerable populations neither have regular access to a health care provider nor can afford to pay medical treatments. Despite being the largest economy in the world, the United States ranks 174th out of 222 countries in infant mortality (Smith & Medalia, 2014). Mental health statistics are not much brighter. According to the Centers for Disease Control and Prevention (Reeves et al., 2011), the prevalence of mental illness is the highest ever at 25% (one in every four Americans experience a mental health illness). Most of these mental health issues (e.g., depression, anxiety, and suicidality) go unchecked. Regrettably, we are experiencing the highest drug use, drug morbidity, and suicide deaths among teenagers in our history (Curtin, Tejada-Vera, & Warner, 2017).

Immigrant communities experience social injustices, including poor health outcomes and low student academic achievement (Halgunseth, Ispa, & Rudy, 2006). Communities that receive present-day immigrants are also considered risk factors for newly arrived families because they often settle into disadvantaged, underprivileged neighborhoods that coincide with schools that are, in turn, underfunded and poorly performing (Suarez-Orozco & Suarez-Orozco, 2001). This environment poses a risk to youths assimilating into a culture defined by underachievement and lack of engagement, thereby impeding the potential for upward mobility. Individuals from socioeconomically disadvantaged backgrounds tend to perform poorly in school and often live in impoverished, high-crime communities, which further limit their access to services, as well as their motivation and ability to prioritize educational attainment (Harris, Jamison, & Trujillo, 2008; Henry, Merten, Plunkett, & Sands, 2008).

Economically speaking, the Great Recession of 2008 is well over, and the American economy has significantly rebounded. In 2017, the American economy was strong, showing high home and commercial investments and the lowest unemployment rate in 30 years—less than 4% (US Bureau of Statistics Data, 2018). Notwithstanding this strong economic boom, the homeless situation in America continues to increase. In 2017, the West Coast, for example, had more than 1 million homeless individuals living in the streets on a daily basis. Most of the members of this vulnerable population lack a fixed, regular, and adequate nighttime residence, and homeless individuals and families rely on public shelters and assistance to survive. Approximately 85,000 of these homeless individuals suffer from a chronic mental illness that is not treated regularly and live without proper medical supervision (US Interagency Council on Homelessness, 2018).

HEALTH AND HUMAN SERVICES ORGANIZATIONS

Throughout this book we use the term health and human services fields and human services organizations to refer to public and/or private agencies addressing immediate-, intermediate-, and long-term social needs. Health and human services organizations exist to ameliorate the social problems described earlier and combat many other issues challenging our communities. Health and human services organizations are financed with public and/or private dollars, providing a safety net of basic services and programs. These organizations fall under two large areas: public sector (government agencies) and private sector (for-profit or nonprofit) organizations.

Public agencies constitute the largest health and human services group when it comes to both dollars amounts and numbers of people served. Public agencies are financed by taxpayers, and they can be organized in federal, state, and county structures. For example, some of the federal public agencies that provide assistance in the health and human services fields include the US Departments of Health and Human Services, Housing and Urban Development, Health, Justice, Labor, Veterans Affairs, Education, Federal Emergency and Management Agency, and Social Security Administration. A large percentage of the federal funding is matched with state and local taxes to support state, county, and local agencies dealing with social needs at the local level. Among others, some of the county and city public agencies working on health and human services include Departments of Mental Health, Health and Human Services, Public Health, Children and Families Services, Probation, Public Defender, Education, Parks and Recreation, Homeless Services, Sheriff and Police, Regional Centers, and Social Services. These federal, state, county, and city agencies employ millions of health and human services practitioners nationwide who support people in need regularly.

The private sector also contributes immensely to fund, design, implement, and evaluate programs and services to support basic social needs. Generally, the for-profit and nonprofit organizations fall under three main categories: education and research, corporate and private foundations, and service delivery. First, many colleges and universities have private, nonprofit status, which exempts them from paying taxes like a regular company or business corporation. The mission of these educational institutions is to educate and advance research agendas for the public benefit by soliciting private funding and/or applying for public tax-based dollars from national foundations like the National Science Foundation and National Institutes of Health. Second, the nonprofit sector has significantly benefited from the private sector's financial contributions by the creation of thousands of corporate and private foundations, including the Bill and Melinda Gates Foundation, Howard Hughes Medical Institute, Lilly

Endowment, Ford, MacArthur, United Way, Annie E. Casey, Robert Wood Johnson, William and Flora Hewlett, Irvine, and others. Foundations are very powerful because they set goals and guidelines for funding. Finally, the private sector has millions of organizations that provide direct services to vulnerable and marginalized populations. About 80% of these service-oriented nonprofit organizations have an annual budget of $2 million or less and employ 20 to 80 people (Hwang & Powell, 2009). These service-driven organizations develop their expertise in specific areas, including mental health services for children, homelessness, veterans with posttraumatic stress conditions, children's health, food banks, American Red Cross units, emergency and temporary shelters, domestic violence, community clinics and hospitals, faith community charity programs and services, and so on.

Although this health and human services system of agencies and organizations is rich, is full of experience, and has an adequate amount of resources (depending on who you ask), it is far from fulfilling its potential. These complex systems can be bureaucratic and dysfunctional, making social issues more difficult to tackle directly. Regrettably, health and human services organizations often become defensive and territorial, competing for the same resources instead of collaborating to improve systems of care and their service delivery. Innovative leaders must disrupt these dysfunctional systems and begin providing new and viable solutions to create positive organizational and social change.

SOCIAL ARCHITECTS

Innovative leaders can no longer tolerate social injustices around them. They see and feel the struggles and suffering from homeless individuals, low-income working families without quality health care, minority groups being discriminated against, inequality among poor people, domestic violence victims, and so on. As a result of these persistent problems, leaders sense the negative energy permeated in their communities, and yet they have the ability to channel these undesirable feelings into an opposite direction. In other words, innovative leaders are positively fueled by the precarious living conditions of vulnerable populations, and they become energized to fight against these injustices. Thus, *innovative leaders uses their passion to empower themselves and others to become the positive change agents in their communities.* Leaders who use innovation learn how to channel negative events into positive energy to improve their communities. These leaders thrive on the notion that the eradication of grand challenges not only is attainable but also for many is a matter of survival. Goals and objectives guide the process to achieve end results, and innovative leadership is the true mechanism to affect successful organizational and social outcomes. This is one of the most important skills as a leader, channeling passion as a key driver to inspire and lead others toward achieving the desired change, often described as leaders being *agents of change.*

You are a leader! The fact that you are reading this book and that the issues around your community truly concern you, makes you a natural leader. You have an inner passion, *a calling*, to help others—you know deep inside that the conditions vulnerable people live with on a daily basis are unacceptable, and you want their lives to improve. Whether you will work for the government, a nonprofit organization, a foundation, a for-profit company, or any other health and human services organization, your thoughts and feelings place you in a unique position to truly make a difference. Innovation can take different shapes and forms, and a leader does not necessarily always have to hold a top position in an organization. For example, any health and human services professional can lead others by finding effective ways to communicate with partners and stakeholders, advocating for those who have no voice, drafting a plan to improve service delivery, educating clients on how to increase their knowledge and skills, participating in program evaluation, and leading others to accomplish new goals. It is important that passion, innovation, and diversity are at the center of how leaders formulate and deliver potential solutions. These qualities should not be seen as separate units, but rather as parts of the whole.

Innovative leaders are social architects. We should clarify that the term "social architecture" was introduced by Bolman and Deal (2008) as a conceptualization of leadership under their Four Frame Model (i.e., the structural, human resource, political, and symbolic frames) wherein the structural frame reflects the architecture of the organization. However, we define social architects a bit differently than Bolman and Deal. Bennis and Nanus (1985) also used the term "social architect" in describing transformational leaders who shape the shared meanings of values in their organizations. However, unlike our predecessors, we refer to social architects as innovative leaders, those individuals who want to change current social systems to improve people's lives. The social architect's purpose is to ensure that effective programs are sustainable and communities become self-reliant. To accomplish these desired goals, successful social architects apply the I.D.D.E.A. (Innovation, Design, Diversity, Execution, and Assessment) Leadership Framework. This proposed leadership framework includes the following five elements (Figure 1.1):

1. *Innovation.* Social architects first visualize and then draft the necessary blue prints to build stronger organizations and communities. This daunting achievement depends on identifying

Figure 1.1 The I.D.D.E.A. Leadership Framework.
Graphic designed by Brian Goodman and Samantha Becker, University of Southern California.

innovative strategies to make health and social services available to those people in need. Additionally, innovative leaders never work alone; they form social networks to advance their causes and achieve social change.

2. *Design.* The social architect shapes the organizational and social landscape so that resources are used to their full extent, services are better delivered, and risks are minimized. During the formulation and development of innovations, innovative leaders must consolidate positive collaborations and partnerships with the goal of designing the path for the implementation of improved programs and services.

3. *Diversity.* As social architects formulate their innovative strategies, they must take into consideration the diversity of the population. A single innovative strategy can neither fit all groups in need nor have the same impact for everyone; knowledge and adaptation to meet the demands of diverse vulnerable and marginalized populations are paramount. Innovative leaders are culturally proficient, and they have the ability to identify and allocate resources that are pertinent to the needs of unique clients.

4. *Execution.* Successful social architects draft a feasible, realistic, and innovative plan to put into place and manage accordingly. This new effort, and in many ways an experiment, is tested repeatedly by the existing pulling forces in our communities. The implementation phase

must show direction, strength, and flexibility. Innovative leaders and their teams will need to exercise multiple competencies, skills, and abilities to achieve the desired goals.

5. *Assessment.* Successful social architects are constantly assessing internal and external factors during the innovation process. Internally, innovative leaders look inward to gauge their self-capacity, well-being, and motivation to continue the work ahead, as well as gauging the internal climate of the organization and stakeholder groups. Only the strongest organizational patterns and social arrangements will come to fruition and expand. By using formal and informal evaluation methods, the innovative leader can assess the progress of the innovation initiative and eventually determine improved organizational arrangements and social norms. Externally, the leader is always keeping an eye on the societal, political, and environmental forces that are at play beyond the agency walls and making adjustments as needed.

WHAT IS AHEAD?

In the pages ahead, we will describe key innovative strategies, leadership styles, competencies, and skills successful leaders apply to improve human conditions. There are a few key features of this book. First, we highlight exemplary health and human services professionals who are currently providing innovative leadership applications in their practices. Each chapter has a leadership profile, which includes the leader's biography and their responses to our interview questions. Each leadership profile showcases each social architect's perspective on how successful practitioners engage in effective leadership, apply their strengths to build partnerships and support systems, motivate themselves and others to continue their services, and change organizational patterns and systems to improve the lives of those who are less fortunate. Along with the leader profile each chapter features a case scenario from the leader for discussion and application. Each case demonstrates the application of an aspect of the chapter's content in real life. Second, at the end of each book section, the reader will find brief leadership assessments to guide his or her own self-efficacy and professional development within each of the five elements of the I.D.D.E.A. Leadership Framework. The book concludes with an epilogue, a bonus chapter, showcasing the Latino Educational Attainment (LEA) Initiative as an example of how this leadership framework has been successfully implemented in the real world.

Book Organization

The book is organized into five major sections. Each section is based on each of the five I.D.D.E.A. Leadership Framework elements: innovation, design, diversity, execution, and assessment. Each section features chapters discussing specific content, aiming to enhance the understanding and application of this leadership framework. For instance, Section I (Innovation) contains Chapters 2 and 3. Chapter 2, "The Power of Innovation in Organizational and Social Change," highlights innovation as a necessary and powerful tool to improve programs and services in the health and human services fields. This chapter also recognizes that innovative strategies must follow ethical standards when working with clients. Innovative leaders become social architects who are open to organizational and social innovations, providing guidelines, fostering creativity, and building new systems for social change. The latest innovations in health and human services are described, including new technologies, the use of big data, patient-guided interventions, and proper use of social media.

Chapter 3, "Key Leadership Styles for Social Change and Innovation," describes and analyzes a handful of powerful leadership styles that have been associated with social change causes and initiatives. The leadership literature is somewhat diffused, dating back more than 100 years. Unfortunately, there is not agreement among scholars and practitioners as to what is the best leadership style. Literally, there are hundreds of leadership theories, approaches, and models that have been created or developed to discover the appropriate attributes leaders have, or should have, to successfully affect social change. Therefore, we will concentrate on what we consider to be the most successful leadership styles for health and human services delivery: the tenets, potential benefits, and key elements.

Section II (Design) features Chapters 4, 5, and 6. Chapter 4, "Teamwork, Collaboration, and Motivation," focuses on the impact of building and maintaining positive relationships in the workplace. The quality of interaction with others guides the attitudes and behaviors of all participating parties. The nature of these relationships can significantly affect our lives, including levels of work engagement and satisfaction, well-being, motivation, and commitment. Building positive working relationships by understanding others' perspectives and being able to effectively share our points of view are very important skills for social architects to craft and master. This chapter reviews key aspects of human psychology, relationships, collaboration, and motivation that can be applied when working with others.

Chapter 5, "Leadership and Communication Strategies," demonstrates the power of the communication process. Sharing information successfully requires paying special attention to what information is being shared, how it is delivered, and how it is received. Communication forms include verbal, visual, written, and nonverbal messages, which can be perfected through systematic learning and skill practice. Additionally, the chapter highlights the importance of understanding others' emotional expressions as a way to better improve working relationships. A discussion on cross-cultural communication is included because interaction with individuals from different cultures or diverse groups has become part of our daily lives. Social architects are constantly building bridges, fostering relationships, and establishing successful collaborations with effective communication.

Chapter 6, "Networking, Community Partnerships, and Social Media Messaging," highlights the various approaches that the health and human services leader can use to build partnerships with other organizations to address service needs and social problems that are larger than one single organization can accomplish. The use of technology, and particularly social media, can be a powerful tool for communication, networking, and reaching out to others beyond one agency. The social architect, in coordination and cooperation with other innovative leaders, can be highly effective through a multitude of ways that are both innovative and instrumental in bringing about positive organizational and social change.

Section III (Diversity) includes Chapters 7, 8, and 9. Chapter 7, "Race and Ethnicity: Past and Present," provides a brief historical background on the socially constructed notion of race and ethnicity and how certain groups continue to experience greater challenges and disadvantages in our society. Social architects work toward building an equitable and just society, and they influence others to embrace a social justice framework in their everyday lives. The charge for health and human services leaders is to facilitate and empower others to improve the human conditions we see as unfit and unjust in our communities.

Chapter 8, "Cultural Proficiency, Equity, and Diversity," demonstrates methods and approaches that innovative leaders can use to promote individuals and organizations to be accountable in advancing equality through personal and institutional practices. This chapter introduces the reader to the Cultural Proficiency Continuum as a tool for social architects to identify attitudes and behaviors in themselves and others with the goal of both reducing discriminatory practices and promoting diversity in the workplace. The multiple facets of intersectionality (i.e., multiple and interrelated identities) are discussed, including convergence issues with race, gender, and sexual orientation. Additionally, leadership models that are aligned with diversity considerations and social equity are reviewed, demonstrating how organizational policies and practices can foster equitable working conditions for all.

Chapter 9, "Women in Leadership," examines theoretical, systems, and institutional gender issues in the workplace. We point out that as long as health and human services organizations are set up to make it difficult for women to be promoted, they will continue to turn down leadership opportunities. Currently, the system is set up to make it almost impossible to accommodate lifestyle choices. Many organizations acknowledge the importance of work-life balance and can tie the benefits to a healthier workforce. Yet, women still report feeling guilty for putting their family ahead of work, while employees who put work ahead of family are acknowledged for their dedication and loyalty. We discuss how social architects can create more leadership opportunities for women and that the existing patriarchal power models must be broken down and rebuilt in a form that promotes unity without sexism and has the support of all groups.

Section IV (Execution) features Chapters 10, 11, 12, and 13. Chapter 10, "Organizational Strategic Planning," sets the basis of how innovative leaders envision the proper structure and management of effective organizations. Innovative leaders acknowledge the enormous value of using a strategic planning process to accomplish desired organizational goals and objectives. The strategic planning process can be complex, guiding the current organizational state to be examined and the one desired to be planned and properly executed. Social architects are designers, stewards, and coaches who have the task to build the capacity and capability of the organization to continuously adjust and thrive in its environment. The key components of a successful organizational strategic plan include a broad *vision* of what the organization should be (aspiration), organization's *mission* or core values (identity), specific *goals* (direction) and operationalized *objectives* (benchmarks).

Chapter 11, "Leadership and Effective Supervision," explores one of the most difficult tasks for leaders and supervisors, that of building and maintaining positive working relationships with team members. Effective supervision is cumbersome because employees have their own needs, making general organizational policies and practices somewhat limited. The innovative leader should pay special attention to their employee's behavior, motivation, and expectations in the workplace. Additionally, we will analyze positive approaches to handling problematic human resource situations with a fair and balanced approach. This chapter also reviews supervisory models and skills applied in the field, explores the supervisor and supervisee roles, and shares coaching and training strategies to improve working relationships and performance in health and human services organizations.

Chapter 12, "Conflict Resolution and Negotiation Strategies," explores how difficult it can be to deal with conflict. Most people are conflict averse and prefer not to deal with disagreements because they can be emotionally charged. The innovative leader sees conflict as a natural part of life and makes a habit of developing negotiation skills and strategies to resolve conflict more effectively. If handled properly, conflict can trigger many positive results. Social architects do not shy away from conflictive situations; instead, they are comfortable tackling interpersonal or organizational issues as early as possible. This chapter also explores stages of the conflict resolution process and how effective leaders can apply several related models to improve working relationships in health and human services organizations.

Chapter 13, "Leadership and Crisis Response," contains the latest emergency procedures and practices leaders and crisis teams can apply during crisis management situations. Unfortunately, the number of human-made (e.g., terrorism and shootings) or natural disasters (e.g., wild fires, earthquakes, and violent storms) has significantly increased, and we need to be more vigilant and better prepared to deal with crisis situations. Key emergency resources, response models, and organizations are highlighted, including the standardized emergency management system, incident command center, food and shelter emergency funding boards, and American Red Cross products and services. Crisis response operations are constantly practiced and assessed so that first responders have the tools to identify the potential events or circumstances that could significantly improve their performance and save lives.

Section V (Assessment) includes Chapters 14, 15, and 16. Chapter 14, "Avoiding Burnout and Promoting Job Engagement," highlights the need for helping professionals in the health and human services fields to understand their own limits and capacities, recognizing issues related to professional fatigue. Burnout is a significant problem in the workplace, especially among health and human services team members. As innovative leaders, we are always thinking and working to support others. This constant use of emotional energy can lead to stress and exhaustion. It is very important to recognize the symptoms of work stress and burnout and take care of ourselves and our team members accordingly. This chapter examines this problem from a theoretical and practical perspective, highlighting a few evidence-based interventions and solutions that address the elements of burnout in the workplace.

Chapter 15, "The Mindful Leader," is complementary to the previous chapter on avoiding burnout and coping with stress through the use of mindfulness. This chapter encourages health and human services professionals to self-assess their internal states and use mindfulness exercises as part of their daily routines. Mindfulness is the art of staying mentally, emotionally, and spiritually in the present moment; a type of meditation that can help social architects cope and thrive in a fast-paced environment. Most of us who practice mindfulness regularly find it extremely helpful in enduring daily stressors, formulating solutions to problems, and strengthening our passion to help others. Incorporation of mindfulness as another evidence-based practice could support your ability to experience life in its fullest form.

Chapter 16, "Assessing Interventions and Evaluating Programs," outlines the multiple methods to assess interventions with clients and evaluate health and human services programs. The goal of this chapter is not for readers to become formal program evaluators, but instead to truly understand and value assessment tools and evaluation methods as key essentials of the innovation process. We expect social architects to apply these qualitative and quantitative evaluation methods as they visualize, formulate, and execute their innovations.

Finally, Section VI (Epilogue) contains Chapter 17, "Putting It All Together: Application of the I.D.D.E.A. Leadership Framework to Achieve Social Change," which is a bonus chapter presented as an epilogue that highlights the LEA Initiative case study. For more than 10 years, the success of the LEA Initiative can be attributed to innovative business, school, and community leaders partnering to increase parent involvement and academic achievement, first with Latino parents and children, and now with Korean, Vietnamese, Chinese, and non-immigrant families and communities. The LEA Initiative puts into practice the five elements of the I.D.D.E.A. Leadership Framework—innovation, design, diversity, execution, and assessment—reaching more than 50,000 low-income parents to engage in their children's education to both gain higher academic outcomes and reduce the minority educational achievement gap.

It is our hope that the pages ahead will educate, motivate, and inspire you in your journey to become an efficacious social architect. There is no greater calling and personal satisfaction than helping other human beings achieve their full potential. The information provided in this book will allow you to continue your personal and professional drive in a more intentional and structured way. Innovation and an appreciation of diversity are essential ingredients to achieving social change. As your knowledge, experience, and expertise strengthen, you will become a more effective agent of change.

REFERENCES

Bennis, W. G., & Nanus, B. (1985). *Leaders: The strategies for taking charge.* New York, NY: Harper & Row.

Bolman, L. G., & Deal, T. E. (2008). *Reframing organizations: Artistry, choice, and leadership.* San Francisco: John Wiley & Sons, Inc.

Carson, A. E., & Sabol, W. J. (2017). *Prisoners in 2011.* Retrieved from http://bjs.gov/index.cfm?ty=pbdetail&ciid=4559,2

Curtin, S. C., Tejada-Vera, B., & Warner, M. (2017). Drug overdose deaths among adolescents aged 15–19 in the United States: 1999–2015. *NCHS Data Brief, Aug*(282), 1–8.

Halgunseth, L. C., Ispa, J. M., & Rudy, D. (2006). Parental control in Latino families: An integrated review of the literature. *Child Development, 77*(5), 1282–1297.

Harris, A. L., Jamison, K. M., & Trujillo, M. H. (2008). Disparities in the educational success of immigrants: An assessment of the immigrant effect for Asians and Latinos. *Annals of the American Academy of Political and Social Science, 620*(1), 90–114.

Henry, C. S., Merten, M. J., Plunkett, S. W., & Sands, T. (2008). Neighborhood, parenting, and adolescent factors and academic achievement in Latino adolescents from immigrant families. *Family Relations, 57*(5), 579–590.

Hwang, H., & Powell, W. W. (2009). The rationalization of charity: The influences of professionalism in the nonprofit sector. *Administrative Science Quarterly, 54*(2), 268–298.

Reeves, W. C., Strine, T. W., Pratt, L. A., Thompson, W., Ahluwalia, I., Dhingra, S. S., . . . & Morrow, B. (2011). Mental illness surveillance among adults in the United States. *MMWR Surveill Summ, 60*(Suppl 3), 1–29.

Smith, J. C., & Medalia, C. (2014). *Health insurance coverage in the United States: 2013*. Washington, DC: US Department of Commerce, Economics and Statistics Administration, Bureau of the Census.

Suarez-Orozco, C., & Suarez-Orozco, M. (2001). *Children of immigration*. Cambridge, MA: Harvard University Press.

US Bureau of Labor Statistics Data. (2018). *Labor data*. Retrieved from https://data.bls.gov/timeseries/LNS14000000

US Interagency Council on Homelessness. (2018). *Ending chronic homelessness in 2017*. Retrieved from https://www.usich.gov/resources/uploads/asset_library/Ending_Chronic_Homelessness_in_2017.pdf

Innovation

2

The Power of Innovation
in Organizational and
Social Change

Logic will get you from A to B. Imagination will take you everywhere.
—Albert Einstein

CHAPTER OBJECTIVES

1. Review ethical challenges and standards for leaders as they design
   and implement innovative strategies to improve programs and service
   delivery for clients;
2. Learn the application of health and human services innovations to
   achieve social change;
3. Explore how innovation is applied to advance organizational
   expansions and social movements; and
4. Gain insights on innovative leadership from a social architect.

INTRODUCTION

Health and human services organizations provide support, programs, and services to disadvantaged and underprivileged children and families in a variety of
structures, including public (government) and private (for-profit and nonprofit)
settings. The design and implementation of these programs and services can
be daunting because of the complexities and barriers encountered by service

providers coupled with the individuals' or families' significant economic, social, and psychological needs. Social architects in the health and human services fields understand that the individuals' and families' health and mental health essentials may be further complicated by both the high levels of bureaucracy experienced in the public sector and the lack of resources in the nonprofit sector. Thus, creating innovative strategies as potential solutions to these immense challenges has become the new leadership imperative at all organizational levels in order to achieve positive social change. This chapter will first review ethical standards as innovative leaders design, implement, and evaluate new programs and services. Then, we will describe the most successful social innovations, highlighting replicable strategies, schemas, and models, including design thinking. We will close the chapter exploring how innovation and diversity principles and practices are applied to advance organizational and social movements.

ETHICS AND INNOVATION

As leaders begin to think and create new ways to treat clients and deliver services, it is critical that they first and foremost adhere to ethical standards and practices. Innovation requires leaders and practitioners to take risks. Organizational leaders are concerned with the ramifications of risky actions and that they could lead to negative consequences. Nonetheless, taking risks is necessary and should not be the reason practitioners shy away from exploring new possibilities. Cels, De Jong, and Nauta (2012) posit that innovations disrupt the status quo and thus are often "opposite of evidence-based solutions" (p. 24); yet client safety and legitimacy of a proposed program are necessary components. For example, if a leader proposes to treat homeless families with a new intervention or program, such as when the Housing First Program (often referred to as a rapid rehousing intervention) was first implemented, the organization's leaders must consider all the ethical aspects and potential program consequences of the proposed strategy. Several key questions must be answered ahead of time; for example: How much is the new program going to cost? What new training will the staff need? How many clients will participate? What other agencies should partner with us in this new program? What kind of data do we need to collect? Are there any ethical or safety concerns?

The first step is to be aware of the numerous ethical challenges facing the health and human services professions, including, but not limited to, the following: practitioner competence, client privacy and confidentiality, accuracy in initial assessments and treatments, technology breaching, videoconferencing and telephone counseling, informed consent, supervisory interactions, conflicts of interest, boundaries and dual relationships, consultation and client referral, termination and/or interruption of services, social media communications, and keeping proper documentation (Reamer, 2013). Understanding these ethical challenges will help social services leaders be (1) more knowledgeable and competent about ethical principles, values, and practices and (2) better prepared to avoid ethical mistakes and/or misconduct.

Generally, ethical theorists and philosophers agree that there are three basic types of ethical frameworks that decision makers and leaders should explore as they think about decisions that affect organizational members and/or clients (Beckett & Maynard, 2005):

1. *Meta-ethics.* Meta-ethics studies critical and analytical thinking about the definition of moral terms, including "right," "good," "duty," and how moral judgments should or should not be justified.
2. *Normative ethics.* Normative ethics tries to answer moral questions and ethical dilemmas, focusing on the morality of the person. For example, is "lying" justifiable sometimes?
3. *Descriptive ethics.* This framework studies moral opinions and belief systems to see if they fit within a moral compass. For example, trying to answer if it is ethically appropriate to euthanize a person suffering from a terminal illness.

Ethical principles are usually coupled with personal core values. Values are specific types of beliefs that each individual possesses and are often generated from ideology, religion, attitudes, principles, opinions, and/or preferences. These values are very important and worthy because they are synonymous with the leader's identity, reputation, and integrity.

In essence, health and human services organizations, leaders, and practitioners are in the business of improving people's lives. As individuals have their values and ethical principles, so do organizations and institutions. Generally, organizational values are often influenced by the broader societal values, reflecting certain beliefs, codes of conduct, cultural affiliations, and political positions. Key values in the health and human services fields include ameliorating individual and family suffering, improving people's functioning in society, and producing social change that can positively affect the institutional and systemic structural flows and foster constructive cultural changes (Dombo, Kays, & Weller, 2014). The central five human and social services ethical principles are:

1. *Social justice.* Because of structural flows, some individuals live at a pervasive disadvantage, confronting crime, drug use, unemployment and/or underemployment, health and mental health access,

educational achievement gap, discrimination, and marginalization.
A few examples of grand social justice efforts to improve living
conditions are the Settlement House Movement in the 1930s, the New
Deal in the 1940s, the War on Poverty in the 1960s, and the American
Disability Act in the 1980s.

2. *Benevolence.* Human nature is to do good. At a personal level,
individuals have a desire to do good for others, engaging in acts of
kindness and causing no harm. For example, people offer to care for
the sick, donate time and expertise (e.g., the international organization
Doctors Without Borders), donate money for the less fortunate, and
so forth.

3. *Dignity and respect.* Every person—regardless of background,
economic status, culture, or sexual orientation—deserves and
expects to be respected. As we work with clients who come from
vulnerable, stigmatized, and marginalized populations, many times
they feel disrespected and segregated. It is important to incorporate
empowerment and self-determination principles in our practices to
best engage and support individuals and families.

4. *Cultural proficiency.* Health and social services professionals recognize
the importance of not only understanding but also embracing
differences in culture, age, race, sexual orientation, gender identity,
immigration status, cognitive abilities, and physical disabilities.
Unfortunately, organizational and institutional barriers created by any
type of individual or group are still present in our society, and we must
continue working together to end them.

5. *Competence and integrity.* A key ethical standard in human services
fields is to treat patients and/or clients with integrity, competence, and
the best available tools at our disposal. Leaders and practitioners need
to continuously update, learn, educate, and evaluate themselves and
their efforts with new interventions and services that can best improve
the functioning of patients and clients.

SOCIAL INNOVATION IN HEALTH AND HUMAN SERVICES

Presently, health and human services programs and services appear to produce
limited results because it seems that major social problems like homelessness,
drug addiction, crime, suicide, economic inequalities, health and mental health
access, and other social injustices continue to be widespread and pervasive.
Thus, successful leaders are open, able, and willing to try new strategies and
practices by designing and implementing social innovations. There are many

definitions of social innovation. For example, GreenHouse defines social innovation as the "systematic disruption of a social norm to affect positive social change" (GreenHouse Guide, 2017, para. 3); the Center for Social Innovation (C4) looks at social innovation as new strategies, programs, and practices that improve the lives of marginalized and vulnerable populations (Center for Social Innovation, 2017); Boston College's Center for Social Innovation refers to social innovation as a new paradigm for sustainable change (Boston College, n.d.); and Cels et al. (2012) define it as "improving social outcomes and creating public value" (p. 4). Furthermore, "an innovation does not have to be new in the world; it just has to be new to the local situation. Innovations differ from 'ideas' in the sense that they have actually been made operational" (Cels et al., 2012, p. 4). In sum, the process of social innovation has four basic steps: (1) identify what needs to be changed, (2) generate a set of new ideas or norms to replace the dysfunctional ones, (3) implement and evaluate these new ideas to cause a disruption in the current faulty system, and (4) create social change by developing and establishing a new system.

Social innovations start with the leaders' empathy to understand a social problem, the knowledge and ability to design a potential solution, and the character to embrace and energize others to join the social change effort. Social innovations are transformative, and either they can occur on a small scale (e.g., change within a program or organization) or take shape on a larger scale (e.g., change within countywide mental health delivery system or new national strategies to "fight the war on drugs"). Whether the changes are small or large in magnitude, social innovations need committed leaders to implement and advance the proposed innovative strategies. We refer to these leaders as *social architects* or *champions*. Social architects can be leaders on top of the organizational hierarchy or in any other position in health and human organizations. Health and human services innovators—social architects— have the willingness and ability to influence social change throughout organizations and institutions. These social architects can be program advisers, middle managers, board members, directors, elected officials, nurses, school psychologists, CEOs, case managers, therapists, social workers, and anyone else who is considered a health and human services practitioner and cares enough to make a difference.

Social architects must identify and obtain the necessary tools to implement innovations and encourage everyone around them to consistently and effectively use these tools. The first step is to engage the organization and/or network to actively participate in and promote the social innovation. Social architects need to actively involve other organizational leaders to determine the scale (size and scope) of the innovation and whether the organization will embrace the innovative idea(s) as a common goal. It is critical that all stakeholders see the social innovation as a key part of their organizations' vision and mission statements. Second, the innovation has to disrupt the current structure and/or system. It is a new way of doing business, and most people may feel uneasy or unsure about the uncertainty triggered by implementing the innovation. All stakeholders must be in agreement with the innovation process, which includes: (1) creating a new tool, program, service delivery, and/or business model; (2) developing entrepreneurial models, strategies, or approaches; and (3) implementing the innovative idea as a separate unit from the rest of the organization to determine viability and effectiveness. Third, social innovations do not happen by one organization working alone. It is critical that partnerships, networking, and collaborations take shape and be productive throughout the different stages of the innovation process (see Chapter 6). Finally, social architects must get ready to accept shortcomings because not all social innovations succeed. The word *failure* is not in the social architect's vocabulary. Not succeeding is part of innovating; it is just a piece of the process. The next social innovation iteration by a leader will be informed by a higher level of experience and result in a greater likelihood of success.

Based on the writings of Mark Moore (1995; as cited in Cels et al., 2012), the challenges that often face a socially innovative leader in the public sector include "securing legitimacy and support in one's authorizing environment [stakeholders and funders]; building sufficient operational capacity, and making a compelling public value opinion" (Cels et al., 2012, p. 13).

A key instrument for overcoming challenges and successfully designing and implementing innovations is through communication or *information dissemination*. Birken, Lee, and Weiner (2012) suggest that effective communication is a great tool to keep high levels of commitment from all stakeholders and that leaders should organize information dissemination into a four-step process: (1) diffusing information (disseminate facts and updates appropriately); (2) synthesizing information (integrate and interpret facts, making general information about innovation implementation relevant to unique organizations and employees); (3) mediating between innovation and daily activities (identify tasks required for implementing innovations, giving employees the necessary tools to implement innovations); and (4) selling innovation implementation (justify innovation implementation, encouraging employees to consistently and effectively use innovations). Cels and colleagues (2012) provide the following words of wisdom with regard to using communication to appeal to constituents:

> Social innovators do a lot of talking—not necessarily because they want to but because they have to. An innovative idea rarely speaks for itself. It needs to be articulated and polished to appeal to constituents. This

involves more than simply selling the idea or crafting a perfect sales pitch. It requires talking with all the key stakeholders in the authorizing environment whose resources and other kinds of support the innovator needs, such as government officials, private donors, leaders of nonprofits, elected politicians, opinion makers, union leaders, members of the public that the innovation aims to address—in short, everyone who can help or hinder the project. And it is not a simple one way communication. Talking about change involves opening up to the ideas and concerns of others, taking in their views and suggesting, and modifying or even reimagining the innovation in terms of what is valuable or feasible. (p. 44)

Additionally, it is critical for social architects to use formal evaluations to gauge the progress of innovation initiatives by collecting and analyzing data. In essence, data are used to measure evidence and levels of success. One effective data analysis method is the application of formative and summative evaluations (Dudley, 2014). Formative evaluations are designed to explore the process of the innovation. These types of evaluations seek to answer the following questions: Were the right partners actively participating? Was the information disseminated appropriately? What other tools were needed to successfully implement the innovative ideas? These process outcomes will be complemented by the summative evaluation results, which seek to describe the level of innovation effectiveness. Some of the questions summative evaluations intend to answer are: Did the innovation reach its goals? What are the differences in programs and clients because of the new intervention/program/structure? Is there strong evidence that the innovation caused the desired social change? (Refer to Chapter 16 for more information). Next, we will review innovative strategies in technology, big data, client-centered interventions, and social media to generate social change.

Technology

Technological advances in the late part of the 20th century and the beginning of the 21st century have been nothing but remarkable. The health and human services fields have experienced significant technological innovations, including medical devices, data analysis software, communication tools, client records, and information technology. It is hard to believe that in our time, the human heart can be monitored from a mobile phone, billions of data bits can be computed in seconds, psychotherapists living in one city can conduct virtual counseling sessions with clients residing in another city, patient medical records can be stored and retrieved almost immediately, and information technology can be extracted to expedite administrative, service, and marketing tasks. Indeed, we live in an automated world and have become dependent on technology in every aspect of our lives.

These new technologies are being used effectively to advance social justice movements. Ordinary people now have the ability to record videos of un-warranted exchanges on their smartphones and post them onto social media outlets, where millions of citizens can watch almost instantly (a social phe-nomenon known as "going viral"). This documentation of unjust encounters between persons of power and victims serves as a social justice platform to demand social change. For example, the issue of police brutality (i.e., use of excessive force) became public knowledge after dozens of videos have shown evidence of misconduct and abuses by peace officers, often resulting in criminal convictions against the perpetrators. Most likely, without videotape evidence, offenders would have walked free without punishment. Furthermore, the use of social media, email, and text can expedite the information exchanges to ener-gize millions of people in a very short amount of time. These new technologies are revolutionary, and leaders must learn how to intentionally harness these innovative devices for the public good.

Information technology (IT) is an area of innovation that has dramati-cally evolved in past decades. The majority of IT innovations have the poten-tial to provide numerous positive benefits in the health and human services fields. Jaskyte (2012) argues that IT innovations are associated with benefits for (1) clients and programs (increasing the number of clients served and service hours and improving client outcomes); (2) internal and external functioning (increasing the staff efficiency and productivity, data collection processes, and partnership efficiency); (3) fundraising and financial aspects (increasing donor donation funds and earned income); and (4) public image and relationships with stakeholders (improving connectivity, communications, and public image). These IT innovations can be directly related with positive client outcomes, such as increasing client's knowledge of prevention, access, and health outcomes, along with individual and family self-sufficiency, inde-pendence, and self-reliance.

One of the major technological developments of our time is the use of the Internet to treat clients with health problems and mental health disorders. Because of the Internet, we have much greater access to information, re-sources, and support than ever before. For example, there have been advances in the effectiveness of therapist-guided Internet treatments for psychiatric disorders (e.g., depression, bipolar disorder, social phobia, anxiety, patho-logical gambling, and posttraumatic stress [PTSD]), other life conditions (e.g., work stress, relational problems, burnout, grief, body dissatisfaction among others), and the provision of couples' therapy. Andersson (2016) suggests that "these treatments require (*a*) a secure web platform, (*b*) robust assessment procedures, (*c*) treatment contents that can be text based or offered in other formats, and (*d*) a therapist role that differs from that in face-to-face therapy" (p. 164). Moreover, Kazdin (2015) advises that before implementing technology-based interventions, leaders first consider important features, such as scalability, affordability, reach, convenience, expansion, acceptability, flexibility, and partnerships.

A very interesting technological innovation is integrating socially assistive robotics (SARs) into mental health interventions. Feil-Seifer and Matarić (2005) refer to SARs as a specific area of robotics created by the intersection of assistive robotics (e.g., mobility assistants, teachers/instructors) and intelligent interactive robotics (e.g., robotic toys, robotic games, information input/output). There is growing variety of clinically relevant functions robots can serve, including companionship (SAR systems function in a way that is analogous to a trained therapy animal, such as a therapy dog); therapeutic play partner (robots as play partners who aid children in practicing or building clinically relevant skills, often in children diagnosed with autism spectrum disorders); and coach (a robot that has the knowledge and capacity to help stroke victims by guiding them through physical and mental exercises). Rabbitt, Kazdin, and Scassellati (2015) conclude that the demand for SARs will significantly increase as millennials feel more comfortable with automatized and robotics applications.

Enock and McNally (2013) argue that these innovative mobile apps and Internet-based interventions or treatments have the capacity to transform how we deliver mental health services. The development of these Internet-based treatments and interventions generally follows four key steps: (1) development (from traditional intervention to a more self-directed psychotherapeutic intervention format); (2) testing (test novel treatments against existing empirical Internet-based interventions); (3) dissemination (share process and results with patients and clinicians seeking fidelity and quality improvement); and (4) clinical practice and continued research (empirical research studies that continue to evaluate efficacy and effectiveness). Expanding into this new frontier also brings potential concerns with regard to direct-to-patient treatment and research, such as proper diagnosis, patient safety and confidentiality, private sector engagement, and conflict of interest. Nonetheless, innovative Internet treatments can be as effective as traditional face-to-face treatments (as long as clients are willing to use this medium), lead to sustained improvements, work in clinical-like conditions, reach remote clients, and be cost-effective.

Big Data

What is big data and how can it be applied in the health and human services fields? Big data is a set of large and complex amounts of information collected and stored in different data bases or computer software. Because of advances in technology, most everyone has daily access to relatively inexpensive and numerous devices (e.g., mobile phones, cameras, and Internet use), contributing an immense amounts of data at an exponential growth. The creation of database management systems has boomed in the past decades with the goal of finding the appropriate strategy to handle big data challenges and possibilities. Imagine storing all the information from people who receive benefits from federal and state programs, such as Medicaid, Social Security income, or food stamps. Another type of big data is capsulated into electronic medical records from large private health care providers like BlueCross and BlueShield Health Systems. These large data sets store billions of pieces of information about individuals, their behaviors, drug prescriptions, doctors' notes, medical tests, money allocation, and so forth.

How did big data become a major innovative strategy? An analysis provided by McKinsey Global Institute (n.d.) revealed that a series of converging trends in bringing multiple industries to a tipping point propelled the collection of big data as a social innovation initiative. There are four major forces that created a positive change for innovation: demand (demands for better data, lower prices, showing impact, and accuracy of information); supply (supply relevant and accessible data at scale); technology (technical capability advances in analytical tools); and government (government catalyzing market change and deregulation). For example, in the health care industry, demand for lower costs, improvement in data collection, creation of new software, and the call for integration in medical services by new federal policies contributed to the integration of primary data pools. Health care providers now integrate four major primary big data pools: clinical data from providers, pharmaceutical research and design data from companies, patient behavior data from clients, and cost data from health care companies.

As leaders contemplate the potential applications of big data as an innovative strategy to achieve social change, Kayyali, Knott, and Kuiken (2013) suggest that leaders follow four guiding principles:

1. *Improving the core services first.* Before looking at investing in new big data initiatives, leaders should look at what else they can do to improve what they are already doing without diving into expensive ventures. Then, do a thorough assessment to fully understand what the organization is about to embark on.

2. *Playing to win.* Big data initiatives have the potential to optimize services, attract best talent, and move quickly ahead of others in the field. To be successful, the entire leadership team must be in agreement about taking on the innovative big data effort.
3. *Promoting transparency as a cultural norm.* Leaders must be honest and share communication throughout the innovation. Without transparency, other organizational members will begin to move away from actively participating and endorsing the big data initiative.
4. *Setting a top-bottom vision and stimulating the bottom-up innovation.* Successful leaders embrace active participation from all the organization members. The leadership provides the vision and resources, while the health and human services practitioners and other organizational members provide the talent, expertise, and application.

Implementing big data initiatives is a transformative process. Leaders understand that the organization is about to go through a cultural transformation and that everyone will be affected one way or another. Keiler and Price (2011) explain that the role of the leader in big data initiatives is to accomplish five major goals:

1. *Aspire.* Setting the performance goals and defining organizational aspirations. Leaders must answer and communicate clearly: where do we want to go?
2. *Assess.* Determining gaps across the organization units and understanding the organizational culture. Leaders should know: how ready are we to go there?
3. *Architect.* Developing key innovative strategies to improve performance and designing the implementation by identifying roles and responsibilities for key organizational members. Leaders must answer: what do we need to do/build to get there?
4. *Act.* Designing how the big data initiative will unfold, engaging broad participation, and measuring the impact. Leaders have to know: how do we manage the big data initiative and evaluate outcomes of use?
5. *Advance.* Setting up the organizational structure to accomplish the desired social change and developing leaders throughout the organization to implement the innovation. The key question leaders should answer here is: how do we keep succeeding?

There are negative and positive aspects to big data innovation. One of the major challenges for organizations managing big data is their ability to collect and sustain this mammoth amount of information. Big data maintenance requires substantial resources, constant update, and keeping it secure and private. Unfortunately, these big data sets can be hacked at any time and used for illegal purposes, including extortion and bribery. A great number of public and private organizations have experienced big data breaches, being hacked by terrorist organizations demanding ransom demands and/or payments, including organizations such as Sony Studios, BlueCross Health Systems, Equifax, Facebook, and many others. Thus, organizations and their leaders must guard this information judiciously and vigorously. On the positive side, the use of big data has the potential to predict and analyze mass behavior, spot epidemiologic illnesses, prevent diseases, combat crime, improve health care access, advance mental health interventions, and so on. Scientists and computer analysts do invest significant amounts of time and money to find new statistical associations or correlations among variables to detect relevant characteristics in an effort to advance natural science simulations, complex biological configurations, behavioral patterns, and environmental trends.

Patient-Centered Interventions

One key innovative strategy in health and human services organizations is a new approach to providing patient-centered interventions. Patient-centered interventions first and foremost address patient needs and goals, such as improved access, treatment continuity, communication and coordination, cultural proficiency, and individual- and family-focused care (Hernandez et al., 2013). There are six primary determinants for initiating a patient-centered innovation:

1. *Effective leadership.* Leaders must craft the vision for the proposed innovation, coordinate technical and professional expertise, and foster creative skills. Leaders welcome ambiguity, unconventionality, proactivity, and change, showing self-confidence, determination, and initiative.
2. *Strong internal and external motivation to change.* Organizational internal motivations can be leveraged to improve services, meet the client at their level, and save costs; and external motivations can be economic, cultural, political, ecological, and technological.
3. *Clear and consistent organizational mission.* The organizational vision and mission serve as inspiration, motivation, aspiration, and direction for all stakeholders. Leaders must communicate how the mission and values align with the innovative idea to solicit and secure support and commitment from everyone.

4. *Alignment with organizational strategy.* The proposed innovation must be aligned with the overall organizational strategy to reach the desired performance, attain its targeted outcomes, and have the ability to compete and/or collaborate with other organizations.
5. *Robust organizational capability.* The organization must take a close look at itself and determine whether it has the appropriate size, financial assets, human resources, and information systems to engage in a new innovative initiative and/or strategy.
6. *Continuous feedback and organizational learning.* As the innovative initiative gets implemented, leaders must observe the process and welcome ongoing feedback from stakeholders. Changes may be needed, and leaders need to stay close to the strategic process and make the necessary adjustments along the way.

Patient-centered innovations need internal actors to shape organizational processes and be aware of the external financial incentives and government regulations that may shape the innovation application. Kazdin and Rabbitt (2013) argue that patient-centered innovative interventions should be appraised on the following six characteristics: reach, feasibility and flexibility, scalability, expansion of workforce, affordability, and expansion of settings. For example, some of the new evidence-based models for delivering health and mental health services and reducing the burdens of physical and mental illnesses that can be considered patient-centered innovations include:

- *Task shifting.* Task shifting is a method of expanding the health care workforce by allowing the patient care and service delivery in the hands of a broader range of individuals with less training and fewer qualifications (nonprofessionals, i.e., lay individuals) rather than exclusively relying on professional health care providers such as physicians, nurses, and social workers. For example, a family member of a child suffering from autism can provide the necessary care at home. This redistribution allows an increase in the total number of health workers (e.g., nonprofessionals, lay individuals) to scale up the scope of providing services. It is patient-centered because the family member may best know the individual's needs.
- *Disruptive innovations.* Disruptive innovations are changes in products or services that do not use an incremental or logical approach to be implemented, but rather provide disruptive approaches to care for people in need. An example of a disruptive innovation is a psychotherapist using tele-mental-health (virtual counseling) to provide mental health services to a patient who lives in a remote area.

- *Interventions in everyday settings.* This innovative patient-centered model expands care beyond the typical settings: clinics, hospitals, and outpatient offices—and instead provides therapy or other care that is embedded into everyday settings where people regularly spend time (e.g., home, shopping malls, workplaces, churches, hair salons).
- *Best-buy interventions.* Best buy refers to an intervention for which "there is compelling evidence that is not only highly cost-effective but also feasible, low-cost (affordable), and appropriate to implement within the constraints of a local health system" (World Health Organization [WHO], 2011, p. 2). For example, nurse technicians providing care in pharmacies instead of clinics or hospitals, $2 generic eyeglasses, and generic/store brand prescription drugs. Low-income individuals and families residing in poor neighborhoods or emerging economies benefit the most from best-buy interventions.
- *Lifestyle changes.* Lifestyle changes refer to innovative intervention efforts that modify high-risk behaviors to reduce disease mortality and morbidity. For this model to work, people must be engaged in having the goal of positively affecting their health outcomes. For example, a few companies have started to provide monetary incentives to motivate their employees to control their diet, exercise, reduce or eliminate consumption of alcohol and nicotine, and participate in activities that can reduce stress.
- *Massive open online interventions (MOOIs).* MOOIs provide evidence-based behavioral interventions to millions of people, having the potential to increase reach and scalability. Whether it is tobacco cessation strategies or reducing alcohol and other drugs dependency, MOOIs provide people worldwide with evidence-based behavioral interventions at minimum or no cost. Additionally, digital interventions, such as websites and apps, can be used repetitively by individuals and families worldwide at any time that is convenient without losing their therapeutic effectiveness (Muñoz et al., 2016).
- *Cyber counseling.* With the increased use of the Internet and mobile devices, cyber counseling has becoming more popular in the past few years. More universities and agencies are offering introductory and advanced training on virtual counseling to expand therapeutic techniques to the online realm, including online communication strategies, creating virtual communities, sharing cognitive and emotional needs, and maintaining a strong virtual rapport with clients. Competencies have been established and operationalized by creating cyber counseling competency rating scales, which indicate the ability

level of the counselor to assess and intervene, build and terminate therapeutic relationships, and enhance virtual presence (Mishna, Levine, Bogo, & Van Wert, 2013).

Social Media

Social media refers to content and information that is publically available on specific Internet sites, including weblogs (e.g., blogs), social networking websites (e.g., Facebook, Instagram, and LinkedIn), collaborative projects (e.g., Wikipedia), and user-generated content communities (e.g., YouTube and Twitter). For example, in health and human services, public health officials and emergency responders can use Facebook or Twitter to track flulike symptoms, predict outbreak patterns, and use information to mitigate potential dangers. Millions of individuals can reach out to others by using social networking sites to share and communicate with various types of online support groups for physical and mental health conditions (e.g., breast cancer, diabetes, alcohol dependence, depression). Social networking sites have become virtual communities, where individuals from all over the world can connect and exchange information, provide product and services feedback, and deliver interventions with one another almost instantly. Services and interventions can now be brought to individuals and families wherever they are through these social media connections.

Sage and Sage (2016) advise us that we must be highly conscious of e-professionalism standards when using social media. First, health and human services organizations must develop clear and practical social media policies that align with their vision, mission, and values. Using social media can be risky for both the health care provider and the client or patient. It is important to have guidelines to minimize the risks and maximize positive client outcomes. Hrdinová, Helbig, and Peters (2010, p. 3) outline the following eight elements of an effective social media policy to be organizationally instituted:

1. Employee access to social media websites
2. Account management (e.g., who can develop and manage changes in accounts)
3. Acceptable use of social media (e.g., language, schedule)
4. Responsible employee conduct
5. Content management (e.g., who is able to post content on behalf of the agency)
6. Security concerns (e.g., the use of passwords, confidentiality, and safety from viruses)

7. Legal issues (e.g., disclaimers, conflict of interests, sharing controversial personal and political views)
8. Citizen conduct (e.g., employee expectations and commitment to social media policy)

These social media policies must be in tandem with ethical decision making and guidelines. The health and human services leader must provide decision-making and ethical guidelines for employees that virtually interact with partners and clients on a regular basis. Besides the ethical principles described at the beginning of the chapter, Congress and McAuliffe (1999, p. 155) offer a simple, but powerful, ethical decision-making framework for all health and human services practitioners called E.T.H.I.C., which stands for:

- Examine personal, societal, agency, and client values
- Think and apply code of ethics, laws, and case decisions
- Hypothesize about decisional consequences
- Identify who could be harmed, with the most vulnerable in mind
- Consult with supervisors and colleagues

Finally, social media policy, procedures, and decision-making guidelines should be evaluated continuously. Kraft and Furlong (2012) provide eight elements that leaders in their respective organizations can use when assessing social media policies and procedures: Effectiveness, efficiency, equity, liberty, political feasibility, social acceptability, administrative feasibility, and technical feasibility.

Design Thinking

The last component to social innovation is derived from design thinking or human-centered approach to innovation (Brown, 2009). Borrowing from the creative strategies of designers in producing products and services (i.e., industrial designers, graphic designers, and others), social architects can utilize the creative methods of those that design automobiles or video games toward the design of innovative health and human services. Brown (2009) describes design thinking as moving from *inspiration,* or the problem or opportunity that drives an innovative solution where insights are gathered from multiple sources, to *ideation,* which is the process of developing ideas, to *implementation* (i.e., concrete plan for action). The first step in departing from the status quo is to understand constraints in terms of *feasibility* (what is possible), *viability* (what is sustainable over time), and *desirability* (in terms of human needs). An innovative leader and his or her team should engage in both *convergent* and *divergent thinking* (multiple options to create choices) and then convergent thinking (analyze options and derive a solution).

According to Brown (2012) there are certain elements that must be created by the innovative leader in the organization in order to engage in design thinking, and these include "a culture of optimism" (where team members must believe in their power to affect change or create something new) (p. 76); judgment of ideas has to be deferred; encouragement of "wild ideas" should be supported while staying focused on the topic (p. 78); and "building on the ideas of others" (p. 78). Ways to express ideas and brainstorm innovative solutions in design thinking include the use visual techniques such as creating prototypes (or models) using art, ceramics, Legos, or Post-Its and/or using narrative or qualitative thinking through storytelling and many other activities. The principle behind design thinking is that it is a way to engage in integrative, nonlinear, "both/and" thinking rather than the "either/or" alternatives (p. 85). Brown (2012) summarizes design thinking as "the ability to spot patterns in the mess of complex inputs; to synthesize new ideas from fragmented parts; to empathize with people different from ourselves—can all be learned" (p. 86).

Keeping in mind leadership with regard to innovation, according to Kouzes and Posner (2012), "leadership is inextricably connected with the process of innovation" (p. 160); and a social architect has to enlist others in this process and make incremental changes through small wins and learning from experience. A few general tips for the social architect on generating innovative ideas are provided by Grant (2016), who posits that "the hallmark of originality is rejecting the default and exploring whether a better option exists" (p. 7). To innovate, a few of the following strategies are proposed (Grant, 2016, pp. 245–252):

- Question the default
- Triple the number of ideas you generate
- Immerse yourself in a new domain
- Procrastinate strategically
- Seek more feedback from peers
- Invite employees from different functions and levels to pitch ideas
- Hire not on cultural fit, but on cultural contribution
- Welcome criticism

Finally, a chapter on innovation would not be complete without *The Guide to Innovation Dynamics* from the GreenHouse Center of Social Innovation

(GreenHouse, 2017). As was mentioned in the beginning of this chapter, in this model, social innovation is defined as "the systematic disruption of a social norm to effect social change" and comprises three steps: "revealing the social norm that holds the undesirable conditions in place; identifying or creating a deviant from that norm; and diffusing the deviance through a sufficient number and breadth of reference groups" (GreenHouse Guide, 2017, para. 3). This model goes beyond creativity (although it requires the use of imagination); the core principle is about addressing social norms to change the way people behave, and through this mechanism, social innovation is possible.

In conclusion, innovation is a necessary and powerful method to improve programs and services in the health and human services fields. Innovative strategies should follow ethical and organizational standards to maximize positive client outcomes and minimize organizational risks. Innovative leaders are social architects who are responsible for delivering client support and are placed throughout the organizational ladder, from interns to executive directors to board members. Social architects are always open to organizational and social innovations, providing guidelines, fostering creativity, and building new systems for social change. Innovations can be designed (e.g., through design thinking) and implemented in different forms, including new technologies, the use of big data, patient-guided interventions, and proper use of social media.

CHAPTER DISCUSSION QUESTIONS

1. As you have learned, social innovation speaks to a disruption of the status quo. Comment on the considerations to disrupting services as usual?
2. Explain the ethical principles associated with health and human services provision. Think of a scenario where you might see a violation of ethics in an organization and how you would address it from a leadership perspective.
3. The benefits of using big data are clear; however, what are the associated concerns, and how can a leader mitigate the potential risks?
4. Think of a social innovation that you would like to implement. What strategies would you use to ensure buy-in from all stakeholder groups?
5. Experiment with design thinking techniques to formulate a social innovation.

6. Read the leader profile and case study located in the Appendix to this chapter. Note innovative ideas and practices and see what aspects of the case you can connect to contents of the chapter and/or the overall book.

REFERENCES

Andersson, G. (2016). Internet-delivered psychological treatments. *Annual Review of Clinical Psychology, 12*(1), 157–179.

Beckett, C., & Maynard, A. (2005). *Values and ethics in social work: An introduction.* New York, NY: Taylor & Francis, Sage.

Birken, S. A., Lee, S. Y. D., & Weiner, B. J. (2012). Uncovering middle managers' role in healthcare innovation implementation. *Implementation Science, 7*(1), 28–39.

Boston College, (n.d.) Center for Social Innovation. Retreat from: https://www.bc.edu/schools/gssw/csi.html

Brown, T. (2009). *Change by Design.* New York, NY: HarperCollins Publishers.

Brown, T. (2012). *Change by design: How design thinking transforms organizations and inspires innovation.* New York, NY: HarperCollins.

Cels, S., De Jong, J. & Nauta, F. (2012). *Agents of change: Strategy and tactics for social innovation.* Washington, DC: Brookings Institution Press.

Center for Social Innovation in the US. (2017). *Social Innovation.* Retrieved from http://www.bc.edu/schools/gssw/csi.html

Center for Social Innovation C4. (2017). *What is innovation?* Retrieved from http://center4si.com/

Congress, E., & McAuliffe, D. (1999). Social work ethics. *International Social Work, 49*(2), 151–164.

Dombo, E. A., Kays, L., & Weller, K. (2014). Clinical social work practice and technology: Personal, practical, regulatory, and ethical considerations for the twenty-first century. *Social Work in Health Care, 53*(9), 900–919.

Dudley, J. R. (2014). *Social work evaluation: Enhancing what we do* (2nd ed.). Chicago, IL: Lyceum Books.

Enock, P. M., & McNally, R. J. (2013). How mobile apps and other web-based interventions can transform psychological treatment and the treatment development cycle. *Behavior Therapist, 36*(3), 56–66.

Feil-Seifer, D., & Mataric, M. J. (2005, June). Defining socially assistive robotics. In *Rehabilitation Robotics, 2005. ICORR 2005. 9th International Conference on Rehabilitation Robotics* (pp. 465–468). Chicago, IL: IEEE.

Grant, A. (2016). *Originals: How non-conformists move the world.* New York, NY: Viking.

GreenHouse. (2017). *Innovation dynamics.* Retrieved from http://ghouse.org/

GreenHouse Guide. (2017). *The GreenHouse guide to innovation dynamics.* Retrieved from http://ghouse.org/category/innovation/

Kayyali, B., Knott, D., & Kuiken, S. V. (2013). The big data revolution in health-care: Accelarating value and innovation. McKinsey & Company Health Systems & Services. Retrieve from: https://www.mckinsey.com/industries/healthcare-systems-and-services/our-insights/the-big-data-revolution-in-us-health-care

Kraft, M. E., & Furlong, S. R. (2012). *Public policy: Politics, analysis, and alternatives.* Thousand Oaks, CA: Sage.

Hernandez, S. E., Conrad, D. A., Marcus-Smith, M. S., Reed, P., & Watts, C. (2013). Patient-centered innovation in health care organizations: A conceptual framework and case study application. *Health Care Management Review, 38*(2), 166–175.

Hrdinová, J., Helbig, N., & Peters, C. S. (2010). *Designing social media policy for government: Eight essential elements.* Albany, NY: Center for Technology in Government, University at Albany.

Jaskyte, K. (2012). Exploring potential for information technology innovation in non-profit organizations. *Journal of Technology in Human Services, 30*(2), 118–127.

Kazdin, A. E. (2015). Technology-based interventions and reducing the burdens of mental illness: Perspectives and comments on the special series. *Cognitive and Behavioral Practice, 22*(3), 359–366.

Kazdin, A. E., & Rabbitt, S. M. (2013). Novel models for delivering mental health services and reducing the burdens of mental illness. *Clinical Psychological Science, 1*(2), 170–191.

Keller, S., & Price, C. (2011). Beyond performance: How great organizations build competitive advantage. Hoboken, NJ: John Wiley & Sons.

Kouzes, J., & Posner, B. (2012). *The leadership challenge: How to make extraordinary things happen in organizations* (5th ed.). San Francisco, CA: The Leadership Challenge, Wiley.

McKinsey Global Institute (n.d.) Retrieve from: https://www.mckinsey.com/mgi/overview

Mishna, F., Levine, D., Bogo, M., & Van Wert, M. (2013). Cyber counselling: An innovative field education pilot project. *Social Work Education, 32*(4), 484–492.

Muñoz, R. F., Bunge, E. L., Chen, K., Schueller, S. M., Bravin, J. I., Shaughnessy, E. A., & Pérez-Stable, E. J. (2016). Massive open online interventions: A novel model for delivering behavioral-health services worldwide. *Clinical Psychological Science, 4*(2), 194–205.

Rabbitt, S. M., Kazdin, A. E., & Scassellati, B. (2015). Integrating socially assistive robotics into mental healthcare interventions: Applications and recommendations for expanded use. *Clinical Psychology Review, 35*, 35–46.

Reamer, F. G. (2013). Social work in a digital age: Ethical and risk management challenges. *Social Work, 58*(2), 163–172.

Sage, M., & Sage, T. (2016). Social media and e-professionalism in child welfare: Policy and practice. *Journal of Public Child Welfare, 10*(1), 79–95.

World Health Organization. (2011). *Global status on alcohol and health.* World Health Organization. Retrieve from: http://apps.who.int/iris/bitstream/handle/10665/44499/?sequence=1.

APPENDIX
Featured Leader: Alfredo Aguirre

Alfredo Aguirre, LCSW, is the Director of Behavioral Health Services of San Diego County and has served in the capacity of Mental Health Director since 1999. He serves on the Board of Directors of the National Network of Social Managers and as a co-chair of the Cultural Competence, Equity, and Social Justice Committee of the California Mental Health Directors Association. He also serves on the Child, Adolescent, and Family Branch Council, a national advisory committee to the Children's Branch of the Center for Mental Health Services under the Substance Abuse and Mental Health Services Administration (SAMHSA).

Mr. Aguirre has worked in the mental health field for more than 34 years as a psychiatric social worker, staff supervisor, manager, and executive. He is the recipient of many prestigious awards, including Mental Health Person of the Year in 2008 and the 2011 Hope Award for his leadership in the County of San Diego's Mental Health Stigma Reduction Media Campaign, "It's Up to Us."

Alfredo received his master's degree in Social Welfare in 1978 from the University of California at Berkeley, and he has a special interest in cultural competence development in systems and communities. He authored a chapter titled, "Community Mental Health Services in a Managed Care Environment: 10 Key Issues in Promoting Cultural Competence," published in *Promoting Cultural Competence in Children's Mental Health Services* (edited by Mario Hernandez & Mareasa R. Issacs, 1999).

LEADERSHIP PROFILE FOR ALFREDO AGUIRRE

Share your professional background and experience

In my family, I am a first-generation professional. My parents are immigrants, and they raised five children. I was the middle child. I went to Community College. I got my bachelor's degree in sociology at California State University, Hayward; now it's called Cal State East Bay. I then went on to get my master's degree in Social Welfare at UC Berkeley. My concentration was organization, planning, and administration, but while I was there I realized that I needed to incorporate more "on the ground" direct experience to facilitate my growth professionally and give me the credibility to eventually be a leader by at least getting more experience in terms of coursework in my practicum. I was one of the few that did a kind of a dual placement. It was approved, and I appreciate the flexibility at UC Berkeley.

My first job after getting out of graduate school was as a social worker for a county adolescent community mental health program in San Mateo County. I then became a supervisor and then a program manager, and I just kind of slowly climbed the organizational chart. I worked at a community mental health clinic that served both adults and kids in the northern part of the county, which actually borders San Francisco County. I got my first real experience of working with a community advisory board and working with a diverse communities, significantly Latino and Filipino populations, in the region that our organization covered. Ultimately, my calling, so to speak, was really getting involved in leadership positions with working with children, youth, and families. While overseeing a clinic, I became the Deputy Director for children, youth, and families. I reported as the a mental health director and was able to get a federal grant to help develop our system of care in San Mateo County, so I was able to bring that experience to San Diego where I was recruited in 1999 to be the first-ever children's Mental Health Director.

At the time, the mental health systems were more of an adult centric system in San Diego. Bob Ross, who's now the executive director of the California Endowment or the CEO California Endowment, brought me in to become the first director of the children's mental health system. We had our own budget, and we had our own administration, which was quite an experience. I was able to learn from my colleagues who were more traditional mental health directors, but I was part of that peer group at the state level. Then as our children's system developed in San Diego, there was an opportunity because our mental health director for the adult system left, and I was asked to be the interim mental health director for adults, as well as the children's mental health director.

Ultimately, we merged with alcohol and drug services to form a behavioral health services department. We brought in a seasoned leader from New York, and we worked very well with her, Jennifer Schaeffer, for five years until she retired. After she retired, I was appointed Behavioral Health Director, and that goes back about six years. I've been in this position seven years. That's my management experience. Along the way I've had experiences on various boards and on various associations and leadership roles that helped shape who I am as a manager and who I am as a leader.

For example, I'm on the board of the Network of the Social Work Management Organization. I'm on the National Board, and I've been on that board for a while. I've had the opportunity to work with leaders in the social work field, whether it's in academia or in the field. We've striven to develop our leadership capacity among our social workers or aspiring social workers. That's been a great opportunity to give back. I've been involved in mentoring programs in San Diego, as well as with the county.

In your experience, what are the top three to five leadership attributes someone in the health and human services field should develop? Share an example of when you have used one or more of these attributes/skills in your work

I have four attributes that have served me well. I think I've done well in terms of the whole area of managing the skill set that's within being an adaptive leader, and I can see those at different levels.

Adaptivity. I went from one county system to another county with different politics, different structures, and different service providers. I went from a county-operated system to a contracted-operated system. The politics were different. Certainly, we had a very engaged and vocal advocacy community here in San Diego, and that was something I had to adapt to because I came from a system that was more administrative and bureaucratic. I worked with other departments and with the school, but it didn't have the kind of level of community engagement that I experienced in San Diego, so I was able to adapt to that. Also by adapting to different supervisors, I had an understanding of what's important to them, what their priorities are, and how to balance my priorities and accomplish what I think is imperative to move our system forward while working within the structure of a larger agency and with the priorities and the style of the director of the agency. At the top of the list is being adaptive: adapting to change, adapting to new policy initiatives, getting out in front of those initiatives, and helping staff understand the importance of those initiatives, whether it's our system of care here in San Diego or anywhere else in the country. We also received a federal grant, which helped everyone—from the line staff, to our providers in the community, to our advocates—to embrace the principles and values of the system of care. Then, the adoption of *Live Well San Diego*, helped our staff and our providers understand how they can live out or incorporate the values and principles and the goals of *Live Well San Diego* around promoting wellness, safety, and building thriving communities. It's been a journey of taking on challenges and seeing the importance of bringing people together toward achieving goals, whether they came from within or came from our larger system, working with our staff to embrace these changes.

Emotional intelligence. Closely related to making a move from one county to another is having emotional intelligence and understanding what your values and your passion are as well as knowing how to modulate those— in other words, compromising without forfeiting your core values. How does someone achieve goals that satisfy a diverse community, where you have different priorities and agendas? In San Diego County, for example, I worked with our justice system and education system, which have their own ideas about what's needed, and was able to bring my experience and expertise to find a way in which those needs mesh with the needs and priorities of these other organizations. Part of that is not "dying on my sword" but instead understanding that we can we can achieve our goals and our priorities, even by working in different contexts. Emotional intelligence has come in handy because I work with people to help them understand the difference between being a great advocate and being a great leader and knowing how to be strategic with the advocacy. Timing is everything in terms of getting what you want accomplished.

Recognizing your strengths and building a team with individuals who complement your strengths. This has served me well in that I don't expect to know everything. I don't believe my primary source of power and influence is expertise. I think it's there, but it's not my primary source. I think about how to motivate my team and how to encourage their growth toward the greater good by helping them with their own emotional intelligence and helping them to understand the difference between being an effective manager, an effective leader, and being an effective advocate. The sum is greater than the individual parts, and bringing all those parts together toward achieving a goal is most important.

Engaging and building partnerships with the community. This has always been more natural for me, perhaps because I'm from a large family and have a strong social network and extended family. Engaging and building partnerships with the community, understanding that people bring different experiences and different biases, and being a good listener are valuable leadership attributes. Even with my friends, whose political views might differ, it is important to create a space and be able to listen to each other and to say, "you know I'm not going to convince you that I'm right, you're not going to convince me, but let's agree to find some common ground." I think I've always taken that attitude when engaging with the community; ultimately it's all about serving our community, and without hearing their voices, without informing our services through their experiences, we're going to fall short. I actually relish the fact that our community members are so diverse, with different needs, and think it's important to understand their experiences. An example of that is working with our refugee community. I don't go to a refugee community meeting and say we can't meet your needs because you don't meet our target population. They don't know what that means. They have needs, and they have issues of trauma, isolation, and adjustment to a foreign land, and for them that brings behavioral health challenges to them. So how do I understand? How does that fit into our overall behavioral health system? How do I help mobilize resources that maybe aren't conventional resources but are other resources in the community? How do we meet the needs of a community? By being a catalyst, by being a leader? Engaging and building partnerships with the community are important.

A CASE STUDY BY ALFREDO AGUIRRE

I try to focus on looking at a need, a community, or a behavioral health challenge in a community and on how to address that need in an innovative way. One of the components of the Mental Health Services Act is something called *innovation funds*. Local communities, specifically counties, have to develop innovative solutions to address a challenge in the community that is not currently being met. This innovation approach relates to the design thinking concept. What can we learn from that strategy? Can that strategy be adapted, and can we learn from it and make some changes, such as midcourse corrections, to address the need more effectively? Ultimately, how do we incorporate that into our community? Do we take this strategy as a whole and find a way to sustain it? Or should we take elements of that strategy and incorporate them into our system of care? Innovation projects are data-driven: a significant number of adults and children go through our crisis system and then get referrals to our outpatient system, whether mental health or alcohol and drug services, a crisis stabilization unit in a hospital, or a mobile crisis team in the community. We have found that many of these people who experience a crisis, emergency, or hospital service don't connect to those outpatient resources for various reasons. There are a lot of data on why people don't engage in mental health care who have behavior health challenges; some are not aware of their illness, don't feel the services are meeting their cultural or linguistic needs, are afraid of medications, feel that there is a stigma to seeking care, have problems with transportation, or have other logistical barriers. So we know what the reasons are, but could we do something that's different from the usual response of, "here are your referrals, here are the numbers, and good luck"? What we came up with was a program called TeleMental Health, and this isn't brand new, the concept of using telecommunications to connect people remotely to providers. You're probably more familiar with telemedicine and telepsychiatry, which are often used in remote, rural communities that do not have access to a clinic. What's different about this is the idea of using TeleMental Health to connect people to outpatient care so that they begin to initiate and seek care remotely without having to go into a clinic. Particularly with younger people, who like their devices and social media, the data are showing that they tend to reject the more conventional and traditional modes of providing outpatient treatment. The idea is that we would offer this as a connection to their referral, and it would be completely voluntary. We would provide devices if they didn't have one, and we would ensure that their privacy and confidentiality are secure, but the idea is that this is arranged while they are at a crisis clinic. We would have a specialist or even a peer who would help them understand how to use the technology. It would be established at the site, and then there would be follow-up care by, in essence, a case manager, but it could be a peer, who would be helping them use the equipment once they leave the hospital. They would partner up at the site, and then they would follow up and connect with a mental health clinician, who would provide the services through telecommunications.

The idea originated from the academic world, and I learned about it from the School of Social Work at San Diego State University. It was originally proposed that TeleMental Health be used to connect people with social workers, mental health clinicians, and case managers, but the idea was centered on the question: Have we used it before and thus what would be innovative about it? We've used telepsychiatry, but we really haven't used it in the broadest sense with other professional disciplines like social workers, mental health clinicians, peer specialists, and case managers. It's use was been very limited not only in San Diego but also in a lot of other places; our research showed that it was not being used anywhere to connect people who left emergency crisis clinics.

The innovative part is using TeleMental Health on the front end for people who historically have not connected for all the reasons I mentioned. How do we get past that barrier? It's just one more tool. We do a lot of different kinds of outreach and engagement strategies. We have an in-home outreach team, for example. We have a lot of tools in our toolkit, but this is a new one, making that connection upfront while the clients are receiving emergency services before they are discharged back into the community.

The other key players were our councils because any innovative project has to be vetted with our community councils, which are essentially collaborative. For example, we have a Child Youth System of Care Council and a System of Peer Counsel, which were the two key councils with which we vetted this program. Each council is a collaborative consisting of providers, advocates, and people with lived experience, including consumers and family members, representatives from other serving agencies, and schools as partner agencies. Whether it's the justice system or child welfare, social services, public health, pediatric community, or people representing hospitals, it's all part of a community effort. Through those councils we vetted the idea, and they helped us to further develop the idea and gave their support.

Our role as the behavioral health authority was as the elite administrator. We were obviously the "thunder" that drove the initiative. We used our innovation funding, and we are the convening entity. Now it's going to be the procurement process and then ultimately the execution of this project. We have the main role here, but we had to take this proposal to the California Mental Health Service Act Oversight and Accountability Commission. We first took it to our County Board of Supervisors in San Diego. They have approved it, but it will not get funding unless the Oversight and Accountability Commission supports it. We were able to secure a unanimous Commission vote in supporting the use of our funds for this program.

What were the goals? Most important is the increased engagement with our outpatient system. Clearly an outpatient system is going to look different that involves TeleMental Health to reduce the use of emergency and crisis services and hospitalizations, so we're going to be tracking these outcomes. We want to take that subset of clients who have a history of rehospitalizations and multiple visits to crisis services without engaging in outpatient care and reduce the number who use crisis services, emergency department–based services, and psychiatric hospitalizations. That's of consequence to clients because when a client goes through a crisis or goes to a hospital, it can be pretty traumatic, and often the person is involuntarily detained. There's a lot of good treatment that happens, but it's not necessarily pleasant for the individual. In terms of the impact on the individual, it reduces the strain and potential for retraumatization of something they've been struggling with that has contributed to their behavioral health condition. It empowers individuals to manage their own care. We invite them to engage in a different way to get on top of their issue, to feel like they can take on this challenge and be the leader in their own care. They will have their own device and will be in an environment that's more comfortable to them and less threatening. For those with transportation issues or those who are employed and trying to keep their job, it's not always easy to leave their job and to drive to a clinic. By having a device, they could check in with their mental health provider during their lunch break. They can bring that device with them, whether it's to work, home, a library, or any secure place where they can speak. It just provides many more options.

In terms of the resolution, we won't know until we see our outcomes. We plan to learn from this. When we look at the role of the case manager, to help people feel comfortable with the technology and their specific activities, their approach, or their technique around helping individuals, what can we learn? Can we develop a workflow for the case managers? If they run into some issues, who can they go to for technical assistance to help them with their client? On the other end, we would expand the field of telecommunication, as it relates to treatment, by expanding the number of disciplines that will be engaged in this kind of tiered approach. We want to recognize where the field is going—that is, for people to be more comfortable ultimately with digital platforms and new ways of serving individuals—but also to recognize that we shouldn't just give up the personal or interpersonal touch and the connection people make when they see a provider face to face. If we can work with clients to seek in-person services, that's great. We want to facilitate that, but we may find that those clients are comfortable continuing to get care through TeleMental Health. It's going to be interesting to see if we can help people bridge that gap and feel comfortable coming into care or continuing to rely on TeleMental Health as their treatment approach.

Our next step is the procurement stage. We are developing a statement for people to respond to this resource. This is recent; we haven't even rolled it out yet. We were approved within the past month. I think the expectation is not only to build and develop the learning in your community but also to share it with the state. The State of California in particular is very interested in the use of technology and being aligned with where we are going in terms of the future of behavioral health and the different platforms that are going to be used to reach people, help them in their recovery, make a difference in their lives, and be of value to them.

CASE DISCUSSION POINTS

1. What is innovative about using technology for client care such as the TeleMental Health program?
2. What aspects of the case were data driven? How were data an important part of the innovative solution?

3. Discuss all of the stakeholders that were involved and continue to be involved in order for this program to come to fruition, In what way would a social architect best position this idea with regard to the funding sources?
4. Explore the feasibility, viability, and desirability of TeleMental Health (using the ideas of design thinking as outlined in the chapter).

3
—

Key Leadership Styles for Social Change and Innovation

> With realization of one's own potential and self-confidence in one's ability, one can build a better world.
>
> —DALAI LAMA

CHAPTER OBJECTIVES

1. Understand the background of key leadership styles that successfully apply for social change and innovation;
2. Explore leadership style applications in the health and human services field;
3. Learn how innovative leaders contribute to the public good; and
4. Gain insights on innovative leadership form a social architect (see Appendix to this chapter).

INTRODUCTION

The leadership literature covering theories and styles is comprehensive and extensive. Since the 1960s, when the idea of leadership became a hot topic of analysis, thousands of authors and institutions have spent a great deal of time and resources formulating and describing the most effective leadership theories, styles, models, and approaches. In the 1970s, there was an intentional effort to separate leadership studies from management and organization theory, looking more in depth to individuals' traits and skills and how they affect followers and populations. Generally, these studies had a tendency to espouse a specific school of thought or philosophy, including positivism, human relations, modernism, postmodernism, or others. As a result, the leadership field in terms of theory has mostly been diffused, and its vast information has become overwhelmingly bulky.

It is important to point out that this chapter is not a summary of leadership theories/styles—that, in our estimation would not be very useful to human services practitioners. Instead, we focus on the following five leadership theories/styles that have been historically utilized for social change and innovation: transformational leadership, authentic leadership, servant leadership, social entrepreneurship, and building public good. Each of these leadership styles will be discussed in detail, describing their background, key tenets, field application examples, and general implications. The goal for the reader is to grasp these key leadership styles, learn their impact, understand key elements, and think about how utilize these styles in practice.

We offer several notes to the reader. First, we are making a distinction between a leader (as in leadership styles) and a manager (as in managerial approaches or models discussed in Chapter 10). Although our definition of a leader as a social architect can be fulfilled by anyone, regardless of position in an organization, here we are making a distinction between the terms "leader" (as in a formal leader, like a CEO or director) and "manager." Thus, in this context, a formal leader is someone who holds one of the top positions in an organization who focuses on agency improvement and change, looks to the future, and seeks innovative ideas, versus a manager, who is typically more involved in the day-to-day administrative activities, including agency policy and procedures (Harley-McClaskey, 2017). However, keep in mind that in most small or mid-sized health and human services nonprofit organizations, the leader and manager are typically the same individual (Golensky, 2011). Thus, for some, the distinctions that we make may seem somewhat arbitrary. Second, we are making the implicit assumption that successful leaders (regardless of the particular style) have competence in emotional intelligence (EI), that is, "are intelligent about emotions" ; and, as Goleman and associates posit in their most recent writing on EI, the "primal job of leadership is emotional" (Goleman, Boyatzis, & McKee, 2013, p. xiii). Thus, we are working on the premise that the reader is aware of EI and, if not, would need to further investigate it.

TRANSFORMATIONAL LEADERSHIP STYLE

Great leaders have the ability to transform organizations and systems. In short, transformational leadership is the process by which people, and potentially cultural norms and even entire systems, are transformed. Although first described by Downton (1973), transformational leadership became popular in the early 1980s. Mainly, it focuses on the charismatic and personal traits of individual leaders and how they interact with their followers. James MacGregor Burns is credited for developing it in a more empirical form. He defined transformational leadership as "the process whereby a person engages with others and creates a connection that raises the level of motivation and morality in both the leader and the follower" (Northouse, 2016, p. 162). It involves a soul-searching effort on the leader's part, focusing on how individuals and groups can evolve by changing their values, belief systems, ethics, and cultural norms.

It is important to point out the difference between transformational and transactional leadership. Transactional leadership focuses on the tangible exchanges between leaders and followers. Basically, the leader decides and communicates what needs to be done and what actions need to be taken to achieve the desired vision, for example, launching a new social media campaign to reduce police brutality or collaborating with key constitutes/advocacy groups to pass new laws. These transactions or mechanisms are necessary to pursue social change, but the relationship between leaders and followers is short-lived and most of the time yields limited results. On the other hand, the transformational leader searches to connect with the follower at an emotional, value-driven level—they are bound together working to achieve a profound common purpose.

A transformational leader's guidance and decision-making are associated with followers having a more positive attitude toward the leader-follower relationship and the workload (Aarons, 2006). Transformational leaders evaluate themselves first and then their followers by looking at their motivations, perceived needs, and interactions with other groups in society. They subscribe to a democratic process as opposed to an authoritative environment (Mary, 2005). Thus, the quality of interaction between the leader and their followers is critical to attaining goals. This relationship is symbiotic in nature—one does not exist without the other, where both the leader and the follower motivate and inspire each other to reach their desired vision.

Transformational Leadership Studies and Application

In recent decades, transformational leadership studies and applications have concentrated in three main areas: the leader's individual traits and characteristics, leader relationships in teams and organizations, and impact in community and systems. All these studies emphasize the nature of the relationship between leaders and followers. Individuals who become effective transformational leaders truly connect with their followers in a deep manner, exploring each other's intrinsic motivations. Inspiration and empowerment become key ingredients to support this fundamental personal evolution for both the leader and follower.

The research on individual attributes within transformational leadership emphasizes the need to better understand a leader's charismatic attributes. For example, Schilling (2010) investigated the leadership attributes of six well-known global leaders: Mahatma Gandhi, Martin Luther King, Jr., Nelson Mandela, Mikhail Gorbachev, John F. Kennedy, and Lech Walesa. These charismatic leaders were instrumental in obtaining the commitment of their followers to generate successful social changes. They showed six common leadership attributes: inspirational motivation, communication skills, EI, empathy, modeling the way, and trustworthiness.

When exploring leaders and their influences within groups or organizations, Jung and Sosik (2006) examined the relationship between five personal attributes of leaders (self-monitoring, self-actualization, motive to attain social power, self-enhancement, and openness to change) and four work performance outcomes from followers (extra effort, self-actualization, collectivistic work motivation, and organizational citizenship behavior). Results indicated that people who exhibit these high charismatic leadership attributes were able to increase the performance outcomes from their followers. Moreover, followers reported that their charismatic leader showed and maintained high levels of self-monitoring, self-actualization, motivation to attain social power and self-enhancement values than the non-charismatic leaders.

One of the key lessons from teams and groups that spouse transformational leadership is measuring the charismatic leaders' ability to bring out the best in themselves and in their followers. Kovjanic, Schuh, and Jonas's (2013) research study integrated the importance of self-determination and work engagement as part of the follower's basic psychological needs. Work engagement is best brought out by the positive relationship between leader and follower. Additionally, studies found that this positive relationship will result in greater knowledge sharing, team creativity (Cai, Jia, You, Zhang & Chen, 2013; Mittal & Dhar, 2015), team commitment to mission follower identification with supervisors (Yang, Wu, Chang, & Chien, 2011), utilization of thinking and action learning strategies (Trautmann, Maher, & Motley, 2007), and better outcome measurement experiences (Fisher, 2005).

As human services organizations continue to evolve and promote internal and external change, they can greatly benefit from transformational leadership approaches. For example, trauma-informed organizational interventions promote inspiration, optimism, encouragement, honesty, motivation, respect, team orientation, and effective communication. These interventions are very similar to the qualities of transformational leadership. Middleton, Harvey, and Esaki

(2015) found that "[g]iven the emphasis transformational leadership places on the importance of an organization's mission and outcomes, as well as embedded principles of participatory leadership, empowerment, and pro-action, this style of leadership may be particularly useful in human services organizations, as such organizations have strong service- and community-oriented missions" (p. 162). Furthermore, a study with social workers in Sweden strongly suggests that employees' knowledge of their assignments and level of commitment toward both their supervisors and the organization were greater when transformational leadership was permeated throughout the workplace (Tafvelin, Hyvönen, & Westerberg, 2014). As organizations continue to improve their services using transformational leadership and focusing on employees' commitment and role clarity can bring their goals to fruition.

Although understanding transformational leadership at the micro and mezzo levels is important, the focus for human services practitioners should also be in its impact in macro practice. Denning (2012) emphasizes that most leadership writing today advises readers on how to prosper *within* the system or even flourish *despite* the system. He recommends that what is missing is focusing on *transforming* the system. Denning adds, "Leadership is not merely about success. Abraham Lincoln and Martin Luther King were great leaders, not because they were successful *within* their different worlds, or even because they were successful *despite* the constraints of their worlds. They were great leaders because they *transformed* their worlds" (p. 47). Moreover, the transformational leader deeply identifies with democratic values and the role of citizens to formulate shared goals (Denhardt & Campbell, 2006). Although building relationships is costly, time-consuming, and difficult to achieve in both organizations and communities (Currie & Lockett, 2007), the public good and other community outcomes are greatly dependent on the quality of interaction between leaders and followers.

Much evidence suggests a strong alignment between human services' outcomes and transformational leadership. Both are about improving the quality of life for all. Transforming organizations and systems requires a strong relationship between leaders and followers. Trust, perseverance, commitment, empathy, and desire to achieve social change are key elements to embrace positive transformation. Leaders in human services fields can continue building these skills by being close to vulnerable populations, listening to their experiences, seeking a deeper understanding of their needs, and improving relationships.

AUTHENTIC LEADERSHIP STYLE

Although there is no agreement as to a single definition for authentic leadership, many authors compliment this style because of its transparency and authenticity—what you see is what you get. People who are authentic leaders are genuine, open, and sincere. They are highly aware of their self-knowledge, are able to self-regulate, have positive self-concepts, and operate within multiple perspectives, including intrapersonal, interpersonal, and developmental aspects (Northouse, 2016). These leaders utilize constant nurturing of relationships, based on self-reflection and a life-learning approach, emphasizing continuing self-development from life events and interactions with others. Much as transformational leadership, authentic leaders have a reciprocal process with their followers. According to Vlachoutsicos (2012), authenticity can be described as an ongoing open message that leaders share with their followers. This open messaging uses language, behaviors, and attitudes to communicate constant shaping and evolving of self and others. Authentic leaders are on a quest to build and advance their "true self."

Many scholars support the notion that leaders can achieve this personal development in multiple dimensions. For example, Ladkin and Taylor (2010) argued that it is through the embodiment of a true self that leaders are perceived by others as authentic. This evolution can be achieved by a leader's self-exposure, ability to relate to others, and leadership decision-making. Rosh and Offermann (2013) highlight that this personal journey requires an open self-disclosed plan, which should include building a foundation of self-knowledge, considering relevance to desired goals, keeping revelations genuine, understanding organizational culture, and avoiding very personal disclosures. Furthermore, ongoing support and regular coaching for leaders can be central aspects of personal improvement and relationship building with followers and others (Fusco, O'Riordan, & Palmer, 2015).

Authentic Leadership Studies and Application

George (2007) described authentic leaders as people who have the ability to connect purpose with passion, values with behavior, relationships with connectedness, self-discipline with consistency, and heart with compassion. Key elements of authentic leadership include self-awareness, moral perspective, balanced processing, and relational transparency. Because authentic leaders are shaped and greatly influenced by life events and the desire to improve people's lives, followers see them with greater authenticity. Authentic leaders are easy to recognize, and followers tend to have a greater and longer attachment to their visions and causes.

The impact of authentic leadership has been studied in multiple health and human services disciplines. For example, when looking at emerging leaders working with disabled individuals, Brady, Fong, Waninger, and Eidelman

(2009) used an authentic leadership framework to learn that constituents highly value the leader's key personal attributes such as their values, communication skills, and conflict resolution abilities. Furthermore, in the medical field, nurses have higher job satisfaction and improve work engagement when doctors and administrators show genuine care for their staff and patients (Wong, Laschinger, & Cummings, 2010). The perception of fairness also becomes an essential characteristic of the relationship between the authentic leader and his or her followers. In organizational settings, when followers feel their leaders make fair decisions, they tend to stay longer and be more committed to the organization's mission (Kiersch & Byrne, 2015).

Authentic leadership can also be very effective within organizations. For instance, Lyubovnikova, Legood, Turner, and Mamakouka (2015) found that teams perform at a higher level when they adopt a self-regulatory process of reflexivity. As regular reflection becomes the team norm, the leader can help to shape members' behavior more positively and improve overall performance. Other studies have focused on the impact of authentic leadership on employees' well-being. Authentic leadership has a role in (1) reducing attachment insecurity in followers, lessening levels of perceived stress and stress symptoms (Rahimnia & Sharifirad, 2015); (2) increasing the positive effects of employees' organizational citizenship behaviors such as moral perspective and relational transparency (Valsania, Moriano, Alonso, & Cantisano, 2012); and (3) promoting psychological ownership in followers (i.e., positive attachment to the organization) and relational transparency (Alok, 2014).

SERVANT LEADERSHIP STYLE

Servant leadership was first introduced by Robert Greenleaf in the 1970s. Greenleaf explained that individuals who espouse servant leadership have a strong ethical compass, a desire to improve their society at large, and a focus on developing their followers' knowledge and skills. Servant leaders embody several characteristics, such as good listening skills, empathic responses, healing attitudes, awareness of self and others, ability to be persuasive, ability to conceptualize ideas clearly, ability to demonstrate foresight, stewardship, and a commitment to the growth of people and building community (Northouse, 2016). In a very altruistic fashion, they perceive that the needs of the followers must come first, and these needs should dictate the leader's actions. Moreover, servant leaders build and monitor their self-efficacy by their followers' response and progress. By serving others, servant leaders build and shape their self-identity and purpose. Therefore, public service motivation is an important element in servant leadership, and it is used to measure the followers' commitment and engagement (Schwarz, Newman, Cooper, & Eva, 2016).

The connection between servant leadership attributes and the leader's values in organizations and communities is strong. Values openly become part of the leader's code of ethics, conduct, and decision-making styles. For example, Mertel and Brill (2015) demonstrated that health care leaders could gain insights they needed to change their habits and improve working with others. They "sought out to explain and demonstrate how the key to helping leaders reframe how they think about the 'soft, emotional stuff' is by having them focus on values—specifically, focusing on values in the context of serving their employees" (p. 234). Moreover, Winston and Fields (2015) developed a measurement to gauge essential behaviors that servant leaders should demonstrate when working with others. The measurement revealed that the leader's values are perceived as one of the most critical attributes for followers' response and to obtain effective leadership outcomes.

Servant Leadership Studies and Application

Similarly to transformational and authentic leadership, servant leaders pay attention to the follower's perceptions, provide feedback regarding their attributes, and aim to build healthy relationships. Servant leader practitioners tend to refine their relational skills toward a more conducive affinity with their followers. The goal for the leader is to develop a constant integration of his or her cognition (thoughts), behaviors, and expectations associated with serving others. The focal point for the leader is the follower and how the follower's conditions can be improved.

Servant leadership goes hand in hand with the helping professions. For example, Cullen (2013) studied social workers while performing palliative care with older adult patients. The study results indicate that social workers exercise their leadership skills to influence patients' decision-making with the goal of achieving greater results during treatment. Garber, Madigan, Click, and Fitzpatrick (2009) learned that attitudes and actions toward collaboration among nurses, residents, and physicians were significantly higher and more positive when servant leadership characteristics were implemented among colleagues and work groups. Similarly, in the public health field, where much the emphasis is placed on generating outcome-based results, servant leadership is well-established and applied. The leading areas across top public health institutes include leaders that emphasize community and organizational responsiveness, develop an ability to inspire others, focus on results, have high social intellect (i.e., EI), be authentic, and demonstrate composure and balance (Grimm, Watanabe-Galloway, Britigan, & Shumaker, 2015).

It is clear that the servant leaders' impact on their followers can rise above hierarchical power and positions within organizations. Sousa and Dierendonck (2015) found that this strong bond is due to two important leadership characteristics: moral virtue and humility. Their study found that leaders who are perceived with lower levels of moral virtue and humility do not connect closely with people around them. Ideally, Mayer, Bardes, and Piccolo (2008) argue, successful leaders create innovative mechanisms to improve job satisfaction and commitment by building organizational justice. These workplaces invite dialogue, create problem-solving apparatuses, and avoid retaliation, making the follower and/or employees feel they are being heard and their needs are being addressed properly. More important, the employees' needs come first, making them the central focus of an unprejudiced and just organization.

The positive impact of servant leadership has also been measured with other professions and internationally. When trying to understand how servant leadership affects employee attitudes and behaviors, Ozyilmaz and Cizek (2015) concluded that servant leadership is positively related to organizational citizenship behavior, job satisfaction, and healthy psychological climate. Additionally, Thumma and Beene (2015) explored servant leadership attributes in the judicial system. They learned that the more successful judges tend to exhibit similar servant leadership attributes as previously mentioned. When comparing servant leadership between Ghana and the United States, one study found that Ghanaians experienced servant leadership behaviors significantly less than Americans. However, when there was a servant leadership situation, then the leader's vision had a significantly stronger relationship with leader effectiveness from Ghanaians compared with Americans. Both Ghanaians and Americans related service and humility with leader effectiveness (Hale & Fields, 2007).

SOCIAL ENTREPRENEURSHIP

Health and human services leaders have been working to expand their vision and mission to achieve social change by increasing visibility and resources. One effective leadership model that has largely evolved in the past decades is social entrepreneurship. The definition of social entrepreneurship is putting innovative ideas in motion to promote and achieve social change. Alvord, Brown, and Letts (2004) argue that social entrepreneurship leads to significant changes in the social, political, and economic contexts for poor and marginalized groups. Furthermore, it can (1) generate propositions about core innovations, leadership, and organizations to produce societal transformation; and (2) explain the social value in organizational performance of nonprofit social organizations. In a favorable context, social entrepreneurship provides more significant support of social values having a positive effect on organizational performance (Felicio, Martins, Goncalves, & da Conceicao Goncalvez, 2013).

As change agents, we are also interested in understanding how innovative leaders affect community entrepreneurship efforts. Community entrepreneurship strives to improve our understanding about how community-based leaders practice social change. Selsky and Smith (1994) defined community entrepreneurship: "[A]s a method of inquiry, community entrepreneurship may help to provide critical knowledge by examining active engagements with complex social systems. As a method of intervention, community entrepreneurship may provide better guidance to change agents attempting to mobilize commitments, build systems of events, and develop collective capacities for action in issue domains" (pp. 294–295). One great example of social and community entrepreneurship is Goodwill Industries International Inc. This giant nonprofit organization wanted to implement social innovation by creating a new sustainable funding stream to help disabled individuals. Goodwill receives tens of thousands of donated goods annually from households and/or businesses and then sells them at discounted prices in their own thrift stores. Millions of dollars in revenue are invested to support the advancement of people with mental and physical disabilities.

Social Entrepreneurship Studies and Application

Nandan and Scott (2013) explain the value and application of social entrepreneurship training and development in human services administration. It is a matter of organizational self-preservation, focusing on management goals and objectives, including product development, appropriate and timely messaging and marketing, understanding the competition, offering excellent customer service and effective programming, and considering revenue and expenses. These skills can create innovative solutions to emergent problems and understand and create new markets. Future leaders, Birchall and Love (2013) argue, must be social entrepreneurs who will know how to prepare, integrate, recognize, monitor quality, and empower others.

Community leaders implement social entrepreneurship strategies to bring sustainability, autonomy, and other resources to their organizations and causes. Moreover, Savaya, Packer, Stange, and Namir (2008) argue that social entrepreneurship must become a mandatory capacity building exercise for workers in public human services agencies. When social entrepreneurship is institutionalized (becoming an ongoing and regular practice in the organization), the role of the leader is to advocate for these practices to continue.

Because of its powerful potential to raise funds and resources to sustain organizations, social entrepreneurship has been introduced to other disciplines and sectors. For example, venture philanthropy and social entrepreneurship are being used in the public sector, including community redevelopment efforts. Van Slyke and Newman (2006) studied how public-private partnerships have created sustainable economic transformation within disadvantaged inner-city areas. When analyzing the redevelopment of the East Lake area in Atlanta, they learned that the leader applied social entrepreneurship featuring four key skills: "(1) identifying and renovating the community's prized asset, (2) innovatively leveraging his own personal networks for social gain, (3) developing partnerships that were financially, socially, and symbolically important, and (4) listening, demonstrating sensitivity, and holding himself accountable to the very constituencies he was attempting to serve" (p. 363).

Social entrepreneurship characteristics have also been studied in different academic fields. In the area of organizational psychology, for example, key leadership attributes include the personality traits of entrepreneurs, the psychopathology of entrepreneurs (i.e., toxic leaders), entrepreneurial thinking, entrepreneurship education, and international entrepreneurship (Hisrich, Langan-Fox, & Grant 2007). Additionally, when analyzing leading social entrepreneurs working in the mental health field, Kidd et al. (2015) found that mental health executives and managers who exhibited social entrepreneurship characteristics and skills had more positive outcomes with employees and clients. Finally, gender in social entrepreneurship seems to be connected with identity. For female entrepreneurs, leadership and entrepreneurship are part of their identity in the workplace (Lewis, 2015).

BUILDING PUBLIC GOOD

The basic definition of a public good is a good or service that is both nonrivalrous and nonexclusive, and it can be used by every individual in society. In theory, the use of the public good or service by one individual does not reduce its availability to others. Examples include access to K–12 education and to public recreation areas, such as parks, rivers, oceans, and mountains, as well as roads, freeways, street lights, and other vital infrastructure goods. These goods and services are usually financed by taxpayers and/or private/government projects, without a direct cost to the consumer. All individuals have the same right to use public goods, and sharing is considered a common benefit with the goal to improve living standards for all. The key dual role of the leader is to build new common goods and improve existing ones.

Even though public goods are outstanding and most often meet the public needs for all community members, they inheritably have several problems. First, public goods are used daily, and their overuse can affect individuals in multiple ways. For example, infrastructure goods like streets and bridges deteriorate with time, forcing the government to maintain them regularly. This ongoing care can be expensive and overwhelming. Second, the "free-rider" problem occurs when some individuals use public goods without providing any contribution. Case in point: most people pay taxes and may access the freeways and roads, while others do not pay taxes but still use this public good. Third, not all regions in our US society have the same resources; therefore, differences are notorious and in many cases generate social injustices. Take, for example, public education. Theoretically, all schools should have similar resources and produce the same quality of education for all students. However, for the most part it is widely accepted that students attending inner-city and rural schools do not receive the same resources or perhaps quality of education as schools located in more privileged urban and suburban areas, thus contributing to an achievement gap that is inescapable and pervasive.

Building Public Good Studies and Application

Building public good leadership focuses on strengthening the community. When looking at the management of common goods, Lorenzi (2004) explains that prosocial behavior enhances community development. He defines prosocial leadership as a positive mechanism to influence and engage constructive goals to service all. Schweigert (2007) argues that community building and development throughout public goods requires five elements: community leadership, community interaction, focus on qualities of social settings and processes, addressing the needs that require and facilitate authoritative action, and acquiring practical wisdom as a core quality required of community leaders. As with the other four leadership models, building public good requires the leader to maintain a close connection with the followers.

The preferences for social architects when making important decisions depend not only on the feedback group members provide but also on the type of dilemma they are facing. More important, when the community or membership feedback to the leader is ambiguous, Van Dijk, Wilke, and Wit (2003) argue that leaders will have to base their decisions on personal gains or losses, explaining: "We suggest that group members are especially likely to evaluate their decisions as personal losses (in the public good dilemma), or as personal gains (in the common resource dilemma), after feedback that their group has failed" (p. 175). Additionally, leaders must also be concerned with how they will be perceived by the community. McAllan and MacRae (2010) advocate to measure social services leaders on the impact their decisions have on the individual leadership practice, the participants' teams, and the provision of services through attempting to evidence observable performance outcomes, concluding that "the findings support that leadership development has to take place on the job; people learn to lead by leading" (p. 68).

Building public good can also be achieved by philanthropy and research. Businesses involvement in social causes is very strong in the United States. There is an increase of successful businessmen and women engaging in philanthropy to help ameliorate social problems. Businesses actively participate in corporate social responsibility to create, implement, sustain, and include socially responsible behaviors within business settings. Moreover, Christensen, Mackey, and Whetten (2014) studied corporate social responsibility firms, finding that their leaders' characteristics, traits, values, and attitudes positively relate to other corporate colleagues enacting social responsibility behaviors in the workplace. In other words, leaders make a significant difference when looking for broader corporate support and legitimacy.

After interviewing prominent philanthropists, Goldman (2016) learned that corporate leaders like to invest for impact and look for measureable results that have the potential to shape existing business systems around social goods. Ongoing research to have a better understanding of forces around big data (see Larson, 2013) and complex systems can build trust among the public and business communities. For example, Larson (2013) argues that using big data for research to serve the public good provides a great potential for useful knowledge to achieve the "triple aim" in health care: provide better care for individuals, provide better care for all, and save more dollars.

The advancement of public goods and social change requires a great deal of ethical compass, collaboration, and connectedness. The leaders must establish a firm moral compass for themselves and those around them. Unfortunately, in highly bureaucratic organizations and with tenured employees, ethical climate sometimes tends to worsen over time. The internal and external perception of these bureaucratic organizations is that ethical behavior declines where workers are no longer held to the same high ethical standard. Raile (2013) strongly suggests that ethics training, interaction with ethics officials, and perceived knowledge about ethics topics consistently be used horizontally or vertically in the workplace.

Finally, social change organizations engage in processes of collaborative governance. Ospina and Foldy (2010) identified five leadership practices to facilitate collaboration and connectedness: prompting cognitive shifts, naming and shaping identity, engaging in dialogue about difference, creating equitable governance mechanisms, and weaving multiple worlds together through interpersonal relationships. The goal is to reach the highest level of connectedness among multiple people and organizations, pulling knowledge and resources to build and improve public goods and services. Table 3.1 summarizes the various

Table 3.1 LEADERSHIP STYLES FOR SOCIAL CHANGE AND INNOVATION CHIEF DESCRIPTORS

Descriptor/ Leadership Style	Transformational Leadership	Authentic Leadership	Servant Leadership	Social Entrepreneurship	Building Public Good
Purpose	Transformation	Sincerity	Service	Accomplishment	Improvement
Definition	Revolution	Relationship	Value-driven	Capitalistic	Benefit all
Strengths	Development	Trustworthy	Self-awareness	Sustainable	Access/usage
Limitations	Overwhelming	Practicality	Paradoxical	Market status	Maintenance
Application	Social change	Positive impact	Group building	Innovation	Social gain

leadership models according to purpose, definition, strengths, limitations, and application.

A last thought about leadership and a word of caution. In some rare instances, there are leaders in health and human services and in other sectors who are toxic or destructive to both the organization and their followers. Although this is beyond the scope of this chapter, the reader is referred to Lipman-Blumen (2005) for further information.

In conclusion, this chapter covered several key leadership theories and styles that in our estimation represent the most often utilized approaches to leadership in the health and human services fields. These leadership styles overlap in many respects, and the most salient characteristics have to do with innovative leaders whose primary mission is to seek to improve the lives of those they serve while engaging their team members in ways that promote integrity, justice, and advocacy toward a shared vision of impact for the greater good. Social architects identify with one or more of these leadership styles as they begin to formulate and design their innovations. Furthermore, once social architects are ready to execute their innovations, they can apply one or more of the managerial approaches described in Chapter 10.

CHAPTER DISCUSSION QUESTIONS

1. What are the strengths and limitations of each of the leadership models presented in this chapter? Provide a rationale for your answers.
2. How would you put your selected leadership style into practice?
3. Utilizing what you have learned in this chapter about the various types of leadership models, what type of leadership style or styles does the leader highlighted in this chapter's Leadership Profile (in the Appendix) have? Be prepared to explain how and why that leader fits that leadership style or styles.
4. Read the case located in the Appendix to this chapter. Note any innovative ideas and practices that you can connect to the contents of the chapter and/or the overall book.

REFERENCES

Aarons, G. A. (2006). Transformational and transactional leadership: Association with attitudes toward evidence-based practice. *Psychiatric Services, 57*(8), 1162–1169.

Alok, K. (2014). Authentic leadership and psychological ownership: Investigation of interrelations. *Leadership & Organization Development Journal, 35*(4), 266–285.

Alvord, S. H., Brown, L. D., & Letts, C. W. (2004). Social entrepreneurship and societal transformation: An exploratory study. *Journal of Applied Behavioral Science, 40*(3), 260–282.

Birchall, A., & Love, C. (2013, February 20). What social entrepreneurs can teach your company's future leaders. *Harvard Business Review*. Retrieved from https://hbr.org/2013/02/what-social-entrepreneurs-can

Brady, L. T., Fong, L., Waninger, K. N., & Eidelman, S. (2009). Perspectives on leadership in organizations providing services to people with disabilities: An exploratory study. *Intellectual and Developmental Disabilities, 47*(5), 358–372.

Cai, Y., Jia, L., You, S., Zhang, Y., & Chen, Y. (2013). The influence of differentiated transformational leadership on knowledge sharing and team creativity: A social network explanation. *Acta Psychologica Sinica, 45*(5), 585–598.

Christensen, L. J., Mackey, A., & Whetten, D. (2014). Taking responsibility for corporate social responsibility: The role of leaders in creating, implementing, sustaining, or avoiding socially responsible firm behaviors. *Academy of Management Perspectives, 28*(2), 164–178.

Cullen, A. (2013). "Leaders in our own lives": Suggested indications for social work leadership from a study of social work practice in a palliative care setting. *British Journal of Social Work, 43*(8), 1527–1544.

Currie, G., & Lockett, A. (2007). A critique of transformational leadership: Moral, professional and contingent dimensions of leadership within public services organizations. *Human Relations, 60*(2), 341–370.

Denhardt, J. V., & Campbell, K. B. (2006). The role of democratic values in transformational leadership. *Administration & Society, 38*(5), 556–572.

Denning, S. (2012, July 27). The key missing ingredient in leadership today. *Harvard Business Review*. Retrieved from http://www.forbes.com/sites/stevedenning/2012/07/27/the-key-missing-ingredient-in-leadership-today/#117388a32c9c

Downton, J. V. (1973). *Rebel leadership: Commitment and charisma in a revolutionary process*. New York, NY: Free Press.

Felício, J. A., Martins Gonçalves, H., & da Conceição Gonçalves, V. (2013). Social value and organizational performance in non-profit social organizations: Social entrepreneurship, leadership, and socioeconomic context effects. *Journal of Business Research, 66*(10), 2139–2146.

Fisher, E. A. (2005). Facing the challenges of outcomes measurement: The role of transformational leadership. *Administration in Social Work, 29*(4), 35–49.

Fusco, T., O'Riordan, S., & Palmer, S. (2015). Authentic leaders are . . . conscious, competent, confident, and congruent: A grounded theory of group coaching and authentic leadership development. *International Coaching Psychology Review, 10*(2), 131–148.

Garber, J. S., Madigan, E. A., Click, E. R., & Fitzpatrick, J. J. (2009). Attitudes towards collaboration and servant leadership among nurses, physicians and residents. *Journal of Interprofessional Care, 23*(4), 331–340.

George, B. (2007). *True north: Discover youth authentic leadership*. San Francisco, CA: Jossey-Bass.

Goldman, P. (2016, February 29). How a new generation of business leaders views philanthropy. *Harvard Business Review*. Retrieved from https://hbr.org/2016/02/how-a-new-generation-of-business-leaders-views-philanthropy

Goleman, D., Boyatzis, R., & McKee, A. (2013). *Primal leadership: Unleashing the power of emotional intelligence*. Boston, MA: Harvard Business School Publishing.

Golensky, M. (2011). *Strategic leadership and management in nonprofit organizations: Theory and practice*. Chicago, IL: Lyceum Books, Inc.

Grimm, B. L., Watanabe-Galloway, S., Britigan, D. H., & Schumaker, A. M. (2015). A qualitative analysis to determine the domains and skills necessary to lead in public health. *Journal of Leadership Studies, 8*(4), 19–26.

Hale, J. R., & Fields, D. L. (2007). Exploring servant leadership across cultures: A study of followers in Ghana and the US. *Leadership, 3*(4), 397–417.

Harley-McClaskey, D. (2017). *Developing human service leaders*. Thousand Oaks, CA: Sage.

Hisrich, R., Langan-Fox, J., & Grant, S. (2007). Entrepreneurship research and practice: A call to action for psychology. *American Psychologist, 62*(6), 575–589.

Jung, D., & Sosik, J. J. (2006). Who are the spellbinders? Identifying personal attributes of charismatic leaders. *Journal of Leadership & Organizational Studies, 12*(4), 12–26.

Kidd, S. A., Kerman, N., Cole, D., Madan, A., Muskat, E., Raja, S., Rallabandi, S., & McKenzie, K. (2015). Social entrepreneurship and mental health intervention: A literature review and scan of expert perspectives. *International Journal of Mental Health and Addiction, 13*(6), 776–787.

Kiersch, C. E., & Byrne, Z. S. (2015). Is being authentic being fair? Multilevel examination of authentic leadership, justice, and employee outcomes. *Journal of Leadership & Organizational Studies, 22*(3), 292–303.

Kovjanic, S., Schuh, S. C., & Jonas, K. (2013). Transformational leadership and performance: An experimental investigation of the mediating effects of basic needs satisfaction and work engagement. *Journal of Occupational and Organizational Psychology, 86*(4), 543–555.

Ladkin, D., & Taylor, S. S. (2010). Enacting the "true self": Towards a theory of embodied authentic leadership. *Leadership Quarterly, 21*(1), 64–74.

Larson, E. B. (2013). Building trust in the power of "big data" research to serve the public good. *JAMA: Journal of the American Medical Association, 309*(23), 2443–2444.

Lewis, K. V. (2015). Enacting entrepreneurship and leadership: A longitudinal exploration of gendered identity work. *Journal of Small Business Management, 53*(3), 662–682.

Lipman-Blumen, J. (2005). *The allure of toxic leaders: Why we follow the destructive bosses and corrupt politicians and how we can survive them*. New York, NY: Oxford University Press.

Lorenzi, P. (2004). Managing for the common good: Prosocial leadership. *Organizational Dynamics, 33*(3), 282–291.

Lyubovnikova, J., Legood, A., Turner, N., & Mamakouka, A. (2015). How authentic leadership influences team performance: The mediating role of team reflexivity. *Journal of Business Ethics, 141*(1), 59–70.

Mary, N. L. (2005). Transformational leadership in human service organizations. *Administration in Social Work, 29*(2), 105–118.

Mayer, D. M., Bardes, M., & Piccolo, R. F. (2008). Do servant-leaders help satisfy follower needs? An organizational justice perspective. *European Journal of Work and Organizational Psychology, 17*(2), 180–197.

McAllan, W., & MacRae, R. (2010). Learning to lead: Evaluation of a leadership development programme in a local authority social work service. *Social Work and Social Sciences Review, 14*(2), 55–72.

Mertel, T., & Brill, C. (2015). What every leader ought to know about becoming a servant leader. *Industrial and Commercial Training, 47*(5), 228–235.

Middleton, J., Harvey, S., & Esaki, N. (2015). Transformational leadership and organizational change: How do leaders approach trauma-informed organizational change . . . twice? *Families in Society, 96*(3), 155–163.

Mittal, S., & Dhar, R. L. (2015). Transformational leadership and employee creativity: Mediating role of creative self-efficacy and moderating role of knowledge sharing. *Management Decision, 53*(5), 894–910.

Nandan, M., & Scott, P. A. (2013). Social entrepreneurship and social work: The need for a transdisciplinary educational model. *Administration in Social Work, 37*(3), 257–271.

Northouse, P. G. (2016). *Leadership: Theory and practice.* Thousand Oaks, CA: Sage.

Ospina, S., & Foldy, E. (2010). Building bridges from the margins: The work of leadership in social change organizations. *The Leadership Quarterly, 21*(2), 292–307.

Ozyilmaz, A., & Cicek, S. S. (2015). How does servant leadership affect employee attitudes, behaviors, and psychological climates in a for-profit organizational context? *Journal of Management and Organization, 21*(3), 263–290.

Rahimnia, F., & Sharifirad, M. S. (2015). Authentic leadership and employee well-being: The mediating role of attachment insecurity. *Journal of Business Ethics, 132*(2), 363–377.

Raile, E. D. (2013). Building ethical capital: Perceptions of ethical climate in the public sector. *Public Administration Review, 73*(2), 253–262.

Rosh, L., & Offerman, L. (2013, October). Be yourself, but carefully. *Harvard Business Review.* Retrieved from https://hbr.org/2013/10/be-yourself-but-carefully

Savaya, R., Packer, P., Stange, D., & Namir, O. (2008). Social entrepreneurship: Capacity building among workers in public human service agencies. *Administration in Social Work, 32*(4), 65–86.

Schilling, L. M. (2010). *A historical analysis of the relationship between charisma and the making of great leaders* (Order No. AAI3397897). Available from PsycINFO. (817617140; 2010-99190-464).

Schwarz, G., Newman, A., Cooper, B., & Eva, N. (2016). Servant leadership and follower job performance: The mediating effect of public service motivation. *Public Administration, 94*(4), 1025–1041.

Schweigert, F. J. (2007). Learning to lead: Strengthening the practice of community leadership. *Leadership, 3*(3), 325–342.

Selsky, J. W., & Smith, A. E. (1994). Community entrepreneurship: A framework for social change leadership. *Leadership Quarterly, 5*(3–4), 277–296.

Sousa, M., & Dierendonck, D. (2015). Servant leadership and the effect of the interaction between humility, action, and hierarchical power on follower engagement. *Journal of Business Ethics, 141*(1), 13–25.

Tafvelin, S., Hyvönen, U., & Westerberg, K. (2014). Transformational leadership in the social work context: The importance of leader continuity and co-worker support. *British Journal of Social Work, 44*(4), 886–904.

Thumma, S. A., & Beene, S. (2015). The judge as servant-leader. *Judges' Journal, 54*(1), 9–13.

Trautmann, K., Maher, J. K., & Motley, D. G. (2007). Learning strategies as predictors of transformational leadership: The case of nonprofit managers. *Leadership & Organization Development Journal, 28*(3), 269–287.

Valsania, S. E., Moriano León, J. A., Alonso, F. M., & Cantisano, G. T. (2012). Authentic leadership and its effect on employees' organizational citizenship behaviours. *Psicothema, 24*(4), 561–566.

Van Dijk, E., Wilke, H., & Wit, A. (2003). Preferences for leadership in social dilemmas: Public good dilemmas versus common resource dilemmas. *Journal of Experimental Social Psychology, 39*(2), 170–176.

Van Slyke, D. M., & Newman, H. K. (2006). Venture philanthropy and social entrepreneurship in community redevelopment. *Nonprofit Management and Leadership, 16*(3), 345–368.

Vlachoutsicos, C. (2012, December 7). What being an "authentic leader" really means. *Harvard Business Review.* Retrieved from https://hbr.org/2012/12/what-being-an-authentic-leader-really-means

Winston, B., & Fields, D. (2015). Seeking and measuring the essential behaviors of servant leadership. *Leadership & Organization Development Journal, 36*(4), 413–434.

Wong, C. A., Laschinger, H. K. S., & Cummings, G. G. (2010). Authentic leadership and nurses' voice behaviour and perceptions of care quality. *Journal of Nursing Management, 18*(8), 889–900.

Yang, F., Wu, M., Chang, C., & Chien, Y. (2011). Elucidating the relationships among transformational leadership, job satisfaction, commitment foci and commitment bases in the public sector. *Public Personnel Management, 40*(3), 265–278.

APPENDIX
Featured Leader: Linda Rosenberg

Linda Rosenberg is a national expert in the financing and delivery of mental health and substance abuse services. Under her leadership, the National Council for Behavioral Health has become our nation's most effective advocate for behavioral health prevention, early intervention, science-based treatment, and recovery. Harnessing the voices of the 10 million adults, children, and families served by the National Council's 2,500 member organizations, Rosenberg helped secure passage of the federal parity law, expanded integrated behavioral and primary care services, introduced Mental Health First Aid in the United States, and built an array of organizational, clinical, and workforce improvement initiatives. The National Council's strong support of the Mental Health Excellence Act will result in the first comprehensive effort to establish community accountability for the health of people with serious mental illnesses and addictions, the consistent utilization of evidence-based practices, and the standardized measurement of outcomes. Rosenberg was Senior Deputy Commissioner of the New York State Office of Mental Health before joining the National Council. She has more than 30 years' experience in designing and operating hospitals and community housing programs and implemented New York's first Mental Health Court. Rosenberg serves on an array of boards of directors and is a member of the Executive Committee of the National Action Alliance for Suicide Prevention.

LEADERSHIP PROFILE FOR LINDA ROSENBERG

Share your professional background and experience

My name is Linda Rosenberg. I've been a social worker since I graduated in 1974. Soon after my undergraduate education, I went to work for a State Hospital in New York City, and I was able to take advantage of the ability to go to school in the next few years. I started as a case aide and probably have held every position particularly focused on mental health. Right now I'm the president and CEO of the National Council for Behavioral Health, which is an association of about 3,000 not-for-profit organizations, mental health centers, addiction centers, and hospitals, all serving the safety net population in every state and in every community and all focused on delivering mental health and addiction services to people affected by those disorders, including children, adults, and families—everything from inpatient services to housing. I've been doing that for 13 years. Before that, I was the Senior Deputy Commissioner for mental health in New York State. I had responsibility for the operations of about 27 state hospitals and a $4 billion community-based budget and had risen to that position through the ranks, basically in New York, in the office of mental health where I started out. I went on to do many things, mostly in the community, which also included running the state hospital at some point. I had a lot of hands-on experiences.

In your experience, what are the top three to five leadership attributes someone in the health and human services field should possess? Share an example of when you have used one or more of these attributes/skills in your work

This is a complicated question because depending on situations, you need different strengths. That's why you'll see someone who is a wonderful leader of the startup but is not able to take it to the next level when it has to become a larger bureaucracy. It's not simple in that there is one set of characteristics that will take you through every situation, but I think there are some basic things if you want to do well in the field that are important. I think if you possess or develop some of these characteristics, you're going to do well.

Passionate curiosity. Most certainly one is passionate curiosity. I think that often, particularly in the not-for-profit sector and in human services, we tend to develop a set of beliefs, and we don't let much interfere with that, and sometimes that is very detrimental because we believe things that aren't necessarily based in fact. I think you want to be an avid lifelong learner. You always want to be questioning. You always want to be reading, and you always want to be learning. Passionate curiosity is something that you're going to need in any situation.

Enjoyment of solving problems. I think the other thing is that if you're a leader, whether you're a leader growing an organization or taking over a situation that's in bad shape that needs to be changed and refocused, I think you need to enjoy solving problems. I don't think some people can talk a good game. I think you have to really enjoy figuring out what the problem is and how you can solve it.

Tenacity. You've got to be willing to work hard. I don't know successful people who are not tenacious and who don't work very hard.

Social intelligence. You need a connectedness to people. You want to have social intelligence. You want to understand that everybody wants to win in most cases. It does not mean that you always have to reach that consensus. I think we're often a field that gets stuck in this notion of consensus, which usually leads to bringing things down to the lowest common denominator that people can agree on, and that doesn't solve many problems. I think you have to understand that most people need to get something out of the negotiation. They have to come away with some kind of a win, and I think that is part of social intelligence.

Generosity. This is connected to social intelligence in that everybody needs to feel good, and you want to celebrate the people around you, the people you work with, the people you negotiate with. You are seen as somebody who not only wants to do well but also wants to be surrounded by talented stars. You are going to do well, and those people around you deserve to do well, and it's your job to help promote them.

Particularly in mental health, in my current leadership position it has become important to appreciate that I am part of a very political world. I have many responsibilities and a fair degree of authority by managing funding that goes out to organizations through contracts, through Medicaid, and through grants. I am part of a complex system, and I expect to meet with resistance. You have to understand that just because you want something to happen, that doesn't mean it's going to happen and is not going to meet tremendous resistance as there are different stakeholder groups. I think there are a number of interventions and programs that evidence has shown to work, whether it is supportive housing or assertive community treatment—they're all interventions for people suffering from mental illnesses. There is a housing and mobile treatment, or a program called Pros, which is a rehabilitation program, but to get those programs to actually happen is a challenge. They're all based on funding and monies, including state money and Medicaid money. You're navigating the governor's office, the division of budget, the provider world, the organizations out there, the not-for-profits that can't turn on a dime and you want them to turn. To create new kinds of programs, you've got to understand that you've got to help them do that. So there has to be something in it for them. Some money to help run that turnaround period. You have to negotiate with the governor's office so that they some of what they want in terms of PR that's positive, even though you may not totally agree. It's that political skill of understanding what people need and then being gracious enough and generous enough to try to deliver that, but understand you do it for yourself too and the people you serve. The bottom line is that if these groups don't feel included, if they're not going to emerge from this in decent shape, it's not going to happen.

A CASE STUDY BY LINDA ROSENBERG

I think we're in the middle of a case study right now actually. It's been interesting. When you run an association in Washington, DC, you don't have the same kind of authority you have when you're running an office of mental health in the state. In fact, your authority comes from a bully pulpit, from your member organizations and members who support you, so there's a lot of engagement and understanding the world from that point of view. I also think that your job is *never justice served, it's a justice plead*. That means being able to have a vision and problem-solving skills, where you come up with a vision of what will work.

I think the problem we have today in the United States is that although we have a lot of interest in mental health and addictions in that we have some money being appropriated at the federal and state levels, through grants, which are time-limited, we're all talking about solving the opioid crisis–what we're not talking about as much is that it's very hard to get any kind of mental health or addiction treatment unless you can pay cash. A child psychiatrist, for example, costs $500 for an evaluation. It is not just a rural problem; in fact, in some ways the problems are also in cities, which have lots of psychiatrists and psychologists, but where private pay is the norm, and it's probably the only medical specialty where it's become primarily private pay. Access is a huge issue. In the 1960s, we created mental health centers supposedly that were available at little to no cost, on a sliding scale. We were dedicated to cover some of the costs for people to go and get services. For example, children with behavior problems, marriage issues, schizophrenia, bipolar disorders, and addictions—but they were never fully developed. In fact, we have become dependent on Medicaid rates that don't cover the cost of skilled staff that can deliver interventions. What government has done in some cases, again because we start to believe things that aren't necessarily true, is staff them with people with very few skills. Probably the most skilled person you'll find is someone just out of graduate school, and it's just not enough. You need more skilled social workers, nurses, doctors, occupational therapists, and a whole host of things. We came up with a model, which got named in Congress as the Certified Community Behavioral Health Centers (CCBHCs), which takes that old notion of mental health treatment and upgrades it with standardized and evidence-based practices. We were able with our champions in Congress to get a bill introduced, with a demonstration in eight states underway now, and we are working with our champions in Congress to expand that. I think that going to meetings about workforce development, which I could do every day, and of unloading the lack of evidence-based treatments is understanding that finance has to be aligned with the services you expect people to get and that we need standardization of modern practices across the country. This is my example of being passionately curious. What is the problem? How do you solve it? We have been tenacious and have worked on this now for many years, and we knew that we had to work with the administration and that we had to work with organizations that would actually qualify to be a CCBHC. We also knew that this wouldn't help every organization, but the most important thing is that it would help patients and their families get better care, and that's the real problem—this has been the driving force behind the vision. How do you help people along the way who are all involved but keep your eye on the people who need the real help? I think we are trying to be generous and to be inclusive, but not to lower our standards.

CASE DISCUSSION POINTS

1. This innovative leader talks about a "justice plead." What does she mean by that?
2. From what you have read in the case and from what you know, what are the challenges associated with funding of services, and how can a social architect address these?
3. How does an innovative leader navigate the political forces and meet the needs of various stakeholders without losing sight of those that need services the most?
4. How can a social architect maintain his or her vision in times of change and competing interests? Does the vision need to be adapted?

Appendices: Leader Assessment Instruments

A. LEADERSHIP ORIENTATIONS

Name:_____

Instructions: This questionnaire asks you to describe yourself as a manager and leader. For each item, give the number "4" to the phrase that best describes you, "3" to the item that is next best, and on down to "1" for the item that is least like you.

1. My strongest skills are:

   _____ a. *Analytic skills*
   _____ b. *Interpersonal skills*
   _____ c. *Political skills*
   _____ d. *Flair for drama*

2. The best way to describe me is:

   _____ a. *Technical expert*
   _____ b. *Good listener*
   _____ c. *Skilled negotiator*
   _____ d. *Inspirational leader*

3. What has helped me the most to be successful is my ability to:

   _____ a. *Make good decisions*
   _____ b. *Coach and develop people*

_____ c. *Build strong alliances and a power base*
_____ d. *Inspire and excite others*

4. What people are most likely to notice about me is my:

_____ a. *Attention to detail*
_____ b. *Concern for people*
_____ c. *Ability to succeed in the face of conflict and opposition*
_____ d. *Charisma*

5. My most important leadership trait is:

_____ a. *Clear, logical thinking*
_____ b. *Caring and support for others*
_____ c. *Toughness and aggressiveness*
_____ d. *Imagination and creativity*

6. I am best described as:

_____ a. *An analyst*
_____ b. *A humanist*
_____ c. *A politician*
_____ d. *A visionary*

_____ST   _____HR   _____PL   _____SY   _____Total

Computing Scores

Compute your scores as follows:

$$ST = 1a + 2a + 3a + 4a + 5a + 6a$$
$$HR = 1b + 2b + 3b + 4b + 5b + 6b$$
$$PL = 1c + 2c + 3c + 4c + 5c + 6c$$
$$SY = 1d + 2d + 3d + 4d + 5d + 6d$$

LEADERSHIP ORIENTATIONS SCORING

The Leadership Orientations instrument is keyed to four different conceptions of organizations and of the task of organizational leadership.

Plot each of your scores on the appropriate axis of the chart below: ST for Structural, HR for Human Resource, PL for Political, and SY for Symbolic. Then read the brief description of each of these orientations toward leadership and organizations.

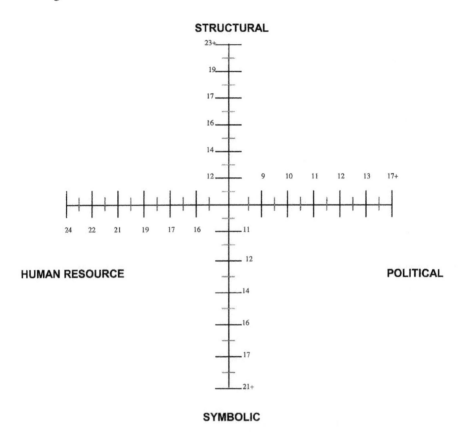

[Scales are adjusted to represent percentile scores. The lowest number for each frame represents the 25th percentile; the highest number represents the 90th percentile. The table below shows percentiles for each frame, based on a sample of more than 700 managers from business, education, and government. For the structural frame, for example, 25% of managers rate themselves 12 or below, and only 10% rate themselves 23 or above. The percentiles for each frame are shown in the following table, based on a sample of more than 700 managers in business, education, and government.]

In a sample of more than 700 managers:	Structural	Human Resource	Political	Symbolic
10% rated themselves at or above:	22	24	17	21
25% rated themselves above:	19	22	13	17
50% rated themselves above:	16	19	11	14
75% rated themselves above:	12	16	9	11

Interpreting Scores

1. **Structural** leaders emphasize rationality, analysis, logic, facts, and data. They are likely to believe strongly in the importance of clear structure and well-developed management systems. A good leader is someone who thinks clearly, makes the right decisions, has good analytic skills, and can design structures and systems that get the job done.
2. **Human resource** leaders emphasize the importance of people. They endorse the view that the central task of management is to develop a good fit between people and organizations. They believe in the importance of coaching, participation, motivation, teamwork, and good interpersonal relations. A good leader is a facilitator and participative manager who supports and empowers others.
3. **Political** leaders believe that managers and leaders live in a world of conflict and scarce resources. The central task of management is to mobilize the resources needed to advocate and fight for the unit's or the organization's goals and objectives. Political leaders emphasize the importance of building a power base: allies, networks, and coalitions. A good leader is an advocate and negotiator who understands politics and is comfortable with conflict.

---

4. **Symbolic** leaders believe that the essential task of management is to provide vision and inspiration. They rely on personal charisma and a flair for drama to get people excited and committed to the organizational mission. A good leader is a prophet and visionary, who uses symbols, tells stories, and frames experience in ways that give people hope and meaning.

B. SERVANT LEADERSHIP QUESTIONNAIRE

Instructions: Select two people who know you in a leadership capacity, such as a coworker, fellow group member, or follower. Make two copies of this questionnaire, and give a copy to each individual you have chosen. Using the following seven-point scale, ask them to indicate the extent to which they agree or disagree with the following statements as they pertain to your leadership. In these statements, "he/she" and "him/her" are referring to you in a leadership capacity.

Key: 1 = strongly disagree; 2 = disagree; 3 = disagree somewhat;
       4 = undecided; 5 = agree somewhat; 6 =agree; 7 = strongly agree.

1.	Others would seek help from him/her if they had a personal problem.	1 2 3 4 5 6 7
2.	He/she emphasizes the importance of giving back to the community.	1 2 3 4 5 6 7
3.	He/she can tell if something work-related is going wrong.	1 2 3 4 5 6 7
4.	He/she gives others the responsibility to make important decisions about their own jobs.	1 2 3 4 5 6 7
5.	He/she makes others' career development a priority.	1 2 3 4 5 6 7
6.	He/she cares more about others' success than his/her own.	1 2 3 4 5 6 7
7.	He/she holds high ethical standards.	1 2 3 4 5 6 7
8.	He/she cares about others' personal well-being.	1 2 3 4 5 6 7
9.	He/she is always interested in helping people in the community.	1 2 3 4 5 6 7

		1 2 3 4 5 6 7
10.	He/she is able to think through complex problems.	1 2 3 4 5 6 7
11.	He/she encourages others to handle important work decisions on their own.	1 2 3 4 5 6 7
12.	He/she is interested in making sure others reach their career goals.	1 2 3 4 5 6 7
13.	He/she puts others' best interests above his/her own.	1 2 3 4 5 6 7
14.	He/she is always honest.	1 2 3 4 5 6 7
15.	He/she takes time to talk to others on a personal level.	1 2 3 4 5 6 7
16.	He/she is involved in community activities.	1 2 3 4 5 6 7
17.	He/she has a thorough understanding of the organization and its goals.	1 2 3 4 5 6 7
18.	He/she gives others the freedom to handle difficult situations in the way they feel is best.	1 2 3 4 5 6 7
19.	He/she provides others with work experiences that enable them to develop new skills.	1 2 3 4 5 6 7
20.	He/she sacrifices his/her own interests to meet others' needs.	1 2 3 4 5 6 7
21.	He/she would not compromise ethical principles in order to meet success.	1 2 3 4 5 6 7
22.	He/she can recognize when others are feeling down without asking them.	1 2 3 4 5 6 7
23.	He/she encourages others to volunteer in the community.	1 2 3 4 5 6 7
24.	He/she can solve work problems with new or creative ideas.	1 2 3 4 5 6 7
25.	If others need to make important decisions at work, they do not need to consult him/her.	1 2 3 4 5 6 7
26.	He/she wants to know about others' career goals.	1 2 3 4 5 6 7
27.	He/she does what he/she can to make others' jobs easier.	1 2 3 4 5 6 7
28.	He/she values honesty more than profits.	1 2 3 4 5 6 7

Scoring

Using the questionnaires on which others assessed your leadership, take the separate scores for each item, add them together, and divide that sum by two. This will give you the average score for that item. For example, if person A assessed you at 4 for item 2, and person B marked you as a 6, your score for item 2 would be 5.

After you have averaged each item's scores, use the following steps to complete the scoring of the questionnaire:

1. Add up the scores on 1, 8, 15, and 22. This is your score for emotional healing.
2. Add up the scores for 2, 9, 16, and 23. This is your score for creating value for the community.
3. Add up the scores for 3, 10, 17, and 24. This is your score for conceptual skills.
4. Add up the scores for 4, 11, 18, and 25. This is your score for empowering.
5. Add up the scores for 5, 12, 19, and 26. This is your score for helping followers grow and succeed.
6. Add up the scores for 6, 13, 20, and 27. This is your score for putting followers first.
7. Add up the scores for 7, 14, 21, and 28. This is your score for behaving ethically.

Scoring Interpretation

- *High range:* A score between 23 and 28 means you strongly exhibit this servant leadership behavior.
- *Moderate range:* A score between 14 and 22 means you tend to exhibit this behavior in an average way.
- *Low range:* A score between 8 and 13 means you exhibit this leadership below the average or expected degree.
- *Extremely low range:* A score between 0 and 7 means you are not inclined to exhibit this leadership behavior at all.

The scores you receive on the Servant Leadership Questionnaire indicate the degree to which you exhibit the seven behaviors characteristic of a servant leader. You can use the results to assess areas in which you have strong servant leadership behaviors and areas in which you may strive to improve.

Source: Reprinted (adapted version) from Liden, R. C., Wayne, S. J., Zhao, H., & Henderson, D. (2008). Servant leadership: Development of a multidimensional measure and multi-level assessment. *Leadership Quarterly, 19,* 161–177. Copyright © with permission from Elsevier Science.

Design

4

Teamwork, Collaboration, and Motivation

We cannot walk alone. And as we walk, we must make the
pledge that we shall always march ahead. We cannot turn back.

—Dr. Martin Luther King, Jr.

CHAPTER OBJECTIVES

1. Review the importance of positive relationships, collaboration, and motivation in health and human services organizations;
2. Learn effective group dynamics strategies to increase individual productivity and team performances;
3. Learn innovating norms of collaboration to improve working relationships;
4. Explore how social architects motivate individuals and groups to affect their attitudes and behaviors in the workplace; and
5. Gain insights on innovative leadership from a social architect (see Appendix to this chapter).

INTRODUCTION

Human beings accomplish their goals and objectives through relationships. Whether we want to pursue personal goals or professional objectives, the quality of interaction with others guides the attitudes and behaviors of everyone involved. The nature of these relationships can significantly affect our lives, including levels of work engagement and satisfaction, well-being, motivation, and commitment. Therefore, building positive working relationships by understanding others' perspectives and being able to effectively share our points of view are very important skills for the leader to craft and master. This chapter will review key aspects of human psychology in the workplace and how they interrelate with relationships, collaboration, and motivation. To describe and understand how effective leaders influence and motivate followers, build and maintain constructive relationships, and collaborate positively with others, we will next review the features of effective relationships, norms of collaboration, and teamwork dynamics.

EFFECTIVE RELATIONSHIPS IN THE WORKPLACE

Innovative leaders have the ability to shape the quality of the work environment, setting the tone and guiding the processes to accomplish the organization's vision and mission. Since the amount of interactions among team members and internal and external groups is frequently high, establishing positive and supportive relationships that can make significant and positive differences in work attitude, behavior, and satisfaction should be a priority. Social exchange theory explains that the impact of positive workplace relationships on employee engagement, well-being, and commitment to the organization is negatively associated with employment dissatisfaction and turnover rates (Brunetto et al., 2013). This important fact should be considered when making decisions that can directly or indirectly affect individuals and teams in the workplace. Leaders in the health and human services field must promote prosocial behaviors and problem-focused strategies among their team members, which have a direct effect in reducing employee anxiety and increasing job satisfaction.

As social architects create and manage work environments, they should pay special attention to the emotional cues that employees, group members, and consumers display throughout the organization. One key ingredient to highlight is workplace stressors, including interpersonal conflict, work overload, failure, role ambiguity, and change. Chung and Chun (2015) explain that individuals in the workplace are exposed to personal protective factors (e.g., personal positive relationships, stress and emotion regulation, and resiliency) and organizational protective factors (e.g., rapport with supervisor and clients, support systems, and breaks from work). When managed properly, these protective factors from both personal and organizational perspectives can reduce workplace stressors as long as the organization habitually fosters a positive culture and the leadership actively promotes positive interactions among group members.

Innovated leaders consistently build work environments where team members are encouraged and supported to develop the following five personal protective factors:

1. *Mindfulness.* Mindfulness is a thought process that helps individuals keep their state of mind in the present. Organizations promote mindfulness by avoiding past experiences and not putting pressure on future expectations. Workplace mindfulness is positively associated with job satisfaction and job performance and negatively associated with turnover intention (Dane & Brummel, 2014). Furthermore, employees who engage in mindfulness practices as a habit experience greater job engagement capacity, which includes dedication, absorption into the work, and vigor. It is important for leaders to not only promote mindfulness in their employees but also practice it themselves (see Chapter 15).

2. *Work-life balance.* As we are more technologically interconnected, individuals take their personal lives from home to work and their workload from work to home. This blurring of work and life boundaries can affect the ability to create a healthy balance between work and personal life. Basically, the 9 AM to 5 PM jobs are less common today than in previous generations. Job satisfaction and organizational commitment are affected by personal attributes and the role of work-life balance. Deery (2008) recommends that leadership in the organization establishes not only minimum working hours but also maximum hours, showcases good role modeling of healthy work-life balance at the workplace, allows flexible working hours, provides employees with training and professional development opportunities, and launches family-friendly work policies. At the same time, each individual should focus on improving how to gauge and assess workload impact on their quality of life (Jang, 2009).

3. *Resiliency.* Resiliency is the ability to bounce back from negative and challenging life situations. All of us go through physical and emotional ups and downs in our lives. Tough situations that can set us back include health changes in ourselves or someone we love, organizational uncertainty, changes in leadership or programming, or client negative outcomes. Therefore, individuals and team members should have a strong resiliency base and know how to bounce back from adversities. Winwood, Colon, and McEwen (2013) studied resiliency models in the workplace, concluding that providing support systems within the organization is highly beneficial to improving employee resiliency.

4. *Emotion regulation.* Leaders monitor individual and collective emotional shifts (i.e., emotional ups and downs) by designing mechanisms in which group members can detect and interpret signs of displayed emotions. Organizations with high job satisfaction rates intentionally create conduits for employees to safely express positive emotions and trust the process without fear of retaliation. These organizational structures have been shown to help improve group member interactions and reach organizational outcomes (Wong, Tschan, Messerli, & Semmer, 2013).

5. *Coping strategies.* When employees exhibit positive occupational attributional styles and skills (e.g., problem-solving, conflict resolution, win-win negotiations, and/or cognitive restructuring), they are more likely to create habitual coping strategies to deal with daily situations and improve job satisfaction. The leaders in the organization should systematically train their workforce to apply these coping strategies to avoid fatigue, burnout, and unnecessary disagreements (Welbourne, Eggerth, Hartley, Andrew, & Sanchez, 2007).

The quality of relationships and team performances highly depends on personality types, social exchanges, prior experiences, and ongoing interactions. At the most basic level, individuals are thought to have personality tendencies that fall into two general categories: type A (i.e., achievement-oriented, impatient) and type B (i.e., easy-going, relaxed). When teams are created with individuals having the same or different personality types, the relationships vary and the group dynamics shift positively or negatively. Kamdar and Van Dyne (2007) studied the effects of social interactions in work performance. They learned that the effects of personality types consistently predict task performance and work satisfaction. Interestingly, workplace interactions characterized by high-quality social exchange relationships have the power to weaken the positive association between personality and performance. This point is important because it strongly suggests that even when people have different personalities, the fact that they have built positive relationships with coworkers means that their work tasks can still be highly productive. Nonetheless, other studies have found that close friendships may get in the way of achieving quality work. These workplace friendships can negatively influence job performance through time-consuming situations and emotional exhaustion (Methot, Lepine, Podsakoff, & Christian, 2015). The social architect must encourage a work and personal relationship balance between team members and model positive working (i.e., professional) relationships.

BENEFITS AND MODELS OF COLLABORATION

Why is collaboration indispensable in the health and human services fields? More important, if we have to work with others, how can we manage and foster positive collaboration? To start, the complex issues we face in our society cannot be resolved by one person or group alone. One organization has neither the means nor the capacity to resolve the wicked problems in our society, such as poverty, educational gaps, immigration, disparities in health access, or discrimination. Collaboration is how we ameliorate these issues and try to find innovative solutions to improve human conditions. Collaboration is another essential skill in leaders' DNA (which can be developed) and involves their ability to work well with others.

We all belong to groups in which we accomplish tasks with relative efficiency, struggle with frequent and unnecessary disagreements, or experience group apathy. Partly because of our Western society's egocentric nature, the idea of collaboration may be a bit difficult to grasp for some people. Individuals tend to pull their own way instead of finding innovative ways to work with others. Nonetheless, once people realize the exhilarating personal and interpersonal benefits of collaboration, they embark on a totally different approach. After you discover your interpersonal style and that of the ones around you, the next step is to better understand the process of collaboration. The collaboration process starts with us. For instance, do you know your own collaboration style? What areas of collaboration do you welcome and what parts you dread? By looking inward and reflecting throughout collaborative opportunities, you can go a long way in your leadership and collaborative development.

According to Ibarra and Hansen (2011) leaders must pay special attention when collaborating with others. In their article entitled, "Are You a Collaborative Leader?" they developed the following key reflective questions (within four areas) that leaders should ask themselves as they implement collaborative efforts:

1. *Play global connector*
   a. Do you attend conferences outside your professional specialty?
   b. Are you part of a global network?
   c. Do you regularly blog or email employees about trends, ideas, and people you encounter outside your organization?
   d. How often do you meet with parties outside your organization (competitors, consumers, government officials, university contacts, and so on) who are not directly relevant to your immediate job demands or current operations?
   e. Are you on the board of any outside organizations?

2. *Engage talent at the periphery*
   a. How diverse is your immediate team in terms of nationality? Gender? Age?
   b. How much time do you spend outside your home country? Have you visited your emerging markets this year?
   c. Does your network include people in their 20s (who aren't your kids)?
3. *Collaborate at the top first*
   a. Do members of your team have any joint responsibilities beyond their individual goals?
   b. Does the compensation of your direct reports depend on any collective goals or reflect any collective responsibilities?
   c. What specifically have you done to eradicate power struggles within your team?
   d. Do your direct reports have both performance and learning goals?
4. *Show a strong hand*
   a. Have you terminated any unproductive collaborative projects in the past six months?
   b. Do you manage dynamically—forming and disbanding teams quickly as opportunities arise?
   c. Do the right people in your organization know they can "close" a discussion and make a decision?
   d. Does your team debate ideas vigorously but then unite behind decisions made?

Models of organizational collaboration can also determine processes and outcomes. Proulx, Hager, and Klein (2014) concluded that there are eight formal nonprofit collaborative models and leaders can choose from the following:

1. *The fully integrated merger*—two or more organizations merging into one
2. *Partially integrated merger*—one organization takes business units from another
3. *Joint program office*—two or more organizations delivering one program in one location
4. *Joint partnership with affiliated programming*—one or more organizations partnering with another organization that has a successful service delivery and/or program implementation record
5. *Joint partnership for issue advocacy*—two or more organizations collaborating to accomplish policy and legislative outcomes
6. *Joint partnership with a new formal organization*—existing organization joining efforts with a new one to accomplish similar goals

7. *Joint administrative operations*—two or more organizations being managed by the same leadership team

8. *Confederation*—multiple organizations coming together to achieve a grand goal

The benefits of collaborating with others are numerous. First, at the individual level, collaboration brings a sense of accomplishment. Often, because of our efforts of working with others and pulling various resources, clients receive more comprehensive services and effective treatments. Simultaneously, we are increasing our individual networks for future opportunities. At the organizational level, different collaborative partnerships may be an innovative approach to reduce costs and employee burnout. Through collaborations, organizations build social capital and stronger safety nets for program and resource delivery. At the systems level, successful collaborative models demonstrate not only the power of partnership outcomes but also the potential for other systems to replicate these innovative collective approaches.

To be successful in collaborative efforts, social architects must become strong team players. Positive collaborative outcomes require all team members to understand their role and have the ability, capacity, and willingness to work and partner with others effectively. How do we become solid team players? Gardner (2015) recommends that innovative leaders consider the following tips for improving collaborative efforts amongst team members:

1. *Don't squeeze your team members.* The leader should be able to sense whether or not followers are willing and capable to participate in a specific role or task. Some people have a tendency to overcommit, which may lead to burnout and poor outcomes. Avoid pushing people to extremes and continue monitoring the quality of relationship displays of emotion. Organizations must put in place mechanisms that allow employees to share their concerns and ideas, emphasizing open communication. Effective leaders stay close to their group members, providing constructive feedback to maximize positive relationships and goal attainment.

2. *Organize for higher value work.* Leaders foster high levels of collaboration among all their team members, acting as facilitators to lower cultural and bureaucratic barriers. As leaders think about the best strategies to engage in collaborative partnerships, they need to consider if this effort has a high value and if it matches the organization's mission. Thus, this investment needs to be carefully assessed before encouraging active participation.

3. *Be a coach.* The best coaches begin with modeling the proper and expected behaviors themselves. Leaders build partnerships by respecting others and earning their respect. These connections are made by showing and leading the way. At times, it is appropriate to communicate that the path to follow has not been determined, but the leader is aware and conscious that decisions are needed. Coaching is not a one-time deal. Building these positive relations is an ongoing process, which takes resources and leaders who are able to manage and foster individuals' professional developments. Top leaders take some simple steps to help those around them build trusting relationships with one another, including engaging in conversations, holding gatherings and retreats that allow them to forge connections, teaching others what they know (while also listening and learning from employees), providing constructive advice and criticism, proposing their vision, modeling expected roles for themselves and those around them, and embracing change.

4. *Improve your abilities and skills as a social architect.* One of the most exciting aspects of leadership is the notion of constant building. Leaders are always creating foundational organizational and social structures, connecting the dots, fostering relationships, communicating processes and outcomes, and rebuilding when needed. By building effective collaborations, innovative leaders are generating great rewards, such as rising levels of client satisfaction, employee retention, and organizational efficiency.

Most successful interdisciplinary or interprofessional collaborations feature a relational system in which individuals from different organizations join in to make decisions. According to D'Agostino (2013), in order for the collaborative process to work as intended, the leader must orchestrate the implementation in several phases. The initial phase requires them to identify the overall partnership goals and to complete a needs assessment to map out (1) current services provided, (2) unmet service needs of the clients or community, (3) resources available to accomplish the desired goals, and (4) potential barriers for implementation. The implementation phase comes next. At this stage, evidence-based interventions are put into practice. The coordination of funding, services, and outcomes will demonstrate how successful the collaborative efforts are at making a difference in clients' lives. Appropriate changes and adjustments will be needed to continue improving the service delivery options. The final phase includes evaluation, reflection, and deciding on next steps.

Ongoing feedback, training, and evaluation can go a long way when leaders are trying to improve collaborative efforts. For example, the collaboration between general practitioners and mental health care professionals has been shown to have strengths and weaknesses. On one side, these collaborative efforts show positive outcomes during consultation of diagnosis, decisions on potential treatments or interventions, and discussions of implementation dilemmas. On the contrary, some of the limitations when medical practitioners collaborate with mental health providers include the lack of mutual knowledge of mental health services and resources (Fredheim, Danbolt, Haavet, Kjønsberg, & Lien, 2011). The innovative leader's training and development should focus on systematic collaborative services, direct means of communication, and additional consultation time.

The Communities of Practice (CoPs) model from the Centers for Disease Control and Prevention (CDC) has been noted to be a successful collaborative model (Mabery, Gibbs-Scharf, & Bara, 2013). The CoPs collaborative model brings staff and professionals together from different organizations and disciplines to share, learn, and address public health concerns. The CoPs model has been documented to improve individual performances and organizational goals, including coordinated daily work efficiencies, expanded infrastructure, increased ability to troubleshoot barriers, and promotion of enhanced relationships among partners (Mabery et al., 2013). Additionally, the great majority of collaborative efforts receive ongoing adaptive collaboration support through training, development, and tutoring, focusing on the co-construction of new knowledge. In essence, the collaborative approaches pursue innovative models and strategies to achieve macro outcomes, mostly because prior approaches and efforts have yielded limited results (Dieglmayr & Spada, 2010). Key training areas include deciding which collaboration skill to support, conceptualizing the individual and collaborative activities underlying the skill, specifying rules for providing adaptive methods based on an online assessment of collaboration indicators, and evaluating collaboration support.

Although collaboration benefits are promising and organizations can experience significant results, at times collaborative efforts can hit roadblocks and barriers. A potential problem is the amount of competition for the same resources among human services organizations. For example, in the past, the nonprofit sector was mostly raising funds by competing against other organizations for the same dollars. This competitive funding system encouraged more resentment and less collaboration between organizations. However, more and more public and private funders today are demanding organizations to submit grant applications in collaboration with other agencies, known as "collaboratives funding models." To acquire these funds, leaders should plan ahead by assembling a cadre of individuals from multiple organizations and disciplines who can work together in a collaborative approach and demonstrate successful outcomes. This takes time and effort because each representative from a different discipline must build relationships, learn the jargon of the others, and coordinate delivery of services. Further, Audia (2012) recommends that leaders facilitate ongoing collaboration conversations, emphasizing how people can read and take others' perceptions and ask brief and direct questions for clarification.

Additionally, collaboration efforts can feel overwhelming and demanding. Sometimes too much collaboration leads to unproductivity and lack of decision-making. Thus, successful collaborative efforts should include a balance between engaging group members and implementing solid collaborative practices. These collaboratives also feature strong leadership that model a culture of transparency and accountability. The best way to achieve efficiency among groups, Hensen (2011) argues, is to have clear expectations and common goals, the same agenda from top to bottom, and willingness to learn and compromise as well as share a culture of innovation.

Other barriers when building or managing collaborations include role blurring, lack of knowledge of the expertise of other professionals, and practical, theoretical and value-based differences among group members. For example, when social work and medical teams work together to provide hospice care, physicians and nurses may see the role of the social worker as secondary to medicine. On the other hand, social work values an emphasis on the patient's self-determination above all. These differences may lead to conflict, disagreements, and lack of collaboration. When these challenges arise, Reese and Sontag (2001) propose the following potential solutions that leaders can implement: recognizing areas of convergence, acknowledging conflict through a discussion of differences, being oriented toward solutions, and teaching positive norms of collaboration.

NORMS OF COLLABORATION

Working with others to achieve grand goals takes individual and collective effort as well as commitment. Collaboration can be challenging and demanding because of many factors, primarily the professional diversity and multidisciplinary nature of the team members and varying resource investments like personnel, time, and money. One significant ingredient in successful collaborative opportunities deals with how stakeholders approach the task at hand. Mitchell and Boyle (2015) advise that open-mindedness norms can moderate the group's identity and capacity for innovation. In other words, if individuals and organizations do not come to the table willing and able to actively participate, then it will be very difficult to reach positive results. Some of the effective practices during the collaboration's initial stages and throughout are ongoing and open communication, sharing of resources, and finding common goals and values (Rogers, 2009).

Social architects have the ability and capacity to shape formal and informal team norms (Taggar & Ellis, 2007). When team members disagree, they turn to the leader for guidance and direction. The innovative leader's primary role while creating norms of collaboration is setting high expectations and modeling positive problem-solving behaviors. Some of the key characteristics influential leaders must attain include positive attributes (e.g., attitudes, perceptions, and trust) and interpersonal ties with team members (Tsasis, 2009). Mental health leaders, for example, engage in strategic collaboration by building effective work teams that adhere to positive norms such as working together to minimize institutional pressures and contributing to homogeneity in the participants' responses (Work, 2014). Importantly, collaboration in the health and human services fields is about the setup (beginning), the means (process), and the end (outcome).

Social architects have the capacity and position to affect and influence others at all times. Garmston and Wellman (2000, p. 21) strongly advise that leaders should adopt a collaborative style with the following seven practical norms:

1. *Pausing.* Before asking questions, it is advisable to take a couple of seconds, think clearly about what has been communicated, and then take your turn.
2. *Paraphrasing.* Most times, disagreement escalates because of misunderstandings. To ensure clear communication, leaders should regularly paraphrase in their own words what has been shared by others.
3. *Probing.* Effective leaders use gentle open-ended questions to inquire a bit further and reach deeper understanding.
4. *Putting ideas on the table.* Leaders are more successful when they explain current problems with proposed potential solutions. Be prepared to share how to solve some of the issues discussed and be open to listening to others' suggestions.
5. *Paying attention to self and others.* Impactful leaders try to regulate their own emotions and simultaneously observe others' reactions. Collaboration is about working effectively with others, and paying special attention to people's expressions and reactions is needed.
6. *Presuming positive intentions.* Assuming others bring their best intentions can help the team to reach positive outcomes early in the collaborative process.
7. *Pursuing a balance between advocacy and inquiry.* Part of the collaboration process is to negotiate potential solutions. Successful

leaders do not push their way/priorities/solutions all the time, but instead try to balance their thoughts and feelings with the ideas proposed by people around them.

Maintaining open communication is another powerful norm of collaboration to encourage people to actively engage in workplace discussions about how to enhance productivity and job satisfaction. Martin (2004) suggests that leaders must be proactive and engage in open conversations regarding a variety of topics that may be in their team members' minds, including workplace resilience, authoritarian versus authoritative leadership or management styles, motivation and workplace climates, personal bests, staff morale, flow in work, the value individuals attach to tasks and outcomes, and the centrality of relationships in the performance context. The results of these open conversations are remarkable. A study of more than 600 school personnel employees found that these conversations increase positive relationships, motivation, and enjoyment of work (Martin, 2009). Furthermore, participants increased their workplace participation, workplace resilience, and participation in extra duties. Interestingly, the study found that females reflected a more adaptive pattern of motivation and engagement than their male counterparts. Nonetheless, all participants were cognitively and behaviorally engaged as a result of this open-communication approach (Martin, 2009).

TEAMS AND TEAM BUILDING

Teamwork occurs when two or more people (or organizations) come together to accomplish common goals, usually by exercising concerted efforts, applying interdependent collaboration, and sharing decision-making opportunities. All areas of health care, human services, government, business, and education operate in dynamic environments where leaders have to identify threats, changes, cause-and-effect relationships, and constructive responses to challenges. Effective teams are characterized by having positive attitudes and strong morale, interpersonal and collaboration skills, and problem-solving and conflict resolution mechanisms and by holding diverse values and inclusiveness and focusing on client outcomes (Cleary & Horsfall, 2015).

Team configuration, or bringing people together and building a team, is another key element to successful collaboration and organizational performance. The team composition is a dynamic progression, and it can take many forms and shapes. Effective leaders exhibit flexibility, patience, and understanding of the team members, know characteristics of the task at hand, and foresee potential obstacles and barriers. When working in teams, members should invest in developing group working skills and interventions to positively affect individuals and should learn the factors that lead to a successful translation of learning into practice (Bayley, Wallace, Spurgeon, Barwell, & Mazelan, 2007).

Team building and group dynamics demand effective techniques that aim to normalize emotions. Studies have shown that emotional intelligence and emotional capability are positively associated with teamwork effectiveness, job performance, and job satisfaction (Farh, Seo, & Tesluk, 2012). Mainly this association occurs because human beings place a high value on achieving emotional balance in their lives. Generally, emotions influence personality, cognitive and affective ability, job demands, and interpersonal reactions. Leaders must gauge the collective emotion of those around them, which includes observing interactions among team members, promoting trust in the workplace, making workload adjustments, and providing comfort among colleagues. These emotional variations in the health and human services fields are significantly affected by space and time. Oandasan et al. (2009) found that both the quantity and quality of interprofessional relationships and personal connections in the workplace are related to the degree of success in teams and collaboratives. Social architects working in smaller interprofessional environments where they can build personal and professional relationships are more likely to invest greater time and effort toward making the collaboration outcomes attainable.

Another important variable in building and maintaining solid interorganizational and multidisciplinary teams is culture. First, innovative leaders use language to influence team members to accomplish objectives like improving service delivery and client outcomes, as well as influencing workplace innovation. Furthermore, innovative leaders who are strong communicators use metaphors as a mechanism by which to share team experiences and bring people together. These metaphors are powerful language tools that can relate to family, peers, sports, military, and community (Gibson & Zellmer-Bruhn, 2002). Traditions and norms are also positively related with teamwork culture and patient satisfaction for inpatient care (Meterko, Mohr, & Young, 2004). A great part of organizational culture includes how people go about their day. Interestingly, Tews, Michel, and Stafford (2013) found that using humor at work decreases employee turnover and burnout, and fun activities increase performance and job satisfaction. When team members perceive having a good time, like laughing and smiling, their brains release more endorphins, which increase their sense of pleasure and happiness. Fun activities can include social events, team-building exercises, and public celebration of personal and professional accomplishments.

Simultaneously, diversity in team members brings a special value in accomplishing goals and objectives. The research in organizational behavior strongly suggests that heterogeneous groups outperform homogeneous teams

(Watson, Kumar, & Michaelsen, 1993). Even though diverse groups may take longer to achieve their goals because of differences of opinion among team members, it is well documented that in-group diversity has a significant constructive impact on both the team process and the formulation of innovative ideas (Woehr, Arciniega, & Poling, 2013). To foster diversity and achieve organizational results, Hamel and Price (2011) recommend that innovative leaders create inspired, open, and free (as in liberating versus coercive) organizations. Social architects helping to overcome ongoing challenges in diverse groups are founded on three organizational attributes: external orientation, coordination and control, and motivation.

1. *External orientation.* The environment for organizations is more dynamic, complex, and global than ever. Organizations should create spaces where every individual is equipped to sense emerging trends, where the implications for action are rapidly recognized, and where the necessary resources are quickly brought to bear.
2. *Coordination and control.* Innovative leaders have the position and power to create ways of integrating complex activities with little or no management directives. Diverse teams are more likely to accomplish goals without others micromanaging their activities. Less control, less rules and sanctions, and less judgment inspire people from different walks of life to become more engaged in the process and more likely to innovate.
3. *Motivation.* Leadership teams within organizations must be capable of producing a steady stream of effective service delivery and programs. This requires innovative leaders to bring the best out of those around them by providing spaces where team members can deepen their imagination, passion, and innovation. Most often, innovation doesn't come from unhappy or discouraged employees. Social architects must be creative and rigorous about inspiring passion and unleashing ingenious contributions from their team members.

THE ART AND SCIENCE OF MOTIVATION

Motivation is a precursor to behavior. Motivation is very powerful, and it can intensely influence individuals to accomplish remarkable personal and professional goals. Social architects must know what motivates, influences, and inspires people within and outside their organizations. This is not an easy task, but one of the most important aspects of leadership is to know what motivates others to change or influence their behavior (act, think, and feel differently).

A great deal of theories, concepts, and models have been created and studied to have a better understanding of individual and group motivation. Among others, these include Maslow's hierarchy of needs, Herzberg's two-factor or motivator-hygiene theory, McClelland's trichotomy of needs, McGregor's Theory X – Theory Y, Likert's System 1 – System 4, Blake and Mouton's managerial grid, Hersey and Blanchard's situational leadership, and Atwater and Bass's transformational leadership (Fisher, 2009).

The great majority of studies concerning motivation in the human services fields focus on adding workplace incentives and thereby improving performance, job satisfaction, and retention, as well as encouraging overall wellness, assisting with client functioning, and reducing employee pressures. Intrinsic motivation exists when an individual is able to answer two key questions: "Who am I?" and "What do I want?" Once there is clarity in the essence and the direction you would like to go, then the levels of stress are reduced, and career expectations and job performance follow suit (Bernadette can Rijn, Yang, & Sanders, 2013). For example, a study analyzed data from the National Administrative Studies Project (NASP-III) to conclude that intrinsic motivation is an important aspect of job choice motivation for individuals in the nonprofit workforce (Word & Park, 2015).

Thus, the initial step for leaders is to reflect on their own motivating factors and have a deeper understanding of what motivates others. Emerging leaders ask themselves what motivates them to be a successful helping professional. How much can they push themselves to perform at higher levels? One way to complete this self-analysis, Aguirre and Bolton (2013) suggest, is by self-reflection within the following six human service motivators: internal motivation to make a difference, desire to volunteer, lived experience, internal/personal fulfillment, lack of direction for vulnerable populations, and lack of support to people in need. Leaders are encouraged to reexamine their own thoughts, feelings, and behaviors on a regular basis within each of these six areas and encourage employees to do the same.

Motivating others in the workplace requires a constant and diligent intentional effort on the part of the leader. Lavigna (2015, p. 733) learned that effective leaders can successfully motivate public service employees by applying the following leadership skills:

1. Communicate effectively
2. Manage employee performance
3. Ensure that employees believe that their opinions count
4. Create a more a positive work environment
5. Provide new employees with a positive onboarding experience
6. Enhance employee prospects for career growth
7. Recognize employee contributions that are linked to performance

Part of the leadership challenge in the fields of health and human services is to recognize that employees within the public and private sectors have higher expectations about their involvement in and impact on policy issues and socially desirable outcomes. Often, these helping professionals base their motivation levels on how they identify themselves with the task at hand and the potential outcome and how well the group is performing. Thus, the level of intrinsic motivation and collective efficacy significantly affects the teamwork processes and outcomes. Lewis (2011) found four domains that innovative leaders could actively engage in when looking to increase the group members' motivation: contextual (culture), independent (team identity and efficacy), moderator (team creativity), and dependent (team performance).

Furthermore, in her book *Focus*, Heidi Grant Halvorson (2013) identifies two predominant types of motivational foci that drive behaviors. She groups employees into one of the following two broad categories:

1. *Promotion-focused.* Some individuals are motivated by the type of organizational advancement or promotions available in the workplace. Many human services workers are eager and comfortable taking chances, working quickly, dreaming big, thinking creatively, and working to reach successful outcomes. Promotion-focused individuals are considered to be in the driver's seat.
2. *Prevention-focused.* Other professionals like to take time to think and analyze alternatives, prefer to wait until others go first, and play it safe. They worry about what might go wrong and avoid losing. They work slowly and meticulously and aren't the most creative, but they often present excellent analytical and problem-solving skills. Prevention-focused individuals are usually considered to be in the passenger's seat.

By understanding these two basic motivational foci, social architects can increase their knowledge and capacity to better motivate themselves and everyone around them.

Motivated team members also exhibit lower levels of stress and a more balanced work-life style. Innovative leaders can definitely reduce stress levels by regularly communicating and positively engaging with team members. One way leaders reduce stress in the workplace as a way to motivate employees to improve their performances is by adopting flexible workplace schedules (McNamara, Brown, & Pitt-Catsouphes, 2012). The advantage of flexibility at work helps health and human services employees reduce stress at work and reach a better work-life balance (Morazes, Benton, Clark, & Jacquet, 2010). The work-life balance is important because productivity means optimizing your entire life, not just work. In other words, when there is equilibrium in your life as a whole, your personal life supports your efforts at work, and being strategic about your workload will allow you additional time to have a rich personal life. Stew Friedman (2008) advises that leaders can adopt a four-way win philosophy, investing time and energy in four domains: personal, professional, community or civic, and health (mental, physical, and spiritual).

POSITIVE ORGANIZATIONAL PSYCHOLOGY

Positive organizational psychology is rooted in the field of positive psychology, which is a branch of psychology that looks at optimal human functioning and improving quality of life (Seligman & Csikszentmihalyi, 2000). Empirical studies have demonstrated that leaders can improve employee engagement through a strengths-based approach that is often associated with one of the tenets of positive psychology (Clifton & Harter, 2003). The Clifton StrengthsFinder is a popular Web-based self-assessment that assists individuals in identifying themes associated with talents or strengths. Social architects can utilize this tool to help employees identify their talent areas and further develop these. (For more information the reader is referred to Rath & Conchie, 2008.)

USING POSITIVE ENERGY TO BUILD SUCCESSFUL TEAMS AND COLLABORATIONS

All innovative leaders and team members are characterized by the kind of energy within and around them. Generally, the energy coming from team members can be positive or negative. We all have participated in groups in which everything seems to be going well, people get along, tasks are accomplished, and each individual actively participates with their best intentions. On the other hand, there are some teams that exhibit a negative force, making individuals retreat and avoid engaging because it is psychologically painful to interact with one another. These teams achieve very little, and most times they dissipate because of members experiencing anger and frustration.

Social architects must carefully observe, monitor, and gauge the energy radiated by the group members. Most times, Schwartz and McCarthy (2007) explain, workers discharge negative energy because of a combination of factors, including working long hours, experiencing increasing levels of distraction, dealing with high turnover rates, and having soaring medical costs. To effectively re-energize team members, innovative leaders need to shift their emphasis from taking more out of people to investing more in them. Positive energy can be built by systematically expanding and regulating renewing types of rituals at the workplace. This requires vision, structure, and time, with a deliberate effort to increase positive energy among everyone in the organization.

To achieve the best energy in groups, social architects need to create workplaces where individuals will thrive in four main areas: body (physical domain), emotions, mind, and spirit (Schwartz & McCarthy, 2007). We will take a brief look at each of these next.

1. *The body.* The body is a source of *physical and somatic* energy. The lack of sleep, exercise, and proper nutrition lowers physical energy levels (low energy reservoir) to the point of dysfunction. Individuals need to regulate their body energy by sleeping well, exercising consistently, and eating well.

2. *The emotions.* Emotions dictate the *quality* of energy. Individuals who can best control their emotions feel better about themselves, their resiliency levels, and their workplace. They can better absorb internal and external stressors, managing their negative emotions appropriately. By expressing genuine appreciation for others, leaders affect the team's positive energy immensely.

3. *The mind.* The mind is the source of *focus*. When we get overwhelmed, our mind tends to wonder and lose concentration. Lack of focus because of distractions can be very costly, causing us to miss key opportunities and lowering our ability to be innovative. If you have too many distractions in your life, it is recommended that you create a ritual to train your mind to stay on task. Practice will improve your level of alertness and attentiveness to deal with one issue at a time.

4. *The human spirit.* The spirit is a source of *meaning and purpose*. Why are we doing what we do? A sense of resolve increases our positive energy levels. When team members have meaning and a sense of purpose, they feel effective, engaged, inspired, and fulfilled.

These sources of energy in the workplace are always fluctuating. Social architects must be aware of energy variations and provide structured renewal energy opportunities throughout all dimensions to create positive norms and rituals and improve organizational culture.

Positive energy also increases productivity. Innovative leaders match their focus to the amount of work necessary to accomplish the task. It is about managing your energy, not just your time. Thus, if your energy is low, tasks that require a great deal of effort should be avoided. Also, sleep patterns and nutrition intakes affect concentration and energy levels. Team members should monitor their level of positive energy by getting enough breaks to resume their project—a mental break every 90 minutes is best (Clark, 2016). Friedman (2015, p.12) recommends the following nine tips to increase your productivity:

1. *Own your time.* It is recommended to create a system in which you can take charge of your time. Try to block out time to work away from social media and email, program your phone to receive messages only in emergency situations, and resist looking at and answering messages all the time.

2. *Recognize busyness as a lack of focus.* Innovative leaders learn to prioritize their workloads to invest their time wisely. To be productive, you should monitor your energy during projects and interactions with team members. Think quality instead of quantity.

3. *Challenge the myth of the "ideal worker."* When team members work long hours, they usually become overwhelmed or stressed out. Their performance drops, and the levels of conflict escalate. Traditionally, the ideal worker is the one who works the hardest. However, today, the ideal worker is the one who works the smartest, being flexible, having a life and work balance, and meeting or exceeding expected outcomes.

4. *Intentionally leave important tasks incomplete.* It is ideal to take the right amount of time to complete projects. If we go from start to finish without breaks, our creativity and innovation may not be at its best. Be comfortable to leave tasks or projects incomplete for the appropriate amount of time to have the opportunity to think about it, ruminate over new ideas, and find additional innovated solutions.

5. *Make a habit of stepping back.* Best solutions to complex problems are usually found when we temporarily remove ourselves from the day-to-day tasks. It is recommended we take a few days off, even a short vacation, and then come back with renewed energy.

6. *Help other strategically.* People remember those who helped them, not expecting something in return or without strings attached. This simple act of supporting team members will go the distance to improve positive energy at the workplace and organizational culture. The reward is intrinsic in nature but can have long-lasting positive effects within the organization, and it can help you in the future if you ever need support from that person.

7. *Have a plan for saying no.* Health and human services professionals are wired to help others, but at times we have a hard time turning people down. Unfortunately, if we do this too frequently, we end up overextended. Worst yet, our energy may be reduced, resulting in our

work becoming mediocre. Prioritize your workload and share with others with honesty how much you can contribute so that they can plan accordingly.

8. *Make important behaviors measurable.* Expectations drive behavior. We know when we have accomplished at a higher level of productivity when we can compare the process and results to measurable behavioral standards. Moreover, success breeds success, and we know what success looks like when specific behavioral measurements are met and well communicated.

9. *Do things today that make more time tomorrow.* As we prioritize our workload, we should be mindful of our ability to complete the tasks at hand. Ask yourself: "What can I accomplish today that will allow me to have more time tomorrow?"

In closing, motivated team members show a great deal of positive energy. They are more likely to perform at a higher level, support other members when collaborating, engage in less conflict, and become more creative and innovative. Social architects establish successful health and human services organizations with the goal of increasing motivated individuals and groups. Seppala (2016) recommends that the organization's environment must provide supports and opportunities to motivate people to be inspired (having a strong sense of purpose and meaning), show kindness (enjoying companionship and recognition), and practice self-care (taking care of our own well-being before we help others).

CHAPTER DISCUSSION QUESTIONS

1. How can a leader motivate his or her employees?
2. What strategies can a leader use to create a positive work environment?
3. How do leaders build effective collaborations both within and outside of the organization?
4. What roles do norms play in an organization? Describe norms that support the mission of the organization and those that do not.
5. Read the leader profile and case study in the Appendix to this chapter. Note innovative ideas and practices and see what aspects of the case you can connect to the contents of the chapter and/or overall book.

REFERENCES

Aguirre, R. T. P., & Bolton, K. M. W. (2013). Why do they do it? A qualitative interpretive meta-synthesis of crisis volunteers' motivations. *Social Work Research, 37*(4), 327–338.

Audia, P. G. (2012, November). Train your people to take others' perspectives. *Harvard Business Review.* Retrieved from https://hbr.org/2012/11/train-your-people-to-take-others-perspectives

Bayley, J. E., Wallace, L. M., Spurgeon, P., Barwell, F., & Mazelan, P. (2007). Team working in healthcare: Longitudinal evaluation of a team building intervention. *Learning in Health and Social Care, 6*(4), 187–201.

Bernadette van Rijn, M. B., Yang, H., & Sanders, K. (2013). Understanding employees' informal workplace learning: The joint influence of career motivation and self-construal. *Career Development International, 18*(6), 610–628.

Brunetto, Y., Xerri, M., Shriberg, A., Farr-Wharton, R., Shacklock, K., Newman, S., & Dienger, J. (2013). The impact of workplace relationships on engagement, well-being, commitment and turnover for nurses in Australia and the USA. *Journal of Advanced Nursing, 69*(12), 2786–2799.

Chung, Y., & Chun, J. (2015). Workplace stress and job satisfaction among child protective service workers in South Korea: Focusing on the buffering effects of protective factors. *Children and Youth Services Review, 57*, 134–140.

Clark, D. (2016). 3 Productivity tips you can start using today. *Harvard Business Review.* Retrieved from https://hbr.org/2016/03/3-productivity-tips-you-can-start-using-today

Cleary, M., & Horsfall, J. (2015). Teamwork and teambuilding: Considering retreats. *Issues in Mental Health Nursing, 36*(1), 78–80.

D'Agostino, C. (2013). Collaboration as an essential school social work skill. *Children & Schools, 35*(4), 248–251.

Dane, E., & Brummel, B. J. (2014). Examining workplace mindfulness and its relations to job performance and turnover intention. *Human Relations, 67*(1), 105–128.

Deery, M. (2008). Talent management, work-life balance and retention strategies. *International Journal of Contemporary Hospitality Management, 20*(7), 792–806.

Deiglmayr, A., & Spada, H. (2010). Developing adaptive collaboration support: The example of an effective training for collaborative inferences. *Educational Psychology Review, 22*(1), 103–113.

Farh, C. I. C. C., Seo, M., & Tesluk, P. E. (2012). Emotional intelligence, teamwork effectiveness, and job performance: The moderating role of job context. *Journal of Applied Psychology, 97*(4), 890–900.

Fisher, E. A. (2009). Motivation and leadership in social work management: A review of theories and related studies. *Administration in Social Work, 33*(4), 347–367.

Fredheim, T., Danbolt, L. J., Haavet, O. R., Kjønsberg, K., & Lien, L. (2011). Collaboration between general practitioners and mental health care professionals: A qualitative study. *International Journal of Mental Health Systems, 5*(1), 13–19.

Friedman, R. (2015). 9 Productivity tips from people who write about productivity. *Harvard Business Review.* Retrieved from https://hbr.org/2015/12/9-productivity-tips-from-people-who-write-about-productivity

Friedman, S. D. (2008). *Total leadership: Be a better leader, have a richer life.* Cambridge, MA: Harvard Business Press.

Gardner, H. K. (2015, March). When senior managers won't collaborate. *Harvard Business Review.* Retrieved from https://hbr.org/2015/03/when-senior-managers-wont-collaborate

Garmston, R., & Wellman, B. (2000). *The adaptive school: Developing and facilitating collaborative groups* (4th ed.). El Dorado Hill, CA: Four Hats Seminars.

Gibson, C. B., & Zellmer-Bruhn, M. (2002). Minding your metaphors: Applying the concept of teamwork metaphors to the management of teams in multicultural contexts. *Organizational Dynamics, 31*(2), 101–116.

Halvorson, H. G. (2013). *Focus: Use different ways of seeing the world for success and influence.* Los Angeles, CA: Penguin.

Hamel, G., & Price, C. (2011, October 12). Creating inspired, open, and free organizations. *Harvard Business Review.* Retrieved from https://hbr.org/2011/10/the-beyond-bureaucracy-challen.

Hansen, M. (2011, June 30). What leaders need to know about collaboration? *Harvard Business Review.* Retrieved from https://hbr.org/ideacast/2011/06/what-leaders-need-to-know-abou.html

Ibarra, H., & Hansen M. T. (2011). *Are you a collaborative leader?* Retrieve from: https://herminiaibarra.com/are-you-a-collaborative-leader/

Jang, S. J. (2009). The relationships of flexible work schedules, workplace support, supervisory support, work-life balance, and the well-being of working parents. *Journal of Social Service Research, 35*(2), 93–104.

Kamdar, D., & Van Dyne, L. (2007). The joint effects of personality and workplace social exchange relationships in predicting task performance and citizenship performance. *Journal of Applied Psychology, 92*(5), 1286–1298.

Lavigna, B. (2015). Commentary: Public service motivation and employee engagement. *Public Administration Review, 75*(5), 732–733.

Lewis, T. (2011). Assessing social identity and collective efficacy as theories of group motivation at work. *International Journal of Human Resource Management, 22*(4), 963–980.

Mabery, M. J., Gibbs-Scharf, L., & Bara, D. (2013). Communities of practice foster collaboration across public health. *Journal of Knowledge Management, 17*(2), 226–236.

Martin, A. J. (2004). The role of positive psychology in enhancing satisfaction, motivation, and productivity in the workplace. *Journal of Organizational Behavior Management, 24*(1–2), 113–133.

Martin, A. J. (2009). Motivation and engagement in the workplace: Examining a multidimensional framework and instrument from a measurement and evaluation perspective. *Measurement and Evaluation in Counseling and Development, 41*(4), 223–243.

McNamara, T., Brown, M., & Pitt-Catsouphes, M. (2012). Motivators for and barriers against workplace flexibility: Comparing nonprofit, for-profit, and public sector organizations. *Community, Work & Family, 15*(4), 487–500.

Meterko, M., Mohr, D. C., & Young, G. J. (2004). Teamwork culture and patient satisfaction in hospitals. *Medical Care, 42*(5), 492–498.

Methot, J. R., Lepine, J. A., Podsakoff, N. P., & Christian, J. S. (2015). Are workplace friendships a mixed blessing? Exploring tradeoffs of multiplex relationships and their associations with job performance. *Personnel Psychology, 69*(2), 311–355.

Mitchell, R., & Boyle, B. (2015). Professional diversity, identity salience and team innovation: The moderating role of open mindedness norms. *Journal of Organizational Behavior, 36*(6), 873–894.

Morazes, J. L., Benton, A. D., Clark, S. J., & Jacquet, S. E. (2010). Views of specially-trained child welfare social workers: A qualitative study of their motivations, perceptions, and retention. *Qualitative Social Work: Research and Practice, 9*(2), 227–247.

Oandasan, I. F., Conn, L. G., Lingard, L., Karim, A., Jakubovicz, D., Whitehead, C., & Reeves, S. (2009). The impact of space and time on inter-professional teamwork in Canadian primary health care settings: Implications for health care reform. *Primary Health Care Research and Development, 10*(2), 151–162.

Proulx, K. E., Hager, M. A., & Klein, K. C. (2014). Models of collaboration between nonprofit organizations. *International Journal of Productivity and Performance Management, 63*(6), 746–765.

Rath, T., & Conchie, B. (2008). *Strengths based leadership: Great leaders, teams, and why people follow*. New York, NY: Gallup Press.

Reese, D. J., & Sontag, M. (2001). Successful inter-professional collaboration on the hospice team. *Health & Social Work, 26*(3), 167–174.

Rogers, R. K. (2009). Community collaboration: Practices of effective collaboration as reported by three urban faith-based social service programs. *Social Work & Christianity, 36*(3), 326–345.

Schwartz, T., & McCarthy, C. (2007). Manage your energy, not your time. *Harvard Business Review*. Retrieved from https://hbr.org/2007/10/manage-your-energy-not-your-time

Seligman, M. E. P., & Csikszentmihalyi, M. (2000). Positive psychology: An introduction. *American Psychologist, 55*, 5–14.

Seppala, E. (2016). To motivate employees, do 3 things well. *Harvard Business Review*. Retrieved from https://hbr.org/2016/01/to-motivate-employees-do-3-things-well

Taggar, S., & Ellis, R. (2007). The role of leaders in shaping formal team norms. *Leadership Quarterly, 18*(2), 105–120.

Tews, M. J., Michel, J. W., & Stafford, K. (2013). Does fun pay? The impact of workplace fun on employee turnover and performance. *Cornell Hospitality Quarterly, 54*(4), 370–382.

Tsasis, P. (2009). The social processes of inter-organizational collaboration and conflict in nonprofit organizations. *Nonprofit Management and Leadership, 20*(1), 5–21.

Watson, W. E., Kumar, K., & Michaelsen, L. K. (1993). Cultural diversity's impact on interaction process and performance: Comparing homogeneous and diverse task groups. *Academy of Management Journal, 36*(3), 590–602.

Welbourne, J. L., Eggerth, D., Hartley, T. A., Andrew, M. E., & Sanchez, F. (2007). Coping strategies in the workplace: Relationships with attributional style and job satisfaction. *Journal of Vocational Behavior, 70*(2), 312–325.

Winwood, P. C., Colon, R., & McEwen, K. (2013). A practical measure of workplace resilience: Developing the resilience at work scale. *Journal of Occupational and Environmental Medicine, 55*(10), 1205–1212.

Woehr, D. J., Arciniega, L. M., & Poling, T. L. (2013). Exploring the effects of value diversity on team effectiveness. *Journal of Business and Psychology, 28*(1), 107–121.

Wong, E., Tschan, F., Messerli, L., & Semmer, N. K. (2013). Expressing and amplifying positive emotions facilitate goal attainment in workplace interactions. *Frontiers in Psychology, 4.*

Word, J., & Park, S. M. (2015). The new public service? Empirical research on job choice motivation in the nonprofit sector. *Personnel Review, 44*(1), 91–118.

Work, S. (2014). Strategic collaboration as means and end: Views from members Swedish mental health strategic collaboration councils. *Journal of Interprofessional Care, 28*(1), 58–63.

APPENDIX
Featured Leader: Nick Macchione

With more than 30 years of experience in the delivery, management, and public policy of health, human services, and housing, Nick Macchione serves as San Diego County's Director of the Health and Human Services Agency. He improves the lives of approximately 1.1 million or one in three San Diegans, overseeing a professional workforce of more than 14,000 employees and a $2+ billion annual operating budget, including 166 citizen advisory boards/commissions with more than 500 contracted community service providers. The Agency is one of the largest integrated health and human services networks in the nation and has earned numerous national accolades for its highly innovative and cost-effective solutions in improving the health, safety, and well-being among residents across the region.

As the Agency Director, Macchione utilizes practical innovation to improve the quality of life of local residents. Considered a strategic and visionary leader of systems-wide solutions, Macchione has helped develop, implement, and grow a bold and ambitious county vision for population health and social wellness, called *Live Well San Diego*. This is a broad-based vision to improve outcomes associated with chronic illness, enhance the customer experience in navigating the health system, promote public safety, and support economic re-siliency. Today, *Live Well San Diego* is implemented countywide among more than 325 public-private partnerships that have committed to integrating efforts among all industry sectors toward a population that is building better health, living safely, and thriving.

Macchione holds master's degrees from Columbia University and New York University, where he specialized in leadership, management, and policy.

LEADERSHIP PROFILE FOR NICK MACCHIONE

Share your professional background and experience

My leadership stems primarily from the field of health and human serv-ices. As we always say, leadership starts as a young child, and for me it was immigrating to this country as a child. At first we relied on public assis-tance in terms of education, food, and housing assistance. It really imprinted for me the importance of public service, being the noble good. The path I took even from a young child in terms of getting involved in the commu-nity in college, to being involved in civic activities on campus and surveying the surrounding communities. I went to Rutgers and it was in the city of Newark, New Jersey, during the AIDS epidemic, which really then framed for me, even as an undergraduate student leader, the importance of getting involved in the community and how adversely affected it was in the 1980s and 1990s at the time.

That led into my path going into public service, particularly into public health, working in hospitals and the Newark Health Department and doing broad-based needs strategic planning. We weren't calling it collective im-pact then, we weren't calling it multisector collaboration in the 1990s, but in fact the AIDS epidemic was one of the times in which we really had to take a multisectoral approach and create a health care and human services safety net. That was my upbringing and also my grounding around this public servant leadership that really prized collaboration. I became the youngest Executive Director at the time, running a nonprofit organization spanning a five-county area and dealing with community-based needs assessment and health planning. We were dealing with the AIDS epidemic at that time and communicable diseases. We were making a difference by bringing government and nonprofits together and building an organized and a more coordinated delivery system that was nonexistent primarily for people who were living with or affected by HIV and AIDS.

The work I did in New Jersey, which itself was very gratifying, caught the attention of the Director in San Diego by the name of Bob Ross, who is currently the CEO of the California Endowment. The Health Director asked me to come out to San Diego to continue that work around community collaborative leadership. The Health Department was dealing with a major problem in 1995 or 1996 here in San Diego, which was HIV and AIDS. This was also at the heels of President Clinton, who had passed the Temporary Assistance for Needy Families (TANF) welfare program from the Aid to Families with Dependent Children (AFDC) program. Using that opportunity to redesign their government services, they collaborated across departments to help families achieve self-sufficiency with TANF. That was the catalyst by which they took the separate departments of public health, human services, child welfare, aging, and various commission on children's programs and created this superagency, which we call the Health and Human Services Agency.

I was part of the development of that. I was brought to San Diego because they needed someone who understood how to move from a collaborative leadership model to an integrated leadership model because they were creating an integrative delivery system here with health and human services. Extending beyond being integrative includes understanding how to be visionary and move with new solutions serving a large number of clients and helping them become self-sufficient. We also were dealing with the AIDS epidemic because it was public health and human services coming together. I was able to accomplish that and became a Deputy Director in 1997, for the next 10 years. Currently, we are the largest integrative health and human services delivery system in the nation today. For the first 10 years I was a Deputy Director in the Northern part of our county with many of the operational requirements around self-sufficiency, job protection, health promotion, public health, community collaboration, and developing the public-private partnership. I was now broadening the understanding of building the human capacity of people and the whole-person approach.

The concept back then was called "no wrong door." I don't like that phrase, but we did use it. It meant, how do we treat people irrespective of where they're coming from? From the public health door, safety door, self-sufficiency door, or food assistance door? When they come in, how do we serve them completely?

That leadership led me to success, and in 2008 I was appointed as the Director for the entire Health and Human Services Agency, which I've been doing now for the last nine-plus years. During this time we have accelerated the public-private partnership. The public servant leadership model about having a very defined collective impact and collective vision developed into *Live Well San Diego*, which is a program designed to improve not just the 1.3 million clients we serve in the health and human services but actually to affect positive change in the entire county population of 2.3 million. That's what we've been embarking on for the last seven-plus years. It's become a bona fide social movement.

My leadership transcended from the organizational and multiorganizational to now a multisectoral leadership. How do you bring various sectors, such as businesses, faith-based organizations, nonprofits, and government, working together, to have greater impact on improving people's lives in terms of health, safety, and economic well-being? That brings me up to my now 31 years of working in the public arena and serving the public.

In your experience, what are the top three to five leadership attributes someone in the health and human services field should develop? Share an example of when you have used one or more of these attributes/skills in your work

Purpose and passion. You have to stand for something. That's, I think, innate in our social workers. I think the people we attract in our Master of Social Work programs, they have that strong conviction. We all want to "do good" in the world. I talk about Don Quixote, I talk about Robin Hood, and the Machiavellian principles. You need Don Quixote in you. You need that idealism. For us it's ensuring that we can get every San Diegan living well. Like you and I are living well. You have to have that strong determination, vision, and passion to want to lead and effectuate that vision. I think without that, you're roadless really, if you don't have that notion or vision of where you want to go and how you want to do that, you can't get there.

Integrity and public stewardship. If you're going to come into our space of public service, the noblest motive is the public good. You have to have immense integrity. You have to have this altruism and operate with commitment and in that have the public stewardship. We are right now in San Diego dealing with a hepatitis A outbreak. We are shifting hand-washing stations from well-intended recreational events that we would have them available for and we are putting them into inner-city areas where we have the unsheltered homeless. We need to make sure that they are avoiding getting contaminated with hepatitis A or spreading hepatitis A. Having that ability of public stewardship and of not losing your integrity but knowing that you have to shift resources because there's never enough. So how do we do that in a way that creates a balance? You're always trying to achieve that balance. These are the *Robin Hood principles*, as I call them, with harming no one as best as you can.

Political and organizational acumen. Much of what we do doesn't happen overnight. We think about *Live Well San Diego*, it's taken us two years in the planning and seven years in the implementation. Things take time. The greatest impact we have is changing culture. If you're creating a social movement, it's about culture, it's about beliefs, it's about norms. It's not about more rules and policies because those things get torn down, but people's beliefs don't, they grow and they become contagious. It's about how you have that type of awareness, how you develop deeds beyond words; in some cases you have to walk down mockery lane. Visionary leadership is seeing what everyone is seeing and doing what no one else is doing at the cost of mockery in the present for the betterment of the future. Mockery lane is tough. You need to know how to bring friends with you because you can't do it alone. Those are the Machiavellian principles. It's understanding that when you work for public service, you're working in a political environment. It doesn't mean we have to become political, but you have to understand the political environment: knowing the mechanisms, having the patience, having that type of acumen of knowing the time, place, and stakeholders. All of the things that we do in the political context affect positive change. You can do that in a very conflicted competitive market like we have in San Diego with the Republican board, Republican mayor, and Democratic consulate and still bring everyone together. That is what we need, especially in our polarized national environment right now. That acumen is a core leadership attribute that we need for our emerging leaders and even for our senior leaders, to be candid.

A CASE STUDY BY NICK MACCHIONE

When we embarked on the *Live Well San Diego* initiative in July 2010, that was going down mockery lane. We were saying that we were going to increase life expectancy for all San Diegans. All of this material on *Live Well San Diego* has become a framework that is being replicated across other communities across the country. It's a beautiful design, and what is beautiful is that it's by the people, for the people. Right from the beginning we said with purpose in mind and intentionality, what is it we want to do? We said we want people to live a full life. We only get one chance at that, right? Nothing is more important than that because in their full life they're with their families, their loved ones, and their spiritual beliefs, and they're having the same impact on others.

So we said life expectancy is our first metric, our first indicator. That's why it's mockery lane: people look at you saying, how can you fluctuate life expectancy? We said it is not just life expectancy but also quality of life. Longer and grumpier was not the metric we wanted. Shorter and grumpier was definitely not, but longer and happier, why not? If our European colleagues have been able to affect that, why can't we? Also, other indicators include the reduction of crime, educational opportunities, unemployment, security, the natural environment, the built environment, and dealing with populations in terms of social cohesion and connecting with people.

We heard a lot of laughter as you could imagine. What did Gandhi say? "First they laugh at you, then they spit at you, then they fight you, and then they join you." Now, today, no one laughs and no one fights us. We have never had a negative story in our local paper, and we were mocked on many things. We went through very ugly labor dispute negotiations. I think they never ridiculed *Live Well San Diego* because it has become a core belief.

I share that with you because back in 2010 the second largest school district in California, the Chula Vista Elementary School District, had 25,000 kids in K–12, and they were having a serious problem.

Superintendent Francisco Escobedo was finding that absenteeism was growing. It was very apparent what they were seeing, which was unfit kids, unfit families, and unfit teachers and personnel. When children are absent because they're ill, the school will lose money. More important, because Escobedo is an education reformer, he realized that children weren't learning. He transcended the status quo, and because he heard about what we were trying to accomplish with *Live Well San Diego*, he reached out to us and said, is there any way you can help us? Obviously, we said of course. They were in the Southern part of our county and primarily a Latino and low-income community. We said we believe in whole-person wellness. We believe that to tackle these issues you have to change culture from within. We believe that you're going to have to work with not only the students and the parents but also the teachers and your board. We believe that you have to work with your local city and the business community because of the unhealthy eating choices. We presented the big picture and said if you believe in these things, we want to work with you. Lo and behold, they were trying things before coming to us that weren't working, and they said, "absolutely . . . let's try." I give them full credit because they're the ones really leading it.

We came shoulder to shoulder with our public health nurses, our social workers, and our community partners. We said it's important to also be data driven and data informed because we wanted to make sure that we were going to have an impact. This is one of the most transformative case studies. Sometime in the spring, end of 2010 and beginning of 2011, we started embarking on getting the parent's consent because we needed to do what's called the body mass index (BMI) on the youth. It's just a measure of height, weight, and fat, but we needed that for the whole school district. This was at a very interesting policy moment. There was a backlash by parents, parenting groups, and Parent-Teacher

Associations (PTAs) about this movement. There was this backlash because the concern was that we were going to be singling out, stigmatizing, and potentially traumatizing children. Parents were not giving consent. We presented, the superintendent presented, and the school board presented. They went over their teachers, and they unionized, and they went over parents reportedly, and the student council, that this was not a blame frame but a name frame. That this was about *Live Well San Diego.*

Live Well San Diego came out in phases. First was our building better health phase, then our living safely phase, and third the thriving phase. We were talking about our core formula that we focused on because we wanted to make sure how we were going to connect with almost 3.1 million San Diegans, in terms of what we were trying to do, building better health. We said we had to start somewhere. We came up with the World Health Organization position called 3-4-50, which stands for 3 lifestyles that lead to 4 chronic conditions that contribute to more than 50% of all deaths in every community of this country. Those three lifestyles are poor diet, lack of exercise, and smoking. Those four chronic diseases in the United States are cardiovascular heart disease, followed by cancer, then diabetes, and then respiratory illnesses. The data show that up to two-thirds or three-fourths of those chronic diseases are preventable. The cost is astronomical. There was a study by the Centers for Disease Control and Prevention (CDC) showing that $1.2 trillion was spent on treating diseases in 2012. The whole thing was, wait a minute, by creating a social movement we can prevent the preventable.

We went on the journey, which was about population-based health and wellness. We zoomed in on what they were eating in the 50-gram sugar muffins they were getting for their free breakfast and zoomed out and looked at where they lived, where the access to food was, and how we were creating safe corridors walking to and from school. By zooming in and zooming out the lens, we made policy and environmental changes as well as personal lifestyle changes in ways that were culturally responsive and culturally appropriate. In many cases we had the kids embracing it and bringing it back into their household and helping their parents, many of whom were monolingual, Spanish speaking.

In the course of four years, from 2010 to 2014, there was an almost 21% reduction of BMI. Why is that profound? As the Superintendent said, that's enough to fill several elementary school kids that move from overweight obesity into normal weight. Because of the scholastic concerns of how they ranked, and not wanting to lose kids, he actually saw the curve in terms of their scholastic improvement. Obviously, a kid in class learning, and now happy and learning, is going to have a stronger mind and stronger body.

We said to Chula Vista, in our case, in San Diego obesity and diabetes was our third leading cause of death, and we were giving these kids adult medications because they were coming up with type 2 diabetes. We got over 95% approvals from the parents to get their child's height and weight measured. What we discovered was that 40% of the 35,000 kids were overweight or obese.

For us it was, how do we create adaptive learning? How do we create a learning environment, not only at the organizational level but also at the multisystem level of *Live Well San Diego?* We took the evidence and came up with a *Body Mass Index Surveillance Kit* based on the work we did with Chula Vista. Then we shared how you go about doing this mass number of BMIs and the interventions. Then to accompany that, we recently added the *Tools for Schools Toolkit,* which was all the best practices and approaches used to reduce the childhood obesity, including addressing behavioral health. It transcended beyond just the chronic disease to the whole health and well-being of the child. We took that to our 42 school districts. San Diego has over 600,000 school-aged kids. When you take the mountain to Mohamed, as they say, which is the second largest student body in California, and when you add in the teachers and the parents, we're at 1.2 million. That's the social movement. Not all schools were at abnormal BMIs; the point is we didn't consult with them, we collaborated. The nature of the work is that you want to really help, but you have to understand that you never just consult but also collaborate. When you consult, you're talking to people, which is different from collaboration. When you consult, you won't get their buy-in—it doesn't become sticky and grow.

We have moved into integrative projects with the business communities, working with local businesses and the parks. That's one spoke in the wheel of *Live Well San Diego.* We have 317 *Live Well* partners. One of those partners is the Chula Vista Elementary School District. Another is the Chamber of Commerce, which represents 3,000 businesses promoting worksite wellness. With all of these partners, it's only an exchange of gratitude, and I call it the public handshake of working together; there's no exchange of money. It's not money I'm giving them, but rather it is community that I offer. San Diegans helping San Diegans, people helping people.

I hope that gives you a little bit of insight into one example of how we're really improving lives and saving money, but saving money wasn't really the driver. It was about how we get these kids to have a long full life. I don't even know how to quantify the differences we've made in the lives of the kids that we prevented from becoming obese or overweight, or the kids that we reverted back to healthy. We know that we have achieved a 30% reduction in the number of these kids who develop type 2 diabetic as adults, a condition that has a shorter life expectancy overall.

We took a different leadership approach to local government, where we were the backbone of this collective impact. I tell people it doesn't matter—it could be a school, a university, United Way, a faith group, a city—it doesn't matter who it is, as long as the intent is pure. I think that's why we're going to see localism, particularly in this very conflicted national environment. Localism, the interplay of local communities and states, is going to be driving significant improvements.

CASE DISCUSSION POINTS

1. What was the health and human need that was identified?
2. What were the innovative solution and vision?
3. Describe the barriers or obstacles to the proposed interventions and how the innovative leader able to overcome these.
4. What did the social architect mean by his statement about "going down mockery lane?"
5. Describe the public-private partnership approach that is mentioned by this innovative leader to solving a community problem. What are the strengths and limitations associated with these types of partnerships/collaborations?
6. How did this social architect obtain the buy-in from a variety of stakeholders that had different concerns and needs?
7. What does this innovative leader attribute to his success? In other words, what element(s) were necessary in the adoption of these groundbreaking programs (both the *Live Well San Diego* and the Chula Vista Elementary School District initiative)?

5

Leadership and Communication Strategies

Communication must be H.O.T. That is <u>H</u>onest, <u>O</u>pen, and <u>T</u>wo-way
—Dan Oswald

CHAPTER OBJECTIVES

1. Review major verbal, written, body, and nonverbal communication techniques that social architects use to accomplish social change and innovation;
2. Explore communication strategies and skills applied in the health and human services field;
3. Learn how to share thoughts and emotions, avoiding misunderstandings and potential conflict;
4. Learn how to become a more influential communicator;
5. Review effective cross-cultural communication; and
6. Gain insights on innovative leadership from a social architect (see Appendix to this chapter).

INTRODUCTION

Communication is an art! The ability to meaningfully share thoughts, emotions, and feelings with others requires purpose, experience, and practice. We are constantly exposed to information bombardment and overload, which makes it even more difficult to select information and communicate effectively. Throughout the day, from the time we wake up to the time we go to sleep, we receive messages from several sources, including traditional and social media, roadside advertising, family, work, and friends. All this information must be assessed somewhat rapidly to figure out options and to make decisions. Our brains are constantly receiving messages, pushing our boundaries and testing our capacity to retain, retrieve, and use the messaging properly at any given time. How do we sort out usable information to eloquently share thoughts and ideas with others? What are the most effective communication techniques that will help us achieve our professional goals and those of the organizations we interact with regularly?

On an initial level, the communication process has three elements. First, one person or entity sends the information (sender). Second, that message is sent using a specific conduit or method (channel). Third, another person or entity receives the message (receiver). For example, a supervisor tells a team member on the phone: "work with two clients today." The sender is the supervisor, the phone/voice is the channel, and the employee is the receiver. Although this communication process may seem like a simple schema, it can rapidly become complex when one or more of these elements does not act as intended. Case in point: the team member could have misunderstood the instructions or may not know exactly which two clients the supervisor was referring to. Either way, the communication process as initially intended can be blocked, interrupted, and/ or misunderstood.

Levels of communication play a critical role in determining the effectiveness of the communication process. Figure 5.1 explains these levels from highly effective to least effective. Because nonverbal clues constitute more than 70% of the communication process, sensitive information should be shared in person, when both parties have the opportunity to assess the content of the message by observing each other's nonverbal expressions. Less sensitive and more public

Highly Effective

Type	Method	Modality
Two-way	Live	In-person
Two-way	Video, voice, writing	Video with caption
Two-way	Video & voice	Video-conferencing
Two-way	Voice	Phone, audio
Two-way	Writing	Chat, message
One-way	Video & voice	Video message
One-way	Voice	Phone message
One-way	Writing	Email, letter, text

Least Effective

Figure 5.1 Communication Process Effectiveness.

information can be shared using one-way method and voice (i.e., voice message). More general messages that do not require two-way sensitive exchanges can be communicated using a one-way method and in writing (i.e., email or text message). The leader must find the appropriate method to communicate with others. At times, it is best to use multiple types of communication and modalities to ensure the message is clearly delivered by the sender and appropriately understood by the receiver.

Another basic understanding in the process of communication is how we share information. Social change and innovation take place using carefully planned communication methods and techniques. Positive results depend on a concerted effort to decide what and how information is shared. Social architects observe and analyze internal and external circumstances around their potential decisions, possible reactions from stakeholders, and consequences of how the messaging is conveyed. The decision should focus not only on the three basic elements (who sends the message, what conduits will be used, and who is expected to receive it) but also on how the information is shared. Consideration is given to how much information is shared, including words, phrases, and images, the tone of the message, the emotional side of the information, and how others respond.

This chapter will focus on the current knowledge of effective and ineffective communication. First, we will explore verbal, written, visual, and body language. Then, a section will be dedicated to the power of nonverbal communication, such as gestures, tone of voice, facial expressions, and listening skills. This information will be followed by key leadership communication attributes, including expressing thoughts and emotions, highlighting strategies for efficient and effective communication, exploring cross-cultural communication, and improving communication to build relationships with others.

COMMUNICATION 101

The way we communicate can definitely shape the viewers' impressions and responses. Elected officials, news media broadcasters, instructors, actors, and others are constantly looking for tips to improve their communication skills. They know that verbal, written, and visual cues have significant consequences. For example, Nagel, Maurer, and Reinemann (2012) found not only that political candidates can change their constituents' views and impressions depending on the quality of their verbal, written, and visual skills but also that visual techniques have the greatest influence. These findings are consistent with the notion that human beings are becoming more visual learners and responders. The amount of screen time we spend with television, video, electronic, computer games, and other forms of social media has significantly increased in the past few years.

Furthermore, De Vries, Bakker-Pieper, and Oostenveld (2010) investigated the relationship between leader styles and leadership outcomes for six main communication skills: verbal aggressiveness, expressiveness, preciseness, assuredness, supportiveness, and argumentativeness. This study showed that human-oriented leaders (e.g., transformational, authentic, and servant leaders) communicate more frequently and more positively, whereas task-oriented leaders (i.e., those who are less focused on relational aspects of communication and leadership) are significantly less communicative.

The quality and frequency of communication must be particularly noted. In looking at emotional expressiveness and authenticity effects on team members, Ilies, Curseu, Dimotakis, and Spitzmuller (2013) learned that when leaders expressed emotions genuinely, they were perceived as authentic and were followed more regularly. The team members also engaged with the leader more closely, feeling a greater effectiveness in their overall mission. Therefore, communication is a key tool to build a powerful working relationship because of the influence exercised by the leader, who has the ability to yield an emotional and lasting effect on the follower. This emotional aspect of communication is highlighted in leaders in clinical settings. While exploring the characteristics of effective clinical leaders in mental health practice, Ennis, Happell, Broadbent, and Reid-Searl (2013) surveyed nursing students and junior staff to discover that their relationship with their leaders depended on four communication skills: choice of language, relationship quality, nonverbal communication, and listening and relevance of communication. The positive connection between innovative leaders and team members begins with strong communication skills, leading to a lasting and mutually beneficial professional relationship.

Beyond the visual communication stimuli, the leader is bound to successfully convey information with both verbal and written skills. First, effective oral presentation skills must be part of the habitual exchange of ideas. This is truncated when people do not share their concerns openly and positively with others. A reason for this lack of verbal expression is that public speaking continues to be one of the top fears among people. Individuals are usually hyperconscious of either potential negative consequences or judgment from peers, forcing them to remain silent and never work to develop these verbal communication attributes. Nonetheless, these fears can be reduced or eliminated by preparation and practice. McConnell (2009) suggests that anyone can learn to overcome fears of public speaking by putting into practice the following five steps: researching the topic thoroughly, outlining the points the talk will cover, studying the audience composition, planning specific levels of understanding, and being aware of potential reactions from the audience. Learning and practicing how to successfully communicate verbally has long-lasting positive consequences, such as increasing the individual's promotional abilities, gaining key opportunities for change, and being appropriately understood.

Ideally, high levels of verbal communication skills must be coupled with effective written communication techniques. Writing is a critical means for social change and innovation as the leadership role focuses on advocating for a cause or helping others. Galer-Unti and Tappe (2006) argue that individuals working in the health and human services field can successfully develop effective writing skills by participating in writing-intensive programs, which helps them to engage regularly in writing strategies for planning, implementing, and assessing advocacy efforts. Improving writing skills to convey a message and/or influence others is a specialized process, in which repetition and ongoing guidance lead to the successful application of critical thinking skills. Thus, effective communication becomes a leadership competence, in which the leader engages with the followers in direct dialogue, sharing and seeking feedback, participating in decision-making, and being perceived as open and involved (Johansson, Miller, & Hamrin, 2014).

There are multiple forms of assessing effective communication. Ultimately, communication effectiveness boils down to how the communication is received by others and how much influence/impact the leader has on the followers. For example, when Heaven, Clegg, and Maguire (2006) examined how communication skills taught in training workshops are applied in the workplace, they learned that successful clinical supervisors often engage in a transfer process. Moreover, practitioners showed the ability to use effective communication skills by paying special attention to the patient cues and concerns. For example, primary care workers who experienced supervision showed evidence of being able to transfer communication skills, which they learned both in training and while practicing in a clinical setting. These communication skills are groomed by constant interaction, where the supervised groups use open-ended questions, negotiation skills, and exploration. Similarly, assessing effective verbal and oral communication skills within organizations, Bambacas and Patrickson (2009) learned that without providing communication skills training sessions on a regular basis, organizations are at a disadvantage compared with those workplaces where developing communication skills is explicitly targeted as part of the human resources training.

Ineffective communication is costly and unnecessary. In a *Harvard Business Review* article, Solomon (2015) shows how communication issues can prevent effective leadership. The article examines the Interact/Harris Poll, which is conducted online annually with 1,000 US workers. One key finding is that 91% of employees consider ineffective communication as a big issue that could drag executives down. Among the most ineffective communication skills are not recognizing employee achievements, not giving clear directions, not having time to meet with employees, and refusing to talk to subordinates.

Moreover, Groysberg and Slind (2012) surveyed a group of more than 200 hospital workers to find that 25% of them were "unsure" about whether or not the organization appropriately communicates issues to their employees and does so on a timely basis. These assessments demonstrate that innovative leaders are best communicators not only when they use appropriate visual, verbal, and writing communication strategies but also when they are closer to the people with whom they need to communicate. The largest impacts seem to be when leaders are better listeners, meet with followers in smaller groups, build trust by showing genuine intentions, and become better communicators by being who they are (i.e., authentic).

The Power of Nonverbal Communication

Nonverbal communication is the most influential element in communication and yet it is the least practiced. It involves conscious and unconscious complex exchanges of encoding and decoding messages. This type of communication occurs all the time between people by sending and receiving wordless clues. Nonverbal communication is mostly visual, which includes body language, distance, facial expressions, gestures, physical appearance, and eye contact (e.g., actions of looking while talking and listening, frequency and pattern of glance, pupil dilation, and blink rate). More important, nonverbal communication can also be transmitted by voice (e.g., quality, rate, pitch, volume, stress, intonation, and style), touch, perception, and emotion. The bulk of the literature in nonverbal communication has focused on three specific areas of study: environmental conditions, physical characteristics of the communicators, and behaviors during interactions.

Another area of study is how nonverbal communication influences others. Social architects put a great deal of effort and resources into improving and perfecting the art of effecting and inspiring change in others' behaviors and attitudes. They use trained tones of voices, body language movements, and specific facial expressions to get others to embrace or resist behaviors without using words. Burgoon, Dunbar, and Segrin (2002) explain that this nonverbal influence emphasizes the persuasive power of one person over another in three main elements: attraction (i.e., likelihood to respond positively to another person based on attraction), similarity (i.e., common attitudes, backgrounds, values, knowledge, and communication styles), and intimacy (i.e., the intrinsic motivation created by a strong bond through a close interpersonal relationship).

Historically, innovative leaders have used nonverbal communication skills like patterns of behavior, relationship building, and emotional expressivity to manage multiple social worlds and to advance social movements. Social architects can sense how people are feeling and how they are reacting to current issues. In many ways, these nonverbal communication skills are needed to decipher how the masses are trying to convey their need for change. Patterson (2014) studied historical trends in nonverbal communication over the past 50 years. He concluded that leaders tend to adjust to their environment and to take a systematic approach to change by calculating and influencing key factors, understanding how settings and environments matter to followers, and clarifying patterns of behavior. Moreover, these innovative leaders emphasized the importance of forming relationships by using nonverbal behaviors as a regular form of communication (Montepare, 2005). These historical social architects commonly utilized nonverbal behavior, such as emotional expressivity and trustworthiness, to build and/or maintain ongoing cooperation and social exchanges (Boone & Buck, 2003).

In looking at the workplace today, one can best observe the value and the power of nonverbal communication. Your body language conveys powerful messages to those around you. Vlachoutsicos (2012) suggests that before going to a meeting, members of the group should carefully review their own individual standard drivers of negative body language. For example, the drivers include how food affects their moods; how other team members react to ideas, feedback, and criticism; and even how they prepare for the meeting. These nonverbal messages can influence the meeting process and outcomes. Detert and Burris (2015) argue that leaders or team members, who send unintentional "I'm the boss" signals, not only can prevent others from freely participating but also can make them unapproachable. In order to build a better working relationship, members of the group should get to know each other and engage in informal and ongoing conversations, thus creating trust and making others feel more relaxed.

Powerful nonverbal communication is also associated with psychological, biological, and behavioral changes. We know that a power posture affects neuroendocrine levels and risk tolerance (Carney, Cuddy, & Yap, 2010). Leaders who experience high levels of testosterone showed lower levels of cortisol, yielding an increase in sense of power and risk tolerance. On the other hand, those leaders who tend to show a low-power posture experienced more stress and projected less confidence (Carney et al., 2010). Nonetheless, confidence can be problematic because excessive amounts of confidence may be a turn-off among members of the group. Locke and Anderson (2015) studied confident individuals in positions of power within their own organizations and how the team members' perceptions affect the participative decision-making process.

As it turns out, team members are negatively affected, mostly by participating less, when they perceive that people of power are present. Group members may fear negative consequences of sharing their ideas and opinions. Similarly, if other members of the group exhibit an excessive amount of confidence, then group members reduce their interaction with one another, resulting in less productivity and sharing. Therefore, it is recommended that individuals of any gender use proper stance and sit up straight when they meet people to project confidence, but do this neither excessively nor in a threatening fashion (Carney, Hall, & LeBeau, 2005).

Finally, as previously alluded, nonverbal communication has the power to transmit emotion among group members. Kramer, Guillory, and Handcock (2014) studied how the emotions expressed from one individual on Facebook can affect others. They found that emotional contagion can be transferred by tone of messages and nonverbal cues. If messages were positive, so were the readers' responses. On the other hand, negative messages resulted in expression of feelings such as anger, frustration, and threatening replies. Additionally, Frisch and Greene (2016) found that members of the group who tend not to participate are more likely to transmit dissatisfaction or agreement. Consequently, it is important to encourage participation from all members of the group by applying other tactics, such as offering anonymous polling, breaking down into smaller groups, providing incentives, and emphasizing a "no-retaliation" protocol. These strategies can help the group experience a more positive emotional contagion, reach decisions more effectively, and have stronger working relationships.

Expressing Thoughts and Emotions

As we express ourselves, others pick up visual, written, verbal, and nonverbal clues. A very important part of communication involves the power of intent. Nayar (2013) argues that when leaders communicate, they must be genuine by both making clear what they are trying to achieve during their interaction with others and understanding the intentions of those people around them. Ambiguity is not an option because it leads to misunderstanding and frustration. Intentionality can best be communicated by leaders using confidence, candor, and courage. Ashkenas (2011) argues that by being honest and starting courageous conversations, leaders create safe spaces and promote the flow of dialogue, where members of the group can raise issues without negative consequences. This can be accomplished if members of the group use positive speaking skills at all times, achieving a balance between warmth and competence. This does not mean that team members "sugar-coat" the issues at hand, but rather feel empowered to engage in difficult discussions in gentle ways. In other words, the interactions among members are perceived as solution-driven to achieve their desired goals and not just accusatory or unfavorable (Fiske et al., 2015).

Managing courageous conversations and conflict is not an easy endeavor. Today, two-thirds of managers are uncomfortable communicating with employees. Most people try to avoid conflict, having a tendency to withdraw from situations in which they need to confront others. The idea of giving constructive feedback terrifies most people, especially when improvement and change are needed. One of the reasons people do not engage in these kinds of conversations is that they are emotional in nature. Emotions can run high, prompting members of the group to disengage. Thus, social architects must pay special attention to the emotional displays within and outside the group. Koning and Van Kleef (2015) studied the effects of happy and angry expressions of leaders on their followers' behaviors. They learned that the negative emotions displayed by the leader resulted in followers' increase in anger and discontent toward the organization. One key solution is to focus on how the message is delivered. Solomon (2016) emphasizes that leaders should be direct but kind, listen, not make it personal, be present, and inspire greatness.

During tough discussions or negotiations, emotions like anger, sadness, disappointment, anxiety, envy, excitement, and regret can play a large role. These emotions can directly affect people's behaviors and ability to effectively communicate. Most often, when negative emotions are present, it leads to poor outcomes. Parties do not reach optimization during their negations because they are trapped trying to manage their anger, anxiety, and/or other feelings and emotions. These high-intensity emotions can contribute to mental exhaustion, lowering the ability to think clearly and communicate concisely (Seppala, 2016). Brooks (2015) recommends to plan ahead to be ready for the different stages of the negotiation. Specifically, innovative leaders must learn and practice coping strategies for self and others, including managing anger preparing an emotional strategy, handling disappointment and regret, and tempering happiness and excitement.

As we communicate with others, simultaneously we try to manage our emotions and make sense of the emotions of others. A social architect has the ability to understand the affective dimensions (i.e., emotion around them) and sense-making as a key process in effective communication. According to Steigenberger (2015), the four basic emotions that can shape sense-making are anger, fear, anxiety, and hope. By managing these emotions, social architects can improve the interpersonal communication outcomes. Instead of hiding feelings and emotions, innovative leaders can be more productive by showing their own emotions in a genuine fashion. Communicating vulnerabilities to other members of the group may no longer be considered a weakness. On the contrary, Brendel (2014) argues, leaders who express their vulnerabilities are better respected, have higher rapport with their followers, and are perceived as stronger leaders. This leader approach brings people closer together, encouraging human connection, well-being, and empathy. This is important because cognitive and emotional empathy have shown to positively affect people's perceptions and organizational behavior (Pohl, Del Santo, & Battistelli, 2015).

STRATEGIES FOR EFFICIENT AND EFFECTIVE COMMUNICATION

Efficient and effective communication takes practice. The first step for social architects—and the most important—is to master our own communication style. How do we communicate with others? What are our short fuses? Can we get our point across easily, or does it take some time to share our thoughts and feelings appropriately? How can we improve our communication? Some of the answers to these questions will help us understand our communication styles and how we handle difficult conversations with others. One strategy involves communicating with image-based words that describe a clear vision. Carton (2015) explains that image-based words convey sensory information of a vivid picture of the future. For example, it has been proved that better patient outcomes are reached when leaders communicate their visions using image-based words. When communicating the desired vision, leaders also pay attention to positive working relationships. When studying leadership and communication, Henderson (2015) concluded that building and maintaining strong working relationships are attained "when leaders role-model and encourage staff to use open communication that draws on basic rules such as honesty, consistency, respect, inclusiveness, appropriate recognition, and establishing safety and trust" (p. 694).

Social architects must be ready and comfortable managing stressful conversations. Group members within and between organizations cannot always agree or avoid conflict (nor should conflict be avoided). Often, innovative leaders have to confront delicate situations caused by disagreement, lack of performance, issues with colleagues, workers not following instructions, and many others. Weeks (2016) offers the following strategies to better manage stressful conversations: approaching the situation with greater self-awareness, rehearsing in advance, and applying three proven communication techniques—honoring your partner, disarming by restating intentions, and fighting tactics rather than people. Similarly, when disagreement is present, Gallo (2014) advises to be realistic about the risks, decide on whether it is best to wait to voice your opinion, identify a shared goal, ask permission to disagree, stay calm, validate the original point, not make judgments, stay humble, and acknowledge authority. A key objective in any tense discussion is to de-escalate negative feelings like frustration and anger by setting up collaborative intentions, describing and sharing feeling about facts, identifying why this is important to both parties, and engaging in joint problem-solving (Webb, 2016).

When the nature of the communication is more contentious, such as during conflict resolution discussions, then it becomes a bit more difficult to share and understand each other's perspectives. Nonetheless, the presence of conflict in a group can be positive as long as communication between parties is handled appropriately. Knight (2015) recommends leaders putting in motion the following strategies: challenge your mindset, be calm and centered, plan but do not script, acknowledge your counterpart's perspective, be compassionate, slow down and listen, give something back by proposing alternatives, and reflect. Davey (2016) agrees that conflict is normal even in high-performing teams. Some strategies during high-tension communications are to validate others during arguments and reduce defensiveness tactics by acknowledging each other's points.

The communication between social architects and team members should be transparent and inspirational. To illustrate this point, we know that authentic and charismatic leaders are perceived to communicate more effectively by others because they have already built trust with their followers. Their communication style is usually symmetrical (balanced) and purposeful. Typically, organizations with authentic leaders cultivate high-quality relationship with their employees, characterized by information substantiality, accountability, high employee participation, and fostering trust, commitment, and satisfaction (Men & Stacks, 2014). As team members emotionally connect with their leaders, they build a sense of identity. The type of communication and shared identity within the group reflects their norms and subculture, creating a greater bond among members (Greenaway, Wright, Willingham, Reynolds, & Haslam, 2015). Similarly, the social architect exhibits the ability to communicate a clear, visionary, and inspirational message that captivates and motivates team members. As a practical reference, Antonakis, Fenley, and Liechti (2012, p. 54) created the following Charismatic Leadership Tactics (CLTs):

1. Use metaphors, similes, and analogies
2. Tell stories and anecdotes
3. Use contrasts
4. Ask rhetorical questions
5. Use three-part lists

6. Use expressions of moral conviction
7. Reflect on the group's sentiments
8. Set high goals
9. Project confidence that the goals can be achieved
10. Use animated voice
11. Use facial expressions
12. Use gestures

CROSS-CULTURAL COMMUNICATION

More than ever before, we live in an interconnected world. Because of social media and other technologies, local issues can quickly become national and even global movements. People from different walks of life, affinity groups, nationalities, religions, and subcultures find the need to work closely together. Nonetheless, collaborating with others who may have different values can be daunting because different cultures have their own norms and ways to exchange thoughts and ideas. There is richness in diversity, but heterogeneous groups have to be managed closely to secure successful outcomes. Using the proper communication techniques, speaking the same languages, and securing understanding among parties can be overwhelming for anyone. Thus, the social architect must pay special attention to visual, written, verbal, and nonverbal exchanges, as well as emotional expressions, while communicating with diverse others. The following three general guidelines can improve cross-cultural communications: understanding cultural norms and differences, clarifying intended messages, and recognizing emotional expressions.

Understanding Cultural Norms and Differences

Cross-cultural teams experience success when each group member takes the time to understand and display respect for each other's culture by asking questions and relating to one another on a personal level (Neely, 2014). Innovative leaders first establish norms of collaboration and specific conflict resolution techniques in a proactive fashion before conflict arrives. There is a deliberate effort to improve group dynamics through training and devoting time for people to get to know each other (Molinksky, 2015). Cross-cultural training can include learning and applying communication competencies (Matveev & Nelson, 2004) and culture orientations with verbal and nonverbal reactions (Fernández, Carrera, Sánchez, Paez, & Candia, 2000) and mapping interactions (including behavioral and attitudinal) to enhance positive communication and conflict resolution (Korac-Kakabadse, Kouzmin, Korac-Kakabadse, & Savery, 2001).

Clarifying Intended Messages. Once we have a better understanding of cultural differences, a fundamental step to ensure accurate cross-cultural communication is to be clear in the level of understanding between parties. Team members should ensure comprehension of the information shared and agreement to next steps from each side. Consequently, a key outcome in the communication process is for members of the group to avoid unnecessary conflict by establishing ground rules of communication, ensuring the information is clearly understood by probing and paraphrasing, and sharing successful models of collaboration (Fuld, 2012). Communication must be open, regular, and ongoing, allowing members of the group to ensure accuracy in what they are trying to say and when they are listening to others. The effectiveness of cross-cultural communication depends on having a balance between quality and quantity.

Recognizing Emotional Expressions. Emotional expressions take center stage in cross-cultural communication. Unfortunately, the intent and content of messages often can be easily misunderstood, creating feelings of frustration and anxiety. Social architects must not only need to understand different cultures and subcultures but also learn how to appropriately read their body language and manifestations of happiness, frustration, or anger. As we have previously mentioned, the ability to cognitively and affectively understand the emotions of self and others is called "emotional intelligence" (e.g., EI or EQ) (Scott-Ladd & Chan, 2014). The innovative leaders' objective is to positively engage others by reading and reacting to their emotions promptly and appropriately. These communication skills are extremely helpful when trying to convey sensitive information during organizational changes, social movements, and crisis responses (Ng, 2005).

Improving Communication Skills to Build Relationships with Others

Social architects must establish trust in order to build long-lasting positive relationships with their team members. Most often, the leadership style and the communication style are analogous. For example, transformational, authentic, and servant leaders have the ability to enhance team performances and creativity simultaneously. Boies, Fiset, and Gill (2015) found that these leadership styles tend to have a greater influence on team dynamics and team outcomes through establishing systematic team communications and putting the emphasis on trusting teammates. It is imperative that leaders in the helping professions continuously use open and safe communication practices and basic rules, such as being honest and consistent in communication and in demeanor;

showing respectful attitude and behaviors including an inclusive approach, and appropriately recognizing the efforts of others (Henderson, 2015). Furthermore, Thompson (2009) argues that effective leaders demonstrate presence, engage in reflective and backstage communication, and share in laughter with members of the group, while ineffective leaders often use sarcasm, facilitate unproductive debates, express boredom, and joke about others inappropriately.

As trust and relationships among group members increase, collaboration takes a different tone that is advantageous and expedient. Team members no longer feel coerced to actively participate or have to engage with others in inauthentic ways. Successful collaborations depend on building shared meaning among all group members by creating translucence (i.e., transparency) regularly (Bjørn & Ngwenyama, 2009). Leaders and organizations can also promote and foster this type of collaboration by using social media and other means of communication to share information about individuals, programs, and events to increase the awareness of current affairs among all stakeholders (Livermore & Verbovaya, 2016). This effort leads to building greater competence in collective communication that is characterized by group members spending time together, practicing trust with each other, discussing their similarities and differences, and engaging in team tasks (Thompson, 2009). To study the value of communication practices among helping professional, Propp and colleagues (2010) examined critical team communication processes that enhanced patient outcomes. They learned that the effective and efficient communication process must both ensure quality decisions and promote a synergistic team and that this will affect patient care.

Building relationships through collaboration takes time and requires the right approach. Teams can be more productive by emphasizing and practicing the use of appropriate communication skills. One basic skill, for example, is the ability to listen to one another. Listening carefully can be a powerful tool that unfortunately is not frequently and appropriately practiced and that most often gets overlooked as the conduit to create the right environment for everyone. Daimler (2016) describes three levels of listening: internal (i.e., immersed in your own thoughts, worries, and priorities), focused (i.e., understanding the other person without fully connecting), and 360 listening (i.e., listening to what the other person is saying more attentively and making sense of how it is affecting you). In other words, 360 listening is the best level of listening as we concentrate on how others are sharing information, what words they are using, what emotions they are trying to communicate, and how the combination of these messages and feelings are connecting with the listener. In order to improve your listening habits and concentration when speaking with others, you can look people in the eye, create space in the day to communicate with colleagues, paraphrase more frequently, and ask more clarifying questions.

Another communication skill that social architects should master is how to frame messages that need to be communicated to others. How we express ourselves can have a greater impact on our listeners. Innovative leaders put a great deal of time and weight on multiple factors before deciding how to frame issues. This framing is coupled with messaging. In other words, how a series of messages are going to be delivered, how words are chosen, the types of messages, and how the message will be delivered (e.g., media and other outlets) are all important considerations. Raffoni (2009) argues that the best way leaders can frame messages is by thinking about the metaphor behind the concept, simplifying the obstacles to help others navigate around them, framing issues in a way that puts both parties in a positive light, and encouraging followers to practice their own communication style needed to deal with a particular situation to ensure success. This requires a greater awareness of our own communication skills. For example, if the leader needs improvement in public speaking, it is recommended to start with an effective mindset, and practicing regularly, just like an athlete will approach mastering a sport or an artist will refine their art work. Bubriski (2011) further explains:

To approach speaking as a sport, leaders need to be aware of their own potent skills. They need to know their bodies: their instruments, and how versatile, flexible and capable they are. They need to know how things work. Where does your voice come from? What can you accomplish with gesture and movement? And how do you organize the flow of information through your body so that it has maximum impact? What's the game plan of a particular meeting or presentation, and what tools can you use to make sure it plays out the way you want it to? (p. 63)

As the social architect and team members apply appropriate and effective communication skills, the group begins to strengthen and establish stronger relationships. The communication is less calculated and more sincere. This is important because calculated words and phrases can be perceived as inauthentic. Social architects have greater impact by being open, connecting with their audience, being passionate, and being able to listen to their audience (Morgan, 2008). Furthermore, innovative leaders must be seen as people who put words into action by effectively using the space provided to them and by creating potent nonverbal messages that are consistent and reinforce the verbal and visual ones (Morgan, 2001). Building bonding between the innovative leader and followers as well as between group members utilizes visual, written, verbal, and nonverbal communication forms to establish a basic feeling of connection among group members. In many ways, the leader-follower relationship mirrors the therapist-patient connection, in which both associations bring about complex bonding needs and anxieties that must be negotiated to establish and maintain bonding. Billow (2003) describes this phenomenon as the "dynamics of bonding are continuous and inevitable; they are a source of anxiety and comfort, resistance and growth, despair and inspiration" (p. 25). It is critical that the social architect foster a true feeling of connection among members of the group on an ongoing and deliberate basis.

In closing, we have demonstrated the power of the communication process. Sharing information successfully requires paying special attention to not only what information is shared but also how it is delivered. Communication skills include verbal, visual, written, and nonverbal messages, which can be improved through systematic learning and practice. The chapter highlighted the importance of understanding others' emotional expressions as a way to better improve communication styles and relationships. Cross-cultural communication is part of our daily lives, and we need to continue learning about other cultures to avoid unnecessary misunderstanding and conflict. Social architects are constantly building bridges, fostering relationships, and establishing opportunities for successful collaboration strategies through an array of communication styles.

CHAPTER DISCUSSION QUESTIONS

1. Explain the different ways that leaders can communicate effectively versus the less effective ways.
2. What are the key aspects in effective cross-cultural communication?
3. What is the role of nonverbal communication and why is it considered as powerful?
4. Read the leader profile and case study in the Appendix to this chapter. Note innovative ideas and practices, and see what aspects of the case you can connect to the contents of the chapter and/or the overall book.

REFERENCES

Antonakis, J., Fenley, M., & Liechti, S. (2012, June). Learning charisma. *Harvard Business Review.* Retrieved from https://hbr.org/2012/06/learning-charisma-2

Ashkenas, R. (2011). Speaking up takes confidence, candor, and courage. *Harvard Business Review.* Retrieved from https://hbr.org/2011/08/speaking-up-takes-confidence-c

Bambacas, M., & Patrickson, M. (2009). Assessment of communication skills in manager selection: Some evidence from Australia. *Journal of Management Development, 28*(2), 109–120.

Billow, R. M. (2003). Bonding in group: The therapist's contribution. *International Journal of Group Psychotherapy, 53*(1), 83–110.

Bjørn, P., & Ngwenyama, O. (2009). Virtual team collaboration: Building shared meaning, resolving breakdowns and creating translucence. *Information Systems Journal, 19*(3), 227–253.

Boies, K., Fiset, J., & Gill, H. (2015). Communication and trust are key: Unlocking the relationship between leadership and team performance and creativity. *Leadership Quarterly, 26*(6), 1080–1094.

Boone, R. T., & Buck, R. (2003). Emotional expressivity and trustworthiness: The role of nonverbal behavior in the evolution of cooperation. *Journal of Nonverbal Behavior, 27*(3), 163–182.

Brendel, D. (2014). Expressing your vulnerability makes you stronger. *Harvard Business Review.* Retrieved from https://hbr.org/2014/07/expressing-your-vulnerability-makes-you-stronger

Brooks, A. W. (2015). Emotion and the art of negotiation. *Harvard Business Review.* Retrieved from https://hbr.org/2015/12/emotion-and-the-art-of-negotiation

Bubriski, P. (2011). Improve your public speaking with a more effective mindset. *Harvard Business Review.* Retrieved from https://hbr.org/2011/02/improve-your-public-speaking-w?cm_sp=Article-_-Links-_-Top%20of%20Page%20 Recirculation

Burgoon, J. K., Dunbar, N. E., & Segrin, C. (2002). Nonverbal influence. *Message Features, 23*, 445–473.

Carney, D. R., Cuddy, A. J. C., & Yap, A. J. (2010). Power posing: Brief nonverbal displays affect neuroendocrine levels and risk tolerance. *Psychological Science, 21*(10), 1363–1368.

Carney, D. R., Hall, J. A., & LeBeau, L. S. (2005). Beliefs about the nonverbal expression of social power. *Journal of Nonverbal Behavior, 29*(2), 105–123.

Carton, A. M. (2015, June 12). People remember what you say when you paint a picture. *Harvard Business Review.* Retrieved from https://hbr.org/2015/06/employees-perform-better-when-they-can-literally-see-what-youre-saying

Daimler, M. (2016, May 25). Listening is an overlooked leadership tool. *Harvard Business Review.* Retrieved from https://hbr.org/2016/05/listening-is-an-overlooked-leadership-tool

Davey, L. (2016). When an argument gets too heated, here's what to say. *Harvard Business Review.* Retrieved from https://hbr.org/2016/03/when-an-argument-gets-too-heated-heres-what-to-say?cm_sp=Article-_-Links-_-Top%20of%20Page%20 Recirculation

Detert, J., & Burris, E. (2015). Nonverbal cues get employees to open up—or shut down. *Harvard Business Review.* Retrieved from https://hbr.org/2015/12/nonverbal-cues-get-employees-to-open-upor-shut-down-2

De Vries, R. E., Bakker-Pieper, A., & Oostenveld, W. (2010). Leadership = communication? The relations of leaders' communication styles with leadership styles, knowledge sharing and leadership outcomes. *Journal of Business and Psychology, 25*(3), 367–380.

Ennis, G., Happell, B., Broadbent, M., & Reid-Searl, K. (2013). The importance of communication for clinical leaders in mental health nursing: The perspective of nurses working in mental health. *Issues in Mental Health Nursing, 34*(11), 814–819.

Fernández, I., Carrera, P., Sánchez, F., Paez, D., & Candia, L. (2000). Differences between cultures in emotional verbal and nonverbal reactions. *Psicothema,12*, 83–92. Retrieved from http://libproxy.usc.edu/login?url=http://search.proquest.com.libproxy2.usc.edu/docview/619479844?accountid=14749

Fiske, S. T., Bergsieker, H., Constantine, V., Dupree, C., Holoien, D. S., Kervyn, N., Leslie, L., & Swencionis, J. (2015). Talking up and talking down: The power of positive speaking. *Journal of Social Issues, 71*(4), 834–846.

Frisch, B., & Greene, C. (2016). Before a meeting, tell your team that silence denotes agreement. *Harvard Business Review.* Retrieved from https://hbr.org/2016/02/before-a-meeting-tell-your-team-that-silence-means-agreement?cm_sp=Article-_-Links-_-Top%20of%20Page%20Recirculation

Fuld, L. (2012). Cross-cultural communication takes more than manners. *Harvard Business Review.* Retrieved from https://hbr.org/2012/08/cross-cultural-communication-takes-more?cm_sp=Article-_-Links-_-Top%20of%20Page%20Recirculation

Galer-Unti, R., & Tappe, M. K. (2006). Developing effective written communication and advocacy skills in entry-level health educators through writing-intensive program planning methods courses. *Health Promotion Practice, 7*(1), 110–116.

Gallo, A. (2014). How to disagree with someone more powerful than you. *Harvard Business Review.* Retrieved from https://hbr.org/2016/03/how-to-disagree-with-someone-more-powerful-than-you?cm_sp=Article-_-Links-_-Top%20of%20Page%20Recirculation

Greenaway, K. H., Wright, R. G., Willingham, J., Reynolds, K. J., & Haslam, S. A. (2015). Shared identity is key to effective communication. *Personality and Social Psychology Bulletin, 41*(2), 171–182.

Groysberg, B., & Slind, M. (2012, June 11). Conversation starter: How intimate are you? *Harvard Business Review.* Retrieved from https://hbr.org/2012/06/conversation-starter-how-intim

Heaven, C., Clegg, J., & Maguire, P. (2006). Transfer of communication skills training from workshop to workplace: The impact of clinical supervision. *Patient Education and Counseling, 60*(3), 313–325.

Henderson, A. (2015). Leadership and communication: What are the imperatives? *Journal of Nursing Management, 23*(6), 693–694.

Ilies, R., Curşeu, P. L., Dimotakis, N., & Spitzmuller, M. (2013). Leaders' emotional expressiveness and their behavioural and relational authenticity: Effects on followers. *European Journal of Work and Organizational Psychology, 22*(1), 4–14.

Johansson, C. D., Miller, V., & Hamrin, S. (2014). Conceptualizing communicative leadership: A framework for analysing and developing leaders' communication competence. *Corporate Communications: An International Journal, 19*(2), 147–165.

Knight, R. (2015). How to handle difficult conversations at work. *Harvard Business Review.* Retrieved from https://hbr.org/2015/01/how-to-handle-difficult-conversations-at-work?cm_sp=Article-_-Links-_-Top%20of%20Page%20Recirculation

Koning, L. F., & Van Kleef, G. A. (2015). How leaders' emotional displays shape followers' organizational citizenship behavior. *Leadership Quarterly,26*(4), 489–501.

Korac-Kakabadse, N., Kouzmin, A., Korac-Kakabadse, A., & Savery, L. (2001). Low- and high-context communication patterns: Towards mapping cross-cultural encounters. *Cross Cultural Management, 8*(2), 3–24.

Kramer, A. D. I., Guillory, J. E., & Hancock, J. T. (2014). Experimental evidence of massive-scale emotional contagion through social networks. *PNAS Proceedings of the National Academy of Sciences of the United States of America, 111*(24), 8788–8790.

Livermore, M., & Verbovaya, O. (2016). Doing collaboration: How organizations use Facebook to foster collaboration. *Human Service Organizations: Management, Leadership & Governance, 40*(5), 553–571.

Locke, C. C., & Anderson, C. (2015). The downside of looking like a leader: Power, nonverbal confidence, and participative decision-making. *Journal of Experimental Social Psychology, 58*, 42–47.

Matveev, A. V., & Nelson, P. E. (2004). Cross cultural communication competence and multicultural team performance: Perceptions of American and Russian managers. *International Journal of Cross Cultural Management, 4*(2), 253–270.

McConnell, C. R. (2009). Effective oral presentations: Speaking before groups as part of your job. *Health Care Manager, 28*(3), 264–272.

Men, L. R., & Stacks, D. (2014). The effects of authentic leadership on strategic internal communication and employee-organization relationships. *Journal of Public Relations Research, 26*(4), 301–324.

Molinsky, A. (2015). The mistake most managers make with cross-cultural training. *Harvard Business Review.* Retrieved from https://hbr.org/2015/01/the-mistake-most-managers-make-with-cross-cultural-training?cm_sp=Article-_-Links-_-Top%20of%20Page%20Recirculation

Montepare, J. M. (2005). Marking the past and forging the future in nonverbal research: The importance of forming relations. *Journal of Nonverbal Behavior, 29*(3), 137–139.

Morgan, N. (2001). The kinesthetic speaker: Putting action into words. *Harvard Business Review.* Retrieved from https://hbr.org/2001/04/the-kinesthetic-speaker-putting-action-into-words

Morgan, N. (2008). How to become an authentic speaker. *Harvard Business Review.* Retrieved from https://hbr.org/2008/11/how-to-become-an-authentic-speaker?cm_sp=Article-_-Links-_-Top%20of%20Page%20Recirculation

Nagel, F., Maurer, M., & Reinemann, C. (2012). Is there a visual dominance in political communication? How verbal, visual, and vocal communication shape viewers' impressions of political candidates. *Journal of Communication, 62*(5), 833–850.

Nayar, V. (2013, February 18). The power of intent. *Harvard Business Review*. Retrieved from https://hbr.org/2013/02/the-power-of-intent

Neely, T. (2014). Getting cross-cultural teamwork right. *Harvard Business Review*. Retrieved from https://hbr.org/2014/09/getting-cross-cultural-teamwork-right

Ng, A. T. (2005). Cultural diversity in the integration of disaster mental health and public health: A case study in response to bioterrorism. *International Journal of Emergency Mental Health, 7*(1), 23–31. Retrieved from http://libproxy.usc.edu/login?url=http://search.proquest.com.libproxy1.usc.edu/docview/620739410?accountid=14749

Patterson, M. L. (2014). Reflections on historical trends and prospects in contemporary nonverbal research. *Journal of Nonverbal Behavior, 38*(2), 171–180.

Pohl, S., Dal Santo, L., & Battistelli, A. (2015). Empathy and emotional dissonance: Impact on organizational citizenship behaviors. *European Review of Applied Psychology, 65*(6), 295–300.

Propp, K. M., Apker, J., Ford, W. S. Z., Wallace, N., Serbenski, M., & Hofmeister, N. (2010). Meeting the complex needs of the health care team: Identification of nurse-team communication practices perceived to enhance patient outcomes. *Qualitative Health Research, 20*(1), 15–28.

Raffoni, M. (2009). How to frame your messages for maximum impact. *Harvard Business Review*. Retrieved from https://hbr.org/2009/04/leaders-frame-your-messages-fo

Scott-Ladd, B., Christopher C. A., & Chan, B. (2014). Emotional intelligence and participation in decision-making: Strategies for promoting organizational learning and change. *Strategic Change, 13*, 95–105.

Seppala, E. (2016). Your high-intensity feelings may be tiring you out. *Harvard Business Review*. Retrieved from https://hbr.org/2016/02/your-high-intensity-feelings-may-be-tiring-you-out?cm_sp=Article-_-Links-_-Top%20of%20Page%20Recirculation

Solomon, L. (2015, June 24). The communication issues that prevent effective leadership. *Harvard Business Review*. Retrieved from https://hbr.org/visual-library/2015/06/the-communication-issues-that-prevent-effective-leadership-2

Solomon, L. (2016). Two-thirds of managers are uncomfortable communicating with employees. *Harvard Business Review*. Retrieved from https://hbr.org/2016/03/two-thirds-of-managers-are-uncomfortable-communicating-with-employees?cm_sp=Article-_-Links-_-Top%20of%20Page%20Recirculation

Steigenberger, N. (2015). Emotions in sensemaking: A change management perspective. *Journal of Organizational Change Management, 28*(3), 432–451.

Thompson, J. L. (2009). Building collective communication competence in interdisciplinary research teams. *Journal of Applied Communication Research, 37*(3), 278–297.

Vlachoutsicos, C. (2012). Your body language speaks for you in meetings. *Harvard Business Review*. Retrieved https://hbr.org/2012/09/your-body-language-speaks-for\

Webb, C. (2016). How to tell a coworker they're annoying you. *Harvard Business Review*. Retrieved from https://hbr.org/2016/03/how-to-tell-a-coworker-theyre-annoying-you

Weeks, H. (2016). Taking the stress out of stressful conversations. *Harvard Business Review*. Retrieved from https://hbr.org/2001/07/taking-the-stress-out-of-stressful-conversations?cm_sp=Topics-_-Links-_-Read%20These%20First

APPENDIX
Featured Leader: Patricia Sinay

Patricia Sinay brings more than 25 years of experience working with nonprofits and foundations to Community Investment Strategies, a consulting firm she founded that connects nonprofits, corporations, government agencies, and foundations' passions to action. She has worked with civil society organizations and community leaders from the United States, Middle East, Central Europe, Africa, Latin America and the Caribbean, Mexico, and Canada. Moreover, as the national Director of Policy, Partnerships, and Program Evaluations for Blue Star Families, Patricia has the opportunity to lead a dynamic team of 12 members who build community among active military families and with their civilian neighbors. Patricia lectures on public service at the University of California, San Diego (UCSD). In 2015, she was appointed as a Trustee to the Encinitas Union School District school board where she served for two years.

Before consulting, she launched her career working with various international development and human rights organizations in Washington, DC, before moving on to the American Cancer Society and subsequently the San Francisco Foundation and the San Diego Foundation, where she worked for nearly seven years

Patricia is a founding member of Women Give San Diego and the Latina Giving Circle of San Diego. In 2009, she was appointed to an advisory committee of First 5 San Diego, and in 2011 she served on the community council to Chicano Federation's Head Starts in Encinitas and Solana. As a German Marshall Fund Transatlantic Community Foundation Fellow in 2004, Patricia worked with community foundations in Slovakia. Further, Patricia was named to *San Diego Metropolitan Magazine's* 2003 "40 under 40," an honor roll of young community leaders. In 2015, she was selected as one of 24 Latinas in California to participate in the Hispanas Organized for Political Equity (HOPE) Leadership Development Institute, as well being selected as a finalist for the San Diego Union Tribune Latino Champions.

Patricia was born in Mexico to a Peruvian mother and Argentine father. She earned a master's degree in International Affairs from American University and a bachelor's degree in Political Science with an emphasis in international relations from UCLA. Most important, she is a wife as well as a mother of two wonderful, elementary school–aged children.

LEADERSHIP PROFILE FOR PATRICIA SINAY

Share your professional background and experience

I've worked with nonprofits since the start of my career, which I guess is getting close to 30 years. I started internationally in Latin America. I was working in Washington, DC at a multinational organization and supporting organizations in Latin America. I did international development work. Everything I have done in some ways has been more in that democracy promotion area or civic engagement public service area. I worked at the American Cancer Society, and that was a great opportunity because that was a one-person office and I really figured out what works and what doesn't work. I never knew when someone called if they had just been diagnosed with cancer or they wanted to give us a check. You just had to be ready whenever the phone rang.

Then I got into philanthropy. I started working with the San Francisco Foundation and then from there I went to the San Diego Foundation. After several years with the San Diego Foundation, I started my own consulting business. The main reason I started my consulting business was that San Diego at that time, about 15 years ago, was a small town. After working at a Community Foundation, I was not sure where I wanted to work. As much as we were a border town, I could not find the right fit for me and my international background. There was not much advocacy and community organizing at the time.

A lot of times you think of Community Foundations as they talk about how much money they give out every year, but you did not get any of it. It is hard to understand that to access the funding from Community Foundations, it is about the individual donors who have set up funds, and how do you get access to those individual donors? I try as much as I can when I go to work in the community and talk to nonprofits to say, "Hey, don't look at me just as a cash register," or, "Don't look at me as just a dollar sign, but I have a lot of different tools." They can approach me in a holistic way. I ask, "What are your challenges? What are the opportunities that I may be able to connect to you with?"

One of the things I noticed as I was heading up the civil society working group and the capacity-building working group is that when you are working internationally, you are promoting democracy. It's about getting people to vote, understand democracy and civic literature, and volunteerism, but it is also about building the capacity of the nonprofit sector. For me, doing those two working groups was easy because I understood the situation. People always

asked how I got those two groups because everyone else had one. It was because when I would go in and talk to nonprofits, I had a sixth sense about the
right question to ask. I would come back from meeting with a group and they
would often call me a few days later and say, "You know that one question you
asked? That's still haunting us. That was the most important thing, and we had
not even thought about that." I thought, "Oh, this is kind of fun. Maybe I can
get paid doing this." That is how I got into consulting. Just being able to ask that
sixth-sense question.

When I first started my consulting business, I would meet with anyone who
called me, and I realized fundraising is not where I want to be because everyone
wants someone who used to work at a Community Foundation to help them
with fundraising, and it did not feel ethical. Ultimately, I went into strategic
thinking, planning, and leadership development.

In your experience, what are the top three to five leadership attributes someone in the health and human services field should develop? Share an example of when you have used one or more of these attributes/skills in your work

Have a vision. I don't do very many strategic plans with your traditional
health and human services nonprofit organizations because I found the
first questions are always, "What would success look like?" and "What is
your vision?" For example, "What is your vision for veterans and military
families? What is that big goal?" It always hard to get groups to think that
big because individuals who work in these fields are working on the day
to day. I feel they do not think that they can really resolve these problems,
and to me that's a big issue. If you can't think you can actually achieve
your success, then you might be in the wrong place. I believe the nonprofit
sector has been given this responsibility to have a big vision for our society. I remember when I worked at the American Cancer Society, whenever we were having a bad week, such as when a volunteer died of cancer,
my boss would bring us all together, and we would talk about what we
want to do the day we discover the cure for cancer. It was in our DNA
to think about the day that there would be a discovery for cancer and we
may not be needed. That is a really hard conversation with a lot of groups,
even executive directors. People always talk about the March of Dimes
and how they re-created themselves and how great that is, but I personally
think it's terrible. I think they should have shut their door and started a
new nonprofit for some of these other issues. I would rather have a success
story of a nonprofit that achieved its vision and closed its doors. That is

my bias. I would say a good nonprofit and leader, be it executive, staff, or on the board, needs to have a vision. A vision of where to go and a vision that they can articulate and communicate clearly so that people will want to follow. They need to understand their mission, and their mission needs to be specific. I worked with one group, and I kept saying, "Are you okay just supporting at-risk kids? Don't you want to ensure that at-risk kids thrive?" They responded, "Well we can't guarantee that." No you cannot guarantee it, but they do not want to be held accountable. They are getting this money, and they need to be held more accountable. It is creating a vision that you're feeling comfortable being accountable for.

Collaborate and connect with others. In this day and age, if you're a good leader, you need to understand that it's not about empire-building, but you do need to connect with others. Figure out how to connect with others so that you are looking at a bigger picture of success for your clients, or as I like to call them, "our neighbors." If your vision is in general to make sure that things are better for your sector, then how can you do it all together?

Be a facilitator. Many leaders try to be out in front, and that's not the type of leadership we need any longer. We need leadership that's about facilitating, bringing people together, and bringing the unheard voices into places like a boardroom. I will always tell people that the best board chair is going be your best facilitator. Do not think about whom everyone listens to, but think about the person who listens to everybody and can bring them into the conversations. That goes the same with executive directors and CEOs because they need to be connecting constantly with the private sector, the government sector, and others to make sure that success is being achieved. The truth is that the success of an individual is going to be measured by a lot of different hits versus the number of clients served. If you look at the old model of counting how many clients you serve, nonprofits have a hard time. They think, "If we refer this individual over to this organization, do they now get to call the person their client?" In reality we should look at how many organizations interacted positively with that client to achieve success. The more we can look at how many different groups served a particular client, the better chance we'll have of finding the right formula for different people because we will learn more by looking at the big picture versus looking at just our organization's picture.

Advocacy. You need to understand that you're advocating for your neighbors, your clients, and your staff. That part gets so lost. When I do board retreats, I talk about earning a living wage in San Diego or wherever I am, and I give them all the figures. Board members start taking notes, and they ask a lot of questions. They expect the next slide to explain that the reason I am doing this is for them to better understand their clients, but the next slide says, "My key question today is: Are you paying your staff a living wage?" I want to know if they are part of the problem or part of the solution. They say, "we are part of the solution," but I ask again if they are paying their staff a living wage. It starts a whole new conversation.

A CASE STUDY BY PATRICIA SINAY

When I was serving on a board of an affordable housing organization, I was reading the newspaper, and there was this whole article about a nonprofit affordable housing organization experiencing a conflict of interest. Since the organization had more individuals wanting the affordable housing than the units available, they had to have a lottery, and one of one of their staff members won the lottery. What I found fascinating was that everybody was stuck on a conflict of interest question of should this staff member be allowed to take a unit and should the person have even been allowed to enter the lottery. I believe it should not be about whether the staff member should have gotten it. For me, the question was, *this staff member qualifies for affordable housing, what does it say about the organization that's building this affordable housing?* They are part of the problem because they're not even paying their staff members a living wage. The staff cannot afford to live somewhere that's not affordable housing. I brought it to the board I was sitting at, and they said, "No, Patricia we can't get into that," and I said, "No, as the board we need to ask these questions." This was before I was doing a lot of strategic planning, and I remember the Executive Director looked at me and saying, "This is a very complicated question, Patricia." Fast-forward 10 years, and they hired me to do some consulting. I wasn't on the board anymore, but at that point they had finally gotten to a place where they could offer their staff a living wage. It was interesting to see that they had gotten to a place where they were now leaders in talking about living wages.

Another example is on the consultant side, still on the issue of a living wage. But this time the issue speaks to the tension that exists in leadership in nonprofits. It was the third time I came to work with this one organization that was a workforce development organization, and they were doing their strategic plan. I worked with them each year on their board retreat, and I pushed them a little harder and a little harder, and this year I talked about a theory of change. I wanted to know why they were here and why they are doing this work. Their mission was to help chronically unemployed individuals get a job. I wanted to know whether it any job or is a job that's sustainable for either them as an individual or for their families. How are we defining the quality, not just the quantity, of work the clients are being offered? They explained to me that they cannot do anything about salaries. This was an organization that served the city of San Diego, and I said, "I hear what you're saying, but right now there's a debate going on in our city especially in City Hall around whether we should raise the minimum wage to a living wage. If you look at your mission, what is your mission saying to you? Is it saying to employ a number of people or is it saying more than that?" A woman got up and said, "I don't know about this whole living wage thing. My niece is a teacher, and she has to work on weekends, and I think it's wonderful that her kids see how hard she works on the weekdays and on the weekends to provide them a good quality of life by working. There is nothing wrong with having work more than one job." To me that was a very sad statement that a parent couldn't spend any time with her child.

Later the Executive Director, the Board Chair, and I met, and they told me people were disappointed that I brought this topic up. I responded that I was sorry that they were getting pushback from this, but I will not apologize for bringing this up. It was an issue that goes directly to the heart of their mission, and the board needs to understand that they're there to represent the mission and not their individual needs. When they are sitting around that table, they are the advocates of the mission of the organization and not of their pocketbooks. I told them that it is important for them to have these difficult conversations, and I'm sorry that they didn't want to have it. As a consultant, if I don't bring it up, if I don't communicate, then who's going to bring it up? It would be un-ethical for me not to bring up the elephant that is in the room. I was pushing them to think about their mission and what success would look like for their mission. They never hired me again, but several of the board members have hired me to do retreats for other boards they're on because they knew I would bring up the hard questions. It took me a long time to think of a consultant as being a leader, but the truth is we do have access to different organizations and leaders, and we probably see the ugly in organizations much more than funders or others do. If we are doing our job ethically, we need to bring up some of the difficult conversations that will move not just one organization but a sector forward. I don't think a lot of consultants do that because they don't want to hurt their livelihood. I understand that, there is a need to think through some of these things.

CASE DISCUSSION POINTS

1. The social architect speaks to bringing up the "elephant" in the room and engaging people in difficult conversations. What do think about this? Also, describe a workplace or classroom situation where there was an elephant in the room that people chose to ignore.
2. Innovative leaders challenge the status quo. What are the best ways for such leaders to engage different stakeholders in open and candid communications?
3. What are some ways to lower the audience defensiveness during difficult conversations?
4. How can an innovative leader manage his or her own frustration in situations where important messages are dismissed?

6

Networking, Community Partnerships, and Social Media

LAKEYA CHERRY ■

I can do things you cannot, you can do things I cannot;
together we can do great things.

—MOTHER THERESA

CHAPTER OBJECTIVES

1. Understand the concept of networking for the purpose of partnership and collaboration;
2. Explore community building and innovation models;
3. Learn about technology and social media and their influence on communications; and
4. Gain insights on innovative leadership from a social architect (see Appendix to this chapter).

INTRODUCTION

For an innovative leader to be effective and ensure the success of the health and human services organization, he or she needs to know and be actively engaged not only in the agency's internal environment but also in the environments outside of the organization. Lewis, Packard, and Lewis (2007) refer to this as a leader assuming "boundary spanning roles" that require him or her to interface with the external environment and that will affect the agency's growth and survival. Social architects should also be aware of environmental trends and factors that can influence the success of the organization, such as the broader political, economic, social, and technological contexts that can affect long-term planning (Bryson, 1995; as cited in Lewis et al., 2007) (see Chapter 10 for more information on strategic planning). The importance of the innovative leader interfacing with the environment outside of the agency cannot be overstated. For example, Lewis et al. (2007) recommend that leaders develop relationships with other social services providers, businesses, community members, and advocacy groups that can lead to building collaborations and assisting with problem-solving; additionally, attending national conferences, getting involved with professional organizations, and meeting with state legislators can be advantageous to learning about cutting-edge programs, funding sources, or pending policies that will affect health and human services. There are many ways to interact with the external environment, including networking through a variety of avenues, building coalitions, and utilizing technology and social media.

This chapter will focus on how an innovative leader interfacing with the external environment can be beneficial in building communities, promoting innovative solutions, and enhancing the organization's capacity and ultimate success. We will discuss models of networking across organizations and review several professional organizations that are dedicated to helping innovative leaders network. Lastly, we will call attention to technology, particularly how leaders can use social media platforms as a form of public relations (PR) toward greater impact.

NETWORKING

What is networking and why is it important? Although there are various definitions, Gibson, Hardy, and Buckley (2014) have synthesized the concept of networking as "goal-directed behavior, both inside and outside of an organization that is focused on creating, cultivating, and utilizing interpersonal relationships" (p. 150). Networking allows the social architect to build relationships to expand his or her circle (i.e., network) and develop/join coalitions that in turn expose the organization to new and varied opportunities. A coalition has been defined as "a group of diverse organizations that join together to accomplish a specific objective that is likely to be achieved more quickly and effectively than if the organizations acted independently" (Grobman, 2015, p. 337).

A health and human services innovative leader meets and interacts with people every day, and with each interaction he or she is making some form of impression. With networking, a leader must be intentional and purposeful in interpersonal interactions as well as consistent. An innovative leader must be prepared to talk about the organization, to ask questions about others and their respective organizations, and then to follow up. To establish rapport and develop any type of relationship takes time and nurturing. For some, networking can be awkward and uncomfortable, but ultimately, it will allow a social architect to build bridges and foster connections. If done correctly, it can lead to mutual exchanges of resources that can in turn lead to future partnerships and collaborations, including coalitions (for the purposes of this chapter, the terms partnership, collaboration, and coalition will be used interchangeably).

When people typically think of networking, they think of it in terms of career advancement. While this is a benefit of networking and one not to be taken for granted, there are many other uses for networking, such as creating community awareness, heightening the visibility of the agency, and promoting innovative solutions to social problems. Networking has been shown to reap rewards for all parties involved, especially with regard to organizational effectiveness. Johansen and LeRoux (2013) studied nonprofit managerial networking and its ability to improve outcomes for organizations to see if their findings would be consistent with available research. Their study confirmed that different types of managerial networking can positively affect nonprofit organizations. For example, the researchers found that political networking increases advocacy effectiveness, while networking within the community can improve general organizational effectiveness. The findings further revealed that political networking does not contribute to the organization's effectiveness; and similarly, community networking does not help with advocacy efforts. This study makes a case for leaders of organizations to network because it contributes to the success of their initiatives, but it also demonstrates the necessity for leaders to be strategic in their networking outreach and approaches. Leaders have busy schedules and demanding jobs, so they must determine which networking efforts will lead to the greater overall benefit for their organizations.

Networking Toward Cooperation

Many organizations exist that have similar missions and values, although their methods for achieving results may differ. If these organizations were to collaborate, it is quite plausible that all parties involved would experience greater success in achieving their mission and vision, and most important, the clients that are served could be better helped through coordinated efforts. However, this is not how organizations typically operate. Many leaders of health and human services organizations, for example, work in silos. There is a common phrase that leadership is lonely at the top, but this does not always have to be the case and oftentimes is counterproductive (Gibson et al., 2014). Nonetheless, cooperation both within and across sectors (private, public, and nonprofit, or sometimes referred to as *public-private partnerships, P3s,* or *intersectoral*) showcase the power of networking and community cooperation in achieving social change are entirely possible. One way to accomplish this is through a "collaborative organization," which is defined as two or more organizations from different sectors that partner in a mutual project or program (Clayton, 2013). Clayton (2013) notes that while these partnerships can be highly rewarding, the challenges for leadership are incredibly complex because these types of arrangements do not rely on conventional hierarchical authority structures (instead, they are horizontal in their leadership structure, where power is distributed); and, as result of the fluid and complex nature of the collaboration, they need highly skilled leaders who can truly work together based on interdependence and mutual aid agreements.

As we learned in Chapter 4, when innovative leaders join forces with other leaders, the potential for impact with regard to addressing significant social issues (or wicked problems) could be far greater. For instance, the American Public Health Services Association (APHSA) and the Alliance for Strong Families and Communities (Alliance), realizing they were stronger together, entered into a "generative partnership" to address the creation of a more integrative health and human services system nationwide. These types of partnerships are thought to be "more than collaborative efforts around a single initiative; their aim is something bigger and their potential impact transformative" (Evans & Dreyfus, 2017, para. 2). According to Evans and Dreyfus (2017), the potential benefits of engaging in a generative partnership include:

- "When you commit to a generative partnership, you will more fully leverage each other's assets, expend existing resources more efficiently, and spur innovation and adaptive solutions, which actually generate new resources."
- "You gain 'co-owners' rather than 'renters' of your shared cause. Generative partnerships last beyond individual leaders and have the capacity for achieving population-level results."
- "You gain access to additional perspectives and insights necessary to help all of us understand root causes of the nation's tough societal issues, and systemically address the causes of stressors facing families and communities."

- "When times get tough, these are the partners who are by your side to help keep you focused on the 'north star.'"
- "Sustainable systems change becomes more attainable. When two distinct systems partners come together, the capacity and leadership to create longer-term change are more achievable." (Evans & Dreyfus, 2017, para. 10)

Evans and Dreyfus (2017) proposed six "accelerants" (or factors) that are transferable to organizations intending to enter into generative partnerships. The accelerants include: (1) clarity of each other's role, distinction, and boundaries; (2) authentic positive relations with executives and their teams; (3) partnerships happen gradually and are not rushed; (4) generative partnerships are untraditional and disrupt the status quo, and leaders must pay attention and remain solution-focused; (5) vision, core beliefs, and organizational commitment to getting the work done individually and collectively must be addressed early on; and (6) honesty, transparency, respect, and trust are necessary ingredients for the partnership.

The downsides of coalitions include difficulties in maintaining a focus, organizations having differing agendas, partners not being able to reach consensus, needing more time to make decisions, and requiring extra time to plan and organize (Grobman, 2015). Innovative leaders and their teams need to consider both the pros and cons regarding whether or not to engage in a coalition. Some of the top considerations according to Grobman (2015) include questions such as: Will the coalition solve a problem that one organization cannot solve alone? How much will it cost (time, money, energy)? Who should be invited to participate?

Coalition-building efforts through collaborative organizations or generative partnerships demonstrate how partnering organizations both within and across sectors can make a difference in social action. By coming together as one, organizations have the potential ability to make more of a difference politically, socially, and economically. There is much to be learned through partnerships and collaborations, and organizations can become stronger and achieve significant aims when they work together. It is the job of the innovative leader of an organization to appreciate and commit themselves to networking and such collaborative efforts.

The next section of the chapter will delve into practical ideas regarding how a social architect can network to benefit a health and human services organization and then share the vision, mission, and programs of various networking organizations that support innovative leaders as well as the use of technology and social media outlets as part of network development and communication.

Networking Strategies

As an executive director (ED) or chief executive officer (CEO) of an organization, who do you talk to? Typically, these positions represent the highest level within an organization with the exception of the board of directors. In most organizational structures, team members have someone at their level or higher whom they can establish meaningful relationships with and collaborate with at least on an internal basis. However, at the top echelon leaders typically feel that they are on their own for high-level decision making. There are circumstances in which a leader will lean on his or her executive team and/or board of directors for feedback and brainstorming, but there is much to be said about having a peer group of other executives. As previously noted, it is critical that the organizational leadership cooperate with other organizations, join coalitions, and work with external groups not only to broaden the leader's professional circle but also to expand the opportunities available for the organization that a leader represents.

There are a variety of approaches to networking, and the strategies implemented should consider what the leader is networking for (i.e., what is the intention or purpose?). A social architect would also take into account the opportunities that he or she would create in order to network or make decisions about participating in existing network opportunities. For example, attending professional conferences could be viable settings to network because these typically draw people with similar interests. Whether a leader knows someone at a conference or not, these can be considered as low-risk opportunities for the more introverted leader because beginning conversations about conference-related topics could be an easier entry to engaging others. In every industry, there are organizational affiliates who host conferences about various subject matters. Some conferences are broad in subject matter and have many workshops to choose from, whereas others are very narrow and specific. Nevertheless, the common denominator of all conferences is that there is always an opportunity to network and meet new professionals.

Clark (2015), realizing that conference environments may not be the most comfortable for everyone, recommends the following ways to make conference networking more palatable and perhaps more effective. The author provides the following tips: offering to speak on a panel, hosting a dinner, preparing for a chance encounter, interviewing people, and using wardrobe in a strategic manner. First, speaking on a panel at a conference will provide visibility for the organization and could be a way for a leader to pitch or test an innovative idea. Those in the audience who hear the leader speak may have follow-up questions and in some cases may simply want to meet to get further acquainted. Another option for a leader is to host a lunch or dinner at a restaurant near the conference venue. By hand-selecting people and inviting them to join in a shared meal, people may feel encouraged to attend. Once a leader has people's attention, it is then in the leader's purview to use the moment to build professional relationships and offer himself or herself as a resource for others.

In select conferences, attendees are provided in advance with a list of registrants, sometimes with their accompanying biographies. In these chance situations, Clark (2015) suggests that leaders do research ahead of time on those who are attending the conference and make a wish list of those whom the leader hopes to meet. The leader can either email them ahead of time or, in the case of a chance encounter at the conference, can spark a conversation more freely if he or she had done research on the individuals ahead of time and knew a little more about them or their organization. The final two approaches that Clark (2015) recommends are arranging interviews and selecting conference wardrobe strategically. For some people, it is flattering to be considered worthy of being interviewed. People will remember this and usually do not mind talking about themselves or their organizations. Lastly, leaders encounter new people in their daily lives, but those who stand out are usually those who say, do, or look a certain way. By adding special, different, albeit still professional elements to their attire, the leader can create a persona that makes them more memorable (in a positive way) and may later be a future topic of conversation (e.g., wearing the colors of an alma mater or an usual pin, given it is of good taste of course).

Professionally, conferences can be good avenues for networking; however, there are many other approaches an innovative leader might consider when hoping to establish new working relationships. Other areas might include participating in meet-up groups, alumni networks, social events, and receptions. Of these, alumni networks have great potential because many universities have a strong network of alumni internationally doing unique work. As an alumni, a leader already has something in common with everyone else (i.e., having attended the same college or university). Alumni associations may have directories that can be researched ahead of time, so a leader can do some homework and find out who attended the same school, what they studied, and where they are presently employed. A leader can outreach to them directly or through alumni departments that may assist by making an introduction. It is not a guaranteed mechanism for a new connection, but it is a great resource to consider. Furthermore, becoming involved in interest groups and engaging in activities around personal or professional interests may lead to meeting others that could be included in the leader's professional circle.

According to Gibson et al. (2014), leaders can engage in many networking behaviors and opportunities when looking to establish new relationships, collaborations, and partnerships. In most cases, it just means taking the initiative, being open and straightforward, and realizing that relationships work best when they are reciprocal. Finally, Cels, De Jong, and Nauta (2012) posit that innovative leaders network and befriend people with a certain status and then leverage those associations to lend credibility to their innovative solutions. The authors refer to this as the "social construction of credibility" in order to influence stakeholders to embrace innovative ideas (Cels et al., 2012, p. 30).

EXAMPLES OF PROFESSIONAL ORGANIZATIONS

Professional organizations serve as conduits for networking opportunities and sources of support for social architects. This section of the chapter will introduce the reader to various organizations that are dedicated to such causes.

The Network for Social Work Management (NSWM), which was formerly known as the National Network for Social Work Managers (NNSWM), was established in 1985 by Robert Maslyn and others who felt that social work professionals who had achieved positions of leadership in their organizations needed their own professional home or network of support and knowledge sharing around management and leadership issues (see the NSWM website for more information: https://socialworkmanager.org/). Maslyn and other founders of the NSWM realized that a networking structure might work best to bring cohesion among these executives who were working in nontraditional social work roles while allowing them to remain aligned with the values of their profession. One key component of NSWM was the introduction of social work management conferences. Conferences are great places for networking because they provide a central place for people to come together from various locations to learn, share, and build relationships by both sector and interest areas. NSWM's introduction of conferences did exactly what the founders thought it would do in that it brought social work leaders who had previously worked in silos face to face to collaborate and learn from each other.

Since 1985, NSWM has grown significantly and now has more than 15,000 members internationally who are committed to social work leadership in health and human services. The network's programmatic offerings have extended to a robust academic journal, international trainings, institutes for emerging leaders and doctoral scholars, an international mentoring and policy fellowship program, executive support group, webinars, career resources, and a job bank. Furthermore, members from across the world can form smaller local networks in the form of chapters to continue to develop leaders, expand professional relationships, and search for jobs. What began from an idea based on an identified need is now contributing to the successful training of human services leaders around the world who are learning core human services management competencies and best practices to improve the work they are doing within their organizations and communities. The notion behind the network is that by developing stronger innovative leaders, this will result in hardier communities whose members experience the benefits of improved and more strategic leadership.

Another example of an organization that is dedicated to social services networking is the National Human Services Assembly (NHSA), originally the National Social Work Council (NSWC), which was formed in the early 1920s by leaders of social services agencies to help individual agencies fulfill their missions better through information sharing and networking. NHSA invited representatives from philanthropic organizations as well as government entities to speak to and exchange information with leaders of local agencies about areas of importance for social work. Later, NHSA's functions were further defined to "study problems of broad social policy affecting the needs of people and to plan action to meet these needs and, also, to serve national organizations and local communities in developing effective programs, operations, and administration in the field of social welfare" (http://www.nassembly.org/nhsa). Today, NHSA has more than 55 member agencies of large national human services agencies and strives to strengthen health and human services in the United States through the active involvement and leadership of its member agencies.

The Association for Research on Nonprofit Organizations and Voluntary Action (ARNOVA) was established in 1971 originally as the Association of Voluntary Action Scholars in order to "help scholars gain insight into the day-to-day concerns of third-sector organizations, while providing nonprofit professionals with connections to research they can use to improve the work of their organizations and the quality of life for citizens and communities" (http://www.arnova.org/?page=About). ARNOVA's membership of academics and practitioners who are interested in research on nonprofit organizations, voluntary action, philanthropy, and civil society are connected through an annual conference, publications, and special interest groups.

Additionally, a multitude of other professional associations represent various disciplines that offer networking opportunities for affiliated professionals; among these are the American Public Health Association (www.apha. org), American Psychological Association (www.apa.org), Association for Community and Social Administration (www.acosa.org), American Nurses Association (www.nursingworld.org), and American Counseling Association (www.counseling.org), to name just a few. Most of these organizations offer state or regional chapters as well.

Thus, there is no reason not to be affiliated with such organizations unless it is by choice because there are so many opportunities and resources available for leaders to find their professional niche and organizations waiting to welcome a leader as a member. Gibson et al. (2014) note that the wider the network, the more people and resources that a leader will have available to support the organization, and we would add to support innovative solutions as well.

BUILDING NETWORKS AND CONNECTIONS
THROUGH TECHNOLOGY

Today the use of technology is paramount, and every day there are advances such as driverless cars, artificial intelligence (e.g., robots), and other devices to improve lives and to make daily human routines more efficient. The use of telehealth and other virtual tools for teaching, coaching, training, and the provision of health services, to name a few, are becoming more and more accessible. Technology has and continues to change the way in which people communicate and interact with one another. The World Wide Web, text messaging, email, videoconferencing, electronic mailing lists, podcasts, mobile applications, wikis, and social media (and its various forms, i.e., blogs, microblogs, social and professional networking sites, and media sharing sites) are concepts and tools that most of US society and much of the world are familiar with.

In the past, traveling for workshops and trainings was a must, but now a leader could feasibly sit at a desk at home or in the office and attend a webinar or an online meeting. If an individual wants to learn something, find someone, or connect with anyone in the world, technology can be utilized to facilitate any of these tasks. There are some cautionary issues with the use of technology, including ethics and privacy, as well as instances where face-to-face live contact would be more appropriate. Steven B. Sample (2002), the past president of the University of Southern California, offered the following warning: "Any leader who thinks that a memo is as effective as a face-to-face meeting, or that an email is as effective as a phone call, is still playing in the minor leagues" (p. 149). Thus, there is a place and a time when Internet use or technology is not always the best option, namely dealing with sensitive, difficult, or conflictual situations. (Also, there exist various legal and ethical considerations for the use of technology that are discussed in Chapter 2).

Health and human services organizations are traditionally known for being somewhat behind in their technological methods and practices. Although electronic health records have been available for some time, there are organizations that still use the old familiar paper and file cabinet method. Smart phones, video conferencing, and email are used to stay connected with bosses, colleagues, clients, and external partners; however, health and human services organizations have yet to fully catch up. According to Sommerfeldt, Kent, and Taylor (2012), the Internet is still mostly used as a one-way communication tool by some nonprofits (i.e., to disseminate information) rather than as a two-way interactive tool (dialogic) to engage stakeholders as a form of PR. According to the Nonprofit Technology Enterprise Network (2016) digital report:

> Staff shortages, budget restraints and lack of training for digital strategies and tactics plague nonprofits. Only 60% of respondents have staff dedicated to online / digital strategy. Across the board, organizations are spending about 10-20% of their overall fundraising budget for digital strategy next year. There was not a significant difference between organizations. (p. 8)

As times change, health and human services organizations have to quickly adapt. Social media used as an interactive tool has single-handedly elevated the conversation and changed the way people connect with each other, even with those outside of the customary circles. Social media has been defined as "an Internet-based technologies/tools/concept that allows the creation and exchange of user-generated content while letting users establish (at least one of these) identity, conversations, connectivity (i.e., presence), relationships, reputation, groups, and share contents" (Khan, 2013, as cited in Khan, Hoffman, & Misztur, 2014, p. 572). The next section of the chapter will explore some of the research behind the utilization of social media, as well as a few of the popular platforms.

Social Media Research Findings

Research has shown that health literacy can be improved at the individual level in addition to provision of health services at the institutional level if social media is utilized (Mano, 2014a). Nine out of 10 businesses utilize social media, which has resulted in increased exposure, improved sales, and collaboration inside companies. Silos are being broken down and productivity boosted (Stanko & Sena, 2017). Social media has also had a positive effect on volunteer engagement and monetary contributions (Mano, 2014b). Campbell, Lambright, and Wells (2014) used data from interviews and Internet searches to explore how nonprofit organizations and county departments involved in the delivery of human services in a six-county region in south-central New York State use social media. Their research revealed that Facebook is the most utilized social networking tool among organizations and that nonprofits are more likely to use social media than county departments. Social media, in general, was used for marketing, communication of organizational activities, correspondence with stakeholders, and increasing community awareness. Some barriers to social media use that were identified included institutional policies (e.g., some county agencies block access to certain sites), concern about appropriateness of fit because of population being served (e.g., high-risk youth), client confidentiality, and capacity and staff expertise concerns. It is clear that technology will continue to improve, so leaders should continuously assess their organizational situation, which includes consideration of population, policy, and capacity to decide how best to use social media in a way that will enable them to get closer to reaching the vision for their organizations.

Further studies also indicate various benefits to using social media in health and human services organizations. For example, a study of child welfare workers showed that use of technology (i.e., email, texting, and social media) has made their work with youth easier (Breyette & Hill, 2015), but it also found some challenges in terms of ethics and professional boundaries. Meanwhile, nurses in formal leadership roles are beginning to leverage social media to listen to individuals on a micro level while also positing them as role models through their use of data, social media listening tools, and crowdsourcing (Moorley & Chinn, 2016). Furthermore, a study about public health interventions found short message service (SMS) and social media use to be pervasive among Latino adolescents, and researchers recommend that programs and their staff innovate through the use of technology in order to reach their young clients and spread public health messaging (Vyas et al., 2012). To maximize the benefits of social media, organizations must use it in a strategic manner. Khan et al. (2014) posit that the benefits of social media outweigh the risks, so public-serving organizations should have a strategy in place to mitigate any potential harm, such as training employees on legal issues and limiting access to select social media tools. When an organization decides to use social media, employees must be held accountable for their social media use and understand that the same rules offline apply online, that clients must always come first, and that client confidentiality and privacy are of utmost concern. Those we serve interact with technology in their daily lives, so agencies must determine the best method of meeting them where they are.

Social Media Platforms

Three common social media/social networking platforms used by organizations are Facebook, Twitter, and LinkedIn. Facebook, a technology platform, was created to give people the power to build community and bring the world closer together (www.facebook.com). This platform enables people to connect with family and friends online in addition to virtually meeting complete strangers. Those who have Facebook accounts may share statuses, pictures, videos, news articles, and other information that matters to them. More recently, Facebook has incorporated a live video streaming feature that allows people to share where they are in the moment and what they are doing with those who are connected to them. There are functions to chat; to have private and public groups, company pages, and advertisements; and to have real-time live conversations, sell items, play games, and raise money for various causes. The platform has expanded significantly over the past 10 years to be a one-stop shop that caters to individual's varying needs.

LinkedIn, while also a social networking technology platform, is more career and employment focused. Its mission is to connect the world's professionals and make them more professional and successful (www.linkedin.com). This platform is not used as heavily as Facebook but is a great tool for branding, networking, searching for jobs, and professional development. LinkedIn is also a useful platform for organizations looking to establish themselves online beyond their website.

Twitter is another common platform used by individuals and organizations to communicate and have the ability to reach large numbers of people at once (www.twitter.com). Its mission is to give everyone the power to create and share ideas and information instantly, without barriers. Twitter users are encouraged to do this through the sharing of hashtags, images, commentary, messages ("tweets"), and resources, all within a strict number of characters and a platform that updates every few seconds.

Platforms such as Facebook, LinkedIn, and Twitter allow users to communicate online with stakeholders and to handle all related customer service activities (in the business arena because personal health-related information is protected under privacy laws). If an individual is seeking a job or a manager is looking to hire, the next job or employee might be found through social media. A survey by McKinsey found that there are multiple benefits for organizations using social media, including speedy access to experts and reductions in marketing costs, communications, and travel expenses (Stanko & Sena, 2017). While this research is primarily focused on corporate enterprises, it is worthwhile for the health and human services sector to observe and learn more about social media and to consider whether its benefits surpass its limitations or challenges, especially because most organizations are competing for funding and other resources. Most concerns over these platforms have to do with privacy, security of information, and misuse. Nonetheless, technology is the way of the world, and if an organization hopes to keep up and be competitive, innovative leaders will need to continue paying special attention and understand how to use these technologies in their organizations to network and facilitate communications. Engaging in social media can be time-consuming, so it is important that a person is strategic when establishing a professional online/virtual presence.

Levy (2013) recommends a step-by-step architecture as a transition for implementing social media in organizations to increase knowledge management. These steps go from no social media to full implementation (p. 745):

(0) *No social media implemented in organization.*
(1) *Traditional Knowledge Management (KM) tools include social media visibility.*
   Examples: (a) Portal bulletin boards are named "the wall" and resemble the user experience of the Facebook wall. (b) Important portal items are highlighted using hyperlinks in the format of tag clouds. (c) Portal home pages include pictures of employees, resembling the "Pictures" component of Facebook.
(2) *Traditional KM tools include social media functionality services.*
   Examples: (a) Traditional KM systems include "LIKE" options. (b) Traditional ECMs (Document Management Systems) include "Comment" and "LIKE" options for each document.
(3) *Social media tools are implemented (for various needs), without social media concepts.*
   Examples: (a) A Wiki serves as an organizational dictionary. The tool is enabled to users in "read only" mode. A limited number of people may add values or edit them. (b) Blogs serve as laboratory notebooks. (c) A micro-blog [Twitter] serves to spread organization competitive intelligence information to managers and other employees who need to be informed.
(4) *Social media implemented fully (concepts and tools).*
   Examples: (a) Field manages a Wiki for reporting on faults and causes. Everyone can add, change, and edit, including formatting of a report. (b) Organization uses Wiki in order to write new procedures collaboratively. (c) A manager writes a Blog communicating thoughts, ideas, and trust to employees.

Knowledge-sharing and visibility are important for organizations, and social media can open doors of opportunity. Thus, social architects who are interested in social media or who are only using it partially can consider Levy's step-by-step process for a gradual transition to full implementation. For those innovative leaders in health and social services who seek to increase or improve their organization's technological readiness, the Nonprofit Technology Enterprise Network (https://www.nten.org/) is a resource. This network provides online trainings, online groups, and localized meetings on modern technological marketing techniques and the sharing of best practices in the field.

Lastly, another important and popular venue for a leader to use is a TED Talk (https://www.ted.com/about/our-organization). TED is a way to share ideas both online and at TEDx (independently run) events that are held around the world to facilitate the spread of ideas, typically through inspirational and informative brief talks or presentations given by an individual to an audience. This is yet another way for an innovative leader to reach many people who would not normally be accessed.

In conclusion, this chapter highlighted the various ways that a human services leader can network and build coalitions with other organizations through partnerships or collaborations that can address service needs and social problems. Technology and particularly social media can be powerful tools for networking and reaching others beyond the walls of the organization. Thus, the social architect is highly influential through a multitude of ways that are innovative and instrumental in affecting positive change both in organizational structures and in the broader social context.

CHAPTER DISCUSSION QUESTIONS

1. What sort of social issues could organizations representing different sectors partner to address?
2. What are the pros and cons of entering into a coalition?
3. Look up a professional organization that assists leaders with networking and note what you have discovered.
4. What are the potential benefits and drawbacks of using social media in health and human services settings?
5. Challenge yourself to do a TED Talk.
6. Read the leader profile and case study in the Appendix to this chapter. Note innovative ideas and practices, and see what aspects of the case you can connect to the contents of the chapter and/or the overall book.

REFERENCES

Breyette, S. K., & Hill, K. (2015). The impact of electronic communication and social media on child welfare practice. *Journal of Technology in Human Services, 33*(4), 283–303.

Campbell, D. A., Lambright, K. T., & Wells, C. J. (2014). Looking for friends, fans, and followers? Social media use in public and nonprofit human services. *Public Administration Review, 74*(5), 655–663.

Cels, S., De Jong, J., & Nauta, F. (2012). *Agents of change: Strategies and tactics for social innovation.* Washington, DC: Brookings Institution Press.

Clark, D. (2015, October 13). 5 Ways to make conference networking easier. *Harvard Business Review.* Retrieved from: https://hbr.org/2015/10/5-ways-to-make-conference-networking-easier

Clayton, T. R. (2013). *Leading collaborative organizations: Insights into guiding horizontal organizations.* Bloomington, IN: iUniverse LLC.

Evans, T. W., & Dreyfus, S. N. (2017, September 20). Two national organizations strive to model generative partnership to accelerate their shared visions. *Social Innovations Journal*, online. Retrieved from http://www.socialinnovationsjournal.org/75-disruptive-innovations/2607-two-national-organizations-strive-to-model-generative-partnership-to-accelerate-their-shared-visions

Gibson, C., Hardy, J. H., & Buckley, M. R. (2014). Understanding the role of networking in organizations. *Career Development International, 19*(2), 146–161.

Grobman, G. M. (2015). *An introduction to the nonprofit sector: A practical approach for the twenty-first century* (4th ed.). Harrisburg, PA: White Hat Communications.

Johansen, M., & LeRoux, K. (2013). Managerial networking in nonprofit organizations: The impact of networking on organizational and advocacy effectiveness. *Public Administration Review, 73*(2), 355–363.

Khan, G. F., Hoffman, M. C., & Misztur, T. (2014). Best practices in social media at public, nonprofit, education, and health care organizations. *Social Science Computer Review, 32*(5), 571–574.

Levy, M. (2013). Stairways to heaven: Implementing social media in organizations. *Journal of Knowledge Management, 17*(5), 741–754.

Lewis, J. A., Packard, T. R., & Lewis, M. D. (2007). *Management of human service programs* (5th ed.). Belmont, CA: Brooks/Cole.

Mano, R. S. (2014a). Social media and online health services: A health empowerment perspective to online health information. *Computers in Human Behavior, 39,* 404–412.

Mano, R. S. (2014b). Social media, social causes, giving behavior and money contributions. *Computers in Human Behavior, 31,* 287–293.

Moorley, C., & Chinn, T. (2016). Developing nursing leadership in social media. *Journal of Advanced Nursing, 72*(3), 514–520.

Nonprofit Technology Enterprise Network. (2016). *2016 Digital outlook report.* Retrieved from http://www.care2services.com/hubfs/Digital_Outlook_Report_2016.pdf?t=1510243659648

Sample, S. B. (2002). *The contrarian's guide to leadership.* San Francisco, CA: Jossey-Bass.

Sommerfeldt, E. J., Kent, M. L., & Taylor, M. (2012). Activist practitioner perspectives of website public relations. Why aren't activist websites fulfilling the dialogic promise? *Public Relations Review, 38,* 303–312.

Stanko, T., & Sena, J. A. (2017). Exploring the impact of social networking on communication in organizations. *Journal of Computer Information Systems.* Retrieved from https://www.tandfonline.com/doi/abs/10.1080/08874417.2017.1365667

Vyas, A. N., Landry, M., Schnider, M., Rojas, A. M., & Wood, S. F. (2012). Public health interventions: Reaching Latino adolescents via short message service and social media. *Journal of Medical Internet Research, 14*(4), 31–40.

APPENDIX
Featured Leader: Lakeya Cherry

Lakeya Cherry, MSSW, is the President and CEO of the Network for Social Work Management (NSWM), an international membership organization dedicated to strengthening social work leadership in health and human services. Under her leadership, the Network has grown globally and introduced new, innovative programming that meets the needs of social work and human services leaders everywhere. At her previous position with 2U, Inc., a technology company partnering with prestigious universities to place degree programs online, Lakeya was a Senior Regional Field Manager for the University of Southern California, Suzanne Dworak-Peck School of Social Work's online Master of Social Work program. Cherry was in charge of spearheading national partnerships and managing field education agency development initiatives. She has also held a variety of direct service positions in the nonprofit sector and volunteers during her free time.

She earned her Master of Science in Social Work from Columbia University and her Bachelor of Arts in Psychology and Legal Studies from the University of California at Santa Cruz. Lakeya also holds a Certificate in Nonprofit Executive Leadership from the NHSA in collaboration with The Fund Raising School at the Lilly Family School of Philanthropy at Indiana University, the Executive Education Program at the School of Public and Environmental Affairs at Indiana University, and ASU Lodestar Center for Philanthropy and Nonprofit Innovation.

LEADERSHIP PROFILE FOR LAKEYA CHERRY

Share your professional background and experience

I have more than 10 years of experience in the human services sector. I began my career working as a Senior Case Planner at Harlem Children's Zone (HCZ) in New York City in their preventive services department immediately following my graduation from graduate school. I had learned of Harlem

Children's Zone while an undergrad and was intrigued by their model for providing targeted services within a set community (i.e., Harlem), so I was excited to get the opportunity to work at the organization. During my time at HCZ, I was responsible for a caseload of families in which there was reported truancy. I conducted home visits, assisted the families with a variety of services, and ultimately worked to get the truant youth back in school. I also led parenting classes for mandated parents on a weekly basis. About a year into my role at HCZ, I became licensed with my LMSW in New York City and wanted to obtain more clinical skills. I secured a position as a Therapist/Forensic Evaluator at the New York Center for Children and was a therapist for children who had been abused or when there were allegations of abuse. In this role, I was also responsible for conducting child-friendly forensic interviews of children when there were reported allegations of abuse. I served in this role for about a year before relocating to California, my home state.

I spent two years in California working as a Clinical Social Worker for UC San Diego and the CA Department of Corrections for their Transitional Case Management Program (TCMP). I worked in a parole office in San Bernardino, CA and was responsible for drafting case plans for eligible inmates who would soon parole back into San Bernardino. I had a caseload of high-risk parolees whom I met with regularly, providing minimal counseling, benefit, and housing assistance. After two years with the TCMP program, I began experiencing burnout and desired to obtain new skills that would enable me to go further in my career.

I began applying for nontraditional social work jobs out of state and eventually secured a role at a technology startup company called 2tor (now 2U Inc.) in the Washington, DC metro area. I relocated to Washington, DC and worked as a Field Development Coordinator. I was responsible for establishing partnerships with human services agencies domestically and internationally for the purposes of placing online MSW students in internships. I eventually was promoted to manager and then senior manager in this role, and I managed a diverse team who were responsible for all field placements in the Northeast and Midwest regions of the United States. In addition to this management responsibility, I was responsible for establishing national partnerships with large human services agencies such as Volunteers of America for the entire online program.

While at 2U Inc., I was exposed to a corporate environment, which was new to me as a social worker. As a result of this new exposure, I learned more about technology, higher education, marketing, and business development. As I learned more and grew as a professional, I desired more opportunity. I conveyed this to management at the time, and they introduced me to an opportunity at the NSWM that was hiring for CEO/Executive Director. I applied and was hired and have spent the past four years leading this organization as a new, first-time executive. In four years' time, the organization has managed to grow to more than 17,000 members globally and introduce information and programming for human services leaders looking to learn management competencies, develop themselves as leaders, mentor or be mentored, network, bring about policy change, and be thought of as leaders in the human services management sector. Much of this growth has been through the embracement and utilization of technology for our marketing.

In this role, networking is highlighted as an important and necessary component in self-development. We assist in facilitating networking among our members by our annual conference, local chapters, specialty programming, and online resources (e.g., *Monday Morning Manager*). On Mondays, the profile of a human services manager from around the world is featured; these managers speak about their career path, current projects, and lessons learned. They provide their contact information, which usually leads to informal networking among our members who have interest in what the managers have shared. Furthermore, we advertise and promote these opportunities through social media.

As an executive, I network formally and informally for NSWM. I am very active on social media and have routine communication with members and others interested in the work we're doing through Twitter, LinkedIn, Facebook, and general email. I also attend conferences and workshops routinely and collaborate with other organizations such as the Association for Community Organization and Social Administration (ACOSA) and the Council on Social Work Education (CSWE) by participating and representing NSWM as a committee member.

In your experience, what are the top three to five leadership attributes someone in the health and human services field should develop? Share an example of when you have used one or more of these attributes/skills in your work

Vision and mission. All great leaders are passionate and have a vision of what they would like to accomplish. It is their ability to convey this vision that gets those who work for them to follow and to stand behind the mission of the organization. If followers can feel and see the passion of their leader, then they will rally behind him or her. Human services agencies do very important work and have missions that could truly affect society in a positive manner. However, many times these organizations forget their mission—their overall purpose for doing what they do—and their leaders lack focus and passion for the work at hand. This then trickles down to the followers (or employees) and eventually to the populations served. This cannot happen. Leaders must stay focused, and they must always evaluate their strengths, weaknesses, opportunities, and threats in order to plan for the future of the organization. Then they must passionately convey this to their followers in order to get their buy-in.

Curiosity. Leaders should always strive to learn and improve. This not only benefits them personally but also benefits the entire organization and those they manage. Curiosity has the ability to open new doors and explore avenues that would not be considered if one were content with just how things are. By opening these doors and exploring these avenues, you are opening up the opportunity for new, innovative ideas. Leaders of human services organizations should be reading, learning new technologies, attending conferences, networking, and exposing themselves to people from different industries on a routine basis. They should always be exploring, "Why?" and then moving on to test out inventive and innovative ideas that could potentially improve their organizations.

Resourcefulness. Most human services agencies do not have adequate resources. Leaders of human services organizations must adapt to what they have, while also exploring and diving into new ways of doing things in order to get the job done efficiently and effectively. If you need something, figure out how to get it. When I first came to NSWM, it was as if I was assembling the pieces to a puzzle—a 25+-year-old puzzle. There were many facets of nonprofit management I did not understand and many things about the organization itself I simply did not know, and the information was not readily available. What I did know was that I wanted to grow the organization, and I needed help. I immediately began seeking pro bono assistance from various organizations and companies I found online in order to get done what I needed done. I refused to accept that I was limited to what my assistant and I could accomplish, given the organization's minimal finances. Instead I sought out others with expertise who were willing to give back and donate their services at no cost to organizations such as ours. Since then, the organization has a robust network of volunteers, and many are members of our organization, who are committed to what we do and are willing to do their part to keep us growing.

A CASE STUDY BY LAKEYA CHERRY

NSWM began as a membership association and charged dues for membership. In 2013 before my hiring, the board of directors decided to eliminate dues. As a new executive, I was unsure how we would generate more revenue without dues as an option. Rather than becoming discouraged, I thought about what the organization had to offer and strategized with my board to establish some products that may assist in revenue generation. Organizations need money to survive, so it was imperative that my board and I come up with a solution that could potentially sustain the organization over time. One solution was to establish a Human Services Management Certificate Program. NSWM has a set of 21 management competencies that many schools of social work have utilized in drafting their macro social work curricula. Many macro social workers do not desire to do clinical work upon graduation, yet they often are limited in their job choices if they are not licensed to practice. We saw our Human Services Management Certificate as a suitable alternative for these graduating students who would need additional credentials as they pursued more macro-focused types of jobs. In the human services sector, professionals are no longer just competing with each other. They are competing with those from other disciplines, such as business, for the same management roles in nonprofit and human services organizations. This certificate and preparation from their schools would allow them more opportunities to get the jobs they wanted and were trained for. Furthermore, it provided our organization an additional method of revenue generation. By charging various fees for the administration and issuing of the certificate for qualifying schools, our organization created an additional source of guaranteed income. This initiative was a win-win or two-for-one situation because it offered a management and leadership competency framework for our members and at the same time provided the organization with a new way to raise funds.

CASE DISCUSSION POINTS

1. In the leader profile, there are several references to the use of technology and networking. Please speak to the benefits of networking in general and of some potential drawbacks.
2. The social architect from the case speaks about developing an innovative solution to generate revenue for the organization. What other innovative solutions could also help this organization or their members to increase visibility and membership?
3. Discuss new fundraising ideas this organization can put into motion to increase sustainable revenue.

Appendices: Leader Assessment Instruments

A. THE WILDER COLLABORATION FACTORS INVENTORY

The Wilder Collaboration Factors Inventory is a useful tool for leaders to assess collaborative strengths and identify weaknesses to improve upon. This is an assessment tool to evaluate how well interagency collaboration is functioning through 20 tested factors comprised of six categories, including: Environment, Member Characteristics, Process and Structure, Communication, Purpose and Resources. This assessment is free for public use and available from:
Website access: http://wilderresearch.org/tools/cfi/form.php

B. HUMAN SERVICES COMPETENCIES ASSESSMENT CHECKLIST

Assessing Your Ratings and Next Steps

Once the human services leader/manager has completed the self-assessment, he/she should review the areas by rating. Many of the leadership competencies referenced in the assessment tool refer to performance indicators that are more likely to be expected in seasoned professionals. Here's what you can expect in your ratings and what that means:

- New management professionals are likely to have less experience in these areas and therefore rate themselves as a (1) or (2).

- As experience grows, those completing the assessment are likely to score in the (2) range.
- The most seasoned leaders are more likely to score (3).

The next step for those completing the self-assessment is to create their own development plan to be used as a blueprint for improving their skills in management and leadership. Generally, less experienced leaders/managers may want to seek out more formal education through graduate or continuing education courses in the specific areas in which skill improvement is needed. Often these are technical skill areas such as finance, human resources management, and technology. It is also essential for new leaders/managers to attend conferences related to their work and identify workshops and lectures that focus on management issues. They should take advantage of any opportunity that will make them feel more comfortable and skilled with their work.

Leaders rating themselves at the (2) level may also need some of this coursework but would also benefit from specific training in management because strong interpersonal skills begin to become more important as professionals move up in an organization. Graduate courses in organizational management are offered in most large universities and through training institutes and webinars, which are offered by institutions and organizations like the Network for Social Work Management. At this level, networking becomes extremely necessary as leaders begin to grow their professional relationships and develop a cadre of colleagues with whom they can share challenges and successes.

The work of leaders scoring themselves as (3) is more interpersonal than technical and requires strong social and emotional skills. Although there are courses available to assist with honing these skills, it is more likely that executive coaching and mentoring will be more beneficial to senior-level managers/leaders. Awareness of emotional intelligence and self-reflection are key to ensuring a high level of functioning in all of these domains. Completing a 360 evaluation can help these managers to identify areas in need of development.

The key to improved management competency is to combine soft and hard skill development. Most important, all leaders have to be willing to examine their own performance and behavior to create a plan that will maximize their effectiveness.

✓ ASSESSMENT CHECKLIST

Now that you have read about the competencies, **assess where you stack up**. This will be helpful in gauging where to improve your skills. This is also a great tool for staff evaluation.

Rate your degree of experience for each NSWM Competency and their performance indicators (PI) and provide an example to illustrate your rating.

KNOWLEDGEABLE
Exposed to the (PI) through education/training/observation

SKILLED
Operational experience with PI at team/unit level.

MASTERED
Operational experience with PI at the organization level.

Start Assessing Your Skills On the Next Page

NSWM COMPETENCY	SELF-ASSESSMENT	SUPERVISOR ASSESSMENT
DOMAIN: EXECUTIVE LEADERSHIP		
1. Competency: *Establishes, promotes, and anchors the vision, philosophy, goals, objectives, and values of the organization*	① ② ③ Example	① ② ③ Example
1.1 Creates, communicates, and anchors a vision for the organization.	① ② ③ Example	① ② ③ Example
1.2 Works to ensure that all programs align with the overall organizational mission.	① ② ③ Example	① ② ③ Example
1.3 Reviews the mission periodically to determine its relevance to client and community needs.	① ② ③ Example	① ② ③ Example
1.4 Works closely with management staff to establish benchmarks to show alignment with vision, mission, philosophy, and goals.	① ② ③ Example	① ② ③ Example
1.5 Identifies potential organizational drift from vision, mission, philosophy, and goals.	① ② ③ Example	① ② ③ Example
1.6 Demonstrates the manner in which the vision, philosophy, and values are applied in making organizational decisions.	① ② ③ Example	① ② ③ Example
2 Competency: *Possesses interpersonal skills that support the viability and positive functioning of the organization*	① ② ③ Example	① ② ③ Example
2.1 Establishes and maintains an organizational culture that recognizes and rewards professionalism, quality customer service, employee engagement and empowerment, and programs and services that further social justice.	① ② ③ Example	① ② ③ Example

NSWM COMPETENCY

SELF-ASSESSMENT

SUPERVISOR ASSESSMENT

DOMAIN: EXECUTIVE LEADERSHIP (CON'T)

NSWM COMPETENCY	SELF-ASSESSMENT	SUPERVISOR ASSESSMENT
2.2 Inspires the workforce to move beyond cynicism and complacency and to perform and produce in a superior manner.	① ② ③ Example	① ② ③ Example
2.3 Demonstrates the ability to assume different leadership styles as appropriate to the situation.	① ② ③ Example	① ② ③ Example
2.4 Possesses strong skills in emotional intelligence, self-awareness, self-mastery, etc.	① ② ③ Example	① ② ③ Example
2.5 Is able to find common ground with others and form positive relationships easily.	① ② ③ Example	① ② ③ Example
2.6 Is able to inspire confidence in others, both internally and externally.	① ② ③ Example	① ② ③ Example
2.7 Demonstrates commitment to the work of the agency.	① ② ③ Example	① ② ③ Example
2.8 Demonstrates and communicates deep knowledge about the work of the agency, using current performance data to discuss successes and challenges.	① ② ③ Example	① ② ③ Example
2.9 Recognizes the value of optimizing the human potential of staff and ensures that the organization develops healthy and productive practices that develop staff in all ways.	① ② ③ Example	① ② ③ Example
2.10 Demonstrates the ability to assemble a leadership team of individuals whose skills and abilities supplement one's own and to be a "team player."	① ② ③ Example	① ② ③ Example

NSWM COMPETENCY   **SELF-ASSESSMENT**   **SUPERVISOR ASSESSMENT**

DOMAIN: EXECUTIVE LEADERSHIP

NSWM COMPETENCY	SELF-ASSESSMENT	SUPERVISOR ASSESSMENT
3. Competency: Possesses analytical and critical thinking skills that promote organizational growth	① ② ③ Example	① ② ③ Example
3.1 Demonstrates a working knowledge of budget and finance, human resources, communication and marketing, applications of information technology, fundraising, and external relations; and an understanding or "feel" for the core work of the organization.	① ② ③ Example	① ② ③ Example
3.2 Demonstrates an entrepreneurial spirit and attitude.	① ② ③ Example	① ② ③ Example
3.3 Makes creative use of agency resources to serve the needs of diverse clients.	① ② ③ Example	① ② ③ Example
3.4 Understands and makes use of historical and current data to inform decision-making about the agency.	① ② ③ Example	① ② ③ Example
3.5 Demonstrates strong skills in turning around dysfunctional organizations.	① ② ③ Example	① ② ③ Example
3.6 Demonstrates strong critical thinking and problem-solving skills.	① ② ③ Example	① ② ③ Example
3.7 Manages ambiguous and complex organizational situations.	① ② ③ Example	① ② ③ Example
3.8 Monitors economic and political trends, shifts in trends, values, and more.	① ② ③ Example	① ② ③ Example
3.9 Displays keen skills in strategic thinking.	① ② ③ Example	① ② ③ Example
3.10 Conceptualizes innovative partnerships to maximize agency resources.	① ② ③ Example	① ② ③ Example

NSWM COMPETENCY	SELF-ASSESSMENT	SUPERVISOR ASSESSMENT
DOMAIN: EXECUTIVE LEADERSHIP		
4. Competency: Models appropriate professional behavior and encourages other staff members to act in a professional manner	① ② ③ Example _____	① ② ③ Example _____
4.1 Engages in and promotes ethical conduct.	① ② ③ Example _____	① ② ③ Example _____
4.2 Protects the integrity and reputation of the organization.	① ② ③ Example _____	① ② ③ Example _____
4.3 Creates and supports an organizational culture that values professionalism, service, and ethical conduct.	① ② ③ Example _____	① ② ③ Example _____
4.4 Encourages staff to become involved in the identification and planning of their own professional development.	① ② ③ Example _____	① ② ③ Example _____
4.5 Displays the ability to carry on effectively in the face of adversity, ambiguity, uncertainly, and anxiety.	① ② ③ Example _____	① ② ③ Example _____
4.6 Encourages staff to engage in a variety of activities including inquiry research, workshops, institutes, and observation/feedback (e.g., peer coaching and mentoring).	① ② ③ Example _____	① ② ③ Example _____
4.7 Demonstrates the ability not to be "consumed" by executive responsibilities and helps others to achieve the balance and maintain a sense of humor and perspective.	① ② ③ Example _____	① ② ③ Example _____
5. Competency: Manages diversity and cross-cultural understanding	① ② ③ Example _____	① ② ③ Example _____
5.1 Publicly acknowledges the diversity of the staff and clients and creates a climate that celebrates the differences.	① ② ③ Example _____	① ② ③ Example _____
5.2 Provides opportunities for staff to learn about different groups to enhance their practice, and encourages open discussion about issues to promote sensitivity.	① ② ③ Example _____	① ② ③ Example _____

NSWM COMPETENCY

SELF-ASSESSMENT

SUPERVISOR ASSESSMENT

DOMAIN: EXECUTIVE LEADERSHIP

5.3 Seeks to employ a diverse workforce to align with clients served by the organization.

(1)—(2)—(3) Example   (1)—(2)—(3) Example

5.4 Seeks input from all levels of staff, listens attentively, demonstrates fairness and consistency, and conveys information fully and clearly.

(1)—(2)—(3) Example   (1)—(2)—(3) Example

5.5 Invites different perspectives to all client-related and management discussions within the organization.

(1)—(2)—(3) Example   (1)—(2)—(3) Example

5.6 Encourages and allows opportunities for staff to confer and present issues and problems affecting program-related services.

(1)—(2)—(3) Example   (1)—(2)—(3) Example

5.7 Takes steps necessary to assure that all services provided by the organization are culturally competent.

(1)—(2)—(3) Example   (1)—(2)—(3) Example

6. *Competency: Develops and manages both internal and external stakeholder relationships*

(1)—(2)—(3) Example   (1)—(2)—(3) Example

6.1 Consistently and effectively motivates governance body members, employees, volunteers, clients, and other key constituencies to work toward achieving the organizational mission.

(1)—(2)—(3) Example   (1)—(2)—(3) Example

6.2 Communicates effectively to multiple constituencies, through various means and media, the mission, vision, and values of the organization along with organizational programs, policies, and performance so as to promote organizational transparency and enhance support and understanding from internal and external constituencies.

NSWM COMPETENCY	SELF-ASSESSMENT	SUPERVISOR ASSESSMENT
DOMAIN: EXECUTIVE LEADERSHIP		
6.3 Plans, thinks, and acts strategically in concert with key stakeholders to position, evolve, and change the organization to assure success in the current and future environments.	①—②—③ Example	①—②—③ Example
6.4 Successfully advocates at the national, state, and local levels for the organization, its clients, and issues promoting social justice for vulnerable populations.	①—②—③ Example	①—②—③ Example
7. *Competency: Initiates and facilitates innovative change processes*	①—②—③ Example	①—②—③ Example
7.1 Remains current on trends and identifies shifts that require an innovative response.	①—②—③ Example	①—②—③ Example
7.2 Presents innovations to appropriate decision makers and stakeholders and makes decisions that are aligned with their feedback.	①—②—③ Example	①—②—③ Example
7.3 Assists staff with implementing positive change and supports risk-taking.	①—②—③ Example	①—②—③ Example
7.4 Supports innovative practices to improve program-related issues and services.	①—②—③ Example	①—②—③ Example
8. *Competency: Advocates for public policy change and social justice at national, state, and local levels*	①—②—③ Example	①—②—③ Example
8.1 Strategically disseminates information about unmet needs and program accomplishments.	①—②—③ Example	①—②—③ Example
8.2 Participates in professional organizations and industry groups that advocate for client social justice, equity, and fairness.	①—②—③ Example	①—②—③ Example

NSWM COMPETENCY	SELF-ASSESSMENT	SUPERVISOR ASSESSMENT

DOMAIN: EXECUTIVE LEADERSHIP

8.3 Engages and encourages staff and clients/customers to be active advocates for social justice issues.

Self-Assessment: ① ② ③ Example
Supervisor Assessment: ① ② ③ Example

8.4 When appropriate and in line with organizational mission, promotes their organization as a well-recognized advocate on public policy topics.

Self-Assessment: ① ② ③ Example
Supervisor Assessment: ① ② ③ Example

8.5 Challenges broad regulatory expectations and advocates for efficient and well-tailored policies with potential to affect clients' welfare.

Self-Assessment: ① ② ③ Example
Supervisor Assessment: ① ② ③ Example

8.6 Advocates for an organizational culture that recognizes and rewards professionalism; quality customer service; employee engagement and empowerment, programs, and policies that further social justice; and efforts to achieve diversity in customers, employees, and ideas.

Self-Assessment: ① ② ③ Example
Supervisor Assessment: ① ② ③ Example

9. *Competency: Demonstrates effective interpersonal and communication skills*

Self-Assessment: ① ② ③ Example
Supervisor Assessment: ① ② ③ Example

9.1 Is able to articulate the mission and vision of the organization both orally and in writing to staff of the agency.

Self-Assessment: ① ② ③ Example
Supervisor Assessment: ① ② ③ Example

9.2 Is able to articulate the mission and vision of the agency to those outside the agency to ensure understanding of the work of the organization.

Self-Assessment: ① ② ③ Example
Supervisor Assessment: ① ② ③ Example

9.3 Ensures that all written and oral communication in the agency is carefully planned and articulated so that it is clear in its message and sensitive to the various audiences that receive it.

Self-Assessment: ① ② ③ Example
Supervisor Assessment: ① ② ③ Example

NSWM COMPETENCY

SELF-ASSESSMENT

SUPERVISOR ASSESSMENT

DOMAIN: EXECUTIVE LEADERSHIP

9.4 Manages communication in conflict and crisis situations in a competent and sensitive manner.

① ② ③ Example

① ② ③ Example

9.5 Engages in emotionally intelligent communications with all stakeholders.

① ② ③ Example

① ② ③ Example

10. *Competency: Encourages active involvement of all staff and stakeholders in decision-making processes*

① ② ③ Example

① ② ③ Example

10.1 Provides opportunities for internal and external stakeholders to give feedback before significant program changes are implemented.

① ② ③ Example

① ② ③ Example

10.2 Shows evidence of stakeholder buy-in through such means as meetings of representative groups and program surveys to the community.

① ② ③ Example

① ② ③ Example

10.3 Delegates authority and decision-making to appropriate entities and supports their decisions.

① ② ③ Example

① ② ③ Example

10.4 Uses collaborative teams and other strategies to identify outcomes, design programs, share intervention strategies, conduct assessments, analyze results, and adjust intervention processes.

① ② ③ Example

① ② ③ Example

10.5 Encourages consumers and underrepresented stakeholders to actively participate in decision-making processes.

① ② ③ Example

① ② ③ Example

10.6 Displays the ability to work with people and institutions to achieve creative compromises and "win–win" solutions.

① ② ③ Example

① ② ③ Example

NSWM COMPETENCY

SELF-ASSESSMENT

SUPERVISOR ASSESSMENT

DOMAIN: EXECUTIVE LEADERSHIP

NSWM COMPETENCY	Self-Assessment	Supervisor Assessment
11. *Competency: Plans, promotes, and models lifelong learning practices*	① ② ③ Example	① ② ③ Example
11.1 Positions the organization as a "learning organization," providing ongoing opportunities for all staff to receive professional development to assure quality service delivery.	① ② ③ Example	① ② ③ Example
11.2 Ensures that the organization offers competent and regular supervision to staff at all levels of the organization.	① ② ③ Example	① ② ③ Example
11.3 Assumes a mentorship role for less experienced managers.	① ② ③ Example	① ② ③ Example
11.4 Keeps up to date with research on instructional practices, management, and leadership, as well as on effective practices in professional development, and shares those practices with staff.	① ② ③ Example	① ② ③ Example
11.5 Engages in a variety of activities to foster the manager's own learning, such as participating in collegial networking and subscribing to journals and listservs.	① ② ③ Example	① ② ③ Example
11.6 Whenever possible, offers staff an opportunity to learn from experts, as well as make presentations themselves, at outside conferences and meetings.	① ② ③ Example	① ② ③ Example
11.7 Whenever possible, allows staff to take classes or work on advanced degrees, with the support of the agency. If agency funds are not available, flexibility in scheduling or other nonmonetary support should be offered to support learning.	① ② ③ Example	① ② ③ Example
11.8 Demonstrates self-confidence in leading the organization, capitalizing on his/her own strengths and compensating for his/her own limitations.	① ② ③ Example	① ② ③ Example

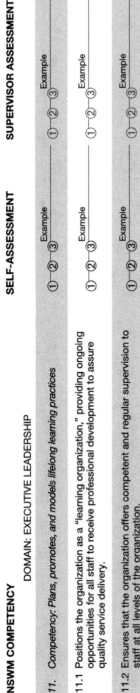

NSWM COMPETENCY

SELF-ASSESSMENT

SUPERVISOR ASSESSMENT

DOMAIN: RESOURCE MANAGEMENT

NSWM Competency	Self-Assessment	Supervisor Assessment
12. *Competency: Effectively manages human resources*	① ② ③ Example	① ② ③ Example
12.1 Designs and manages the workplace to ensure a positive and supportive culture and climate for staff and clients.	① ② ③ Example	① ② ③ Example
12.2 Designs and manages employee relations policies and practices that are fair, adhere to law, and are implemented in a consistent manner.	① ② ③ Example	① ② ③ Example
12.3 Supervises recruitment, hiring, training, performance assessment, and promotion/termination based on established criteria.	① ② ③ Example	① ② ③ Example
12.4 Creates, maintains, and fosters a discrimination- and harassment-free work environment for employees, clients, and the general public.	① ② ③ Example	① ② ③ Example
12.5 Successfully recruits and retains a diversity of employees to reflect the communities and constituencies served by the organization.	① ② ③ Example	① ② ③ Example
12.6 In settings with Civil Service and Unions, works within existing systems to ensure that the most qualified employees are selected to carry out agency responsibilities.	① ② ③ Example	① ② ③ Example
13. *Competency: Effectively manages and oversees the budget and other financial resources to support the organization's/program's mission and goals and to foster continuous program improvement and accountability*	① ② ③ Example	① ② ③ Example

NSWM COMPETENCY	SELF-ASSESSMENT	SUPERVISOR ASSESSMENT

DOMAIN: RESOURCE MANAGEMENT

NSWM COMPETENCY	SELF-ASSESSMENT	SUPERVISOR ASSESSMENT
13.1 Manages utilization of resources to ensure that they are in line with the organization's mission and goals.	① ② ③ Example	① ② ③ Example
13.2 Ensures that expenditures are allowable and appropriate and that allocated funds are available throughout the fiscal year.	① ② ③ Example	① ② ③ Example
13.3 Monitors revenue and expenditures at regular intervals to ensure that budget assumptions are consistent with anticipated income and expenses.	① ② ③ Example	① ② ③ Example
13.4 Ensures that financial activities are consistent with organizational policies and are sufficiently documented for audit.	① ② ③ Example	① ② ③ Example
13.5 Oversees equitable allocation of funds based on such indicators as visits, outcomes, and historical precedent.	① ② ③ Example	① ② ③ Example
13.6 Monitors expenditures to ensure that operating units have sufficient resources to offer quality services, using dashboards and other visual tools to link expenditures to outcomes.	① ② ③ Example	① ② ③ Example
14. *Competency: Establishes and maintains a system of internal controls to ensure transparency, protection, and accountability for the use of organizational resources*	① ② ③ Example	① ② ③ Example
14.1 Prepares and manages organizational budgets in a manner that maximizes utilization of available funds for client service and complies with requirements of funders.	① ② ③ Example	① ② ③ Example
14.2 Develops and implements a system of internal controls that adequately safeguards the resources of the organization.	① ② ③ Example	① ② ③ Example

NSWM COMPETENCY

SELF-ASSESSMENT

SUPERVISOR ASSESSMENT

DOMAIN: RESOURCE MANAGEMENT

14.3 Demonstrates effective actions to protect the organization and its employees from liability by both managing and ensuring risks incurred within the scope of discharging established responsibilities.

Self-Assessment: ① ② ③ Example
Supervisor Assessment: ① ② ③ Example

14.4 Assures the maintenance of financial records that comply with generally accepted accounting standards.

Self-Assessment: ① ② ③ Example
Supervisor Assessment: ① ② ③ Example

14.5 Assures the appropriate safety, maintenance, protection, and utilization of other organizational resources, such as facilities and equipment.

Self-Assessment: ① ② ③ Example
Supervisor Assessment: ① ② ③ Example

14.6 Helps design and manage a process of succession planning to assure the organizational continuity of executive, professional, and service leadership.

Self-Assessment: ① ② ③ Example
Supervisor Assessment: ① ② ③ Example

14.7 Establishes strong systems of accountability for revenues received from various sources.

Self-Assessment: ① ② ③ Example
Supervisor Assessment: ① ② ③ Example

15. *Competency: Manages all aspects of information technology*

Self-Assessment: ① ② ③ Example
Supervisor Assessment: ① ② ③ Example

15.1 Identifies and utilizes technology resources to enhance the organization's processes.

Self-Assessment: ① ② ③ Example
Supervisor Assessment: ① ② ③ Example

15.2 Uses resources to promote the effective use of technology for clients and staff.

Self-Assessment: ① ② ③ Example
Supervisor Assessment: ① ② ③ Example

15.3 Remains current with developments in technology and upgrades the organization accordingly.

Self-Assessment: ① ② ③ Example
Supervisor Assessment: ① ② ③ Example

15.4 Encourages adaptation of technology for service tracking and for other purposes that enhance efficiency and quality.

Self-Assessment: ① ② ③ Example
Supervisor Assessment: ① ② ③ Example

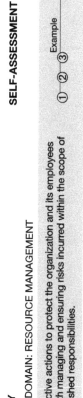

DOMAIN: RESOURCE MANAGEMENT

16. Fundraising Competency: Identifies and applies for new and recurring funding while ensuring accountability with existing funding systems

	Self-Assessment	Supervisor Assessment
	①—②—③ Example	①—②—③ Example

16.1 Creates a culture of philanthropy that engages the organization's governing body, employees, volunteers, and actual and potential donors.

	Self-Assessment	Supervisor Assessment
	①—②—③ Example	①—②—③ Example

16.2 Works closely with public and private funding sources to ensure positive relations and confidence in the organization.

	Self-Assessment	Supervisor Assessment
	①—②—③ Example	①—②—③ Example

16.3 Develops and implements a successful fundraising plan that includes a diverse funding mix and utilizes a strong marketing focus.

	Self-Assessment	Supervisor Assessment
	①—②—③ Example	①—②—③ Example

16.4 Establishes strong systems of stewardship with donors/funders.

	Self-Assessment	Supervisor Assessment
	①—②—③ Example	①—②—③ Example

16.5 Seeks partnerships with other programs funded under federal/state/local authorities and other interest groups.

	Self-Assessment	Supervisor Assessment
	①—②—③ Example	①—②—③ Example

16.6 Maintains active awareness of and pursues potential grant and funding sources in local, regional, or national community.

	Self-Assessment	Supervisor Assessment
	①—②—③ Example	①—②—③ Example

16.7 Demonstrates innovative approaches to resource development at all levels of the organization.

	Self-Assessment	Supervisor Assessment
	①—②—③ Example	①—②—③ Example

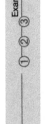
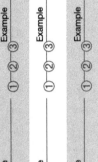

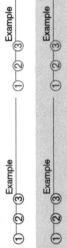

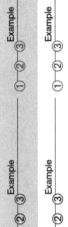

NSWM COMPETENCY

SELF-ASSESSMENT

SUPERVISOR ASSESSMENT

DOMAIN: RESOURCE MANAGEMENT

17. *Marketing and Public Relations: Engages in proactive communication about the agency's products and services*

① ② ③ Example   ① ② ③ Example

17.1 Consistently establishes and maintains positive external relationships with key organizational constituencies such as the media, public governance bodies, actual and potential donors, the business community, professional and service organizations, and the public at large.

① ② ③ Example   ① ② ③ Example

17.2 Builds and conveys to multiple constituencies an organizational brand that reflects competence, integrity, and superior client/customer and community service.

① ② ③ Example   ① ② ③ Example

17.3 Develops and implements a successful marketing plan that dovetails with the fundraising activities of the organization.

① ② ③ Example   ① ② ③ Example

17.4 Ensures that the work of the agency is featured in various public relations venues to build and maintain visibility, access, and credibility and to ensure maximum usage of program resources.

① ② ③ Example   ① ② ③ Example

17.5 Develops clear guidelines for managing interactions with the press to ensure client confidentiality and accurate representation of agency performance.

① ② ③ Example   ① ② ③ Example

17.6 Maximizes the use of electronic media to communicate the work of the organization and deepens the public's understanding of the mission.

① ② ③ Example   ① ② ③ Example

NSWM COMPETENCY

SELF-ASSESSMENT

SUPERVISOR ASSESSMENT

DOMAIN: STRATEGIC MANAGEMENT

NSWM COMPETENCY	SELF-ASSESSMENT	SUPERVISOR ASSESSMENT
18. *Competency: Designs and develops effective programs*	① ② ③ Example	① ② ③ Example
18.1 Guides program staff in designing and implementing interventions consistent with the mission of the organization that respect all types of clients from diverse circumstances.	① ② ③ Example	① ② ③ Example
18.2 Supports and assists staff in planning evidence-based programs, based on performance standards, assessments, client data, research on effective practice, community and user needs, demographics, resources, and economic and technological trends.	① ② ③ Example	① ② ③ Example
18.3 Develops and enforces procedures for collecting, reporting, and analyzing data to measure program quality and achievement of defined outcomes.	① ② ③ Example	① ② ③ Example
19. *Competency: Manages risk and legal affairs*	① ② ③ Example	① ② ③ Example
19.1 Protects the agency from undue risk by ensuring that appropriate policies and procedures exist in all areas of operation.	① ② ③ Example	① ② ③ Example
19.2 Establishes systems for monitoring all areas of the organization where there may be potential risk (e.g., client services, record-keeping, accounting, purchasing).	① ② ③ Example	① ② ③ Example
19.3 Ensures adherence to all laws, regulations, contracts, and legal agreements.	① ② ③ Example	① ② ③ Example

NSWM COMPETENCY

SELF-ASSESSMENT

SUPERVISOR ASSESSMENT

DOMAIN: STRATEGIC MANAGEMENT

20. *Competency: Ensures strategic planning*

20.1 Understands the organization's relationship to its environment, the emerging internal and external forces affecting the organization, and the ability to position the organization within that environment for future and current success.

① ② ③ Example   ① ② ③ Example

20.2 Directs staff effectively in identifying areas of future growth and development in all areas of agency operations to be used in a strategic planning process.

① ② ③ Example   ① ② ③ Example

20.3 Demonstrates competence in the ability to orchestrate and support an inclusive and organization-wide strategic planning process designed to position the organization for success in achieving its mission in the mid- and long-term future.

① ② ③ Example   ① ② ③ Example

20.4 Constructs or directs the construction of an adequate business plan that details the pathway, timelines, and accountability for the accomplishment of identified strategic objectives.

① ② ③ Example   ① ② ③ Example

NSWM COMPETENCY

SELF-ASSESSMENT

SUPERVISOR ASSESSMENT

DOMAIN: COMMUNITY COLLABORATION

21. *Competency: Builds relationships with complementary agencies, institutions, and community groups to enhance the delivery of services*

① ② ③ Example

① ② ③ Example

21.1 Establishes partnerships and allliances with businesses, institutions of higher learning, local educational agencies, child care centers, health and human services, employment and job training centers, boards, and other agencies to assess needs, enhance program resources, and improve services to service users.

① ② ③ Example

① ② ③ Example

21.2 Collaborates with other health and human services organizations to better serve clients in ways that work toward the enhancement of client well-being and the achievement of the organizational mission.

① ② ③ Example

① ② ③ Example

21.3 Identifies opportunities for partnerships, acquisitions, and mergers, where applicable, that promote the achievement of the organizational mission and the well-being of clients served.

① ② ③ Example

① ② ③ Example

21.4 Effectively manages policy advocacy coalitions dedicated to issues of social justice and client well-being

① ② ③ Example

① ② ③ Example

Diversity

7

Race and Ethnicity

Past and Present

> If we cannot now end our differences, at least we can help make the
> world safe for diversity.
>
> —PRESIDENT JOHN F. KENNEDY

CHAPTER OBJECTIVES

1. Review historical and theoretical divisions of race and ethnicity;
2. Learn about past and present racial/ethnic facts to increase
   understanding of vulnerable populations' struggles in the United
   States;
3. Review and recognize current race/ethnicity inequalities on the four
   well-being outcomes of health, education, income, and housing; and
4. Gain insights on innovative leadership from a social architect (see
   Appendix to this chapter).

INTRODUCTION

As an innovative leader, it is important to understand the origins of race and
ethnicity differences, the main struggles some groups have endured for generations, and the current moral and political debate over race relations in the
United States. Successful leaders are empathetic to historical and contemporary
issues that vulnerable populations have experienced both in the past and in the
present. Unfortunately, there has been an enormous amount of debate, con-
frontation, and animosity when it comes to race concerns in the United States.

Throughout history, wars around the world have been fought because of racial, ethnic, or religious inequality and intolerance, resulting in millions of people being killed. One of the main reasons for this separation is that race, ethnicity, and religious affiliation are strong components of a person's identity and value system. Additionally, when people are categorized into certain groups, divisiveness and resentment can be generated. The goal of this chapter is to highlight issues of difference in the United States, with particular emphasis on race/ethnicity, focusing on how those in power have systematically oppressed certain groups for their own political and economic advantage. This chapter lays the foundation for the next Chapter 8 on developing greater cultural proficiency in health and human services organizations.

HISTORICAL BACKGROUND

The concept of race is illegitimate in that it has no biological or genetic grounding; it was conceived centuries ago by one group to take advantage of other groups. Its invention is purely political and economic, one that positions one group ahead of another. The *Stanford Encyclopedia of Philosophy* explains that the original ontological status of race, *race naturalism,* is no longer accepted. Race naturalist social scientists once thought of adjudicating the biological conceptions of race by depicting races as bearing bio-behavioral essences or genetic differences that explain behavioral characteristics, physical characteristics, and cultural predispositions of individuals from a certain race. Instead, today we spouse to *racial skepticism,* which holds the notion that racial naturalism is false and that races of any type do not exist (except for the human race), and *racial constructivism,* which refers to the argument that races have come into existence, and continue to exist, through human culture and group decisions (*Stanford Encyclopedia of Philosophy,* 2016). Additionally, the *Oxford Dictionary* defines race as an unscientific social construct; that is, the concept of race is created from prevailing social perceptions and is without scientific foundation (Witzig, 1996).

Although the terms *race* and *ethnicity* are often used interchangeably, each is defined differently. Cornell and Hartmann (1998) provide a helpful definition of the differences between race and ethnicity. On one hand, race is "a human group defined by itself or others as distinct by virtue of perceived common physical characteristics that are held to be inherent. . . . Determining which characteristics constitute the race . . . is a choice human beings make. Neither markers nor categories are predetermined by any biological factors" (p. 24). Ethnicity, conversely, is defined as "a sense of common ancestry based on cultural attachments, past linguistic heritage, religious affiliations, claimed kinship, or some physical traits" (p. 19). Thus, race and ethnicity clearly differ in the individual's identity acknowledgment. In many ways, individuals can rarely have any choice over their racial identity because of the physical traits associated with race, but ethnicity is more a choice because it is based on context, culture, tradition, origin, and language. Nonetheless, there is fine line between race and ethnicity for some groups in the United States, including Hispanics/ Latinos, African Americans, Native Americans, and Asians. Regardless of race/ ethnicity, successful leaders have the moral responsibility and ability to empower people to define themselves rather than labeling them according to a social construct that is concealed as scientific fact.

It is also interesting to point out the historical and theoretical sociological dimensions of race. Most sociologists define race as a concept that signifies and symbolizes sociopolitical conflicts and interests to different types of human characteristics. Therefore, because race has no biological scientific meaning, its implications have become more aligned with the ideas of Herbert Spencer, Karl Marx, and Max Weber's concepts of *class* and *status*. Historically, the origins of race had a deep interconnection between the development of the modern world economic systems (e.g., capitalism, empire building, and slavery). The more modernist view is shaped by political and economic processes. Modern and contemporary theories of race are entangled with (1) political upheaval focusing on racial themes like decolonization, civil war, *apartheid*, civil rights, and equity; and (2) economic implications addressing poverty, urbanization, underdevelopment, and financial inequalities (Winant, 2000). The academic works of Du Bois (at the beginning of the 20th century) and the extensive body of knowledge published by the Chicago School of Sociology (from the 1930s to the 1970s) were oriented by pragmatism and progressivism. Some of the most significant sociological work for the social sciences was establishing evidence that race was socially, and not biologically, constructed.

Even after the immense struggles of the civil rights movement in the 1960s, to date we continue to experience a sociopolitical crisis of race. Unfortunately, there is a persistence of racially based distinctions across organizations, institutions, and communities that are pervasive and detrimental to vulnerable populations that traditionally have experienced exploitation and/or oppression. Minority individuals encounter prejudiced attitudes because of their ethnicity, class, and nationality. First, ethnicity-oriented theories of race have tried to end the racial divide by creating laws and regulations, but results have been limited because of the difficulties of integration and assimilation as the white dominant culture creates obstacles and minority cultures prefer to continue with both acculturation and their own race-conscious identity. Second, class-based theories of race pursue the end of inequality among racially defined groups, but the effects of discrimination continue to be significant, and they even have a growing impact on inequality within racially defined minority groups, which weakens their political and economic progress and strengthens white commitments to racial privilege (i.e., persistent racism). Third, nation-oriented views of race have tried to combine international heterogeneity and improve conditions for developing countries. However, the growth of cultural nationalism and the decline of international racial sociopolitical solidarity have forced individuals and families in poor countries to migrate or seek asylum in more developed countries.

THEORIES OF RACE AND ETHNICITY

In this section we will explore several contemporary theories of race and ethnicity, which include the following: social dominance theory, critical race theory, eugenics today, stereotype threat, model minority, symbolic interactionism, social control theory, implicit bias, and institutional racism. The goal of describing and briefly analyzing these theoretical models is to illustrate the complexity of race and racial dynamics in American society.

1. *Social dominance theory.* Social dominance theory is a multilevel approach to explaining how certain groups or societies maintain their dominance. Nearly all societies have group-based dominance hierarchies, in which one group based on religion, race, or ethnicity exercises more power than others, maintains a perceived higher status, and enjoys greater amounts of privileges (including legal, political, and economic). Group dominance also intersects with oppression, namely sexism. In many societies around the world, men still hold disproportionate amounts of power and freedom compared with women. Social dominance theory describes how processes take place at different levels of organizations and institutions, explaining how cultural ideologies and institutional discrimination of gender roles and the psychology of prejudice interact to produce stable group-based inequality (Pratto, Stewart, & Zeineddine, 2013).
2. *Critical race theory.* Critical race theory explores and challenges the prevalence of racial inequality in society. The basic notion of critical race theory is that race and racism are products of social thought and power relations. This theory discards the idea that racism may be understood and assumed as a normal feature in human nature (Tate, 1997).
3. *Eugenics today.* Eugenics is a set of beliefs and practices that aims to improve the genetic quality of a human population. The eugenics philosophy espouses the notion that human characteristics or desired traits, such as intelligence and health, can be improved by keeping

a race that would be exempt of various diseases and disabilities. To create the perfect humans, eugenics argues that is best to eliminate the "unhealthy"—known as *negative eugenics*. Eugenic practices were widely accepted from the 19th to the first half of the 20th century. Initially, eugenics practices included compulsory sterilization of the handicapped, diseased, and "lower" classes (including Jews and Gypsies), which resulted in tens of thousands being sterilized and millions being exterminated during the period of Nazi Germany. Currently, new biological and genetic scientific developments have now enabled eugenic ideals to reappear under the spotlight, creating new moral and ethical dilemmas (Guvercin & Arda, 2010). Nonetheless, Hayden (2013) discards genetics-based notions by demonstrating how levels of intelligence, violence, and sexuality cannot be scientifically linked to any specific race or group.

4. *Stereotype threat.* In the 1990s, Steel and Aronson introduced the concept of stereotype threat, which explains how societies consciously or unconsciously continue to use negative stereotypes to judge and set low expectations for minority groups. As members of society judge certain minority individuals or communities, those who identify with the domain to which the stereotype is relevant may engage in a self-fulfillment prophecy, forming enclaves and marginalizing themselves from the dominant culture (Lewis & Sekaquaptewa, 2016).

5. *Model minority theory.* The model minority theory became popular during the 1960s by proclaiming that Asian cultures are the perfect minority group to assimilate into the American culture. However, this view erroneously postulated that all Asian cultures are the same, further stereotyping the image of Asian Americans and discrediting the protest and demands for social justice of other minority groups. Osajima (2005) argued that the model minority image has misled people to think of the alleged success story of Asian Americans as evidence of triumph in terms of meritocracy in American society (Wong, Lai, Nagasawa, & Lin, 1998).

6. *Symbolic interactionism.* Symbolic interactionism seeks to explain some of the insights of race and ethnicity from the lenses of each actor and the settings where it occurs. The main tenet of this theory focuses on the quality and quantity of behaviors and interactions between actors to explain and analyze collective action (Lal, 1995).

7. *Social control theory.* Social control theory seeks to understand the link between individuals and social institutions in order to explain delinquent behavior. Originally, Hirschi (1969) argued that a strong social bond to social institutions, such as schools, promotes conformity to conventional norms. Individuals who possess weak or broken social

bonds to conventional institutions are more likely to engage in deviant behavior. However, this theory has been challenged because of the evidence that white color crimes are mostly committed by individuals who do have strong social bonds, but simply commit crimes for personal gain (Peguero, Pop, Latimore, Shekarkhar, & Koo, 2011).

8. *Implicit bias.* Implicit bias theory seeks to explain the persistent racial discrimination and inequality observed in today's society. An implicit bias is a social condition passed to individuals that unconsciously triggers a belief in the inferiority of a group. As people are falsely told that one group is superior to another, it creates a bias by (1) manipulating their expectation and (2) dissenting negative beliefs and feelings about racial or ethnic minority groups (Clair & Denis, 2015).

9. *Institutional racism.* First defined by Stokely and Hamilton in the 1960s, institutional racism refers to instances of racial discrimination, inequality, and exploitation within organizations and/or institutions. Although institutional racism can be overt (e.g., organizational norms that excludes a particular race), most frequently cases of discrimination are more subtle or concealed and hidden to protect the perpetrators.

INEQUALITIES AMONG MINORITY POPULATIONS

The persistent racial disparities in the United States with regard to health care access, education, income, and housing are concerning. There is mounting evidence showing disparities in these four areas for minorities groups. Particularly, Native American, African American, and Latino/Hispanic American populations present widespread gaps in health care access and quality of treatment, educational outcomes in mathematics and English, more blue collar jobs and lower wages, and less housing ownership compared with Caucasian and Asian Americans. Minorities continue to experience organizational isolation and exclusion from the dominant group. In this section, we will present the current inequalities and racial/economic divides so that the reader can begin to consider how effective leadership can generate positive social and institutional change that aims to even the playing field from an equity perspective.

A note to the reader, while we are using the terms Hispanic/Latino, we are no way intending to exclude gender considerations with not using terms such as Latina and Latinx, as we wish to be inclusive, however, we are only using traditional terms for convenience. Additionally, although we make generalizations about particular ethnic groups, we also recognize that there are differences within groups that a leader should always consider.

Health Disparities

When looking at racial disparities in health and mental health, there are four conceptual models that may shed light on this problem's, fundamental cause, pathways, and interaction. First, the genetic model supports the notion that genetic differences are important drivers of health disparities. Specific races and ethnicities may be more prone to certain illnesses. This school of thought continues to decipher genetic clues through the Genome Project with the purpose of finding solutions to health disparities of not only minority groups but also all races/ethnicities. Second, the fundamental cause model of health disparities highlights the importance of social and economic forces that alienate certain race groups from accessing quality health and mental health treatments. Third, the pathways model considers various types of mediating mechanisms (factors that explain relationships between other factors) that influence behaviors, such as smoking, dietary, and physical activity patterns. These mediating factors include resources (time, talent, and treasure), environments (culture and organizational contexts), life course history (early-life factors, generational precursors), culture (social norms and traditions), and other social processes (such as institutional discrimination and prejudice policies and practices). The fourth and final approach is the interaction model, which focuses on the importance of interaction among factors, including the intersectionality between race and other variables (Diez Roux, 2012).

For instance, Hispanics/Latinos have one of the largest gaps in health care access and quality in the United States. The key health care barriers include health insurance affordability (40% uninsured); selection of a usual health care provider (27% of adults lack a usual health care provider); oral care insurance affordability (54% of children do not receive dental care); mental health underutilization (often due to a cultural stigma against seeking mental health services); native language preferences (lack of Spanish-speaking health care professionals); and unauthorized legal status (not going to the hospital because of fear of deportation) (Perez-Escamilla, 2010). Additionally, Hispanics/Latinos are much less likely to have any health spending (68%) and more likely to pay out-of-pocket (6%) compared with the Caucasian population (Vargas Bustamante, & Chen, 2012). Kim et al.'s (2011) research study with Latinos and Asians with limited English proficiency show that these groups are less likely to access mental health services for psychiatric disorders.

African Americans are also at a disadvantage. Using nationally representative data from 1998 to 2009, Mehta and associates (2013) tested 17 indicators of child health (overall health status, disability, measures of specific illnesses, and indicators of the social and economic consequences of illnesses) and found little evidence that racial/ethnic disparities in child health have changed over

time. In general, African American children had the highest reported prevalence across the health indicators, and Asian children had the lowest. Moreover,
when looking at asthma indicators, African American children were twice as
likely to be readmitted for hospital stays as white children. As to what explains
these health inequities? One of the major barriers is financial hardships/soci-
oeconomic status (which explained more than 40% of this disparity). Other
factors include cultural stigma, behavioral preferences (with regard to nutrition
and physical exercise), stress, pollution, tobacco exposure, and housing quality
(Beck et al., 2014).

Educational Achievement Gap

The impact of education inequalities is devastating. Among other associated problems with low academic performance include lower employment
and earnings, general issues with child and adult well-being, individual and
family hardships, neighborhoods affected by concentrated poverty and deprivation, propensity to exploitation and dominance, lack of social capital, and
truncated intergenerational mobility (Barton & Coley, 2010). The achievement
gaps and inequities in educational settings start at an early age in the United
States. The *Inequalities at the Starting Gate: Cognitive and Noncognitive Skills
Gaps between 2010–2011 Kindergarten Classmates* report explores gaps by social class and race/ethnicity in both cognitive skills—math, reading, and executive function—and noncognitive skills such as self-control, approaches to
learning, and interactions with teachers and peers. The study refers to these
skills gaps as gaps in school readiness, demonstrating that minority groups, particularly African American and Hispanics/Latinos, lag behind their Caucasian
counterparts (Garcia & Weiss, 2015).

Students from historically underserved groups continue to be dispropor-
tionately identified and placed in unchallenged "educational tracks" and special education settings. Implementation and support for cultural proficiency
practices and policies can improve racial disproportionality in special education and signal a retrenchment to deficit views about students from historically
underserved groups. Part of the problem is that research and practice in special education have been based on limited views of culture that rely on proxy
indicators such as race and ethnicity. The limitations of equating culture with
people's traits are significant (Gutiérrez & Rogoff, 2003) and have potentially
damaging implications for school policies and practices that disproportionally
affect minority populations (Artiles, Kozleski, Trent, Osher, & Ortiz, 2010).

Unfortunately, racial and ethnic patterns in school discipline sanctions,
suspensions, and expulsions, particularly with African American and

Hispanic/Latino youths, continue to be grossly disproportionate, contributing to their achievement gap (Gregory, Skiba, & Noguera, 2010). Simultaneously, African American and Hispanic/Latino students are underrepresented in gifted education, proposing that social inequality contributes to the unbalanced segregated programs. Underrepresentation trends of minority groups are common, along with methods and practices for calculating underrepresentation and inequity. These racial biases fall under the larger umbrella of achievement gaps and inequities in school settings with attention to "de jure segregation" (Ford, 2014).

A more recent study published by the Education Trust-West (2018) entitled, *The Majority Report: Supporting the Educational Success of Latino Students in California,* provides a comprehensive assessment of educational outcomes, demonstrating that while more than 3 million Latino students in K–12 schools are the majority of California's 6.2 million K–12 population, and nearly 1 million Latino students attend public colleges and universities, they continue to face troubling inequities from early learning through higher education. The report concludes that California's Latino students:

- Attend the nation's most segregated schools;
- Are often tracked away from college-preparatory coursework;
- Are sometimes perceived as less academically capable than their white or Asian peers;
- Have insufficient access to early childhood education;
- Are less likely to feel connected to their school environment; and
- Are more likely to be required to take remedial courses at colleges and universities. (p. 4)

The racial inequalities in higher education are no different in primary and secondary schools across America. Bailey and Dynarski's (2011) study used national longitudinal surveys of youths to illustrate the inequalities in postsecondary education for the past 70 years (from 1979 to 1997). They found growing gaps between children from high- and low-income families in college entry, persistence, and graduation and substantial gender differences in educational attainment with women outpacing men in every demographic group. This systemic achievement gap is institutional. More important, Hillman (2016) used county data to demonstrate that the number of local colleges varies along lines of race and class. Communities with large Hispanic and African American populations and low educational attainment have the fewest educational alternatives nearby, while white and Asian communities tend to have more. This systemic institutional problem perpetuates the existence of racial enclaves and education deserts, denying poor students of color the same opportunities that wealthier and whiter communities have (i.e., those in more privileged positions).

Income Inequities

Occupational segregation has existed in America since its inception. Minority groups have been exploited first through slavery and then by the continuation of discriminatory policies and practices. To date, the income and career racial disparities are significant among Native Americans, immigrants, and people of color. Stewart and Dixon (2010) used the 2000 census to study income inequalities. They found that minority groups and immigrants receive fewer wage returns to years spent in the United States and that their wage disparities are magnified by the percentage of immigrants in a metropolitan area, whereas their Caucasian counterparts receive a wage premium when living in an area with a larger share of immigrants. This income inequality has existed and still is present to date, between genders, showing that the occupational sorting of women is still worse than that of men of the same race/ethnicity. For some groups the income disparities are more extensive. For example, Del Río and Alonso-Villar (2015) concluded that segregation reduction programs that women experienced between 1940 and 1990 did not allow any of them to reach a sustainable position in the labor market; the consequences of segregation were negative for women more than men.

Simultaneously, the intersectionality between gender and race has affected African American females harder than any other group. While 69% of African American women would have had to switch occupations to achieve zero segregation in 1940, this percentage fell to about 40% in 1970, 36% in 1990, and 33% in 2000, remaining without significant positive change in more than 40 years. This occupational segregation has persisted, resulting in Caucasian men maintaining their advantage in the occupational hierarchy, and only Caucasian women have made more progress than any other group (Mintz & Krymkowski, 2010).

The criminal justice system has also played an integral role in suppressing people of color from attaining employment and livable wages. Newell (2013) argues that the 1980s and 1990s "tough on crime" policies have resulted in a backlash against the race inequality progress made during and after the Civil Rights Movement of the 1960s. Furthermore, racially charged political rhetoric has fueled the rising incarceration rates of African Americans and Hispanics/Latinos (e.g., school-to-prison pipeline), particularly mandatory minimum sentencing laws, resulting in racially disparate outcomes by allowing employers to indiscriminately screen candidates on the basis of their criminal backgrounds. This discriminatory practice in the labor market goes beyond criminal records. Studies have shown that when people of color attempt to get a job, they are more successful when they conceal or downplay racial cues in job applications (known as "résumé whitening"), whereas when employers are looking for a more diverse pool, job seeker minorities engage in minimal résumé whitening. Race seems to matter during job interviews, which shows that diversity statements are not necessarily associated with the reduction of discriminatory policies and practices (Kang, DeCelles, Tilcsik, & Jun, 2016).

Housing Inequalities

The presence of income inequality creates segregation in housing. Because minority groups have lower incomes, they do not have the means to own a house. For example, Dickerson vonLockette and Johnson (2010) found that segregation has a deleterious effect on Hispanics/Latinos employment; for example, in cities where housing segregation is worse, their employment rates are lower; and as cities where Latinos live become more segregated, their employment rates decrease. And even if a small minority have greater income levels than the majority of people of color, they may have the ability to only purchase homes/condominiums in neighborhoods that have higher crime rates, lower educational outcomes, and fewer resources (Araque & Vergara, 2016). There is a clear intersection of neighborhood racial segregation with poverty, urban dwelling (i.e., "urbanicity"), and availability of quality goods and services. Using US Census tracks, Bower and colleagues (2014) show that poor neighborhoods have fewer supermarkets, whereas the number of grocery and convenience stores is greater in economically advantaged areas.

Residential segregation instigates predatory lending, foreclosure concentrations, educational dwindling, and pollution exposure, and this where many African American and Hispanics/Latinos reside. The foreclosure crisis after the 2009 economic recession took place along racial lines. Racially integrated neighborhoods, mostly with African American and Hispanics/Latinos, had exceptionally high foreclosure rates (Hall, Crowder and Spring, 2015). When examining data from the *Panel Study of Income Dynamics* and the decennial censuses, Quillian (2014) learned that poor—non-poor segregation (the have's and have not's) is associated with lower rates of high school graduation among adolescents from poor backgrounds, but has no effect on rates of graduation for students from non-poor backgrounds. African American and Caucasian segregation is associated with lower rates of high school graduation and college graduation for African American students, but has no effect on graduation rates for Caucasian students. At the same time, Jones et al.

(2014) learned that residential segregation leads to more exposure to ambient air pollution.

Housing inequalities and segregation continue to be positively associated with discrimination and marginalization. Spivak and Monnat (2013) used data from the Metropolitan Statistical Areas to find that dissimilarities in neighborhoods depend on household income. For example, African American and Hispanic/Latino households with higher household incomes live in urban areas and neighborhoods with greater resources and experience lower isolation from Caucasians than do African Americans and Hispanic/Latino households with lower incomes. Sadly, people with different levels of education get sorted into housing and jobs with different degrees of exposure to housing and workplace attributes that contribute to poor health. Goh, Pfeffer, and Zenios (2015) conclude that 40% of the difference in life expectancy across demographic groups can be explained by the different housing and job conditions these minority groups experience.

In conclusion, this chapter provides a brief historical background on the socially constructed notion of race and highlights the current-day challenges that disadvantaged groups in the United States continue to face, despite progress in aspects of civil rights. An equitable society is what any responsible leader would aspire to while simultaneously influencing others to embrace a social justice framework in their everyday lives. The charge for health and human services leaders is to facilitate and empower themselves and others to improve the human condition for all of humanity. In the next chapter we will delve into ways that leaders can promote organizations to be accountable in advancing equality through personal and institutional practices.

CHAPTER DISCUSSION QUESTIONS

1. Compare and contrast two theories of race and how these affect current institutional policies and practices in the United States.
2. Provide a contemporary example of disparity in the United States from any of the areas discussed in the chapter (health, education, income, and housing).
3. What are some of the systemic (or institutional) barriers or challenges in the criminal justice arena that are most salient in today' society? (even beyond those mentioned in this chapter).
4. Identify your experience with privilege.
5. Read a current news report and be ready to briefly describe any policy, law, or social program that can result in potential racial or ethnic divisiveness and counteract that with an innovative idea or

solution that is antidiscriminatory and from a social justice or social equity lens.

6. Read the leader profile and case study in the Appendix to this chapter. Note innovative ideas and practices and see what aspects of the case you can connect to the contents of the chapter and/or overall book.

REFERENCES

Araque, J. C., & Vergara, A. (2016). Effectiveness of service-enriched programs in affordable housing to low income Latino families: It is about quantity and quality. *Journal of Sociology and Social Work, 4*(1), 119–133.

Artiles, A. J., Kozleski, E. B., Trent, S. C., Osher, D., & Ortiz, A. (2010). Justifying and explaining disproportionality, 1968–2008: A critique of underlying views of culture. *Exceptional Children, 76*(3), 279–299.

Bailey, M. J., & Dynarski, S. M. (2011). Gains and gaps: Changing inequality in US college entry and completion. *National Bureau of Economic Research*. Retrieved from http://www.nber.org/papers/w17633.pdf

Barton, P. E., & Coley, R. J. (2010). The Black-White achievement gap: When progress stopped. *Educational Testing Service*. Retrieved from http://files.eric.ed.gov/fulltext/ED511548.pdf

Beck, A. F., Huang, B., Simmons, J. M., Moncrief, T., Sauers, H. S., Chen, C., Ryan, P. H., Newman, N. C., & Kahn, R. S. (2014). Role of financial and social hardships in asthma racial disparities. *Pediatrics, 133*(3), 431–439.

Bower, K. M., Thorpe, R. J., Rohde, C., & Gaskin, D. J. (2014). The intersection of neighborhood racial segregation, poverty, and urbanicity and its impact on food store availability in the United States. *Preventive Medicine, 58*, 33–39.

Clair, M., & Denis, J. S. (2015). Sociology of racism edited by James D. White *International Encyclopedia of the Social and Behavioral Sciences, 19*, 857–863.

Cornell, S., & Hartmann, D. (1998). Mapping the terrain: Definitions. *Ethnicity and race: Making Identities in a Changing World, 23*, 15–38.

Del Río, C., & Alonso-Villar, O. (2015). The evolution of occupational segregation in the United States, 1940–2010: Gains and losses of gender–race/ethnicity groups. *Demography, 52*(3), 967–988.

Dickerson vonLockette, N. T., & Johnson, J. (2010). Latino employment and residential segregation in metropolitan labor markets. *Du Bois Review: Social Science Research on Race, 7*(01), 151–184.

Diez Roux, A. V. (2012). Conceptual approaches to the study of health disparities. *Annual Review of Public Health, 33*(1), 41–58.

Du Bois, W. E. B. (1940). *Dusk of dawn: An essay toward an autobiography of a race concept: The Oxford WEB Du Bois* (Vol. 9). Oxford University Press on Demand.

The Education Trust-West. (2018). *The majority report: Supporting the educational success of Latino students in California*. The Education Trust-West.

Ford, D. Y. (2014). Segregation and the underrepresentation of Blacks and Hispanics in gifted education: Social inequality and deficit paradigms. *Roeper Review, 36*(3), 143–154.

García, E., & Weiss, E. (2015). Early education gaps by social class and race start US children out on unequal footing: A summary of the major findings in "Inequalities at the starting gate." *Economic Policy Institute.* Retrieved from http://files.eric.ed.gov/fulltext/ED560364.pdf

Goh, J., Pfeffer, J., & Zenios, S. (2015). Exposure to harmful workplace practices could account for inequality in life spans across different demographic groups. *Health Affairs, 34*(10), 1761–1768.

Gregory, A., Skiba, R. J., & Noguera, P. A. (2010). The achievement gap and the discipline gap two sides of the same coin? *Educational Researcher, 39*(1), 59–68.

Gutiérrez, K. D., & Rogoff, B. (2003). Cultural ways of learning: Individual traits or repertoires of practice. *Educational Researcher, 32*(5), 19–25.

Guvercin, C., & Arda, B. (2010). Eugenics concept: From Plato to present. *Human Reproduction and Genetic Ethics, 14*(2), 20–26.

Hall, M., Crowder, K., & Spring, A. (2015). Neighborhood foreclosures, racial/ethnic transitions, and residential segregation. *American Sociological Review, 80*(3), 526–549.

Hayden, E. C. (2013). Taboo genetics. *Nature, 502*(7469), 26–28.

Hillman, N. W. (2016). Geography of college opportunity: The case of education deserts. *American Educational Research Journal, 53*(4), 987–1021.

Hirschi, T. (1969). *Causes of Delinquency.* Berkeley, CA: University of California Press.

Jones, M. R., Diez-Roux, A. V., Hajat, A., Kershaw, K. N., O'Neill, M. S., Guallar, E., Post, W.S., Kaufman J.D., & Navas-Acien, A. (2014). Race/ethnicity, residential segregation, and exposure to ambient air pollution: The Multi-Ethnic Study of Atherosclerosis (MESA). *American Journal of Public Health, 104*(11), 2130–2137.

Kang, S. K., DeCelles, K. A., Tilcsik, A., & Jun, S. (2016). Whitened resumes: Race and self-presentation in the labor market. *Administrative Science Quarterly, 61*(3), 469–502.

Kim, G., Loi, C. X. A., Chiriboga, D. A., Jang, Y., Parmelee, P., & Allen, R. S. (2011). Limited English proficiency as a barrier to mental health service use: A study of Latino and Asian immigrants with psychiatric disorders. *Journal of Psychiatric Research, 45*(1), 104–110.

Lal, B. B. (1995). Symbolic interaction theories. *American Behavioral Scientist, 38*(3), 421–441.

Lewis, N. A., & Sekaquaptewa, D. (2016). Beyond test performance: A broader view of stereotype threat. *Current Opinion in Psychology, 11*, 40–43.

Mehta, N. K., Lee, H., & Ylitalo, K. R. (2013). Child health in the United States: Recent trends in racial/ethnic disparities. *Social Science & Medicine, 95*, 6–15.

Mintz, B., & Krymkowski, D. H. (2010). The intersection of race/ethnicity and gender in occupational segregation: Changes over time in the contemporary United States. *International Journal of Sociology, 40*(4), 31–58.

Newell, W. (2013). The legacy of Nixon, Reagan, and Horton: How the tough on crime movement enabled a new regime of race-influenced employment discrimination. *Berkeley Journal of African-American Law & Policy, 15*(1), 3–35.

Osajima, K. (2005). Asian Americans as the model minority: An analysis of the popular press image in the 1960s and 1980s. *A companion to Asian American studies, 1*, 215–225.

Peguero, A. A., Popp, A. M., Latimore, T. L., Shekarkhar, Z., & Koo, D. J. (2011). Social control theory and school misbehavior: Examining the role of race and ethnicity. *Youth Violence and Juvenile Justice, 9*(3), 259–275.

Perez-Escamilla, R. (2010). Health care access among Latinos: Implications for social and health care reforms. *Journal of Hispanic Higher Education, 9*(1), 43–60.

Pratto, F., Stewart, A. L., & Zeineddine, F. B. (2013). When inequality fails: Power, group dominance, and societal change. *Journal of Social and Political Psychology, 1*(1), 132–160.Quillian, L. (2014). Does segregation create winners and losers? Residential segregation and inequality in educational attainment. *Social Problems, 61*(3), 402–426.

Race. (2016). *Stanford Encyclopedia of Philosophy*. Retrieved from https://plato.stanford.edu/entries/race/

Spivak, A. L., & Monnat, S. M. (2013). The influence of race, class, and metropolitan area characteristics on African-American residential segregation. *Social Science Quarterly, 94*(5), 1414–1437.

Stewart, Q. T., & Dixon, J. C. (2010). Is it race, immigrant status, or both? An analysis of wage disparities among men in the United States. *International Migration Review, 44*(1), 173–201.

Tate IV, W. F. (1997). Critical race theory and education: History, theory, and implications. *Review of Research in Education, 22*(1), 195–247.

Vargas Bustamante, A., & Chen, J. (2012). Health expenditure dynamics and years of US residence: Analyzing spending disparities among Latinos by citizenship/nativity status. *Health Services Research, 47*(2), 794–818.

Winant, H. (2000). Race and race theory. *Annual Review of Sociology, 26*(1), 169–185.

Witzig, R. (1996). The medicalization of race: Scientific legitimization of a flawed social construct. *Annals of Internal Medicine, 125*(8), 675–679.

Wong, P., Lai, C. F., Nagasawa, R., & Lin, T. (1998). Asian Americans as a model minority: Self-perceptions and perceptions by other racial groups. *Sociological Perspectives, 41*(1), 95–118.

APPENDIX
Featured Leader: Nahla Kayali

Nahla Kayali, a *2014 White House Champion of Change* recipient, is described as an advocate and a leader who inspires, elevates, and empowers underserved individuals and families because she believes that every human being has the right to lead a dignified life. Nahla arrived in the United States as a married Palestinian refugee from Syria at the age of 16 with only having finished ninth grade. In 1997, as a result of her divorce, Nahla sought out counseling services but unfortunately could not find a culturally sensitive organization to provide her with the services she needed. Thus, Nahla made it her goal to establish a social services organization to enrich the lives of the underserved community with a focus on the Arab American and Muslim American communities.

Through a borrowed book from the public library on *How to Start a Non-Profit in California*, Nahla taught herself how to establish a nonprofit organization. As Nahla began learning, she started networking with different agencies and other community-based organizations to learn how to bring services to her community. Upon establishing the 501(c)3 nonprofit organization in 1998, which is now Access California Services (AccessCal), Nahla was awarded her first $2,000 grant from Community Action Partnership of Orange County (CAPOC), which served as seed money to support AccessCal.

Out of a one-room office with a folding table and chair, Nahla became the first volunteer of AccessCal and started serving the community. As Nahla began serving, she realized the needs were only growing. This sparked Nahla's curiosity to learn more about her community's needs, and with that, she solicited funding to conduct a needs assessment for community members. The results of the assessment opened the path for further funding/resources to establish wraparound programs that would encourage economic, linguistic, civic, and community integration for the community.

AccessCal has a come a long way from its humble beginnings in 1998, evolving into one of the most trusted community-based organizations serving newcomer immigrants and refugees in the State of California. As of 2016, AccessCal had 40 staff members delivering 50,000 health and human services in 16 languages to more than 10,000 individuals annually.

AccessCal's programs include Case Management & Client Advocacy, Counseling & Support Services, Employment Readiness & Placement, Emergency Financial Assistance, English as a Second Language Classes, Computer Classes, Parenting Classes, Citizenship Classes, Home Daycare Licensing Training, Enrollment in Government Health Coverage, Refugee Social Services, Refugee Health Services, Citizenship & Immigration Services, Tax Preparation Assistance, After School Enrichment Program, Youth Group Program, Community Service & Recreational Activities, and Civic Engagement Activities.

Nahla's work at the local and national levels has awarded her multiple recognitions from federal, state, county, and city public officials, foundations, corporations, and service providers. In addition to her leadership role at AccessCal, as of 2018, Nahla serves as the President of the Orange County Refugee Forum, holds the State Refugee Forum Seat for the State Advisory Council on Refugee Services, and also holds a seat with the State Office of

Health Equity. Nahla serves on 20 different boards and advisory and steering committees at both the national and local levels with passion to be an advocate for the underserved communities.

LEADERSHIP PROFILE FOR NAHLA KAYALI

Share your professional background and experience

I was born in Syria, got married at the age of 16, and have no formal education beyond ninth grade. I have worked in school administration, banking, and business (I had started a meat processing plant production factory under the sponsorship of the US Department of Agriculture [USDA]). My family and I went through a great deal of hardships. We needed counseling and other supports, but there was no therapist who could understand my culture to properly help me—this gap made me wonder how other community members were addressing these challenges, and then this motivated me to establish a human services organization for my community.

I always had a passion to serve my community—I committed and dedicated my time to organizations like the Palestine Children Relief Fund, and I also cofounded the Palestinian American Women's Association (PAWA). It is with this love and passion for my community and the nonprofit sector that I had the vision to establish Access California Services—a health and human services agency to serve the underserved with a focus on the Arab American/Muslim American communities in an effort to preserve their dignity and enrich their lives. I have been the Executive Director of Access California Services since 1998.

In addition to my role as an Executive Director, I also serve as the chairwoman for the *Refugee Forum of Orange County* and hold a state refugee forum seat for the *State Advisory Council on Refugee Assistance and Services and the Office of Health Equity Advisory Committee*. I also serve on the following boards/committees:

- Arab American Institute
- California State University, Fullerton's Public Health Board at the Department of Health Sciences
- Community Action Partnership of Orange County and Orange County Food Bank
- Community Health Council for Covering Kids and Families Statewide
- Mental Health Services Act Steering Committee (MHSA)
- National Network for Arab American Communities (NNAAC) Advisory Council

- Shura Council of Southern California
- Southern California Edison Advisory Committee
- University of California Irvine's Department of Clinical and Translational Science, Community Action Planning Group

I have also had the honor of being the recipient of several awards at the federal, state, county, city, and community levels, but my most significant honor was the Champion of Change Cesar Chavez Award in 2014 from President Barak Obama for which I was recognized at the White House.

In your experience, what are the top three to five leadership attributes someone in the health and human services field should develop? Share an example of when you have used one or more of these attributes/skills in your work

> *Be a team player.* This involves demonstrating to coworkers that we are all part of one team and that it doesn't take just one leader to have the vision or make a difference. I always pride myself on working directly with people and not over them. We all sit together to address needs and challenges and to come up with solutions. I really feel it has helped motivate them to represent the organization and better serve the community. This gives them a sense of ownership. I also recognize that the smallest acts make the biggest impacts. So whether I do my part to take out the trash or mop the floor at our organization, or represent my community at the White House, it is all about making a difference, big or small.
>
> *Be empathetic.* This means understanding the other person's needs, whether client or staff, to better serve them. Be there for them and let them know how much you care and understand.
>
> *Be accountable.* This means taking responsibility for shortcomings and knowing when and where to make things better. Be ready to have solutions and also be proud to recognize the accomplishments of others.

A CASE STUDY BY NAHLA KAYALI

One particular case that AccessCal took ownership of was one that really shook our community to its core. Our involvement with this case started when I received a call from a local shelter asking for our help in finding a culturally appropriate home for three young children who were identified as Arab American. After learning more about the situation of these children, I found out that they were taken away from their mother, Fatima (fictitious name). She was a recent refugee who has just arrived in the United States. Sadly, she lost her husband in her home country as a result of the war.

One day when Fatima went to school to pick up her children, the police department was present at the school site holding her kids. The children were being taken away because it was reported that Fatima committed an act of abuse toward her son. It turns out the day before her son had stolen money from his mom's purse and she reprimanded him by hitting him. This particular son was the eldest, and he was used to acting as the head of household back home and in the United States because there was no father figure in the picture. The teacher noticed a bruise on his body and reported this to the police department. As a result, the police came to the school to take the kids away from Fatima. Fatima's third child, who was under the age of 2, was in her arms at the time she came to pick up her kids from school. The police tried to take away the baby from her, but she resisted, and the officer used a Taser on her face. Although the police officers were trying to explain to the mother why this was happening, she did not know any English and neither understood what was been said nor had the ability to speak. Fatima was an Arab refugee who only had recently arrived to the United States and started to learn about the American system. The police ended up taking the three kids away from Fatima and placed them in a local children's shelter.

Fatima and her children, Orange County Children and Family Services Department, police department, court system, and AccessCal were all involved. As a representative for AccessCal, I was the main point of contact for this case. I served as an advocate, cultural broker, translator, and supporter. I was there for her and did my best to advocate for her before, during, and after the court hearing, with Children and Family Services meetings, and with other community members.

Because the nature of this case is very sensitive and it involves alleged child abuse, we were worried that AccessCal would be seen as an organization that is trying to break the law or condone acts of child abuse. AccessCal only took on this case and advocated for this mother because we knew it was a case of cultural barriers and not knowing or understanding the laws in the United States. We did not believe that this was a case in which a mother was abusive. Upon conducting an initial conversation and client intake with Fatima, she demonstrated to be a very kind, caring, and a loving mother to her kids. Her kids were attached to their mother and did not complain about her parenting. We knew from our own experience growing up in this culture that hitting our kids was considered "normal" back home. Nonetheless, our intention was to really show that this mother meant well for her kids and wanted to do the right thing, which is why we advocated for her and educated her on proper parenting skills and those that would be accepted in the United States. Otherwise, the mother could have permanently been separated from her kids and/or have gone to jail.

First, our staff and I completed a comprehensive needs assessment of the mother's case to gauge the situation at home. After speaking with Fatima and witnessing the home environment, we determined that she was a very caring and loving mother—not an abusive person. During the initial interview, she stated that she grew up in a society in which hitting was normal, but if she had known this would result in her kids being taken away from her in America, there was no way she would have hit her son.

Second, I intervened by placing out a call to the community in an effort to help find a suitable and temporary home for these children, which I eventually did find. During this time, I also received a call from the Orange County Children and Family Services Department inviting me to attend a team decision meeting (TDM) regarding Fatima's case. I attended this meeting to clarify that this was a case of a helpless woman who did not know any better. She simply did not know the system nor the potential consequences. I begged to the team that Fatima needed a second chance. I explained that she was coming from a country where hitting a child as a form of punishment was considered a cultural norm, and she grew up in that environment.

After several meetings it was decided that Fatima needed to receive parenting classes at AccessCal as a condition to get her kids back. Fatima took the required parenting classes at our agency and received additional services, including individual counseling, emergency financial assistance to assist with rent, English as a second language classes, and a women's empowerment class to increase her self-esteem. It was all in an effort to help her to become a more suitable mother according to American cultural standards. In the end, Fatima was empowered, received her kids back (four months later), improved her English language skills, learned appropriate parenting skills, and became a more independent and able person.

CASE DISCUSSION POINTS

1. Describe the cultural and linguistic barriers that were present in this case and whether or not the outcomes would have been any different.
2. From this case, what is your interpretation of the systems' attitudes toward a minority refugee such as Fatima?

3. How does this case assist you in understanding the critical issues that an innovative leader might face in a diverse context and the dilemmas that he or she may face?

4. How did the leader's own identity affect her perception of Fatima and the situation?

5. What roles do worldviews and cultural values play in influencing health and social services provision?

8
—

Cultural Proficiency, Equity, and Diversity

I learned that courage was not the absence of fear, but the triumph over it. The brave man is not he who does not feel afraid, but he who conquers that fear.

—Nelson Mandela

CHAPTER OBJECTIVES

1. Discover the true meaning of cultural proficiency and how leaders can foster behavior to expand equity and diversity within organizations;
2. Understand how issues of equity and diversity have systematically affected vulnerable populations;
3. Learn how effective leaders can be inclusive and proactive to improve organizational behavior and culture; and
4. Gain insights on innovative leadership from a social architect (see Appendix to this chapter).

INTRODUCTION

Discrimination of any kind is immoral and deplorable and must not be tolerated! As the reader can see, we dive into leadership from a social justice values-driven perspective. It all starts with leaders creating and nurturing a safe environment for all. Although predilection and biases are inescapable and pervasive in human nature, everyone in the organization has the capability and ethical responsibility to foster respectful behavior and maintain positive working relationships. We know that classifying individuals into categories, such as race/ethnicity, creates nothing but division. As children, we do not necessarily judge others on the playground, but once we learn that others may "belong" to a different category than ours, then we begin to pass judgment, and many times, hate starts to take form. For those who may be considered "different" from the mainstream group, even the idea of feeling like an outcast or being judged by others brings excessive personal doubt and stigma. To date, there is growing evidence of the association between stigma and multiple negative health outcomes, including mental illness, anger, depression, and stress (Hatzenbuehler, Phelan, & Link, 2013). Minority stress is considered particularly harmful and a strong indicator of how discrimination can negatively affect a person's health. Stress caused by discriminatory policies and practices deeply affects individuals for long periods of time, and it can lead to heart disease and other physical health problems (Williams, Neighbors, & Jackson, 2003).

Successful and socially responsible leaders have the ability to bring people together by clearly stating and modeling with their own actions that hatred and bigotry are not accepted. In this chapter, we will continue the discussion from Chapter 7 on how equity and diversity issues have systematically affected vulnerable populations. We will share cultural proficiency tools to add to your knowledge and practice as emerging leaders. You will discover the true significance of accepting and advocating for others and how you can be a change agent when it comes to eliminating implicit biases and prejudices in the workplace. Finally, we will discuss key dimensions of intersectionality when it comes to race/ethnicity, gender, income, health access, education, and sexual orientation. To achieve a more equitable and diverse organization, it is imperative that you reflect on your own biases (as well as sources of privilege) and put forward a committed effort to reach your own cultural proficiency so that you can then lead others in disrupting the status quo.

THE PERSONAL AND COLLECTIVE QUEST FOR CULTURAL PROFICIENCY

We all are greatly influenced by our environment, cultural norms, and people around us. For the most part, our belief system is regularly shaped by forces out of our control. Therefore, achieving cultural proficiency is not easy. It truly requires digging deep within our hearts and souls, reflecting on how groups that we have belonged to have conditioned our thinking and belief system since birth. Social architects must look inward to identify their own biases (unconscious or conscious), prejudices, and forms of privilege to advocate for others regardless of their backgrounds or situations. This is neither a one-time exercise nor a superficial lesson on cultural competency. To reach cultural proficiency really means the elimination of preconceptions or preferences toward or against any individual or group. Indeed, it is a different way of being, resulting in new ways to sense, feel, and see the world around us.

Cultural proficiency is the ability to respond positively by knowing how to learn about other individuals' and organizations' cultures and being able to interact effectively in a variety of cultural environments. Lindsey, Nuri-Robins, and Terrell (2003) define cultural proficiency as "a way of being that enables one to effectively respond to a variety of cultural settings to the issues caused by diversity" (p. 84). Leaders who are culturally proficient know and respect other cultures, know how to interact with people who may be considered by some as outside of the norm, know how to speak other people's languages and slang phrases, know how to ask questions without offending or insulting, and most important, know how to successfully advocate for the well-being of all individuals. Since cultural proficiency is a personal journey, there is not a silver bullet or magic pill approach for people to work on toward becoming culturally proficient. Nonetheless, there are a few strategies to follow for those who are willing to take a hard look at themselves and are ready for a personal transformation. Ask yourself, what would it take for me to become culturally proficient?

Terry Cross (1989), from Georgetown University's Child Department Program, was one of the first authors to illustrate appropriate strategies to meet the needs of culturally diverse mental health clients. He and his colleagues developed the Cultural Proficiency Continuum (CPC) to help illustrate different cultural stages based on responses to diversity. Throughout the years, the CPC has become an equity and diversity building tool and action model that has entered other disciplines, providing a common language for describing both healthy and unhealthy attitudes, behaviors, practices, and policies. The following six points along the CPC include unique means of seeing and responding to perceived differences among people and cultures (Figure 8.1):

1. *Cultural destructiveness.* This includes any policy, practice, behavior, or attitude that functions toward the elimination of other cultures. Leaders have the power to revise organizational policies and practices with the goal of shaping behaviors and attitudes that will preserve everyone's culture (e.g., destroying Native American tribes during the colonial era).
2. *Cultural incapacity.* This belief system perpetuates the notion that one culture is superior to others; the policy or practice of one culture subordinates another (e.g., white supremacy groups claiming superiority over other racial/ethnic groups).
3. *Cultural blindness.* This is the idea that all people are the same, without paying attention to uniqueness. Cultural blindness ignores differences in culture and tries to put everyone in the same box. Differences are important, and they need to be respected and celebrated (e.g., failing to recognize prior struggles and differences of minority groups).
4. *Cultural precompetence.* Individuals and organizations understand differences but do not do much about changing the status quo. These

Continuum of Cultural Competency

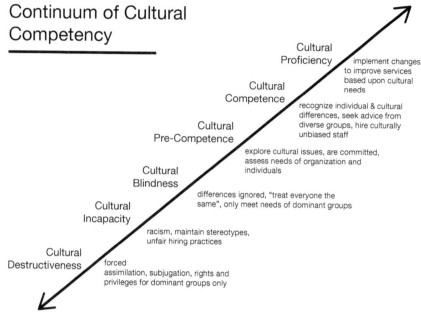

Figure 8.1 The Cultural Proficiency Continuum.
Adopted from Cross, T. (1989). Toward a culturally competent system of care.
Washington DC: Georgetown University Child Department Program, Child and
Adolescent Service Program.

individuals see differences but prefer not to get involved or act to
change injustices and prejudices. Their role is more like a bystander
who feels slightly empowered to make a difference (e.g., celebrating
diversity day once a year).

5. *Cultural competence.* Individuals and organizations at the competence
level have a great awareness of the differences among cultures.
However, policies, practices, behaviors, and attitudes remain marginal.
Advocacy may be almost nonexistent, allowing the status quo to
continue (e.g., acknowledging differences associated with sexual
minorities, i.e., LBGTQA, from the dominant group, but not doing
anything about supporting those individuals).

6. *Cultural proficiency.* The individual's awareness of differences in
culture are moved into action. Culturally proficient leaders not
only realize the differences among people but also celebrate these
differences as strengths. Culturally proficient individuals advocate
for others, and culturally proficient organizations are open learning
environments that promote and encourage equity and diversity at all
times (e.g., advocating for disabled individuals to receive the same
education as anyone else).

The application of the CPC is a regular, ongoing, and intentional personal and collective process. Leaders can use this tool as part of their skill and attitude development. Prejudices can run deep in many regions and subcultures, and eradicating them from the individual's values and beliefs requires deep reflection, practice, and commitment. People tend to stay in the blindness and/or precompetence stages because they may perceive that it is easier to dismiss differences, or even acknowledge differences, but without responding or taking action with regard to discrimination or inequities. The quest for cultural proficiency is a genuine personal and collective journey to live free of hate and bigotry and to truly accept/respect and start advocating on behalf of people with diverse backgrounds, gender identifications, races/ethnicities, nationalities, and sexual orientations. However, the reader should keep in mind that models that propose mastery or proficiency with regard to addressing diversity and systemic inequities are not without critics. For instance, in the field of medicine, Tervalon and Murray-Garcia (1998) originally developed an alternative narrative that they framed as *cultural humility*. This is a term that the authors defined as "a lifelong commitment to self-evaluation and critique, to redressing the power imbalances in the physician-patient dynamic, and to developing mutually beneficial and non-paternalistic partnerships with communities on behalf of individuals and defined populations" (p. 123). Thus, as the discourse and language in addressing culture and diversity shift over the years (and not intending to underestimate the power of language), the point is that a social architect should be self-aware, humble, and action-oriented toward ending social injustices based on race, ethnicity, gender, class, and other forms of diversity.

DIVERSITY AND INCLUSION: CURRENT STATE WITH REGARD TO MINORITY GROUPS

As we move toward cultural proficiency, it is important to understand that a number of vulnerable groups have been marginalized and/or stigmatized for decades, or even hundreds of years. Historically, in the United States, groups that have held less power or have gotten very few decision-making opportunities are recognized as "minority groups." (Although the term *minority* is a misnomer given the population and demographic trends toward greater racial and ethnic diversity in the United States.) Nevertheless, the term *minorities* in our society is inclusive of groups with diverse racial/ethnic backgrounds, women, families in poverty, and individuals with various forms of sexuality that are not exclusive to heterosexuality, gender beyond binary classifications, and disabilities, to name a few. The leader must (1) understand and empathize with the struggles minority groups have historically endured and (2) learn how to become an advocate for equality. Next, we will review how health and human services leaders apply innovative policies and practices in diverse organizations to bolster equity and inclusion.

Gender

Organizations that promote antidiscrimination strategies and fairness, access and legitimacy, and integration among all gender groups are more successful in becoming inclusive. These organizations employ an integration and learning approach, one that encourages dialogue and education and condemns judgment and separation (Bernstein & Bilimoria, 2013). Nonetheless, cultural norms and stereotypes still persist, both continuing the beliefs of gender differences in leadership and influencing how diversity policies and initiatives are implemented. To overcome organizational gender biases, the first step is to assess the organization's board of trustees' composition. Does the board reflect gender diversity? A diverse and balanced board membership is essential because greater gender diversity can improve organizational culture and even mitigate negative impacts of racial disparities. In an empirical study of 1,456 nonprofit board chief executive officers (CEOs), Buse and associates (2016) found that board governance practices are directly influenced by the gender and racial diversity of the board and that board inclusion behaviors, together with diversity policies and practices, play a significant role in the influence of the board's gender and racial diversity on internal and external governance practices.

Next, social architects should assess how the organization perceives gender and leadership within three lenses: gender-blind (there are no gender differences in leadership); gender-conscious (leadership varies depending on gender); and perception creates reality (believing is seeing). Often, the gender-conscious approach is the most appropriate of these three lenses. For example, one method to improve gender equity in leadership is seen when organizations provide gender-based leadership training sessions that are created and adapted to meet specific needs of women in the workplace (Ely, Ibarra, & Kolb, 2011). Buse et al. (2016) argue that adhering to gender-conscious perspectives will influence how diversity is managed, policies are created, and practices are realized. It is recommended to increase employee satisfaction by eliminating relational sources of bias and creating heterogeneous groups to work together with the goal of reducing interpersonal bias and conflict (Nishii, 2013).

Simultaneously, innovative leaders should observe carefully how male and female employees interact with each other. Although both men and women perceive microaggression types of behaviors (subtle forms of discriminatory behaviors) equally, women tend to detect greater discrimination than men, particularly when subtleties are present. Both genders expect microaggressions to generate more negative work outcomes (Basford, Offermann, & Behrend,

2014). Fostering proper norms of collaboration and at least minimizing microaggression (ideally extinguishing it altogether) can avoid gender biases and improve collegiality in the workplace. Sexual harassment in the workplace is another area that desperately needs attention (see Chapter 9).

Gender stereotypes pervasively constrain women's access to power positions, causing a gender effect (Yang & Aldrich, 2014). Therefore, women not only are underrepresented as leaders of private social enterprises but also take lower paying managerial jobs in nonprofit organizations and participate in more volunteer hours than men (Teasdale, McKay, Phillimore, & Teasdale, 2011). There is a discrepancy between the numbers of women in high positions in business compared and those in the nonprofit sector. For-profit businesses have more women in part-time positions and in jobs that are marginal to the organizational purpose, whereas the proportion of women in full-time mission-driven organizations is much higher. Women may be attracted to the public and nonprofit sectors because of favorable human resources policies (e.g., flexible hours, generous paid leave, and less stress environments), inclusive work processes, mission-driven work groups, and smaller gender pay gaps (Faulk, Edwards, Lewis, & McGinnis, 2013; Mastracci & Herring, 2010). Chapter 9 explores in greater depth the gender issues raised in this section.

Race/Ethnicity and Nationality

Racial differences in America have produced a confrontational environment among race groups since the very beginning of the republic. Minorities, including Native Americans, African Americans, Asian Americans, and Latinos/Hispanics, have historically been exploited and marginalized to enrich businesses owned by Caucasian individuals and families for generations. From land adjudication, to slavery, to railroad construction, farming, and internment camps, race struggles have had long historical roots in the American story. Until the civil rights movement in the 1960s, these groups continued to be separated and ostracized as detached groups from the dominant Caucasian privileged business owners. Serious consideration of diversity in the workplace is relatively new in our history (about three or four decades), and it continues to evolve. For many individuals and organizations, collaborating with diverse groups is a work in progress. Social architects know and understand their team members' values and perceptions and create safe and brave spaces for diverse individuals to come together to perform at the highest levels possible.

The perception or organizational justice for minority groups really matters. A positive diversity climate has the power to affect organizational commitment and reduce turnover intentions. When people feel welcomed and perceive the organizational leadership to be fair, then diverse individuals perform at a higher level and think less about leaving the organization, thus raising productivity and reducing turnover rates (Buttner, Lowe, & Billings-Harris, 2010). These findings were corroborated in a study by Hwang and Hopkins (2015) on child welfare workers. They learned that minority groups in the child welfare workforce tend to demonstrate higher levels of organizational commitment and job satisfaction and lower levels of turnover rates when their perceptions of organizational inclusion are fair and consistent.

Managing diversity can be more complex when intersectionality issues cross paths. For example, when examining gender and race in the workplace, Hall, Everett, and Hamilton-Mason (2012) found that African American women cope with stress much differently than other groups of women. Racism and sexism are found to be sources of stress for African American women. Generally, these women examine race and gender inequalities within five domains: (1) being hired or promoted in the workplace, (2) defending one's race and lack of mentorship, (3) shifting or code-switching to overcome barriers to employment, (4) coping with racism and discrimination, and (5) being isolated and/or excluded. Another example occurs when issues of gender and age interact, which brings a further complex diverse intersection into the workplace, one that should be studied in more detail (Choi & Rainey, 2010). Leaders who espouse transformational and authentic leadership models see inclusion, equity, and diversity as value added and as having a positive association with higher performance, self-esteem, and collaboration (Cottrill, Denise Lopez, & Hoffman, 2014).

Sexual Orientation (LGBTQA)

The lesbian, gay, bisexual, transgender, questioning—and more recent, *ally* (LGBTQA)—movement has significantly advanced in America in the past decades. As younger generations become more culturally proficient, groups with diverse sexual orientations are more welcomed and accepted by families, organizations, and communities. Government and other institutions have also initiated removing detrimental and separatist policies and practices, like eradicating the Defense of Marriage Act (DOMA) at the federal level, repealing the "Don't ask; don't tell" policy in the US military, and no longer prohibiting same-sex marriages across states in the union. Nonetheless, many organizations are still lagging behind when it comes to providing forums for LGBTQA individuals to voice their concerns in the workplace. Bell and associates (2011) argue that heterosexist environments can foster organizational climates of silence, where sexual minorities feel that speaking up is dangerous; and they recommend human resources managers facilitate the expression of voice for LGBTQA employees in today's increasingly diverse organizations. Social architects are compelled to foster an environment where everyone is respected and free to share their concerns without fear of retaliation, discrimination, or punishment.

Inspired by the feminist movement and then the civil rights movement, the LBGTQA crusade took off by leading a campaign to legitimize same-sex marriage in the 1970s. Hagai and Crosby (2016) explain that the victory of same-sex marriage rights in the United States was based on two legal justifications: first, judges and people justified same-sex marriage based on procedural justice reasoning (government should not police marriage); and second, judges and individuals justified same-sex marriage based on restorative justice reasoning (marriage is a human right). Nonetheless, because of the religious and conservative origins since the formation and foundation of the United States, many groups have challenges accepting the idea of same-sex relationships. Therefore, disclosure practices and hierarchies based on race, social class, and sexual orientation continue to influence hate crimes (particularly physical and sexual assault) and discrimination against individuals who identify as LGBTQA (Cramer, McNiel, Holley, Shumway, & Boccellari, 2012; Swank, Fahs, & Frost, 2013).

Discrimination in the workplace is particularly troublesome. Part of the problem, Ozeren (2014) argues, is that social institutions, legal frameworks, and cultural norms are still the key pillars of sexual orientation discrimination in the workplace. Tilcsik (2011) demonstrated that there is a regional difference employers have when hiring gay applicants, for example. Companies in the southern parts of the United States tend to show significant discrimination hiring practices against gay applicants—which appears to have an association with local attitudes and disagreement with antidiscrimination laws. Interestingly, businesses who emphasized the importance of stereotypically male heterosexual traits were particularly likely to discriminate against openly gay men as well. Additionally, Mize (2016) used data from the General Social Survey (N = 13,554) and the National Longitudinal Study of Adolescent to Adult Health (N = 14,714) to conclude that perceptions of prejudicial treatment partially explain the wage gaps between LGBTQA and other groups. McDonald (2016, p. 27) argues that one method to improve occupational segregation that is based specifically on sexual orientation is to develop a strong research agenda to follow a four-step queer theoretical approach:

1. Examining occupational segregation beyond the multiple binaries on which extant occupational segregation research is premised;
2. Conceptualizing and operationalizing difference as being "performatively" accomplished in everyday occupational and organizational life;
3. Articulating a politics of occupational segregation that challenges dominant notions of group identity and exposes within-group inequalities and marginalization; and

4. Expanding the repertoire of methods through which we conduct occupational segregation research.

In addition to discriminatory practices in the workplace, LGBTQA populations generally live with an internal stigma—*minority stress*—that negatively affects their health and mental health outcomes. Lifetime victimization, financial barriers, access to appropriate health care, obesity, and limited physical activity accounted for poor general health, disability, suicidal ideation, and depression among LGBTQA youth, adults, and older adults (Dilley et al., 2010; Edmiston et al., 2016; Fredriksen-Goldsen et al., 2013). Even with well-intentioned initiatives, LGBTQA patients are vulnerable to being misled into believing that their rights extend further than they do, giving them a false sense of security with regard to specific arenas of medical practice (Wahlert & Fiester, 2013).

However, innovative leaders have positively affected the integration of LGBTQA individuals into organizations and communities. Baker and Beagan (2014) showed that cultural proficiency health approaches with LGBTQA patients require health and human services practitioners to learn *with*, rather than learn *about*, LGBTQA people's particular health care concerns, paying explicit attention to pervasive power relations and normative contexts. To ensure organizational progress, Cavico, Muffler, and Mujtaba (2012) advocate for human resources departments to amend their policies and practices to include the following clause:

Amending Title VII of the Civil Rights Act to encompass protection against discrimination against gay, lesbian, bisexual, sexually transitioning, and transgender individuals will ensure that all people have equal access to the same employment opportunities, benefits, and protections, as well as fair and unbiased treatment in the employment environment. In order to achieve the goals of fair and equal treatment, as well as to promote diversity, inclusion, and mutual understanding and respect, all employees must have the full protection of civil rights law. (p. 17)

WORKING TOWARD INCLUSION, EQUITY, AND DIVERSITY

As social architects build an inclusive and equitable work environment, they must assess the cultural context in which work groups function. Individuals' behaviors and attitudes are greatly influenced by practices and norms within organizations. The environment and culture can affect how people conceptualize inputs and outcomes, practice their equity preferences, and react to inequities (Bolino

& Turnley, 2008). Thus, workplaces must provide their diverse workforce a sense of inclusion that involves the satisfaction of the needs of both belongingness and uniqueness (Shore et al., 2011). Unfortunately, many organizations are far from reaching this goal, and much work needs be done. Mor Barak's (2015) study of employees in the health and human services concluded that even though the employees considered their workplaces to be free of racial and gender biases, they still felt *excluded* from the dominant group. Employees perceived that they were not consulted regularly when it came to important decisions that affected them, and they were often avoided by key network members within the organization.

Innovative and effective leaders can certainly guide social change. Four distinct leadership styles seem to be best suited to advance equity and diversity in the workplace and to capture the importance of adapting to more caring and inclusive climates: ethical, authentic, servant, and spiritual leadership (i.e., the incorporation of spiritual principles in the workplace) (Gotsis & Grimani, 2016). Boekhorst (2015) argues that authentic leaders are naturally attracted to transmit social information about the importance of inclusion in organizations through inclusive leader role-modeling and reward systems that foster a culture of learning about "inclusive conduct" by followers. In other words, authentic leaders and followers who share cooperative goals related to developing a climate for inclusion can prompt the ongoing learning opportunities of inclusive behaviors by followers, thereby facilitating both individual and organizational goal attainment.

Furthermore, transformative leaders embrace notions of social justice and social change. Thus, transformative leadership focuses on advancing justice and democracy, critiques inequitable practices, and addresses both individual and public good (Shields, 2010). Groves and Feyerherm's (2011) study of 99 leaders and 321 followers demonstrated that leaders who embrace diversity have a strong sense of *cultural intelligence* and can predict the follower's perceptions of the leader's performance and team's performance beyond the effects of other leadership competencies.

Health and human services organizations have the capacity to implement successful managerial models to advance positive equity and diversity in the workplace. The Diversity and Equality Management System has shown successful results that are positively associated with higher labor productivity and workforce innovation and lower voluntary employee turnover (Armstrong et al., 2010). Another successful model is the categorization-elaboration model (CEM), in which the leader's consideration addresses the negative group processes that can result from categorizing perceptions of diversity and how diverse teams operate. The CEM allows the leaders to work with the diverse group members and establish their own norms of collaboration. These models indicate that participants who are challenged with the prospect of working in a diverse team had a higher preference for *considerate leadership* than participants expecting to work in a homogeneous team. Simultaneously, the ability of the leader to treat members as unique individuals is a key variable to explain the positive effects of considerate leadership in the functioning of diverse teams (Homan & Greer, 2013).

Organizational practices have successfully proved the advancement of equity and inclusion in a diverse workplace. Leadership is the most powerful means we have to generate organizational and social change. Groysberg and Connolly (2013) interviewed 24 CEOs from around the world who had a reputation of integrating and embracing people from all kinds of backgrounds. They found that successful leaders have a habit of promoting the following specific organizational values and practices: holding managers accountable, supporting flexible work arrangements, recruiting and promoting from diverse pools of candidates, providing leadership education, sponsoring employee resource groups and mentoring programs, offering quality role models, and creating a chief diversity officer position.

In conclusion, this chapter introduced the reader to the CPC as a tool for innovative leaders to identify attitudes and behaviors in themselves and in others in order to promote diversity in workplace environments. Diversity was also examined with regard to gender and sexual orientation as well as the intersectional issues (i.e., What happens when an individual's race and gender identity interact?). Leadership models that are aligned with diversity considerations and social equity were also reviewed in addition to the organizational policies and practices that foster equitable working conditions for all.

CHAPTER DISCUSSION QUESTIONS

1. Apply the CPC to yourself and to a leader you know and reflect where you and the leader fall within the continuum and where you aspire to be.
2. What steps do you need to take in order to become a more culturally proficient leader?
3. Take any of the free Web-based implicit bias tests offered by Harvard University to learn more about your own potential implicit biases (https://implicit.harvard.edu/implicit/).
4. Read the leader profile and case study in the Appendix to this chapter. Note innovative ideas and practices, and see what aspects of the case you can connect to the contents of the chapter and/or overall book.

REFERENCES

Armstrong, C., Flood, P. C., Guthrie, J. P., Liu, W., MacCurtain, S., & Mkamwa, T. (2010). The impact of diversity and equality management on firm performance: Beyond high performance work systems. *Human Resource Management, 49*(6), 977–998.

Baker, K., & Beagan, B. (2014). Making assumptions, making space: An anthropological critique of cultural competency and its relevance to queer patients. *Medical Anthropology Quarterly, 28*(4), 578–598.

Basford, T. E., Offermann, L. R., & Behrend, T. S. (2014). Do you see what I see? Perceptions of gender microaggressions in the workplace. *Psychology of Women Quarterly, 38*(3), 340–349.

Bell, M. P., Özbilgin, M. F., Beauregard, T. A., & Sürgevil, O. (2011). Voice, silence, and diversity in 21st century organizations: Strategies for inclusion of gay, lesbian, bisexual, and transgender employees. *Human Resource Management, 50*(1), 131–146.

Bernstein, R. S., & Bilimoria, D. (2013). Diversity perspectives and minority nonprofit board member inclusion. *Equality, Diversity and Inclusion: An International Journal, 32*(7), 636–653.

Boekhorst, J. A. (2015). The role of authentic leadership in fostering workplace inclusion: A social information processing perspective. *Human Resource Management, 54*(2), 241–264.

Bolino, M. C., & Turnley, W. H. (2008). Old faces, new places: Equity theory in cross-cultural contexts. *Journal of Organizational Behavior, 29*(1), 29–50.

Buse, K., Bernstein, R. S., & Bilimoria, D. (2016). The influence of board diversity, board diversity policies and practices, and board inclusion behaviors on nonprofit governance practices. *Journal of Business Ethics, 133*(1), 179–191.

Buttner, E. H., Lowe, K. B., & Billings-Harris, L. (2010). Diversity climate impact on employee of color outcomes: Does justice matter? *Career Development International, 15*(3), 239–258.

Buttner, E. H., Lowe, K. B., & Billings-Harris, L. (2012). An empirical test of diversity climate dimensionality and relative effects on employee of color outcomes. *Journal of Business Ethics, 110*(3), 247–258.

Cavico, F. C., Muffler, S. C., & Mujtaba, B. G. (2012). Sexual orientation and gender identity discrimination in the American workplace: Legal and ethical considerations. *International Journal of Humanities and Social Sciences, 2*(1), 1–20.

Choi, S., & Rainey, H. G. (2010). Managing diversity in US federal agencies: Effects of diversity and diversity management on employee perceptions of organizational performance. *Public Administration Review, 70*(1), 109–121.

Cottrill, K., Denise Lopez, P., & C. Hoffman, C. (2014). How authentic leadership and inclusion benefit organizations. *Equality, Diversity and Inclusion: An International Journal, 33*(3), 275–292.

Cramer, R. J., McNiel, D. E., Holley, S. R., Shumway, M., & Boccellari, A. (2012). Mental health in violent crime victims: Does sexual orientation matter? *Law and Human Behavior, 36*(2), 87–95.

Cross, T. (1989). *Toward a culturally competent system of care*. Washington DC: Georgetown University Child Department Program, Child and Adolescent Service Program.

Dilley, J. A., Simmons, K. W., Boysun, M. J., Pizacani, B. A., & Stark, M. J. (2010). Demonstrating the importance and feasibility of including sexual orientation in public health surveys: Health disparities in the Pacific Northwest. *American Journal of Public Health, 100*(3), 460–467.

Edmiston, E. K., Donald, C. A., Sattler, A. R., Peebles, J. K., Ehrenfeld, J. M., & Eckstrand, K. L. (2016). Opportunities and gaps in primary care preventative health services for transgender patients: A systematic review. *Transgender Health, 1*(1), 216–230.

Ely, R. J., Ibarra, H., & Kolb, D. M. (2011). Taking gender into account: Theory and design for women's leadership development programs. *Academy of Management Learning & Education, 10*(3), 474–493.

Faulk, L., Edwards, L. H., Lewis, G. B., & McGinnis, J. (2013). An analysis of gender pay disparity in the nonprofit sector: An outcome of labor motivation or gendered jobs? *Nonprofit and Voluntary Sector Quarterly, 42*(6), 1268–1287.

Fredriksen-Goldsen, K. I., Emlet, C. A., Kim, H. J., Muraco, A., Erosheva, E. A., Goldsen, J., & Hoy-Ellis, C. P. (2013). The physical and mental health of lesbian, gay male, and bisexual (LGB) older adults: The role of key health indicators and risk and protective factors. *Gerontologist, 53*(4), 664–675.

Gotsis, G., & Grimani, K. (2016). Diversity as an aspect of effective leadership: Integrating and moving forward. *Leadership & Organization Development Journal, 37*(2), 241–264.

Groves, K. S., & Feyerherm, A. E. (2011). Leader cultural intelligence in context: Testing the moderating effects of team cultural diversity on leader and team performance. *Group & Organization Management, 36*(5), 535–566.

Groysberg, B., & Connolly, K. (2013). Great leaders who make the mix work. *Harvard Business Review*. Retrieved from https://hbr.org/2013/09/great-leaders-who-make-the-mix-work

Hagai, E. B., & Crosby, F. J. (2016). Between relative deprivation and entitlement: An historical analysis of the battle for same-sex marriage in the United States. In: K. Sabag & M. Schmitt (Eds.), *Handbook of social justice theory and research* (pp. 477–489). New York, NY: Springer.

Hall, J. C., Everett, J. E., & Hamilton-Mason, J. (2012). Black women talk about workplace stress and how they cope. *Journal of Black Studies, 43*(2), 207–226.

Hatzenbuehler, M. L., Phelan, J. C., & Link, B. G. (2013). Stigma as a fundamental cause of population health inequalities. *American Journal of Public Health, 103*(5), 813–821.

Homan, A. C., & Greer, L. L. (2013). Considering diversity: The positive effects of considerate leadership in diverse teams. *Group Processes & Intergroup Relations, 16*(1), 105–125.

Hwang, J., & Hopkins, K. M. (2015). A structural equation model of the effects of diversity characteristics and inclusion on organizational outcomes in the child welfare workforce. *Children and Youth Services Review, 50*, 44–52.

Lindsey, R., Nuri-Robins, K., & Terrell, R. (2003). *Cultural proficiency: A manual for school leaders* (2nd ed.). Thousand Oaks, CA: Corwin Press.

McDonald, J. (2016). Occupational segregation research: Queering the conversation. *Gender, Work & Organization, 23*(1), 19–35.

Mastracci, S. H., & Herring, C. (2010). Nonprofit management practices and work processes to promote gender diversity. *Nonprofit Management and Leadership, 21*(2), 155–175.

Mize, T. D. (2016). Sexual orientation in the labor market. *American Sociological Review, 81*(6), 1132–1160.

Mor Barak, M. E. (2015). Inclusion is the key to diversity management, but what is inclusion? *Human Service Organizations: Management, Leadership & Governance, 39*(2), 83–88.

Nishii, L. H. (2013). The benefits of climate for inclusion for gender-diverse groups. *Academy of Management Journal, 56*(6), 1754–1774.

Ozeren, E. (2014). Sexual orientation discrimination in the workplace: A systematic review of literature. *Procedia—Social and Behavioral Sciences, 109,* 1203–1215.

Shields, C. M. (2010). Transformative leadership: Working for equity in diverse contexts. *Educational Administration Quarterly, 46*(4), 558–589.

Shore, L. M., Randel, A. E., Chung, B. G., Dean, M. A., Holcombe Ehrhart, K., & Singh, G. (2011). Inclusion and diversity in work groups: A review and model for future research. *Journal of Management, 37*(4), 1262–1289.

Swank, E., Fahs, B., & Frost, D. M. (2013). Region, social identities, and disclosure practices as predictors of heterosexist discrimination against sexual minorities in the United States. *Sociological Inquiry, 83*(2), 238–258.

Teasdale, S., McKay, S., Phillimore, J., & Teasdale, N. (2011). Exploring gender and social entrepreneurship: Women's leadership, employment and participation in the third sector and social enterprises. *Voluntary Sector Review, 2*(1), 57–76.

Tervalon, M., & Murray-Garcia, J. (1998). Cultural humility versus cultural competence: A critical distinction in defining physician training outcomes in multicultural education. *Journal of Healthcare for the Poor and Underserved, 9*(2), 117–125.

Tilcsik, A. (2011). Pride and prejudice: Employment discrimination against openly gay men in the United States. *American Journal of Sociology, 117*(2), 586–626.

Wahlert, L., & Fiester, A. (2013). A false sense of security: Lesbian, gay, bisexual, and transgender (LGBT) surrogate health care decision-making rights. *Journal of the American Board of Family Medicine, 26*(6), 802–804.

Williams, D. R., Neighbors, H. W., & Jackson, J. S. (2003). Racial/ethnic discrimination and health: Findings from community studies. *American Journal of Public Health, 93*(2), 200–208.

Yang, T., & Aldrich, H. E. (2014). Who's the boss? Explaining gender inequality in entrepreneurial teams (Summary). *American Sociological Review, 79*(2), 303–327.

APPENDIX
Featured Leader: Steven Kim

Steven Kim, MSW, cofounded a nonprofit organization, *Project Kinship,* in 2014 to serve individuals affected by gangs and incarceration, with the aim of successfully reintegrating them back into our communities. His dedication to breaking cycles of incarceration, gang membership, and community violence stems from more than 15 years of working with traumatized and abandoned youth throughout Orange County, CA. Steven is highly regarded for his human rights work in the field of forensic social work, where he led multidisciplinary teams to identify early childhood traumas on high-profile death penalty cases. He is sought out for his expertise on understanding root causes of violence and has facilitated training on the state and federal levels of the criminal justice system. He has held teaching appointments with the University of Southern California (USC), lecturing on best practices that focus on adolescent gang prevention and intervention strategies.

LEADERSHIP PROFILE FOR STEVEN KIM

Share your professional background and experience

I engaged in outreach work in the community for formerly incarcerated youth, adults, and gang members. I did that for many years, in different capacities, such as helping develop programs, doing faith-based outreach, and collaborating with partner agencies.

I spent a few years working on death penalty cases with amazing folks across the nation in a small cohorts; they call themselves "abolitionists" and are top-tier academics and attorneys. For example, some of them worked on the Unabomber, Tookie Williams, Boston Marathon Bomber, and Guantanamo Bay cases. We were just trying to figure out what happened in a person's life to try to explain why these individuals committed such heinous crimes. I did that through an organization called Center for Capital Assistance.

For the past 12 to 13 years, I've been engaged in private work while simultaneously working at the Orange County Department of Education, where I develop programming and engage in administrative, juvenile justice, school, and community work. And then in 2014, although I never thought it would come to fruition, I was able to start Project Kinship. I began the program with Mary Vu, and with Father Greg's (Rev. Greg Boyle, the founder of Homeboy Industries) blessing, it has been growing. Project Kinship represents what all of my experiences have prepared me for. The organization began in 2014 with $25,000 and two part-time staff members working about 5 hours a week. It has since grown to 15 full-time staff members, has just reached more than $1 million dollars, and now operates in school sites, jails, and communities around the county.

In your experience, what are the top three to five leadership attributes someone in the health and human services field should develop? Share an example of when you have used one or more of these attributes/skills in your work

Relationships and empathy with your staff, clients, and partners. I think these are the most important aspects of leadership. That's what I've learned, even in my three years with Project Kinship, while managing and trying to run this organization. I have been reminded that not everyone thinks like me or even likes me and that I have to slow down and really value relationships, know each person's strengths, and learn how to place people according to their strengths while at the same time providing growth opportunities. I have realized that this takes time and that it doesn't always move on my time frame.

Organizational culture. I think setting the organizational culture is big for us and really grounded in strengths-based perspectives. I feel like the majority of folks are very happy here, which I think in turn also helps the culture.

Accountability and structure. Looking at the present, now that we're so large, I question how to create a structure that doesn't compromise too much of our culture, while allowing space for relationships. Then there are strategies for different stakeholders. For example, the way we connect with probation or parole may be different from the way we connect with a community or faith-based organization or university. Being very strategic on relationships and how you maneuver every single step of the way is a big deal.

A CASE STUDY BY STEVEN KIM

At the very beginning of starting the organization, we knew we wanted to empower formerly incarcerated individuals to be part of our agency's DNA along with our team and staff. When we first started, we received another $20,000, and we were able to have a first cohort of training sessions in partnership with USC for formerly incarcerated folks to become community intervention workers as paraprofessionals. At that time, it was a huge risk. People were wondering why we were training formerly incarcerated individuals through such a prestigious university. We took a big chance to train them, and eventually the stakeholders started to come around and buy into the idea. Strategizing to utilize the leverage of USC to provide training, but also leveraging name recognition in the community in hindsight, turned out to be huge benefit. I think it is very helpful to form partnerships with credible institutions, and we needed visibility and a way to "de-demonize" our highly stigmatized population.

My role was to create a free-of-charge training program with other individuals that we provided to our cohort of the formerly incarcerated folks. The program could have worked out badly and failed, but it did not. In the Santa Ana Unified School District, a few months after the training was completed, at one of the schools with a significant population of at-risk Latino/a youth, there was a sexual assault, a stabbing, a riot, and five fights all in one week, and they asked for our help. These situations were not anything new for the school, but what happened is that the news hit the media. Once it hit the media, they needed help, and they asked for help from us. We said, "we've got trained community folks ready to intervene through our training that was conducted in partnership with USC," and the district agreed. We brought in three members of the cohort and were able to turn the school violence around. As a result of this success, we have partnered with two other organizations to bring in folks who have "lived experience" (again formerly incarcerated individuals and prior gang members) to become community interventionists on school campuses, and at least 10 schools participate in this program.

One thing about leadership is being able to have the confidence when you believe in something and in yourself, and at the same time have the humility to follow the steps of other leaders. I think it is also about developing your own identity as a leader. I think I'm in a place now of maturing into a leadership role, and there is no turning back. I have been open-minded to integrating leadership styles of the folks that have influenced me. I have tried to lead like other leaders before me, but it felt foreign, and I stopped having fun. So, in the end, it is important to be true to yourself, that is, be authentic.

CASE DISCUSSION POINTS

1. This social architect talked about taking risks with a highly stigmatized population. What are your thoughts about this type of risk-taking?
2. From a cultural perspective, do you think it was a good idea for the innovative leader to involve formerly incarcerated individuals to become community interventionists in schools with at-risk youth? Please elaborate on your response.
3. Is the empowerment of formerly incarcerated individuals that could lead to gainful employment a type of social justice intervention? If so, why? If not, why not?
4. The development of a "leadership identity" was described as something important. How would you go about developing your own innovative leader identity?

9

Women in Leadership

Men, their rights, and nothing more; women, their rights, and
nothing less.

—SUSAN B. ANTHONY

CHAPTER OBJECTIVES

1. Explore gender gaps in leadership and in compensation;
2. Understand the challenges associated with integrating work, personal,
   and family life;
3. Gain an appreciation of the organizational and societal structures that
   maintain the status quo; and
4. Obtain insights on innovative leadership from a social architect (see
   Appendix to this chapter).

INTRODUCTION

According to *Fortune* magazine's 2017 annual list of the World's Greatest
Leaders, it appears that more women leaders are getting the recognition
they deserve. The list includes 50 honorees, 25 of whom are women leaders
representing various organizations, including business, government, the
military, activism, and philanthropy (Belstrom, 2016)—an increase from 23
women who made the list last year and 15 women the year before. Although
these are promising figures, the *Fortune 500* list of female chief executive
officers (CEOs) is much less impressive: as of 2017, 32 women represent
6.4% of CE's (up from last year's 21 women), and out of the 32 only two

of these are women of color (Zarya, 2017). Women are underrepresented in leadership positions both in the public and private sectors. Although women represent a large number of workers in human services, men tend to gravitate toward the upper echelons of leadership (Golensky, 2011). There are a variety of complex reasons and theories behind the gender gap in leadership, and this chapter is not meant to be an exhaustive review of the literature, but rather to offer the innovative leader a few compelling issues to consider.

Women in the workplace continue to compete with one of the earliest 20th-century theories of leadership known as the "great man theory." This theory assumed that leaders were born with masculine-type characteristics such as being dominant, ambitious, self-confident, decisive, clever, achievement-oriented, persuasive, and intellectual (Lazzari, Colarossi, & Collins, 2009). This theory is still ingrained in society despite the lack of research confirming that these traits separate male leaders from female leaders. In fact, leadership traits are more individualized than gender-specific. Most women who are senior executives today have been in the workforce for a while and have seen and experienced gender-based discrimination. Women executives are more likely than male executives to recognize the signaling that goes along with gender and sexual harassment and have a heightened awareness to the warning signs (Benko & Pelster, 2013).

This chapter will outline several areas with regard to women in leadership, including topics of self-confidence, motivation, balancing work and family, time management, decision-making, and issues with regard to workplace sexual harassment. A caveat for the reader: unfortunately, most of the research on women in leadership is conducted in the corporate arena rather than in human services. Thus, many of the studies cited in this chapter tend to slant toward the for-profit sector. Many of the issues are similar regardless of sector; however, there are differences that should be pointed out. Gardella and Haynes (2004) note that women leaders in health and human services should not attempt to fit into the mainstream, that is, transform themselves; instead, they have the responsibility of transforming the organization. Additionally, the missions associated with publically operated health and human services agencies can be markedly different from corporate objectives, and thus the leader holds an onus of responsibility toward social justice, making sure to mitigate against discrimination in the workplace as well as mentoring and encouraging other women into leadership roles (Gardella & Haynes, 2004). With these principles in mind, a social architect can think about how to best promote and support women leaders in health and human services.

BACKGROUND

The literature reveals that although women make up more than half the work-force, they face many obstacles their male counterparts do not when it comes to obtaining executive leadership positions (Kellerman, 2010; O'Neil & Hopkins, 2015; Slaughter, 2012). This remains an ongoing problem because the focus is erroneously placed on the individual when the root of the problem is systemic; most organizations still operate under the traditional male leadership model (O'Neil & Hopkins, 2015). This type of structure maintains the status quo because it works for those in charge, most of whom are men. Additionally, women who may be in a position to move up the ladder are often juggling multiple work and family roles. They realize that many organizational policies and procedures are not conducive to their real-life situations and eventually opt-out of leadership opportunities rather than continue to fight the system.

Studies show that women striving for top leadership positions still contend with negative biases, attitudes, behaviors, and perceptions, mostly from their male colleagues who believe women are the weaker sex and not equipped for tough decision-making (O'Neil & Hopkins, 2015). During a 2011 commencement speech to Barnard College graduates, Facebook's chief operating officer (COO), Sheryl Sandberg, pointed out that with 190 heads of state, only nine are women, and only 13% of the world parliaments include women; the number of women in the corporate world occupying board seats and executive roles is about 16% (Slaughter, 2012). Under closer examination, Slaughter (2012) notes that the women who do make it to the top seem to have in common one shared circumstance: privilege. They are all scholars who graduated from prestigious universities. Sandberg herself was one of Harvard's top students of economics and won a Pulitzer Prize—a tough standard for any man or woman to compete with. Many women in executive leadership roles are single with no children, but their male colleagues typically all have families. O'Neil and Hopkins (2015) posit that women in senior leadership positions serve as role models and have the positional authority to change organizational norms that have been in place since the middle of the last century when social norms, economic realities, and women's roles were different from what they are today. Something that could increase more women's potential for advancement into executive leadership positions would be if women leaders at the top advocated for other women. All organizations, including those in the not-for-profit sectors, have a responsibility to eliminate the bias and discrimination that undermine women at all levels and to break down and rebuild systems and structures to foster a more inclusive environment for all workers (O'Neil & Hopkins, 2015).

As previously discussed in the chapters relating to culture and diversity, intersectionality (i.e., multiple identities) can present additional challenges for marginalized groups. For instance, in the case of gender, women who identify as African American and lesbian tend to be undercompensated compared with women who identify as heterosexual white or African American (Bateu, 2014). In fact, when addressing compensation, the gender pay gap continues to be an ongoing issue of inequity in the workplace. The pay gap issue based on gender is very straightforward: women earn less money for the same position as men (at the time of this writing, estimated at 76 cents to the dollar) (see www.payscale.com). The Institute for Women's Policy Research predicts that women will not have equal pay with men until 2059, and Latina women not until the year 2233 (www.iwpr.org). Women are also less likely to be promoted than their male counterparts with similar credentials and work experience (males are 30% more likely to be promoted) (see Sheryl Sandberg's website, www.LeanIn.org).

SELF-CONFIDENCE AND MOTIVATION

It has been noted that some women self-sabotage their own success because of a phenomenon referred to as "imposter syndrome" (Kanazawa, 2009). Imposter syndrome has been described as an individual feeling that eventually someone will find out they are a fraud and that they do not genuinely belong in their role despite their high motivation, qualifications, and effective leadership skills. Attribution theories posit that women often credit their success to luck (i.e., external locus of control), whereas men do not usually experience imposter syndrome because they are more likely to associate success with their abilities and effort (i.e., internal locus of control) and to attribute their failings to bad luck.

While the competitive male leadership model remains unchallenged for the most part, it perpetuates the idea that women have something to prove (O'Neil & Hopkins, 2015). The opinion that more women are not in leadership positions because they lack confidence or motivation implies that women need to be fixed when in fact the problem is systemic (O'Neil & Hopkins, 2015). Women have reported that they believe they need to work harder and often sacrifice personal or family life to prove they are cut out for demanding leadership positions (Schuh et al., 2014). In 2012, BIC (the pen manufacturer) received backlash on social media and was accused of sexism when it released an advertisement with the slogan, "Look like a girl, act like a lady, think like a man, work like a boss" to recognize National Women's Day in South Africa (Davies, 2015).

Women, more often than men, are scrutinized for the way they dress, especially in the corporate world (Bell, 2016). This is particularly notable in news reports of women political leaders compared with men in equivalent positions of power and authority in which women are accused of dressing too sexy for work or too masculine. Consultants hired to help women improve their chances of landing high-profile positions advise women to be careful not to appear too authoritative or not feminine enough (Bell, 2016). Others argue that the trick is to know exactly when a woman should exert the so-called masculine traits for the sake of fitting in among the traditional male leaders and when to be more feminine in their approach; thus, knowing this balance will result in greater leadership potential (Leo, Reid, Geldenhuys, & Gobin, 2014). This behavior is not so different from an individual knowing how and when to alter his or her interpersonal skills to establish rapport and build trust with different personality types; however, it also suggests that women need to change and not the system and thus places an unjust onus of responsibility on the woman.

BALANCING WORK AND FAMILY LIFE

Women who make the personal choice to leave or opt-out of leadership positions do so because the traditional path to the top does not support women being accomplished professionals and responsible caregivers simultaneously (Slaughter, 2012). Some of the most accomplished female executive leaders acknowledge that social policies need to change to accommodate a woman's right to be all she can be and stop accepting the traditional male leadership model as the only mechanism for success. Slaughter's (2012) article in *The Atlantic* magazine, entitled, "Why Women Still Can't Have It All," claims that the traditional male leadership model will remain detrimental to women and organizations until society decides to value the choice a woman makes to put family ahead of work. If society valued the choices women made to combine work and family, organizations would do everything possible to alter their structures so that women felt supported and thus would be less likely to opt-out of leadership positions (O'Neil & Hopkins, 2015). In fact, Slaughter (2012) suggests that a work structure that is more conducive to modern lifestyles could improve conditions for all employees by implementing policies that are fair for everyone. Case in point: some employers offer paid maternity leave to mothers, while paternity leave is often viewed less seriously (Sherwin & Meyer, 2017).

While women who have given birth need time to recover and spend time with their newborns, limiting full or partial paid leave to mothers and not fathers in some states perpetuates the notion that only women can or should care for children (Sherwin & Meyer, 2017). The American Civil Liberties Union fights hard to combat stereotypes that perpetuate gender inequality, and the Equal Employment Opportunity Commission has warned that unequal leave policies for men and women are discriminatory (Sherwin & Meyer, 2017).

Recognizing that families look different today than they did years ago, there have been some policy shifts introduced with regard to leave. For example, the Family and Medical Insurance Leave Act (FAMILY Act) was introduced in February 2017 by Democratic Senator Kirsten Gillibrand of New York and Representative Rosa DeLauro of Connecticut, and at the time of this writing it is still being considered by the 115th Congress (S.337). The FAMILY Act would provide spouses, domestic partners, same-sex couples, and adoptive parents with 12 weeks of partially paid leave to care for a new baby or a sick family member or for their own serious health condition. No one can argue that caregiver roles are changing as more and more men share parenting responsibilities for various reasons. Slaughter (2012) reported an example of how Deputy Secretary of State James Steinberg, who shared the parenting of his two young daughters equally with his wife, made getting access to classified information at home a priority so that he could leave the office at a reasonable hour and participate in important meetings through videoconferencing if necessary. While this is commendable, many women in similar positions would be perceived as less committed to their jobs (Slaughter, 2012).

Another factor that could support women with children to strive for or remain in leadership positions would be to alter school schedules to match work schedules (Slaughter, 2012). Policy makers and employees (specifically female teleworkers with families) suggest that working from home is an effective solution to balancing work and family (Hilbrecht, Shaw, Johnson, & Andrey, 2008). At first glance working from home seems like the perfect opportunity to manage responsibility in the context of marriage, family, and social networks. However, a study that examined the experiences of a group of employed mothers who worked from home found these women to be even busier because they were expected to—or felt like they had to—volunteer at schools and pick up and drop off their children and their children's friends because the other mothers were out "at work." Hilbrecht et al. (2008) found no evidence that women attained a better work–life balance by working from home: a break at the office meant a true break away from work, whereas a break at home meant doing the laundry. Alternatively, men who worked from home spent time on personal leisure or obtained more paid work, not typically engaging in caregiving or domestic chores. Thus, flexible work hours by working from home made it easier for women to assume total domestic responsibility, and thus these findings suggest that flexible scheduling from home does not necessarily result in better time management or assist women to build support (Hilbrecht et al., 2008). Slaughter (2012) argues that some women give in to the feeling that there really is no choice but to opt-out because they experience both the social expectation and for some the maternal instinct to be caregivers first.

Decades of observations and writings about traditional roles and stereotypes contend that men are socialized to be breadwinners and women are socialized to care for their children; in addition, where men seem more likely to choose a job at a cost to the family, women feel obligated to choose their family over work (Hilbrecht et al., 2008; O'Neil & Hopkins, 2015; Slaughter, 2012).

TIME MANAGEMENT AND SUPPORT SYSTEMS

Despite the seemingly unequal gender division of labor at home, women continue to want to work from home because it allows them to feel like they are being more efficient and productive in both roles. Over the past decades, men have become more involved with parenting; in fact, Deputy Secretary of State James Steinberg and Deputy Secretary of Defense William Lynn resigned after two years with the Obama administration so that they could spend more time with their children (Slaughter, 2012). Stepping down from a position of power, even temporarily, contradicts the expectations of top executives that anyone would voluntarily leave a position of power for parenthood. These attitudes contrast with campaign commitments to support family values. Women in top positions have the authority and arguably a responsibility to support efforts to implement changes that increase a woman's chance to obtain leadership roles—not be exploited by a work–life imbalance (Slaughter, 2012). Another factor that could increase women's potential for executive leadership is to appoint a pool of successful women mentors to coach, guide, and encourage other women to continue their advancement toward top leadership positions (O'Neil & Hopkins, 2015). Interestingly, Martha Minow, the Dean of Harvard Law School, noted that many young men are now asking for information on how they can manage a work–life balance, and this may be a new generational trend (Slaughter, 2012).

Advancing technology is another factor that increases a woman's potential for leadership by making participation in meetings less burdensome. For instance, videoconferencing is an alternative to long business trips and a factor in reducing time-management obstacles that might otherwise cause a woman to opt-out (Slaughter, 2012).

Additionally, women who do have flexible schedules and are able to work from home can increase their potential for leadership positions by knowing how they are spending time at home and at work. Knowing how time is spent helps one determine the type and amount of support that may be needed from hiring someone to help with certain chores or from a spouse, partner, or other family member. This can help an individual rebalance priorities and spend time on high-profile projects or participate in important business decisions, thereby showcasing leadership skills.

DECISION-MAKING

Women have a propensity to engage in what has been described as a collaborative type of leadership style (Shambaugh, 2016). In contrast to authoritarian leadership styles, a collaborative leader takes time to build relationships, is inclusive, enlists consensus building, handles conflict, and yet shares control (Martin, Chrispeels, & D'Emedio-Caston, 1998). For example, Meg Whitman, President and CEO of Hewlett-Packard, is said to have contributed her success to knowing when to shift from being inclusive and having a sense of humor to being strong-willed and direct (Shambaugh, 2016). Shambaugh (2016) suggests that collaborative types of leadership are found to be more effective than exclusively command-and-control leadership styles, especially now that organizations are becoming more global; thus, women in or seeking leadership roles must be able to convey that consensus building is an advantage over the authoritarian way of giving orders. Women can take steps to help move their careers forward by knowing how they are spending their time, flexing their leadership styles while incorporating a collaborative approach and maintaining an open dialogue about the costs and benefits of collaboration.

In terms of perceptions of risk-taking decisions at work, according to Sundheim (2013), people—usually men—who appear physically stronger and taller receive more support from others for engaging in risky decisions, whereas women are perceived by others to be strong in behaviors like standing up for what's right in the face of opposition or taking the ethical path when there is pressure to stray away from ethics. However, because these behaviors do not fit the perception of what are typically considered risk-taking actions, women often do not receive credit for being decisive leaders in terms of assuming risks (Sundheim, 2013). The author claims that broadening the definitions of risk-taking in organizational contexts is an important factor in increasing a woman's potential for leadership. Additionally, when it comes to decision-making, female senior executives have reported that their male counterparts take a somewhat patronizing, "Don't worry, we'll take care of it" approach. This is an approach that male leaders are less likely to accept from other men (Benko & Pelster, 2013).

Interviews conducted with female executives in the field of human resource management revealed that the level of involvement they had with business strategy and decision-making varied based on different factors (Waitman, 2015). For example, the female executives were aware of their contributions to organizational success but felt they were not always taken seriously as decision makers and would often have to assert themselves to be heard (Waitman, 2015).

So, what do the women who have made it to the top have in common that other professional women lack? A common element shared among women in executive leadership roles is known as *identity integration* (Mor, 2014). Identity integration is the unification of gender identity with professional identity, as opposed to separate entities, and this is viewed as essential for leadership success. Financial feminist Sallie Krawcheck is the CEO and co-founder of Ellevest, a recently launched innovative digital investment platform for women designed to close the gender gap in investing (Clifford, 2017). Krawcheck believes that after professional women in their 30s have proved that they are good at their job, they stop networking. This is a huge mistake because it allows men to move past them. Men are making important business connections at cocktail parties, and women in their 30s with children do not make business or work-related networking a priority (Clifford, 2017). Networking is even more critical for women who take time off to have children because they have to make up for lost time. It is even more difficult if a woman's partner disagrees with the notion of her going out to meet new people, even though that partner supported the woman's career path in the beginning.

Arguably one of the more controversial positions on the success of women leaders was presented by college president Mary Sue Coleman, who believes that women who get ahead are *relentlessly pleasant* and advises women asking for a pay raise to do so with a smile (Mor, 2014). According to Coleman, to be pleasant and smile is good advice for anyone but typically not the kind of advice given to men. However, she failed to mention how her hard work and dedication contributed to her success. She is recognized as a higher education leader at the national level; *Time* magazine named her one of the nation's 10 best college presidents, and the American Council on Education honored her with its Lifetime Achievement Award (Bloomberg.com, 2017).

HARASSMENT IN THE WORKPLACE

The 1964 Civil Rights Act, Title VII established that employers cannot discriminate employees based on sex, race, color, national origin, or religion. Sexual harassment has been defined by the US Equal Employment Opportunity Commission (EEOC) as follows: "unwelcome sexual advances, requests for sexual favors, and other verbal or physical conduct of a sexual nature constitute sexual harassment when this conduct explicitly or implicitly affects an individual's employment, unreasonably interferes with an individual's work performance, or creates an intimidating, hostile, or offensive work environment" (n.d., para. 1). Sexual harassment in the literature is typically described as two types: *quid pro quo*, which involves engaging in sexual relations in exchange for a job or promotion (i.e., sexual favors) and in which the victim is often feeling under pressure or coercion; and the type that represents a hostile work environment, such as being the target or witness of offensive or sexually inappropriate jokes, exposure to pornographic material at work, and so forth (MacKinnon, 1979).

Unfortunately, both men and women are subjected to these types of harassment (with women typically taking the brunt of it). Sexual harassment had been historically socially acceptable for the most part (or ignored or silenced) in the United States until more recent times. It was not until 1986 that the Supreme Court ruled that sexual harassment was a form of sexual discrimination (Austin, Solic, Swenson, Jeter-Bennett, & Marino, 2014). It is estimated that one-fourth of all women have experienced workplace sexual harassment, keeping in mind that this figure is likely an underestimation of cases as a result of lack of reporting or filing of complaints by victims (National Women's Law Center, 2016). Fear of retaliation, loss of employment, embarrassment, and fear of not being believed are common reasons for victim hesitancy to report harassment.

At the time of this writing, high-profile cases of sexual assault and harassment by male leaders in various industries, such as media, film, government, sports, higher education, and what seems to be in every sector of society, have fueled a women's social media campaign, the *Me Too movement* ("Me Too," 2017), to bring public awareness to the issues and encourage destigmatization of reporting. Leaders, regardless of gender identification, need to confront this issue in the workplace and be intolerant of harasser conduct. The EEOC recommends that prevention of workplace harassment through training programs for all employees and having a formalized complaint or grievance process in place are key elements to avoiding or decreasing the incidence of harassment (although sexual harassment training programs have had limited empirical study in terms of evaluation of their effectiveness). Nevertheless, leaders need to act quickly and responsibly to ensure that they are doing all they can to ameliorate this social ill.

CONCLUSION

As discussed in this chapter, there are factors that may increase women's potential for gaining and succeeding in leadership positions. First and foremost, the literature surrounding this subject contends that the system must be restructured to catch up with the way people live in the 21st century. The challenge is that men are in most of the executive decision-making roles, and as long as the system is working for them, there is no motivation to change (O'Neil & Hopkins, 2015). It can be argued that the gender gap in leadership roles will continue as long as organizations operate under the traditional patriarchal types of leadership models (O'Neil & Hopkins, 2015).

Women are educated and equipped with skills and traits required to effectively manage challenges within a global economy and in their own communities. Women realize that balancing work and family in the current systemic structures affects both men and women in terms of economic and social issues (Slaughter, 2012). Women opt-out of leadership roles because of the need for frequent travel, conflicts between their children's school and work schedules, and the lack of flexible work schedules that require work be done in the office. Changing the system requires more than commencement speeches that applaud the efforts of women as if that should satisfy their need to be appreciated. These issues, according to Slaughter (2012) and others, need to be addressed in organizations, through legislation, and in the media on a continuous basis so that they are no longer seen as a feminist rant or inconvenience to some, but instead as a necessary improvement to the overall health and well-being of all members of our communities.

Women will continue to turn down promotions and leadership opportunities as long as the system is set up to make it difficult or impossible to accommodate lifestyle choices. Many organizations acknowledge the importance of work–life balance and can tie the benefits to a healthier workforce. Yet women still report feeling guilty for putting their family ahead of work, while employees who put work ahead of family are acknowledged for their dedication and loyalty. The culture is changing, but like every step along the way toward gender equity and equality, the process is painfully slow (Slaughter, 2012). Society continues to make efforts toward achieving greater diversity (and acceptance of diverse individuals) in a variety of contexts, yet a gender gap remains in terms of realizing that women have the potential to be excellent leaders especially if organizations ensure and maintain a diverse workforce with family-friendly policies.

What may be perceived as women's lack of confidence is in reality a pervasive, systemic disadvantage that women face in the work environment that serves to undermine them as they seek to advance into leadership positions (O'Neil & Hopkins, 2015). In order to create more opportunity for women, the existing patriarchal power models must be broken down and rebuilt in a form that promotes unity without sexism and has the support of all groups, not only of men but also of other women, transgendered, and intersexed people alike (Lazzari, Colarossi, & Collins, 2009).

CHAPTER DISCUSSION QUESTIONS

1. What are some of the workplace gender gap disparities described in this chapter and that you have heard of or read about elsewhere?
2. What challenges do women leaders tend to face with regard to stereotypes?
3. How can women and men address work–life balance?
4. What is something that you can personally do to effect change with regard to sexual harassment and gender discrimination in the workplace?
5. Familiarize yourself with Malala Yousafzai's website about the importance of educating girls from a global perspective (https://www. malala.org/girls-education). Report back on the evidence of benefits resulting from secondary education for girls (see https://www.malala. org/brookings-report) and how that translates to the betterment of women and societies.
6. Read the leader profile and case study in the Appendix to this chapter. Note innovative ideas and practices, and see what aspects of the case you can connect to the contents of the chapter and/or overall book.

REFERENCES

Anyikwa, V. A., Chiarelli-Helminiak, C., Hodge, D. M., & Wells-Wilbon, R. (2015). Women empowering women. *Journal of Social Work Education, 51*(4), 723–737. Retrieved from http://libproxy.usc.edu/login?url=http://search.proquest.com. libproxy1.usc.edu/docview/1777157867?accountid=14749

Austin, S., Solic, P., Swenson, H., Jeter-Bennett, G., & Marino, K. M. (2014). Anita Hill round-table. *Frontiers: A Journal of Women's Studies, 35*(3), 65–74.

Bateu, A. M. (2014). Equal pay for (some) African-American women. *Reproductive Health*. Retrieved from www.rhrealitycheck.org.

Bell, E. (2016). Why workplace dress codes have troubled women for decades. *Newsweek*. Retrieved from http://www.newsweek.com/high-heels-and-workplace-460312

Belstrom, K. (2016, March). Meet the world's latest female leaders. *Fortune*. Retrieved from http://fortune.com/2016/03/24/greatest-female-leaders/

Benko, C., & Pelster, B. (2013). How women decide. *Harvard Business Review*. Retrieved from https://hbr.org/2013/09/how-women-decide

Bloomberg.com. (2017). Company overview of University of Michigan. Mary Sue Coleman, Ph.D. Retrieved from https://www.bloomberg.com/research/stocks/private/person.asp?personId=588949&privcapId=3758920&previousCapId=3758920&previousTitle=University%20of%20Michigan

Clifford, C. (2017). Ex-Wall Street titan Sallie Krawcheck on the no. 1 mistake professional women in their 30s tend to make. *CNBC Make it.* Retrieved from https://www.cnbc.com/2017/01/23/sallie-krawcheck-on-the-mistake-professional-women-in-their-30s-make.html

Davies, C. (2015, August). "Look like a girl . . . think like a man": Bic causes outrage on National Women's Day. *Guardian.* Retrieved from https://www.theguardian.com/society/2015/aug/11/look-like-a-girl-think-like-a-man-bic-outrage-south-africa-womens-day#top

Gardella, L. G., & Haynes, K. S. (2004). *A dream and a plan: A woman's path to leadership in human services.* Washington, DC: NASW Press.

Golensky, M. (2011). *Strategic leadership and management in nonprofit organizations: Theory and practice.* Chicago, IL: Lyceum Books.

Hilbrecht, M., Shaw, S. M., Johnson, L. C., & Andrey, J. (2008). "I'm home for the kids": Contradictory implications for work-life balance of teleworking mothers. *Gender, Work and Organization, 15*(5), 454–476.

Kanazawa, S. (2009). The imposter syndrome: Why do so many successful women feel they are frauds? *Psychology Today.* Retrieved from https://www.psychologytoday.com/blog/the-scientific-fundamentalist/200907/the-imposter-syndrome

Kellerman, B. (2010). The abiding tyranny of the male leadership model—a manifesto. *Harvard Business Review.* Retrieved from https://hbr.org/2010/04/the-abiding-tyranny-of-the-mal

MacKinnon, C. (1979). *Sexual harassment of working women: A case of sex discrimination.* New Haven, CT: Yale University Press.

Martin, K. J., Chrispeels, J. H., & D'Emidio-Caston, M. (1998). Exploring the use of problem-based learning for developing collaborative leadership skills. *Journal of School Leadership, 8*(5), 470–499.

"Me Too." (2017, October 17). Me Too: Why are women sharing stories of sexual assault and how did it start? *Independent.* Retrieved from http://www.independent.co.uk/news/world/americas/me-too-facebook-hashtag-why-when-meaning-sexual-harassment-rape-stories-explained-a8005936.html

National Women's Law Center. (2016). *Fact sheet: Sexual harassment in the work place.* Retrieved from https://nwlc.org/wp-content/uploads/2016/11/Sexual-Harassment-Fact-Sheet.pdf

O'Neil, D. A., & Hopkins, M. M. (2015). The impact of gendered organizational systems on women's career advancement. *Frontiers in Psychology.* Retrieved from http://journal.frontiersin.org/article/10.3389/fpsyg.2015.00905/full

Lazzari, M. M., Colarossi, L., & Collins, K. S. (2009). Feminists in social work: Where have all the leaders gone? *Affilia: Journal of Women & Social Work, 24*(4), 348–359.

Leo, L., Reid, R., Geldenhuys, M., & Gobind, J. (2014). The inferences of gender in workplace bullying: A conceptual analysis. *Gender & Behaviour, 12*(1), 6059–6069.

Mor, S. (2014). Why some women negotiate better than others. *Harvard Business Review.* Retrieved from https://hbr.org/2014/10/why-some-women-negotiate-better-than-others

Pratch, L. (2011). Why women leaders need self-confidence. *Harvard Business Review.* Retrieved from https://hbr.org/2011/11/women-leaders-need-self-confidence

Schuh, S. C., Hernandez Bark, A. S., Van Quaquebeke, N., Hossiep, R., Frieg, P., & Van Dick, R. (2014). Gender differences in leadership role occupancy: The mediating role of power motivation. *Journal of Business Ethics, 120*(3), 363–379. doi:10.1007/s10551-013-1663-9.

Shambaugh, R. (2016). The time-consuming activities that stall women's careers. *Harvard Business Review.* Retrieved from https://hbr.org/2016/03/the-time-consuming-activities-that-stall-womens-careers

Sherwin, G., & Meyer, K. (2017). In Trump's "maternity leave" plan,—the devil—and the stereotypes are in the details. *American Civil Liberties Union (ACLU).* Retrieved from https://www.aclu.org/blog/womens-rights/womens-rights-workplace/trumps-maternity-leave-plan-devil-and-stereotypes-are?redirect=blog/speak-freely/trumps-maternity-leave-plan-devil-and-stereotypes-are-details.

Slaughter, A. (2012, July/August). Why women still can't have it all. *The Atlantic.* Retrieved from https://www.theatlantic.com/magazine/archive/2012/07/why-women-still-cant-have-it-all/309020/

Sundheim, D. (2013). Do women take as many risks as men? *Harvard Business Review.* Retrieved from https://hbr.org/2013/02/do-women-take-as-many-risks-as

US Equal Employment Opportunity Commission (EEOC). (n.d.). *Facts about sexual harassment.* Retrieved from https://www.eeoc.gov/eeoc/publications/fs-sex.cfm

Waitman, H. R. (2015). Female HR executives' contributions to firm performance: The effects of gender on decision-making and strategic-planning (doctoral dissertation). Retrieved from http://libproxy.usc.edu/login?url=http://search.proquest.com.libproxy3.usc.edu/docview/674699201?accountid=14749

Zarya, V. (J2017, June 7). The 2017 Fortune 500 includes a record number of women CEOs. *Fortune.* Retrieved from http://fortune.com/2017/06/07/fortune-women-ceos/.

APPENDIX
Featured Leader: Maricela Rios-Faust

As Chief Executive Officer, Maricela Rios-Faust, MSW, LCSW, provides vital leadership, support, and vision to the continued growth and success of Human Options, Inc. Since 2006, she has capitalized on her 20 years' experience working with vulnerable populations and has been a key driver to Human Options becoming the most comprehensive domestic violence service providers in Orange County, CA. Her commitment comes from a desire to raise her daughter in a world where domestic violence is not tolerated. Recognized as a leader in the field, Maricela is past President of the Board of Directors for the California Partnership to End Domestic Violence. She co-chairs the Orange County Domestic Violence Death Review Team and serves on the Orange County Women's Health Project Advisory Board. Maricela was named one of *Orange County's Most Influential of 2014* for her leadership on increasing awareness of health impacts of domestic violence.

LEADERSHIP PROFILE FOR MARICELA RIOS-FAUST

Share your professional background and experience

If I look before my social work beginnings, I think macro practice always worked with the way that I think. My brain is naturally wired to think in systems. I did a lot of work from a systems perspective, and I really felt like I gravitated toward social work. More specifically, I gravitated toward a balance of both micro and macro work. For instance, what you know about the family dynamic you can apply to organizational dynamics. Communication is important, and how you manage change and how you set up systems and processes are all critical elements for a leader. When there is an issue that starts within the system, understanding what is creating that and then really tending to people's emotions around how the system is getting in the way or enhancing it are crucial to the survival of an organization. That was something I remember really gravitating toward because organizations feel very real and alive to me.

I graduated with my Master of Social Work degree and got into more community work. I was still doing organizational work but was also doing more in the community, trying to build and strengthen communities, and seeing how social issues and systems work hand in hand.

When I came to work at Human Options, it was a real opportunity for me to look at an issue like domestic violence, one that was very much framed around being a family issue and an individual issue, and think about it more from the lens of a societal and more specifically a social justice issue. I realized that some of the very systems that have been put in place to protect women and children may in fact be harming families. Through this job, I was able to get connected at the state level on the board of directors for the statewide coalition and the leadership development program. We do everything to provide services for individuals and families, but we have to understand the underlying root causes and the larger societal issues that are affecting these individuals and families in order to address domestic violence in a systems kind of way.

In your experience, what are the top three to five leadership
attributes someone in the health and human services field
should develop? Share an example of when you have used
one or more of these attributes/skills in your work

Openness to listening and learning. What I have found is that although I feel
knowledgeable, there's always something new to learn. As a leader, if you
are tied to one way of doing things, "No, we have to do it this way," then
you lose the ever-changing issues and how these affect your goals. If you
are willing to listen, learn, and grow from the stories that are being shared
with you from your staff or from community members and especially
from those affected, you are able to develop more responsive techniques
and strategies. Listening and learning are very key leadership attributes.

Be a change agent. It is essential to be in relationships with people in a way that
helps them move through change. We live in a world that's ever-changing;
some people work really well with that, and others do not. Attending to
and acknowledging that change is difficult while still moving things along
is important. There needs to be an honoring of the historical context in
which problems have evolved and successes have been achieved. Honor
what has worked in the past and what has not worked in the past, while
also applying today's contextual factors. You need to help teams of people
look at the past and the present and then into the future. This will not necessarily ensure that every single person will have a buy-in, but it will help
people contextualize when change is needed, why it's needed, and what
you're hoping to gain. Understand that some people will readily make that
change and others will not, but do not make this personal. Some people
have reached where they're going to reach, and others may join at different
stages of their journey.

Stay humble. I learned this from a mentor of mine. We have a society that
celebrates accomplishments. As wonderful as it is to be honored and
recognized, one of the things he said was, "Never believe your own hype."
I think the intention behind that message was that there needs to be humility in leadership. Just because you're in a leadership seat, that does not
mean you're the one doing all of the work. Remember that you just happen
to be the person in the forefront, but it's the team that really makes a difference. I think that this requires a certain level of emotional intelligence
from a leader. There are moments in which there are huge successes and
you want to celebrate, but also there is more work to be done. At times
there are disappointments, and as the leader your responsibility is to keep
forging through and to contain those feelings to help everyone move
through and keep doing the work.

Good communication skills. Sometimes there will be imperfect communications, but it is important to really understand and own when you haven't communicated something well. Always make sure that you are checking to see if the things that needed to be communicated have been. As leaders, there is information we have to keep confidential, but we also should understand that transparency is important and that holding that standard for ourselves and for others is key.

What are challenges you have experienced being a Latina woman in leadership?

Social work and helping professions are predominantly female until you get to the nonprofit and governmental systems, particularly in leadership roles, in which there are more men. I look at those places and wonder how often women are at the table. And how often do women have an opportunity to be involved in dialogue that creates the change that needs to happen at the local and state levels? Throughout my career, even early on, I remember working with government entities, and it would take some time and effort to have your voice heard. When you are trying to create change, as a female, my inclination is to pull at heartstrings and really make an emotional appeal. As a female leader, I have to learn to adapt that model when I'm in circumstances where there are more males. I have to get more factual, and it doesn't necessarily mean that they aren't tied to it emotionally, but there's a different level of healing, and you are often talking about a bottom line that's different. There is a different way of getting people to enter into a conversation. It is more factually based, statistically driven, and bottom-line driven when you start to engage and then you can gradually bring in the heartstrings on the emotional piece of it. You can still honor both the sides of the story, but you are entering into that dialogue differently. I have felt very fortunate to have had a number of different mentors and role models who I think have helped me grow and learn.

I also realize that my lived experience is very different from that of others. It is important to understand when you are setting policies and as you're running an organization and there is dialogue around, "Let's just do this one-size-fits-all solution." I try to have others understand my perspective because it may vary from that, and I'm trying to bring different voices to the forefront in a way that is meaningful. I think it is important as a Latina in leadership that I realize I have a certain amount of privilege because I am at the table. I am able to talk and represent some perspectives, but also realize that I don't represent every Latina. Honoring that I am one voice, I am not all voices.

There are not a lot of Latinas in leadership. There are some, and those that are in leadership positions are very strong leaders. Before I was serving in a formal position of leadership, I was a therapist and a gang prevention specialist, and I remember being a part of this conversation about leadership opportunities, and all these Spanish-speaking therapists, who had great leadership skills, were not getting promoted or offered those opportunities because they needed bilingual people working directly with clients. Since they had Spanish-speaking skills, they were stuck in a way because giving them leadership opportunities would take them away from direct service.

I have also seen as you build your leadership potential and as people start to see more Latinos, or even more females, I think they tend to be drawn to organizations that have that diversity that they're looking for. From that perspective I've found that if your leadership is diverse, your staff is going be diverse, and vice versa. You want to balance that inclusion because anytime you focus on one population, you exclude another. It is a fine line. I think as a Latina leader, I have more awareness of the tremendous opportunity and responsibility and privilege to give back to others. I have been successful because people have supported me in my success and people have believed in me, so I am mindful that I have an opportunity to give back to other leaders who have potential.

A CASE STUDY BY MARICELA RIOS-FAUST

I have been at Human Options for a little over 11 years and in the CEO role for about a year and a half now. When I came to Human Options, I started as a program director, and within 6 months I had been promoted to the COO position. That position was new to the organization. Anytime you create a new position, people kind of wonder: *What is it? Do you really need it? What is it supposed to do?* The position was intended to help provide a succession plan for the long-time founding executive director and also to support the executive director in switching to a more external view of the organization. She was going to begin to do more in terms of our donors, fundraising, and community presence, so in order to free up more of her time, there needed to be somebody doing the internal day-to-day operations of the organization. Everyone who had a long-term relationship with her was going to experience a change. All of a sudden they have this new person, who happens to be me, who is redefining the systems or processes that hopefully will help move the organization into this next iteration. There was a huge learning opportunity for me because as I reflect back, the founding executive director and I kept all the processes the same and made no substantial changes, yet the feedback from a couple of key supervisors said, "Why are things changing? Why can't they stay the same?" It took me time to realize that I was the change. I myself was different from the founding executive director, we were different people. She was very charismatic and a ball of energy, and she had developed these long-term relationships over years. Then here I was, jumping into a world where I hadn't had the time to develop these long-standing relationships, where trust can be formed. Through this process, I learned I needed to keep the day-to-day operations going, but I also needed to invest the same amount of time and energy in relationship building and trust building and understanding people's loss. Not loss in the tactical things that were happening, but loss in their relationships. Now there was someone in between them and the person that they valued as their leader.

I talked about changes in a mindful way. I said, "We're moving in this direction not because it's broken, but because this will help us continue to grow." I would say it wasn't a perfect thing from the beginning, but now it's being mindful again to always honor what was there before and then also look at the context of how things are different. Since things in the environment have changed, we need to look at moving things differently. Then recognizing that as an individual, how I learned, how I process, and how I take things were very different from my predecessor. When I am learning, I ask a lot of questions, it's just the way I process things, and I realized my way of learning was making people feel like I was questioning their abilities. I learned to acknowledge my judgment and state things out loud, such as, "I like to ask a lot of questions, that's how I learn. I am not asking questions because I do not believe this is how you should be doing this, I'm actually asking questions because it helps me understand it in a way that then we can talk about it later." For me that was the process of change. In creating the COO position and then partnering with the founding executive director, it took a lot of negotiation and then renegotiation. It was important to make sure that we were providing the right training and support with plenty of room for dialogue while still not letting all of that get in the way of our progress. There was a lot of dialogue with the executive director on what that change looked like and what we wanted the culture of the organization to look like. We looked at the organizational structure and the positions from a strengths-based perspective. We learned about strengths-based leadership as part of a leadership development program called the Strong Field Leadership Development program that was put on by Blue Shield against violence. In that program, we learned about strength-based leadership, and we did the Strengths Finder activities and discussed our top talents. I learned how to talk about my learning style. I thought this had made me really understand myself as a leader, so I was going to bring this back to my leadership team.

At the time, I had 12 individuals, and some of them had been struggling in their positions, but I thought this was going to get us on the same page and we were going be able to have this shared language around strengths. It helped us talk about when a position is a good fit and when it is not in terms of strengths, instead of saying, "You're not doing this effectively." So we have a half-day meeting and go through this leadership journey to find our strengths. Everybody is into it and excited about sharing some of the key concepts and strengths because these are tied to different positions. For instance, if your skill set or strength does not include being detail-oriented and you're more relationship-driven, being in a financial position is going to be hard because there are deadlines and information that need to be timely and accurate. Everybody understood the language, and everybody learned a lot about each other. Two days later, I had three resignations on my desk. That was not at all the intent, but during that process there were conversations along the lines of, "I have been unhappy in my position for a long time and for the first time I now know why. It is because it's not the right position for me." One of them was a very artistic and creative person, and he happened to be in a rigid contractual role. The reason the conversations were so meaningful is that they were not re-volving around how the organization was not adapting the jobs to fit their skills, but instead were about these positions were not fulfilling for them. There are no jobs in which you're going be 100% fulfilled. There's no job in which you don't have to spend at least some percentage of your time in a space that you don't really appreciate that much, but you should at least enjoy and be excited by your work most of the time.

As an organization, we began to talk about strengths and to think about the strengths and talents that are necessary for our positions so that when we recruit people, we aren't setting them up in positions in which they would feel like they are not contributing in a meaningful way. Those people that moved on were able to find positions that did fit their passions, and they still stay connected to the organization albeit in a different way. They send us referrals, or we work with them as partners at other agencies. There is mutual respect because as hard as it was to lose people, it was liberating for them to be in that place to understand that the jobs were just not the right jobs for them.

Even though we believe in strengths, you have to manage your weaknesses. For me, it took me a while to love budgeting, but I am a strong storyteller. I love stories, and I love to understand how things sit within the larger context, so I took responsibility to learn how the budget numbers sit within the larger context of the organization or the larger context of the program. By using my strengths and tying budgeting to storytelling, I began to see what questions I needed to ask to be able to do my job effectively. It allowed me to look at my team and find a person who loves numbers and loves the details so that I can partner with that person very effectively to get the story that I need to be able to communicate out. Learn how to partner with another person so that you don't have to be experts in everything, but know each other's strengths. You can be a leader who knows how to tune into individual needs and help your staff work together by saying, "I have found that this person really does well with praise."

I am still a work in progress. This is something I try to live up to all the time, but I'm not perfect. When you are in the nonprofit world, change becomes the constant, and then when you're in leadership, sometimes you forget to pause. The way I handle this is that I hire people I know are willing to tell me that I'm wrong or that I missed something. When you hire too many people like you, you create your own blind spots. Remember to hire people who aren't exactly like you.

I remember that a mentor of mine asked me when I was trying to fill a po- sition, "Have you ever thought to ask the people who work for you what they think is the biggest skill they need to have in order to work for you or with you?" I try my best, and I am human, but through that conversation it was also very clear to me that my team members should always be part of the in- terview process when I am hiring new people. They have the ability to tell me, "I think this person could really work with you, and this is where this person may struggle. This person may not be willing to tell you what you need to hear, or this person actually can tell you and will do it in a way that we can all really benefit from." What I am trying to verbalize to my team is that I never want to create an environment where people are chronically stressed or fearful. We have a responsibility to those we serve. It is okay to be uncomfortable sometimes when you are not 100% sure that what we're doing is the correct solution. Being uncomfortable as we work through an important issue is different than feeling unsafe. It is important that we honor that notion of safety, especially with the work that we do because we work with individuals who are unsafe, and that's not the same as us being uncomfortable during difficult situations. To get the best results, you should talk through a struggle in a way that is still respectful and promotes growth. Not only will you have worked through something to- gether, but you will also have grown.

CASE DISCUSSION POINTS

1. In the leadership profile, the social architect spoke about being a Latina leader. What insights did you derive from the telling of her story?
2. How did the leader's own personal experience of being a Latina woman inform her perspectives on service provision?

3. In the case, organizational and leadership change was described as a challenge. How did the innovative leader attempt to address the change in leadership with the team members?
4. How should a social architect cope with his or her imperfections as well as those of her team members?
5. How can a strengths-based approach to leadership be utilized to foster a positive organizational climate?

Appendices: Leader Assessment Instruments

A. THE MOR BARAK INCLUSION-EXCLUSION SCALE

Scale Items

1	2	3	4	5	6
Strongly disagree	Moderately disagree	Slightly disagree	Slightly agree	Moderately agree	Strongly agree

1. I have influence in decisions taken by my work group regarding our tasks. ☐1 ☐2 ☐3 ☐4 ☐5 ☐6

2. My coworkers openly share work-related information with me. ☐1 ☐2 ☐3 ☐4 ☐5 ☐6

3. I am typically involved and invited to actively participate in work-related activities of my work group. ☐1 ☐2 ☐3 ☐4 ☐5 ☐6

4. I am able to influence decisions that affect my organization. ☐1 ☐2 ☐3 ☐4 ☐5 ☐6

5. I am usually among the last to know about important changes in the organization (R). ☐1 ☐2 ☐3 ☐4 ☐5 ☐6

6. I am usually invited to important meetings in my organization. ☐1 ☐2 ☐3 ☐4 ☐5 ☐6

7. My supervisor often asks for my opinion before making important decisions. □ 1 □ 2 □ 3 □ 4 □ 5 □ 6

8. My supervisor does not share information with me (R). □ 1 □ 2 □ 3 □ 4 □ 5 □ 6

9. I am invited to actively participate in review and evaluation meetings with my supervisor. □ 1 □ 2 □ 3 □ 4 □ 5 □ 6

10. I am often invited to contribute my opinion in meetings with management higher than my immediate supervisor. □ 1 □ 2 □ 3 □ 4 □ 5 □ 6

11. I frequently receive communication from management higher than my immediate supervisor (i.e., memos, emails). □ 1 □ 2 □ 3 □ 4 □ 5 □ 6

12. I am often invited to participate in meetings with management higher than my immediate supervisor. □ 1 □ 2 □ 3 □ 4 □ 5 □ 6

13. I am often asked to contribute in planning social activities not directly related to my job function. □ 1 □ 2 □ 3 □ 4 □ 5 □ 6

14. I am always informed about informal social activities and company social events. □ 1 □ 2 □ 3 □ 4 □ 5 □ 6

15. I am rarely invited to join my coworkers when they go for lunch or drinks after work (R). □ 1 □ 2 □ 3 □ 4 □ 5 □ 6

Overview

The Mor Barak Inclusion-Exclusion scale (MBIE) (Mor Barak, 2005) measures the degree to which individuals feel a part of critical organizational processes such as access to information, involvement, and participation with the organization and influence in the decision-making process. It uses a matrix system of five work-organization system levels (work group, organization, supervisor, higher management, and social/informal) intersected by three inclusion dimensions (decision-making, information networks, and participation/involvement). The measure thus includes 15 items that evaluate a worker's sense of inclusion in relation to the following five work-organization system levels:

1. Work group (items 1–3)
2. Organization (items 4–6)
3. Supervisor (items 7–9)
4. Higher management (items 10–12)
5. Social/informal (items 13–15)

In each of these levels, the respondent is asked to assess his or her inclusion across the following three dimensions:

a. The decision-making process (items 1, 4, 7, 10, 13)
b. Information networks (items 2, 5, 8, 11, 14)
c. Level of participation/involvement (items 3, 6, 9, 12, 15)

The 15 scale items are summed to create a composite inclusion-exclusion continuum score with three reverse-scored questions (items 5, 8, 15—noted by the letter R) to prevent response sets from systematically answering the questions. Higher scores on the scale reflect a higher sense of inclusion.

B. THE MOR BARAK AND COLLEAGUES' DIVERSITY CLIMATE SCALE

Scale Items

1	2	3	4	5	6
Strongly disagree	Moderately disagree	Slightly disagree	Slightly agree	Moderately agree	Strongly agree

1. I feel that I have been treated differently here because of my race, gender, sexual orientation, religion, or age (R).   ☐ 1 ☐ 2 ☐ 3 ☐ 4 ☐ 5 ☐ 6

2. Managers here have a track record of hiring and promoting employees objectively, regardless of their race, gender, sexual orientation, religion, or age.   ☐ 1 ☐ 2 ☐ 3 ☐ 4 ☐ 5 ☐ 6

3. Managers here give feedback and evaluate employees fairly, regardless of employees' race, gender, sexual orientation, religion, age, or social background. □1 □2 □3 □4 □5 □6

4. Managers here make layoff decisions fairly, regardless of factors such as employees' race, gender, age, or social background. □1 □2 □3 □4 □5 □6

5. Managers interpret human resource (HR) policies (such as sick leave) fairly for all employees. □1 □2 □3 □4 □5 □6

6. Managers give assignments based on the skills and abilities of employees. □1 □2 □3 □4 □5 □6

7. Management here encourages the formation of employee network support groups. □1 □2 □3 □4 □5 □6

8. There is a mentoring program in use here that identifies and prepares all minority and female employees for promotion. □1 □2 □3 □4 □5 □6

9. The "old boys' network" is alive and well here (R). □1 □2 □3 □4 □5 □6

10. The company spends enough money and time on diversity awareness and related training. □1 □2 □3 □4 □5 □6

11. Knowing more about cultural norms of diverse groups would help me be more effective in my job. □1 □2 □3 □4 □5 □6

12. I think that diverse viewpoints add value. □1 □2 □3 □4 □5 □6

13. I believe diversity is a strategic business issue. □1 □2 □3 □4 □5 □6

14. I feel at ease with people from backgrounds different from my own. □1 □2 □3 □4 □5 □6

15. I am afraid to disagree with members of other groups for fear of being called prejudiced (R). □1 □2 □3 □4 □5 □6

16. Diversity issues keep some work teams here from performing to their maximum effectiveness (R). □1 □2 □3 □4 □5 □6

Overview

The diversity perception scale examines employees' views about the diversity climate in the organization (Mor Barak, Cherin, & Berkman, 1998). It includes 16 items with two dimensions: the organizational and the personal, each containing two factors, as follows:

I. Organizational dimension
   a. Organizational fairness factor (items 1–6)
   b. Organizational inclusion factor (items 7–10)
II. Personal dimension
   c. Personal diversity value factor (items 11–13)
   d. Personal comfort with diversity (items 14–16)

The *organizational dimension* refers to the perception of management's policies and procedures that affect members of minority groups and women— such as discrimination or preferential treatment in hiring and promotion procedures (factor a). It also refers to management actions that affect inclusion or exclusion of women and members of minority groups—such as mentorship programs or the preservation of the "old boys' network" (factor b). The personal dimension refers to individuals' views of the importance of diversity to work groups and to the organization (factor c) and their level of comfort in interactions with members of other groups (factor d).

The 16 scale items are summed to create a composite diversity perceptions score with four reverse-scored questions (items 1, 9, 15, 16, noted by the letter R) to prevent response sets in answering the questions. Higher scores on the scale reflect a positive perception of diversity climate. The dimensions and factors can be separately summed and analyzed to gain insight into the composition of employees' views of the diversity climate.

Execution

10

Organizational Strategic Planning

Before anything else, preparation is the key to success.
—ALEXANDER GRAHAM BELL

CHAPTER OBJECTIVES

1. Review historical and innovative organizational strategic planning processes in the health and human services fields;
2. Learn how successful leaders formulate compelling vision, mission, and values and how they lead their organizations to accomplish goals and objectives;
3. Analyze how organizational culture can be a conduit to accomplish performance expectations and organizational purposes; and
4. Gain insights on innovative leadership from a social architect (see Appendix to this chapter).

INTRODUCTION

Innovative leaders acknowledge the enormous value of using a strategic planning process to accomplish desired organizational goals and objectives. The strategic planning philosophy in health and human services comes from the ideology that organizations, just like people, are living and dynamic entities that can improve by ongoing learning opportunities. First developed in the 1960s by Mintzberg's *Organizational Systems Approach*, and later by Senge's *The Learning Organization*, strategic planning is a process in which the complex current organizational state is examined and the desired state is carefully planned and executed (McKelvey et al., 1999). Under this school of thought, leaders are designers, stewards, and teachers who have the task of building the capacity and capability of the organization to continuously adjust and thrive in its environment.

In a nutshell, strategic planning is a process in which the organizational leadership identifies their strategic intent in four levels: a broad *vision* of what the organization should be (aspiration), an organization's *mission* or core values (identity), specific *goals* that are operationalized (direction), and *specific objectives* (benchmarks, evaluation) (Reid, 1989). Senge describes that learning organizations must evolve within five domains (as cited in Goding, 2005):

1. *Systems thinking*—learning is a process by which organizations maintain and develop strong relationships and networks with others
2. *Personal mastery*—embracing people's growth and development to master their individual traits and expertise
3. *Mental models*—knowing the organizations' strengths and weaknesses and working with their teams to manage these dynamic environments
4. *Shared vision*—fostering everyone's awareness and having a meaningful participation to accomplish its purpose, mission, and vision
5. *Team learning*—identifying interactive patterns that lead to collective learning and increased productivity

Generally, strategic planning has four main stages: formulation, development, implementation, and evaluation. First, leaders formulate their vision based on experience, field/environment observations, current state of affairs, and organizational capacity. Second, the development stage brings together the organization's stakeholders (in this case, board members, executive team, and key partners) to discuss and write the strategic plan, which functions as the blueprint of agreed goals and objectives for the next two to four years. Third, the organization members implement the plan, trying to accomplish all the desired goals and objectives. During the final stage, a third party (typically through a contract with an external evaluator) engages the organizational members in completing a formative and summative evaluation, which assesses what worked well and what did not during the implementation process. Measuring organization progress on its strategic objectives is critical to short-term adjustments in strategy and long-term success (Blatstein, 2012). The strategic planning process and implementation outcomes are coupled with organizational values and culture. This chapter provides a detailed description and analysis of how leaders apply successful strategic planning practices in organizational settings, develop capacity in their workforce, and monitor their organizational culture. We also provide a few managerial approaches to complement leadership styles that are covered in Chapter 3.

VISION, MISSION, AND STRATEGIC PLANNING

Every organization has to have a clear sense of purpose that is shared and agreed on by its members. Strategic planning has a significant value of positively influencing the shape of the organization's environment and future direction. It serves as a great opportunity for leadership teams to provide feedback of the current state of affairs and discuss potential steps to improve internal and external policies and practices. Building the strategic plan with a shared vision, mission, goals, and objectives is not an easy task; it takes concerted and thoughtful effort from leaders and their teams to craft and execute a successful plan. Social architects have to formulate and identify the following five strategic elements: stakeholders, customers, or clients the organization intends to serve; products and services the organization intends to provide; technologies needed to accomplish the goals; fundamental accomplishments to achieve; and how the organization is innovative (Dutton & Duncan, 1987).

When working on strategic planning, social architects are cautious of the kind of ambiguity that can cause confusion and make sure to pay attention to it. Abdallah and Langley (2014) describe three types of ambiguities that can lead to frustration, exhaustion, and rethinking: duality (dual structure combining the social and commercial nature of the organization), equivocality (linguistic; the use of equivocal words with various meanings), and expansiveness (wide variety of mission-related action proposals). With this being said, a leader who is innovative has to also avoid binary thinking and instead should engage in "thinking free" (i.e., free from prior restraints in order to take innovation to the next level) (Sample, 2002). Therefore, a leader should balance ambiguity with free thinking, and this is not always easy to accomplish. The use of data and evaluation results has the potential to avoid confusion, but it needs to be purposeful. Information comes in two ways: formal (rational) and informal (implicit or intuitive). Unfortunately, many health and human services strategists tend to use and analyze data that are collected from formal methods and mostly ignore the informal sources, which can paint an incomplete scenario (Daake, Dawley, & Anthony, 2004).

It is critical that strategic plans also include ways and means to improve internal organizational cultures. For example, Darnell and Kuperminc (2006) demonstrated that public mental health agencies that (1) include culturally competent mission and vision statements and (2) provide ongoing cultural proficiency training have significantly higher member perceptions of both cultural competence within the organization and greater acceptance for diversity. Denton (2001) argues that leaders must go beyond formulating and writing mission statements and work with their teams to focus on both the environmental issues affecting the organization and the task at hand so that goals and objectives can be accomplished. Studies have shown that characteristics of strategic situations and environments (e.g., complexity, uncertainty, orientations, performance), rather than a manager's psychological type, determine configuration of the strategic planning process. Jennings and Disney (2006) explain that there is evidence that successful organizations spend about 90% of their time keeping people focused and engaged and the other 10% figuring out how to get there. Ineffective organizations tend to spend 90% of their time making rules, regulations, and procedures and only 10% working on their goals.

Nonprofit organizations and public agencies in the health and human sector invest time and effort to actively participate in strategic planning processes with the goal of addressing challenges, refining mission and main goals, and obtaining feedback from the members and clients in order to better meet their needs and move the organization forward in a unified and decisive manner (McHatton, Bradshaw, Gallagher, & Reeves, 2011). O'Neil and Willis (2005) suggest that organizations strategically engage in five important elements as they plan for the future: being aware of important shifts and innovations; being responsive to member needs and demographic shifts; employing a strategic planning process; assessing progress toward specific goals; and using marketing strategies to reach possible new members.

A technique that is often implemented in strategic planning is the use of a SWOT analysis as an environmental scan of the organization or often referred to as a gap analysis between the current realities of the organization and its desired future direction (Harley-McClaskey, 2017). The acronym SWOT stands for internal strengths, internal weaknesses, external opportunities, and external threats.

Nordqvist and Melin (2008) recognize that the role of the leader in crafting the vision and mission statements during the strategic planning process is vital. The social architect is the key individual who introduces, promotes, and guides the strategic planning process in an organization. An innovative leader has two specific roles: the social craftsperson and the artful interpreter. These leaders understand and respect the specific values, interests, and concerns that form and run the rules of the game for the work of strategy practitioners. Equally important is considering that a meaningful vision and mission statements can be effective strategic tools as long as employees' purpose is aligned with the organizations' values. In other words, organizational commitment may be seen as the result of a complex influence of other organizational dynamics, such as the sense of mission, purpose, and positive relations (Macedo, Pinho, & Silva, 2016).

Crafting a mission statement takes careful consideration. Health and human services organizations must have a clear and effective strategy, or uniqueness, to be able to attract resources, such as funds and action partnerships. When the strategy is effective, it can provide a path for competitive advantage, resulting in appropriate growth and development. Pandolfi (2011) encourages innovative leaders to think of three fundamental components when crafting mission statements:

1. *The mission statement must clearly describe the agency's strategy—* articulating clearly the actions that make the agency unique.
2. *A well-crafted mission statement allows agencies to operate with focus and discipline—*providing consistency in decision-making over both time and geography.
3. *The process of creating the mission statement is as important as the end result—*fostering the opportunity for the leadership group to come together to define their purpose, what success looks like, and how they plan to get there.

In actually writing a mission statement (or the purpose of the organization), it is typically recommended that it is brief and contains three basic elements, for example, what an organization does, who the organization serves, and how the organization does what it does (Harley-McClaskey, 2017). The vision statement also should be brief and should address the organization's core ideology along with guiding values, purpose, and the envisioned future (Collins & Porras, 2011).

Lastly, leaders working in the nonprofit sector of health and human services will be engaging with a board of directors that also assists with the strategic planning and setting the mission and vision of the agency. Boards typically approve agency budgets and plans for fundraising as well as engage in public relations. These board members also advise and evaluate the executive director or leader of the agency. In fact, the authority over the organization (or the "governance") is entrusted to the board of directors (sometimes referred to as "the board of trustees") (Grobman, 2015, p. 98). A board member is not just filling an honorary or volunteer position, but the position also carries legal duties toward the organization, and these duties vary from state to state. However, in the majority of states, these duties typically involve duty of care, duty of loyalty, duty of obedience, and duty to avoid conflicts of interest (Grobman, 2015, p. 89). Thus, a social architect also needs to work cooperatively with his or her board of directors and draw on their strengths. The notion behind a "shared leadership" (between the board of directors and the executive director) is "to establish a meaningful division of labor between the board and the top management to maximize the talents and expertise of both" (Golenski, 2011, p. 266).

ORGANIZATIONAL DEVELOPMENT AND
ORGANIZATIONAL CULTURE

Individuals have an aspiration to work in organizations that have earnest leaders, and the organization's purpose is aligned with their personal values. Simultaneously, leaders know that one way to attract and retain a successful, loyal, and engaged workforce is by creating and maintaining sustainable organizations. The mutual goal is to foster and nurture a happy employee who values retention, empowerment, and work performance (Howard & Gould, 2000). Thus, success is often measured by the organizations' accomplishments, reputation, and culture. Organizational culture has a direct influence on work attitudes and an indirect effect on the organizational climate. Aarons and Sawitzky (2006) learned that work attitudes significantly predicted one-year staff turnover rates and that both culture and climate affect work attitudes and subsequent staff turnover. A constructive organizational culture has individualism and supportiveness features, whereas a defensive culture is characterized by submissiveness and conformity. Innovative leaders appreciate when team members' job satisfaction, work attitudes, and organizational commitment are more positive and sustainable, creating a productive organizational culture.

One method highlighted on constructive organizational cultures is strategy visualization. The organizational leadership, as a team, has the ability to see and put pieces into motion to execute short- and long-term goals in multiple dimensions: cognitive, social, economic, and emotional. Eppler and Platts (2009) developed a conceptual framework for strategic visualization in which three elements are considered: use visualization at different organizational levels; deliberate the potential solutions to the expected challenges involved during the execution of the strategic plan; and communicate clearly the goals, accomplishments, and barriers before, during, and after the strategic planning process.

Additionally, constructive organization cultures are established and maintained throughout positive organizational development practices. Resnick and Manefee (1993) suggest that if organizational development interventions can help "transform an organization's culture from one focused on maintenance and survival to one concerned with growth and success . . . the impact on these organizations, their clients, and our communities would be truly remarkable" (p. 441). Organizational development practices in health and human services organizations are established on individual and social change that is based on strong humanitarian and democratic philosophies and the belief that individuals must be treated with inherent value and dignity. Furthermore, well-established organizational development practices become a safeguard to protect the organization from internal threats, including lack of staff, management, and board engagement; an inability to escape the crisis mode; undefined or ill-defined values; and low staff compensation and morale (Steiner et al., 1994).

The social architect is aware that human services organizations create a social context for the services they provide and that climate and culture have a direct effect on the quality and outcomes of the services in a variety of ways (Hemmelgarn, Glisson, & James, 2006). Stable organizational cultures have the capacity to provide a very important ingredient to the organization's employees and clients—namely, a high sense of safety and security. Fox (2013) indicates that at any given time, there are four major external threats to any organization: changing political priorities; competing human services organizations; increasing demands for services and accountability; and disconnecting program evaluation from the organizational values. These external issues can create a temporary vacuum, which the leader must manage properly to be able to continue providing effective services to needy individuals and families.

There is a strong relationship between organizational culture and innovation in the health and human services fields. Leaders with innovative ideas have to be willing to take calculated risks. On one hand, they understand the environment around them, current and potential political and social uncertainties, and external pressures that can rapidly destabilize the organization. On the other hand, leaders open to innovation allow their employees to think out of the box, try something new or different, and nurture ingenuity. At times, when conservative values are highly expected, such as cohesion, status quo, and lack of conflict, these organizational policies and practices may not foster but instead hinder innovation efforts. For example, in a study focused on the relationships between organizational culture and innovation with nonprofit human services organizations in the State of Alabama, Jaskyte and Dressler (2005) concluded the following: (1) organizational innovativeness was positively associated with the aggressiveness value dimensions and negatively associated with the stability value dimension; (2) cultural consensus was the only significant predictor of conservative organizational values; and (3) innovative employees have to be given enough leeway to express their creativity, be allowed to take risks, and take advantage of opportunities.

Two other studies have shed light on the value of constructive organizational culture in the health and human services fields. First, when measuring community-based mental health organization's culture and climate, Petterson and colleagues (2011) found that the perceptions of culture have a direct impact on employees' behavior. Moreover, the frequent use of intraorganizational events, group discussions, and training sessions can help increase stability and positive organizational development. Second, Willis et al. (2014) found that improving organizational capacity for delivering health services had a positive direct relationship with organizational culture. In other words, as employees improved their service delivery, they felt better about their workplace, felt a positive impact on their organization's capacity, and felt that the services received by their clients were more effective. The strategies used to improve organizational capacity and culture may be classified into three domains: (1) government action—policies to reinforce social norms and standards for education, research, and program evaluation; (2) organizational action—appropriate models of leadership (both government engagement and shared leadership); and (3) partnership action—for instance, collaborations with media outlets, community organizations, and school-based programs.

In closing, health and human services organizations in particular can be subject to funding changes, new leadership, market fluctuations, and other reasons that drive them to constantly adapt and adjust. Organizational cultures are affected by these changes, being forced to reconfigure business units and to strategize for innovative service delivery alternatives. Schreter (1998) recommends that social architects embark on a clinical and administrative re-engineering process, by taking the following steps:

- Identifying the leadership team
- Formulating a mission statement and strategic plan
- Creating a legal entity capable of achieving the organization 's goals
- Drawing up an organizational chart
- Developing the provider network
- Enhancing the continuum of services offered
- Developing administrative capability
- Dealing with managed care and/or other services
- Paying attention to fundamental business practices
- Integrating key services into the organization
- Marketing current and new services

KEY ORGANIZATIONAL DEVELOPMENT MODELS IN HEALTH AND HUMAN SERVICES

This section will review strategic planning process applications. The design, implementation, and evaluation of these organizational development models have produced positive cultural transformation results in multiple settings.

1. *Leadership development.* This organizational model involves designing, implementing, and evaluating leadership development interventions targeted at behaviors essential to an innovative and adaptive culture (Barriere, Anson, Ording, & Rogers, 2002). Leadership development

programs include a multisource feedback component and are targeted for all health and human services managers. The social architect and the leadership team must ensure the following steps are completed:

- Tailor the leadership developmental training to the specific context of the organization.
- Involve all employees in the process of defining strategic initiatives.
- Secure and maintain a commitment by senior staff with the necessary financial resources being provided.
- Create a sense of urgency among all employees.
- Conduct ongoing formative and summative evaluations of all improvement initiatives using organizational surveys and interviews to modify or create innovative initiatives.
- Ensure that the leadership development process provides an unbiased viewpoint to help build trust at all levels of the organization and to add specific expertise in change management.

2. *Organizational learning capacity.* Organizational learning capacity is defined as the alignment of internal and external organizational systems to promote cultural learning. The key tenants of learning capacity are exploration of information, open communication, staff empowerment, and professional development (Bess, Perkings, & McCown, 2011). For example, Marin County Health and Human Services Department in California has implemented an organizational learning capacity model, in which agency leaders create a culture where communication is encouraged both vertically and horizontally, frontline-level workers are engaged and their voices heard, cross-departmental problem-solving is practiced, innovative ideas are supported, and evidence-informed practice are regularly implemented (Lindberg & Meredith, 2012).

3. *Strategic review.* Periodically, organizations engage in comprehensive performance assessments with the purpose of identifying strategies to improve their effectiveness. These assessments use data-informed practice and knowledge management (Harrison, 2012). For example, the organization may gather information on staff perceptions, perceptions of external stakeholders, changing citywide and neighborhood demographics, policy mandates, and budget and workload issues. The strategic review reports generally have five areas: introduction (background and overall state of affairs), emerging trends (current issues affecting the organization), agency performance (data on services and client outcomes), resources (workforce, workload, and budget), and conclusion (next steps and new benchmarks).

4. *Train the trainer.* Disseminating expertise can be a highly valuable service delivery model. It is generally used by organizations with a smaller capacity and a willingness to partner with community groups to share information with clients. A successful example is the *promotoras de la salud* (community health workers) model in Spanish-speaking communities. Neighborhood residents are trained by health technicians and nurse practitioners to canvas (door to door) their neighborhoods and share information with other residents about nutrition, cooking habits, prevention, fitness, physical activity, and health outcomes. This peer-to-peer model tends to have greater client engagement than a professional-client approach (Marks, Sisirak, & Chang, 2013).

5. *Staff training and development.* Successful organizations believe that their team members are their greatest resource and capitalize on their training and development. This is a trait leadership approach, in which group members are prepared and coached in certain attributes and characteristics, including determination, self-confidence, communication, sociability, and empathy. Staff development requires an ongoing investment—competency-based training, supervision congruent with the service vision and mission, accountability through performance evaluation, and opportunities for growth. A comprehensive staff training and development program is designed to (1) enhance the 3 C's: capacity, commitment, and culture (Seibold & Gamble, 2015); and (2) improve motivation, social identity, and emotional resources (Suh, Houston, Barney, & Kwon, 2011).

Planning and Executing: Managerial Approaches to Achieving Goals and Expectations

Strategic planning processes and organizational development execution are mostly implemented and monitored by the social architect and the organization's leadership team, in collaboration with the human resources departments. How team members perceive human resources management practices can determine their behavioral outcomes (e.g., motivation and engagement). First, social architects select one or more leadership styles that best describe them (key leadership styles are addressed in Chapter 3). Whether they select to be transformational, authentic, or another leadership style is a personal choice that mostly depends on the individual's drive, passion, attributes, and skills. After the innovative leaders select one or more leadership styles, they can choose from several managerial approaches to execute their innovation and strategic plan. Next, we will review the five most well-known managerial approaches and their applications in the health and human services fields: leader–member exchange (LMX) theory, adaptive management, psychodynamic approach, the managerial grid, and team management models.

Leader–Member Exchange Theory

The LMX theory tries to understand the value and meaning of the interactions between leaders and followers as a dyadic relationship. The LMX theory was originally developed by Dansereau, Graen, and Haga (1975), and it has morphed in multiple ways in the leadership literature throughout the years. The main idea is that by improving the value and quality of interactions between people, innovative leaders will increase the effectiveness of their relationships and productivity. Under the LMX lenses, leaders must work together with their team members to achieve the proposed strategic outcomes. The LMX theory suggests that in-group members must be paired with their leaders depending on their attributes, characteristics, skills, and adaptability. When there is a high quality of LMX interactions between the leader and the followers, in-group members feel more empowered and able to reach greater engagement, trust, and productivity (Harris, Wheeler, & Kacmar, 2009).

The LMX theory is designed for the leader to pay special attention to, and work closely with, their team members. For example, transformational, authentic, and servant leadership approaches (described in Chapter 3) have a natural alignment with the LMX theory features because of the emphasis on positive dyadic relationships.

Adaptive Management

Under adaptive management (also known as adaptive leadership), the innovative leader is expected to encourage and guide the followers to continuously adapt to organizational changes (internal) and environmental factors (external). Drawn from systems theory and Darwinism, adaptive management focuses on developing policies and practices that help retain and train talented team members to build organizational commitment through adaptation—or survival of the fittest. The original adaptive management framework was first introduced by Heifetz in the 1990s, who thought that the leaders' key role is to effectively mobilize people and resources to accomplish a common purpose (Heifetz, 1994).

Adaptive management has three major components: situational challenges, leader behavior, and adaptive work. First, situational challenges are mostly technical and adaptive challenges in the organization and/or community that can usually be resolved by acquiring the needed resources and putting in place favorable policies and procedures. The three main situational challenges are technical challenges (technology), technical and adaptive challenges (organizational structure and support systems), and adaptive challenges (client response and adaptation). Second, the innovative leader must properly assess the challenges and begin exploring potential solutions. The role of the innovative leader is to successfully lead and manage the workforce adaptation within an uncertain environment. The final stage is the adaptive work, in which the innovative leader and team members engage in ongoing and regular interactions to tackle challenges (Northouse, 2016).

Psychodynamic Approach

The psychodynamic approach seeks to better comprehend the behavior dynamics of leaders and followers. In essence, human behavior is very complex to comprehend and decipher with 100% accuracy. Leaders deal with human intricacies, trying to understand what motivates individuals to behave in certain ways, what structures can best provide support to group members, and how to inspire others to contribute with their best effort. This "energy" can easily be disrupted by internal or external factors, forcing the leader to find strategies that will assist with harnessing and levering the different human complexities and organizational functioning. Applying psychodynamic clinical knowledge, leaders embrace human nature and create platforms for positive team member interactions.

The psychodynamic model has its origins in Sigmund Freud's theory of human behavior and personality. Freud believed that the mind had three levels of awareness: conscious or rational self (the ego), unconscious or irrational self (the id) and the mediator between the rational and the irrational parts (the superego, based on higher order societal rules). He argued that dysfunctional behavior was a manifestation of the struggle between the unconscious (desires, feelings, and emotions) and the conscious (rational and appropriateness) states of mind. Much theoretical work has been published within the psychoanalytic and psychodynamic schools of thought; among the most notable in organizational behavior are developmental psychology, anthropologic cultural discoveries, motivational theories, neuroscience, cognitive and affective theories, and individual and group psychotherapy. Social architects have been able to apply knowledge extracted from psychodynamic approaches within organizations and with their clients, particularly to better understand specific behaviors, such as motivation, interests, drive, and aspiration.

The Managerial Grid

The Managerial Grid is one of the most common tools used to influence and understand leadership and managerial behaviors. Originally developed by Blake and Mouton (1964) as the managerial grid, and later changed to the leadership grid, this model is concerned with people (team members) and results (production). On one hand, concern for people assesses how the leader attends to individuals and groups in the organization. The innovative leader should be (1) promoting people's motivation, commitment, and trust, and (2) providing a sense of security, good working conditions, fair compensation practices, and social relationship. On the other hand, concern for results focuses on how the leader is achieving the vision, mission, goals, and objectives of the organization. Measuring outputs and outcomes takes into consideration internal and external policies and practices put forward by the leader to best position the organization and services in their environment.

The Managerial Grid joins concern for people and concern for results in two intersecting axes. The vertical axis denotes the leader's concern for people, and the horizontal axis represents the leader's concern for results. Each of the axes has a nine-point scale on which 1 represents *least concern* and 9 represents *most concern*. The model illustrates five managerial styles, depending on the level of the leader's concern for people and results:

1. *Impoverished management (1,1)*. The 1,1 style demonstrates poor leadership in both task accomplishments and interrelationships. This type of leader has a small number of followers and is considered apathetic, indifferent, and noncommittal.
2. *Authority-compliance (9,1)*. The 9,1 style places a great deal of energy and resources to accomplish the tasks at hand. This leader is most concerned about results rather than people's needs, motivations, or concerns. These leaders tend to be demanding, authoritarian, and controlling.
3. *Country-club management (1,9)*. The 1,9 style of leadership has a high concern for people and their feelings. These leaders want to please people and make them feel appreciated. People's experiences are more important than the product or service. These leaders are very friendly, avoid conflict, and are comforting.

4. *Middle-of-the-road management (5,5).* The 5,5 leader is always trying to find a balance between people and results. These leaders have a compromising approach to conflict, which focuses on quality and quantity. Leaders in this category are seeking win-win conflict resolution outcomes, equality, and common ground.

5. *Team management (9,9).* The 9,9 style encourages a high degree of participation, commitment, and teamwork, coupled with high standards of service delivery. This leader is involved, active, and mindful of people's perceptions. Innovative leaders who espouse to the team management style are open-minded, communicative, and committed to find the best strategies to improve work systems and results.

Most leaders have a dominant/preferred grid managerial style and a backup style.

The preferred managerial model is applied regularly, whereas the backup model is mostly utilized under pressure. Social architects in the health and human services work toward reaching the 9,9 managerial style because it involves the opportunity to find more effective programs and services to help those in need. At the same time, this managerial approach values emotional intelligence (EQ)—people's feelings, perceptions, and emotions—as a key factor to get the work done.

Team Management Models

Health and human services organizations best function when individuals work together in groups and teams. Generally, teams are created to design and implement programs and to monitor service delivery systems. Social architects have the ability to create and handle effective teams. Although empirical studies focusing on team performance originated in the 1960s, team leadership was first introduced by Zaccaro and colleagues in the 1990s. They were interested in the leader–team dynamics through the lens of "functional leadership" (which asserts that the leader's main job is to do whatever functions are not being handled adequately in terms of group needs). A key point that these authors considered was the reciprocal influence between leadership and team processes (Zaccaro, Rittman, & Marks, 2000).

The literature regarding team leadership has significantly expanded in the past 20 years, and many models have been created and analyzed. Nonetheless, one popular team leadership model, which focuses on team effectiveness, is best illustrated with Hill's model for team leadership. Team effectiveness is measured by performance (task accomplishment and quality) and development (team maintenance and support). In this team leadership model, the leader's decision-making is imperative. Decisions involve taking actions that have immediate, intermediate, and long-term internal and external consequences. As decisions are made, the leader must monitor and adjust internally and externally using the team's resources to best adapt to their tasks, relations, and environment.

Team management is a practical and beneficial model that allows the innovative leader to make decisions and take action as needed. This model clarifies the leader's role as the person who will complement the team. The quality of the relationship between the leader and group has to be effective and efficient. To accomplish high efficacy, the leader formulates cognitive maps to identify team needs, offer potential solutions as next steps, and suggest appropriate corrective actions. Most teams apply this team management model to improve the productivity, programming, and service delivery systems.

In closing, strategic planning and organizational development models are key elements of successful leaders. As iniquitous societal problems continue, a great deal of innovation is required during the strategic planning processes. Conducting business as usual is not an option because the current funding, programs, and services are not significantly improving human conditions. Formulating innovative strategic processes, creating new programs, and implanting services differently are highly needed to achieve better results.

CHAPTER DISCUSSION QUESTIONS

1. Why is strategic planning important?
2. Write mission and vision statements for a health and human services agency that you currently work for or aspire to create one day.
3. Conduct a SWOT analysis of the health and human services organization that you are affiliated with.
4. Choose two of the managerial approaches described in this chapter and compare their strengths and limitations.
5. Read the leader profile and case study in the Appendix to this chapter. Note innovative ideas and practices, and see what aspects of the case you can connect to the contents of the chapter and/or the overall book.

REFERENCES

Aarons, G. A., & Sawitzky, A. C. (2006). Organizational climate partially mediates the effect of culture on work attitudes and staff turnover in mental health services. *Administration and Policy in Mental Health and Mental Health Services Research, 33*(3), 289–301.

Abdallah, C., & Langley, A. (2014). The double edge of ambiguity in strategic planning. *Journal of Management Studies, 51*(2), 235–264.

Barriere, M. T., Anson, B. R., Ording, R. S., & Rogers, E. (2002). Culture transformation in a health care organization: A process for building adaptive capabilities through leadership development. *Consulting Psychology Journal: Practice and Research, 54*(2), 116–130.

Bess, K. D., Perkins, D. D., & McCown, D. L. (2011). Testing a measure of organizational learning capacity and readiness for transformational change in human services. *Journal of Prevention & Intervention in the Community, 39*(1), 35–49.

Blake, R., & Mouton, J. (1964). *The Managerial Grid: The key to leadership excellence.* Houston, TX: Gulf Publishing.

Blatstein, I. M. (2012). Strategic planning: Predicting or shaping the future? *Organization Development Journal, 30*(2), 31–38.

Collins, J. R., & Porras, J. I. (1994). *Built to last: Successful habits of visionary companies.* New York, NY: HarperCollins.

Daake, D., Dawley, D. D., & Anthony, W. P. (2004). Formal data use in strategic planning: An organizational field experiment. *Journal of Managerial Issues, 16*(2), 232–247.

Dansereau, F., Graen, G., & Haga, W. J. (1975). A vertical dyad linkage approach to leadership within formal organizations: A longitudinal investigation of the role making process. *Organizational Behavior and Human Performance, 13*(1), 46–78.

Darnell, A. J., & Kuperminc, G. P. (2006). Organizational cultural competence in mental health service delivery: A multilevel analysis. *Journal of Multicultural Counseling and Development, 34*(4), 194–207.

Denton, D. K. (2001). Mission statements miss the point. *Leadership & Organization Development Journal, 22*(7), 309–314.

Dutton, J. E., & Duncan, R. B. (1987). The influence of the strategic planning process on strategic change. *Strategic Management Journal, 8*(2), 103–116.

Eppler, M. J., & Platts, K. W. (2009). Visual strategizing: The systematic use of visualization in the strategic-planning process. *Long Range Planning: International Journal of Strategic Management, 42*(1), 42–74.

Fox, H. L. (2013). The promise of organizational development in nonprofit human services organizations. *Organization Development Journal, 31*(2), 72–80.

Goding, M. (2005). Strategic planning and public mental health services. *Australasian Psychiatry, 13*(2), 116–119.

Golensky, M. (2011). *Strategic leadership and management in nonprofit organizations: Theory and practice.* Chicago, IL: Lyceum Books.

Grobman, G. M. (2015). *An introduction to the nonprofit sector: A practical approach for the twenty-first century.* Harrisburg, PA: White Hat Communications.

Harley-McClaskey, D. (2017). *Developing human service leaders.* Thousand Oaks, CA: Sage.

Harris, K. J., Wheeler, A. R., & Kacmar, K. M. (2009). Leader–member exchange and empowerment: Direct and interactive effects on job satisfaction, turnover intentions, and performance. *Leadership Quarterly, 20*(3), 371–382.

Harrison, L. (2012). Linking an agency strategic review to increase knowledge management: San Francisco county human service agency. *Journal of Evidence-Based Social Work, 9*(1–2), 43–56.

Heifetz, R. A. (1994). *Leadership without easy answers* (Vol. 465). Cambridge, MA: Harvard University Press.

Hemmelgarn, A. L., Glisson, C., & James, L. R. (2006). Organizational culture and climate: Implications for services and interventions research. *Clinical Psychology: Science and Practice, 13*(1), 73–89.

Howard, B., & Gould, K. E. (2000). Strategic planning for employee happiness: A business goal for human service organizations. *American Journal on Mental Retardation, 105*(5), 377–386.

Jaskyte, K., & Dressler, W. W. (2005). Organizational culture and innovation in nonprofit human service organizations. *Administration in Social Work, 29*(2), 23–41.

Jennings, D., & Disney, J. J. (2006). Designing the strategic planning process: Does psychological type matter? *Management Decision, 44*(5), 598–614.

Lindberg, A., & Meredith, L. (2012). Building a culture of learning through organizational development: The experiences of the Marin County health and human services department. *Journal of Evidence-Based Social Work, 9*(1-2), 27–42.

Macedo, I. M., Pinho, J. C., & Silva, A. M. (2016). Revisiting the link between mission statements and organizational performance in the non-profit sector: The mediating effect of organizational commitment. *European Management Journal, 34*(1), 36–46.

Marks, B., Sisirak, J., & Chang, Y. (2013). Efficacy of the HealthMatters program Train-the-Trainer model. *Journal of Applied Research in Intellectual Disabilities, 26*(4), 319–334.

McHatton, P. A., Bradshaw, W., Gallagher, P. A., & Reeves, R. (2011). Results from a strategic planning process: Benefits for a nonprofit organization. *Nonprofit Management and Leadership, 22*(2), 233–249.

McKelvey, B., Mintzberg, H., Petzinger, T., Prusak, L., Senge, P., Shultz, R., . . . Lebaron, D. (1999). The gurus speak: Complexity and organizations. *Emergence: Complexity and Organization, 1*(1), 73–91.

Nordqvist, M., & Melin, L. (2008). Strategic planning champions: Social craftspersons, artful interpreters and known strangers. *Long Range Planning: International Journal of Strategic Management, 41*(3), 326–344.

Northouse, P. G. (2016). *Leadership: Theory and Practice* (7th ed.). Los Angeles, CA: Sage.

O'Neil, S. L., & Willis, C. L. (2005). Challenges for professional organizations: Lessons from the past. *Delta Pi Epsilon Journal, 47*(3).

Pandolfi, F. (2011, March 14). How to create an effective non-profit mission statement. *Harvard Business Review.* Retrieved from https://hbr.org/2011/03/how-nonprofit-misuse-their-mis

Patterson, D. A., Maguin, E., Dulmus, C. N., & Nisbet, B. C. (2011). Measuring a community-based mental health organization's culture and climate scores stability. *Social Work in Mental Health, 9*(6), 435–444.

Reid, D. M. (1989). Operationalizing strategic planning. *Strategic Management Journal,* *10*(6), 553–567.

Resnick, H., & Menefee, D. (1993). A comparative analysis of organization development and social work, with suggestions for what organization development can do for social work. *Journal of Applied Behavioral Science, 29*(4), 432–445.

Sample, S. (2002). *The contrarian's guide to leadership.* San Francisco, CA: Jossey-Bass.

Schreter, R. K. (1998). Reorganizing departments of psychiatry, hospitals, and medical centers for the 21st century. *Psychiatric Services, 49*(11), 1429–1433.

Seibold, M., & Gamble, K. (2015). Capacity, commitment, and culture: The 3 Cs of staff development in a learning organization. *Psychiatric Rehabilitation Journal, 38*(3), 286–287.

Steiner, J. R., Gross, G. M., Ruffolo, M. C., & Murray, J. J. (1994). Strategic planning in non-profits: Profit from it. *Administration in Social Work, 18*(2), 87–106.

Suh, T., Houston, M. B., Barney, S. M., & Kwon, I. G. (2011). The impact of mission fulfillment on the internal audience: Psychological job outcomes in a services setting. *Journal of Service Research, 14*(1), 76–92.

Willis, C. D., Saul, J. E., Bitz, J., Pompu, K., Best, A., & Jackson, B. (2014). Improving organizational capacity to address health literacy in public health: A rapid realist review. *Public Health, 128*(6), 515–524.

Zaccaro, S. J., Rittman, A. L., & Marks, M. A. (2002). Team leadership. *Leadership Quarterly, 12*(4), 451–483.

APPENDIX
Featured Leader: Marvin Southard

Dr. Marvin Southard is a Professor of Practice and the Director of the Doctor of Social Work program at the University of Southern California (USC), Suzanne Dworak-Peck School of Social Work.

A licensed clinical social worker, Southard is a nationally renowned expert in the areas of mental health, homelessness, and substance abuse. From 1998 to 2015, he was director of the Los Angeles (LA) County Department of Mental Health, serving more than 250,000 clients annually in one of the most ethnically diverse counties in the nation. During his tenure, he focused on developing community-based partnerships and initiating children's mental health programs. Before that, he served in a similar capacity as director of mental health in Kern County, overseeing mental health, substance abuse, public conservatorship, and mental health-related HIV services. His past appointments also include seven years as vice president of mental health programs and director of clinical services at El Centro Human Services Corporation in LA.

He served as senior fellow of public policy at the University of California Los Angeles (UCLA) School of Public Policy and Social Research; as associate clinical professor at the UCLA School of Medicine's psychiatry and bio-behavioral sciences department; and as clinical associate professor of psychiatry and the behavioral sciences at the Keck School of Medicine of USC. Southard is past president of the California Social Work Education Center Board of Directors as well as past president of the County Behavioral Health Directors Association of California. He was also a commissioner on the LA County Children and Families First – First 5 LA Commission.

Among his many achievements are the 2016 Social Welfare Alumnus of the Year Award from UCLA in recognition of his contributions and dedication to the field of mental health and the 2015 Inter-Agency Council on Child Abuse and Neglect Award for his commitment to protect the most vulnerable children in LA County. He is currently a board member of the California Institute for Behavioral Health Solutions, a member of the American College of Mental Health Administration, and a board member of the Network for Social Work Management.

LEADERSHIP PROFILE FOR MARVIN SOUTHARD

Share your professional background and experience

My original thought for my career was that I was going to be a Catholic priest. I went to the seminary and studied there for years. Two years before I would have been ordained, I decided to take a leave of absence and enrolled in the UC Berkley Master of Social Work program in community organization and social planning. Then, when I finished my schooling, I was encouraged to apply for a job as the director of a brand-new federal drug treatment program sponsored by Catholic Social Services. Much to my surprise, because I was a newly graduated student, I got the job. I was hired to implement this innovative substance abuse treatment program that was focusing on five small towns in the rural areas of San Joaquin Valley in Kern County, CA. It was going to be a mobile program for which we would use a Winnebago as our counseling vehicle parked in each of those towns and then would see what came. In order to really make that work, there was a lot of infrastructure that needed to be done. We first had to reach out to the communities so that they knew who we were. We met with churches, businesses, and schools to form that community relationship. We then began the program, and it worked remarkably well. The main challenge for the program that I was working in was that in many of these towns, we were the only social services agency; therefore, even though we were there for the treatment of drug addiction, people came to us with a variety of problems. These problems included issues with domestic violence, mental illness, child exploitation, and other issues. What I learned from this first job is that people do not come to see you for a specific problem, they come to you as a full person with many different issues that tie together. If you are going to be successful, you really need to look at all of those problems the best you can. I was in that role for four years, and then I realized all the stuff I did not know, and so I decided to go back to school.

I enrolled at UCLA in the doctorate of social work program. My first year, I entirely focused on my studies. The second year, I got a job at a community mental health center in East LA called El Centro Mental Health. In that agency, I was hired as a forensic specialist. I did not know what forensics had to do with mental health at that time, so I had to do research in the library. I did my research well, and I got the job. As it turned out, I ended up being used for my writing skills. I was sent to meetings to conceptualize the topics and do reports. I started out as a forensic specialist, and I ended up being promoted, through the 10 years I worked there, to the director of clinical services for that agency. This was an exciting program. It was premiere Latino mental health organization in California and one of the top two or three in the country. I met a cadre of friends in that context, including faculty who work at USC right now. This job taught me a lot about what is necessary to meet the demands of communities. I learned some of that in my first job, but I learned even more of that in this second job. I worked for El Centro for about 10 years, and then I fell in love with a woman from Bakersfield, CA. She had two small children, so rather than having them move to LA, I moved up there and looked for a job.

I got a job as program chief for the Kern County Mental Health Department, which meant being in charge of both mental health and substance abuse services in that county. I did that for a year as program head, and then the director retired and I was selected as the director, so I became the director of Kern County Mental Health. I served in that role for about seven years, and it came at a really interesting time because that's when mental health consolidation took place. There was an opportunity to reinvent the mental health system with a new set of funding sources. I was persuaded to put my résumé in for the director of LA County Mental Health. This was a job I did not want but applied to as a favor to the previous director who wanted a good pool of resumes. I put in my application and didn't worry about the interviews. Ordinarily, I overprepare for job interviews, but not for this interview. I was surprised to find out I was one of the three finalists. I did no preparation for the final interview and had a major panic attack when I got the call that offered me the job. I told the director of personnel that I had to talk to my wife, which is not what the board wanted to hear. She and I spoke about it and decided that this was probably what I was called to do . . . so I did it. I served as the LA County Mental Health Director for 17 years. I retired from that job two years ago and have since been a Professor of Practice at USC.

In your experience, what are the top three to five leadership attributes someone in the health and human services field should develop? Share an example of when you have used one or more of these attributes/skills in your work

Balance between impatience and patience. For somebody in our role, we need to be impatient with the need for change and make these systems that serve our clients better. We need to be filled with the energy that the change needs to take place. At that same time, we need to be patient with the people who work for and with us. Be sure the impatience for results in the community does not degenerate into impatience with the team that you need to get anything done in the long run. My learning in this regard began in my first job because I was hired as the director of a substance abuse program and frankly I knew about community organization from my education but knew very little about substance abuse treatment. I needed to listen to and learn from the staff who were hired, so I ended up learning effective treatment from my staff. The hallmark of what I have tried to do is to be idealistic about what it is we want to do and what we're called to do in these leadership roles, but at the same time to be able to carefully learn and listen to the lessons from the people that you're working with. Sometimes they will say things that are wrong and not helpful, and even then you need to be careful to listen. I'll give you an example: When I became the mental health director in Kern County, I had this incident in which a guy came to me to tell me that he was having a problem and asked if I could help. In the previous clinic he visited, the mental health services and the substance abuse services were in the same place—one was on the righthand side of the lobby and the other one was on the left. He said that he went to the mental health facility and tried to get some help, but when he described his problem which included an addiction, they said, "No, you need to be clean and sober for 30 days before we can help you. You go over across the lobby." So he went across the lobby and was interviewed over there, and they said, "No. You need to be stable on your medication for 60 days before we can enroll you in the addiction program." He said, "Doctor, you've got to help me. What am I supposed to do?" I was new, full of energy, and impatient for those results, so what I did was I thought, "*Oh I'll fix this. I'll just put mental health people on the substance abuse treatment teams and substance abuse treatment on the mental health treatment team. That fixes it right?*" I was wrong. Since I had not prepared patiently for the system that I wanted to make, the immune systems (metaphorically speaking) of each of those cultures organized to expel the outsider. In one of those instances, it went so far as to have my tires slashed. When I became the mental health director in LA County, I had learned from that experience that I needed to be patient. The goal was still the same, but what I ended up doing is telling my staff that if we don't treat the substance abuse issues of our mental health clients, we are just wasting our health dollars because nobody will get better. If our real goal is not just providing treatment but also having people recover, we need to make sure that they get the substance addiction treatment. If they don't get it because it's not available, we need to provide it. I stated a process of building-in the treatment. In the end the goal was to explain to all of the staff who work for the LA County Mental Health Department and also our contract providers that a clinician treating the seriously mentally ill can't say, "I don't do addictions" any more than a licensed provider can say, "Oh, I'm a clinician but I don't do depression." It really is an essential element for any clinician's tool box that they have the ability to begin interventions with addiction or they are not providing quality clinical work. That took time, about a decade, but that change in culture took place within a large system. That's why I say you need a balance between patience and impatience if you are going to be an effective leader.

Customer-focused. Think of the experiences of the people who are coming to you for assistance. In your imagination, be able to put yourself and your family in the position that they are experiencing. In my case, that was easy because I ended up having a family member with a mental illness and a substance abuse problem. Knowing what he and we as a family went through trying to get the right kind of services helped me make better decisions. I have very good insurance, so I could get access to really high-quality places, but just because you're paying a lot of money for insurance doesn't necessarily mean you'll get a customer-focused quality service. I learned some things I already knew about what needed to change in order to make services more acceptable. Many of these are easy things. For example, if the receptionist who greets you is unfriendly, looks down on you, or is not eager to assist you, you do not feel welcomed. Even with all the obstacles and barriers to receiving mental health or substance abuse care, all it takes is an unwelcoming and unfriendly receptionist, and you will not come back. One of the surprising things is how many mental health contacts are one-time-only events. That is a clear indicator that something is not going right. I think the ability to imagine and then make changes based on what you believe to be good customer service is the way to go. A way to do this is to meet and talk to customers and have relationship with clients in such a way that they'll tell you what's wrong. That is one of the things I always did. I think it would be important for anyone in a leadership role to have an ability to connect with the core clientele in such a way that there's a personal relationship. That way they are willing to tell you exactly what is going on.

Ability to be creative with rules and structures. In any organization, whether it is governmental, nonprofit, or academia, there are rules and structures. It is important to know those rules and structures and to be able to fulfill them. It is also important to be flexible and creative. You need to be able to work around the rules in order to accomplish the mission. If you know the rule structures well, you can learn how to play them like an instrument to get those core items done. Ultimately, if you can show the outcomes are what you needed them to be, you can use that as a vehicle for changing policies and structures that may impede the mission that everybody is trying to accomplish. I'm not saying to just disregard rules and structures because that is not a good thing to do. You have to honor rules and structures, and then you find a deeper way of honoring them by making sure they're in tune with the mission that they are meant to accomplish. I think that's a really important balance to accomplish.

A CASE STUDY BY MARVIN SOUTHARD

The situation I am thinking of happened early in my 10-year role at the LA Department of Mental Health. At that time, when resources became available or cuts became necessary, there was always a tension between the community agency providers and their advocates and the county-operated programs and the unions that supported them. The challenge would be to say, "Does extra money go to the community agencies or does it go to adding to the county workforce?" Obviously there was a political dimension involved, too. Another county agency had tried to do some significant curtailments for their community agency, and the L.A. County Board of Supervisors room was full of advocates for the community agencies. Out of the turmoil that came from that process, the interim director at that time ended up losing his job. I had a relatively small curtailment coming my way, about $5 million, and again the board room was full of community agencies that didn't want the community agencies to suffer that cut. I had a plan that allocated some of that money to the department and some of that money to the community agencies. I made my presentation of my plan, and the chairman of the board asked me, "What's your budget?" I said it was about $1.2 billion, and he said, "Are you telling me that with a budget of $1.2 billion, you have no other way of covering that curtailment but by cutting these community agencies?" I said, "Yes sir," and he said, "Well you better think again." I did, and I produced a new plan in which community agencies were unharmed. My budget people told me that I had a deficit of $37 million dollars. I knew I could not do the planning process like I did before, which is all internal, so what I ended up doing as a solution was to create a stakeholder process to determine how we would make these cuts. The stakeholders included:

- Community agencies
- The unions
- Other county departments that would be affected if we had a curtailment, for example, a cut that would affect the health department because the emergency rooms would be more full
- Ethnic communities, whose concerns were different from each community
- Law enforcement because what happens in our mental health services has a rollover effect for law enforcement issues
- Clients and family members of clients, the most important stakeholders

The first remarkable thing we did in this process is not to make a plan until there was a consensus of all the stakeholders in participation. Second, we made the voices of the client and the family member central. The reason that was important is because typically in the past it had been a "tug of war" over who's going to get more or, in this case, who's going to get hurt. Is it going to be layoffs within the county, or is it going to be curtailments for the contract agencies? Instead, we said, "Let's listen to the clients and families, and if we have to restructure our system so it's $37 million smaller, what would they want it to look like?" Then the competition changed from, "cut them not me" to, "What do we need to do to reduce the budget and still fulfill the desires of our clients?" That became the dialogue, and since it was consensus based, it was sometimes really long and painful. There was a whole process that we developed for coming to consensus, so we had a variation from, "I can't live with it" to "I completely agree with it."

Until everyone agreed, we would not move on. Eventually, we developed a complete consensus plan and prepared to present that to the LA County Board of Supervisors. Then the books closed for that fiscal year, and there was no deficit. It was not all for nothing because that was in the end of 2004, in which in Mental Health Services Act passed. It required a local planning process, and we already had this vehicle that had been developed for the budget deficit. We decided to use the vehicle in order to strategically plan for the Mental Health Services Act. Even though we're the largest and most unwieldy county, we were the second of the 58 counties in California to produce a Mental Health Services Act plan. Stanislaus County beat us by a day. It was approved completely without any hesitation by the LA County Board of Supervisors. Instead of being this wrangling event about who's going to get more, the community agencies or the directly operated programs, we had a consensus plan that was built using those same principles that we used for the budget deficit. That vehicle we ended up calling the *System's Leadership Team* because it was meant to lead the whole system, not just the mental health department, but also the community agencies. We used the System's Leadership Team to make every significant decision that needed to be made in the mental health system of care in LA County. The long-term result was that there were never events in which the community agencies would go to the County Board of Supervisors protesting about "nefarious things" that the Mental Health Department wanted to do because they were a part of making all the significant decisions. It also formed alliances that lasted. We became allies with the Hospital Association, with law enforcement through the Police Chiefs' Association, and with the organizations providing substance abuse treatment because they all ended up playing a role in the decision-making. We could use it as a way of promoting diversity because we had ethnic groups and gay and lesbian populations represented specifically as stakeholders on this board. As I said, I retired two years ago, and the System's Leadership Team still endures to this day as a way the department has of making key significant decisions.

The final thing I would like to add is that the role of being a leader in the health and human services system is both a huge responsibility and a great honor. We have both the responsibility and the ability to make our society a more just, healthier, and happier place for a lot of people. It is a burden, but I don't think there could be any better burden than that.

I think in part I have always been open to innovation. That is the part that's probably my contribution. The other part is that no important goal the social services system is trying to deal with is easy. It is always complicated. We look at whatever circumstance we are in as a puzzle and ask, "How do we solve this puzzle?" If you are trying to solve a puzzle, you need to be willing to try different things and to be creative with it, while being careful. You will end up needing to try some things that don't work or do not work right away, like with my substance abuse idea. Ultimately, it is a good idea to have substance abuse specialists on mental health teams and vice versa, but only after you prepare the culture and the ground for it. Innovation is really something I've learned to appreciate because I found that if you're careful with it, it can produce good results. Another side effect of innovation is that it keeps everyone active and interested. People don't get bored. In both my jobs, in Kern County and in LA County, they hated it if I would go to a conference or a seminar because I would come back with a list of ideas. I would then be giving them ideas and assignments for things that they ought to try. At the Department of Mental Health, they used to tell me the four most dreaded words the director could say is, "Here is an idea!" Clearly I like new ideas, and some of them end up not being practical, but if you persist with those that are really customer focused, good things will happen.

CASE DISCUSSION POINTS

1. The innovative leader in this case was able to involve all stakeholders in planning. How do you think it is possible to engage all of the stakeholders in this process? What did the social architect do and what would you do differently, if anything?
2. Reaching consensus with all of the stakeholders was an important element in this leader's success. Describe the process of consensus building.
3. Talk about the responsibility and honor of being an innovative leader as well as what burden means to someone in this position. In other words, how does one personally balance the honor and the burden that come with leadership?
4. How does a social architect prepare various stakeholders for innovation?

11

Leadership and Effective Supervision

What you are will show in what you do.
What a man's mind can create, man's character can control.
—Thomas A. Edison

CHAPTER OBJECTIVES

1. Explore the roles of the supervisor and supervisees in the workplace;
2. Learn effective supervision methods and performance review approaches in the health and human services fields;
3. Review motivation, coaching, and training strategies to improve working relationships in human services organizations; and
4. Gain insights on innovative leadership from a social architect (see Appendix to this chapter).

INTRODUCTION

One of the most difficult tasks for leaders and supervisors is to build and maintain a positive working relationship with supervisees and/or direct reports. This is a very demanding undertaking for two reasons primarily. First, each employee has his or her own needs, making general organizational policies somewhat limited and adding a degree of difficulty when it comes to managing behavior, motivation, and expectations in the workplace. Policies and practices put forward by supervisors may not be welcomed, or even followed, by all employees. Pleasing all organizational members is almost impossible. Second, the longer people work together, the greater the likelihood that disagreement and conflict will occur. In most cases, people's past negative experiences may trigger undesirable work environments, affecting productivity and performance. Thus, the role of the supervisor is to learn how to handle difficult situations with a fair and balanced approach. In this chapter, we will review supervisory models and skills applied in the field, explore the supervisor and supervisee roles, and share coaching and training strategies to improve working relationships and performance in health and human services organizations. Supervision will be addressed in terms of both administrative (managerial) and clinical (professional) types of supervision; however, the distinctions are not as relevant as the quality of the relationships that a supervisor is able to develop with his or her supervisees (Lewis, Packard, & Lewis, 2012).

CHARACTERISTICS OF THE SUPERVISOR–SUPERVISEE PRODUCTIVE WORKING RELATIONSHIP

Effective supervision starts with a strong supervisor–supervisee working relationship, respecting each other's attributes, perspectives, experiences, and expertise. McPherson, Frederico, and McNamara (2016) describe supervisory relationships within the following eight fundamental themes, corresponding to the contexts of individuals, organizations, and communities:

1. *Safety.* In any positive relationship, for both parties to engage openly and freely, they must feel safe. Safety lies at the heart of effective supervision and is considered vital by all interested parties.
2. *Emotion regulation.* Responding appropriately to the emotional effects of work experiences relates to the empowerment that practitioners and their supervisors share on a daily basis. The supervisor must adjust and be attuned to the particular needs of the direct report.
3. *Learning and growth.* An effective supervisory relationship extends the supervisee's learning and promotes critical reflection on practice, provides constructive feedback, and evaluates performance. An effective leader provides support in all four areas of knowledge: expert theoretical, organizational awareness, practice wisdom, and self-knowledge.
4. *Integrity and justice.* Values such as integrity, honesty, and commitment to social justice principles contribute to a positive working relationship and regular dialogue between both parties.
5. *Balancing supervision functions.* A challenging and complex issue is the potential for tensions to arise between different functions of

supervision. Studies strongly suggest that as effective supervisors are able to integrate a broad range of knowledge, skills, and values into the performance of their role, supervisees do appreciate that this task is challenging.

6. *Organizational culture.* Organizational policies and practices have a significant bearing on supervision practices. Generally, the organizational culture and norms provide supervisory relationship guidelines.

7. *Community support.* Often, employees identify the wider community as lacking an understanding of their work, including the complexity of issues faced by vulnerable children and family populations. Government employees are particularly affected by sensationalized and negative media coverage and recognize that it affects morale and professional identity.

8. *Leadership.* Modeling leadership skills and behaviors is emphasized by supervisors in conjunction with self-regulation and self-awareness. In particular, paying attention to consistency, respectful behavior, transparency, and openness to disagreement is important for building the supervisee's confidence and trust in their supervisors.

The effective supervisor is able to positively navigate these fundamental themes on a regular basis, focusing first on building trust. Individual and organizational trust has been studied thoroughly in the leadership literature for many decades. Trust is significant because it affects behavior, motivation, willingness to take risks and share information, perception of empowerment, and organizational engagement. A meta-analysis conducted by Nienaber, Romeike, Searle, and Schewe (2015) revealed that there were more than 100 studies and more than 50 findings focusing on trust between 1995 and 2011. What we know about building trust in the workplace can be organized in the following four clusters:

1. *Supervisor attributes.* The supervisor's benevolence, competence, and ability to maintain positive relationships are critical to increasing trust and the perception that the supervisee's needs and welfare are taken care of and are a priority.

2. *Subordinate (team member) attributes.* The supervisee's character traits significantly and positively affect trust toward the supervisor. Supervisees with higher organizational commitment are more likely to trust a new supervisor.

3. *Interpersonal processes.* Transactional types of leaders put less emphasis on building and maintaining relationships with supervisees.

Other leadership styles, including active-corrective (i.e., teacher instructing students); laissez-faire, or passive-corrective leadership (i.e., supervisees without an assigned supervisor), produce a decline of trust.

4. *Organizational characteristics*. The supervisee needs psychological safety and reassurance to maintain high levels of trust toward the supervisor. Additionally, organizational support increases trust because supervisees recognize that the organization cares for their well-being and professional development.

Trust is built and maintained by the quality of interactions between supervisors and their team members. If the majority of interactions are perceived as positive by both parties, trust is increased. Most supervisees understand that not all their needs will be met, but they expect their supervisor and the organization practices to be fair and balanced. Liao and Chun (2015) suggest that supervisors engage in observational (looking without comments) and interactional (offering constructive feedback) monitoring to increase positive relationships and innovation with their direct reports. These two monitoring styles are related to subordinates' trust and distrust in their supervisor. Trust and distrust in the supervisor, in turn, are related to the quality of the interactions, motivation and behaviors, and ultimately, innovation. Interestingly, when the supervisor selects observational over interactional monitoring, the supervisees feel less innovative (Liao & Chun, 2015). It seems that innovation is best fostered and nurtured when the supervisor maintains ongoing dialogue with the supervisees, focusing on creativity and inspiration.

Clinical supervision is a common type of management in the health and human services fields, such as social services, social work, nursing, public health, individual and marriage therapy, and psychology. The clinical supervisor is seen as an innovative leader by the organization and the team members, owing to their expertise in the subject matter and experience with those they serve. Pack (2009) argues that effective clinical supervisors are able to provide expertise and continuity in the clinical supervisory relationship by offering: (1) opportunities for engaging in a sustained on-the job reflection, (2) insights into practice that can grow and flourish, and (3) realistic and practical practice environments. Moreover, clinical supervision is about hands-on professional development training, coaching, and directing based on transparent communication, trust, safety, mutuality, equal voice, free disclosure, and regular and timely feedback.

Clinical supervisors offer professional development opportunities by providing ongoing educational workshops. Discussions, exercises, and activities during these training sessions are usually centered on debriefing and identifying challenges and solutions to client needs and building interpersonal skills associated with improving service delivery, communication, power dynamics, working relationships, and conflict resolution strategies (Power & Bogo, 2002). Training sessions on conflict resolution strategies are particularly essential because working relationships tend to be fragile and people are inclined to make mistakes. When the supervisor–supervisee relationship is broken, reconciliation is needed. Repairing working relationships takes time, and it is a process that attempts to restore trust in the offending party and forgiveness on the part of the offended person. Nonetheless, it is an important organizational practice because of its potential to improve employees' attitudes toward their development, recover the supervisor–supervisee relationship, and re-establish trust (Andiappan & Treviño, 2011).

Social architects also engage in organizational monitoring by having their employees provide constructive feedback and/or complete questionnaires on a regular basis with the intention of improving organizational culture and supervisor–supervisee working relationships. Some of the key statements supervisees use to rate their supervisors include: works to improve organizational culture, maintains positive personal relationships, is open to other's opinions, promotes innovation, treats all staff equally, demonstrates trustworthiness, promotes professional development and advancement, and is a pillar of support when needed (Kagan, Kigli-Shemesh, & Tabak, 2006). If the ratings are too low, then this is a sign that the reciprocity of trust in the supervisor–supervisee relationship needs to be rebuilt. One way to enhance supervisor–supervisee reciprocal trust is by increasing supervisees' work-related autonomy and heightening their sense of power. This complementary process for trust building is based on the notion that the leader's behavior has the power to change the employee's own standing, dependence, and vulnerability in the workgroup, and subsequently to encourage cognitive and emotional processes favorable for promoting trust (Seppälä, Lipponen, Pirttila-Backman, & Lipsanen, 2011).

In addition to trust, effective supervisors have the ability to empower their supervisees and promote ownership in their work. For instance, in Participative Decision-Making (PDM), supervisors allow supervisees to have greater decision-making capabilities in the organization, and thus supervisees feel a greater sense of ownership in their work (Likert, 1967; McGregor, 1960). Packard (1989) found that child protective workers had higher performance and job satisfaction having supervisors that used PDM than those who had supervisors who engaged in less PDM. In fact, more recent studies show that some of key variables that affect supervisee empowerment include role ambiguity, role overload, degree of participation, decision-making capabilities, supervisor–supervisee relationships, and peer support. Wallach and Mueller's

(2006) study revealed that these job dimensions account for half of the employee's empowerment. Other predictors are sociodemographic variables, such as a supervisee's age and gender, organizational unit size, and title/position. Simultaneously, the supervisor–supervisee working alliance is strongly associated with the perception of empowerment. Wallach and Mueller (2006) discovered that "paraprofessionals with supervisors who function collaboratively to structure service tasks and build rapport are more empowered" (p. 112).

The final key element in the supervisor–subordinate relationship, in addition to trust and empowerment, is motivation. We know that as motivation increases, purpose and inspiration do, too. Drawing on Herzberg's concept of motivation to work, Smith and Shields (2013) investigated the main characteristics related to job satisfaction among social services workers. They learned that variety and creativity are the most predictive values related to purpose, and the supervisee experiences with their supervisors predicted their levels of motivation and job satisfaction. Thus, the positive experience of meaningful work is linked with perceived capacity to make occupational decisions, locus of control, and organizational engagement (Allan, Autin, & Duffy, 2014). Because motivation influences an individual's behavior and innovation, supervisors can integrate their working relations with supervisees, focusing on four key areas of professionalism: supporting (i.e., "I am here to help you"); motivating (i.e., "you can do it"), referral (i.e., "this new information can assist you"); and rejection (i.e., "let's try a different way"). Study results favor attribution explanations and imply that successful supervisors provide higher levels of supporting, motivating, referring, and rejecting helping statements and behaviors as means to maintain professionalism among team members (Drach-Zahavy & Somech, 2006).

Supervisor–Supervisee Relations Foster Purpose and Inspire Innovation

As supervisors work closely with their supervisees, one of their key goals is to build a strong sense of purpose. To be an effective worker in health and human services is a tall order. Improving clients' conditions and functioning can be intense, mentally exhausting, and emotionally charged, requiring people to truly believe that helping others is the right thing to do. Successful leaders are constantly (1) reminding their followers of the positive reasons that they are doing this work and (2) building their intrinsic motivation and meaning. Lawler (2015) argues that building effective human services workers depends on both having their own self-regulation skills and receiving external supports and guidance. The role of the supervisor is to offer personal and professional growth and development through constant dialogue, direction, reflection, and perspective. Often, strength-based strategies—acknowledging the supervisee's strengths, abilities, and skills, and then intentionally building on them—have proved to be effective when building professional competencies and inspiring innovative practices. Therefore, the quality of the supervisor–supervisee relationship is based on mutual trust and respect.

Generally, purpose and innovation are fostered and nurtured through coaching and mentoring. The quality of the coaching relationship depends on the perceptions of behaviors exhibited by each person. For example, if the supervisee reacts to the supervisor's influence positively, then the coaching relationship will yield encouraging results (e.g., increasing organizational commitment, fostering creativity, and decreasing levels of turnover intention). Michela (2007) summarized eight specific behavioral tactics that supervisors can apply to improve their coaching/mentoring skills and working relationship with their supervisees:

1. *Rational persuasion.* The supervisor uses logic and facts to motivate and encourage the completion of a task.
2. *Inspirational appeal.* The supervisor tries to elevate the supervisee's enthusiasm and excitement by appealing to his or her values and aspirations.
3. *Consultation.* The supervisor seeks the input and participation of the supervisee in the decision-making process and planning.
4. *Ingratiation.* The supervisor seeks to get their supervisees to think positively or get in a good mood before asking or requesting an assignment.
5. *Exchange.* The supervisor offers supervisees an exchange of favors, indicating the willingness to reciprocate at a later time.
6. *Personal appeal.* The supervisor appeals to the supervisee's feelings and emotions of loyalty toward a particular task or charge.
7. *Legitimating.* The supervisor claims authority or uses his or her organizational position to make the request.
8. *Pressure.* The supervisor uses demands, threats, or persistent reminders to influence a specific behavior. However, this tactic rarely produces a long-term positive results.

The positive supervisor–supervisee interactions and their perceptions of commitment are also important factors for a healthy professional development environment. For example, when a clinical supervisor perceives more benefits from a particular clinical supervisory relationship, the supervisee perceives more mentoring support. Simultaneously, clinical supervisors appear to place a greater emphasis on the supervisees' loyalty as a motive for providing mentoring support compared with mentoring being a rewarding experience to improve their job skills. Laschober and Kinkade (2013) argue that mentoring between clinical supervisors and supervisees also depends on the type of social economics at work. In other words, mentoring is a two-way street. On one side are the benefits to the supervisees; on the other side, clinical supervisors are assessing the potential positive or negative impact that providing mentoring support will have on them, and this may drive the type of mentoring behavior toward their supervisees.

Coaches and mentors can be considered social architects because they work with their mentees to build interpersonal and professional skills. These abilities, in turn, are used to improve working relations, service delivery, and care for clients. For example, a comprehensive systematic review of evidence to improve working relationships among health providers summarized four areas: (1) structure (the function of a team requires health providers to exhibit accountability, commitment to the team, and enthusiastic attitude); (2) process (teams must establish specific outcomes to evaluate the team practice and service delivery); (3) collaboration (collaborative structures should integrated to improve services); and (4) functioning (team functioning is established when supervisors and supervisees are engaged in practice and policy decision-making with clear communication patterns and process structures) (Pearson et al., 2006). The overall goal is to build long-lasting team characteristics and values, including accountability, commitment, enthusiasm, and motivation. Social supports within a team coming from a supervisor are likely to increase satisfaction levels among supervisees.

Innovation can take center stage during the supervisor–supervisee working relationship. Because current interventions and service delivery systems can be enhanced, health and human services practitioners are invested in finding new strategies and approaches to improve the way they do their work. The supervisor should encourage and foster the supervisee's creativity by using an approach that provides an educative, safe, and free space—one that allows exploration, support, and validation. For example, when McFadyen, Darongkamas, Crowther-Green, and Williams (2011) studied supervision themes among mental health workers, they learned that five elements are significant to have an effective supervisory relationship and to promote innovation: (1) supervisor's approach (educative, enabler and safety figure, exploring issues of responsibility, and supporting and validating staff); (2) supervision format (advantages and disadvantages of the group, including learning session outcomes and interactions among group members); (3) supervision ingredients (rapport, collaboration, flexibility, and innovative supportive style); (4) supervision function (accountability, training, and quality assurance); and (5) absence of supervision dangers (safety, fear of clients, case overload, and compromising professionalism). Key recommendations to foster innovation between supervisors and their supervisees include supervisors engaging in ongoing training in supervision skills, encouraging theory–practice consolidation, and balancing competency with creativity.

EFFECTIVE AND SUCCESSFUL SUPERVISION MODELS

The literature on supervision and management dates back more than 100 years. During all of this time, several schools of thought and many managerial models have been created and assessed within multiple organizational settings. Since the 1960s, organizational behavior theories and studies have focused on the supervisor–supervisee working relationship as a personal and professional growth prospect. This section reviews the following seven widespread supervision models that have demonstrated a high degree of effectiveness and are considered resourceful for utilization in health and human services: purpose-to-impact, attachment-informed, trauma-informed, cognitive behavioral clinical supervision, empirically supported treatments (as a model for supervision), developing communities of practice, and group consult models.

Purpose-to-Impact Supervisory Model

This model views successful client outcomes as a major purpose of supervision. Supervisors see the process as a rational and systematic tool for safeguarding the standard and quality of service, and supervisees hope that supervision will provide emotional support and foster teamwork. The purpose-to-impact supervisory model has also been implemented international, particularly in Hong Kong and other cities in Asia (Tsui, 2014). The four major cultural themes in this model are time perspective, concept of space, value orientation, and attitudes.

The first component of the purpose-to-impact supervisory model is purpose. To start the process, both parties ask themselves, "What is the leadership purpose of the supervision?" Your leadership purpose defines who you truly are and what makes you unique. It's not *what* you do; it is *how* and *why* you do your job. Purpose clarifies the strengths, passions, and commitment people bring to the organization and to the clients they serve. Human services professionals increase their positivity in serving others by identifying their passions, core beliefs, values, and pursuits. The supervisor can ask the supervisee three basic questions to begin formulating their sense of purpose:

1. What did you especially love doing when you were a child? Describe a
   moment with facts and feelings.
2. Share one or two of your most challenging life experiences. What did
   you learn about yourself?
3. What do you truly enjoy doing in your life?

Once the supervisee identifies key elements of their passion and purpose,
they are asked to write them down in a statement that begins with, "My leadership purpose is. . . ."

The second element is to move this leadership purpose statement into action. To accomplish this essential task, the supervisor and supervisee need to
work together to develop an action plan. The purpose-to-impact plans have a
clear statement of leadership purpose, take a holistic view of professional and
personal life, incorporate meaningful purpose-infused language, and agree on
specific short-, intermediate-, and long-term goals. The purpose-to-impact
planning significantly differs from the traditional development planning. For
example, the traditional development planning focuses on the present and ge-
neric approaches, whereas the purpose-to-impact supervisory model focuses
on the future and unique approaches.

Attachment-Informed Supervision

Originally linked to the research on attachment theory, this type of supervision
model has an emphasis on establishing and maintaining a positive supervisory
working alliance, which is defined as the quality of the relational bond between
the supervisor and supervisee needed to successfully accomplish the mutually
agreed supervision goals (Bennett, 2008). Generally, this model educates social work field instructors and other supervisors about attachment theory and
its usefulness for effective supervision. The attachment-informed supervisory
model has five educational objectives in mentoring students:

1. Examine the supervisor's role in the context of the student's education;
2. Understand the components of a successful working alliance and
   effective supervision;
3. Understand how supervision may generate attachment;
4. Increase the supervisor's skills for reading student attachment
   cues; and
5. Understand the supervisor–supervisee relationship as a circle
   of security facilitating development of the student's professional
   knowledge, skills, and abilities.

Additionally, the attachment-informed supervision training offers the following eight training modules for supervisors:

Module 1—a 6-hour session overview that provides examples of the working alliance between the supervisor and supervisee. This session emphasizes the supervisor as caring and supportive, serving as a positive model by attuning to the supervisee.

Module 2—reviews goals for supervision. During this session, working relationship processes are established, delineating specific steps to accomplish areas of competency in the supervisee.

Module 3—describes the tasks for both the supervisor and supervisee. This session is used to clarify concrete actions (e.g., visits to clients, individual or family interviews, biopsychosocial assessments, treatment plans) and processes (e.g., relationship building, listening, thinking, empathizing, evaluating, reflecting).

Module 4—focuses on the supervisor–supervisee bond. This module reinforces the supervisory circle of security, examining attachment cues as supervisee's need for exploration, advisement, and support.

Module 5—identifies and handles potential disagreements in supervision. When the supervisor–supervisee attachment becomes too strong, it may create the emergence of transference and/or countertransference, which may lead to conflict and separation. Any of these dynamics must be managed by the supervisor in a timely manner.

Module 6—covers the supervisees' developmental stages of learning, promoting the optimal transition of development. Supervisees apply self-reflection, empathy, and intuition to enhance their learning and professional growth.

Module 7—focuses on termination. The feelings of separation or detachment must be clearly understood by both parties by embracing the four basic working relationship stages: beginning, developing, mastering, and ending.

Module 8—addresses the process of giving mutual constructive feedback, defining future boundaries and appropriate professional behaviors.

The following actions by the supervisor make the attachment-informed supervision successful: following a clear structure, linking theory to practice, having supervisees working with clients and staff, and fostering an open and profound learning experience that encourages personal and professional growth. From the perspective of supervisees, this supervisory model increases their confidence, while the supervisor has an opportunity to develop their supervisory skills. Furthermore, participants are able to establish an environment that is conducive to their learning and to build a relationship that serves as a secure base for the student's exploration and innovation (Bennett, 2008).

Trauma-Informed Practice Supervisory Model

Trauma-informed practice care is a specialized set of interventions within the helping professions that can be adapted and applied in a supervisory model to foster the personal and professional growth of supervisees and practitioners. The supervisor using this model uses supervision as "a reflective process that provides a physical and emotional safe space and opportunity to examine the clinical work of the practitioner with the goal to enhance personal and professional growth, shape competence, and promote a high level of services" (Berger & Quiros, 2014, p. 297). The three basic trauma-informed supervisory role functions are (1) educational (linking to theory and policy, teaching about relevant population groups, debriefing challenges and potential solutions, and learning models of practice and strategies for interventions); (2) supportive (providing emotional and professional support to help the supervisee cope with challenges and stressors and identifying personal and professional skills to develop in an effort to improve the supervisee's efficacy); and (3) administrative (advising the supervisee about the organization's policies and procedures, monitoring the appropriate policy application, delegating tasks, and evaluating performance).

According to Berger and Quiros (2014, p. 298), the following four key principles of supervision are applied during the trauma-informed supervisory model:

1. *Providing ongoing and structured supervision*—functions as a protective factor and buffer against vicarious trauma (the supervisee's own trauma symptoms begin to take effect as a result of working with traumatized clients). For example, the supervisee is encouraged to participate in group counseling, weekly supervision, and keeping meeting agendas.
2. *Linking trauma and supervision knowledge*—focuses on the characteristics of the interrelationship between the trauma, the supervisee, and the clinical relationship. For example, the supervisor can use prior cases or theoretical models to explain trauma-related processes.
3. *Navigating within the supervisory functions*—educational (transferring theoretical, empirical evidence and clinical knowledge through teaching, training, and overseeing clinical judgments); supportive (assessing supervisees' vulnerabilities and resilience relative to trauma

knowledge and experience and providing resources to exercise self-care); and administrative (assigning a balanced caseload and following the implementation of organizational policies).

4. *Implementing key practice elements*—The supervisor–supervisee working relationship fosters safety, trustworthiness, innovation, collaboration, and empowerment. Supervisees learn about trauma related to clients and vicarious trauma related to them. Supervisees learn cognitive and affective methods to cope with and also guide clients with trauma issues, maintaining a healthy balance between personal life and workloads.

Emotion Regulation Process Supervisory Model

Developed by Gross in 2001, this supervisory model details emotion regulation processes and strategies for individual and/or group training and supervision (Champe, Okech, & Rubel, 2013). The following five sequential steps are included in the emotion regulation process supervisory model: situation selection, situation modification, attentional deployment, cognitive change, and response modulation.

1. *Situation selection.* Situation selection is the first step in the emotion regulation process and serves as an emotion regulation strategy in group work. The supervisees identify a situation, person, or place that triggers negative emotions and identifies how they would like to change them.

2. *Situation modification.* After the situation is selected, the supervisees can use a number of strategies to enter or avoid the situation, focusing on changing the trajectory of the emotion generation process. These modification strategies are used to move from a current to a desired emotional stage for the individuals and/or others around them.

3. *Attentional deployment.* This step attempts to regulate emotions after the situation has been selected and begins to be modified. There are many variables that can distract or derail the positive emotion regulation process. For example, rumination or excessive thinking can lead the supervisees to choose where, how, and how much to focus their attention. Other distractions can be external in nature, triggering the individual to lose focus and direction. During this time, the individuals must put into practice specific strategies to help them go back and try to accomplish the desired emotional goal.

4. *Cognitive change.* The thinking sequence must change to alter emotional reactions. If the supervisee continues to think the same

way about the situation, most likely the emotions will remain negative and will not change. Changing the interpretation of events, or seeing things differently, will help to regulate emotions more appropriately. This emotion regulation strategy is called *reappraisal,* allowing the supervisee to cognitively change the meaning of the situation followed by the emotional reaction associated with it. Reappraisal strategies can be used to increase or decrease emotional reactions.

5. *Response modulation.* Response modulation strategies can include physical activity, nutrition, meditation, and/or drug treatment with the goals of (1) influencing physiological, experiential, or behavioral responses; (2) achieving expressive suppression; and (3) reducing physiological reactions. During this step, the client is monitored regularly to measure the emotional regulation progress.

In this model, supervisors provide supervisees with information and strategies for each step of the emotion regulation process. This supervisory model requires a significant amount of time involvement and commitment from the supervisor because emotion regulation can change quickly and often.

Cognitive Behavioral Clinical Supervision

The cognitive behavioral clinical supervision model consists of three stages and is based on cognitive behavioral principles: agenda setting, problem-solving, and formative feedback. Cummings, Ballantyne, and Scallion (2015) argue that this supervisory model should be used during each supervision meeting between the supervisor and supervisee. Each stage description follows:

1. *Agenda setting*—This first important step outlines the specific items the supervisor will cover during the meeting with their supervisee. Having a well-structured and organized agenda goes a long way. An effective agenda has input from both the supervisor and the supervisee, and it is put together ahead of time. It covers all the necessary topics, including client progress, strategy implementation, and learning outcomes.

2. *Problem-solving.* Problem-solving cognitive approaches encourage the supervisee to make sense of their initial clinical thoughts and strategies before receiving specific direction or input from the supervisor. This stage can use cognitive coaching as a method to encourage supervisees to propose assessment tools and treatment plans, develop case conceptualizations, begin problem-solving of

client issues, and make decisions about potential treatments before receiving feedback from the supervisor.

3. *Formative feedback.* Supervision requires the provision of ongoing and regular feedback of the supervisee's performance. Constructive criticism should be used as a tool for instruction and professional development. The supervisee should not fear constructive feedback but instead should welcome it to improve their skills and abilities. It is recommended that the supervisor first build a working relationship that is based on trust and sincerity, and any critical feedback should be delivered in a way that is timely, constructive, and specific rather than general. Moreover, Abbott and Lyter (1998) learned that the most effective critical feedback strategies include developing of self, correction of deficits, promotion of learning and innovation, skill development, and creation of a manageable challenge. Simultaneously, criticism that is not well communicated can damage the supervisee's self-confidence and motivation.

Empirically Supported Treatments Supervisory Model

Empirically supported treatments (ESTs) are frequently used in the social work field with a particular focus on organized systems of health care. The supervisor uses a list of ESTs that show the documented interventions with evidence of effectiveness from controlled experimental trials conducted by one or more scientific studies (Hoge, Migdole, Cannata, & Powell, 2014). The ESTs supervisory model's purpose is to restore the consistency and quality of supervision throughout the organization and organized systems of care. This supervisory model involves using evidence-based teaching practices to educate leaders, supervisors, and supervisees about proper and effective supervision and practices. Training and development include following a set of organizational standards and a list of evidence-based interventions, creating a supportive culture of uniformity in service delivery and supervision expectations.

Generally, organizational leaders develop the following six ESTs comprehensive supervisory model standards for all supervisors in the health care organization:

1. *Written supervisory policy.* Each health care organization writes and follows a supervision policy, which is reviewed and updated every two years.

2. *Informed consent.* The organization adopts an informed consent process in which the supervisor–supervisee's working relationship details are delineated, including purpose, frequency and duration, content, roles and responsibilities, rights, evaluation, and confidentiality restrictions.
3. *Documentation of supervision.* The supervisor develops implementation plans, which can include training and consultation techniques, peer learning communities, leadership development, and individual coaching.
4. *Structure of supervision.* The supervisory model will include detailed information about the duration, frequency, and format of supervision. The structure of the supervision must balance four key functions in the supervisory process: quality of care for clients, administrative procedures, support opportunities, and professional development.
5. *Qualifications and preparation.* Every organization develops a minimum set of qualification criteria for supervisors. Usually, organizations look for professionals who have high educational degrees, licenses, certificates, and a minimum of five years of field experience.
6. *Assessing supervision quality.* The final stage is to have an organization-wide assessment or evaluation tool to measure the supervisor's performance. Questionnaires, focus groups, and/or interviews are common performance evaluation techniques.

Developing Communities of Practice Supervisory Model

The Developing Communities of Practice (DCP) supervisory model first originated in the 1980s with the goal of developing learning organizations in which participatory approaches to social services are generated and community results are measured (Adair, 1984). This model focuses on systems change, putting emphasis on creating blue prints for practices across organizations. Gray, Parker, Rutter, and Williams (2010) argue that "successful involvement of people who use services is identified as a key feature of a more advanced approach to leading a community of practice and the effectiveness of supervision is seen as dependent on the development of a community" (p. 24). This model offers a set of strategies to increase team effectiveness and improve service delivery within a larger context.

The DCP supervisory model is well suited to embracing a community of practice in social work and social services fields. The model can be represented in a Venn diagram featuring the following three basic domains that supervisors/

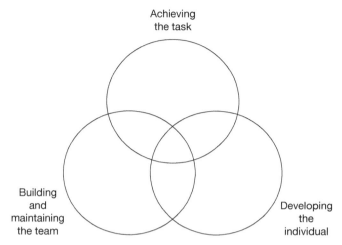

Developing Communities of Practice

Achieving
the task

Building
and
maintaining
the team

Developing
the
individual

Figure 11.1 Developing Communities of Practice Supervisory Model.
SOURCE: Gray, I., Parker, J. Rutter, L., & Williams, S. (2010). Developing communities
of practice: A strategy for effective leadership, management and supervision in social
work. *Social Work and Social Science Review, 14*(2), 20–36, used with permission.

leaders must simultaneously accomplish with their supervisees: achieving
the task, developing the individual, and building and maintaining the team
(Figure 11.1). These three domains/goals can only be realized when each of
them participates in the process. In other words, supervisors cannot achieve the
desired task if they are not developing the individual and building a team simultaneously. Supervisors will need to follow a set of standards to build and maintain trusting relationships and positive team culture, improve the supervisees'
skills and team processes, and meet the task at hand.

Group Consult Supervisory Model

The group consult supervisory model, also known as the action-reflection
approach, was first designed and successfully tested with social services
practitioners during group supervision within child and family services community agencies (Rankine, 2013). This supervisory model offers a structure
and format that has been applied nationally and internationally in community
child and family services to promote reflective practice and support supervisory needs. Typically in this model, the supervisor facilitates the supervisee
groups using a consultation format of exchanges to organize information into
specific domains. Each consult session begins with a definition, purpose, and

case consultation and ends with the supervisee briefly assessing whether the goals have been met. Frequently, the consult sessions are recorded to provide the focal point and a collective task for the group and utilize a visual aid, such as a whiteboard or computer screen.

The consult session starts recording information with the use of a genogram (a diagram or graphic depiction), organized into categories or headings, including danger/harm, strengths/protective factors, limitations/risk factors, safety, and so forth. By identifying the child or youth within these categories, the group can start having a deeper understanding of the client's issues. To restore the clients' functioning, the group members begin sharing potential interventions and solutions. After the group selects an action path, the assigned clinician to the discussed case can move forward, implementing the ideas produced during the group consult. This model is also helpful as a reflective tool to support critical thinking, supplement individual supervision, and assist collaborative decision-making in practice. Simultaneously, the group consult supervisory model shows flexibility in that it can be adapted in a number of ways, depending on the clinical concerns the group members are working to ameliorate.

OTHER EFFECTIVE STRATEGIES IN SUPERVISION

Supervisors and innovative leaders balance the use of formative and summative feedback to express their thoughts and feelings appropriately and succinctly while working with supervisees. Formative feedback focuses on teaching, educating, and demonstrating the subject matter to a supervisee. Supervisors use their practice experience and expertise to inform their supervisees with the goal of training their abilities and strengths in the workplace. On the other hand, summative evaluation aims to provide information regularly to assist the supervisees in developing the skills, knowledge, and attitudes needed to become competent health and human services practitioner. Summative feedback takes place while the practitioner works with clients as a form of continuous improvement evaluation (Chur-Hansen, & McLean, 2006). When providing feedback, efficacious supervisors use the following guiding principles:

1. *Maintain professional practices.* Provide feedback one on one, either in writing or verbally, sharing clearly what is incorrect or inappropriate and what specific steps to take to improve the behavior or action. For example, feedback should never be humiliating, embarrassing, or intimidating to anyone; on the contrary, appropriate feedback must be direct and constructive.

2. *Foster interpersonal factors.* The type of feedback depends on the maturity of the supervisee and their level of training. Formative and summative feedback strategies should be shared in a direct and balanced fashion. The supervisor must maintain a high level of mutual trust and respect.
3. *Focus on improving performance.* The feedback must be adequate to improve the supervisees' performance, increasing their skills, abilities, and knowledge to build rapport and behavioral functioning levels with clients and their families.

Supervisees also appreciate positive working supervisory relationships that begin with structured agreements. The supervisor–supervisee relationship becomes a working alliance that is based on mutual expectations and deliverables. Kavanagh, Spence, Wilson, and Crow (2002) concluded that supervisors can customize the following effective supervision strategies:

- *Procedures for direct observation of clinical skills.* Demonstration of new procedures and skills practice with detailed feedback are critical to the supervision's impact on practice.
- *Capacity and access.* Have the minimum number of personnel and resources to support both the supervisor and supervisee. Compatibility with the values and procedures of both parties are necessary with access to supervision training and formal and informal consultation.
- *Adopt effective procedures.* Supervision has to deal with practical field issues and concern, having the ability to adapt when needed. Organizational policies and processes must be structured but not rigorous. For example, agenda items can be negotiated ahead of time to support current needs of supervisees.
- *Address problems with routine implementation.* Client problems and needs must often be met with innovative approaches and interventions. The supervisor–supervisee working relationship must be regular and continuous to best support the client's progress as well as the supervisee's.
- *Provide effective training and consultation in supervision.* Most supervisors learn how to supervise by reading cases and/or by participating in brief training sessions. The organization's leaders must invest in the development of their workforce by offering extensive in-service training sessions on supervision skills to their supervisors.

Interestingly, the *Harvard Business Review* recently published an article on the importance of leadership and supervisory competencies (Giles, 2016). More than 195 leaders/supervisors in 15 countries shared 74 competencies they think are important when supervising employees. The 10 most recurrent competencies were grouped into the following five major themes: strong ethics and safety (high morals), efficient learning (flexibility to change options), connecting and belonging (open and ongoing communication, creating a feeling of group success or failure), self-organizing (provision of goals and objectives with structure and direction), and nurturing growth (committed to employee's training and development). When developing supervisees, successful supervisors have the ability to equally influence multiple personality styles, including introverts and extroverts. Knight (2015) suggests that supervisors take the following steps to ensure that everyone receives the supervisory benefits: know all team members and their personalities, keep frank and open conversations, rethink agendas and workdays to match people's personalities with job requirements, promote privacy, and encourage introverts to speak out and extroverts to listen.

Additionally, health and human services supervisors work closely with different types of individuals, including volunteers and external employees who may not be as knowledgeable about the intricacies of the organization's programs and practices. In these cases, social architects must make an extra effort to properly engage these different team members into the workforce. McCannon and Han (2016) suggest that supervisors should implement the following supervisory practices while working with volunteers and/or external employees:

- *Make their dreams and goals come true.* This requires listening closely by engaging in one-to-one, personal conversations in which values and beliefs are shared.
- *Create fellowship.* Show how their impact will make a difference in others by highlighting the kind of meaningful, transformative experiences that will be provided.
- *Build easy on-ramps.* Provide time and resources to support specific ways to get started and continue developing their skills and confidence
- *Get rhythm.* Structure their roles and workloads depending on the ultimate goal or purpose, debriefing their failures and celebrating their successes.
- *Motivate with data.* Create specific personal and professional benchmarks to measure progress. People need to know how their work and effort are making a difference.

In conclusion, social architects are effective supervisors. They gain the experience and ability to work positively with others in multiple capacities.

Supervisors provide training, direction, coaching, support, motivation, and appropriate feedback. The supervisor–supervise relationship is fostered by mutual trust, respect, and fairness. This chapter also reviewed several supervisory models being utilized by health and human services organizations that have shown to be effective.

CHAPTER DISCUSSION QUESTIONS

1. What is the role and function of supervision?
2. What makes an effective supervisor?
3. Choose three of the supervision models presented in this chapter and compare and contrast these.
4. Which of the models are you more likely to use as a supervisor and why?
5. Read the leader profile and case study in the Appendix to this chapter. Note innovative ideas and practices and see what aspects of the case you can connect to the contents of the chapter and/or overall book.

REFERENCES

Abbott, A. A., & Lyter, S. C. (1998). The use of constructive criticism in field supervision. *Clinical Supervisor, 17*(2), 43–57.

Adair, J. G. (1984). The Hawthorne effect: A reconsideration of the methodological artifact. *Journal of Applied Psychology, 69*(2), 334.

Allan, B. A., Autin, K. L., & Duffy, R. D. (2014). Examining social class and work meaning within the psychology of working framework. *Journal of Career Assessment, 22*(4), 543–561.

Andiappan, M., & Treviño, L. K. (2011). Beyond righting the wrong: Supervisor-subordinate reconciliation after an injustice. *Human Relations, 64*(3), 359–386.

Bennett, C. S. (2008). Attachment-informed supervision for social work field education. *Clinical Social Work Journal, 36*(1), 97–107.

Berger, R., & Quiros, L. (2014). Supervision for trauma-informed practice. *Traumatology, 20*(4), 296–301.

Champe, J., Okech, J. E. A., & Rubel, D. J. (2013). Emotion regulation: Processes, strategies, and applications to group work training and supervision. *Journal for Specialists in Group Work, 38*(4), 349–368.

Chur-Hansen, A., & McLean, S. (2006). On being a supervisor: The importance of feedback and how to give it. *Australasian Psychiatry, 14*(1), 67–71.

Cummings, J. A., Ballantyne, E. C., & Scallion, L. M. (2015). Essential processes for cognitive behavioral clinical supervision: Agenda setting, problem-solving, and formative feedback. *Psychotherapy, 52*(2), 158–163.

Drach-Zahavy, A., & Somech, A. (2006). Professionalism and helping: Harmonious or discordant concepts? An attribution theory perspective. *Journal of Applied Social Psychology, 36*(8), 1892–1923.

Giles, S. (2016, May 15). The most important leadership competencies, according to leaders around the world. *Harvard Business Review.* Retrieved from https://hbr.org/2016/03/the-most-important-leadership-competencies-according-to-leaders-around-the-world

Gray, I., Parker, J., Rutter, L., & Williams, S. (2010). Developing communities of practice: A strategy for effective leadership, management and supervision in social work. *Social Work and Social Sciences Review, 14*(2), 20–36.

Gross, J. J. (2001). Emotion regulation in adulthood: Timing is everything. *Current Directions in Psychological Science, 10*(6), 214–219.

Hoge, M. A., Migdole, S., Cannata, E., & Powell, D. J. (2014). Strengthening supervision in systems of care: Exemplary practices in empirically supported treatments. *Clinical Social Work Journal, 42*(2), 171–181.

Kagan, I., Kigli-Shemesh, R., & Tabak, N. (2006). "Let me tell you what I really think about you"—evaluating nursing managers using anonymous staff feedback. *Journal of Nursing Management, 14*(5), 356–365.

Kavanagh, D. J., Spence, S. H., Wilson, J., & Crow, N. (2002). Achieving effective supervision. *Drug and Alcohol Review, 21*(3), 247–252.

Knight, R. (2015, November 16). How to be good at managing both introverts and extroverts. *Harvard Business Review.* Retrieved from https://hbr.org/2015/11/how-to-be-good-at-managing-both-introverts-and-extroverts

Lawler, J. (2015). Motivation and meaning: The role of supervision. *Practice: Social Work in Action, 27*(4), 265–275.

Laschober, T. C., Turner de Tormes Eby, L., & Kinkade, K. (2013). Mentoring support from clinical supervisors: Mentor motives and associations with counselor work-to-nonwork conflict. *Journal of Substance Abuse Treatment, 44*(2), 186–192.

Lewis, J. A., Packard, T. R., & Lewis, M. D. (2012). *Management of human service programs* (5th ed.). Belmont, CA: Brooks/Cole.

Liao, E. Y., & Chun, H. (2015). Supervisor monitoring and subordinate innovation. *Journal of Organizational Behavior, 37,* 168–192.

Likert, R. (1967). *The human organization: Its management and value.* New York, NY: McGraw-Hill.

McCannon, J., & Han, H. (2016, March 2). A guide to managing a volunteer workforce. *Harvard Business Review.* Retrieved from https://hbr.org/2016/03/a-guide-to-managing-a-volunteer-workforce

McFadyen, K. M., Darongkamas, J., Crowther-Green, R., & Williams, O. (2011). Primary-care mental-health workers' views of clinical supervision. *The Cognitive Behaviour Therapist, 4*(3), 101–113.

McGregor, D. (1960). *The human side of enterprise.* New York, NY: McGraw-Hill.

McPherson, L., Frederico, M., & McNamara, P. (2016). Safety as a fifth dimension in supervision: Stories from the frontline. *Australian Social Work, 69*(1), 67–79.

Michela, J. L. (2007). Understanding employees' reactions to supervisors' influence behaviors: A community sample predicting employee commitment, turnover, and stress. *International Journal of Organizational Analysis, 15*(4), 322–340.

Nienaber, A., Romeike, P. D., Searle, R., & Schewe, G. (2015). A qualitative meta-analysis of trust in supervisor-subordinate relationships. *Journal of Managerial Psychology, 30*(5), 507–534.

Pack, M. (2009). Clinical supervision: An interdisciplinary review of literature with implications for reflective practice in social work. *Reflective Practice, 10*(5), 657–668.

Packard, T. (1989). Participation in decision making, performance, job satisfaction in a social work bureaucracy. *Administration in Social Work, 13*(1), 59–73.

Pearson, A., Porritt, K. A., Doran, D., Vincent, L., Craig, D., Tucker, D., Long, L., & Henstridge, V. (2006). A comprehensive systematic review of evidence on the structure, process, characteristics and composition of a nursing team that fosters a healthy work environment. *International Journal of Evidence-Based Healthcare, 4*(2), 118–159.

Power, R., & Bogo, M. (2002). Educating field instructors and students to deal with challenges in their teaching relationships. *Clinical Supervisor, 21*(1), 39–58.

Rankine, M. (2013). Getting a different perspective: Piloting the "group consult" model for supervision in a community-based setting. *Practice: Social Work in Action, 25*(2), 105–120.

Seppälä, T., Lipponen, J., Pirttila-Backman, A., & Lipsanen, J. (2011). Reciprocity of trust in the supervisor–subordinate relationship: The mediating role of autonomy and the sense of power. *European Journal of Work and Organizational Psychology, 20*(6), 755–778.

Smith, D. B., & Shields, J. (2013). Factors related to social service workers' job satisfaction: Revisiting Herzberg's motivation to work. *Administration in Social Work, 37*(2), 189–198.

Tsui, M. (2004). Supervision models in social work: From nature to culture. *Asian Journal of Counselling, 11*(1–2), 7–55.

Wallach, V. A., & Mueller, C. W. (2006). Job characteristics and organizational predictors of psychological empowerment among paraprofessionals within human service organizations: An exploratory study. *Administration in Social Work, 30*(1), 95–115.

APPENDIX
Featured Leader: Thenera Bailey

Thenera Bailey is the President/CEO of the SISGI Group. In this capacity she serves as the Interim Director of the SISGI Beyond Good Ideas Foundation, the organization's non-profit charitable division, and as the Editor of the social research blog, NotEnoughGood.com.

She has an accomplished career as a consultant, trainer, and technical assistance provider to programs, organizations, government agencies, nonprofits, corporations, schools, and school districts. She has extensive experience in social entrepreneurship and started a nonprofit organization immediately on completion of her undergraduate degree. Over the past decade, she has continued to assist other individuals and organizations in developing their nonprofit organizations, grant writing, fundraising, strategic planning, financial management, and general startup and expansion.

She has a Master of Social Work degree from the University of Maryland with a concentration in Management and Community Organizing and a specialization in Social Action and Community Development. She also has a Master of Arts with a concentration in globalization, sustainable development, and tourism from New York University, where she was a Gallatin Koppenaal Scholar. She is currently completing a Doctorate in Business Administration in Strategy and Innovation.

As the CEO of the SISGI Group, Bailey has developed key programs and organization initiatives for the organization's nonprofit division, with the assistance of the board of directors, key partners, and volunteers. Since 2011, she has served as the director of the organization's cutting-edge virtual internship program, overseen the increase in free trainings offered by the organization, and established the organization's strategies around collective impact and collaboration in youth development.

She has conducted research and fieldwork around the globe on topics as varied as Afro-Brazilian tourist traditions in the celebration of Carnival, international perspectives of higher education reform, the impact of sustainable tourism initiatives on local communities in Costa Rica, Black South African identity post-apartheid, the tourism industry in South Africa post-apartheid and leading up to the 2010 World Cup, and research on strategies for increasing outcomes in global social entrepreneurship. She is also a featured blogger for the *Huffington Post* on topics related to social change and the nonprofit sector.

She has served with the Corporation for National and Community Service (CNCS) Office of Leadership Development and Training as a member of their Training and Technical Assistance Workgroup and as a consultant assisting large multistate grantees and applicants. Bailey is a Certified Grants Manager and has received certification in crisis intervention for Domestic Violence and Sexual Assault. She also has received training in federal grants management and monitoring. She has worked as a community organizer in Baltimore, MD, has worked as a social worker in public schools, and has served on the board and advisory groups for a variety of charitable organizations.

LEADERSHIP PROFILE FOR THENERA BAILEY

Share your professional background and experience

I like to say I am a nonprofit professional and a social entrepreneur. My entire career has been in the nonprofit sector. I started as an undergraduate student working for a national organization called *Junior Achievement*, which provides an economic curriculum through volunteers from local businesses to public schools around the country. I worked in the national office as an intern during the summers and in a local office during the school year in the city where my college was located. When I graduated with my Bachelor of Social Work degree, I worked in a local office as the Special Events Manager planning fundraising events and managing donors.

I really entered the nonprofit sector because I knew I wanted to make a difference. I chose social work because I wanted to understand how individuals, groups, and organizations make a difference around social issues. I've worked for a mix of mostly large organizations, either on the state level or national level. I think the majority of my career has really been looking at large-scale issues. I've worked for a state-based mentoring organization that provided training and technical assistance to individuals who were interested in either starting a mentoring program, serving as mentors, or providing mentoring programming in their community.

I moved after that into a role at a national organization looking at literacy and education work across the country. I managed about $2 to $3 million of grant funds as a Program Officer. That included providing training and providing support to programs in how to manage our curriculum in a way that met our brand requirements and produced the best outcomes. It included visiting programs and assuring that their program operations matched what was required in the grants. In addition, I did a lot of startup work, going to organizations and communities who were interested in our program model and helping them think through the strategies to get their program started.

When I decided to return for another master's degree and leave the organization, I was asked by one of the funders to serve as a consultant helping new programs to write strong proposals and implement their programs once funded. That helped me understand a little bit about consulting and the ways that I might be able to take my expertise to the nonprofit sector, running and managing programs, and transition more to helping new programs start up.

I think my core role, even though it was in different organizations, has always had this basis of strategy. How can you think about creating change in new ways? How can you incorporate innovation, program design, and best practices to move programs forward?

This is actually my second round of entrepreneurship. I'm just an entrepreneur by nature. I've always been that way. I finished my Master of Social Work degree in 2000 and started a nonprofit at the same time called SOS. We provided in-school assistance to African American students to help lower the achievement gap and to address issues that were affecting African American students in the public school system. I learned a lot about running an organization from this experience especially about the challenges of being an Executive Director.

I knew when I finished my second master's degree that I did not want to work for another organization. I really liked working for myself and doing consulting. I also liked the idea of going and working with an organization for a short period of time. Of course, the social worker in me is still very interested in creating change, so I knew I didn't want to create something that would not have some sort of social impact. That is when I ended up founding The SISGI Group. Our core mission is strategic resources for mission-driven work. SISGI is a hybrid social venture, which means we're part for-profit and part nonprofit. Though I knew I wanted to make a difference in the sector in the same way that nonprofits do, I did not want the burden of having the financial responsibility of fundraising. I created the organization in a way that the for-profit would sustain the nonprofit. The other thing I didn't want to do was compete with my clients. For example, if we are trying to do a training program and they're also trying to do a training program, I didn't want to compete with them for funding because they're 100% grant funded and we would be going after the same grants.

The consulting group works with nonprofits predominantly, and like I said, I'm really interested in strategy, so much of our work includes some strategic work. For example, things like, how do we take something that we are doing in this one community and expand it across the country? After finishing my master's degree, I spent a lot of time as a trainer, and that is also another big part of our work at SISGI. A lot of the work that I would do with clients sits in that space of training and knowledge management and thinking about how we can train people better.

Our nonprofit side is the *Beyond Good Ideas Foundation*, and the goal is to go beyond good ideas. There are a lot of organizations that are doing good things that feel good, but they're not necessarily the best way to solve a problem. Our focus is always on solution-based strategies, how to think about solving the social issue, not just addressing the Band-Aid things that are at the surface. We use three pillars to do that:

- *Preparation.* We have an internship program because we saw with our clients that one of the biggest challenges that they were having was hiring management level staff, people who were coming in to manage their programs and organizations, with limited management experience. Our program is about giving people the autonomy, the skills that they need to run programs, to immediately enter an organization and be able to think about problems that they're having strategically and to answer that with little oversight because we know most organizations are often understaffed.

- *Education.* Professional development, we know, is one of the ways that industries improve and ensures that innovation happens. One of the things we have learned through research is that most nonprofits do not invest in professional development, unless you work for a national organization. So, wanting to address that leadership and knowledge gap, we provide free training and low-cost training.
- *Collaboration.* If you are running a mentoring program and you happen to be at *Big Brothers, Big Sisters*, you're learning all the best practices that the *Big Brothers, Big Sisters* organization has mastered as one of the leaders in that space. If you have a small faith-based men's mentoring program through the small church, you're not accessing that same training and that same information. So, we try to create a way for that to be shared. We do that through our social media and through our blogs and programs. We want people to see what is working and how to replicate what works well. With that last pillar of collaboration, we try to help people work better to move the needle on social problems because we don't think anything related to social change can happen alone.

Ultimately, I think our work is focused on just understanding some of the needs that are in the sector and trying to address those in a way that's not competitive to the people who are doing the really hard day to day work.

In your experience, what are the top three to five leadership attributes someone in the health and human services field should develop? Share an example of when you have used one or more of these attributes/skills in your work

Problem solving. One of the things that I think is important for people who are in a leadership role is to know how to problem-solve. No one is going to tell you how to find a solution. They are going to expect you to be able to find solutions on your own. The thing I learned is that just because something has been done one way and was written one way into the grant, it doesn't mean that you have to implement it exactly that way. You can be thoughtful about solving the problem in unique ways.

Autonomy. I think people come into leadership roles assuming that they're going to have this great supportive supervision that happens, particularly in the health and human services. People in a leadership role are very isolated. When I work with executive directors or I work with people who are in program leadership, this is kind of the big shock. It is so important for leaders to learn to trust their own voice and viewpoint, and having that independent ability to work by yourself, to think by yourself, and to manage by yourself. It doesn't mean you don't include people. You're thoughtful about how you include people. You recognize that at the end of the day there are going to be some times and some places in your work that you really are just going to have to figure it out. If you're the leader, then you've been hired to do a specific task and role and have to get comfortable in that autonomy and in working independently and thinking independently about the work. If you're waiting for someone to tell you what to do, you will fail. That's where I see organizations start to crumble, when their leadership wasn't prepared for that level of autonomy and that level of independence in thinking and problem-solving.

Innovation. At SISGI, we do a lot of things in a more forward-thinking, tech-driven way. For nonprofits, mostly because of budget, technology is limited. We know funders don't invest in tech. There is this push back about thinking about doing things differently. We still rely on in-person meetings, conferences, and face-to-face site visits too much for collaborating and learning in the sector. Today you can do videoconference webinars, so why are so much time and effort wasted in older strategies? You can double your outcomes because no one has to drive and no one has to get in a car. Now we can use our time and resources in another way because we aren't held to the same expensive systems of operation. Every leader should be asking how he or she can think about innovation in the work that they are doing. Particularly, I think about social progress.

Collaboration. One of the challenges is that there has been a bit of a competitive mindset that has been created by the funding shortage in the nonprofit sector. Which is something like, "Well, our tutoring program is better than that tutoring program because of A, Y, and Z. So you should fund our tutoring program." Instead of saying, "There are 800 kids in this school system. We serve 300, and they serve 200. That's 500 students that get additional academic support. How can we think about doing this together? How can we share resources? How can we share strategies? How can we think about how our curriculum manages and captures fluency better in readers and how yours captures the student comprehension? Well then, let's train together and let's work together." Then kids are getting fluency and comprehension. It is also recognizing that competition will never get us toward solutions. Leaders, particularly, have to be thinking like that. Not, "How are we better than X, Y, and Z organizations in our space?" but instead, "How can we think together and work together, and solve together?" I don't think you can do this work without being collaborative.

Understanding the difference between leading and managing. It's really about this notion that too often the people who are put in these leadership roles are managing the program, managing the staff, and managing things. *They are not leading.* They do not trust the people they hired to do the work, accepting their outcomes and not worrying about their paths to the solution. People learn through experience, trial and error, and failure. Failure, we look at as this huge negative thing, but until we fail we don't understand how to modify and change and succeed. So, it's important for your staff to have failures, just as much as it's important for your organization to move forward. As I look at it, my role is to lead the organization. That means that sometimes things are not going to be the way I would have done them, but we meet our mission. I do very rigorous thinking about hiring decisions. I bring people to my team whom I can trust. If you can't make that decision in the hiring, don't hire people whom you can't trust to do the job. Otherwise you end up managing, and that's not what you're there to do. You're there to think strategically, to problem-solve, to be innovative, and to collaborate, and there is no time for that if you're in the weeds managing the day-to-day and the minutia.

A CASE STUDY BY THENERA BAILEY

The team was led by a program director, and this individual served as the face of the program. She was responsible for grants management and operational responsibilities. The program manager had more operational responsibilities related to staffing, program design, and implementation in the many schools and volunteers she working with. She had a small team of five to six people who covered several schools in a particular part of the city. We're talking about the San Francisco, California area. They covered Oakland, San Francisco, and San Mateo. So, they were working in a very large geographic spread and many schools.

The challenge was that they had high staff turnover of those site coordinators. Literally almost every year resulted in new people. They also had a training manager who did the training of the volunteers, and they had a recruiter who brought people in. No one was really talking or interacting together. Staff were not in well-paying positions when you think about the cost of living in the Bay area. There was low to no investment in the program outside of the grant funding they received from us. The host organization appeared not very interested in sustaining, maintaining, and investing in the program in any way, whether with internal talent and knowledge or external partnerships, collaborations, or individuals who might be able to benefit the program. This program was operating as its own 501(c)3 but within this very huge 501(c)3.

Within a few months of my assignment to this program, the program director left. He held all of the institutional knowledge. The host organization, in an effort to save money, was very slow to fill that position. The program manager suddenly had to take on these executive leadership–based roles that she had never been exposed to, such as grant writing and being the face of the program. She also had to deal with about three or four of her six site coordinators leaving and being replaced. Again, this was a very slow process, and because of the huge nature of the host organization, the hiring process was a little bit slow. I think there was an effort to try to also keep and spend the money a little bit differently in the grant cycle rather than fill the positions again quickly.

My role was to help them think about why they were having so many problems, to address the staffing turnover issue, to make sure they got the resources from the local organization, and to help them think better about their program operations. Since they weren't meeting the metric that we had set out for number of volunteers or program outcomes, I also was asked to assist them in thinking how they might be able to do those things better. My challenge was in six months to try to get them to a place that we could meet our standard and improve the organization.

The consequence for the organization if changes did not happen would be to lose their funding. They were really on the line of not being able to continue to receive the funds because a lot of the funds that we were giving to them were federal funds and had to be spent in a particular way as well as matched in a particular way. It wasn't a dollar-for-dollar match, but you had to match it with certain resources and in a certain timeline. They were not doing that. They risked having to return the funds that they had received, with not meeting and getting funds going forward.

They had somewhere between 75 and 100 school partnerships that looked to this intervention as a way to meet their academic outcomes. If the program folded or if they didn't get the right staffing in place and didn't get enough people on the ground, the schools that were looking for certain outcomes also wouldn't get them.

One of the things that I really started with was the program manager. She was not innovative, and she could not work autonomously. She wanted everything to be a group discussion. When thrown into this leadership role, you need to be able to make decisions and move forward. I was able to be a sounding board, allowing her to process her challenges without overburdening or oversharing with her staff.

One of the challenges was that the site coordinators weren't speaking to the trainers and the trainers didn't know what to train the people about based on issues that the site coordinators were aware of. We needed to think about her staffing in a different way so that there was more overlap, such as even though you are a site coordinator, you also have some training responsibility to help make training more specific to the site-based challenges. The overlap in job descriptions would allow for people to leave or join the organization, and work could still happen because everybody was handling bits and pieces of every role.

The other thing I implemented was moving them toward developing an annual program plan. They had performance measures that they had to meet: the number of volunteers, number of academic gains, and number of schools for their grants. In our new program plan, each staff person would sit with the program manager and talk through his or her connection to the larger program goals. It might be something like, "As an organization we have to be in 100 schools. You're in the South Bay. You have 20 schools in that area. How many volunteers do you think you can manage and recruit?" The staff was then charged to think about the larger goal, too.

The other piece she asked was, "What is something, a talent or a strength that you have that you have not been able to use in our organization?" Through that process of questioning and seeing how they'd like to use their talents and strengths, she learned that there were people who were really interested in training and never had that opportunity. There were people who were interested in learning more about grants management, and since they didn't have a program director, this was a place to be able to provide some training and some support while meeting a program need. *The purpose was to really assess not the tasks and the duties that had to be done, but the talent and the strengths of the team that she had to do it.* It shifted the way they operated a little bit. Then they had some checkpoints: I believe a 30-day, a 90-day, and then a 6-month check in. They came back to the plan and saw where they were failing and then adjusted.

There was also this cross-training that happened, so in the event that someone did leave, there wasn't a gaping hole. It was a hole, but it was easier to fill in with bits and pieces of people's work because everybody had been cross-trained across the organization.

The program manager felt less stressed because she knew what people were expected to do. She had a check-in point, so she didn't have to check on the progress throughout. She got more time to spend thinking about the big ideas. She was able to look at the full picture for the full year at one time and to get the level of detail that she needed to be successful but not be pulled completely into the day-to-day weeds. For my part, I just helped to design it and helped them think through what they needed to include in the program plan and how they managed that and served as the sounding board for the program manager.

CASE DISCUSSION POINTS

1. How did the social architect understand the challenges that the organization was having?
2. What were the proposed solutions to the challenges?
3. This social architect describes the importance of an innovative leader being able to be autonomous and yet be able to work with others. How does a leader balance the two?
4. The innovative leader recognizes the importance of identifying strengths in team members. How was this element important through the use of supervision to effect change in this particular case?
5. What is the difference between leadership and management?

12

Conflict Resolution and Negotiation Strategies

If you want to bring an end to long-standing conflict,
you have to be prepared to compromise.

—Aung San Suu Kyi

CHAPTER OBJECTIVES

1. Review positive strategies when dealing with conflict, including finding common ground and compromise;
2. Learn and apply new conflict management and negotiation skills;
3. Explore how leaders use strategies to improve problem-solving in the health and human services fields;
4. Learn the definition of strategic abandonment and how to best manage conflict during organizational change; and
5. Gain insights on innovative leadership from a social architect (see Appendix to this chapter).

INTRODUCTION

It is fair to say that we all have experienced the unwelcome feeling of partaking in uncooperative discussions and disagreements. When people argue, they often take opposite sides of an issue or situation, which leads to contentious practices and undesired outcomes. Individuals and organizations tend to defend their thoughts, values, and positions at all costs, leaving little room for compromise and resolution. Some individuals even think that if they remain stubborn and unwilling to change their position, this strategy will give them more leverage during negotiations. In more extreme cases, some of us have to deal with individuals who believe that bullying others is a way to show their strength. These types of conflict resolution approaches are unhealthy, limited, short-lived, and unnecessary. A great deal of conflict can be resolved positively as long as it is managed swiftly and properly. Keeping in mind that an innovative leader is not looking for "yes" men and women (i.e., those that easily conform) but instead is looking for people to challenge assumptions and offer dissenting points of view in order to make room for innovation. It is rather more about how the leader manages conflicting points of view and reaches consensus by creating a safe territory within a brave space to explore new ideas. In this chapter, you will explore and learn positive conflict resolution strategies, negotiation skills, win-win solutions, and problem-solving techniques to de-escalate negative emotions and resolve disagreements confidently.

FINDING COMMON GROUND

Solutions to conflicts and disagreements are most often reached through negotiations. Negotiation is a process in which both sides are pulling their own way to achieve their anticipated expectations. Successful negotiations should focus on goals and cooperation throughout the negotiation stages, keeping in mind that positive relations from the onset are a key path to more desirable outcomes (Halpert, Stuhlmacher, Crenshaw, Litcher, & Bortel, 2010). Social architects have the ability to negotiate with others by focusing on solutions and finding common ground. Innovative leaders influence both the mode of interaction between groups and the outcome of these interactions. The first step for the group members is to carefully and strategically choose who is going to take the lead and represent them during the negotiation process (Hamlin & Jennings, 2007). After leaders are chosen, Malhotra (2015) suggests that successful outcomes can be achieved by applying the following four strategies: negotiating process before substance, normalizing the negotiation process, mapping out the negotiation space, and controlling the frame of the negotiation. Additionally, as the negotiation is underway, innovative leaders should consider the following: balance values versus costs, own alternatives versus those of others, and dominance versus equity.

Finding common ground can be achieved in different ways. One popular negotiation and conflict resolution strategy is called "interest-based negotiation." The analogy of this strategy is of a person taking "a walk in the woods." In order to not only survive but also thrive, the person in the woods must foster self-awareness, cultivate curiosity, and understand the importance of worldviews (Marcus, Dorn, & McNulty, 2012). This strategy can even be employed in severe value-driven cases. For example, Jackson, Wilde, and Williams (2003) studied how practitioners use clinical empowerment and interest-based negotiations to negotiate end-of-life choices between terminally ill patients and their family members. Negotiation processes are reached, breached, and regained, allowing all sides to finally attain consensus and agree on next steps.

Another strategy to find common ground focuses on how to conduct a successful negotiation process as the primary aim. Without the right elements and suitable environment, opposite parties will tend to disagree more often and begin dealing with frustration and uncomfortable discussions. Malhotra and Malhotra (2013) advise that health and human services leaders can prepare ahead of time and manage discussions by applying the following three negotiation strategies:

1. *Focus on interests, not positions.* Positions are *what* people want, interests are *why* they want it. Positions can be incompatible and contradictory, whereas interests are more flexible and likeminded.
2. *Framing matters.* Not only *what* we say but also *how* we express ourselves is critical to build a strong negotiation frame. Leaders should prepare and be aware of the quality of messages shared, which includes the tone and type of exchanges.
3. *Negotiation space.* All *relevant* parties must be taken into account during the negotiation process. If someone of interest is left out, the agreement most likely will be short-lived because all stakeholders will be affected by the decisions.

Social architects engage frequently in negotiations during community collaboration efforts. It is important that conflict is identified early and managed appropriately. Otherwise, conflict has the potential to escalate and be disruptive when trying to achieve collaboration and program outcomes. A key strategy involves a continuous assessment of the quantity and quality of conflict resolution training programs that are provided within an organization. Conflict management skills can improve through systematic training and supervision (Leon-Perez, Notelaers, & Leon-Rubio, 2016). To illustrate this point, Blanch and associates (2015) completed a four-year study examining conflict in two federally funded children's systems of care organizations. They mapped the differences of how each provider conceptualized and managed conflict. The study revealed that when conflict is left unaddressed, it can negatively affect the development and sustainability of each service provided as well as the quality of their service delivery.

There may be a few factors that can derail or disrupt the flow of the negotiation process. First, teams may consist of members who have cognitive diversity (disagree about process or solutions). When personal differences are present, it is critical that the leader gets involved earlier in the process, focusing on team cohesion and viability (Mello & Delise, 2015). Second, power struggles can affect the symmetry of the conflict resolution process. One strategy to combat an unbalanced perception of power is to build integration and interdependence between the groups involved (Coleman, Kugler, Mitchinson, & Foster, 2013). Third, negotiations can become frozen because of constant misunderstanding of cultures and norms within and between cross-cultural groups. Posthuma (2011) recommends reducing the negotiations to two-person dyads as opposed to multiple people representing each side. This strategy allows for positive relationship building and greater innovation. Fourth, a toxic environment will not be conducive to a successful negotiation. The social architect concentrates on finding and eliminating small details that may cause further conflict escalation, problem repetition, and insulation (Gallicano, 2013). The three most common conflict management styles are avoidance, forcing, and negotiation. Negotiation should always take precedence before turning to avoidance or force (Skjørshammer, 2001). The innovative leader will have a greater chance to reach common ground and long-lasting positive outcomes through negotiating than through avoiding or forcing others to take a specific position or direction.

CONFLICT RESOLUTION MODELS

When disagreements are constant, individuals and groups are more likely to engage in ongoing unhealthy discussions. These informal arguments can be detrimental to maintaining positive working relationships and can destabilize the organizational environment. Thus, a more formal systematic process to resolve differences is needed. Conflict resolution is a communication process in which both parties agree to engage in formal and organized discussions. Conflict theory reveals that there are two types of conflict episodes when leaders are trying to resolve differences between people: (1) behavioral strategies, seeking individual change; and (2) multiple simultaneous conflicts, concerning collective issues within organizations (Speakman & Ryals, 2010). The majority of conflict resolution models focus on three key themes: workplace conflict and conflict management, cultural differences in conflict management, and conflict management in practice (Ma, Lee, & Yu, 2008). Next we will describe a few conflict resolution models within each of these three themes.

Workplace Conflict and Conflict Management Models

1. *Seeking compromise.* Baldoni's (2012) compromise approach
   includes two key principles. First, both parties have to agree that

the organization and/or institution come first. The stability of the organization must be above anything else. Although leadership can be seen as an individualized effort, the leader must focus on identifying and improving the organization's needs. Second, the only way compromise can work is if both parties understand each other's points of view. To better appreciate others' points of view, leaders should emphasize the use of open-ended questions and statements, designed to stimulate conversation. For example:

- Tell me about _____.
- Why do you feel that way?
- How can we do it better?
- Help me understand the issue more clearly.

By using this approach, leaders will be more prepared to share their own perspectives and better understand the other person's views and interests. Each side should practice how to share respectful statements, build mutual trust, allow people to disagree without animosity, and make compromise easier.

2. *Improving relationships.* Ashkenas' (2013) conflict resolution approach focuses on relationships instead of friendships. The leader should encourage individuals to form positive working relations, demonstrating that they can work together effectively and efficiently. Positive working relationships are manifested by developing trust with potential members and listening to each other. This model has two simple relationship-building steps:
    - Identify people in your organization and adjacent organizations who might have differing views and whom you might need to collaborate with.
    - Develop a tailored way to reach out to each person on the list (a few at a time) with the simple goal of getting to know each other.

3. *Focusing on interests*—Dorn, Marcus, and McNulty's (2013) conflict management approach focuses on sharing and identifying interests. The authors argue that fragmented and complex structures, such as the health care and human services systems, can benefit by bringing all key stakeholders to the table simultaneously. When all the representatives are actively participating, this conflict resolution strategy includes the following four steps (Dorn, Marcus, & McNulty, 2013, p. 341):
    - Articulate *self-interests* so that everyone will hear one another.
    - Look at where the overlap among these self-interests reveals agreement, what they call the *enlarged interests.*

- Collaborate to develop solutions to the remaining disagreements, or *enlightened interests.*
- Certify what has now become a larger set of agreements, or *aligned interests.*

4. *Interactive problem-solving.* Cross and Rosenthal's (1999) study demonstrates the potential of the interactive problem-solving model. Their experiment was designed to evaluate three conflict and mediation models: distributive bargaining, integrative bargaining, and interactive problem-solving. The latter proved to be the most effective when dealing with value-based disputes and long-term disagreements. Problem-solving techniques focus on how each side defines the problem; each person then shares how he or she feels about it and proposes a potential solution. The interactive problem-solving model was shown to have the greatest positive attitudes and behavioral changes compared with the other two models. Moreover, Kelman (1999) describes this type of negotiation as coming to an agreement that addresses the needs and fears of both parties, using four phases: identifying and analyzing the problem, joining and shaping ideas for solution, influencing the other side, and creating a supporting environment.

5. *Community-powered problem-solving.* Gouillart and Billings (2013) argue that organizations that engage in co-creating through communal innovation are more likely to ameliorate and even solve large systemic problems. The community-powered problem-solving model, also known as the co-creation model, has the following four implementation steps:
   - *Problem identification.* Identify a large problem that the organization cannot solve alone. Select one that may require people from different groups to actively participate in improving the organization's ecosystem.
   - *Leader selection.* Develop hypotheses about the internal and external leaders who could get involved and have both the resources and leadership potential to begin solving the problem.
   - *Pilot-testing.* Conduct experiments to test one or two hypotheses on a smaller scale. The solutions should have the potential to be implemented on a larger scale after their effectiveness is proved. Goals and objective should systematically be assessed and evaluated.
   - *Data-driven implementation.* The continuous generation of data will provide new insights and ideas. Data sharing should be organized, and rules regarding data sharing must be in place to avoid unnecessary conflict among stakeholders.

The community-powered problem-solving model has the potential to increase the size and richness of the community and to expand the individuals' networks.

Cultural Differences in Conflict Management

1. *Transnational conflict resolution.* Yarn (2002) defines the transactional conflict resolution model as any emerging guidelines, protocols, or best practices that are useful in aiding the recipient society's efforts to structurally adapt the mediation techniques of individuals from opposing groups conducted during the conflict resolution process. This international conflict resolution model tries to export the American strategies to resolve disagreements. Negotiation procedures take center stage, applying these concepts and conflict-handling patterns in other societies and cultures. The successful integration of this model depends on cultural appropriateness, transferability options/channels, and conflict-handling capacity.

2. *Culturally based negotiation.* Tinsley (1998) argues that each country's norms and traditions are key ingredients in defining individual methods to resolve differences. The culturally based model indicates that cultures are powerful mechanisms for filtering information and guiding their members toward a particular conflict resolution model. For example, when looking at differences among Japanese, German, and American cultures, the three dimensions of cultural variation are hierarchical differentiation, explicit contracting, and poly-chronicity (time-use preference). The normative conflict models among these three cultures are predetermined more intensely by these three cultural variations than other conflict resolutions models, such as deferring to status power, applying regulations, and integrating interests. The importance of culture was corroborated in a study about conflict management behaviors of welfare practitioners with respondents from Sydney and Hong Kong. Results strongly suggest that these two cultures' approaches to integrating and dominating modes of conflict management behaviors were very different (Wan, 2007).

3. *Collective conflict resolution.* Ma, Erkus, and Tabak (2010) explore the benefits and impact of collectivism on conflict management styles. The collective conflict management model features collaboration and accommodating each side as needed. It is based on the following four principles:

- Competitive success leads to preference for a competing style.
- The value of working alone leads to less collaboration.
- The norms of subordination of personal needs to group interests are positively related to more collaborating and accommodating.
- The effects of personal interventions on group productivity are positively related to more compromising.

The collective conflict resolution model has been successful in de-escalating interorganizational conflict. For example, health and human services organizations participating in the Systems of Care Networks for children with mental, emotional, or behavioral problems and their families across the United States have been involved with constant struggles, characterized by incompatible goals, competing interpersonal relations, and overlapping authority. A collective approach to resolving these differences in their development stages has proved to improve working relationships and patient outcomes (Boothroyd, Evans, Chen, Boustead, & Blanch, 2015). Ohbuchi and Suzuki (2003) review three dimensional structures of conflict in Japanese organizational settings: correct–incorrect (collaborative strategies), right–wrong (confrontational strategies), and gain–loss (avoiding strategies). Their findings imply that if the leader's management style applies collective methods and mediation, then it can greatly contribute to constructive settlements during organizational conflicts. Finally, Gil (2001) found that the best collaborative conflict resolution leaders foster and monitor the following: relationship building, participatory planning, collective decision-making, coordinating and sharing of tasks, problem-solving, and facilitative leadership.

Conflict Management in Practice

1. *Individual conflict styles.* The three main individual conflict resolution styles are compromising, avoidant, and confrontational. To find out their personal conflict style, leaders should have a clear idea of their goal orientations and outcome preferences. Zarankin (2008) argues that there is a clear path from motivational antecedents (what got you there) to goal orientation (where you want to go) to conflict style (how you want to get there). Goal orientation is relatively stable and appropriate to unique situations. Having this constant assists in determining which conflict style best suites the leader. To avoid misunderstandings due to egocentric personalities in conflict, the leader must be aware of (1) the priorities of the group members, and (2) the compatibility of both parties when participating in

the negotiation (Chambers & De Dreu, 2014). Moreover, Moberg (2001) links personal attributes and behavioral patterns with conflict resolution techniques. At the onset, the relationship of individual personality preferences for approaching and managing conflict is considered a factor in workplace settings. In this model, individual differences in personality and stylistic behavioral preferences greatly influence how conflict is managed. For example, when collaboration is preferred, leaders with more interpersonal skills should be selected. On the other hand, when a more confrontational approach is needed, individuals with stronger personalities should represent the group. To this end, Sportsman and Hamilton (2007) demonstrated that the prevalent conflict resolution style for nursing students was compromising. whereas accommodation was preferred by allied health students.

2. *Social action task group.* This conflict resolution model intends to transform the essence and purpose of the conflict at hand, focusing on community macro goals as a key objective. First, community members are organized in the social action task groups to achieve specific objectives. Then, participants use a collective process to ensure all voices are heard. Most likely, conflict will be present at this stage as concerned citizens diverge in their perceptions and proposed solutions, but all of them are united to accomplish the same community purpose and outcomes. Because all members have the same grand goals, the negotiation becomes less challenging, and members may have an easier time reaching consensus. When the task groups apply social action as a conflict resolution process, this can yield a very positive transformation. For example, Clemans (2010) studied the application of social action task groups in the school social work field. When supervisors used this model to work with families during their economic hardships, the clinical supervision process changed its trajectory because of the social action group intervention, resulting in a school-wide community transformation to more positively assist children and families.

3. *Organizational justice.* Tatum and Eberlin (2006) showed how organizations' justice concepts can be applied during conflict resolution and negotiations. The key idea of this approach is to demonstrate the value of organizational justice, the negative consequences for leaders who fail to attend to the social and structural elements in their organizations, and the fair and just treatment of employees. For example, as conflict is characterized with emotional exhaustion, an organizational justice conflict resolution model will

take into consideration gender. The conflict resolution may feature different approaches for males than females. Furthermore, when men use an avoidant conflict management style, the association between negative emotions and emotional exhaustion is mitigated, whereas among women, avoiding conflict did not diminish this relationship (Bear, Weingart, & Todorova, 2014).

4. *The U.S.A. method: understanding, suggestions, and agreement.* A simple and popular conflict resolution model is the U.S.A. method: understanding, suggestions, and agreement. The first phase, understanding, requires both parties to listen to one another, understand each other's positions, ask questions for clarification, and even paraphrase each other's key points. Then, the conversation can move to the second phase, which is suggesting alternative solutions. Each party shares how they see the problem or issue being addressed properly. After all the potential solutions are shared and understood, the final step is to come to an agreement where both sides will take action (Johnson & Johnson, 1996).

General Recommendations to Manage Conflict More Effectively

Because conflict is inevitable, it is essential that organizations and leaders continue to improve their conflict resolution processes and skills. Constructive conflict resolution strategies, like the ones presented earlier, can be useful in understanding the nature of disagreements, in sensing how people act/react in certain situations, and in reaching desired outcomes. The tenants of constructive conflict assume that opposing parties will structure their negotiations in a more collaborative approach than a confrontational one. For example, better solutions or outcomes are attainable when integrative negotiation procedures are put into place to address disputes that arise during the conflict resolution process (Stevahn & King, 2005). Innovative leaders willing to participate in constructive conflict resolutions need to affirm their confidence and self-relevant values to reduce negative perceptions and secure collaboration between parties to conflict resolution (Ward, Atkins, Lepper, & Ross, 2011).

One successful strategy to improve our knowledge about how the conflict resolution process is unfolding is to intentionally evaluate individual and collective efforts to resolve problems. The innovative leader should closely monitor the players, processes, and outcomes by considering the different roles individuals play within teams and organizations. Aritzeta, Ayestaran, and Swailes (2005) classify these team roles into five conflict resolution preferences or styles: dominating, integrating, avoiding, compromising, and obliging. The sooner the innovative leader can effectively evaluate the preferences of the individuals in both parties, the greater the likelihood that he or she is able to improve the conflict resolution process and outcomes.

This identification of individual roles becomes more multifaceted when dealing with interprofessional conflicts. When individuals come from various disciplines, often they encounter a variety of problems, including differences in their responses to conflict, different language (lingos), goal mismatches, and unbalanced negotiation approaches. According to Aritzeta et al. (2005), social architects manage these differences by evaluating the situation within three main themes: sources of team conflict (e.g., role boundary issues, scope of practice, and accountability); barriers to conflict resolution (e.g., lack of time, power struggles, unfair recognitions, lack of motivation); and strategies for conflict resolution (integrative responses, structure protocols, active listening). When the evaluation reveals patterns, the leader can focus on implementing individual strategies such as open and direct communication, willingness to find solutions, showing respect to everyone, and humility (Brown et al., 2011).

Finally, social architects should think ahead and be able to envision the emotional aspect of the conflict resolution process before starting negotiations. Emotions can easily run high as the conflict process evolves. As emotions shape behavior, the leader can better anticipate and predict the group members' reactions if the structure of the conflict resolution is appropriately designed and executed. Usually, individuals who are engaged in conflict management are likely to display positive or negative emotions. Positive emotions are more demonstrative with verbal and nonverbal cues, and negative emotions can be somewhat invisible because members may want to hide their anger and frustration (Obeidi, Hipel, & Kilgour, 2005). Thus, the leader should consider key emotional variables, including tasks, relationships, trust, forgiveness, and venting. Posthuma (2012) concludes that the proper regulation of emotions such as anger, enthusiasm, excitement, guilt, and remorse can significantly increase a more viable conflict management process and preferred outcomes.

Conflict Resolution during Strategic Abandonment

Organizations evolve all of the time for two main reasons: economic or strategic. Commonly, lack of funding forces organizations to decrease services, reduce personnel, and/or change course of action, including the closure of the organization. This is troublesome for those organizations that depend only on one or two large sources of income, forcing them to seek a more diversified donor-based funding stream. As these extreme organizational funding shifts occur, AbouAssi (2013) recommends for the leader to follow four modes of response: exit (suspending relationship if needed), voice (reaching common ground with affected group members), loyalty (executing the organizational mission and interests), and adjustment (adjusting to the situation voluntarily and deliberately). Furthermore, Major (2013) acknowledges that the decision-making process during strategic abandonment is overwhelming and leaders should consider the following steps: own your personal values; consider values and demands of those around you; think about the quality of work and the aesthetic and utilitarian purposes of each affected unit, as well as the economic value of each unit; and consider contributions made by group members.

The second reason for organizational transformation is strategic in nature. New leaders and/or board of trustees implies that the organization may take a new direction and that change is around the corner. Whether the organization is projecting growth (e.g., providing new services, opening new locations, adding new departments) or decline (e.g., reduction of workload, less personnel), a shift in leadership will result in sweeping organizational changes. Any of these adjustments brings conflict. The innovative leader must decide what pieces of the organization will be kept, which ones need to be adjusted, and which ones will be let go. This is what is known as "strategic abandonment."

Strategic abandonment is a challenging process because of the multiple views and perceptions that come into play during stormy organizational changes, adding complexity and sophistication to the leadership role. Malekoff and Ppell (2012) advise that leaders in these situations must remain empathetic to others and lead with a social justice compass in mind and spirit. They remind us of the admirable leadership of a remarkable social architect, Jane Adams, while she was leading Hull House in Chicago at the beginning of the 21st century. For her, it was imperative that the community, and especially elected officials, witness the devastating immigrant health conditions that so they could empathize with this human condition. The entire community needed to engage in a social justice movement to address significant demographic changes and secure health, social services, and other basic resources for immigrant children and their families.

During the strategic abandonment process, leaders are expected to (1) collaborate with other individuals and organizations, and (2) advocate for specific strategic and policy changes. During this time, effective leadership encompasses a process of constant analysis and vigilant restructuring, which fosters a better understanding of the diversity of programming, operational challenges, and professional development needs (Pardasani & Sackman, 2014). These leadership skills are evident when either the organization takes over another or two organizations decide to merge. Benton and Austin (2010) recommend that during merging situations, leaders carefully manage a three-part process (premerger, implementation, and postmerger), monitoring closely the following collaborative and advocacy developments: communication styles; staff morale, involvement, and satisfaction; and organizational identity and commitment. The rule of thumb is that the closer leaders are to the people affected during organizational changes and/or mergers, the higher the likelihood that they will be able to de-escalate conflict.

A powerful example to illustrate the complexity of change and strategic abandonment is when private companies, public agencies, and nonprofit organizations had to implement the new Patient Protection and Affordable Care Act (ACA) after 2011. Many health care companies and agencies encountered a dramatic shift in operations, which forced them to merge with other agencies and/or abandon services. The hardest part was to connect long-term goals to short-term actions, partially because of gaps in the new policy, ongoing legal challenges, and variation in the implementation state by state. One particular company, MedStar, which operated nine hospitals, had a strategic plan until the year 2020, but it was obvious that it needed serious revisions that included merging with other agencies and letting go a few of their business units. Johnson (2015) explains that leaders in this company focused on strategic changes in three business portfolios: future state (goals 10 years into the future), innovation (new service delivery), and investment (core business budgets).

In closing, we realize how difficult conflict can be. Many of us don't even like to deal with disagreements or prefer to avoid situations that can be emotionally charged. Nonetheless, conflict is a natural part of life, and effective leaders make a habit of developing negotiation skills and learning to integrate strategies to resolve conflict more positively. We should not shy away of conflictive situations; instead, we need to be more comfortable tackling interpersonal or organizational issues as early as possible. Social architects constantly evaluate their self-efficacy as predictors of positive (compromise, negotiation) or negative (attacking or power assertion) conflict resolution processes and outcomes (Field, Tobin, & Reese-Weber, 2014). We need to keep in mind that part of the conflict resolution process is to have an appropriate closure. Whether there is final agreement reached (sufficing mutual interests) or absence of resolution (no agreement), the innovative leaders must provide a level of cognitive closure to all the involved parties (Bélanger et al., 2015). Like any other ability, improving our conflict resolution management and negotiation skills requires the leader to practice, practice, and practice.

CHAPTER DISCUSSION QUESTIONS

1. Name three conflict resolution strategies and why you think these are the most important for a leader to utilize.
2. How can cultural differences among individuals affect negotiation skills?
3. What is strategic abandonment and how is change best managed?
4. Read the leader profile and case study in the Appendix to this chapter. Note innovative ideas and practices and see what aspects of the case you can connect to the contents of the chapter and/or the overall book.

REFERENCES

AbouAssi, K. (2013). Hands in the pockets of mercurial donors NGO response to shifting funding priorities. *Nonprofit and Voluntary Sector Quarterly, 42*(3), 584–602.

Aritzeta, A., Ayestaran, S., & Swailes, S. (2005). Team role preference and conflict management styles. *International Journal of Conflict Management, 16*(2), 157–182.

Ashkenas, R. (2013, January 22). Compromise requires relationships (not friendships). *Harvard Business Review.* Retrieved from https://hbr.org/2013/01/compromise-requires-relationsh.html

Baldoni, J. (2012, October 12). Compromising when compromise is hard. *Harvard Business Review.* Retrieved from https://hbr.org/2012/10/compromising-when-compromise-i

Bear, J. B., Weingart, L. R., & Todorova, G. (2014). Gender and the emotional experience of relationship conflict: The differential effectiveness of avoidant conflict management. *Negotiation and Conflict Management Research, 7*(4), 213–231.

Bélanger, J. J., Pierro, A., Barbieri, B., De Carlo, N. A., Falco, A., & Kruglanski, A. W. (2015). Handling conflict at work: The role of fit between subordinates' need for closure and supervisors' power tactics. *International Journal of Conflict Management, 26*(1), 25–43.

Benton, A., & Austin, M. (2010). Managing nonprofit mergers: The challenges facing human service organizations. *Administration in Social Work, 34*(5), 458–479.

Blanch, A. K., Boustead, R., Boothroyd, R. A., Evans, M. E., & Chen, H. (2015). The role of conflict identification and management in sustaining community collaboration: Report on a four-year exploratory study. *Journal of Behavioral Health Services & Research, 42*(3), 324–333.

Boothroyd, R. A., Evans, M. E., Chen, H., Boustead, R., & Blanch, A. K. (2015). An exploratory study of conflict and its management in systems of care for children with mental, emotional, or behavioral problems and their families. *Journal of Behavioral Health Services & Research, 42*(3), 310–323.

Brown, J., Lewis, L., Ellis, K., Stewart, M., Freeman, T. R., & Kasperski, M. J. (2011). Conflict on interprofessional primary health care teams—Can it be resolved? *Journal of Interprofessional Care, 25*(1), 4–10.

Chambers, J. R., & De Dreu, C. K. W. (2014). Egocentrism drives misunderstanding in conflict and negotiation. *Journal of Experimental Social Psychology, 51*, 15–26.

Clemans, S. (2010). The transformation of the purpose of a school-based supervision group during tough economic times: Challenges and considerations for the worker. *Social Work with Groups, 33*(1), 41–52.

Coleman, P. T., Kugler, K. G., Mitchinson, A., & Foster, C. (2013). Navigating conflict and power at work: The effects of power and interdependence asymmetries on conflict in organizations. *Journal of Applied Social Psychology, 43*(10), 1963–1983.

Cross, S., & Rosenthal, R. (1999). Three models of conflict resolution: Effects on intergroup expectancies and attitudes. *Journal of Social Issues, 55*(3), 561–580.

Dorn, B., Marcus, L., & McNulty, E. J. (2013, October 31). Four steps to resolving conflicts in health care. *Harvard Business Review.* Retrieved from https://hbr.org/2013/10/four-steps-to-resolving-conflicts-in-health-care

Field, R. D., Tobin, R. M., & Reese-Weber, M. (2014). Agreeableness, social self-efficacy, and conflict resolution strategies. *Journal of Individual Differences, 35*(2), 95–102.

Gallicano, T. D. (2013). Internal conflict management and decision making: A qualitative study of a multitiered grassroots advocacy organization. *Journal of Public Relations Research, 25*(4), 368–388.

Gouillart, F., & Billings, D. (2013, April). Community-powered problem solving. *Harvard Business Review.* Retrieved from https://hbr.org/2013/04/community-powered-problem-solving

Gil de Gibaja, M. (2001). An exploratory study of administrative practice in collaboratives. *Administration in Social Work, 25*(2), 39–59.

Halpert, J. A., Stuhlmacher, A. F., Crenshaw, J. L., Litcher, C. D., & Bortel, R. (2010). Paths to negotiation success. *Negotiation and Conflict Management Research, 3*(2), 91–116.

Hamlin, A., & Jennings, C. (2007). Leadership and conflict. *Journal of Economic Behavior & Organization, 64*(1), 49–68.

Jackson, W. C., Wilde, J. O., Jr., & Williams, J. (2003). Using clinical empowerment to teach ethics and conflict management in ante mortem care: A case study. *American Journal of Hospice & Palliative Care, 20*(4), 274–278.

Johnson, M. (2015). What to do when your future strategy clashes with your present. *Harvard Business Review.* Retrieved from https://hbr.org/2015/04/what-to-do-when-your-future-strategy-clashes-with-your-present

Johnson, D. W., & Johnson, R. T. (1996). Conflict resolution and peer mediation programs in elementary and secondary schools: A review of the research. *Review of Educational Research, 66*(4), 459–506.

Kelman, H. C. (1999). Interactive problem solving as a metaphor for international conflict resolution: Lessons for the policy process. *Peace and Conflict: Journal of Peace Psychology, 5*(3), 201–218.

Leon-Perez, J., Notelaers, G., & Leon-Rubio, J. (2016). Assessing the effectiveness of conflict management training in a health sector organization: Evidence from subjective and objective indicators. *European Journal of Work and Organizational Psychology*, *25*(1), 1–12.

Ma, Z., Erkus, A., & Tabak, A. (2010). Explore the impact of collectivism on conflict management styles: A Turkish study. *International Journal of Conflict Management*, *21*(2), 169–185.

Ma, Z., Lee, Y., & Yu, K. (2008). Ten years of conflict management studies: Themes, concepts and relationships. *International Journal of Conflict Management, 19*(3), 234–248.

Major, M. L. (2013). How they decide a case study examining the decision-making process for keeping or cutting music in a K–12 public school district. *Journal of Research in Music Education, 61*(1), 5–25.

Malekoff, A., & Papell, C. (2012). Remembering Hull House, speaking to Jane Addams, and preserving empathy. *Social Work with Groups, 35*(4), 306–312.

Malhotra, D. (2015, December). Control the negotiation before it begins. *Harvard Business Review*. Retrieved from https://hbr.org/2015/12/control-the-negotiation-before-it-begins

Malhotra, D., & Malhotra, M. (2013, October 21). Negotiation strategies for doctors— and hospitals. *Harvard Business Review*. Retrieved from https://hbr.org/2013/10/negotiation-strategies-for-doctors-and-hospitals

Marcus, L. J., Dorn, B. C., & McNulty, E. J. (2012). The walk in the woods: A step-by-step method for facilitating interest-based negotiation and conflict resolution. *Negotiation Journal, 28*(3), 337–349.

Mello, A. L., & Delise, L. A. (2015). Cognitive diversity to team outcomes: The roles of cohesion and conflict management. *Small Group Research, 46*(2), 204–226.

Moberg, P. J. (2001). Linking conflict strategy to the five-factor model: Theoretical and empirical foundations. *International Journal of Conflict Management, 12*(1), 47–68.

Obeidi, A., Hipel, K. W., & Kilgour, D. M. (2005). The role of emotions in envisioning outcomes in conflict analysis. *Group Decision and Negotiation, 14*(6), 481–500.

Ohbuchi, K., & Suzuki, M. (2003). Three dimensions of conflict issues and their effects on resolution strategies in organizational settings. *International Journal of Conflict Management, 14*(1), 61–73.

Pardasani, M., & Sackman, B. (2014). New York City senior centers: A unique, grassroots, collaborative advocacy effort. *Activities, Adaptation & Aging, 38*(3), 200–219.

Posthuma, R. A. (2011). Conflict management and performance outcomes. *International Journal of Conflict Management, 22*(2), 108–110.

Posthuma, R. A. (2012). Conflict management and emotions. *International Journal of Conflict Management, 23*(1), 4–5.

Skjørshammer, M. (2001). Co-operation and conflict in a hospital: Interprofessional differences in perception and management of conflicts. *Journal of Interprofessional Care, 15*(1), 7–18.

Speakman, J., & Ryals, L. (2010). A re-evaluation of conflict theory for the management of multiple, simultaneous conflict episodes. *International Journal of Conflict Management, 21*(2), 186–201.

Sportsman, S., & Hamilton, P. (2007). Conflict management styles in the health professions. *Journal of Professional Nursing, 23*(3), 157–166.

Stevahn, L., & King, J. A. (2005). Managing conflict constructively in program evaluation. *Evaluation: The International Journal of Theory, Research and Practice, 11*(4), 415–427.

Tatum, B. C., & Eberlin, R. J. (2006). Organizational justice and conflict management styles: Teaching notes, role playing instructions, and scenarios. *International Journal of Conflict Management, 17*(1), 66–81.

Tinsley, C. (1998). Models of conflict resolution in Japanese, German, and American cultures. *Journal of Applied Psychology, 83(2)*, 316–323.

Wan, H. K. (2007). Conflict management behaviors of welfare practitioners in individualist and collectivist culture. *Administration in Social Work, 31*(1), 49–65.

Ward, A., Atkins, D. C., Lepper, M. R., & Ross, L. (2011). Affirming the self to promote agreement with another: Lowering a psychological barrier to conflict resolution. *Personality and Social Psychology Bulletin, 37*(9), 1216–1228.

Yarn, D. H. (2002). Transnational conflict resolution practice: A brief introduction to the context, issues, and search for best practice in exporting conflict resolution. *Conflict Resolution Quarterly, 19*(3), 303–319.

Zarankin, T. G. (2008). A new look at conflict styles: Goal orientation and outcome preferences. *International Journal of Conflict Management, 19*(2), 167–184.

APPENDIX
Featured Leader: Dave Coplan

Dave Coplan is the Executive Director of the *Human Services Center* and Director of the *Mon Valley Providers Council*. The Human Services Center was honored as the recipient of the 2004 Wishart Award for Excellence in Nonprofit Management awarded by The Forbes Funds of The Pittsburgh Foundation. In 2012, Dave was the inaugural recipient of the statewide CAAP Sargent Shriver Community Service Award. In 2017, the Network for Social Work Management nationally recognized Dave with its Exemplar Award for commitment to Leadership and Management Competencies. In 2010 the University of Pittsburgh's School of Social Work honored Dave as its Outstanding Field Instructor, an honor of great meaning to him for his role as a mentor to those entering the field. In 2009 the University of Pittsburgh's Graduate School of Public and International Affairs honored Dave as one of its inaugural 4 Under 40 recipients, and in 2007 Dave was recognized as one of Pittsburgh's 40 Under 40 by PUMP and *Pittsburgh Magazine*.

Before his promotion to Executive Director, he held the position of MVPC Director and was the Associate Director of the Center for 11 years. He started with the agency as an intern in 1990 and has worked in many facets of community organizing such as with the Pantry Network of Eastern Suburbs, coordinating an Affordable Housing Bank Project, and working with the member agencies of the Mon Valley Providers Council to fill gaps in services and on a variety of special initiatives.

In 2006, Dave launched a separate college access nonprofit—*Advancing Academics*. In his part-time role as Director, Dave assists low-income, high-achieving youth to gain entry into and financial assistance for college. The initiative currently boasts an 87.5% college graduation rate.

He has worked for the United Way and United Jewish Federation and has performed consulting for The Forbes Funds, University of Pittsburgh Medical Center Braddock and McKeesport, Auberle, McKeesport Hospital Foundation, Pittsburgh Partnership for Neighborhood Development (now Neighborhood Allies), and many others.

Currently, Dave is on the Partner4Work Board (the workforce development board for the City of Pittsburgh and Allegheny County) and is Chair of the Personnel Committee and serves on the Governance Committee, the Family Support Policy Board, and the Executive Committee of APOST. He is Secretary of the Board of the Pantry Network of Eastern Suburbs and served recently nationally on a committee for Grantmakers for Effective Organizations. Previously he served on the founding Advisory Team for the Greater Pittsburgh Nonprofit Partnership (past Chair of the Public Policy Committee) for its first seven years. In 1997, Dave was selected as one of five international fellows by the Indiana University Center on Philanthropy in Indianapolis, for which he published a manuscript on endowments for small nonprofits and under contract gave speaking engagements across the country for 18 months to other development professionals. Since 1997 and currently, he has taught courses at the University of Pittsburgh on nonprofit management, fundraising, human resources, public policy, and advocacy and lobbying for the School of Social Work, as well as in the undergraduate program in public administration (for GSPIA). Dave has conducted dozens of presentations on advocacy and lobbying throughout Pennsylvania.

A native of both Washington, DC, and Pittsburgh, Dave graduated from the University of Pittsburgh with a master's degree in Social Work, Community Organizing, and a master's degree in Public Administration, along with a Certificate in Nonprofit Management and a Bachelor of Arts degree in Social Work. He has also received Executive Training at Harvard Business School. He is an alum of the Leadership Development Initiative (LDI I), Leadership Pittsburgh (LP XIII), and the Human Services Executive Academy. Dave prioritizes family in his busy life, spending as much time as possible with his wife and three sons.

LEADERSHIP PROFILE FOR DAVE COPLAN

Share your professional background and experience

I have been in the human services field for 27 years, and 24 of them have been in senior management. I developed a small nonprofit called Advancing Academics that has won countless awards that are up on our website, including management awards and awards for our advocacy for low-income people across the state. I have been teaching classes now for 20 years in nonprofit management. I have done some consulting work with a variety of nonprofits.

In your experience, what are the top three to five leadership attributes someone in the health and human services field should develop? Share an example of when you have used one or more of these attributes/skills in your work

First and foremost, in our sector, when I think of leadership attributes, possibly the one that is most important is *ability to deliver*. We're constantly evaluated, and leaders in this field are constantly evaluated on their ability to deliver. Three simple words. The things that keep nonprofit leaders up at night, especially those that run 501(c)3s, typically are *fundraising or finance, human resources, and working with a board*. You could summarize human resources and working with a board as part of managing and leading people through political acumen, which of course starts with a very rudimentary base of having a network.

I'll end with the three skills. I get asked to do these interviews by students, and they always ask, what are three skills you use in your work? There are my leadership skills. These are not bad words but may elicit some negative feelings on your behalf. These three words are actually skills we apply all the time in our network and outside of our network to exude pressure to get things done for positive outcomes to benefit people. They're so underplayed in our sector and yet so essential. I teach advocacy and lobbying and I teach fundraising and these permeate those aspects, which are important to our work. Those three skills are *persuasion, manipulation,* and *coercion*.

I don't mean coercion in the sense that we're seeing it so horribly depicted in multiple arenas right now. I don't mean a coercive environment as a negative thing; I mean coercion toward a positive end for the people we serve. I could give multiple examples and illustrations where there's a continuum. These skills have benefited thousands of people through my work. Indeed, it's not a bad word. Sometimes coercion toward a good end is a good thing.

I will tell you how I used all three in a case. Years ago, we needed to try to bring a Career Expo of 600 people for half a day, in a community where the only space to do it was a brand-new beautiful facility, and basically the person in charge didn't want us to do it. So, of course we start with the usual persuasive tactics with the person, like, "here's all the benefits to you and here's how it will help you." Well then we're trying to manipulate the circumstance. Do we need to reach out to his board? I'm fast-tracking a long story over protracted weeks, and we're losing precious time, and he says, the real issue is if we use our senior space for this job fair, we probably won't get our per diem from our funding source because our per diem will be down because people who come here will be bused to another site and won't want to come and I will get less money. It's pretty coercive if I'm saying to you, "so if I call your funder, who I know, and I can guarantee you that you will receive the average number of seniors on a Friday in March for you to meet your per diem, and even if you don't reach the number, you will still get paid." I mean who wants to be told, "I'll speak to your funder on your behalf?" "I can make this happen by this afternoon" Then he looked at me like with a blank look like he still didn't get it because actually at that point the right thing to do would have been for him to say, "I'll do it my-self, I can take care of myself." I don't think he understood, but you know when you have a network like I do, and can you imagine this funding source saying we're not going to let 600 other people benefit and get this career fair and that's how many people showed up (589), and we helped about half of them get jobs. So anyway, I made the call and by that afternoon, that's that. It was a done deal. They signed on the dotted line.

You build this network of social capital or human capital. You build a net-work where someone says, well we don't really want to move forward unless we know where this person is at with a particular issue, well I can find that out for you. Just give me five minutes and if I can reach them, we'll have an an-swer. I mean that was coercive, but not with negative end. I mean trying to help people get jobs. You can't say that if you don't have the ability to deliver. These things are interrelated. You couldn't say any of that unless you were certain you could get the result. I had to call the one person, and if she had said no, I would have talked to her boss, and if she said no, I would have talked to their mutual boss, and there's no way he would have said no. I knew they didn't want it to have to go that far.

Building a network is vital. As I was starting in this field, I went to every meeting I could before having a family of my own, to meet new people. That is just something very basic that people are always astonished when I say this, but

I'll just give you an example. If you go to a meeting, whether you're new this year or you've been in this field a long time, when do you arrive at the meeting? I arrive early and I talk to everyone as they come in. I meet the people I don't know. Twenty-seven years later, I know a lot of people in Pittsburgh. If I know the list of attendees in advance, I'll look to see who I don't know and I'll make a point to try to meet them before the meeting starts. When you pick a seat in a meeting, usually someone sits to your left or to your right, maybe if you're lucky even across from you, but if you get there early, you get a chance to pick at least one person to sit with. Pick that one person you want to sit with because you want to know them. I went to a meeting where there were 22 guests on the list. I was one of them, so there were 21 other people, and I knew 19 of them. I still went to the meeting early, talked with everybody I could, and continued to build rapport with people, even if I have a relationship with them, and then picked one of those two people I did not know and tried to take a seat next to that person. I think when you've established a network, it takes time to cultivate that, get together with people for lunch, breakfast, coffee. I go to lunch with a lot of these folks throughout the year, lunch or breakfast, and continue to nurture those relationships, and most of the time with no agenda. Just, "hey, haven't seen you in a while, let's get lunch or breakfast." I don't drink coffee, that's why I don't go for coffee. Spend the time building a relationship, and that keeps those doors open and then it's a more natural interaction when you actually need to turn to somebody versus "hey, haven't talked to you in five years and I need something." That's not helpful. I go out to as many meetings as I can fit in my schedule.

If you read the Network for Social Work Managers, I was featured in July in the Monday Morning Leader thing, and I'm going to have more than 2,000 contacts of real people. I'm not on any social media platform, but certainly those who choose to do that, yes it will help, but nothing replaces real face-to-face conversations, phone conversations, and really getting to know a person. I've chosen to avoid those platforms personally and professionally. I am unique in that way.

I think one of the key things, when you think of what I said, is that you have a network if people trust you and respect you and you lead with integrity and you feel you're being evaluated based on your ability to deliver. But sometimes it requires the courage to say, "this is not going well and we're pulling the plug on this." Just own up to what is not going well. I'll give an illustration of that because the illustrations always tell the story well better than just a statement.

We created a partnership years ago when distance learning first came out with the workforce provider to do distance learning because no one was doing it in our region. We took the offer because it was funded by a couple of major funders and we figured they vetted it; and they had two other partners, and we figured those partners vetted it. They came in to do this distance learning, and the audio didn't work. It's really hard to teach someone banking fundamentals or computer repair with no audio. One week the video didn't work. They were supposed to have a technology (IT) coordinator on-site, but they couldn't fill that position because they weren't paying a good wage. Eventually, we had to pull the plug on the project and have the courage to look people in the eye and say "this isn't working." Consumers were also complaining because if fewer than six people showed up, they wouldn't run the distance learning. They said it wasn't worth the expense for six people. Well those six people went to a lot of trouble, got transportation and child care, and *holy moly our reputation was now on the line.* We basically dissolved our partnership with this group. One of the funders, the biggest funder, who knew us wanted to know why. I had to tell them everything that went wrong on this very large investment they were making. That's a hell of a challenge—*do you just to ride out a bad situation for all the wrong reasons or do the right thing?* And you are considering maintaining future relationships and partnerships.

We got asked some questions recently by a major funder who was looking at an incredibly large gift to our organization and really wanted to vet our agency completely. One of the things they asked us was to talk about some of our "misses"; that is, where we didn't end up delivering. I had board members in this meeting, and some of them asked, "Do we have a situation like that?" This was the story I told. I said I think it's a pretty big one and acknowledging that our relationship with that one large funder is probably never going to be the same, but it had to be done. The risk of reputation alone when our agency was growing was a great concern. When you think of true risk management, risk of income, goodwill, property, and people, with the exception of property, but with the other three, we're all being compromised. That's something we don't see a lot of. Not many folks are willing to admit when they made a mistake. Just taking the loss is better than trying to see this out when we're not going to get to a great end. The good end is all about the people were serving. If they're not getting a good product, I don't really care who's paying for it.

As an aside, I tell people, including funders, "If you go to a bakery and your baked product is stale, you probably take it back. Maybe you get another one. If your second or third one is moldy, I mean at some point, do you really want to do business there?" Low-income people that we serve, no matter who's paying the bill, they don't have an appetite for moldy food, and they sure don't deserve that. At some point, even if everything else was held equal, we should be putting the consumers' interests first. I think we did the right thing, but it took a lot of courage to do that.

A lot of what I tell people is when you've been doing this work, it's like you've seen not just this movie, but you've seen most of these movies. I'm not saying you've seen everything, as a matter of fact, I can tell you lots of stories of things I would have never believed in my lifetime, but you know some of these stories have recurring themes. People don't want to admit when they've made a mistake. They think it's going be catastrophic, but if you are known for your ability to deliver, you've established this network, people know you to be honest and have integrity, that you're making decisions for the betterment of people, I don't understand why people have a hard time saying, "This isn't going well and we've made a mistake." I think it serves you so much better. We tried this program, but we're not getting the results we expected so we're not going compromise the people we consider with a half-baked deliverable. Pun intended to the bakery.

A CASE STUDY BY DAVE COPLAN

At the very beginning of my career, I'm interning for an organization that develops a "special needs" task force in 1990s. The special needs task force is doing work in the religious community to encourage folks to be more accommodating of people with disabilities and special needs. This is about sanction, if you will, and real leadership, and the special needs task force is advocating that folks do whatever possible to improve facilities for those with special needs, particularly during a major fundraising campaign of more than $50 million to improve a building in a faith-based program. The special needs task force is trying to make sure that some of the funding goes toward accommodations. Obviously in the 1990s, around the time that the American with Disabilities Act (ADA) came out, organizations were making changes to improve access for the disabled. However, because of this particular organization's religious affiliation, they weren't required by law to make full accommodations. Yet you have a special needs task force of your entity advocating for this, perhaps you would lead by example? The initial plans called for an elevator in the building, and when cost overruns began to hit, they decided to eliminate the elevator because they could have all meetings on the first floor to avoid an elevator cost to the second floor. How do you think that made that committee look at its work? They were up in arms, and the task force was composed of very powerful people in the community. And somehow, "I'm like the go-between of the higher-ups in the agency who are fixated on sparing a $50,000 cost for the elevator and the special needs task force who are fixated on how this is undermining the intent of the task force." It all gets back to relationships, people working together and folks compromising, having the ability to deliver, and speaking with each other with honesty and integrity. Although the end outcome was not one that anyone was happy with because they put a chairlift in from the side of the building instead of an elevator. And of course you get people who aren't in a wheelchair, and they would not be using the chairlift. A person using a walker doesn't want to sit on a chairlift. They would rather be in an elevator to the second floor. It was a terrible compromise, but at one point the president of the organization and board chair spoke to the two committee co-chairs and said to them that they were "corrupting a young mind" (mine). I went to breakfast with the co-chairs of the task force, and they asked me, "Does it feel like we are corrupting you? Anyway, you need to be very clear about where your allegiances lie." You could argue that I get my check from the agency, so therefore I should follow whatever the mother ship wants; the school places me at the agency as an intern, and I am there to serve the people. So whose interests are you most representing?

It was a very interesting time and in many ways I think emblematic about when I opened this conversation about boards and networks and that relationships matter. And being very clear about where you stand when something's controversial. On what side of the issue are you? I was consistently on the side for the people that we were there to serve. Believe me, I make decisions all of the time for the agency in my role, but we use a strategy screen, and several of the questions we're always asking about include the impact on the people we serve. *Are we doing well by the people we're here to actually help?* If we're not, one of my humorous lines is, they should reinstate the smiley face stickers at Walmart and we should get a job giving those out because at least when people got the smiley stickers, like a little kid or a senior, they at least usually smiled about it. Are we there for the people or not? I don't want to sound totally altruistic. I'm not on a soapbox. There are some things I just don't understand. Like, "how can you create a special needs task force asking to make accommodations and your mothership is saying we're running a $50 million campaign and we can't spend $50,000 on an elevator and lead by example?" Unbelievable. I am astonished by people's actions. Why have a task force then? Just say, "we don't care about that group of folks with special needs." "We've got plenty of other work we care about, and focus on what you're really going do." I call it "mission hypocrisy." That's the term. I'm not saying I'm the only one who's coined this term, but I use it all the time. For example, how do you have a nonprofit that has a mission to improve the quality of life of everyone else but pays villains to treat employees like garbage, gives them no health insurance and no pension, or gives them the cafeteria plan with only a few grand to spend on them. This is true mission hypocrisy. That's the learning example for emerging leaders here. What are we even doing if we're not doing the most basic things to benefit the people we're here to help?

CASE DISCUSSION POINTS

1. What is mission hypocrisy? Provide an example from real life.
2. What happens when there is conflict and a consensus is reached, but the agreed-on solution is far from meeting the needs of the people who were intended to be represented?
3. How can an innovative leader overcome the challenge of reaching an unsatisfactory compromise?
4. In the leadership profile, the social architect mentions tactics such as coercion and manipulation toward the public good. Are these tactics justified? Can you provide of other examples of when such persuasive techniques have helped those in need?
5. How important is it for an innovative leader to admit to mistakes and do so publicly and at the risk of losing a funding source? Do the benefits outweigh the costs? Why or why not?

13

Leadership and Crisis Response

Concentrate all your thoughts upon the work at hand.
The sun's rays do not burn until brought to a focus.
— ALEXANDER GRAHAM BELL

CHAPTER OBJECTIVES

1. Explore the role of health and human services leaders during disasters and emergencies;
2. Learn how to respond in every phase of a crisis situation: preparation, response, and recovery;
3. Learn effective triage models and other crisis response techniques to help people dealing with stressful situations during difficult times; and,
4. Gain insights on innovative leadership from a social architect (see Appendix to this chapter).

INTRODUCTION

In today's world, both human-made and natural disasters are unfortunately a common occurrence. Human-made disasters have increased 10-fold in the United States in the last decade, including incidents that involve gun violence and shootings (murders, suicides, and unintentional shootings kill more than 30,000 people every year), domestic and international terrorist attacks (more than 10 attacks in 2017 alone, killing more than 80 people), and infrastructure malfunctions (e.g., gas leaks, oil spills, explosions). In addition, we are enduring continuous natural disasters, including earthquakes, hurricanes, tsunamis, wildfires, public health or pandemic outbreaks, and extreme climate changes. These occurrences are mostly lethal, forcing all of us to prepare the best we can to ameliorate the human death and suffering toll and reduce material damage costs.

Innovative leaders must be ready at any given moment to confront a crisis. The *Harvard Business Review* published six simple guidelines that leaders can put into practice in their workplaces as they experience a disaster or catastrophe (Baldoni, 2011):

1. *Take a moment to figure out what's going on.* Leaders who experience a major disruption in service to their organizations must replace the excessive nervous response of employees with delegating responsibilities and then call for a subsequent meeting in an hour's time. This also helps to impose order in a chaotic situation.
2. *Act promptly, not hurriedly.* An effective leader must provide direction and respond to the situation in a timely fashion, but acting hurriedly only makes people more nervous.
3. *Manage expectations.* Communicate that in times of crisis, quick resolutions are not possible. It falls to the leader in charge to address the size and scope of the crisis. You don't want to alarm people, but do not be afraid to share the magnitude of the situation.
4. *Demonstrate control.* The effective leader must assume control of how to respond to the situation. Leaders put themselves into the action, bringing people and resources to bear.
5. *Keep loose.* An effective leader can never afford to lose composure. Flexibility and ability to change quickly are paramount. First responses may not be final. Leaders put in place channels of communication to receive information on an ongoing basis, listen carefully, and consult with the frontline staff members who know what's happening.
6. *Provide perspective.* Effective leaders can often do more by participating from the "balcony" and engaging in the front lines as necessary.

As leaders in health and human services organizations, we have a greater responsibility to be prepared and be competent to assist people who experience crises or calamities. There are several definitions for crises and disasters. We understand disasters as events that cause greater losses than a person, organization, or community can handle, including personal and financial losses, the loss of life and/or property, and irreparable damage to current human conditions. Besides grand disasters, organizations also sustain crises and emergencies for many reasons. Pearson and Clair (1998) define "an organizational crisis as a low-probability, high-impact event that threatens the viability of the organization and is characterized by ambiguity of cause, effect, and means of resolution, as well as by a belief that decisions must be made swiftly" (p. 60).

The two key organizations responsible to mobilize resources, the Federal Emergency Management Agency (FEMA) and the American Red Cross (ARC), have developed a number of effective systems to deploy first responders, resources, and relevant information during emergency situations. First, FEMA's mission is to provide training, support, and resources to all citizens and first respondents so that we can improve our capability to prepare, protect, respond, and recover from all hazards, emergencies, and disasters. FEMA's five strategic priorities are:

Priority 1: Be survivor-centric in mission and program delivery;
Priority 2: Become an expeditionary organization;
Priority 3: Posture and build capability for catastrophic disasters;
Priority 4: Enable disaster risk reduction nationally; and
Priority 5: Strengthen FEMA's organizational foundation.

FEMA offers a package of tools and resources built on the National Preparedness System to help citizens and crisis teams to prepare before disasters occur. The key four tools are:

1. *Threat and hazard identification and risk assessment (THIRA)*—risk assessment tool of any threat or emergency
2. *Operations plans*—strategic, operational, and tactical plans depending on the type of crisis or disaster
3. *National incident management system*—a standardized method of crisis management, assisting multidisciplinary teams to identify roles and train to mitigate a disaster
4. *National planning system*—provides a unified approach and common terminology to support the implementation of the National Preparedness System through plans that support an all threats and hazards approach to preparedness

These emergency preparedness tools enable the whole community to build, sustain, and deliver the core capabilities identified in the National Preparedness Goal.

FEMA works in collaboration with other public agencies, mainly the Departments of Homeland Security, Health Services, and Housing, Urban Development, as well as USA.gov and DisasterAssistance.gov. Simultaneously, FEMA has partnerships with nonprofit organizations, mainly with the ARC, which offers emergency preparedness kits, first aid kits and supplies, training materials, and other goods. Some of the key emergency items ARC distributes include survival kits, 72-hour emergency kits, emergency radios, emergency flashlights, and sandless sandbags. More important, one of the main priorities of the ARC is to manage the blood supply needed for health emergencies and unexpected catastrophes.

Organizations that provide vital health and human services (such as hospitals, clinics, mental health institutions, food supply centers, senior centers, and shelters) need to be ready to deal with any catastrophe at any given moment in three main capacities: prepare, respond, and recover. First, preparation is critical. Health and human services professionals must be clear about how to respond to any crisis situation by writing an action plan in collaboration with law enforcement, first responders, and other agencies. Second, organizations and teams must have a response plan during the crisis situation, usually applying the Standardized Emergency Management System (SEMS), which contains the role of each person in the organization, triage techniques to help those immediately affected, and steps to take depending on the type of disaster. Finally, most of the health and human services organizations must bear the bulk of the crisis aftermath, which includes short-, intermediate-, and long-term medical, shelter, food, mental health, and other services. This chapter will review the role of leaders in the health and human services, explain components of effective safety plans, and introduce the latest crisis response interventions and techniques to utilize during emergencies.

ROLE OF HUMAN SERVICE LEADERS
AND ORGANIZATIONS DURING EMERGENCIES

The main role of the innovative leader before, during, and after an emergency or crisis situation is to assess the capacity of the organization and its personnel. To best assess their personnel, leaders should map out the safety and crisis response knowledge and abilities of key individuals in the organization. Then, the organization must put together a training plan and disaster guidelines on how to proceed during an emergency, identifying mental health and crisis interventions that will be activated. Everly (2002) highlights that in the past, psychologists, psychiatrists, social workers, and other helping professionals have found themselves thrust into situations in which they have been expected to provide emergency mental health services in the absence of formalized training. Thus, health and human services professionals must acquire training and expertise in five core competencies: providing realistic preparation, fostering group cohesion and social support, fostering positive cognitions, building self-efficacy and hardiness, and training in applying collaborative models. Training sessions must be practical and should use case studies from past emergencies (i.e., the lessons learned approach). Gelman and Mirabito (2005) recommend that the trainers provide guidelines for discussion and teaching points to structure didactic and collaborative problem-based learning, using examples from their own and their students' practice.

Smith (2012) explored the issues and challenges that nonprofit organizations endured during the devastating Hurricane Katrina in 2005. This catastrophic event alone affected 93,000 miles across 138 counties. As a consequence of the storm, 80% of New Orleans, a city built under sea level, was flooded because of the levee failures. The flooding destroyed New Orleans, the Nation's 35th largest city, displacing hundreds of thousands of people. The lessons learned were reported in the following five broad categories:

1. *Clients*
   - Do not presume to know the needs of clients. Clients' needs could change daily.
   - Service needs for traditional clients tend to be lost after a catastrophe, with the focus on the needs of new clients.
   - A plan for clients in need of long-term services (e.g., older adults, disabled people, people with diabetes) needs to be followed up on immediately.
2. *Organizational*
   - Be prepared to absorb programs of nonprofit organizations going out of business.
   - Organizations and relationships change overnight. Your entire database and understanding of community resources may disappear.
   - Have electronic backup files for everything and consider using national firms for banking and payroll management.
   - Nonprofit organizations need to have sufficient financial reserves to carry them for three to six months in an emergency.
   - Keep extensive and updated lists of staff home phone numbers, emergency phone numbers, and email addresses, including locations outside the area that they are most likely to evacuate to in an emergency.
   - Staff members are victimized as well and have to deal with personal needs along with client needs and seeing vicarious trauma throughout the city.
3. *Funding*
   - Short-term funding after a disaster is important, but those funds will disappear at some point.

- Locally responsive private funders such as United Way and community foundations can be very helpful and flexible following a catastrophe.
- Be ready to look outside the geographic area for funding.
4. *Collaboration and competition*
   - There is a tremendous need to collaborate on a centralized intake process.
   - Collaborations among small organizations, when the executive is directly involved, tend to work better than larger collaborative efforts with executives simply planning and delegating.
   - After a catastrophe, organizations try to work together. As short-term funding goes away and private contractors emerge, competition returns.
5. *Leadership*
   - Innovative leaders must realize that the old way of doing business no longer exists after a disaster. Thus, leaders must have a new vision, think outside the box, and be innovative.
   - Innovative leaders must have the mindset of responding and rebuilding.
   - Innovative leaders will be affected too, and they need to take care of themselves to be effective leaders with all the complexities involved in disaster response and recovery.
   - Innovative leaders must drive the reconfiguration of core staff to shape a new way of doing business following a disaster.

The current effort of preparedness and training has significantly improved in the past few years. Today, health and human services professionals receive targeted crisis response preparation at the workplace and while attending college. For example, the Council for Social Work Education (CSWE) offers accreditation to social work programs across the country, ensuring that students receive a strong foundation in crisis response and learn how to work effectively with populations increasingly affected by bio-psycho-social stressors. Professionals become competent in four key elements to crisis interventions: (1) definition of a crisis as a state of disequilibrium; (2) delineation of the phases of a crisis: the hazardous event, vulnerable state, precipitating factor, state of active crisis, and reintegration or crisis resolution; (3) discussion of common and expectable emotional, cognitive, physical, and interpersonal responses to trauma; and (4) immediate, active, and direct interventions such as education, clarification, and reassurance about reactions to trauma designed to reduce symptoms, provide support, and return clients to functioning.

Vulnerable populations under the responsibility of mental health practitioners and law enforcement personnel need to have special considerations during emergency management care. One successful model, the crisis intervention team (CIT), is designed to improve both police officers and first responders to safely intervene, link patients with the appropriate mental health and other services, and, when possible, divert them from the criminal justice system (Watson, & Fulambarker, 2012). Individuals participating in CIT are carefully trained and coached, owing to the unpredictability of mental health patients going through crisis episodes. Training includes the recognition of symptoms of mental illness, mental health treatments, co-occurring disorders, legal issues, and de-escalating techniques.

Another cutting-edge method for avoiding and managing crises is the scenario-based training (SBT) model. The SBT model uses three components: scenario development (creating scenarios based on prior crisis events), delivery (teaching and demonstrating), and after-action reviews (discussion and learning). Moats, Chermack, and Dooley (2008) advise that the delivery components have a five-step approach: present the scenario, engage participants through discussions and role play, extract participants' reactions, note observations and highlight new learning, and coordinate adjustments. The SBT is a teaching method that provides a context in which individuals and groups can experience and interact during crisis response training.

One of the most exciting advances in crisis management and response is focusing on engineering new technologies. The most recent information and communication technology (ICT) instruments and methods are carefully designed by engineering research and tested by health care providers and practitioners. The purpose of ICT tools is to minimize the potential for bias, misinterpretation, or mistakes caused by human error when using and reading health devises. Frequently, ICT methods identify with ambulatory care risks to patients, and they are used in high-hazard work settings and rural and urban community clinics (Nemeth, Wears, Patel, Rosen, & Cook, 2011). The most current ICT learning practices and instruments utilized to improve the efficacy of treatment and patient management among health and human services professionals include:

1. *Cognitive tasks analysis (CTA)*. CTA has several techniques that can be used to assist human performance in cognitive work (i.e., problem-solving and decision-making). CTA methods are used to determine specific information requirements. The most common CTA methods are:
   a. *Cognitive walkthrough*. Scenarios are generated in order to simulate the problem-solving process that an individual follows.

   b. *Verbal protocol analysis.* A subject is asked to perform a task and say out loud what thoughts come to mind.

   c. *Critical decision method.* Knowledge elicitation methods such as retrospection, response to probe questions, and timeline construction serve as frameworks that can be reconfigured during the emergency situation.

2. *Interviews.* Structured or semistructured interviews apply the strength of interpersonal interaction in order to build a knowledge base.

3. *Artifact analysis.* Artifact analysis is a retrospective method to identify critical features of care when working with clients or in clinics. Cognitive artifacts (e.g., patient orders, laboratory test orders, transfer orders, computers and software applications, white board displays, schedules, checklists, and information system displays) are typically electronics based and are used to support important and difficult activities.

4. *Work domain analysis.* Constraint-based work domain analysis is used to depict the goals and constraints of diabetic care and other work domains that the observation data produce.

5. *Process tracing.* Process tracing is used to extract patterns from the phenomena of daily operations, followed by distilling those patterns into descriptions of functions that occur in the care settings.

6. *Rapid prototyping.* In rapid design prototyping, project teams create hard-copy examples of the cognitive aid concept and review them with patients and clinicians. Repeating this cycle frequently maximizes the fidelity of the representation design to patient and clinician needs.

7. *Evaluation.* Project teams frequently apply outcome-oriented evaluations, which assess the effectiveness of hard-copy prototype concepts. The lead researchers invites clinicians to obtain their guidance on what they find clinically relevant. This participatory design approach incorporates representative users in the design process.

8. *Telehealth.* Telehealth or tele-mental-health services are offered virtually through smart phone and/or computer as part of an emergency response (e.g., during bush fires, earthquakes, and mass shootings) with the goal of providing victims with access to counseling and crisis support centers. Structured phone callback models may be of limited value in the aftermath of disasters, and there is a need to support counselors by (1) refining existing models and (2) offering multiple virtual service delivery options.

9. *Computer-supported cooperative work (CSCW).* This innovated technology is drawn from the fields of crisis informatics and disaster

sociology to develop new computer models to assist during crisis management. A good example of CSCW is the Crisis Crowdsourcing Framework computer software, which features a systematic, problem-driven approach to determining the social, technological, organizational, and policy interfaces that could be involved and coordinated to manage a disaster (Liu, 2014).

10. *Videoconferencing technology.* Curricular development and training are key to building crisis intervention skills and appropriate emergency management coordination. One valuable technological method of delivering training and information is by videoconferencing. Videoconferencing is successfully used domestically and internationally. For example, US officials set up a series of videoconferences to train Chinese social work faculty and practitioners to develop capacity for relief efforts during earthquakes. Chinese crisis teams learned sociocultural theories of learning, theories of disaster management, crisis intervention theory, and crisis in context theory (Wyatt & Silver, 2015). These teams were able to quickly mobilize resources and knowledge to train other mental health professionals in China in techniques of disaster response, including Psychological First Aid (PFA) and SEMS.

A noteworthy source for training, research, and information is the Centers for Disease Control and Prevention (CDC). Among other activities in crisis management, they have created a model to prepare and build capacity within communities during a potential pandemic or other crisis emergency situations, which is called *crisis and emergency risk communication* (CERC). Quinn (2008) describes CERC as an effective model that has the capability to (1) increase community engagement, disaster risk education, and crisis and emergency risk communication; (2) prepare minority communities and government agencies to work effectively in a pandemic; (3) build the response capacity of each responder's organization and community; and (4) strengthen the trust among stakeholders during crisis response and recovery stages. When using CERC, emergency responders activate the following three intervention stages:

1. *Pre-event.* Focus is on building community partnerships, conducting needs assessments, and assessing the ability to respond to emergencies.
2. *Event.* Emphasizes appropriate response from each partner, coordinating services, and managing messaging and media outlets as well as evaluating damage caused by the crisis.

3. *Postevent.* Concentrates on developing the appropriate evaluation of services, conducting debriefings on the success of communication channels, and establishing future protocols.

Paying special attention to low-income and marginalized communities is particularly important because they exhibit health access gaps during pandemic outbreaks and other emergency circumstances. These communities have differences in social positions owing to lower income, education achievement, and occupation, which trigger disparities in exposure to viruses, susceptibility to contracting diseases, and receiving improper treatment, resulting in higher illness and death rates.

Information dissemination has become one of the major components during crisis management. During disasters, leaders must have the ability to share information with stakeholders and the general public promptly and fluently. This is not an easy task because events move rapidly, and there are a large number of organizations and stakeholders to coordinate efforts on a continuing basis. Seeger (2006) summarizes from field experts the 10 best crisis communication practices and processes before, during, and after emergencies:

1. *Process approaches and policy development.* Communication should not merely involve communicating decisions after they have been made; rather, risk and crisis communication is most effective when it is part of the decision process.
2. *Pre-event planning session.* Planning assists with identifying risk areas and corresponding risk reduction, presetting initial crisis responses, and identifying necessary response resources.
3. *Partnering with the public.* Public concerns about risk are legitimate. During a crisis, the public should be told what is happening, and organizations managing crises have a responsibility to share this information quickly and accurately.
4. *Understanding the audience.* Organizations managing risks or experiencing a crisis must listen to the concerns of the public, take these concerns into account, and respond accordingly.
5. *Honest, candid, and open approach.* Honesty builds credibility and trust before, during, and after a crisis. Openness about risks may promote an environment of risk-sharing, in which the public and agencies mutually accept responsibility for managing a risk.
6. *Collaboration and coordination with credible sources.* Establish strategic partnerships before a crisis occurs. These collaborative relationships allow agencies to coordinate their messages and

activities more effectively. It is important to maintain networks, and crisis planners and communicators should continuously seek to validate sources, choose subject-area experts, and develop positive relationships with stakeholders at all levels.

7. *Meeting the needs of the media and remaining accessible.* Best practices of crisis communicators are grounded in effective communication with multiple media outlets. The media are the primary conduit to the public and, during a crisis, are obligated to report accurately and completely. Use the media as a strategic partner and resource to manage the crisis.

8. *Communicating with compassion, concern, and empathy.* The designated spokespersons should demonstrate appropriate levels of compassion, concern, and empathy. These characteristics significantly enhance the credibility of the message and the messenger.

9. *Accept uncertainty and ambiguity.* Risks always include some level of uncertainty. Warnings and recalls often must be issued regularly and consistently.

10. *Messages of self-efficacy.* The self-efficacy communication can help restore some sense of calm and control over an uncertain and threatening situation.

One final successful public health infrastructure and communication model we will briefly review is the New Jersey Department of Health and Senior Services' Health Educator/Risk Communicator (HERC) program. HERC was formed after the September 2011 terrorist attacks by a trained diverse group of health and communications professionals in emergency communication. These individuals provide crisis information regarding public health threats and their role has expanded from bioterrorism to all-hazards approach and emerging infections public health preparedness, including pandemic influenza (Taylor, Miro, Bookbinder, & Slater, 2008).

Building Support Systems Before Disasters Occur

Innovative leaders prepare to manage crises effectively by first producing an emergency and safety plan, which will define the organization's own internal readiness and its commitment and role when partnering and networking with other agencies to respond to a crisis. Cavanaugh et al. (2008) recommend that leaders and organizations prepare for disasters centering on five key elements: people (focus on keeping people safe), experience (know what to do during the crisis), planning (create a plan with other organizations), decisiveness (be decisive and use clear communications), and execution (invoke the safety and emergency plan and monitor developments).

The emergency and safety plan identifies the roles of key respondents within organizations. Most agencies use SEMS, which is a fundamental structure for the response phase of emergency management. SEMS unifies all elements of emergency management responders into a single integrated system and standardizes the following four key elements:

1. *Incident command system (ICS)*—a field-level emergency response system based on management by objectives. Usually one person/ organization is selected to lead each ICS position (Figure 13.1).
2. *Multiple interagency coordination*—agencies working together to coordinate allocations of resources and emergency response activities
3. *Mutual aid*—a coordinated system for obtaining additional emergency resources from nonaffected jurisdictions
4. *Operational area concept*—in which each region or subdivision coordinates damage information, resource requests, and emergency response

Nonetheless, converting safety and emergency plans into practice can be difficult and cumbersome. According to McConnell and Drennan (2006), leaders can encounter four key difficulties as they prepare for a catastrophe or disaster: (1) large demands are placed on resources (time, talent, and treasure); (2) responding to crisis is not a linear situation, and chaos usually erupts before plans can be put into place; (3) integration of multiple parts and organizations can be fragmented because competing interests; and (4) preparing through

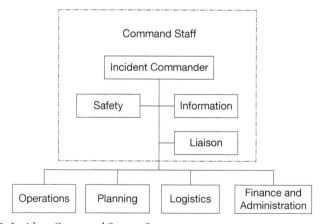

Figure 13.1 Incident Command System Structure.

training and exercises becomes costly and time-consuming, and many organizations may not have adequate resources to invest on an ongoing basis.

Today, because of the safety issues concerning terrorism and other threats in the workplace and public institutions, each safety and emergency plan can be adapted to the type of organization. For example, public and private schools write their comprehensive safety and emergency plans in collaboration with other agencies to prepare for a natural or human-made disasters. To be able to revise plans annually, school personnel must partner with other agencies regularly. This preparation effort includes establishing a cohesive multidisciplinary crisis team that is in constant communication throughout the year. Brock (2013) suggests that crisis teams focus on increasing competency in eight safety and emergency elements:

1. Develop a comprehensive safety and emergency school plan, including drills to prepare for disasters;
2. Integrate planning with community-based emergency response services;
3. Assess vulnerabilities and the traumatic potential of crisis events to school personnel, children, and families;
4. Protect physical and psychological safety;
5. Promote recovery and a return to learning through school-wide, classroom-based, and individualized interventions;
6. Provide care for school staff and caregivers;
7. Align crisis prevention and intervention services with existing delivery models; and
8. Support ongoing positive behavior and school culture.

Furthermore, crisis response teams must partner with mental health professionals during the planning, management, and postdisaster phases. Any catastrophic event produces traumatic symptoms in both victims and responders. Simultaneously, we must take care of those individuals who have already been diagnosed with severe mental illnesses. These individuals may be living at home under the care of family members or residing in mental health boarding institutions. Milligan and McGuinness (2009) suggest that organizational leaders and crisis teams keep in mind four issues during the emergency planning process. Victims and/or patients during a disaster often (1) experience acute mental distress and exacerbation of their illness, (2) need to re-establish a connection with a stable social environment and a sense of community, and (3) must be assessed by mental health clinicians and have access to their medications; in addition (4), those individuals with more severe conditions, including suicidal ideation and other high-risk behaviors, should be prioritized in receiving the appropriate care.

Social workers also play a key role during crisis management. These helping professionals receive supervised training addressing a continuum of local, national, and international dimensions of practice, as well as individual, family, organizational, community, and policy-based interventions. Rogge (2003) explains that social workers' unique knowledge, skills, and abilities can be utilized during a crisis as follows:

1. Define disaster and traumatic events and understand their nature;
2. Help communities assess, plan, and act to reduce damage and loss;
3. Respond to disaster and traumatic events with knowledge and skill sets that minimize error;
4. Engage in service delivery systems and community actions to improve the quality of life;
5. Apply disaster and traumatic event–related knowledge and experience to improve crisis responses;
6. Create disaster management strategies at the individual, local, organizational, national, and international levels; and
7. Account for the needs of culturally diverse people and of vulnerable populations before, during, and after disasters.

In conclusion, it is critical that crisis teams evaluate and assess their performance regularly. One of the tools utilized to assess the reliability of public safety and emergency management systems is called Failure Mode Effects and Criticality Analysis (FMECA). The FMECA assessment model is built on the frameworks of probabilistic risk analysis, high-reliability organizations, and normal accidents. This model should be used by leaders and organizations during the preparedness phase as they put together their crisis response teams. According to Jackson, Sullivan, and Willis (2011), applying FMECA to a large-scale emergency or disaster response operation involves the following four steps:

1. *Define and map the system.* Identify what it means for each individual and organization to perform effectively.
2. *Identify failure modes.* Decipher which different parts of the system could break down and reduce their response performance.
3. *Assess the failure mode probability.* Estimate what can go wrong using empirical evidence based on the occurrence of failures from past responses.

4. *Assess failure mode severity and effect.* Assess how much failure damages crisis response outcomes and potential impact size to victims and responders.

Effective Crisis and Emergency Management Models

A main component of crisis and emergency management is the coordination of response and services before, during, and after disasters. Building successful multidisciplinary coalitions and crisis teams takes experience and resources. Participating individuals and organizations must be willing, capable, and able to engage and partner with other agencies. Most crisis and emergency coalitions sign a memorandum of understanding (MOU), delineating each organization's roles and responsibilities. In addition to the rescue and law enforcement involvement, these coalitions also focus on coordinating mental health efforts in response to a community in crisis. For example, Dodgen and associates (2002) summarized the importance of creating the Mental Health Community Response Coalition to support the short- and long-term mental health needs of those affected by the Pentagon attack on September 11, 2001. Coalition members have the opportunity to network and exchange information between military service providers, the ARC, local mental health agencies, and other groups. Key partnership features are inclusiveness of membership, flexibility and responsiveness, fluidity in communication, and a collaborative leadership. The results of these efforts are that individuals and families receive a coordinated response to their mental health needs and that the duplication of services is avoided.

After the coordination of services and emergency response roles become more defined, the next phase for crisis teams is to have the ability to immediate triage or debrief the emergency situation with the victims affected by the disaster. Effective triage or debriefing features a structured group process that responds to the cognitive, emotional, physical, and social reactions resulting from traumatic events. The seven components of an effective triage/debriefing session are to:

1. Assess the impact of the critical incident on survivors and response personnel;
2. Identify the critical issues surrounding the problem, particularly relating to safety and security;
3. Validate the importance of ventilation of thoughts, emotions, and experiences;

4. Anticipate and predict future reactions and responses;
5. Explore and review the event and the responses;
6. Attempt to bring closure to the event and to connect people to community resources; and
7. Emphasize that debriefing sessions assist people with making a re-entry back to their community or workplace (Dodgen, LaDue, & Kaul, 2002, p. 88).

Emergency mental health intervention for victims of disasters begins the moment the first responders arrive. Small details make big differences, including the use of verbal communication, body language, behavioral strategies, and interpersonal styles. The correct intervention strategies in the first few moments and hours of a crisis can profoundly influence the recovery of victims and survivors of catastrophic events. Additionally, Miller (2010) argues that there are six areas of potential debriefing model expansion:

1. Fostering greater connectedness with others;
2. Creating more heterogeneous debriefing groups;
3. Balancing the needs of individuals and different groups;
4. Re-evaluating the structure, sequence, timing, process, and metaphors of debriefings;
5. Fine-tuning the balance between spontaneity and predetermined formats; and
6. Ensuring equal access and services for all.

An innovative tool in crisis and emergency response is the PFA Practice Guide, which was developed to support crisis teams in multiple settings. The National Child Traumatic Stress Network and the National Center for PTSD created PFA with a set of guiding principles and core actions, providing guidance for practitioners who respond to immediate mental health needs of children, adults, and elders who have experienced or are experiencing a disaster. The PFA was created from successful evidence-based interventions with the goal of reducing initial distress caused by catastrophic events and fostering short-, intermediate-, and long-term adaptive functioning. The PFA's four objectives are to be (1) consistent with research-based evidence on risk and resiliency following trauma; (2) applicable and practical; (3) appropriate for developmental levels across the life span; and (4) culturally informed and deliverable in a flexible manner (Vernberg et al., 2008).

The PFA intervention strategies are grouped into the following eight conceptual modules or core actions:

1. *Contact and engagement.* Respond to and initiate contacts in a nonintrusive, compassionate, and helpful manner; maintain a calm presence; and be informed about cultural norms in preparing to interact with affected individuals.
2. *Safety and comfort.* Implement strategies to enhance the survivor's immediate and ongoing safety and to help provide both physical and emotional comfort.
3. *Stabilization.* Provide a variety of strategies to help calm and orient emotionally overwhelmed children, adults, and elders as necessary.
4. *Information gathering.* Collect information to identify immediate needs and concerns following three specific courses of action:
   a. Identify problems that require immediate attention;
   b. Monitor high-risk individuals for future intervention; and
   c. Identify target risk and resilience factors that can be addressed immediately.
5. *Practical assistance.* Apply practical assistance strategies to help children, adults, and elders identify their most immediate needs or problems and where to receive needed services.
6. *Connection with social supports.* Assist children, adolescents, adults, and elders in enhancing their access to primary support persons or other sources of support.
7. *Information on coping.* Provide psychoeducation to survivors about stress reactions and coping to reduce distress and promote adaptive functioning.
8. *Linkage with collaborative services.* Be a liaison for survivors and victims to available services needed at the time and in the future.

A large number of crisis teams also prefer to use the triage assessment system (TAS) to assist during crisis interventions. The TAS is a practical tool to assess affective, behavioral, and cognitive reactions of individuals to crisis events. Myer and Conte (2006) recommend TAS to crisis management participants because it (1) offers clinicians an understanding of their clients' reactions; (2) provides a quick, accurate, and ready-to-use method, which is part of the intervention process; (3) monitors client's progress; and (4) includes the triage assessment form in the package. Furthermore, the TAS primarily focuses on clients' behavioral and cognitive reactions. Behavioral reactions include immobility (feeling stuck in this situation, helpless), avoidance (denying or escaping consequences), and approach (wanting to resolve the situation in the best possible way). The cognitive reactions are transgressional (demeaning offense against oneself), threat (impending catastrophe is approaching), and loss (feeling that the past cannot be recovered). During a crisis, behavioral and cognitive reactions play within four domains: physical/safety, psychological/self-concept, social/community, and moral/spiritual.

The final crisis management strategy to be reviewed in this section is the assessment, crisis intervention, and trauma treatment (ACT) model. The ACT model may be thought of as a sequential set of assessments and intervention strategies following a disaster. It presents a simple conceptual three-stage framework (assessment, crisis intervention, and trauma treatment) and a seven-step intervention model (biopsychosocial assessment, establishment of rapport, problem identification, exploring feelings and emotions, generating alternative solutions, formulating a strategy, and following the plan) that assist mental health professionals in providing acute crisis and trauma treatment services (Roberts, 2002). The ACT integrates various assessment and triage protocols to diffuse stress, anxiety, tension, and other adverse emotions experienced by victims during crisis.

Collaboration and Innovation Elements to Manage Disasters

Crisis management respondents need to develop a special trust with one another. These multidisciplinary teams come together to coordinate emergency efforts under stressful situations, aiming to help victims and survivors get back to normalcy. One of the best strategies for building trust is for people to get to know each other during regular crisis training sessions and emergency response drills. During this time, team members have the opportunity to clarify their roles, which may enable collaborative working practices among organizations involved in emergency management and thus facilitate multiagency coordination (Curnin, Owen, Paton, Trist, & Parsons, 2015). Trust is also built by application of an established collaboration model that aims to develop close cooperation between communities, law enforcement personnel, and local media stations. Granatt (2004) argues that a solid collaborative model with clear communication systems goes beyond protocols and procedures: "[T]hese systems can create a permanent strength essential to successful risk communications: A culture of personal commitment, mutual understanding, realistic expectations, and trust" (p. 361).

Innovative leaders are aware of the remarkable benefits of utilizing strengths-based approaches (SBAs) to crisis management and recovery. Slawinski (2005) explains that there is solid record of SBAs being successfully implemented with vulnerable populations who have experienced trauma. There are eight strength-based practices that can be applied during a disaster:

1. Each individual's response is unique. Be prepared to adapt interventions to meet individual needs.
2. Individuals are expert in their own recovery process. Focus on reassuring coping skills and reconnecting with their support systems.
3. Individual define their own needs. Use natural recovery processes without artificial interventions.
4. Individual should take their own time to express their emotional and psychological experiences.
5. Individual will eventually reconnect with their own past abilities, skills, and strengths.
6. Individuals will determine what level of support and resources is appropriate. Support systems and resources may be used in very different ways and at different times.
7. Individual should be provided with a means of self-evaluation to assess the need for future interventions.
8. Individuals have their own cultural values, and we need to honor them during the recovery process.

Social media has the potential to be utilized as a practical and innovative tool during crisis management. Today's world has become highly dependent and reliant on social media outlets to share information instantly and to mobilize large numbers of people swiftly. One of the major challenges for crisis management during a disaster is integrating and disseminating information (e.g., places to avoid, available resources, list of casualties, lost and found items, affected streets and neighborhood). Affected citizens can become the main source of this information using social media outlets, and then official responders can take that information to disseminate messages through regular channels such as television, radio, SMS (text messages), and Internet websites.

Another example shared by Maresh-Fuehrer and Smith (2016) shows the following benefits and advances of social media's innovative tools for crisis prevention and intervention:

1. Crisis managers are becoming increasingly attracted to social media because of the ability to expand the communication options available to organizations.
2. Studies have identified a variety of benefits and challenges presented by the use of social media for crisis communication.

3. Two new social media mapping applications, SituMap and PhotoSorter, were created to cultivate participation, collaboration, and conversation during a crisis.

Nonetheless, Hiltz, Diaz, and Mark (2011) caution that there is a need to find out how these two modes of communication (traditional media and social media) can be integrated efficiently, taking into account that their information delivery is based on different sources, perspectives, and styles. Thus, crisis management teams need more assurances before they can consider social media a reliable and trustworthy source of information because the content may not be accurate or verifiable at times. For example, Wyatt and Silver (2015) demonstrate how crisis teams collaborate to ensure the safety of affected residents in three domains: individuals, children, and families (Table 13.1).

In closing, innovative leaders and crisis teams are always working to improve their emergency procedures and practices. Nonetheless, the analysis and evaluation of emergency response operations is not an easy task, especially when the operation involves multidisciplinary teams and organizations. Abrahamsson, Hassel, and Tehler (2010) identified four key challenges or issues that crisis response teams have to overcome when building an effective evaluation framework: (1) values governing the evaluation, (2) complexity of the systems involved, (3) validity of the information on which the analysis and evaluation are based, and (4) limiting conditions under which the emergency response system operates. Thus, crisis response evaluations should provide a better understanding of how

Table 13.1 GOALS AND OBJECTIVES FOR INDIVIDUALS, CHILDREN, AND FAMILIES AFFECTED BY DISASTERS

Individuals	Children	Families
• Individual responses to disaster • Phases of disaster recovery • Psychological aid assessment and intervention • Vicarious traumatization • Special problems including suicidality, concrete needs • Do's and don'ts • Experiential role-plays and case scenarios	• Developmental considerations • Symptoms of stress and reactions to trauma in children • Play as a modality for communication and intervention • Intervention skills with children to educate, improve functioning and coping, and mobilize supports	• Issues for families • Family reactions to disasters • Family relationship changes • Loss and mourning • Ill/disabled family members • Family resilience • Steps in recovery for each member of the family

an emergency response system functioned and should identify the potential events and/or circumstances that could significantly improve its performance. A key aspect of evaluating the crisis team response is analyzing and visualizing how the actions of a certain actor in the emergency response operation are related to the performance of the overall crisis response system.

CHAPTER DISCUSSION QUESTIONS

1. This chapter has outlined several models that can be applied in the management of crisis response. Describe one of these and note the strengths and limitations.
2. What do you see as the role of health and human services leaders in emergencies or crisis situations?
3. Collaboration is a key element to responding to a crisis or emergency situation. Discuss what elements are necessary in order to have successful collaborative partners.
4. Innovative models that use social media and technology can facilitate the coordination of services and information sharing. What do you see as the potential challenges with these types of interventions?
5. Describe your organizations' emergency preparedness plan and the assigned roles and responsibilities of leaders as well as personnel.
6. Describe your own (personal) emergency preparedness plan for home and workplace. If you do not have one, consider developing one.
7. Read the leader profile and case study in the Appendix to this chapter. Note innovative ideas and practices and see what aspects of the case you can connect to the contents of the chapter and/or the overall book.

REFERENCES

Abrahamsson, M., Hassel, H., & Tehler, H. (2010). Towards a system-oriented framework for analysing and evaluating emergency response. *Journal of Contingencies and Crisis Management, 18*(1), 14–25.

Baldoni, J. (2011, January). How a good leader reacts to a crisis. *Harvard Business Review*. Retrieved from https://hbr.org/2011/01/how-a-good-leader-reacts-to-a

Brock, S. E. (2013). Preparing for the school crisis response. *Handbook of crisis counseling, intervention and prevention in the schools, 3*, 19–30.

Cavanaugh, J. C., Gelles, M. G., Reyes, G., Civiello, C. L., & Zahner, M. (2008). Effectively planning for and managing major disasters. *Psychologist-Manager Journal, 11*(2), 221–239.

Curnin, S., Owen, C., Paton, D., Trist, C., & Parsons, D. (2015). Role clarity, swift trust and multi-agency coordination. *Journal of Contingencies and Crisis Management, 23*(1), 29–35.

Dodgen, D., LaDue, L. R., & Kaul, R. E. (2002). Coordinating a local response to a national tragedy: Community mental health in Washington, DC after the Pentagon attack. *Military Medicine, 167*, 87–89.

Everly, G. (2002). Thoughts on training guidelines in emergency mental health and crisis intervention. *International Journal of Emergency Mental Health, 4*(3), 139–142.

Gelman, C. R., & Mirabito, D. M. (2005). Practicing what we teach: Using case studies from 9/11 to teach crisis intervention from a generalist perspective. *Journal of Social Work Education, 41*(3), 479–494.

Granatt, M. (2004). On trust: Using public information and warning partnerships to support the community response to an emergency. *Journal of Communication Management, 8*(4), 354–365.

Hiltz, S. R., Diaz, P., & Mark, G. (2011). Introduction: Social media and collaborative systems for crisis management. *ACM Transactions on Computer-Human Interaction, 18*(4), 1–6.

Jackson, B. A., Sullivan Faith, K., & Willis, H. H. (2011). Are we prepared? Using reliability analysis to evaluate emergency response systems. *Journal of Contingencies and Crisis Management, 19*(3), 147–157.

Liu, S. B. (2014). Crisis crowdsourcing framework: Designing strategic configurations of crowdsourcing for the emergency management domain. *Computer Supported Cooperative Work (CSCW), 23*(4–6), 389–443.

Maresh-Fuehrer, M., & Smith, R. (2016). Social media mapping innovations for crisis prevention, response, and evaluation. *Computers in Human Behavior, 54*, 620–629.

McConnell, A., & Drennan, L. (2006). Mission impossible? Planning and preparing for crisis. *Journal of Contingencies and Crisis Management, 14*(2), 59–70.

Miller, L. (2010). On-scene crisis intervention: Psychological guidelines and communication strategies for first responders. *International Journal of Emergency Mental Health, 12*(1), 11–19.

Milligan, G., & McGuinness, T. M. (2009). Mental health needs in a post-disaster environment. *Journal of Psychosocial Nursing and Mental Health Services, 47*(9), 23–30.

Moats, J. B., Chermack, T. J., & Dooley, L. M. (2008). Using scenarios to develop crisis managers: Applications of scenario planning and scenario-based training. *Advances in Developing Human Resources, 10*(3), 397–424.

Myer, R. A., & Conte, C. (2006). Assessment for crisis intervention. *Journal of Clinical Psychology, 62*(8), 959–970.

Nemeth, C., Wears, R. L., Patel, S., Rosen, G., & Cook, R. (2011). Resilience is not control: Healthcare, crisis management, and ICT. *Cognition, Technology & Work, 13*(3), 189–202.

Quinn, S. C. (2008). Crisis and emergency risk communication in a pandemic: A model for building capacity and resilience of minority communities. *Health Promotion Practice, 9*(4), 18S–25S.

Pearson, C. M., & Clair, J. A. (1998). Reframing crisis management. *Academy of Management Review, 23*(1), 59–76.

Roberts, A. R. (2002). Assessment, crisis intervention, and trauma treatment: The integrative ACT intervention model. *Brief Treatment and Crisis Intervention, 2*(1), 1–21.

Rogge, M. E. (2003). The future is now: Social work, disaster management, and traumatic stress in the 21st century. *Journal of Social Service Research, 30*(2), 1–6.

Seeger, M. W. (2006). Best practices in crisis communication: An expert panel process. *Journal of Applied Communication Research, 34*(3), 232–244.

Slawinski, T. (2005). A strengths-based approach to crisis response. *Journal of Workplace Behavioral Health, 21*(2), 79–88.

Smith, S. L. (2012). Coping with disaster: Lessons learned from executive directors of nonprofit organizations (NPOs) in New Orleans following Hurricane Katrina. *Administration in Social Work, 36*(4), 359–389.

Taylor, L., Miro, S., Bookbinder, S. H., & Slater, T. (2008). Innovative infrastructure in New Jersey: Using health education professionals to inform and educate during a crisis. *Health Promotion Practice, 9*(4), 88S–95S.

Vernberg, E. M., Steinberg, A. M., Jacobs, A. K., Brymer, M. J., Watson, P. J., Osofsky, J. D., Layne, C.M., Pynoos, R.S., & Ruzek, J. I. (2008). Innovations in disaster mental health: Psychological first aid. *Professional Psychology: Research and Practice, 39*(4), 381–388.

Watson, A. C., & Fulambarker, A. J. (2012). The crisis intervention team model of police response to mental health crises: A primer for mental health practitioners. *Best Practices in Mental Health: An International Journal, 8*(2), 71–81.

Wyatt, J., & Silver, P. (2015). Cross-cultural crisis intervention training via videoconferencing. *International Social Work, 58*(5), 646–658.

APPENDIX
Featured Leader: Kristi Batiste

If we are a product of our environment, then Kristi Hofstetter Batiste is a product of Orange County, CA. Kristi is third generation to Orange County. As a graduate of local schools and programs, Kristi has always been involved in her local community. Kristi "works to support her volunteer habit."

As program director for the Orange County Department of Education Crisis Response Network, Kristi strives to support of continuum of care for the student population. When a traumatic event or emergency happens in the community, she enables networks to support the student, family, and school communities, helping to provide better coping mechanisms and healing as those affected begin to move forward.

In 2011 Kristi became one of the Crisis Team Managers for the Trauma Intervention Program (TIP) in Orange County. Kristi works with volunteers to develop training, support, and efficiency when dealing with daily disasters in Orange County. TIP Orange County collaborates with area law enforcement in the county to support the victims and families of tragedy. TIP serves 23 jurisdictions in the county, including the Orange County Sheriff's Department and the Orange County Coroner. TIP volunteers are on call 24/7/365 to respond within 20 minutes of dispatch to the survivors and family of any traumatic event. TIP acts as a force multiplier, allowing first responders to focus on the scene, investigation, and victim while knowing the family, bystanders, and witnesses are being supported. TIP volunteers respond to any situation, any time of day, and anywhere that local agencies deem safe. They support survivors of suicide, overdose, accidents, and any other traumatic event that may occur in the county.

Kristi started volunteering in Trauma Intervention Program Inc. in 2005, doing community outreach, mentoring new volunteers, dispatching teams, and briefing first responders in and around Orange County. She brought her crisis dog to TIP, where together they created and implemented the model for dog teams to help serve in the program. She believes that no one should have to be alone during certain times, and for those times there is TIP.

Kristi is a retired educator who taught adjudicated minors for the Orange County Department of Education, implementing and developing award-winning service learning projects with her students in and around Orange County. During this tenure Kristi collaborated on a daily basis with program and agency partners (Health Care Agency, Orange County Probation, and local law enforcement, among others) to ensure success of the students and program. Kristi worked as a freelance writer at the University of Santa Clara, infusing character and ethics into the curriculum.

Kristi is currently working on her master's degree in Emergency Services and Disaster Management at California State University, Long Beach. She resides in Southern California with her family and two dogs.

LEADERSHIP PROFILE FOR KRISTI BATISTE

Share your professional background and experience

My background is in a couple of different fields. I come from a background in business and being self-employed doing consulting work and then a lot of experience from the nonprofit human services side. I also went into educating minors, and on top of that I have written curriculum and development. I have been working with the Trauma Intervention Program (TIP) organization for the past 15 years. I started as a volunteer doing trauma response and for five years have managed the trauma team, and now I'm with the Crisis Response Network (CRN), managing the network side.

The objective of our program (TIP) is that we put a volunteer to work side-by-side with law enforcement within 20 minutes of a crisis call coming into our center. It can be any sort of traumatic situation. Whether someone wakes up in the morning to find that their loved one has passed away, or a mass critical event, or a traffic accident, but I would say that 80% of what we do is helping someone when they wake up in the morning to find that their loved one is deceased.

I am a founding member of TIP. We train volunteers who are paraprofessionals. We conduct training for our volunteers, and our founder was a clinician and so he founded the organization from the mental health side of it. We do 55 hours of training for our volunteers to even walk out the door and start taking calls. Once they are able to start going out on calls, they're paired with a mentor, and then they're also in a three-month field training where they're always taking a call with a partner or another veteran volunteer. As part of that program, once they're done with a call, they have to go through a brief debriefing session within 24 hours of taking a call. So we make sure our paraprofessionals and even the professionals with mental health backgrounds go through the same debrief regardless of whether it's a very small basic call or a really big call (as in large disaster or shooting).

In your experience, what are the top three to five leadership attributes someone in the health and human services field should develop? Share an example of when you have used one or more of these attributes/skills in your work

> *Trust.* I think the biggest one is trust, and trusting one's team, and trusting yourself as a leader to make the right call for the situation. Trusting your team or whomever is working with you to go out to fulfill the obligation of whatever situation or whatever framework is in place. I have a team of volunteers and people who all have roles to fulfill, and if I start to get in-volved, I can sometimes mess up the system instead of just trusting that they're going do what they need to do and communicate it back to me and letting things unfold the way that they're supposed to.

Communication. Communication, communication, communication. The biggest one that stumps me every time is always communication issues. I can think that I'm communicating clearly, but unless somebody is hearing or receiving my messages clearly, there's a communication issue. I think that's where I get into the biggest stumbling block.

Flexibility. Need to be flexible at all times.

Collaboration. The ability to collaborate. Collaboration in terms of working with other groups, working with other networks, and having the trust that others are going to fulfill their roles and everybody can stay focused.

Knowing yourself and being open to feedback. I think being open, being honest, and knowing oneself, and really looking at every given situation as an opportunity. For example, where we have a response, we have a call, and I try to go back and just evaluate how the situation went. Not just from an organizational standpoint, but also as an individual. What did I do well, and even taking that one step forward, what worked, what didn't work, where were our opportunities, so basically doing a SWOT (strengths, weaknesses, opportunities, and threats) evaluation, but then also trying to take it one step forward and having my team evaluate me. It's easy for me to evaluate other people, but if I give them the opportunity to look at what I did well as a leader and what I could have done better, this provides an opportunity for dialogue, as well as an opportunity to just see something from a different person's perspective.

A CASE STUDY BY KRISTI BATISTE

Our world is changing, and it seems that things are getting larger and more complex and sometimes more intense. I think one of the challenges that we have is overlooking the smaller situations. An example is that in the last couple months, we had a mass shooting, which had a trickledown effect of what was massive in terms of the direct victims at the scene and the secondary and third victims as they came back into our region and county. Followed by two or three fires that came up, and I think that we started overlooking the smaller situations. While there are major events, there are still daily events that we can't lose sight of because if we can't handle those, it is going to be harder to handle the bigger picture.

Here is a recent example. Orange County right now seems to be having a massive amount of suicides, and statistically I can't even go into it, but a school-based suicide is hugely traumatic to a family and to a system. Sometimes these situations might get overlooked when all of the other big events are going on.

Consider a child's suicide, this is a hugely traumatic event for the family, but the response, systemically speaking, was maybe not as big as it could have been because the world was literally on fire this fall. So I think just mainly making sure that victims are heard and putting little bit more emphasis in the system to respond with a greater sense of urgency to their needs. If a person is going through a crisis, that's their personal experience of that crisis at that one given time. The system is used to handling crises, and yet people who feel like they're being overlooked by the system may not be able to recover from that crisis as well. I'm thinking this fall of the shootings and all of the things that were going on, that this particular family's crisis with the suicide was almost being overlooked by the system because massive events were happening at the same time.

Response wise, I think that there are a couple of different things that need to be happening. First and foremost is getting people connected with the services that align to their needs as quickly as possible, if the people are accepting of services. We can refer people through the roof, but if they're not accepting of that, that's one challenge that goes with destigmatizing reaching out for help. Stigma often prevents people from reaching out for any sort of therapeutic help or social service help because people don't understand the merits of it. I think a lot of education on that side and also helping our responders desensitize to the big events, that is, helping them not overlook the smaller events that occur to people on a daily basis, are necessary. If we start to consider that large events are the norm, then we forget that is not our norm, nor should it be our norm. Trying to change our mindset as to what are the normal events that are happening, those that are not in the media, that we don't hear about every day, and putting some more focus on that to help people recover from the smaller events a little bit better.

It is hard because when there are big events that are occurring, when we go to the gym or wherever and it's on the news 24/7, you sometimes can't get away from it. We forget that all over our counties and in our daily lives, people are being affected by things that aren't insignificant, they're very significant events, but they kind of get overshadowed by the large events. I think this has other consequences as well, where people feel like they can't stand up and say, *hey, this is happening to me* because this bigger media event is occurring, so then there's that challenge of feeling, like, *well, why should I reach out for help when all of these other people were just involved in something that was massive and critical?* You start looking at other people and you forget, but it's like, *well, I'm still hurting, I just had a big loss, I just had a big event happen in my world,* and that this is still something that people need to reach out for. It is almost like people don't feel worthy of help. And this also happens to our first responders and team members, where something happens to them, but they're comparing themselves to some other larger traumatic event that happened on their shift, and they say to themselves, *gosh, you know I really got nothing on my plate in comparison to these other people*. But I remind them that they still have to reach out and take care of themselves, even if they think that the event is comparatively speaking not as bad.

How does a person get referred to TIP and to the Crisis Response Network?

There are two ways. I will answer this from two different programmatic standpoints. On the TIP side of things, we are solely invited by first responders and by emergency personnel. So, if the first responder is going to an accident, to a home, or an emergency room, we may get called in by the hospital or by a surgical floor. If the first responders see something that might be considered traumatic to an individual or family, or they just see that a family needs additional support, they'll call in our team. We are there within 20 minutes of that call to be on the forefront of the intervention. The TIP program is more like the paramedics' response because we're not there for long-term support, we're there to stabilize the individual or family, to get them to a point that they can start accepting resources, and get them to their next step. We may stay until the individual's family members arrive or until their support system gets there. Our volunteers on the front end with a family work probably four to six hours in the initial hours after the traumatic event. Now, if its something's big, like the Las Vegas shooting, our chapter in Vegas, they were there for three or four days. It just kind of depends on the situation, but for the basic stuff, our team members are there for four to six hours, and they're referred by law enforcement.

On the CRN side of things, referrals come in a couple of different ways. They may get a call from the county coroner or law enforcement, if the coroner is going out on a death that relates to a student, once they've done their investigation, they'll refer the student's school information to CRN. Our agency (TIP) partners with others out with CRN and others in the field. So on the TIP side, we go out on a call that relates to a student or a young person who has passed away, or if it's a critical event, we will call CRN to alert them of that event so that they can talk to the school. CRN is school based. So they only respond to calls that are related to school-aged kids in Orange County. Not only do they train school-based responders to do responses, but then they'll also go in and help the school respond if something's happened to one of their students. Just to clarify, TIP and CRN are two different organizations, but because in recent years with the ability to network and build relationships, we realized there is a greater continuum of care if we have a combined response. So if TIP is working on the scene with a student, or teacher, if we can get that information to the

CRN as quickly as possible, they can then be reaching out to the school some-times in real time. So then the school as a whole is able to better prepare them-selves and respond almost immediately. That intervention can sometimes go on for two or three days while they are talking with affected students, and they follow the students' day, so they are interacting in every class that the students are in and talking to the kids in those classes, and then also working with the staff to support them. Sometimes they can be on-site for two, three, or four days consecutively.

CRN is funded by the Orange County Health Care Agency. They are grant funded and based out of the Orange County Department of Education, and they are part of the Safe Schools Division. Not only are they doing the work of crisis response, they also do antibullying campaigns, run drug and alcohol programs, so there are multiple programs that they offer such as suicide pre-vention, parenting programs, and mental health clinicians on-site. CRN has a big network of professionals and paraprofessionals who go into schools for a variety of different reasons. While TIP is a nonprofit and it's funded through contract cities. They get their funding from the cities that they serve, as well as from grants and donations.

How do you personally cope with all of these crises?

It is hard. I try to stay as mentally healthy as much as I possibly can. It is kind of one of those situations where it's "do as I say, not do as I do." I have to re-ally make a concerted effort to make sure that I have support and a "dumping ground" of my own. I also need to make sure that I am doing positive things for myself and really hitting that self-care side of things because unless I do that, I am not going to have longevity in this field. For me, it is hard to look at the various situations that are going on; however, I have the ability to compart-mentalize, which is probably not the best thing in the world to do, but where I get the most concerned is for the volunteers and the staff that respond. I go out on responses, too, and I typically get the big ones, but it's harder for me just to watch our volunteers deal with some of the crazy things that they go out on. I try to support them, but I also make sure that I shift myself in, that is, I make sure that I take calls myself, because it takes me back to the roots as to why I got into this in the beginning and that's just to support somebody who's in the midst of a tragedy and they don't know what to do next. To be able to go in, and walk them through that process, and be a support network for them, it keeps me grounded. It is fulfilling to me. I try to shift myself in at least once a month, if not twice a month, just to stay grounded in the why am I here and why I do this, to interact with responders, to interact with our public, and to know that they have resources that they wouldn't have if somebody wasn't there for them.

CASE DISCUSSION POINTS

1. This innovative leader describes the large traumatic events, mass critical events, versus the everyday traumatic events that could affect an individual or a family. She speaks to responders focusing on the larger events and sometimes losing sight of the smaller events that need just as much attention. What are some ways that a social architect would help the responders to focus on the smaller everyday events so that everyone feels that they are deserving of help?
2. Self-care is mentioned as being important in this line of work. What are some of the self-care activities that you engage in on a regular basis?
3. This innovative leader is concerned about her staff's reactions to responding to crises. How would you support your staff?
4. Interagency collaboration (e.g., between TIP and CRN) and how each organization can offer different services in the context of a traumatic event are described. Think about an organization that you know or work for, that could partner with another to provide more comprehensive and responsive services. What would be the challenges and how can a social architect overcome these?

Appendices: Leader Assessment Instruments

A. LEADER–MEMBER EXCHANGE (LMX) SURVEY

LMX 7 Questionnaire

Instructions: This questionnaire contains items that ask you to describe your relationship with either your leader or one of your subordinates. For each of the items, indicate the degree to which you think the item is true for you by circling one of the responses that appear below the item.

1. Do you know where you stand with your leader (follower) . . . [and] do you usually know how satisfied your leader (follower) is with what you do?

Rarely	Occasionally	Sometimes	Fairly often	Very often
1	2	3	4	5

2. How well does your leader (follower) understand your job problems and needs?

Not a bit	A little	A fair amount	Quite a bit	A great deal
1	2	3	4	5

3. How well does your leader (follower) recognize your potential?

Not at all	A little	Moderately	Mostly	Fully
1	2	3	4	5

4. Regardless of how much formal authority your leader (follower) has built into his or her position, what are the chances that your leader (follower) would use his or her power to help you solve problems in your work?

None	Small	Moderate	High	Very high
1	2	3	4	5

5. Again, regardless of the amount of formal authority your leader (follower) has, what are the chances that he or she would "bail you out" at his or her expense?

None	Small	Moderate	High	Very high
1	2	3	4	5

6. I have enough confidence in my leader (follower) that I would defend and justify his or her decision if he or she were not present to do so.

Strongly disagree	Disagree	Neutral	Agree	Strongly agree
1	2	3	4	5

7. How would you characterize your working relationship with your leader (follower)?

Extremely ineffective	Worse than average	Average	Better than average	Extremely effective
1	2	3	4	5

By completing the LMX 7, you can gain a fuller understanding of how LMX theory works. The score you obtain on the questionnaire reflects the quality of your leader–member relationships and indicates the degree to which your relationships are characteristic of partnerships, as described in the LMX model.

You can complete the questionnaire both as a leader and as a subordinate. In the leader role, you would complete the questionnaire multiple times, assessing the quality of the relationships you have with each of your subordinates. In the subordinate role, you would complete the questionnaire based on the leaders to whom you report.

Scoring Interpretation

Although the LMX 7 is most commonly used by researchers to explore theoretical questions, you can also use it to analyze your own leadership style. You can interpret your LMX 7 scores using the following guidelines: very high = 30–35, high = 25–29, moderate = 20–24, low = 15–19, and very low = 7–14. Scores in the upper ranges indicate stronger, higher-quality leader–member exchanges (e.g., in-group members), whereas scores in the lower ranges indicate exchanges of lesser quality (e.g., out-group members).

Source: Reprinted from Graen, G. B., & Uhl-Bien, M. (1995). Relationship-based approach to leadership: Development of Leader–Member Exchange (LMX) Theory of leadership over 25 years: Applying a multi-level, multi-domain perspective." *Leadership Quarterly,* 6(2), 219–247. Copyright © 1995. Reprinted with permission from Elsevier Science.

B. IMPLEMENTATION LEADERSHIP SCALE

Implementation Leadership Scale (ILS)

The ILS, developed by Gregory A. Aarons (gaarons@ucsd.edu), Mark Ehrhart (mehrhart@mail.sdsu.edu), and Lauren Farahnak (lfarahnak@ucsd.edu), assesses the degree to which a leader is proactive, knowledgeable, supportive, and perseverant in regard to evidence-based practice implementation. There are two versions of the ILS: one for staff to report about their supervisor/leader, and another for supervisors/leaders to report about themselves.

Source: Aarons, G.A., Ehrhart, M.G., & Farahnak, L.R. (2014). The Implementation Leadership Scale (ILS): Development of a Brief Measure of Unit Level Implementation Leadership. *Implementation Science.* For information contact Gregory Aarons at gaarons@ucsd.edu.

Staff Version

Please indicate the extent to which you agree with each statement.

0	1	2	3	4
Not at all	Slight extent	Moderate extent	Great extent	Very great extent

PROACTIVE

1. [Name of Supervisor] has developed a plan to facilitate implementation of evidence-based practice. 0 1 2 3 4

2. [Name of Supervisor] has removed obstacles to the implementation of evidence-based practice. 0 1 2 3 4

3. [Name of Supervisor] has established clear department standards for the implementation of evidence-based practice. 0 1 2 3 4

KNOWLEDGEABLE

4. [Name of Supervisor] is knowledgeable about evidence-based practice. 0 1 2 3 4

5. [Name of Supervisor] is able to answer my questions about evidence-based practice. 0 1 2 3 4

6. [Name of Supervisor] knows what he or she is talking about when it comes to evidence-based practice. 0 1 2 3 4

SUPPORTIVE

7. [Name of Supervisor] recognizes and appreciates employee efforts toward successful implementation of evidence-based practice 0 1 2 3 4

8. [Name of Supervisor] supports employee efforts to learn more about evidence-based practice. 0 1 2 3 4

9. [Name of Supervisor] supports employee efforts to use evidence-based practice. 0 1 2 3 4

PERSEVERANT

10. [Name of Supervisor] perseveres through the   0   1   2   3   4
    ups and downs of implementing evidence-based
    practice

11. [Name of Supervisor] carries on through the   0   1   2   3   4
    challenges of implementing evidence-based
    practice

12. [Name of Supervisor] reacts to critical issues re-   0   1   2   3   4
    garding the implementation of evidence-based
    practice by openly and effectively addressing the
    problem(s). . . . . . .

Supervisor Version

Please indicate the extent to which you agree with each statement.

0	1	2	3	4
Not at all	Slight extent	Moderate extent	Great extent	Very great extent

PROACTIVE

1. I have developed a plan to facilitate implemen-   0   1   2   3   4
   tation of evidence-based practice.

2. I have removed obstacles to the implementation   0   1   2   3   4
   of evidence-based practice.

3. I have established clear department standards   0   1   2   3   4
   for the implementation of evidence-based
   practice.

KNOWLEDGEABLE

4. I am knowledgeable about evidence-based   0   1   2   3   4
   practice.

5. I am able to answer staff's questions about   0   1   2   3   4
   evidence-based practice.

6. I know what I am talking about when it comes to   0   1   2   3   4
   evidence-based practice.

SUPPORTIVE

7.	I recognize and appreciate employee efforts toward successful implementation of evidence-based practice.	0	1	2	3	4
8.	I support employee efforts to learn more about evidence-based practice.	0	1	2	3	4
9.	I support employee efforts to use evidence-based practice.	0	1	2	3	4

PERSEVERANT

10.	I persevere through the ups and downs of implementing evidence-based practice.	0	1	2	3	4
11.	I carry on through the challenges of implementing evidence-based practice.	0	1	2	3	4
12.	I react to critical issues regarding the implementation of evidence-based practice by openly and effectively addressing the problem(s).	0	1	2	3	4

Interpretation of Scores:

Higher scores in each domain: Proactive, Knowledgeable, Supportive, and Perseverant means the staff and the supervisor have high levels of evidence-based practice implementations.

Assessment

14

Avoiding Burnout and Promoting Job Engagement

FRED P. STONE ■

With realization of one's own potential and self-confidence in one's ability, one can build a better world.

—DALAI LAMA

CHAPTER OBJECTIVES

1. Review the problems of job stress, engagement, and burnout in the workplace;
2. Analyze theories of burnout;
3. Examine practical solutions to burnout and ways to promote job engagement; and
4. Gain insights on innovative leadership from a social architect (see Appendix to this chapter).

INTRODUCTION

The problem of burnout and lack of job engagement reaches across the entire workforce. A 2015 Gallup survey found that only 32% of employees were engaged on the job, while 50.8% were unengaged (Gallup, 2016). These unengaged workers put forth minimal effort and were "checked out." The same survey found that 17.2% of workers were actively disengaged. These workers were not only unhappy at their jobs but also expressed their displeasure and undermined the ability of others to do their work. These workers were burned out—a feeling of being overworked, stressed, and exhausted with little sense of accomplishment.

The helping professions and innovative leaders are far from immune from burnout and the factors related to it. A study by Shanafelt et al. (2015) estimated that more than half of the physicians in the United States are burned out. Burnout among nurses has been estimated to be as high as 50% (Aiken, Clarke, Sloane, & Sochalski, 2001). In a study of 460 mental health professionals, Acker (2011) found that 56% had moderate to high levels of emotional exhaustion. Seventy-three percent reported moderate to high levels of role stress, defined as role conflict or role ambiguity, and 50% were considering leaving their jobs. Siebert (2006) discovered in a sample of 751 social workers that 39% were currently burned out, and 75% reported being burned out at some time in their career. Beder (2012) found that 66.2% of Department of Defense social workers surveyed reported being burned out.

In this chapter, we will look at the problem of burnout and examine how social architects can create work environments to reduce it and promote self-care. We will also discuss ways to equip health and human services professionals with the tools to create work–life balance and find personal and professional fulfillment. Of the many challenges leaders face, few are more difficult than creating productive work environments that promote self-care and personal growth, yet helping workers feel energized, engaged, and fulfilled in their jobs is the surest way to create a workforce that can fulfill an organization's vision and accomplish its goals.

BACKGROUND

Numerous studies have looked at the factors related to stress and burnout among mental health professionals. For example, for social work professionals, these factors include increased workloads, severity of client problems, and paperwork, which were all coupled with decreased supervision and staff support (Lloyd, King, & Chenoweth, 2002; Schwartz, Tiamiyu, & Dwyer, 2007; Siebert, 2006; Smullens, 2015). Other factors include education, age, and gender. In a meta-analysis of mental health professionals, Lim et al. (2010) found that education was modestly inversely related to burnout, suggesting that more knowledge or education does not necessarily lead to more self-care. More educated professionals may also have higher expectations from organizations and themselves. Younger social workers tend to have higher rates of burnout than older social workers (Schwartz, Tiamiyu, & Dwyer, 2007), and age is negatively correlated with feelings of exhaustion (Lim et al., 2010). Experience and better work–life balance may explain this phenomenon, but Maslach (2015) argued that early burnout may force younger workers out of the profession, which skews the data. Men and women appear to have equal rates of burnout in the general population (Maslach, 2015). Likewise, Leiter and Harvie's (1996) literature review found no significant relationship between gender and burnout among mental health professionals. LGBT mental health professionals have been shown to have higher rates of burnout, which may be the result of a lack of support and heterosexism (Viehl, Dispenza, McCullough, & Guvensel, 2017).

Workplace settings also affect burnout. Studies have consistently found that mental health professionals in private practice have lower levels of burnout than those who work in agency settings (Lim et al., 2010). Private practice may offer more autonomy, which may decrease job stress, while agencies not only have less autonomy but also have additional administrative demands. Higher workloads are also associated with higher levels of burnout (Lim et al., 2010).

Acker (2011) noted that the changing mental health landscape, such as managed care, decreasing compensation, and increased workloads, has contributed to increased stress. In particular, mental health professionals are increasingly feeling role stress that involves demands that are inconsistent with their expectations. Along with these factors, mental health professionals may have a high risk for burnout because of the expectations they put on themselves. It is easy to fall into the hero role of wanting to rescue people and to become frustrated when we find that we don't have the tools we need. This can be particularly problematic for new health and human services professionals, who might have unrealistic expectations of themselves and others.

THEORIES

The term *burnout* was coined in 1974 by Herbert Freudenberger, a psychologist. Freudenberg discovered burnout from his own experience. Besides his practice as psychoanalyst, he helped open a number of free mental health clinics in New York City. A devoted family man, he recognized his own increasing irritability at home and lack of fulfillment at work. He was professionally successful, but he realized that he was also burned out, which he defined as a "state of mental and physical exhaustion caused by one's professional life" (Freudenberger, 1974, p. 160).

Around the same time, Christina Maslach, a social psychologist, was studying emotions and job stress among human services workers (Maslach, Schaufeli,

& Leiter, 2001). She found three factors associated with burnout: exhaustion, depersonalization or cynicism, and lack of professional efficacy or fulfillment. These factors are described below:

1. *Exhaustion.* This factor refers to "being overextended and depleted of one's emotional and physical resources" (Maslach & Leiter, 2008, p. 498). This factor does not always include physical exhaustion. A worker might feel physically energized but does not have the emotional resources to deal with work challenges. Some jobs are emotionally exhausting because they require workers to "display emotions inconsistent with their feelings" (Maslach et al., 2001). Exhaustion is the most widely reported factor in burnout (Maslach & Leiter, 2008).

2. *Depersonalization (or cynicism).* Cynical and negative attitudes toward clients are hallmarks of this factor. It can include disengagement, lack of feelings toward others, callousness, and extreme detachment. Workers may go through the motions but care little about their work.

3. *Lack of professional efficacy or lack of fulfillment.* This factor includes feelings of incompetence and a lack of productivity and can be coupled with negative evaluations of oneself. Workers who experience this problem lose faith in their abilities to make a difference, and the feelings of personal fulfillment they once felt are gone.

Human services professionals' mental relationship to their work runs along a continuum of positive experiences such as energy, involvement, and efficacy to the negative factors of burnout—exhaustion, depersonalization, and inefficacy (Maslach, Leiter, & Jackson, 2012). While most workers will occasionally experience one or more of these elements, it is the chronic form of all three that results in burnout.

Maslach and her colleagues (2012) continued to expand their theory and "increasingly recognized that social and organizational conditions are primary correlates of burnout" (p. 297). Maslach and Leiter (1997) integrated individual and situational factors and focused on the relationship workers have with their jobs and the psychological contract that exists between employers and employees in six domains—workload, control, reward, community, fairness, and values. Significant mismatches between worker expectations and an organization provision in these areas results in burnout (Maslach et al., 2012).

Workload

Workload applies to the quantity and quality of work, and mismatch occurs when workers do not have the personal or organizational resources to meet workload demands. Work overload and time pressures have consistently been found to be correlated with burnout, in particular, the exhaustion dimension (Maslach & Leiter, 2008). Workload consists of two factors—quantitative and qualitative. Both of these factors can deplete energy and lead to exhaustion. Quantitative workload is simply the amount of work, such as caseload, number of administrative duties, and production quotas. Assessing quantitative workload means comparing the amount of work to previous periods and the amount of work required in similar organizations. It requires realistic assessment of what can be accomplished given the time and resource requirements. Social architects should also consider other obligations that workers have, such as additional job requirements, and inquire about after-work obligations. For example, a director of a medical clinic was approached by a few medical providers and mental health professionals who complained of feeling exhausted and overworked. The director compared the workload of these personnel with their coworkers and found no difference. The director soon found out that these workers were employed at other jobs after hours, which ended up being the primary source of their work exhaustion.

Qualitative stress occurs when workers do not have the proper skills, experience, or training to do their jobs. Qualitative stress usually results from a lack of job training, which is a leading cause of turnover. An IBM survey found that one in four workers quit because of a lack of on-the-job training (IBM, 2014). Too often, new workers are blamed for failing to meet standards that other workers with more experience and training meet easily.

Control

This dimension relates to the ability to access resources and the authority to direct work (Maslach et al., 2001). Problems related to control can be seen in team members who have been given the responsibility to achieve objectives but not the authority to access resources to accomplish them. Control also includes autonomy. Workers who have the autonomy to make their own schedules and act with a modest degree of independence experience less stress. Workplaces that focus on accomplishing goals but allow autonomy for team members to achieve them as long as goals are being met are called "bottom-line" organizations (Maslach & Leiter, 1997). These organizations contrast with micromanagement organizations, in which workers feel constantly watched and given direction with little freedom to act on their own.

Reward

Team members expect to be compensated for their efforts, and unfair compensation is a leading cause of burnout. In a survey of 614 human resources leaders, unfair compensation was rated as the leading cause of burnout (41%), followed by unreasonable workload (32%) and long work days (32%) (Kronos, 2017). Compensation includes salary and wages but also includes benefits such as health care and time off. Human services providers usually earn modest salaries, which adds to the high burnout rates. While financial compensation is important, rewards also include recognition. When efforts are not recognized and appreciated, workers feel devalued, which results in feelings of inefficiency (Maslach et al., 2001). Many join the helping professions not for extrinsic rewards such as money but for the intrinsic rewards that come from making a positive difference in people's lives. They take a feeling of pride and a sense of accomplishment in their work. When they cannot see that they are making a difference or feel ineffective in their jobs, the intrinsic rewards of helping are lost.

Community

Workplaces are social environments in which workers seek belongingness, nurturing, and esteem (Day & Leiter, 2014). Workers hope to share "membership in a group with shared values" (Maslach, 2001, p. 415), make friends among coworkers, and have emotional investments in their jobs. Workplaces, however, also include competition between workers and inevitable personal conflicts. These conflicts do not necessarily lead to burnout, but a workplace characterized by chronic incivility can. Porath and Pearson (2010) defined workplace incivility as "the exchange of seemingly inconsequential inconsiderate words and deeds that violate conventional norms of workplace conduct" (p. 64). A few examples are taking credit for other's work, blaming others for our own mistakes, checking social media during meetings, belittling coworkers, and engaging in passive-aggressive behaviors. These behaviors may appear minor, but incivility has a profound effect on workers. In a poll of more than 9,000 workers, Porath and Pearson (2010) found that incivility results in less work effort. Eighty percent reported losing work time worrying about an incident of incivility, and 66% reported a decline in workplace performance. The result of these uncivil behaviors was significant turnover, although few workers reported the behavior problems.

Fairness

A number of studies have found a relationship between fairness and burnout (Kroon, Van de Voorde, & Van Veldhoven, 2009). When pay, benefits, and other rewards are not delivered fairly, workers can become cynical and upset. Fairness in the workplace conveys respect and appreciation and promotes a sense of community, which can reduce burnout. Fairness is displayed in a number of ways. Informal fairness is the way that leaders act toward workers. Leaders who show clear favoritism toward some workers, such as giving them desirable projects or benefits, undermine the fairness of their organizations. But it is more than these obvious shows of favoritism. Leaders who engage in exclusionary talk, such as discussing sports or activities with certain coworkers, can send subtle messages about who is favored in the organization. These factors alone, however, do not necessarily lead to burnout, although they may result in worker turnover. One element of fairness that has been linked with burnout is procedural and organizational justice (Kroon et al., 2009). Team members expect organizational policies to be implemented fairly and consistently. They want the processes, such as those that determine pay and promotion, to be clearly stated and followed. Organizational justice gives workers a greater sense of control (Maslach et al., 2001) and provides consistent boundaries and expectations that can reduce uncertainty.

Fairness speaks to the inherent trust in an organization and fosters communication. Unfair practices lead to cynicism and distrust as if some people are privileged to information that others are not. For example, as one social worker noted about the unfair distribution of information, "I never get the feeling that I am being told the truth around here" (Maslach & Leiter, 1997, p. 53).

Values

A mismatch in personal and workplace values predicts exhaustion, cynicism, and inefficacy (Leiter, Frank, & Matheson, 2009) and has been associated with a number of negative outcomes such as poor performance and lower quality services (Dylag, Jaworek, Karwowski, Kozusznik, & Marek, 2013). The mismatch of values can occur in a number of ways. When an organization's stated values are inconsistent with the daily experience of workers, they can grow cynical. For example, many organizations promote slogans like, "people are our most valuable asset," but then cut pay and benefits or lay off workers with little notice or compensation.

A mismatch in values may occur between personal and professional values. In human services organizations, it is challenging when clients engage in behaviors that are inconsistent with the worker's personal moral standards. The problem of mismatched values may also be a conflict between self-transcendent values and self-enhancement values. In a study of 512 Israeli social workers, Tartakovsky (2016) found that social workers value benevolence and helping others, especially those who lack resources or suffer discrimination. These values, however, conflict with social status values of seeking dominance, prestige, and control. For example, Tartakovsky (2016) found that social workers whose values were congruent with social work values (high self-transcendent values, low self-enhancement values) were less likely to burn out.

The Six Domains and Burnout

Maslach et al. (2001) emphasized that domains create "a conceptual framework for the crises that disrupt the relationships people develop in their work" (p. 416). The theory might be summarized this way. Workers are more likely to be engaged in their jobs when the workload matches their capabilities and the time and resources available. They will be more engaged when they perceive a higher level of control in their work environment and are rewarded appropriately for their contributions. Because workplaces are social environments, workers are less likely to burn out if they have friendships or at least positive professional relationships in the workplace and are treated with consideration and fairness. Most important, workers are less likely to burn out when their personal values align with the values of the workplace.

Other Factors to Consider

Personal Characteristics and Burnout. People with some personality traits may be more susceptible to burnout. In a meta-analysis of personality, burnout, and work outcomes, Swider and Zimmerman (2010) compared the Five-Factor Model of personality traits with job burnout dimensions and job-related factors. The personality traits included emotional stability, extraversion, openness to experiences, agreeableness, and contentiousness. When compared against dimensions of exhaustion, depersonalization, and inefficacy, the researchers found that team members with lower levels of extraversion, conscientiousness, and agreeableness and higher levels of neuroticism were more likely to experience burnout. Maslach (2015) argued that workers who are prone to burnout struggle in relating to others, are inpatient and intolerant, and lack confidence. She wrote, "Such a person has neither a clearly defined set of goals nor the determination and self-assurance needed to achieve them" (p. 105). The literature on personality and burnout focuses on personal faults, but as Freudenberger (Freudenberger & Richelson, 1980) maintained, burnout may be the result of a healthy and natural desire for approval that drifts to an unhealthy demand. Likewise, a natural desire for accomplishment can become an overweening need. The personality traits of burnout have two important elements for innovative leaders to consider. First, leaders should consider job demands and personality traits in hiring. They also need to be concerned that workers who have a healthy desire to help others are not overcome with unhealthy needs for approval and achievement. The stress of work can bring out the worst in people, and their reactions are seen as personal failings rather than the reaction to work demands. Mentoring and burnout prevention education can help these workers cope better with workplace stressors.

Individual and Outside Concerns. Workplaces consist of people who have lives outside of work that have a profound effect on them. Workers who experience health issues, marital strife, financial worries, and other factors will likely be less productive and more difficult to work with. Life stressors such as divorce, illness, and past trauma have been associated with burnout as well as depression (Plieger, Melchers, Montag, Meerman, & Rueter, 2015).

Team members can also have unreported mental health problems. The US National Comorbidity Survey found that 18% of workers "experienced symptoms of a mental disorder in the previous month." (Mental health problems in the workplace, 2010, n.p.). The survey also found that more than 6.4% of workers met the criteria for major depressive disorder in the previous month (Kessler et al., 2006). Because burnout and depression share many of the same characteristics, such as exhaustion, feelings of failure, and social withdrawal or isolation, some researchers believe that burnout and depression are closely related and that the link is underestimated (Bianchi, Schonfeld, & Laurent, 2014).

One advantage for social architects in health and human services organizations is their familiarity with the impact of stress as well as mental illness. They should consider making reasonable accommodations for workers to resolve life stress and recommend professional help if appropriate. Leaders should talk about employee assistance benefits on a regular basis and encourage employees to use the service as needed. Innovative leaders, however, need to be cautious. Suggesting that workers who express workplace concerns seek mental health care can be construed as minimizing or retaliation. The Americans with

Disability Act may also apply, so leaders should consult with human resources specialists or lawyers before recommending care.

Secondary Trauma. Mental health professionals who are exposed to the trauma of their clients may experience secondary trauma or compassion fatigue (Craig & Sprang, 2009). Compassion fatigue results in many of the symptoms of posttraumatic stress disorder (PTSD), including hyperarousal, avoidance, and re-experiencing (Bride & Figley, 2009). It shares some of characteristics of burnout but is different. Burnout relates to the larger context of a worker's environment, such as those in the six domains. Compassion fatigue focuses exclusively on the relationship between the person providing care and the person receiving it (e.g., physician and patient)) and includes symptoms of PTSD.

Ways in which social architects can avoid compassion fatigue include many of the same elements that can reduce burnout. Craig and Sprang (2009), in a study of 539 trauma treatment therapists, found that similar to burnout, mental health workers with more experience and adequate training report lower levels of compassion fatigue. They also found that practitioners using evidence-based practices suffered less compassion fatigue. Leaders need to keep in mind that compassion fatigue may indicate PTSD, and workers may need professional mental health services to deal with it.

PRACTICAL STRATEGIES TO PREVENT BURNOUT

Despite decades of research, scholars have found few evidence-based practices that reduce burnout (Maslach & Leiter, 2015). The burnout literature, however, does offer a host of practical recommendations that draw on the job stress and wellness literature. In this section, we will look at two of these areas—self-care and job engagement.

Promoting Self-Care

The first step to establishing a self-care program is for workers to realize the importance of self-care, the hazards of self-neglect, and the significant dangers that being burned out can have personally and professionally. Thus, an awareness campaign is the first step to reducing burnout. Innovative leaders also need to set up the conditions for self-care—time, permission, and place (Smullens, 2015). Allowing time for workers to engage in self-care activities is crucial. Too often, self-care is considered almost a luxury, and time is allotted only when other "more important" tasks have been taken care of. Allotting time is not enough if workers do not give themselves permission to use the time. This may be their own reluctance to take time, but workers may neglect taking this time because they do not trust that the leadership is sincere in its support for self-care. This is one reason that leaders need to model self-care behavior. Promoting self-care also requires a supportive place. Because burnout occurs at workplaces, providing a respite at work for self-care should be considered (Smullens, 2015). Some workplaces have provided exercise areas or walking paths. Other workplaces have designated breakrooms and other areas that are relaxing and allow workers to engage in non–work-related conversations.

An increasing amount of research is being done on resilience. Resiliency training, which has been used extensively in the US military, focuses on four areas: physical, mental, social, and spiritual. Taking self-care actions in these areas may reduce burnout.

Physical. The first step is taking care of our physical needs. These needs include adequate rest, a healthy diet, and exercise. An abundance of research shows that attending to these elements helps with host of stress-related problems (Lopresti, Hood, & Drummond, 2013).

Mental. Our mental attitudes play an important role in self-care. Collins (2008) argued that positive emotions and optimism help increase work satisfaction and reduce job stress. These positive emotions include gratitude, hope, and joy, among others, and have been shown to reduce negative emotions (Fredrickson, 2013). Positive reappraisal or reframing can also help with difficult situations and frustrations, as can establishing goals and using problem-solving strategies (Collins, 2008). Emphasizing positive emotions as a self-care strategy is not without its critics (Power, 2016). The so-called "bright-siding" (Ehrenreich, 2009) of difficult circumstances can skew our perception of reality and lead to denial of problems. A better approach is to practice self-acceptance—accepting ourselves as fallible human beings who have limits to our abilities (Ellis, 2001). Each day presents a limited amount of time to accomplish goals, and everyone has limits on their experience or knowledge. Too often, workers engage in self-abuse for their inability to accomplish impossible tasks.

Along with self-acceptance, workers need to engage in other-acceptance. Workplaces require us to sometimes work with people we dislike. As human services providers, we sometimes work with clients or patients who are often resistant to help and sometimes hostile. Viewing coworkers and customers as fallible human beings like ourselves and expecting some obstruction every day can help with inevitable frustrations that come with working with others.

As Marcus Aurelius famously said, "Begin each day by telling yourself: Today I shall be meeting with interference, ingratitude, insolence, disloyalty, ill-will, and selfishness—all of them due to the offenders' ignorance of what is good or evil" (Hammond & Clay, 2006). Maybe he was a bit too pessimistic for modern tastes, but his attitude made it easier to deal with the challenges presented by working with others.

It is very important for social architects to maintain work–life balance as a major strategy to avoid burnout. While there are different definitions of work–life balance, most agree it means that workers need to recognize that they have a life outside of the office. Work can be consuming, which leads to neglecting family and friends. The modern workplace makes this even harder because supervisors and coworkers can always reach out and contact a worker at almost any time or place. The key to developing work–life balance is establishing boundaries. Workers should try to create a home environment that acts as a sanctuary from work. Some steps include not checking work emails and not responding to nonemergency calls.

Spiritual. In the context of preventing burnout, the term *spiritual* refers to meaning and purpose. Workers who are burned out often find the initial passion that they once had for their work has been lost. Workers need to take some time to reassess the reasons that they entered their profession as well as their long-term goals and aspirations. Some questions human services organizations workers can ask are:

1. What were some of my values that made me choose this profession?
2. What values are the most important to me that I am not expressing at work?
3. What are some things in my current job that do reflect my highest values?
4. What is one step I can take to better align my values with my work?

Finding a mentor or trusted coworker to discuss these questions may help restore a sense of purpose and meaning. Taking an inventory of accomplishments can help restore a sense of purpose.

Engaging Workers

The concept of *job engagement*, also called *work engagement,* has become increasingly popular, and some studies show that it increases job performance and improves attitudes (Christian, Garza, & Slaughter, 2011). Job engagement research, however, has been hampered by a lack of an agreed-on definition. Kahn (1990) provided one of the earliest and most cited definitions, although he used the term *personal engagement*. Personal engagement involved workers who "employ and express themselves physically, cognitively, and emotionally during their role [work] performance" (Kahn, 1990, p. 694). Schaufeli, Salanova, Gonzalez-Roma, and Bakker (2002) defined work (job) engagement as "a positive, fulfilling, work-related state of mind that is characterized by vigor, dedication, and absorption" (p. 74). They argued that job engagement was a separate concept from burnout.

Maslach and Leiter (1997), on the other hand, viewed job engagement as a positive alternative to burnout. It is "an energetic state of involvement with personally fulfilling activities that enhance one's sense of professional efficacy" (Maslach & Leiter, 2008, p. 498). Job engagement counters exhaustion with energy, cynicism with involvement, and inefficacy with efficacy (Maslach & Leiter, 2008).

Based on this model, Maslach and Leiter (1997) offered "Six Paths to Engagement" that addressed the mismatches in six domains discussed earlier. These paths are:

1. Sustainable workload
2. Feelings of choice and control
3. Recognition and reward
4. A sense of community
5. Fairness, respect, and justice
6. Meaningful and valued work

In a review of the research, Bakker, Schaufeli, Leiter, and Taris (2008) found that resources including social support, feedback, autonomy, and learning opportunities increase job engagement. These elements provide both intrinsic and extrinsic motivation because they may foster personal growth as well as help workers attain organizational goals. Resources are especially important to engagement when job demands are high.

The concept of job engagement has its critics. Garrad and Chamorro-Premuzic (2016) argued that high levels of job engagement may push employees to burnout, reward workers with certain personality characteristics, and discourage negative thinking and feedback. Wefald and Downey (2009) criticized the lack of rigorous research on the topic and the significant differences between organizational goals of engagement (e.g., performance, retention, and commitment) and academic researchers' focus on construct development.

STRATEGIES FOR INNOVATIVE LEADERS TO REDUCE BURNOUT AND INCREASE JOB SATISFACTION

The key factor to reducing burnout is applying leadership skills to action. In the previous sections, we have looked at the importance of self-care and job engagement—both important concepts that innovative leaders should encourage and support. In this section, we will consider some other ideas to reduce burnout.

1. *Reward doing less.* Jim Collins (2001) in his bestselling book, *Good to Great,* found that the best organizations focus on core activities. They essentially do less, better. Unfortunately, performance reports tend to reward workers who do more or have innovative ideas. While being more productive and innovative is important, Collins argues that leaders also need to reward workers who figure out what organizations need to stop doing. He endorsed a "stop doing" list as opposed to the expanding "to do" list (Collins, 2001, p. 139). Eliminating tasks and projects that have little value promotes focus on priorities that result in higher quality work, a greater sense of accomplishment, and a calmer atmosphere. Workers usually recognize programs and tasks that have little value, and continuing in them leads to cynicism and frustration.

2. *Provide necessary and adequate training.* In the modern workplace, workers are often thrust into positions with minimal and in some cases no training at all. Workers are expected to learn their jobs on the job, and leaders assume that coworkers will help new workers gain experience. New workers are castigated for failing to meet the demands of their jobs when they lack the proper training to do their work. Experienced workers may criticize new workers, noting that they, the experienced workers, could do the job easily. This fails to consider that experienced workers know the tasks well. Leaders also do not realize how much training and experience are necessary for workers to learn new skills and thus may assume that an hour of instruction is adequate to understand complex systems. New workers feel incompetent and blamed when in reality they have not acquired the necessary skills to do their jobs. Leaders need to recognize that workers need time to learn new programs and systems, and they need feedback mechanisms to measure their skill acquisition.

3. *Make goals, roles, and priorities clear.* Innovative leaders need to ensure that workers clearly know their priorities and the goals. A simple test is to ask workers what the priorities of the organization are and

what the workers' goals are. If the worker can provide one or two priorities and three or four goals, he or she is less likely to get burned out. Roles and responsibilities also need to be clear. As organizations have focused on flattening out hierarchies, many workers are confused about their roles and responsibilities. They can feel tasked by multiple supervisors who assign duties that are inconsistent with the workers' view of their job or their job descriptions. The term *job description* is often used as the punch line of a joke because many workers are regularly expected to do things outside of their job description. While fluid responsibilities and roles may have some advantages in rapidly changing environments of fast-paced companies, they sometimes leave workers confused.

4. *Promote autonomy and control.* One of the best ways to reduce burnout is to let team members exercise some autonomy and control. The ability to exercise autonomy and control may be one reason mental health workers in private settings have lower rates of burnout than those in public settings (Lim et al., 2010). Although some jobs offer little opportunities for autonomy and control, social architects need to let workers make decisions and control their work schedules and duties. Leaders also should avoid micromanaging workers.

5. *Respect boundaries.* In the modern information age, there are few boundaries between work and home life. This constant sense of being on call increases worker stress. Even when bosses tell workers that they are not expected to check emails or respond from home, there is an inherent pressure that the "good workers" will respond and be ready to take action. This constant feeling of being on call leads to activation of the central nervous system that pours stress onto workers who will become exhausted and anxious and ultimately burned out. Social architects need to establish firm boundaries for themselves as well as their team members. While every job is different, innovative leaders should refrain from contacting team members outside of the workplace except in emergencies. Even if workers are told not to check email, some will. Leaders, therefore, should avoid emailing after hours.

6. *Deal with toxic environments.* If innovative leaders want to maintain a healthy workforce, they must create a healthy work environment. This means creating an environment that not only lacks hostility but also is safe. One social architect had a simple phrase that became his leadership mantra—*dignity and respect*. Leading a human services organization, he would tell his team members, "If we cannot treat each other with dignity and respect, then we cannot be expected to

treat our clients with dignity and respect." His point was that how people treated each other in the workplace was practice for how to treat clients. Treating people with dignity and respect in the workplace requires leaders to quickly address issues of racism, sexism, and other discriminatory elements. They should not be afraid to remove workers who fail to treat others well. Social architects should also welcome ideas and disagreement.

Porath and Pearson (2010) offered innovative leaders a number of suggestions to deal with incivility in the workplace. The first is for leaders to set the tone for civility and to make an honest self-assessment of their own behavior. A 360 feedback exercise can be helpful in this regard. Social architects should also consider civility in hiring. One of the primary considerations in hiring should be whether a worker will be a good fit with other workers and the organizational culture. The standards for civility need to be taught, and incivility needs to be addressed. As with other workplace complaints, reports of incivility need to be taken seriously. Offensive behavior should not be tolerated or excused (Porath & Pearson, 2010).

Civility, Respect, and Engagement in the Workforce (CREW), a program developed by the Veterans Health Administration, has been found to substantially improve civility in the workplace (Osatuke, Moore, Ward, Dyrenforth, & Belton, 2009). One of the hallmarks of the program is that it treats civility in the workplace as a vital part of increasing job performance, not an add-on that meets a human resources requirement.

7. *Provide support and community.* Research consistently shows that support from leaders reduces burnout (Day & Leiter, 2014). A meta-analysis of 114 studies found that workplace support that includes coworkers and supervisors can help reduce feelings of exhaustion (Halbesleben, 2006). Two interventions have been shown to reduce burnout used group training that focused on workplace dynamics, personal motivations, and interpersonal relationships (Rabin, Feldman, & Kaplan, 1999; Scarnera, Bosco, Soleti, & Lancioni, 2009).

8. *Have fun.* Social architects deal with difficult problems. It is sometimes difficult to find humor, yet a workplace devoid of humor is not one that anyone wants to work in. Social architects know how to bring appropriate humor to the office to lighten the mood. This is admittedly challenging and should be done with caution.

A CHAPTER CASE STUDY

Phil was recently named as the director for a local community mental health clinic that provides low-fee mental health services. It also runs therapy groups for court-ordered clients. The staff includes a psychiatrist, three psychologists, and eight social workers, along with a dozen support staff.

The previous director was fired after a workplace climate assessment found the staff suffered from low morale and many were considering leaving. During Phil's first meeting with the staff, it was clear that the clinic had problems. The staff complained of being exhausted from heavy caseloads. Some of the staff did not feel they had enough training to take on the numerous complex cases. One social worker commented, "I don't think I am making any difference and might actually be hurting some of my clients."

The staff also had conflicts with each other. The staff psychiatrist often showed up to work late and left early, but the previous director had never addressed this problem with her. When support staff showed up late, however, the previous director would yell at them in front of everyone. One of the psychologists was clearly "checked out" and spent the first meeting scrolling through his cell phone and making snide comments to other workers such as, "you are lucky just to have a job."

Phil recognized his staff was burned out and that he needed to act quickly. His first step was to make the staff feel supported. He did this by listening to their concerns with real interest and without judgment. The priority for the group was clearly workload, so he contacted other local community mental health clinics to see how his staff's workload compared. When he was able to show that his clinic had a significantly higher caseload, he was able to persuade his supervisor to hire additional staff. He was also able to provide in-house training for some of the staff to improve their clinical skills.

The mission of the clinic was to provide quality care to its clients at an affordable price. Phil recognized that the staff was often being tasked with additional assignments that had little to do with client care. Phil asked the staff to create a list of "crazy makers"—things that made little sense but took up a lot of time. On the top of the list was a weekly 3-hour staff meeting that usually involved conversations that only applied to two or three people. Phil was able to cut the meeting to 30 minutes by creating a strict agenda and eliminating discussions on topics that did not apply to the entire staff, such as specific case problems.

Phil established rules for civility in the workplace. He counseled the staff psychiatrist about the need for her to show up on time and stay at work as needed. Phil was pleasantly surprised that she took the feedback well and changed her behavior. He also counseled the psychologist on his lack of civil behavior, but the psychologist continued acting out. Phil soon learned that the psychologist had been telling sexually suggestive jokes and making other inappropriate comments. Phil let him go, much to the relief of rest of the staff.

Finally, Phil brought in an expert in workplace burnout to conduct weekly group sessions after work. The sessions were voluntary, but most of the staff decided to stay. The sessions focused on workplace dynamics, personal motivations, and interpersonal relationships.

Six months after taking over, the clinic had an entirely new atmosphere. There were still occasional problems with personal conflicts and feelings of being overworked, but a climate assessment showed that the workers were more energized, felt good about working with their clients, and had a greater sense of personal accomplishment.

CONCLUSION

Burnout is a significant problem in the workplace, especially among health and human services leaders and team members. In this chapter, we looked at the extent of the problem and some theories that help us understand it. We also saw that there are few evidence-based interventions to avoid burnout, demonstrating a number of practical solutions that address elements of the problem. Further research in this area is needed. The next chapter will address self-care through the use of mindfulness.

CHAPTER DISCUSSION QUESTIONS

1. How is burnout defined and how do you know if you or a colleague is experiencing it?
2. What is the difference between burnout and compassion fatigue?
3. What are some practical strategies to prevent or mitigate burnout in yourself and in others?
4. What role does a leader play in instigating or reducing the possibility of burnout in employees?
5. Describe the workplace challenges and solutions provided by the leader in the case study. Are there additional considerations and other innovative solutions that you can think of as an emerging leader?
6. Read the leader profile and case study in the Appendix to this chapter. Note innovative ideas and practices and see what aspects of the case you can connect to the contents of the chapter and/or the overall book.

REFERENCES

Acker, G. A. (2011). Burnout among mental health providers. *Journal of Social Work, 12*(5), 475–490.

Aiken, L., Clarke, S., Sloane, D., & Sochalski, J. (2001). Nurses' reports on hospital care in five countries. *Health Affairs, 20*(3), 43–53.

Bakker, A., Schaufeli, W., Leiter, M., & Taris, T. (2008). Work engagement: An emerging concept in occupational health psychology. *Work & Stress, 22*(3), 187–200.

Beder, J. C. (2012). Social work in the department of defense hospital: Impact of the work. *Advances in Social Work, 13*(1), 132–148.

Bianchi, R., Schonfeld, I. S., & Laurent, E. (2014). Is burnout a depressive disorder? A reexamination with special focus on atypical depression. *International Journal of Stress Management, 21,* 307–324. doi:10.1037/a0037906.

Bride, B., & Figley, C. (2009). Secondary trauma and military veteran caregivers. *Smith College Studies in Social Work, 79*(3-4), 314–329.

Cable News Network. (2009). *Stressful jobs that pay badly.* Retrieved from http://money.cnn.com/galleries/2009/pf/0910/gallery.stressful_jobs/index.html

Christian, M. S., Garza, A. S., & Slaughter, J. E. (2011). Work engagement: A quantitative review and test of its relations with task and contextual performance. *Personnel Psychology, 64*(1), 89–136.

Collins, J. (2001). *Good to great: Why some companies make the leap—and others don't* (1st ed.). New York, NY: Harper Business.

Collins, S. (2008). Social workers, resilience, positive emotions and optimism. *Practice, 19*(4), 255–269.

Craig, C. D., & Sprang, G. (2009). Exploratory and confirmatory analysis of the trauma practices questionnaire. *Research on Social Work Practice, 19*(2), 221–233.

Craig, C., & Sprang, G. (2010). Compassion satisfaction, compassion fatigue, and burnout in a national sample of trauma treatment therapists. *Anxiety, Stress & Coping, 23*(3), 319–339.

Day, A. & Leiter, M. (2014). The good and bad of working relationships. In M. P. Leiter, A. B. Bakker, & C. Maslach (Eds.), *Burnout at work: A psychological perspective* (pp. 57–79). New York, NY: Psychology Press.

Dylag, A., Jaworek, M., Karwowski, W., Kozusznik, M., & Marek, T. (2013). Discrepancy between individual and organizational values: Occupational burnout and work engagement among white-collar workers. *International Journal of Industrial Ergonomics, 43*(3), 225–231.

Ehrenreich, B. (2009). *Bright-sided: How the relentless promotion of positive thinking has undermined America* (1st ed.). New York, NY: Metropolitan Books.

Ellis, A. (2001). *Overcoming destructive beliefs, feelings, and behaviors: New directions for rational emotive behavior therapy* New York, NY: Prometheus Books.

Fredrickson, B. L. (2013). Positive emotions broaden and build. In P. Devine & A. Plant (Eds.). *Advances in experimental social psychology* (Vol. 47, pp. 1–53). Burlington, MA: Academic Press.

Freudenberger, H. (1974). Staff burnout. *Journal of Social Sciences, 90*(1), 159–165.

Freudenberger, H., & Richelson, G. (1980). *Burn-out: The high cost of high achievement* (1st ed., Anchor Press ed.). Garden City, NY: Anchor Press.

Gallup. (2016, January 13). *Employee engagement in U.S. stagnant in 2015.* Retrieved from http://money.cnn.com/galleries/2009/pf/0910/gallery.stressful_jobs/index.html

Garrad, L., & Chamorro-Premuzic, T. (2016, August 16). The dark side of high employee engagement. *Harvard Business Review.* Retrieved from https://hbr.org/2016/08/the-dark-side-of-high-employee-engagement

Halbesleben, J. R. B. (2006). Sources of social support and burnout: A meta-analytic test of the conservation of resources model. *Journal of Applied Psychology, 91*(5), 1134–1145.

Hammond, M., & Clay, D. (2006). *Meditations* (Penguin classics). London, UK/New York, NY: Penguin Books.

IBM. (2014). *The value of training.* Retrieved from https://www-03.ibm.com/services/learning/pdfs/IBMTraining-TheValueofTraining.pdf

Kahn, W. (1990). Psychological conditions of personal engagement and disengagement at work. *Academy of Management Journal, 33*(4), 692.

Kessler, R. C., Akiskal, H. S., Ames, M., Birnbaum, H., Greenberg, P., Hirschfeld, R. M. A., . . . Wang, P. S. (2006). The prevalence and effects of mood disorders on work performance in a nationally representative sample of US workers. *American Journal of Psychiatry, 163*(9), 1561–1568. http://doi.org/10.1176/appi.ajp.163.9.1561

Kronos. (2017, January 9). *The employee burnout crisis: Study reveals big workplace challenge in 2017 workplace study.* Retrieved from https://www.kronos.com/about-us/newsroom/employee-burnout-crisis-study-reveals-big-workplace-challenge-2017

Kroon, B., Van de Voorde, K., & Van Veldhoven, M. (2009). Cross-level effects of high-performance work practices on burnout: Two counteracting mediating mechanisms compared. *Personnel Review, 38*(5), 509–525.

Leiter, M., & Harvie, P. (1996). Burnout among mental health workers: A review and a research agenda. *International Journal of Social Psychiatry, 42*(2), 90–101.

Leiter, M. P., Frank, E., & Matheson, T. J. (2009). Demands, values, and burnout: Relevance for physicians. *Canadian Family Physician, 55*(12), 1224–1225.

Lim, N., Kim, E., Kim, H., Yang, E., & Lee, S. M. (2010). Individual and work-related factors influencing burnout of mental health professionals: A meta-analysis. *Journal of Employment Counseling, 47*(2), 86–96.

Lloyd, C., King, R., & Chenoweth, L. (2002). Social work, stress and burnout: A review. *Journal of Mental Health, 11*(3), 255–265.

Lopresti, A. L., Hood, S. D., & Drummond, P. D. (2013). A review of lifestyle factors that contribute to important pathways associated with major depression: Diet, sleep and exercise. *Journal of Affective Disorders, 148*(1), 12–27.

Maslach, C. (2001). What have we learned about burnout and health?. *Psychology & Health, 16*(5), 607–611.

Maslach, C. (2015). *Burnout. The cost of caring.* Los Altos, CA: Malor Books.

Maslach, C., & Leiter, M. (1997). *The truth about burnout: How organizations cause personal stress and what to do about it* (1st ed.). San Francisco, CA: Jossey-Bass.

Maslach, C., & Leiter, M. (2008). Early predictors of job burnout and engagement. *Journal of Applied Psychology, 93*(3), 498–512.

Maslach, C., & Leiter, M. (2015). It's time to take action on burnout. *Burnout Research, 2*(1), iv–v.

Maslach, C., Leiter, M., & Jackson, S. (2012). Making a significant difference with burnout interventions: Researcher and practitioner collaboration. *Journal of Organizational Behavior, 33*(2), 296–300.

Maslach, C., Schaufeli, W., & Leiter, M. (2001). Job burnout. *Annual Review of Psychology, 52*, 397–422.

Mental health problems in the workplace. (2010, February). *The Harvard Mental Health Letter.* Cambridge, MA: Harvard Health Publications.

Osatuke, K., Moore, S., Ward, C., Dyrenforth, S., & Belton, L. (2009). Civility, Respect, Engagement in the Workforce (CREW). *Journal of Applied Behavioral Science, 45*(3), 384–410.

Plieger, T., Melchers, M., Montag, C., Meermann, R., & Reuter, M. (2015). Life stress as potential risk factor for depression and burnout. *Burnout Research, 2*(1), 19–24.

Porath, C. L., & Pearson, C. M. (2010). The cost of bad behavior. *Organizational Dynamics, 39*(1), 64–71.

Power, M. (2016). *Understanding happiness: A critical review of positive psychology.* New York, NY: Routledge.

Rabin, S., Feldman, D., & Kaplan, Z. (1999). Stress and intervention strategies in mental health professionals. *British Journal of Medical Psychology, 72*(2), 159–169.

Scarnera, P., Bosco, A., Soleti, E., & Lancioni, G. (2009). Preventing burnout in mental health workers at interpersonal level: An Italian pilot study. *Community Mental Health Journal, 45*(3), 222–227.

Schaufeli, W. B., Salanova, M., González-Romá, V., & Bakker, A. B. (2002). The measurement of engagement and burnout: A two sample confirmatory factor analytic approach. *Journal of Happiness Studies, 3*, 71–92.

Schwartz, R., Tiamiyu, M., & Dwyer, D. (2007). Social worker hope and perceived burnout. *Administration in Social Work, 31*(4), 103–119.

Shanafelt, T. D., Gorringe, G., Menaker, R., Storz, K., Reeves, D., Buskirk, M. D, Sloan, J. A., &. Swensen, S. (2015). Impact of organizational leadership on physician burnout and satisfaction. *Mayo Clinic Proceedings, 90*(4), 432–440.

Siebert, D. (2006). Personal and occupational factors in burnout among practicing social workers. *Journal of Social Service Research, 32*(2), 25–44.

Smullens, S. (2015). *Burnout and self-care in social work: A guidebook for students and those in mental health and related professions.* Washington, DC: NASW Press.

Swider, B. W., & Zimmerman, R. D. (2010). Born to burnout: A meta-analytic path model of personality, job burnout and work outcomes. *Journal of Vocational Behavior, 76*(3), 487–506.

Tartakovsky, E. (2016). Personal value preferences and burnout of social workers. *Journal of Social Work, 16*(6), 657–673.

Viehl, C., Dispenza, F., McCullough, R., & Guvensel, K. (2017). Burnout among sexual minority mental health practitioners: Investigating correlates and predictors. *Psychology of Sexual Orientation and Gender Diversity, 4*(3), 354–361.

Wefald, A., & Downey, R. (2009). Job engagement in organizations: Fad, fashion, or folderol? *Journal of Organizational Behavior, 30*(1), 141–145.

APPENDIX
Featured Leader: Fred P. Stone

Fred P. Stone is a retired US Air Force Colonel, a licensed clinical social worker, and Clinical Associate Professor at the University of Southern California Suzanne Dworak-Peck School of Social Work. He holds a doctoral degree in Social Work and a master's degree in Public Administration from the University of Utah. He also has a master's degree in Social Work from the University of Texas at Arlington. Dr. Stone spent 29 years in the US Air Force and held a number of leadership positions, including Director of Social Work Services, Director of Behavioral Health, Air Force Medical Doctrine Development section chief, Medical Operations Squadron Commander, Director of Research at Air Command and Staff College, Chief of Air Force Family Advocacy, and Deputy Medical Group Commander. He has lectured extensively on leadership and has taught leadership courses for the Air Force since 2007.

LEADERSHIP PROFILE FOR FRED STONE

Share your professional background and experience

I graduated from the Virginia Military Institute in 1983 with a Bachelor of Arts in Economics and was commissioned as a Second Lieutenant through AF ROTC. From 1985 to 1990, I was a C-130H navigator for the 772 Tactical Airlift Squadron and 463rd Tactical Airlift Wing, where I served as a Wing's Chief Navigator for Standardization and Evaluation. Then I left the active Air Force from 1990 to 1992 and became a member of the Texas Air National Guard. I served at the 181st Tactical Airlift Wing as a Tactical Officer while attending the University of Texas at Arlington Graduate School of Social Work. I received my Master of Science degree in 1992 and that summer returned to active duty in the Air Force as a clinical social worker. My first social work job was as a case manager in the 20th Medical Group hospital. In 1993, I transferred to the 2nd Medical Group, where I served as the chief of social work services and supervised a staff of eight. I was named the 1993 Medical Group Company Grade Officer of the Year.

In 1995, I was selected to attend the Air Force Institute of Technology advanced civilian degree program. Then I graduated with a Doctorate of Philosophy in Social Work and a Master of Public Administration in 1998 from the University of Utah. I was next assigned as the Director of Behavioral Science at the Eglin AFB Family Practice Residency Program, where I was selected as the Air Force Material Command Field Grade Social Worker of the Year. I served as Chief of Medical Doctrine Development, Office of the Air Force Surgeon General, in Washington, DC, where I authored numerous publications on the deployment of medical assets. Later I served as the commander of the 43rd Medical Operations Squadron at Pope Air Force Base (AFB) and supervised more than 80 personnel. I served as the President of the Air Force Cadet Officer Mentor Action Program (AFCOMAP) at Pope AFB, which was selected as the top AFCOMAP program in the Air Force. In 2005, I attended Air War College in-residence and was awarded the Thomas Dutch Miller Award for outstanding research in the field of counterproliferation. After Air War College, I was assigned as the Director Research and Publication at Air Command and Staff College and taught a research elective, leadership seminar, and regional studies course. In my next assignment, I served as the Chief of the Air Force Family Advocacy Program and oversaw a budget of more than $35 million dollars and directly supervised a staff of 35. My final assignment was as the Deputy Medical Group Commander of the 374th Medical Group at Yokota Air Base, Japan. I retired from active duty effective October 1, 2012.

I have published and lectured extensively on a wide variety of subjects, including airdrop techniques, patient safety, health care communication, leadership, stress management, and health service support lessons learned from Operation Iraqi Freedom.

In your experience, what are the top three to five leadership attributes someone in the health and human services field should develop? Share an example of when you have used one or more of these attributes/skills in your work

A *growth mindset*. Too often people believe they are either leaders or not, and this fixed mindset hinders their leadership development. They need to view leadership as a skill not a trait, and like any skill, it requires a process for improvement, practice, and feedback. Almost anyone can become a competent leader if open to learning the best leadership theories and practices.

Know your job and the organization. Successful leaders know their jobs, and they study their organizations intensely and understand the people, programs, and missions.

Develop good organizational habits and processes. Work habits and processes will produce positive work environments and move organizations toward accomplishing goals. Leaders who develop good organizational habits provide a consistency that workers can rely on. Successful leaders also develop personal habits that help them to ward off burnout and to become more efficient and effective.

Create an atmosphere of dignity and respect. Successful human services organization leaders develop an atmosphere of dignity and respect. As one social work leader asked me, "If we cannot treat each other with dignity and respect, then how can we be expected to treat our clients this way?"

In my professional life, all of these attributes helped me to prevent burnout. In my first leadership positions, I made a lot of mistakes, which could have discouraged me, but seeing leadership as a skill helped me to learn from my mistakes and motivated me to become a better leader. I worked hard to learn my job and consulted regularly with mentors. I also developed some personal habits that helped reduce my stress, including a meditation practice, daily exercise routine, and time management system. Finally, I always tried to keep our clients and patients in mind. It is a privilege to be asked to help another person, and keeping the nobility and importance of my organization's mission in my mind always helped me deal with its challenges.

My biggest challenge as a leader was reprimanding and firing people. It is hard to look someone in the eye and take actions that can hurt their careers and cause them and their family hardship. I learned a few things that made handling these situations easier. The first step was to separate the person from the action. I had a number of employees who were likeable and often did their jobs well, but these same employees got involved in drugs or other problems, which required me to take actions. Even though I often felt deep disappointment and some anger, to the best of my recollection, I never personally berated any of these employees, but solely focused on their actions. In many cases, these employees remained in my organization, and I did my best to treat them with dignity and respect. After reprimanding someone, I considered the matter closed and was ready to move on. Focusing on actions also helped navigate firing people. A phrase that I often used with someone who was being fired was that they were "not a good fit" for their current position. Their removal was not about them personally so much as their skill set and job requirements.

Finally, in many cases, I supported those who were forced to leave the organization as a result of my disciplinary actions. In one case, I had one individual who had consistently failed to meet the fitness and weight requirements for being in the Air Force. Previous commanders had demoted and reprimanded her on several occasions, but despite her best efforts, she was unable to meet the standards. After some consideration, I elected not to let her re-enlist. I told her that it was unlikely that she would ever meet the standards, and another commander might discharge her under less than honorable circumstances. I, however, said that I would be glad to write a letter of recommendation and support her finding a civilian job. She separated from the service and quickly found a civilian job. She wrote me a letter thanking me for the support and said that she was happier than she had ever been.

A CASE STUDY BY FRED STONE

On March 11, 2011, a 9.0 earthquake off the northeastern coast of Japan created a tsunami that streaked across the low-lying coastal areas along the northeastern shore of the nation. The Great East Japan Earthquake resulted in more than 18,000 deaths/people missing, hundreds of thousands of people displaced, and $360 billion in damage. At the time, I was the Deputy Medical Group Commander of the 374th Medical Group at Yokota Air Base, Japan, but the commander was moved to 5th Air Force, and I was put in charge. The 374th Medical Group had more than 400 personnel assigned and was responsible for the health of more than 5,000 base personnel.

Within a few hours, we learned that one of the cooling units at the Fukushima power plant had failed. A 40-foot-high wall of water had breached the plant and caused an explosion in reactor 4, resulting in iodine and cesium being released into the atmosphere. We did not know the consequences of this event but assumed the worst. Someone in the command post muttered, "China syndrome." The implications of this event were unclear. We received conflicting reports, and the "what if's" were frightening. Leaders at every US military base in Japan were concerned about the welfare of the men, women, and children who lived on their bases. Panic was a real concern and potentially threatened the ability of the bases to complete their missions. As the acting medical group commander, I was concerned about the health of the base, especially after the media reported the potential problems that the radiation leak might pose. I was also worried that the base population would demand answers and medical care we could not provide.

Our direction from higher headquarters was to limit the amount of information we shared with the base because too much was unknown. This approach, however, posed a problem. In the absence of information, the base personnel would "fill in the gaps" that would likely result in panic. The Wing Commander and I realized this potential danger and began an aggressive information campaign. Our approach was to provide crisis communication. Crisis communication means communicating all of the information that is known and accepting that some if not much of it will be inaccurate. This sounds like a mistake—to give information that will likely be proves wrong—but in the absence of communication, the population will come up with its own answers that are at least as equally ill-informed.

At Yokota AB, the leadership team regularly communicated whatever they knew about the crisis. I held daily meetings with my staff and met with personnel across the base to answer questions and allay concerns. The leadership team kept the base informed through radio and press interviews and social media. One example of this was the daily radiation level report, which always included a comparison of Yokota's radiation with a city in the United States. For example, on March 29, Public Affairs posted this statement on the base's Facebook page: "Today's radiation levels in the air average 37 μR. This is the equivalent to every day levels in Spokane, WA." The 374 Airlift Wing (AW) Public Affairs made an active and public effort to discover and openly discuss rumors with the community. On March 13, they posted on the base Facebook page, "What rumors are you hearing? Let us know and we will try to find the answers." The responses ranged from fears of a nuclear meltdown to an eruption of Mount Fuji, and for each fear, the 374 AW leadership was able to provide reassurance and reliable information.

As a result, the base population was remarkably calm. One senior leader who visited the base was surprised that during the height of the crisis, Yokota AB was a picture of relaxed "business as usual" as opposed to the anxiety-laden bases that he had witnessed elsewhere. He called it, "the Yokota miracle."

CASE DISCUSSION POINTS

1. In the leader profile, the innovative leader talks about attributes or skills assisting him in preventing burn out. Which attributes or skills do you currently possess and what needs to be further developed in your own leadership?
2. In what ways did the social architect in the case provide support to his team and community in order to decrease anxiety and stress?

3. Do you think it was an appropriate solution to provide information to a community in a situation of crisis, even if that information was not completely accurate or fully known at the time? Why or why not? What were the risks? Would you have done the same or something different? If so, what?

15

The Mindful Leader

GOLNAZ AGAHI ∎

Time passes unhindered. When we make mistakes, we cannot turn
the clock back and try again. All we can do is use the present well.

—DALAI LAMA

CHAPTER OBJECTIVES

1. Explore the use of mindfulness for innovative leaders to self-assess
   their internal states of being and to continue learning to avoid
   workplace burnout and excessive stress as discussed in the previous
   chapter;
2. Understand the various mindfulness practices;
3. Gain an appreciation of the benefits associated with mindfulness,
   particularly for social architects in the health and human services
   fields; and
4. Gain insights on innovative leadership from a social architect (see
   Appendix to this chapter).

INTRODUCTION

In today's workforce, "mindfulness" has become a popular buzzword.
Organizations pursue opportunities to help their leaders become mindful in
order to be better at their jobs. Mindfulness is defined as being aware of the
moment and accepting nonjudgmentally (Kabat-Zinn & Davidson, 2012).

Mindfulness practice is an approach to reduce stress and serves as a venue for self-care (McCollum & Gehart, 2010). It improves well-being and behavioral regulation and positively affects attention, cognition, and stress management, which are all important factors in being an effective leader (Creswell & Lindsay, 2014; Keng et al., 2011; Smallwood & Schooler, 2015). In a recent survey conducted by the American Management Association, more than half of respondents indicated that their organizations were negatively affected by experiencing high stress levels (American Management Association, 2014). The Gallup employment engagement study identified that a majority (70%) of employees were not engaged or were actively disengaged. The study suggests that a contributing factor affecting disengagement is the employees' relationship with their supervisor (Gallup, 2017). Thus, creating a mindful workplace can help mitigate the negative consequences associated with stress for both leaders and employees.

This chapter will provide the reader with some of the research behind the utility of mindfulness practice particularly as it relates to leadership. Simple mindfulness techniques will be presented that can be applied on a daily basis. A case study also illustrates the daily life of an innovative leader in a health and human services organization who incorporates mindfulness to assist her to stay focused and in the moment in order to be the best that she can be in her leadership role while balancing her daily personal life at home. Finally, as already mentioned, this chapter is meant not only to help readers assess their internal states (including thoughts, emotions, physical perceptions, etc.) but also to complement the material presented in the previous chapter (Chapter 14) in finding innovative and evidence-based methods to address stress in the workplace.

BACKGROUND

An individual holding a leadership role is particularly vulnerable to occupational stress, and for women leaders, it is a double burden as they try to balance work, home demands, and, for some, motherhood (Barsh, Cranston, & Craske, 2008; Bryant & Constantine, 2006; Burke, 2006; Schueller-Weidekamm & Kautzky-Willer, 2012). When this occupational stress level is continuously elevated for leaders, their ability to fully use both cognitive and emotional intelligence to make timely and effective decisions is significantly impaired (Thompson, 2009). For women innovative leaders, it has been argued that the added burden of maintaining their femininity while remaining competent and assertive in their leadership role significantly increases stress levels (Rudman & Glick, 1999).

As leaders juggle multiple roles, there is a need to practice self-care to be an effective leader and to avoid burnout (Wicks & Buck, 2013). Balancing multiple roles and job satisfaction are positive predictors of overall life satisfaction (Bryant & Constantine, 2006). And who doesn't want satisfaction in both their work and personal lives? Additionally, how can innovative leaders slow down to make better decisions? The solution may be in the practice of mindfulness. With even a small amount of effort, mindfulness allows us to stay focused in the moment and provides space to make better decisions. More organizations have begun to recognize the importance of mindfulness and how it can improve work productivity for their managers and employees. According to the American Management Association's (2014) recent survey, about 50% of the firms interviewed incorporated some aspect of mindfulness resource or training and 85% found that incorporating mindfulness is beneficial. Many of these organizations are well known, including Google, Aetna, Mayo Clinic, General Mills, Intel, and the US Army (Jha et al., 2015; Tan, 2012; West et al., 2014; Wolever et al., 2012). A study on middle managers and mindfulness found that training of mindfulness for middle managers improved supervisor-rated job performance (Shonin, Gordon, Dunn, Singh, & Griffiths, 2014). So not only can we as social architects incorporate mindfulness exercises in our daily routine, but we can also develop opportunities within our organizations to become an agent of change and develop opportunities for our team to practice mindfulness. The Mindfulness-Based Stress Reduction program is one such training program with validated success and has been adapted for the workplace (Good et al., 2016).

Various factors contribute to successful innovative leadership, such as capacity for stress management, resilience under stress, cognitive resilience, emotional intelligence, and positivity (Barsh, Cranston, & Craske, 2008; Thompson, 2009). Mindfulness practice improves the factors noted because it helps individuals to remain engaged in their day-to-day work. It is a development of lifestyle balance that includes acceptance, nonjudgment, trust, and patience (Kabat-Zinn, 2012). Mindfulness can help connect one's actions with the organization's purpose by helping the leader turn off "autopilot" functioning and focus on the present, with the intent to be a better leader.

A recent comprehensive analysis on mindfulness by Good and colleagues (2016) found five areas in which mindfulness positively effects individual functioning: physiology, behavior, cognition, emotion, and attention. Specifically, with attention, it was shown that individuals were able to remain focused longer on both visual and listening tasks. The study also suggests that mindfulness improves interpersonal behavior and workgroup relationships. There is also recent research that specifically shows a strong correlation between mindfulness and higher ethical and prosocial behavior, while reducing hostile feelings (Krishnakumar & Robinson, 2015; Reb, Narayanan, & Ho, 2015).

Other studies have found that mindfulness activates the anterior region of the brain, which in turn increases positive affect and compassion and reduces anxiety and negative effects (Evans et al., 2011). According to Davidson, a neuroscientist who has conducted significant research in the field of mindfulness, 1.5 hours of mindfulness practice per day can lead to positive structural changes in the brain. Additionally, there is preliminary research showing that leaders who practice mindfulness can remain engaged on a task and better disengage from an interrupting task that can negatively affect thoughts and emotions (Long & Christian, 2015). A five-minute mindful exercise has shown to help reduce the residue, that is, thinking about the last stimuli from ongoing interruptions, instead of focusing on the new tasks at hand (Kuo & Yeh, 2015).

MINDFULNESS PRACTICE

So, what do you think about giving mindfulness a try? On an individual level, consider the activities that can be incorporated into your daily routine to practice mindfulness. Ask yourself what can be done now to stay focused. For each of us, this may look a little different based on our individual preferences. Some may focus attention on deep breathing; others on the monitoring of various sensory stimuli such as a body scan (Lutz et al., 2008). These activities require mini-pauses in one's daily routines. They are simple mediation tools that can be done at work or at home and do not require fancy equipment, clothing, or materials. Although varied, each of these exercises begins with a relaxed physical posture, followed by engagement in an activity that helps clear a mind that is typically racing at the speed of light.

Mindfulness Techniques

There are several mindfulness techniques that can be practiced while breathing, eating, being aware of your body, and walking.

Mindful Breathing. This is a meditation practice that can be done anytime and anywhere. One such method outlined by Elisha Goldstein (2012) is called STOP:

1. The "S" in "STOP" stands for the intention to engage in mindfulness by stepping away from the routine and fully engaging in the STOP practice. Hence, prepare to take a second to break away from current thoughts or activities.

2. The "T" stands for "Take a Breath," which is the action of focusing attention on your breathing and identifying the part of the body through which the breathing takes place. It is awareness of the breath as it flows in and out of the body.
3. The "O" stands for "Observe," which indicates attention to be paid to the present experience. It is an opportunity to check yourself and explore what you are feeling inside (e.g., your heart rate, body temperature, your mind, and/or your environment). Observe is an opportunity to notice the changes without passing any judgment.
4. The "P" in "Proceed" is the final step, which brings you back to the present situation and the activity that you were engaged in before taking the breath. "Proceed" helps balance the external and the internal cues to avoid negative interaction in your activity/situation and allow you to be in the moment without the anger, resentment, anxiety, or irritation that you may have initially harbored before your STOP exercise.

Mindful Eating. Mindful eating is a commitment to appreciate and enjoy food with the intention of focusing on the food that is placed in one's mouth. Often, we eat to keep functioning and to have fuel to make it through the day. Mindfulness eating is meant to take the time to bite into your food or drink and savor the moment. So here are a few tips to be a mindful eater as recommended by Jenni Grover (2013), a registered dietitian:

- *Eat slower.* When at work, usually eating means sitting in front of the computer, or at a meeting or in-between meetings, stuffing one's mouth as quickly as possible to avoid a growling stomach. But what if at least once a week you take the time to savor your food, or a favorite for many, that piece of chocolate. This is one of the healthiest actions you can take for yourself. When you take the time to eat slower, you chew your food more, resulting in better digestion, but it also allows you to enjoy the flavor of the food and remain present in the moment.
- *Savor the silence.* This means taking just a few minutes away from the hustle and bustle of your day to eat without distractions. It is recommended to take some time to enjoy the silence and to focus on the meal or drink. Savoring the silence can help you to savor the meal.
- *Silence the electronics.* What if for only 1 to 5 minutes you take your eyes away from the TV, computer monitor, laptop, iPad, smart phone,

or any other electronic gadget? Give your mind a rest from all external stimuli to focus on the meal on hand. Make this conscious choice to enjoy your meal without the use of technology.

- *Pay attention to flavor.* When you can create a moment of silence and reduce distractions, you can then focus your attention on the food and start mindful eating. Focus on flavors and textures of the food. What does it taste like and how does it feel (texture)? Is sweet or bitter? Is it spicy or tangy? Is it cold or hot? When was the last time you took the time to truly appreciate the flavor of your meal?

Body Scan. A body scan is a way to get in touch with different parts of your body and to experience how each part feels. It is designed to focus attention and to release emotions. Alidina (2015) describes the body scan as a tool to train the mind to focus on details and then to open to a wider spectrum. For example, start thinking of your toes or start with your head and then move progressively to larger, more complete parts of the body, and eventually to an internal scan of whole body. This practice can be done at work sitting in your chair with your back straight and eyes closed or laying down on the floor in your house or office. Try these steps:

1. Close your eyes and take several deep breaths.
2. Begin to focus your attention from top of your body (your head) and move through different body parts. Notice your cheeks, mouth, neck, arms, hands, chest, abdomen, legs, and feet.
3. Do this scanning several times, moving top to bottom and then bottom to top of your body.
4. The scanning helps to identify any stress or strain, and the deep breathing helps to relieve body tension.

Mindful Walking Meditation. A walking meditation helps develop calmness and awareness. The purpose of mindful walking is to enhance your attention by paying attention. In his book, *The Long Road Turns to Joy*, Hanh notes that to regain peace one must enjoy each step and each breath in difficult moments. The author states, "To have peace, you can begin by walking peacefully. Everything depends on your steps" (2011, p. 5). So here is a simple walking map:

1. Find a space where you can walk, such as outside your office or even in your backyard. Start with standing and taking several deep breaths.

2. Move your feet muscles and feel how they touch the ground. Do a quick body scan with attention to any areas of stiffness in the body and make a conscious effort to relax the stiff body parts.

3. Listen to sounds surrounding you. Notice the air temperature and the environment that you stand in before you begin your walk.

4. Breathe in and take a conscious step, aware of every step taken, each one taken slowly, deliberately.

5. Take the time to be aware of the step taken and how the sole of the foot lifts and lands on the ground.

6. Now focus on the state of your mind. Is it cluttered and busy, cloudy, distracted? Acknowledge it and practice freeing the mind. Clear the mind, aiming to become a blank slate.

7. Then take the next step, and then the next step, until you can bring attention to the now. This process can be 5 minutes or 20 minutes in length. You make the choice.

In the next section, we will make a closer examination of what a busy and often hectic day looks like for a leader. See if you can identify with any parts of the case study and how mindfulness could possibly apply to you.

A CHAPTER CASE STUDY

Nancy is a midlevel manager at a large health care organization. In the following case study, she relates her daily routine both in and out of the clinic.

My daily routine: almost every morning I wake up to a text or a call from an employee who needs an immediate response. This is followed by running in circles, while I prepare breakfast and lunch bags for the family, then dress myself and the family to head out for the day. While all this is occurring, I am checking emails and responding to more texts and phone calls. I arrive to work and don't step more than a foot out of the elevator before I am pulled in different directions by competing employees' needs and/or work demands. It takes about an hour to travel the 50 feet from the elevator to my office, only to turn on the computer to 100 plus emails, while my cell phone is receiving more texts, my work phone is ringing, and I have an employee at my office door needing immediate attention. Meanwhile, a patient is waiting to speak to the manager (me) in the waiting room. YES, I am already exhausted, and I haven't made it beyond the first two hours at work. So how should I balance my day, prioritize my work, meet my report deadlines, while watching my inbox grow exponentially? Still, the requests for attention from employees and patients pile up, my "same time" messaging is blinking angrily on my computer while the line at my office door is growing with disgruntled individuals who need immediate attention, and by the way my family is texting asking what is for dinner? Now I am running into a meeting. Sitting in the meeting, I am so focused on my laundry list of work-related tasks, and I look up and see my colleague moving his mouth but I don't understand the words. And that is when I stop and play one of my favorite movie clips in my head, "Do you understand the words that are coming out of my mouth?" For the movie enthusiast, you may remember this quote from the film Rush Hour, *where the Los Angeles Police Detective Carter (played by Chris Tucker) shouts at the Hong Kong Detective Inspector Lee (played by Jackie Chan) in their introduction to each other. This is where I finally take my first deep breath. It is now 10:05 AM, and back to the present I return. A practice of mindfulness.*

On average, I work 9 to 10 hours a day, so it is pertinent to pay attention to my mood. Am I being irked by an email? Is the present circumstance irritating me? Am I having a difficult time letting go of a situation? It takes practice to condition my mind to identify these moments, pause, and incorporate mindfulness mini-pauses. When I can identify these moments, I stop and take a mindful deep breath, hold, and slowly release. If I am in my office, I am mindful to close my eyes, while taking several deep breaths. Or it may be a simple mindful exercise of rotating the neck or the wrist as part of a body scan. If I am still not able to focus on the task on hand, it is a matter taking a mindful walk around the office to get my steps in for the day. In a meeting or at my desk, it may be grabbing a snack from my lunch box and taking a moment to be mindful of the texture and flavor of a tangerine, cheese string, or the pirate booty. At least once a week, I indulge myself in a midday basketball game. When playing basketball, I must focus on the moment. I need to know where the ball is, where my teammates are positioned, and where they are going. It is all about the NOW. In the game, I am conditioning my mind to focus on the task at hand and let go of my work and emotional turmoil. My peers ask if it is not hard to peel myself from the office to play basketball. My response is, "I don't play ball for a midday exercise . . . I play to keep my sanity.

Can you relate to this leader's experience? Every day, as social architects we lead and/or work in our organizations with every intention to be our best, but we are affected by various challenges and distractions that seem to bog us down. To thrive and be our best, we need to reprogram our brain to focus on the here and now by taking intentional breaks, or mindfulness mini-pauses. This helps to turn off the autopilot behaviors and be more focused and innovative in the moment. When conducting mindfulness trainings for managers, I use the example of a driver on autopilot mode. How many of you have driven to or from work while making a mental checklist of items to be done at home and/or work? And, when you arrive at your destination, you don't recall how you got there? The parallel experience of this at work entails the times we go through the motions to arrive at some end point, but we forget or don't pay attention to the essential components of the process to make it a more rewarding and lived experience.

In conclusion, as noted in this chapter, different exercises, including the use of mindfulness, can help a leader cope (and thrive) in the fast-paced rollercoaster of a busy life and allow him or her to take moments out of the day to focus on what is at hand. Can we always be successful at mindful living? Absolutely, not! But with practice, it becomes more natural to incorporate mindfulness each day. Some popular inspirational quotes on practicing mindfulness from fictional *Star Wars* character, Jedi Master Yoda, include, "Train yourself to let go of everything . . ." followed by, "[M]ind what you learned, save you it can." Incorporation of mindfulness will not take away a leader's daily challenges. However, when combined with at least two to three mini-pauses in the day to formally practice mindfulness and support it over a sustained period, mindfulness can lead to valuable and positive changes that can help an innovative leader to be a better leader and to experience life in its fullest form.

CHAPTER DISCUSSION QUESTIONS

1. Identify the general benefits of mindfulness.
2. Why is it important for a leader to engage in mindfulness and encourage employees to do the same?
3. Which mindfulness techniques can you incorporate in your daily life?
4. Attempt at least one of the mindful techniques today and note how it affects you. Challenge yourself to continue to practice even if you do not feel the immediate effects.
5. Read the leader profile and case study in the Appendix to this chapter. Note innovative ideas and practices and see what aspects of the case you can connect to the contents of the chapter and/or overall book.

REFERENCES

Alidina, S. (2015). *Mindfulness for dummies* (2nd ed.). Chichester, UK: John Wiley & Sons.

American Management Association. (2014). *Stress Management and mindfulness in the workplace executive summary.* Retrieved from http://www.amanet.org/training/articles/stress-management-and-mindfulness-in-the-workplace.aspx

Barsh, J., Cranston, S., & Craske, R. A. (2008). Centered leadership: How talented women thrive. *McKinsey Quarterly, 4*, 35–48.

Bryant, R., & Constantine, M. (2006). Multiple role balance, job satisfaction, and life satisfaction in women school counselors. *Professional School Counseling, 9*(4), 265–271.

Burke, R. J. (2006). Supporting women's career advancement: Challenges and opportunities. *Human Resource Management International Digest, 14*(3).

Creswell, J. D., & Lindsay, E. K. (2014). How does mindfulness training affect health? A mindfulness stress buffering account. *Current Directions in Psychological Science, 23*, 401–407.

Evans, S., Ferrando, S., Carr, C., & Haglin, D. (2011). Mindfulness-based stress reduction (MBSR) and distress in a community-based sample. *Clinical Psychology and Psychotherapy, 18*, 553–558. doi: 10.1002/cpp.727

Gallup. (2017, February) *State of the American workplace.* Retrieved from http://www.gallup.com/services/178514/state-american-workplace.aspx?g_source=ServiceLandingPage&g_medium=copy&g_campaign=tabs

Goldstein, E. (2012). *The now effect: How a mindful moment can change the rest of your life.* New York, NY: Simon and Shuster.

Good D. J., Lyddy C. J., Glomb T. M., Bono J. E., Brown K. W., Duffy M. K., Baer R. A., Brewer J. A., & Lazar S. W. (2016). Contemplating mindfulness at work: An integrative review. *Journal of Management, 42*(1), 114–142. doi: 10.1177/0149206315617003

Grover, J. (2013, September 6). Mindful eating: 5 Easy tips to get started. *Mother Nature Network.* Retrieved from https://www.mnn.com/food/healthy-eating/stories/mindful-eating-5-easy-tips-to-get-started

Hanh, T. (2011). *The Long road turns to joy: A guide to walking meditation.* Berkeley, CA: Parallax Press.

Jha, A. P., Morrison, A. B., Dainer-Best, J., Parker, S., Rostrup, N., & Stanley, E. A. (2015). Minds "at attention": Mindfulness training curbs attentional lapses in military cohorts. *PLoS ONE, 10,* e0116889

Kabat-Zinn, J., & Davidson, R. (Eds.). (2012). *The mind's own physician: A scientific dialogue with the Dalai Lama on the healing power of meditation.* New York, NY: New Harbinger Publications.

Keng, S.-L., Smoski, M. J., & Robins, C. J. (2011). Effects of mindfulness on psychological health: A review of empirical studies. *Clinical Psychology Review, 31*(6), 1041–1056.

Krishnakumar, S., & Robinson, M. D. (2015). Maintaining an even keel: An affect-mediated model of mindfulness and hostile work behavior. *Emotion, 15,* 579–589.

Kuo, C.-Y., & Yeh, Y.-Y. (2015). Reset a task set after five minutes of mindfulness practice. *Consciousness and Cognition, 35,* 98–109.

Long, E. C., & Christian, M. S. 2015. Mindfulness buffers retaliatory responses to injustice: A regulatory approach. *Journal of Applied Psychology, 100,* 1409–1422.

Lutz, A., Slagter, H. A., Dunne, J. D., & Davidson, R. J. (2008). Attention regulation and monitoring in meditation. *Trends in Cognitive Sciences, 12,* 163–169.

McCollum, E. E., & Gehart, D. R. (2010). Using mindfulness meditation to teach beginning therapists therapeutic presence: A qualitative study. *Journal of Marital and Family Therapy, 36*(3), 347–360.

Reb, J., Narayanan, J., & Ho, Z. W. (2015). Mindfulness at work: Antecedents and consequences of employee awareness and absent-mindedness. *Mindfulness, 6,* 111–122.

Rudman, L. A., & Glick, P. (1999). Feminized management and backlash toward agentic women: the hidden costs to women of a kinder, gentler image of middle managers. *Journal of Personality and Social Psychology, 77*(5), 1004.

Schueller-Weidekamm, C., & Kautzky-Willer, A. (2012). Challenges of work–life balance for women physicians/mothers working in leadership positions. *Gender medicine, 9*(4), 244–250.

Shonin, E., Gordon, W. V., Dunn, T. J., Singh, N. N., & Griffiths, M. D. (2014). Meditation Awareness Training (MAT) for work-related wellbeing and job performance: A randomized controlled trial. *International Journal of Mental Health and Addiction, 12,* 806–823.

Smallwood, J., & Schooler, J. W. (2015). The science of mind wandering: Empirically navigating the stream of consciousness. *Annual Review of Psychology, 66,* 487–518.

Tan, C. M. (2012). *Search inside yourself: The unexpected path to achieving success, happiness (and world peace).* New York, NY: HarperOne.

Thompson, H. L. (2009). Emotional intelligence, stress, and catastrophic leadership failure. In M. Hughes, H. L. Thompson, & J. P. Terrell (Eds.), *Handbook for Developing Emotional and Social Intelligence* (pp. 111–138). San Francisco, CA: Pfeiffer.

West, C. P., Dyrbye, L. N., Rabatin, J. T., Call, T. G., Davidson, J. H., Multari, A., Romanski, S. A., Hellyer, J. M. H., Sloan, J. A., & Shanafelt, T. D. (2014). Intervention to promote physician well-being, job satisfaction, and professionalism: A randomized clinical trial. *JAMA Internal Medicine, 174,* 527.

Wicks, R. J., & Buck, T. C. (2013). Riding the dragon: Enhancing resilient leadership and sensible self-care in the healthcare executive. *Frontiers of Health Services Management, 30*(2), 3.

Wolever, R. Q., Bobinet, K. J., McCabe, K., Mackenzie, E. R., Fekete, E., Kusnick, C. A., & Baime, M. (2012). Effective and viable mind-body stress reduction in the workplace: A randomized controlled trial. *Journal of Occupational Health Psychology, 17,* 246–258.

APPENDIX
Featured Leader: Golnaz Agahi

Golnaz Agahi received her dual master's degrees in Public Health and Social Work from San Diego State University. She has more than 20 years of experience working in both public health and social services settings. Presently, she is the Assistant Director at Kaiser Permanente Behavioral Health Department in Orange County and co-chairs the Orange County Kaiser Permanente Family Violence Prevention Program. Also, she teaches part-time at the University of Southern California Suzanne Dworak-Peck School of Social Work and earned her doctorate degree in social work from the University of Southern California.

Her area of expertise is in program planning, implementation, and evaluation. Her past clinical work, research, and publications (including curriculum development) have addressed the following areas: alcohol and drug prevention and treatment, high-risk and homeless youth services, gang prevention and intervention, crisis intervention, intimate partner violence, and stress management.

LEADERSHIP PROFILE FOR GOLNAZ AGAHI

Share your professional background and experience

I grew up with my role models being superheroes, like Superwoman and Storm. I knew when I grew up I wanted to be in a position that I could make a difference in people's lives. I didn't know what that would be exactly. When I was in college, I was trying to pursue medical school, and that's when I got introduced to the field of public health. I said to myself, wow, what a neat concept, not just being able to change and improve the well-being of the individual but also making changes on a community level. So I took a detour from medical school and decided to pursue a master's degree in Public Health and Social Work with a focus on Administration. I realized that's what I wanted to do, to make an impact on a larger macro level. In order to do that, I needed the management and leadership skills that administration studies would provide me with.

I was very fortunate in the past 17 to 20 years. I've worked in different sectors of our service provision community and in the following types of organizations:

- Nonprofits
- For-profits
- Government
- Hospitals
- Community clinics

I have been very fortunate to be able to experience different levels of providing services and care and understanding the different populations so that I could be a better leader. Presently, I'm the Assistant Director for Orange County Kaiser Permanente Behavioral Health Department. In my role, I support the different services that we have, which include addiction medicine, psychiatry, ambulatory care, and inpatient services.

In your experience, what are the top three to five leadership attributes someone in the health and human services field should develop? Share an example of when you have used one or more of these attributes/skills in your work

> *Emotional intelligence.* I would say that one of the most essential pieces, if you're going to be a leader and you want to make a change in your department or position, is the importance of having emotional intelligence. Really being able to engage and connect with your team, with your department, to be able to make a change, which is not always easy to do. From all the models that I have looked at and I've tried to mimic in my life, or actually individuals, like Martin Luther King Jr., as an influential political leader/activist that he was not only able to change history but also able to engage a large population to believe in him. If we're going to improve anything, we're not going to be able to make a successful change, unless we engage the people in this conversation.
>
> *Passion and motivation to make a change.* Leaders and managers are two different things. You can have managers that are not leaders, and you can have employees that are leaders but not managers. I think it is essential to recognize the difference because if you are going to be a manager who is also a leader, you're not just going to follow what's been dictated or try

to get by with just day-to-day operations, you want to think outside the box, you want to be able to improve, you want to be able to inspire your department as part of that. And that's where your passion and energy can be translated. When you can inspire others in your clinic or workplace to not be apathetic but to be involved and engaged.

Professional growth. If you want to be a leader, you constantly have to be in a position in which you are learning. Not only learning from the world of academia, which is essential for understanding what's new, like what are new evidence-based practices that can be incorporated into our work settings, but also learning from peers and employees. Understand where they are coming from and search for opportunities to further foster professional and personal growth together. Your professional and personal interests will always intermingle if you are a leader because your passion becomes your work. It is an essential component to foster those skills rather than remain stagnant and go through day-to-day operations because it's very easy for us to get trapped in that position where, *oh my gosh today I have to come in, I have to review my emails, I have to respond to emails, I have to do A, B, and C, and oh the day is over, alright next day.* So really pushing ourselves and challenging ourselves to strive on that higher level. I also practice mindfulness on a daily basis. I utilize yoga techniques and make sure to breathe, eat, and walk mindfully. This practice has allowed me to face the everyday challenges with greater sense of peace and patience. I also encourage my team members to practice mindfulness and will often conduct some mindfulness activities before a meeting to get everyone in the right frame of mind to be in the present moment.

A CASE STUDY BY GOLNAZ AGAHI

I'm going to speak of my present program, created within a large complex health care system, where it's always challenging to develop new programs because there are so many different dimensions to it. In light of the challenges, we have created our first dual diagnosis clinic to serve individuals with both mental health issues and substance abuse disorders. It is an integrative clinic where we address addiction and psychiatry simultaneously, which is a recommendation from SAMHSA—the Substance Abuse and Mental Health Services Administration.

Even though research supports how important combining treatments for both conditions is, so many of the institutional systems keep these two interventions apart from each other. One of the systems or stakeholders involves health insurance benefits, where certain services are carved out. The Parity Act was supposed to integrate mental health and addictions to be included as part of the overall health care system. But there is continued stigmatization; the common narratives are, for example, "psych medicine is better than addiction medicine, because if you have a drug problem, you are the worst of the worst."

I am very passionate about helping individuals in an integrated fashion because whether it's the chicken or the egg question, both need attention. That is, is it anxiety that came first to then cause the drinking problem? Or is it drinking too much alcohol that produced the anxiety? Creating a program that really treats the whole person rather than just the symptom is what I believe and is supported in the literature. And this is something that when I came in as a leader, four or five years ago at Kaiser, I said, *why is it that someone who has an addiction and mental health disorder can only go through the addiction medicine department? How come a patient has to have 90 days of sobriety before they can get psych treatment? And why can't the therapist in the addiction center address the psych issues simultaneously so the patient is not bouncing back and forth between programs? Or, why does everything shut down in the psychiatry unit as soon as the patient says, "I've been smoking weed once a week," and he or she gets switched to addiction medicine?* I think we have culture in the United States (and in the field of psychiatry) of categorizing people and addressing their symptoms versus looking at the whole person, and this is unsettling for me. I felt very passionate and driven to create a program that really integrated these two components.

I put a business plan together for an integrated clinic type of framework that would consider the clinical perspectives in terms of what the clinicians have to be trained in, that is, what skills they need, what this treatment model is going to look like, and also from a logistics perspective. In other words, *what would it look like to merge these two separate departments, two different insurance benefits, two different federal requirements?* There are the clinical components, the administrative piece, the health insurance piece, and the legality/policy pieces that have to be pulled together to be able to feasibly create and sustain this program. So I had to engage key players at various levels.

1. *Micro level.* I had to get the buy-in of the practitioners that were going to move to a new clinic and get them to agree to do things differently from all of their other colleagues, which meant that they were going to treat the whole patient. You can't bounce a patient from unit to unit just because they have a drug problem; you are going to treat that patient for their addiction and the psychiatry issues simultaneously.
2. *Mezzo level.* I had to work with my manager and my supervisor and the department leadership to get their buy-in for the new program

because they had to invest by providing a budget to create this program, find a facility to house it, and get on board with how the services would be integrated. When I had to recruit for this clinic, I had to find therapists that were willing to do both pieces and have the buy-in from the labor union.

3. *Macro level.* Then there was the regional buy-in. There are multiple services areas in Southern California, from Kern Country to San Diego County, that all report to our behavioral health department in Pasadena. So I had to get the Pasadena leadership team onto the idea of the new clinic and the new concept we were integrating and make sure we were not breaking any laws, rules, or regulations. *Is this even possible??* I had to talk to the director of behavioral health for all of Southern California Kaiser, budget people, IT people, and our ethics and electronic health professionals to help them understand this model and what we were envisioning.

We wanted to be a blueprint for future models across Kaiser. I drafted my vision, my business plan, the purpose, and program needs. Then meeting with all these different players to engage them and get their buy-in for this first ever integrative clinic for Kaiser. I think in terms of potential positive consequences for the organization, we just opened the first clinic in November, so I am still in the process of evaluating it to see if it is meeting the intended goals. I am excited that Kaiser CEO Bernard Tyson came for a visit because he wanted to see what this integrative clinic looked like. We have some challenges, but I think there is opportunity to make changes on a national level. Insurance companies and HMOs that provide these services as separated care can use this model to really change how we treat mental health issues and addictions in silos across the United States.

The best part of this is the delivery service that we provide to our patients because they are not bouncing between clinics anymore and getting lost through the process, but actually they get all of their care in one place (at least the psychological and substance abuse care). It is the beginning of patient-centered care. I feel like it's my baby, my integrative clinic; I think there is more to come of it. I have been meeting with quite a few managers and directors from other service areas who say they are considering a similar model. Many of them ask me, "How did you get your therapists to agree to this?" There are some service areas in which the therapist in addiction medicine won't even talk to the therapist in psychiatry. I tell other leaders that what it all comes down to is your leadership skills, to basically sell your product and your concept. You need to fuel the passion among everyone to believe in what you believe and how it relates to them and supports their passion as well.

CASE DISCUSSION POINTS

1. What was the service need that was identified?
2. What were some of the perceived and/or potential barriers to implementation?
3. What are the different levels of influence (or engagement) that this innovative leader faced when attempting to convince a variety of stakeholders that had different concerns and needs?
4. What does this innovative leader attribute to her success? In other words, what element(s) were necessary in the adoption of this innovative program by the organization?
5. What could be some potential future steps for the social architect in ensuring the sustainability and success of the program?

16

Assessing Interventions and Evaluating Programs

> One of the great mistakes is to judge policies and programs
> by their intentions rather than their results.
>
> —MILTON FRIEDMAN

CHAPTER OBJECTIVES

1. Examine best practices to assess interventions in the health and human services fields;
2. Review the most common program evaluation types, including formative, summative, or outcome evaluation; needs assessment; and cost-benefit analysis, as well as the use of theory for guiding evaluation practice;
3. Explore how public agencies and private organizations promote evidence-based interventions, promising practices, and effective programs; and
4. Gain insight on innovative leadership from a social architect (see Appendix to this chapter).

INTRODUCTION

Unfortunately, many health and human services practitioners and leaders are concerned and anxious about engaging in formal program assessments and evaluations. One of the main reasons that organizations may not like to conduct evaluations is the potential ramifications that negative or insignificant results may have on their team members, clients, and programs. Imagine a health and human services organization investing significant resources (e.g., time, talent, and finances) in a program, to later learn that the assessment or evaluation results demonstrated little or no improvement in the intended client outcomes or, in the worst-case scenario, that the program was demonstrated as being deleterious to client well-being. The consequences can be devastating to the organizational leadership because stakeholders (e.g., board of directors, donors, media) will demand immediate staff and/or programming changes, or it could result in a loss of funding. Nonetheless, instead of experiencing feelings of vulnerability because of the potential for negative evaluation results, innovative leaders must welcome and embrace ongoing measurements that will shed light on their clients' progress and program outcomes. Social architects learn the value of intervention assessments and program evaluations as key routines of their practice. More important, social architects consider assessment and evaluation as part of their core ethical compass because these measurements have the potential to directly benefit the organization's service delivery effectiveness and contribute to the clients' improvement (see ethical standards in Chapter 2).

The content ahead is presented with the goal of increasing your knowledge and understanding of general assessment and evaluation practices; it is not intended to instruct you on how to become a formal program evaluator. For those of you interested in becoming formal applied researchers and/or program evaluators, you will need far more advanced training and education, which includes research methods and statistical analyses (which usually means having to obtain a doctoral degree in a social science discipline from an accredited university). This chapter will provide an overall and brief introduction to measurement applications, outlining key tools for assessing interventions that clinicians can utilize with their clients, program evaluation types and methods, and online resources to find evidence-based interventions and effective programs for your clients.

ASSESSING INTERVENTIONS

The majority of health and human services organizations provide direct interventions to patients and clients to improve their health, well-being, and general functioning. Among many others, examples of health and human services interventions and settings include a community clinic offering health checkups, outpatient surgeries, and prescription drugs to low-income families; a neighborhood pantry providing meals and mental health services to homeless individuals; a behavioral health agency with providers facilitating psychotherapy sessions for individuals diagnosed with clinical depression or anxiety disorders; behavioral interventions rendered by a specialist working in a school to improve behavior and socialization skills for youth diagnosed on the autism spectrum; or a local boys and girls club hosting family counseling sessions to teenage parents struggling with drug dependency issues. Many of these interventions are designed and/or implemented by health and human services clinicians, professionals, paraprofessionals, and even trained volunteers, who are poised to improve people's lives. Innovative leaders understand that not all interventions are created equal, and thus, not all intervention services have the same impact or effectiveness. It is fair to say that intervention results depend on many factors—some under our control, and others out of our control. Consequently, how can we assess interventions appropriately? How do we know that one intervention is more effective than another depending on the clients and their needs? To answer these questions, we will review general definitions along with several types of interventions, proper measurements to apply when assessing the intervention's effects on clients, and key evidence-based intervention elements.

Generally, an intervention is a guided and structured set of actions and/or activities performed by a licensed and/or knowledgeable professional with the purpose of improving another person and/or group with certain characteristics. Although in the West, psychotherapy or the "talking cure" is associated with Sigmund Freud and his predecessors in the late 19th century, more recently, Vernon Johnson is credited with the creation and application of the first formal intervention model in the 1960s. Johnson later established the Johnson & Johnson Institute, which focuses on helping individuals fighting addiction of alcohol and other drugs (see more information on the Johnson & Johnson Institute's interventions and programs in their website at https://jnjinstitute.com/).

Typically, clients with mental health concerns seek help by formally participating in psychotherapy, which serves as a guided process to improve their conditions. For the past half-century, health and human services have significantly increased the number and sophistication of such therapeutic interventions. To date, we have thousands of intervention models and therapies available, most of them tailored to clients exhibiting specific illnesses, disorders, or conditions. For example, some of the most widespread intervention models or therapies include those aimed at alcohol and drug rehabilitation (detoxing and counseling), or those intended to be brief and crisis oriented or time limited and structured, such as those under the umbrella of cognitive behavioral therapies, and so on. Psychotherapy or counseling is also provided in various formats, including individual, family, couples', and group based, and in a multitude of settings (e.g., schools, outpatient clinics, inpatient psychiatric units, hospitals, community resource centers, shelters, home based).

The most effective method to assess the intervention's impact or effect is by collecting and measuring client data. Data are any form of information about the patient or client in question. Typically, data are collected and assessed by the clinician or provider on a regular basis; the more critical the health or mental health condition of the patient, the more frequently data are collected. These data can be quantified (i.e., numbers), such as the patient sharing his or her pain levels between 1 and 10 (where 1 is low-level pain and 10 is high-level pain); or qualified (i.e., words), such as a provider asking the patient, "tell me about your emotions today" or "share what happened." According to Rubin and Babbie (2016), there are five types of data collection:

1. *Instruments or scales.* Instruments or scales are highly refined questionnaires that have been pilot-tested repetitively and have passed rigorous standardization protocols that address their reliability and validity. Generally, instrument developers are social scientists who have published the instrument design, development, and statistical diagnostics in peer-reviewed academic journals. There are thousands of scales or instruments available to assess a patient's condition and measure the effects of an intervention or program. Examples of these client self-report scales are the D.A.S.S. (**D**epression, **A**nxiety, **S**elf-Esteem **S**cale) (Sinclair et al., 2010); the Behaviors After Parental Bereavement Measure (a scale that helps to assess bereavement reactions in youth) (Hirooka et al., 2017), and the more widely recognized Beck Depression Inventory (BDI) (Beck, Ward, Mendelson, Mock, & Erlbaugh, 1961). Information about these instruments and others can be found at the American Psychological Association (APA) website (http://www.apa.org/pubs/databases/psyctests/index.aspx) or any major research university website (see https://www.ebsco.com/products/research-databases/mental-measurements-yearbook).
2. *Archival or records.* Archival sources of data are highly utilized in the health and human services fields. Archival data include prior information from the patient or client in question that have been collected in the past. For example, a nurse can look at the patient's medical chart for blood pressure or heart rate history, or a mental health provider can check another therapist's past notes about a client to better understand the client's behavioral patterns and psychological background.
3. *Biological or physiological.* Biological data include any substance or fluids that derived from the human body. For example, a drug counselor can request a client's urine or blood test to measure drug consumption, or

a health care provider can order saliva tests to find out levels of stress (cortisol hormone) or aggressiveness (testosterone hormone).

4. *Self-report.* This type of information is provided by patients or clients themselves, sharing personal facts and/or feelings. Generally, the health or mental health provider asks questions through client interviews, focus groups, or surveys. For example, before a client begins any intervention, the counselor or therapist requests personal and background information to be shared during the in-take process, or a social worker asks about the client's feelings regarding personal issues or current events. In addition to a client self-report, a parent, teacher or significant other, etc., can also provide a report on the client (with client or parental permission).

5. *Observation.* The health or mental health provider collects information by watching and taking notes (or recording) patients or clients during intervention sessions. The purpose of observation is to identify the clients' behavior, attitudes, and perceptions while they are exposed to certain situations or stimuli. For example, a therapist can carefully observe the parent-child interaction to assess the level of attachment between them.

Innovative leaders know that the more data they collect about an individual, the more informed they are to make decisions about their patient's treatment. Thus, adequate intervention assessments include the collection of more than one source of data to reach a better understanding of the client's condition and monitor their progress. These intervention assessments also include two key measuring principles that were previously alluded to: reliability and validity. Briefly, reliability refers to the consistency of the measurements or data collection sources. If we apply the same measuring technique repeatedly, we will expect no major changes; most likely we will get very similar results time and time again. Concurrently, the intervention assessment should have high validity, which means that the measurements utilized are testing the intended constructs or concepts. For example, we would use a depression scale—not an anxiety scale—to measure someone's levels of clinical depression (Rubin & Babbie, 2016).

In the next section, we will cover a basic research design that can be used by a clinician or evaluator to assess client outcomes. There are a variety of designs when it comes to evaluating client outcomes. Please see Rubin and Babbie (2016) for a comprehensive explanation of research methods and Rossi, Freeman, and Lipsey (1999) for evaluation research and corresponding use of designs. Here we will attempt to synthesize a few concepts and therefore will be oversimplifying. For example, when evaluating outcomes of individual cases or units (a family or community), single-case design (or single-subject or single-system) studies can be used, and when assessing outcomes for groups (larger samples), there are a variety of other designs.

These include:

- *Pre-experimental designs* are usually one group pretest and posttest design, where there is one group that is assessed with a scale before treatment (pretest) and again after treatment (posttest) and statistical analyses are used to see if there were differences in scores from pretest to the posttest.
- *Quasi-experimental designs* often are nonequivalent comparison groups design, where one group has received the experimental intervention (the intervention that is being tested) and the other group has not (comparison group that has received treatment as usual) and pretest and posttest scores are compared for both groups, again with the use of statistical analyses; and lastly, what are considered the most scientifically rigorous designs but are not always feasible in agency settings.
- *True-experimental designs* generally compare the scores of at least two groups, one that received the experimental intervention and the other that did not (control group, for example, those clients on a wait list) and where individuals are randomized into either of the conditions and are all given pretests and posttests. This type of design allows for greater confidence through the use of randomization that there were causal effects, or that the treatment caused changes in client outcomes.

There are strengths and limitations with each of these designs. For the purposes of this chapter, we will only cover the single-case design that can be easily utilized by a clinician with his or her client to assess how the intervention is affecting the client's symptoms or behaviors and that often does not require the use of advanced statistical analyses. In fact, the single-case design is mostly used by clinicians to assess how the individual client is responding to an intervention; this is considered a "clinical-research model" that demonstrates "how research can be merged with clinical practice" (Monette, Sullivan, & DeJong, 2002, p. 298). In the following section we will explain this design and an example of its use.

Single-Case Design Studies

In one option of a single-case study design, for instance, the therapist collects data repeatedly from a client before, during, and after an intervention with the goal of finding patterns or trends of the client's expected outcomes (for example, based on scores derived from a scale or by tallying or keeping track of behaviors). The idea behind collecting data several times is to get a more robust understanding of the thoughts, behaviors, and/or feelings a client is exhibiting. One-time data collection techniques may not be enough to get a true picture of the client's condition, nor decide on what intervention is best fitted for the case. There are many types of single-case designs, but one of the most common measurement techniques is the baseline-intervention single-case design (Rubin & Babbie, 2016).

For example, suppose a therapist is working with a client to improve his or her self-esteem. The clinician decides to utilize the Rosenberg Self-Esteem (RSS) scale (which is an *instrument or scale* data source collection type developed by Rosenberg in 1965) as one method to measure the current self-esteem of the client (called baseline phase, or A) and the progress during the intervention (called intervention phase, or B). In order to find out the client's initial level of self-esteem, the client completes the RSS scale every day for a week before the start of therapy sessions (baseline phase—A). Then, to measure progress, the client completes the RSS scale multiple times during the intervention (intervention phase—B). The data collected can show differences before (A) and during (B) the intervention to assess the client's self-esteem changes and progress. To ensure the effectiveness of the intervention, the baseline data collection procedure can be repeated one more time (baseline phase A again, where the intervention is paused but the client keeps rating him or herself on the scale). If there are no positive changes on the expected behavior or, in this case, the client's level of self-esteem, then the therapist can try a different intervention (phase B again with a different intervention), completing the ABAB single-case

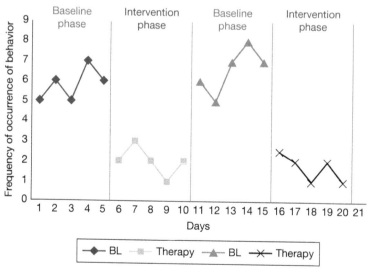

Figure 16.1 Single-Case Design (ABAB) Graph.
SOURCE: https://www.google.com/search?q=single+case+design&source=lnms&tbm=isch&sa=X&ved=0ahUKEwjX5Y7ftZDbAhVGi1QKHSOnDbEQ_AUICygC&biw=1677&bih=919#imgrc=FwIwdU542j2yMM

design intervention measurement. Figure 16.1 illustrates the single-case design graph—ABAB.

The next section will touch on the notion of evidence-based practice (EBP) and how this process can best guide a clinician in delivering and assessing patient or client care.

Evidence-Based Practice

Evidence-Based Practice (EBP) has become the most influential conceptual guide for innovative leaders as they make therapeutic or programming decisions for their clients or help their team members choose which interventions will be most effective while working with patients or clients. The EBP concept has been implemented in the health and human services fields for decades, and the associated definitions and applications differ slightly, depending on the field of study (e.g., medicine, psychology, social work). Generally, the EBP *process* directs the clinician's decision-making based on three components: client's values and expectations, best available evidence and research, and practitioners' expertise. Rubin and Bellamy (2012, p. 7) provide the most current and comprehensive definition of the transdisciplinary model of EPB as follows:

> EBP is a process for making practice decisions in which practitioners integrate the best research evidence available with their practice expertise and with clients attributes, values, preferences, and circumstances. . . . [T]here are six broad categories of EBP questions, as follows:
> 1. What factors best predict desirable or undesirable outcomes?
> 2. What can I learn about clients, service delivery, and targets of intervention from the experience of others?
> 3. What assessment tool should be used?
> 4. What intervention, program, or policy has the best effects?
> 5. What are the costs of interventions, policies, and tools?
> 6. What are the potential harmful effects of interventions, policies, and tools?

Consequently, it is important for health and human services innovative leaders to embrace and foster the utilization of the EBP process in their organizations and choose therapies that are considered as EBPs. Individuals and families from multiple marginalized and vulnerable populations come from diverse situations and have different needs. A particular strategy or innovation may work for one individual but not for another. Also, adaptations to the interventions based on a client's culture, language, and ethnicity must be considered when applying EBPs. The last step in the EBP process includes evaluation of the intervention. Therefore, social architects apply all EBP components by making a habit of understanding the client's circumstances, learning and applying the latest interventions that have evidence and research support behind them, and continuing to improve their practice effectiveness by regularly evaluating their practices.

RESOURCES TO FIND EVIDENCE-BASED INTERVENTIONS AND EFFECTIVE PROGRAMS

There are a number of institutions and organizations that rate or qualify evidence-based interventions and effective programs. Typically, these rating are scientifically-based, focusing on the research design and the level of rigorous methodology used to test the effectiveness of an intervention. Figure 16.2 provides a hierarchy of research designs. This hierarchy provides an illustration

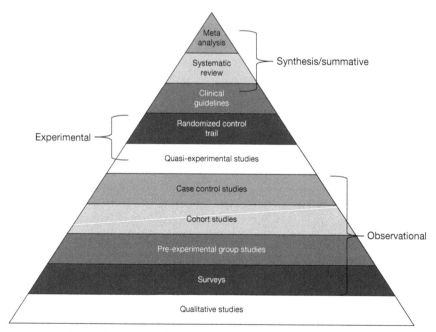

Figure 16.2 Hierarchy of Research Designs.
SOURCE: http://libguides.usc.edu/socialwork/socialworkEBP

of the different ranking levels of research and evaluation. The main three research design levels are:

1. *Synthesis/summative.* Studies published in this category are considered the highest level of research. The two main research designs at this level are meta-analyses and systematic reviews. For example, to understand the best research on treatment for suicide ideation, we would look at a meta-analysis or systematic review research articles that contain the summary of all the empirical study results on this subject.
2. *Experimental.* This level is categorized by empirical studies that use mostly random data collection techniques to measure interventions and program effectiveness. The two key research designs at this level are true-experimental and quasi-experimental empirical studies. Usually, experimental designs have multiple groups and large datasets (number of study participants). These empirical studies are characterized by advanced knowledge in research methods and statistical diagnostics.
3. *Observational.* The lowest level of research design is considered observational. Study designs at this level may not select their samples randomly, and these studies tend not to be as rigorous as experimental research studies. Some of the study approaches at this level include pre-experimental designs, surveys, case studies, and other qualitative studies.

Next, we will present a few institutions and organizations that highlight and/or conduct researched evidence-based interventions and effective programs to be implemented in the health and human services fields.

Substance Abuse and Mental Health Services Administration

The Substance Abuse and Mental Health Services Administration (SAMHSA) is a public agency (funded by taxpayers) located within the US Department of Health and Human Services. SAMHSA's mission is to advance the knowledge and resources of behavioral health efforts and reduce the impact of substance abuse and mental illness throughout the nation (see the SAMHSA website at https://www.samhsa.gov/). Their website contains a significant amount of resources for health and human services leaders in the areas of emergency response, prevention, intervention, and recovery (e.g., research-based treatments, interventions and programs, reports, publication, hotlines, mobile applications). At the time of this writing, one of their divisions, the National Registry of Evidence-based Programs (NREPP), rates evaluation studies based on the quality of the evidence, the size of the program, and the impact on the patient or client outcomes (the

NREPP website is https://www.samhsa.gov/nrepp). Finally, the SAMHSA web-site offers thousands of free reports and publications on health and mental health initiatives, programs, and interventions for diverse populations and conditions (https://store.samhsa.gov/).

National Institutes of Health

The National Institutes of Health (NIH) is also a part of the US Department of Health and Human Services. The NIH receives significant annual funding from the US Congress, and it is considered the nation's health and mental health research agency. The NIH focus is on making new discoveries to improve individuals' health and save peoples' lives (see NIH website at https://www.nih.gov/). The NIH has more than 25 divisions, called *Institutes and Centers*. Each of these institutes or centers has a specific research purpose and agenda, focusing on particular diseases or illnesses. The NIH's main areas of research and evaluation include cancers, human body target areas (e.g., brain, eye, heart, lung), oral and dental science; genome project; alcohol abuse and alcoholism; allergy and infectious diseases; imaging and technology; translational science; integrated health; mental health; and drug abuse.

National Science Foundation

The National Science Foundation (NSF) is an independent agency, also funded by the US Congress. The NSF's mission is not only to promote the progress of science but also to advance the welfare of all Americans (see NSF website at https://www.nsf.gov/). The NSF has many research areas of interest. The two research areas that are particularly important to the health and human services fields are the Divisions of Behavioral and Cognitive Science (BCS) and Social and Economic Sciences (SES). The BCS focuses primarily on research about human cognition, language, social behavior, culture, and interactions between human societies and their environments. The SES research areas include decision-making, risk and management, organizations, technology, and society.

The Office of Juvenile Justice and Delinquency Prevention

The Office of Juvenile Justice and Delinquency Prevention (OJJDP) is an agency of the US Justice Department. The OJJDP's mission is to support local and state efforts to prevent delinquency and improve the juvenile justice system (see the OJJDP website at https://www.ojjdp.gov/mpg). The OJJDP has developed a Model Programs Guide (MPG), which features a list of evidence-based juvenile justice and youth prevention, intervention, and re-entry programs. This resource is available for health and human services practitioners working in organizations and communities to increase juvenile justice, delinquency prevention efforts, and child safety. The MPG has evidenced-based programs in the following categories: child protection, health, and welfare; children exposed to violence and victimization; delinquency prevention; detention, confinement, and supervision; juvenile justice system; juvenile and family courts; law enforcement; offending by juveniles; multiple populations; and schools. MPG uses both expert study reviewers and program review processes to score instruments and programs at three levels: effective, promising, or no effect.

Children's Data Network

The Children's Data Network (CDN) is a data and research partnership that includes government, universities, foundations, and community organizations with the goal of generating research to advance policies that aim to improve the lives of children ages 0 to 21 years (see the CDN website at http://www.datanetwork. org/research/). The CDN contains data, studies, and reports in diverse areas, including health, prenatal care, mental health, substance abuse, education, safety, well-being, maltreatment, parent incarceration, and transition-aged youth.

There are a significant amount of additional local, state, and national resources for measuring intervention and evaluating programs. For example, major universities and private research institutions (i.e., The Rand Corporation) host a variety of research centers to continue exploring targeted health and human services interventions and programs to help people improve their conditions. Additionally, there are other independent clearinghouses, such as the Campbell Collaboration (https://www.campbellcollaboration.org/) and the Cochrane Collaboration (http://www.cochrane.org/), that both maintain and disseminate information on EBPs through libraries of systematic reviews and/or meta-analyses.

The last section of the chapter will briefly cover formal program evaluations that are conducted either in-house (by an internal evaluator) or by an external evaluator (a professional third-party that is contracted by the agency to conduct a formal program evaluation).

FORMAL PROGRAM EVALUATION TYPES
AND METHODS

Innovative leaders are constantly designing, reinventing, and implementing programs to improve people's lives. Innovation and creativity come to fruition as social architects problem-solve situations their clients have to face or endure. Grinnell and Unrau (2005) define program evaluations as "systematic processes of collecting useful, ethical, cultural sensitive, valid, and reliable data about a program's current (and future) interventions, outcomes, and efficiency to aid a case – and program – level decision making in an effort . . . to become more accountable to our stakeholder groups" (p. 117). Before we proceed with a discussion on program evaluation, we will note that many of the health and human services programs fall under three categories:

1. *Prevention.* The programs' purpose is to prevent an undesired condition or situation before it happens—for example, tobacco prevention programs being implemented at school sites after school hours, or parent readiness programs to promote positive parenting (i.e., Early Head Start or Head Start Programs).
2. *Intervention.* Intervention programs take place when an individual's health or behavioral health condition has already started or is in an advanced stage. These programs tend to be comprehensive, using evidence-based interventions (described earlier in this chapter) as part of the multiple services clients receive. For example, a drug facility providing a combination of services, including case management, individual and group counseling, detoxification, medications, and so forth. Most patients or clients participate in these programs on a voluntary basis.
3. *Suppression.* These programs take place when an individual's condition must be suppressed and/or eliminated immediately because of harm that can be caused to the individual or to someone else—for example, gang suppression programs for incarcerated youth who have committed violent gang-related crimes. Most suppression programs have mandatory participation, ordered by the legal system or another law enforcement entity.

Social architects are aware that the quality of these services takes center stage because positive program results truly have the potential to transform people's lives. Then, how do we best plan and conduct program evaluations? Fortunately, we have many evaluation tools at our disposal, depending on the program's purpose, resources, and goals. We will briefly introduce and describe the most common program evaluation types and methods, including logic models, needs assessments, formative evaluations, summative evaluations, outcome evaluations, cost-benefit analyses, and theories that guide evaluation practice.

Logic Models

Logic models have been successfully utilized by health and human services practitioners for many decades. A logic model is a conceptual tool for designing program and evaluation elements together. Dudley (2013) describes logic models as follows: "The logic model is a tool to theoretically analyze a program . . . with this model, it is important to examine the sequence of steps in program development, beginning with the problems of prospective clients and culminating in anticipated client outcomes, which helps stakeholders link the stages together." (p. 104). Throughout the years, logic models have been applied in different disciplines and for multiple purposes. Innovative leaders in health and human services organizations use logic models to design program elements and link them with the expected outputs and outcomes (Figure 16.3). Generally, logic models have the following five stages: input, activity, output, outcome, and impact.

- *Input or planning stage.* The first stage serves to plan and formulate the elements of both the program and the evaluation. At this point, the innovative leader must decide what is the purpose and focus of the program. Once the purpose is envisioned, the leader has to figure out the human and financial resources needed to successfully create and implement the program and its evaluation. For example, to implement a program to help individuals with disabilities become more independent and self-sufficient, several questions must be answered: How many staff members will participate? How much money is needed for implementation? Where it will take place? What curriculum will be used? What method will be utilized to recruit participants? How will the evaluation be conducted? And so on.
- *Activity stage.* The second stage is the first part of the program implementation phase. During this stage, all the activities have to be designed, planned, and prepared accordingly. It has to be clear what activities will take place. It is important to answer questions like: How long will these events last? Who is going to be responsible for carrying out each of the activities and with whom? For example, one behavioral specialist teaching disabled children three independent skills: language acquisition, social competencies, and self-esteem.
- *Output stage.* The third stage is the second part of the program implementation phase and the first part of the evaluation phase. At this point, the program begins, and we start counting and numerically recording all the units of services (outputs), for example: How many children participated? How many classrooms were used? How many

Program Implementation Phase		Program Evaluation Phase		
Input Stage	**Activity Stage**	**Output Stage**	**Outcome Stage**	**Impact Stage**
Identify program purpose and goals; and human capital, financial, and other resources needed to operate the program and evaluation	How the human capital and other resources are utilized	Unit of service resulting from activities—this is counted numerically	Change in either knowledge, perception, behavior, attitude, or skill	Change in organizations, communities, or systems
Examples: Staff Clients Materials Funding Experience Collaboration	Teach children with disabilities independent skills: 1. Language 2. Social 3. Self-esteem	# of children # of classrooms # of instructors # of materials # of instructional hours	1. Higher language acquisition 2. Increase in positive social interactions 3. Increase in self-esteem	More productive, independent, and self-sufficient members of society

Figure 16.3 Logic Model Example.

instructors? How many hours of independent skills workshops? What materials were used for language acquisition, social competencies, and self-esteem?

- *Outcome stage.* The fourth stage serves as the second part of the evaluation phase. Outcomes are changes in knowledge, behavior, skills, perceptions, or attitudes. It is common practice to evaluate these outcome changes to determine whether the program services have made a difference in the short (less than one year), intermediate (one to three years), or long (more than three years) term. For example, we will evaluate the effects of the program by measuring how many disabled students increased or decreased their language acquisition, social competencies, and self-esteem.

- *Impact stage.* The final stage is the third and last part of the evaluation phase. The impact stage is designed to measure the impact of the program on a larger scale, including effects on the organization, community, and/or system levels. For example, we would like to know how much the program contributed to the development of individuals with disabilities becoming more productive, independent, and self-sufficient members of society.

Needs Assessments

Needs assessments have been utilized by health and human services practitioners for many years. Although needs assessments have several definitions depending on the field of study, most agree on their purpose and application. In basic terms, a needs assessment is a systematic approach to identifying what a particular vulnerable group or population lacks or requires. Essentially, the needs of a particular population of interest are acknowledged and measured to determine the scope, prevalence, and severity of the social problem. Social architects' value needs assessments because the results have the potential to show the social needs of individuals and families, and this information can be used to plan and establish programs to address those social needs.

Social needs are often based on Maslow's (1971) hierarchy of human needs shown in Figure 16.4. For example, an evaluator can apply a needs assessment to measure the most pressing human needs (located on the bottom of the pyramid—physiological needs—which include basic survival items like food, shelter, water, and health emergencies) after a natural disaster, such as Hurricane Harvey in Texas or Hurricane Maria in Puerto Rico, both of which occurred in 2017. Needs assessments can be utilized to evaluate physiological needs within vulnerable populations in those states or territories (i.e., children, older adults, low-income families, homeless, etc.).

Maslow's Hierarchy of Needs

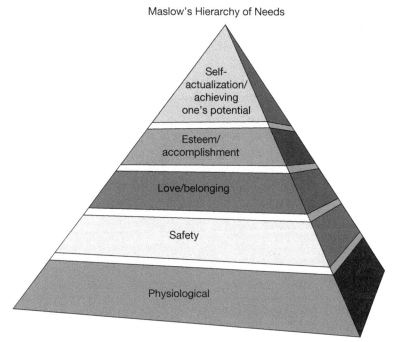

Figure 16.4 Maslow's Hierarchy of Human Needs.
SOURCE: https://www.google.com/search?q=maslow%E2%80%99s+hierarchy+of+human
+needs&source=lnms&tbm=isch&sa=X&ved=0ahUKEwj60ILsuJDbAhWNFXwKHZwT
Cd0Q_AUICigB&biw=1677&bih=919#imgrc=Z_By3kD1zcKZGM

Conducting needs assessments like any of the other evaluation types requires knowledge, expertise, and experience. Needs assessments tend to follow six interrelated steps (Grinnell, Gabor, & Unrau, 2015):

1. *Focus the problem.* Define the specific social need and/or problem. When the definition of the problem is clear, specification is required to know what is going to be counted and measured during the needs assessment process.
2. *Develop needs assessment questions.* Developing key questions will help guide the process and help multidisciplinary groups to work toward the same goals. The questions should be geared to answer the specific social needs identified in step 1.
3. *Identify targets for intervention.* Selecting targets to intervene will facilitate the advancement of solutions to the human needs identified earlier. This step includes what activities and events must take place to improve the current situation. Also, the level of intervention and analysis must be clarified, including individual, family, neighborhood, or larger community.

4. *Develop data collection plans.* At this point, the evaluation team must decide what information is needed. What data are going to be collected? Who is collecting it? And what resources are needed to collect the data?

5. *Analyze and display data.* When the information begins to come in, the evaluators will start analyzing and displaying it for others to see and use. This step should identify how the data will be displayed, so all stakeholders will have access to the information analyzed.

6. *Disseminate and communicate findings.* The final step is to carefully decide who, what, and how the learned data on human needs will be disseminated and communicated. A trusted and knowledgeable source must take this task to avoid confusion and ensure proper information dissemination.

Formative Evaluations

The purpose of formative evaluations is to better understand the development and effectiveness of the program implementation stages (Dudley, 2013). Formative evaluations answer the following questions: Is the program functioning at its highest effectiveness and capacity? What parts of the program need improvement? The evaluator aims to collect data that will reveal what elements of the program are being successfully implemented and which ones need to be revisited. Think of a formative evaluation as a quality improvement process that guides the innovative leader to fine-tune the different elements of the program, particularly, "the type and quantity of program activities and inputs" (Lewis et al., 2012, p. 215). This type of evaluation is exploratory in nature and often applies to fairly new agencies, programs, and/or new clients.

Formative evaluations can take different forms and collect numerous types of data sources, including satisfaction questionnaires; use of structured or semistructured interviews, instruments, and scales; and direct or indirect observations. Dudley (2013) explains that "formative evaluations may examine the interactions between clients and practitioners, management strategies, practice philosophies, or cost associated with the program" (p. 238). For example, suppose an innovative leader is interested in starting a domestic violence program to reduce aggressive behavior among male perpetrators. The program can be planned and set up by applying S.M.A.R.T goals (which stands for goals that are Specific, Measurable, Attainable, Relevant, and Timely) (Figure 16.5). As the implementation of the program takes place, the evaluator will collect data to assess the program processes, including recruitment tools, staff training, curriculum development, client responses to the program elements, and others.

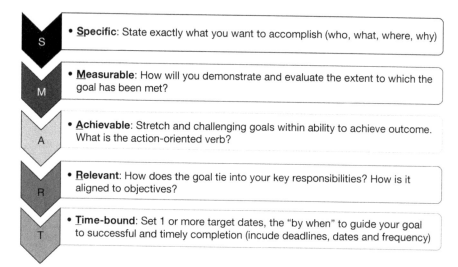

Figure 16.5 S.M.A.R.T. Goals.

SOURCE: https://www.google.com/search?q=s.m.a.r.t.+goals&source=lnms&tbm=isch&s
a=X&ved=0ahUKEwjZ6ruYupDbAhXCzlQKHeZCB5UQ_AUICigB&biw=1677&bih=9
19#imgrc=lF68WlhomGTpCM

The formative evaluation can help demonstrate which areas of the program must be kept or changed, so that the next time the program is implemented, the results may be more successful.

Outcome and Summative Evaluations

Sometimes the terms *outcome* and *summative evaluation* are used interchangeably. Often summative evaluations are described as those conducted at or near the end of a program to determine whether or not a program should be continued (Lewis, Packard & Lewis, 2012). Outcome evaluations relate to the client's goals and outcomes of the program. Both outcome and summative evaluations are mostly conducted by a third party (i.e., external evaluator) to avoid perceived or real biases in the evaluation process, and they are expected to measure how much change clients have experienced due to participating in the program. To determine that a program changed a client's outcome (i.e., a change in behavior, knowledge, skills, perception, or attitude), the evaluator often sets up the evaluation design to demonstrate a cause-and-effect relationship (causality). First, the evaluator must use standardized instruments or scales with high measuring principles, including reliability and validity, and must consider multiple data collection sources, as well as other factors.

Second, the evaluation results must satisfy the following three causality criteria:

1. *Time order.* Cause must occur before the effect—the program must happen first and the change in outcome second, not the other way around;
2. *Correlation or covariance.* As participation in the program increases, the outcomes change; and
3. *No other cause that can explain the outcome change.* Also known as no spurious correlations—the outcome changes are not because of another factor, but only the result of participation in the program.

As already mentioned, the most rigorous research design (from a scientific standpoint) is the true-experimental design, but this is often not feasible in an agency setting or real-world setting for a variety of reasons. The limitations have to do with practically (not enough resources or participants) and ethics (withholding treatment or delaying treatment for the purposes of the evaluation study is not ethical). Therefore, program evaluators often do not use true-experimental designs and instead use more than one method, a design called *mixed research methods.* For example, mixed research methods apply scales or instruments (quantitative data) and interviews or observations (qualitative data) and will often rely on either multiple measures (the use of multiple pretests and posttests) and/or will utilize quasi-experimental designs (as previously mentioned) (see Chen, 2005). The reader can review Chapter 17, which illustrates a summative evaluation that applies a quasi-experimental research design and suggests the Latino Educational Attainment (LEA) Initiative's causal effects on both parent engagement and student academic achievement.

Additionally, to collect data from patients or clients for the purposes of formal program evaluation or research, the health and human services practitioner needs to follow certain ethical standards. It is unprofessional and unethical to ask individuals or families who are receiving an intervention to provide information without properly being advised of their rights and responsibilities. To collect data (any type of information) from clients or patients, Dudley (2013) advises following four basic ethical standards:

- *Informed consent.* Before collecting information, patients and clients have to consent either in writing or verbally. It is best to obtain their signature to ensure understanding of their rights and responsibilities. Additionally, when working with minors (17 years or younger), it is advised to have them and their parents/guardians sign or verbally agree to the information shared (most clinicians use an Assent Form for minors).

- *Confidentiality.* Patients and clients have to be advised that the information they are going to share is confidential. We must maintain a high level of confidentiality for the patients to trust us; otherwise, they will not feel secure or be totally honest when sharing their personal information with us.
- *Right to withdraw.* Treatments and studies must always be voluntary. Also, an individual can opt-out at any time without expecting any negative consequences.
- *Benevolence (do not cause harm).* Patients and clients must be ensured that neither the information they provide, the treatment they are about to receive, nor their participation in a study has the intent to cause harm. It is important that the necessary steps are taken to safeguard that the benefits far outweigh the risks.

According to the American Evaluation Association (AEA), evaluators need to adhere to the following guiding principles (2003, p. 5):

A. *Systematic inquiry.* Evaluators conduct systematic, data-based inquiries about whatever is being evaluated.
B. *Competence.* Evaluators provide competent performance to stakeholders.
C. *Integrity/honesty.* Evaluators ensure the honesty and integrity of the entire evaluation process.
D. *Respect for people.* Evaluators respect the security, dignity and self-worth of the respondents, program participants, clients, and other stakeholders with whom they interact.
E. *Responsibilities for general and public welfare.* Evaluators articulate and take into account the diversity of interests and values that may be related to the general and public welfare.

The aspect of evaluator competence noted above includes having a respect for client diversity, which encompasses self-awareness of cultural assumptions and the selection of evaluation strategies that consider the worldviews of diverse and "culturally-different participants and stakeholders in the evaluation" (AEA, 2003, p. 2). While the principle of respect for people considers the contextual elements of the evaluation, that can include "geographic location, timing, political and social climate, economic conditions and other relevant activities in progress at the same time" (AEA, 2003, p. 3).

Additionally, if the data to be collected are part of a formal research study or evaluation, then the researchers or evaluators must be officially certified to collect data from human subjects (study participants) and apply for the study's approval through an Institutional Review Board (IRB). Often, IRBs are well established within research institutions, such as universities and research-based organizations (public or private), as well as hospital settings that conduct research. The IRB membership consists of experienced researchers in the health and human services fields, and they have the responsibility to approve and oversee the research or evaluation study.

Goals and Objectives in Outcome Evaluations

Outcome evaluations are designed to evaluate the program's goals and objectives. As innovative leaders utilize S.M.A.R.T goals (see Figure 16.5) to design and implement their programs, these goals can be measured by outcome evaluations. Most of the program goals are based on whether or not the patient or client met the expected outcomes. Remember that outcomes are changes in the client's behavior, knowledge, skills, perception, or attitude. To measure potential changes, the evaluator first develops a hypothesis. Suppose a job readiness program has the S.M.A.R.T. goals of (1) teaching former incarcerated youth new job skills and (2) obtaining employment. The hypothesis could be: Job readiness participants will learn job skills in six months, earn a specialized job certificate in nine months, and gain employment within one year of completing the program. The outcome evaluation will determine how successful the program was to the participants depending on how many of them learned the necessary job skills within six months (change in skills), how many of them earned a specialized certificate in nine months (change in knowledge), and how many of them successfully gained employment at the year mark (change in attitudes and/or behavior).

Grinnell and associates (2015) provide an outcome evaluation path with the following six steps:

1. *Specifying program goals and objectives.* Identify clear S.M.A.R.T. goals for patients and/or clients.
2. *Measuring program goals and objectives.* Identify measurements and sources of data for each of the specific goals. This step includes resources needed to collect the information.
3. *Designing a monitoring system.* Data collection is best collected under a systematic approach. Often, not all the patients or clients in the program participate in the outcome evaluation. Sample sizes, specific measurement types, and data collection timelines must be delineated.

4. *Analyzing and displaying data.* Similar to the needs assessment step, the evaluators analyze and display the data for others to use. This step should identify how the data will be displayed so that all stakeholders will have access to the information analyzed. Scientific notation should be discouraged; instead, common language and terms should be used to ensure wide understanding.

5. *Developing feedback system.* As data are collected, evaluated, and shared with internal stakeholders (i.e., program staff, clients, and board members), an outcome evaluations feedback system is set up to learn how the data collection process is developing. This step is critical because we need to know if the information we are collecting truly reflects the realities of what is going on during the program evaluation phase.

6. *Disseminating and communicating results.* The final step is to identify who, what, and how the outcome evaluation results will be disseminated and communicated internally (i.e., team members and administrations inside the organization) and externally (i.e., media, funders, and partners). A third party should assume this task to avoid perceptions of bias and ensure proper information dissemination.

Cost-Benefit Analyses

Also known as efficiency evaluations, cost-benefit analyses measure the program costs and the perceived benefits to the patient and society at large. The cost of major social services (the monetary value of running programs for people in need over long periods of time) can be very high and complex to measure. To date, health and human services organizations feel the need to constantly justify programming costs to their stakeholders. Generally, cost-benefit analysis evaluations have three basic components: (1) determining the costs associated with the program; (2) estimating the expected benefits as a result of participating in the program; and (3) performing the cost-benefit analysis calculation (Monette, Sullivan, & DeJong, 2002). To illustrate an example of a cost-benefits analysis, suppose a human service agency at the state level is interested in learning how much money a universal preschool program can save the taxpayers on incarceration-related costs. The agency may think it is appropriate to make this sizeable investment because longitudinal research studies have shown that children attending preschool programs become more self-sufficient and have better long-term outcomes into adulthood (e.g., higher grades, higher salaries, less incarceration rates, more diverse vocabulary, and so on) compared with those children who did not attend preschool programs

(Barnett & Masse, 2007; Temple & Reynolds, 2007). The state agency can calculate a cost-benefit analysis to find out if designing and implementing a universal preschool program will save money in the long run.

First, the program cost will be based on current and future administrative cost (directors, direct and indirect costs, insurances, etc.), programing costs (number of instructors, salaries, fringe benefits, classrooms, transportation, etc.), and materials and supplies (curriculum, training, other supplies, etc.). After all of this information is calculated, it can be displayed as an annual gross amount or annual cost per participant, which must be adjusted for inflation annually. Second, the benefit has to be determined by calculating the current and future cost of housing adults who did not attend preschool programs as children; in 2018 the annual cost of an incarcerated inmate was about $50,000 (Clear, Reisig, & Cole, 2018). The final step is to calculate if the benefits offset the costs. The reader should be advised that although this is a simplistic example to illustrate the power of a cost-benefit analysis program evaluation, more complexities are involved, including mathematical formulas, assumptions about program implementation, and expected outcomes. Finally, a word about the use of theory in evaluation practice. According to Shadish, Cook, and Leviton (1991), there are several components of evaluation theory, and these include the following: knowledge, value, use, practice, and social programming. These components are interrelated and represent the necessary elements of "good" program evaluation theory.

The *knowledge* component involves questions regarding ontology, epistemology, and methodology. Theory should take into account all three of these parts to assist evaluators in decision-making and setting the standards of what constitutes truth and reality and thus form the basis of setting priorities in evaluation practice.

The *value* component has to do with questions of justice, equality, human rights, and anything else that drives the evaluation process from a values perspective. Under this rubric, evaluators can promote prescriptive (i.e., advocating for one set of values) or descriptive (i.e., describing values but not upholding or claiming to support one value over another) theories.

The *use* component involves the utility of the evaluation findings in terms of solving social problems. Use consists of instrumental, conceptual, and persuasive elements that can foster program changes or improvements or influence stakeholder decision-making. According to Shadish et al. (1991), a good theory of use provides alternatives of use, time frames in which use can occur, and information that is relevant and takes into account political and organizational interests and constraints. All of this should occur in order for stakeholders to actually use or implement the findings derived from the evaluation.

The *practice* component not only addresses the purpose of the evaluation (e.g., formative and summative) and the role of the evaluator but also outlines the strategies and methods that will be used to carry out the evaluation. The practice of evaluation is driven by stakeholder needs along with the identification of resources and limitations that then inform priorities and the methodology (including research design).

The *social programming* component examines internal program structures and functioning as well as external and political constraints that address how program change can incrementally contribute to improvements in a program as well as affect the solving of social problems.

There are various theoretical models that guide evaluation practices. For example, David Fetterman's (2013) empowerment evaluation model is one in which the external evaluator acts as a "coach or critical friend" to the stakeholders. The guiding principles of empowerment evaluation include a social justice perspective, an emphasis on inclusivity, and democratic participation. Here the stakeholders assume leadership of their own evaluation with the "critical friend," who guides the evaluation process through the use of critical questioning. This models seems appropriately suited for empowering communities. Donna Mertens (2009) also proposes an inclusive approach to evaluation that she coined the *transformative-emancipatory framework*. Mertens posits that this approach to evaluation acknowledges diverse viewpoints with an "emphasis on deliberate inclusiveness of groups that have historically experienced oppression and discrimination on the basis of gender, culture, economic levels, ethnicities/race, sexual orientation, and disabilities, and in a conscious effort to build a link between the results of the evaluation and social action" (2009, p. 94).

Again, there are many other guiding theories. For the innovative leader who is interested in learning more about evaluation, the AEA is a good starting point of reference (see the AEA website at http://www.eval.org/).

In conclusion, looking at the I.D.D.E.A. Leadership Framework, this chapter focused on external assessments (evaluation of interventions and programs), complementing the previous two chapters, which covered internal assessments (leader self-assessment). We highlighted the need for social architects to understand the importance of encouraging their team members to measure their practice effectiveness with clients by assessing their interventions and by engaging in formal program evaluation on a regular basis (formative and summative/outcome evaluations). Innovative leaders emphasize the need for team members to utilize EBPs with their patients or clients. Thus, social architects are committed to investing time and effort into career-long learning, sharpening their critical thinking, and practicing their skills. Simultaneously, innovative leaders have knowledge of how interventions are properly measured and where to locate well-researched innovative programs.

CHAPTER DISCUSSION QUESTIONS

1. The innovative leader engages and encourages his or her team members to utilize an EBP *process* in making decisions about client care. What does this process entail?
2. What are the differences between formative and summative evaluations? And when or in what circumstances would it be appropriate to use either?
3. What is the difference between a program output and a program outcome?
4. Utilizing the S.M.A.R.T. approach to developing goals, attempt to create a goal for your client or program with this method.
5. Read the leader profile and case study in the Appendix to this chapter. Note innovative ideas and practices and see what aspects of the case you can connect to the contents of the chapter and/or overall book.

REFERENCES

American Evaluation Association (AEA). (2003). *Guiding principles for evaluators.* Retrieved from http://www.eval.org/p/cm/ld/fid=51

Barnett, W. S., & Masse, L. N. (2007). Comparative benefit–cost analysis of the Abecedarian program and its policy implications. *Economics of Education Review, 26*(1), 113–125.

Beck, A. T., Ward, C. H., Mendelson, M., Mock, J., & Erlbaugh, J. (1961). An inventory for measuring depression. *Archives of General Psychiatry, 4,* 561–571.

Chen, H. T. (2005). *Practical program evaluation: Assessing and improving planning, implementation, and effectiveness.* Newbury Park, CA: Sage.

Clear, T. R., Reisig, M. D., & Cole, G. F. (2018). *American corrections.* Belmont, CA: Brooks/Cole, Cengage Learning.

Dudley, J. R. (2013). *Social work evaluation: Enhancing what we do.* New York, NY: Oxford University Press.

Fetterman, D. M. (2013). Empowerment evaluation: Learning to think like an evaluator. In M. C. Alkin (Ed.), *Evaluation roots: A wider perspective of theorists' views and influences* (2nd ed.) (pp. 304–322). Thousand Oaks, CA: Sage.

Grinnell Jr, R. M., & Unrau, Y. (2005). *Social work research and evaluation: Quantitative and qualitative approaches.* New York: Cengage Learning.

Grinnell, R. M., Gabor, P. A., & Unrau, Y. A. (2015). *Program evaluation for social workers: Foundations of evidence-based practice.* New York, NY: Oxford University Press.

Hirooka, K., Fukahori, H., Ozawa, M., & Akita, Y. (2017). Differences in posttraumatic growth and grief reactions among adolescents by relationship with the deceased. *Journal of Advanced Nursing, 73*(4), 955–965.

Lewis, J. A., Packard, T. R., & Lewis, M. D. (2012). *Management of human service programs* (5th ed.). Belmont, CA: Brooks/Cole, Cengage Learning.

Maslow, A. H. (1971). *The farther reaches of human nature.* New York, NY, US: Arkana/Penguin Books.

Mertens, D. M. (2009). The inclusive view of evaluation: Visions for the new millennium. In S. I. Donaldson & M. Scriven (Eds.), *Evaluating social programs and problems* (pp. 91–107). New York, NY: Psychology Press.

Monette, D. R., Sullivan, T. J., & DeJong, C. R. (2002). *Applied social research* (5th ed.). Orlando, FL: Harcourt.

Rossi, P. H., Freeman, H. E., & Lipsey, M. W. (1999). *Evaluation: A systematic approach* (6th ed.).Thousand Oaks, CA: Sage.

Rubin, A., & Babbie, E. R. (2016). *Empowerment series: Research methods for social work.* Belmont, CA: Brooks/Cole, Cengage Learning.

Rubin, A., & Bellamy, J. (2012). *Practitioner's guide to using research for evidence-based practice.* Hoboken, NJ: John Wiley & Sons.

Shadish, W. R., Cook, T. D., & Leviton, L. C. (1991). *Foundations of program evaluation: Theories of practice.* Newbury Park, CA: Sage Publications.

Sinclair, S. J., Blais, M. A., Gansler, D. A., Sandberg, E., Bistis, K., & LoCicero, A. (2010). Psychometric properties of the Rosenberg Self-Esteem Scale: Overall and across demographic groups living within the United States. *Evaluation & the Health Professions, 33*(1), 56–80.

Temple, J. A., & Reynolds, A. J. (2007). Benefits and costs of investments in preschool education: Evidence from the Child–Parent Centers and related programs. *Economics of Education Review, 26*(1), 126–144.

APPENDIX
Featured Leader: Anthony Hassan

As the inaugural CEO of the Cohen Veterans Network, Dr. Hassan oversees the establishment of 25 mental health clinics nationwide. These clinics are designed to improve the mental health outcomes for post-9/11 veterans and their families, with a particular emphasis on posttraumatic stress, through high-quality, free, and accessible mental health care. In addition, he leads efforts to advance the field through funded research initiatives and training programs to improve care within the network and beyond. Hassan is a veteran of the US Army enlisted and Air Force officer with 30 years of experience in military behavioral health, serving as a military social work officer, leader, clinician, and academic. He served during Operation Iraqi Freedom in 2004 on the first-ever Air Force combat stress control and prevention team embedded with the Army. He also led the largest military substance abuse and family advocacy programs in the Pacific. These programs were recognized as benchmark programs and training sites for all other Pacific bases. He most recently served as the inaugural Director and Clinical Professor of the Center for Innovation and Research on Veterans & Military Families (CIR) at the University of Southern California School of Social Work. During his tenure at CIR from 2009 to 2015, Hassan was instrumental in the exponential growth of the school's military social work program and community-based research on veterans and military families. He has strong relationships with the most senior levels of leadership in the US Department of Defense, US Department of Veterans Affairs, and Washington, DC.

LEADERSHIP PROFILE FOR ANTHONY HASSAN

Share your professional background and experience

I retired from the military in 2009 and so was there for 25 years. I held a variety of leadership positions from small squad level to large company level positions. So I was doing the kind of military traditional leadership. For instance, training and developing people to accomplish military jobs. Then as I progressed in my career, I had a chance to get away from more of the hierarchical leadership and do more vertical leadership and do more horizontal leadership. In that, I started leading like-minded professionals in mental health clinics. Working with psychiatry, psychology, and social work and then leading the professional ranks, if you would, to accomplish a mission.

Then before I retired, I went to the Air Force Academy where I was not only leading within an administrative program but also developing officers to be horizontal. In other words, they were the same rank, but by virtue of my position, I held leadership responsibilities and authority over them. But the whole goal there was to develop them into leaders. So it was interesting leading with a horizontal approach in meeting your peers and trying to influence their thinking around leadership. Developing young leaders as well. So it was interesting in the military, going from more of a vertical into a horizontal leadership position and then leading your peers.

So then, I retired and went to work at USC. There again it was more of a horizontal kind of leadership approach where in higher education everybody's a peer of academic standing. So trying to influence others who are equal, many would have a difficult time with, but it worked out well. Obviously, there was some vertical leadership in the center that I led, but when I stepped away from the center and would lead committees then it was more of a horizontal leadership where you really have to pay attention to the profession, the competencies people bring, and learn how to motivate and inspire people because they're not going to do things just because you tell them to do it.

The center at USC was pretty much something that grew from a project. So we were able to secure a big grant. The grant turned into a big project. The project had many, many team members. As that project grew, opportunities grew for us to do more, to expand new training ideas, to measure training in different ways, to secure additional grants, to advance the work beyond the original product. Eventually, we got to the point where we were feeling like we can be called a "Center." A center that focused a lot on educational intervening. We kind of identified ourselves as a place that developed training curriculum that can be used in the classroom through artificial intelligence and virtual reality. But, we quickly realized we needed more funding, so we started looking for new opportunities that we could grow the center but still stay in our wheelhouse or staying true to the mission of advancing the field of military mental health through educational training. We also became involved in the community. The questions were: How does one build a community collaborative? How does one get community resources that can be leveraged for veterans and military families arriving in Los Angeles? For example, how do you make services better? So we took a large community role of being the quarterback, if you would, of all community resources for veterans and military family members. We evolved, and I think we evolved from our own growth, but also looking for opportunities to have greater impact in the community we serve. And it just happened to be that during the time of our growth, the country was looking for coordinating and collaborating across sectors for the support of veterans and military families. It's one of those things that you started off with one niche and then you evolved, but we're always mindful not to exceed our mission. And not to do mission creep and do things that didn't matter, that didn't influence curriculum, that didn't help advance the pipeline of clinicians to work with veterans and military families. And as social workers we felt that the community approach and being focused on community were a core part of where the center should spend its time, if you would. So, it was an evolving kind of growth, it was a new business. It was kind of like I'm doing now. It's very entrepreneurial startup mentality. Small team bringing together many different types of people. Building a team with a lot of diversity, thought, and competency. So it was really fun growing a small team. Building something new. Identifying the mission and redefining the mission as we grew. I was just so pleased with that work and that type of leadership that requires you not to be the boss but to be the convener, be the person moving the conversation. Allowing people to participate, but at the same time keeping folks focused on goals and objectives.

I'm currently the CEO of the Cohen Veterans Network, which is a network of mental health clinics established across the country to support veterans and military family members with low- or no-cost mental health care. So trying to fill the gap in care whereby many folks aren't eligible for care in the Veterans Administration or family members aren't eligible for care. Many are in the middle of transition out of the military without insurance. Many have insurance. So it's really establishing a national health system focused on veterans' and family members' mental health. I'm really, really proud to be the founding director and founding CEO of this. It has been so rewarding to be able to grow something from the ground up, to have all the resources I need to do it. I think the greatest risk for me is that I have everything I need to be successful. And by golly, I better be successful. I've been able to build a team of people who rallied around the mission. Obviously, for the first two years we were a startup. We started small and got like-minded individuals. We also had diversity in thought. We had met many groups and folks working on our team who really added value. So it's really about building a team and leading it. So that's really been fun.

Now we're about two years in and we're starting to see that some of the startup mentality is not so easy when you have a bigger team and you have teams of teams. We're no longer one team, we're a team of teams that has to interact with each other on a regular basis to accomplish our mission. So, for example, we've got a team that works on network systems, electronic health records, data management, and data analytics. They have to work very closely with our clinical programs team on the actual delivery of care and outcome-based care and measurement-based care. They have to know what has to be measured, so they have to work with the clinical team. The clinical team is working with the risk management team. The finance team is working with everybody. The communications and marketing team has to work with everybody as well. So it's a real dynamic, and it's so much fun. I don't believe in today's day that you can lead vertically anymore. That you really have to be a teams-based kind of organization just because of the dynamic nature of work today with social media and the fast movement of information. The ability to move and scale quickly. You have to work in teams. You can't stand on top of the mountain and bark out orders to people. It really has to be a collaborative team-based approach as we evolve to this era of information exchange. Rapid information exchange, if you would.

In your experience, what are the top three to five leadership attributes someone in the health and human services field should develop? Share an example of when you have used one or more of these attributes/skills in your work

Caring. I think a leader has to show or demonstrate that he or she cares about the people they lead and that this isn't just a job. That these people have lives and other things that we have to consider and take into consideration. I think a leader should show concern and care for the people that work for them. I think a leader needs to be energetic and enthusiastic about their work. They have to lead from a position of energy, of engagement, but not to be too overly excited. So you have to be able to temper your energy and your enthusiasm where it's not too excitable or moody. Being balanced, I think that's really, really helpful.

Be a good listener. I think a leader today has to listen and listen very well, especially as you talk about team dynamics and really appreciating the specialty and nuances of team members. Teams that are quite different and figuring out how to best bring them together is an important element. So I think you have to really listen.

Focus on development. We have to develop the next generation of leaders. We have to give them room to develop. We have to give them voice at the table. What I mean by that is that our relationship development is that we give them a voice at the table and have them share their thoughts because the feedback they get is part of development. We have to instill enough confidence in them that they can share, but also the realization that not every idea is going to be accepted. So that's part of development.

Know who you are. I've always lived with the model of leadership that who you are is how you lead and how you lead determines the effectiveness of your team, which in the end, determines the effectiveness of your organization. I've always been mindful that I've got to be very aware of who I am as an individual. What are my strengths and weaknesses? What are those dark side traits that I have? Where are my areas of weakness? Then ensure I have people around me to compensate for those. It's always about who am I? What are those dark sides about me that I need to worry about? Do I not listen well enough? Do I tend to give too much instead of listening? Am I too excitable? Am I too conscientious, where I'm so rigid? Thinking about who I am would determine how I lead others and how they perceive me. In the end, who I am and how I lead determines how well my team performs. If my team performs well, then the mission is accomplished.

If they don't perform well, then the mission isn't accomplished or it's accomplished in a way that doesn't meet all of our objectives. I really believe leadership starts with the self and I think the higher you are in the leadership chain, the higher you are in that vertical staircase, the more it is you need to be aware of your personality, your communication style, because that's what you're doing. You're no longer the technical expert. You're no longer advising on the micro level. You're dealing with people and you're influencing people. You are making decisions with people. I think you have more people skills as you grow. Why do leaders fail when they get up to the top? What happens? One thing that I know is that when you're given a lot of discretion, a lot of authority, if you don't manage that well you're going to fail. I think the reason why people can't manage discretion well is because they're not focused on themselves. This idea of who you are personally. We see it all the time, leaders fail because they get into inappropriate relationships. They fail because they mismanaged money. They fail because they take it upon themselves to do something that's outside of the scope of their practice of their work because they don't manage discretion well.

A CASE STUDY BY ANTHONY HASSAN

When a leader makes the decision, say on the organizational structure, so you're looking to redesign your organization, sometimes we think of that change only in one area or one aspect. We think of it only as human resources, right? So we're going to restructure our organization. We're going to cut positions. We're going to move people around. We're going to create a more efficient organization, and we're going to think of it only in the sense of human resources. We're going to cut money. We're going to save. We're going to consolidate, and we're going to do that. Everyone thinks that that's the right thing to do, right? We need to save money. We need to be more efficient. We need to consolidate. We need to merge, and I think, I've been guilty of this sometimes, too, in our haste to do that, to reorganize, or to make a sudden change, or an organizational shift, we only think of it through one lens and that is the human resources lens. I'm referring a lot to what we call the Bolman and Deal model, which is a four-frame model of organizations and change that says that when you look at it through only one lens, then you are going to miss a lot. They gave a number of examples in their book.

Sometimes you think about the structural piece, okay what are all the new rules, roles, and responsibilities? So you typically focus on let's do structural, we are going to do human resources, and we are going to figure this out. I quickly learned in my experience, that I've done that a couple of times, is that if you don't consider the political and the symbolic pieces to that, you're going have a lot of people upset. You're not going to have real buy-in. You're going to create a lot of problems if you don't think about the power loss that some might have when that happens or who gains power. Who is going to be in conflict now? Who's in competition? And if you don't think about that as you go about restructuring and realigning roles, some people are going to be very hurt. Some people are going to feel left out. Some of your best leaders are not going to feel rewarded. Some of them who had power will lose power. It's a dynamic shift, and when you don't consider the political piece, you're going to have a lot of angry people and unintended consequences.

Another piece that sometimes is forgotten about is symbolic, which I refer more to the cultural norms of that organization or the way we do business here. The unspoken rules are now violated. Something as simple as when you change the meeting or you change something from Tuesday to Wednesday, you've affected how we do business around here. Every Wednesday, if half the team goes out on the patio for a lunch together, you've disrupted something very important and almost a ritual by doing this shift without really considering. We see that in higher education sometimes, people do events and they do event planning, but it falls on Rosh Hashanah, a religious holy day. How did you not know that, right? So it's taking into consideration the rituals, the storytelling, and the things that are important. What happens when you make this shift and the eldest person in the organization, who may just be the secretary, and say just because that's unfortunately how people define the front desk person, but you take that person out, who's been part of that organization for 20 years, all of a sudden you shift that person and you move them away from that role, that affects everybody. That affects the whole meaning of the organization, the stories behind that individual. I don't want to belabor this one because you get it, but if a leader doesn't sit down with his team and really consider all of the things that happen when you make shift in an organizational process, in the human resources or the structure of your organization, you don't consider the political and the cultural or the symbolic elements, you're really going to miss it. I'm telling you, I've done that a number of times and I didn't pay attention to them, and you don't have to consider them fully, but boy you'd better stop and pause to think about moving someone around or changing a process or changing the routine. I pause all the time to make sure I'm looking at power and organizational culture. I'm pausing to make sure I'm looking at being prepared for the conflict. I would say lessons for leaders, and my own experiences, remind me that when you make organizational shifts, you should consider Bolman and Deal's four-frame model.

CASE DISCUSSION POINTS

1. The innovative leader in this profile spoke about outcome-based care and measurement-based care. What did he mean by that? And how are these important to the organization and to client care?
2. The leader mentioned that it is important to know yourself, including strengths and weaknesses. Create an inventory of your own strengths and weaknesses and what you can do to continue to grow as an innovative leader.
3. As described in the case, consideration of many facets of the organization are important, particularly when making decisions about shifts or changes. Name a few of the considerations that were discussed. Additionally, why would a social architect think these are important and how should each of these facets be addressed?

Appendices: Leader Assessment Instruments

A. 360 DEGREES LEADERSHIP FEEDBACK SURVEY

Instructions: Rate each bullet point with the following: poor (1), below average (2), average (3), above average (4), or excellent (5).

Leadership/Motivation	Character
• Makes a compelling case for his/her point of view • Effectively persuades others in order to build commitment for ideas • Communicates an inspiring vision • Helps people develop passion for their work • Recognizes employee contributions and ideas • Is sensitive to satisfaction and morale in the group • Generates urgency in others • Recognizes and rewards high performers • Provides a positive example; "walks the talk" • Creates an atmosphere that inspires others to achieve at a higher level • Helps staff define clear objectives	• Patient when necessary • Self-confident • Open to feedback and criticism • Avoids negative politicking and hidden agendas • Willing to take a courageous stand • Trusts others appropriately • Respected by others • Sincere and straightforward • Serves others; avoids selfishness • Accepts responsibility for own mistakes • Can be trusted with sensitive information • Eagerly pursues new knowledge, skills, and methods • Knows own strengths and limitations • Avoids bias in attitude or treatment of people

| • Regularly reviews objectives with staff
• Involves employees in decisions
• Delegates enough work
• Delegates authority; encourages independence
• Sets clear deadlines
• Facilitates rather than dominates
• Communicates reasons for changes and decisions
• Conducts effective meetings
• Manages people according to their unique needs
• Tolerates honest mistakes as learning experiences
• Articulates the strategy in plain language | **Interpersonal Skills**

• Recognizes the value of people with different talents and skills
• Brings conflicts into the open for resolution
• Listens effectively
• Adjusts to changes without frustration |

Interpreting the 360 Degree Survey Results:
1–2 = Leadership skills need improvement
2–3 = Leadership skills below average
3–4 = Very good leadership skills
4–5 = Excellent leadership skills

B. BURNOUT SELF-TEST

Maslach Burnout Inventory (MBI)

The Maslach Burnout Inventory (MBI) is the most commonly used tool to self-assess whether you might be at risk for burnout. To determine the risk for burnout, the MBI explores three components: exhaustion, depersonalization, and personal achievement. While this tool may be useful, it must not be used as a scientific diagnostic technique, regardless of the results. The objective is simply to make you aware that anyone may be at risk for burnout.

For each question, indicate the score that corresponds to your response. Add up your score for each section and compare your results with the scoring results interpretation at the bottom of this document.

QUESTIONS	NEVER	A FEW TIMES PER YEAR	ONCE A MONTH	A FEW TIMES PER MONTH	ONCE A WEEK	A FEW TIMES PER WEEK	EVERY DAY
SECTION A	0	1	2	3	4	5	6
I feel emotionally drained by my work.							
Working with people all day long requires a great deal of effort.							
I feel like my work is breaking me down.							
I feel frustrated by my work.							
I feel I work too hard at my job.							
It stresses me too much to work in direct contact with people.							
I feel like I'm at the end of my rope.							
Total score – SECTION A							

Questions	Never	A few times per year	Once a month	A few times per month	Once a week	A few times per week	Every day
Section B	0	1	2	3	4	5	6
I feel I look after certain patients/clients impersonally, as if they are objects.							
I feel tired when I get up in the morning and have to face another day at work.							
I have the impression that my patients/clients make me responsible for some of their problems.							
I am at the end of my patience at the end of my work day.							
I really don't care about what happens to some of my patients/clients.							
I have become more insensitive to people since I've been working.							
I'm afraid that this job is making me uncaring.							
Total score – SECTION B							

Questions	Never	A few times per year	Once a month	A few times per month	Once a week	A few times per week	Every day
SECTION C	0	1	2	3	4	5	6
I accomplish many worthwhile things in this job.							
I feel full of energy.							
I am easily able to understand what my patients/clients feel.							
I look after my patients'/clients' problems very effectively.							
In my work, I handle emotional problems very calmly.							
Through my work, I feel that I have a positive influence on people.							
I am easily able to create a relaxed atmosphere with my patients/clients.							
I feel refreshed when I have been close to my patients/clients at work.							
Total score – SECTION C							

Scoring Results: Interpretation

SECTION A: BURNOUT

Burnout (or depressive anxiety syndrome): testifies to fatigue at the very idea of work, chronic fatigue, trouble sleeping, and physical problems. For the MBI, as well as for most authors, "exhaustion would be the key component of the syndrome." Unlike depression, the problems disappear outside work.

- Total 17 or less: low-level burnout
- Total between 18 and 29 inclusive: moderate burnout
- Total over 30: high-level burnout

SECTION B: DEPERSONALIZATION

Depersonalization (or loss of empathy): rather a "dehumanization" in interpersonal relations. The notion of detachment is excessive, leading to cynicism with negative attitudes with regard to patients or colleagues, feelings of guilt, avoidance of social contacts, and withdrawing into oneself. The professional blocks the empathy he or she can show to patients and/or colleagues.

- Total 5 or less: low-level burnout
- Total between 6 and 11 inclusive: moderate burnout
- Total of 12 and greater: high-level burnout

SECTION C: PERSONAL ACHIEVEMENT

The reduction of personal achievement: the individual assesses himself negatively and feels he or she is unable to move the situation forward. This component represents the demotivating effects of a difficult, repetitive situation leading to failure despite efforts. The person begins to doubt his or her genuine abilities to accomplish things. This aspect is a consequence of the first two.

- Total 33 or less: high-level burnout
- Total between 34 and 39 inclusive: moderate burnout
- Total greater than 40: low-level burnout

A high score in the first two sections and a low score in the last section may indicate burnout.

Leadership assessment developed by Thomas, M; Kohli, V; & Choi, J. (2014). Permission granted by authors on March 15, 2018.

Epilogue

17

Putting It All Together

Application of the I.D.D.E.A. Leadership Framework to Achieve Social Change

> I have not failed. I've just found 10,000 ways that won't work.
> —THOMAS A. EDISON

CHAPTER OBJECTIVES

1. Explore cultural, environmental, and institutional barriers to the Latino educational achievement gap;
2. Learn the application of the I.D.D.E.A. (Innovation, Design, Diversity, Execution, and Assessment) Leadership Framework to achieve social change; and
3. Review program evaluation methods, results, and implications.

INTRODUCTION

This chapter will address various leadership aspects covered in this book, including the I.D.D.E.A. (**I**nnovation, **D**esign, **D**iversity, **E**xecution, and **A**ssessment) Leadership Framework as a working example of innovative programing to meet a social need. The focus of the social issue is empowering ethnic minority parents/families to navigate local school systems in order to increase educational attainment for Latino/a students. The Latino Educational

Adapted from Araque, J. C., Wietstock, C., Cova, H., & Zepeda, S. (2017). Impact of Latino parent engagement on student academic achievement: A pilot study. *School Community Journal, 27*(2), 229–250.

Attainment (LEA) Initiative demonstrates the power of community building and the formation of coalitions and multiagency partnerships toward the public good. The application of the LEA Initiative will be highlighted as a case study that took place in Orange County, CA. The results of the pilot study findings will be provided, as well as implications for social architects who represent various sectors in promoting community-based collaborative efforts.

BACKGROUND: EDUCATIONAL ACHIEVEMENT BARRIERS FOR HISPANICS/LATINOS

Hispanics/Latinos(as) remain the largest minority population in the United States and one of the most rapidly increasing ethnic groups today (Garcia & Bayer, 2005; Kohler & Lazarin, 2007). With increases in immigration, US public schools and other institutions are faced with the immense challenge of identifying and attempting to meet the unique needs of its mounting Latino/a immigrant student population in order to ensure the success of its students and to create a more educated and competitive workforce across the United States. This ethnic group is often characterized by high dropout rates, low college enrollment, and lack of educational attainment, which negatively perpetuates the pervasive Latino/a achievement gap (National Center for Education Statistics, 2014).

According to the US Census Bureau (2014), Latinos/as account for 34% of Orange County's current population, and based on new government population projections, the minority group is expected to grow to nearly 45% by the year 2060. Additionally, when considering the total youth population (under age 18), Latinos/as currently represent 46.7%. Almost 10% of Orange County's residents are undocumented immigrants who work in low-wage jobs. Not surprisingly, Latino/a families have twice the rate of poverty than the rest of the county. Furthermore, nearly three times (43.5%) the number of Latinos/as have attained less than a high school diploma compared with 15.7% of all Orange County residents (Waheed, Romero, & Sarmiento, 2014). In the 2012–2013 school year, Latino/a students in this county represented approximately 48.3% of the public school enrollment, yet maintained one of the highest dropout rates in comparison with other minority and nonminority groups (Kena et al., 2014). This is especially significant given education-based earning differentials contributing to social risk factors—including unemployment, poverty, substance abuse, and crime—negatively affecting the achievement of future generations (Annunziata, Hogue, Faw, & Liddle, 2006; Trusty, Mellin, & Herbert, 2008).

It is important to highlight that external factors play a major role in positive family functioning, health outcomes, and student academic achievement

(Halgunseth, Ispa, & Rudy, 2006). Communities that receive present-day immigrants are also considered risk factors in that newcomer families often settle into disadvantaged, underprivileged neighborhoods that coincide with schools that are, in turn, underfunded and poorly performing (Suarez-Orozco & Suarez-Orozco, 2001). This environment poses a risk to youth assimilating into a culture defined by underachievement and lack of engagement, thereby impeding the potential for upward mobility. Individuals from socioeconomically disadvantaged backgrounds tend to perform poorly in school and often live in impoverished, high-crime communities, which further limits their access to services, as well as their motivation and ability to prioritize educational attainment (Harris, Jamison, & Trujillo, 2008; Henry, Merten, Plunkett, & Sands, 2008; Ramirez & Carpenter, 2005).

Many low-income Latino/a families experience the education system as impersonal and nonresponsive to their concerns (Fine, 2014). As a result, many Latino/a parents are distrusting of the school system and fearful of being perceived as undeserving. This experience has resulted in deep-seated fears and attitudes among many Latino/a parents toward the school, such as the fear of being put down, either overtly or covertly. In addition, few teachers are explicitly trained in working with families, and some may view parents, particularly immigrant and low-income parents, as liabilities rather than assets in children's educational pursuits (Hayes-Bautista, 2004). A study by Ong et al. (2006) found that student grade point average (GPA) increased in relation to persistent parental support and engagement, irrespective of socioeconomic status. Eamon (2002) noted similar results in regard to academic performance, such that greater parent engagement was indicative of higher reading and math achievement among Latino/a students.

APPLICATION OF THE I.D.D.E.A. LEADERSHIP FRAMEWORK

Innovation: The Latino Educational Attainment Initiative

Finding solutions to the Latino/a student achievement gap remains a top priority. The Latino Educational Attainment (LEA) Initiative addresses issues affecting the rising Latino/a immigrant population in the educational system within one of the most populous and wealthiest counties in California: Orange County. Parent engagement represents an important and effective target strategy to support immigrant populations in closing the academic achievement gap, thereby positively affecting the workforce gap as well. Empowering parents, one of the keys to student success, is a critical mechanism to ensure a better educated, better prepared, and more competitive workforce in Orange County and elsewhere.

The LEA Initiative was created in the wake of the *Orange County (OC) Register* series, "Our Children, Our Future" (June 2003–March 2004). A key outcome of this 12-part report was the identification of the inability of immigrant parents to effectively navigate the US education system. These immigrant parents wanted their children to succeed—become doctors, lawyers, business people—but they did not know how to help their children achieve these goals. The *OC Register* acted as a convener to bring a variety of businesses and community groups together to address this issue. Key leader organizations included the Orange County Department of Education; the Orange County Business Council (OCBC); United Way of Orange County; KidWorks, Inc.; the Roman Catholic Diocese of Orange; Santa Ana College; Santa Ana Unified School District; Fullerton Collaborative; Creer, Inc.; Boy Scouts of America, Orange County Chapter; Garden Grove Unified School District; and Saddleback Unified School District.

As a result of this leadership meeting among stakeholders, the OCBC created the LEA Initiative with the focus on building a more competitive workforce and empowering parent coalitions to take a more active role as parent advocates in their children's education. OCBC committed to act as the lead and backbone organization for the LEA Initiative, working on the collective impact efforts and maintaining momentum to provide resource allocation and coordinate program implementation. Currently, OCBC supports new and ongoing parent coalitions that are engaged in the LEA Initiative by providing monthly networking meetings; maintaining the Initiative's website and marketing materials; creating, printing, and translating training materials; and hosting the annual LEA Initiative Awards Reception (for more information about the LEA Initiative go to the OCBC website: https://www.ocbc.org/ocbc-initiatives/latino-educational-attainment-initiative-lea/).

Design and Diversity: Gaining Organizational and Cultural Understanding to Formulate the LEA Initiative Blueprints

The vision of the LEA Initiative was to fill the gaps left by the educational system to address critical issues to improve and maintain Orange County's workforce. The LEA Initiative adopted the following goals:

- Ensure the future of Orange County's highly skilled workforce.
- Assist parents to be more effective advocates for their children's education.

- Improve student performance, lower the achievement gap, and increase enrollment in postsecondary education and training.
- Empower and unify the community by being neighborhood based and school based.
- Foster parent-to-parent social networking opportunities by promoting dialogue—"the good gossip" (speaking and sharing about the benefits of education).
- Align and leverage existing programs rather than creating new ones.

The LEA Initiative began by surveying and interviewing Latino/a parents to assess their knowledge of the education system and how to get involved in their children's education. Results suggested that parents were limited in their understanding of their local education system. To address the identified gaps, the LEA Initiative collaborated with educators at the Orange County Department of Education and youth advocates from different nonprofit organizations to create the parent curriculum, *Ten Education Commandments for Parents*, which is an easy-to-understand, accessible, 33-page guide containing 10 key messages for parents. A train-the-trainer model was designed to train volunteer facilitators from participating organizations to disseminate this information to parents. The majority of these volunteer facilitators were parent educators who had experience with providing training to parents (Box 17.1).

Box 17.1

Ten Education Commandments for Parents

Ten Education Commandment for Parents teaches parents the fundamentals of the American education system and gives parents the tools to become more actively engaged in their children's education. A brief description of each educational commandment follows.

Commandment 1: Commit as a family to be involved in school.

Family engagement in your child/children's education is an important way for you to support your child not only in school but also for future life success. Everyone in the family has a role to play and something to contribute to their child's education.

Commandment 2: Do my part in helping my child study.

Supporting your child's education begins with your interest and support at home. What are you doing at home to support learning at school?

Commandment 3: Understand how grades work (A, B, C, D, & F).

Grades are an important way to communicate to parents how a child is doing in school in both achievement and effort. Monitoring your child's progress from grading period to grading period and year to year gives YOU the opportunity to help your child, seek help if needed, and/or celebrate your child's success in school.

Commandment 4: Learn how schools are structured.

Students need to demonstrate proficiency at each grade level and master the Common Core State Standards, which set grade-level learning expectancies for students in grades K–12 for mathematics, English language arts, and science. These standards were designed to prepare students for success in college and the workplace. They set clear, consistent, and high learning goals.

Commandment 5: Learn what my child needs to graduate high school.

Graduating high school can be a challenging task if you don't know the class requirements needed to graduate. California requires that students must pass a minimum set of required courses and an exit examination. In California, the minimum requirements are three courses in English, two courses in mathematics, two courses in science, three courses in social studies, one course in visual/performing arts or foreign language, and two courses in physical education.

Commandment 6: Support the learning of math, science, and English.

Science, technology, engineering, and math (STEM) education is a critical program focused on ensuring students success in school and the real world. Parents can support their children by engaging in their daily school schedule and finding someone who can provide tutoring in these courses.

Commandment 7: Encourage my child to take honors and advanced courses.

Advanced courses are available in high school to students who excel in core subject areas such as English, math, science, history, foreign languages, and art. These rigorous and challenging courses require commitment on the student's part and support from parents. The advantages to taking these courses include the possibility of earning college credit and a higher and competitive grade point average (GPA).

Commandment 8: Help my child prepare to be college and/or career ready.

Help your child prepare for college early. Planning for college and career begins as early as the elementary years. It is important to plant the seed of a future beyond the classroom. Making the connections between education and careers helps children understand the path toward realizing their career goals.

Commandment 9: College options are affordable.

You don't have to pay for school all by yourself—there are grants, loans, and scholarships that can help you pay some or all of the expenses of college.

Commandment 10: Teach my child to view obstacles as challenges, to hope, and to visualize their future.

Teach your child how to set goals and to pursue them from an early age. Create your plan to support your child/children to reach their full potential. Start early, be intentional, and involve your child as you support them to reach their goals.

To date, the curriculum is in its third edition, and more than 50,000 parents from more than 150 neighborhoods in Orange County have completed the training in a variety of venues; the curriculum is customizable to meet individual setting needs (e.g., schools, community centers, neighborhood association, churches). As previously noted, the long-term goal of the LEA Initiative and its principal sponsor, OCBC, is a better educated, better prepared, and competitive workforce in Orange County. Empowering parents, one of the keys to student success, is a critical mechanism in creating a globally competitive 21st-century workforce (Orange County Business Council, 2017).

Execution: Gaining Participation and Expanding the LEA Initiative

Parent coalitions recruit interested parents from schools, recreational programs, community centers, and other locations to engage in parenting workshops provided by educators, other parents, or community members. Flyers are sent home with students, or announcements are made during school open houses and other school related meetings. Once parents register to participate, they attend 10 hours of training (about three to four hours per week). For every training session, refreshments and child care are provided by the host agency. The *Ten Education Commandments for Parents* curriculum is divided into three parts (usually during three or four days of instruction/sessions). First, parents take the pretest so that the facilitator knows their knowledge and perceptions of the school system. During this first session, parents learn about the first three commandments, focusing on what they can do to help their child improve their academic achievement. During the second session, parents learn the next three commandments, covering expectations and educational outcomes of elementary and middle school. The last meeting covers the final commandments, including financial aid, high school, and beyond. At the end, parents complete the posttest and answer a few open-ended questions to gauge their learning and satisfaction with the program.

Assessment: Program Evaluation Methods, Results, and Implications

The program evaluation (summative evaluation) assessed the impact of the *Ten Education Commandments for Parents* program on (1) parent knowledge of the US educational system (as applied to their local schools), (2) parent engagement in their children's education, and (3) parent engagement's effects in their children's academic achievement (Araque et al., 2017). Applying a mixed-methods study using a nonequivalent comparison group design, (see Chapter 16 for a review on research designs), the evaluation team partnered with the Orange County Department of Education and the Santa Ana Unified School District to conduct the study. Two elementary (Diamond and Adams) and two intermediate (Carr and Spurgeon) schools in Santa Ana Unified School District with similar student demographic composition (Latino/a, low income, moderate/low academic achievement) were chosen for the study (Table 17.1). Using an availability sampling technique, parents from Diamond and Carr schools were recruited (experimental group), and the sample consisted of 68 parents. The control group (made up of students of those parents not receiving the intervention but still participating in the study assessments) comprised a total of 1,628 students. All participating parents (those in the experimental condition) attended the 10-hour parent training over five weeks and completed the *LEA Initiative Engagement and Skills Parent Survey* to assess their knowledge and behavior changes before and after the program. Additionally, parents provided written comments on their learning experience and personal testimonials at the end of the workshops. The goal of this qualitative data (i.e., written comments by parents) collection technique was to give parents the opportunity share their personal views on the impact the training and curriculum had on themselves and their families.

A total of 68 parents of students attending Diamond Elementary ($n = 30$) and Carr Intermediate ($n = 38$) schools participated in the experimental

Table 17.1 School Year 2012–2013 Demographic Information*

Student Demographics	Experimental Group		Control Group	
2012–2013	Diamond Elementary	Carr Intermediate	Adams Elementary	Spurgeon Intermediate
Students enrolled	582	1,589	576	1,144
Socioeconomically disadvantaged	578	1,576	523	1,109
English learners	469	633	407	527
Latino of any race	460	1,559	506	1,078

*California Department of Education, Data and Statistics, 2016.

SOURCE: Araque, J. C., Wietstock, C., Cova, H., & Zepeda, S. (2017). Impact of Latino parent engagement on student academic achievement: A pilot study. *School Community Journal, 27*(2), 229–250.

group. These parents learned the *Ten Education Commandments for Parents* curriculum in a 10-hour training session over five weeks. Parents in the control group did not participate in these training sessions. Participating parents completed the *LEA Initiative Engagement and Skills Parent Survey* before and after the program. This parent survey has 25 items using a five-point Likert scale, including one item consisting of a simple math problem to assess whether or not they know how to calculate GPA, and the following three demographic questions: How old were you when you arrived to the United States? What country are you from? What level of education do you have? (Note: the *LEA Initiative Engagement and Skills Parent Survey* is available from the authors on request.)

Program Evaluation Results: Parents

Parents demonstrated statistically significant improvement in the following six areas: (1) understanding how to navigate the educational system; (2) engagement in their children's education, including role recognition when helping their children study; (3) understanding of the report card and computation of GPAs; (4) appreciating the importance of setting high academic achievement goals for their children; (5) understanding of high school courses and graduation requirements; (6) and increasing awareness of financial aid choices and opportunities. Table 17.2 shows the positive changes of parent behavior and knowledge as a result of the training sessions.

Subsequently, evaluators collected qualitative parent testimonials after the training sessions with the goal of enhancing survey results and capturing personal impact. Parent testimonials showed appreciation for participating, learning, and meeting with other parents. Parent observations were originally written in Spanish and subsequently translated into English. The interrater analysis coded two key categories: increased parent engagement and social network development.

Parent Engagement. The majority of parents wrote how the *Ten Education Commandments for Parents* training sessions affected their involvement in the schools, sparking a greater engagement with regard to their child's academic achievement. Parents shared that they were no longer as intimidated with the educational system and that they gained a better understanding about their own roles when helping their children. Generally, parents explained that increasing their knowledge on how the schools are structured and operate, how to calculate a GPA, and how to access college opportunities has empowered and re-energized them more actively help their child at

Table 17.2 The Latino Educational Attainment Initiative Engagement and Skills Parent Survey Pretest and Posttest Results*

Item #	Item	Pretest Mean (SD)	Posttest Mean (SD)	Correlation	t	df	Sig. (Two-tailed)
1	Do you attend parent-teacher meetings as well as back-to-school nights (open house)?	3.76 (1.04)	4.85 (0.47)	-.103	-7.598	67	.000
2	Do you help your child with his/her homework; or if you cannot help him/her, do you find someone who can?	3.82 (1.09)	4.60 (0.90)	.459	-6.128	67	.000
3	I know my child's teachers or counselors, and they know me.	3.87 (0.93)	4.94 (0.29)	.026	-9.156	67	.000
4	I feel comfortable talking with my child's teachers or counselors about his/her education.	3.68 (1.10)	4.74 (0.84)	.165	-6.885	67	.000
5	Do you feel it is important to visit colleges and/or universities with your child?	3.78 (1.01)	4.43 (0.53)	-.269	-4.260	66	.000
6	It is important for me to know about the free application for the federal student aid (FAFSA) so that my child can receive money to attend a college or university.	3.75 (1.14)	4.84 (0.56)	.029	-7.152	67	.000
7	My child has a quiet place to work on his/her homework.	3.75 (1.20)	4.93 (0.26)	-.156	-7.621	66	.000
8	My child first completes his/her homework before helping with household chores.	3.86 (1.04)	4.95 (0.72)	.042	-8.453	65	.000
9	I discuss with my child his/her future (such as goals and dreams).	4.12 (0.72)	4.84 (0.48)	-.074	-6.638	67	.000

10	I discuss with my child the importance of going to college.	3.69 (1.00)	4.79 (0.53)	-.177	-7.510	67	.000
11	I believe it is important for my child to take mathematics classes every year.	4.13 (0.86)	4.93 (0.26)	.109	-7.497	67	.000
12	I believe it is important for my child to take science classes every year.	4.26 (0.75)	4.93 (0.26)	.177	-7.322	67	.000
13	I will/do encourage my child to take AP and/or honors classes.	4.46 (0.63)	4.94 (0.24)	.181	-6.306	67	.000
14	I verify my child's grades by looking at his/her report card.	4.19 (0.89)	4.91 (0.29)	-.056	-6.900	67	.000
15	Elementary school ends in fifth or sixth grade.	4.34 (0.79)	4.93 (0.40)	-.109	-5.159	66	.000
16	Students need to complete at least 240 credits to graduate from high school.	4.06 (1.09)	4.93 (0.26)	.171	-6.639	67	.000
17	Each student must pass the California High School Exit Exam (CAHSEE) to graduate from high school.	3.84 (1.20)	4.94 (0.24)	.228	-7.750	67	.000
18	Students who get a college degree earn more money and get better jobs than students who just go to high school and do not earn a college degree.	4.00 (0.95)	4.94 (0.24)	-.067	-7.834	67	.000
19	The US educational system is organized as follows: elementary, junior high, high school, and college/university.	3.90 (1.12)	4.94 (0.24)	-.079	-7.393	67	.000
20	Children who attend preschool are better prepared for kindergarten and elementary school than children who do not attend preschool.	4.16 (0.94)	4.96 (0.21)	-.039	-6.747	67	.000

(continued)

Table 17.2 CONTINUED

Item #	Pretest 2012; Posttest 2014 Item	Pretest Mean (SD)	Posttest Mean (SD)	Correlation	t	df	Sig. (Two-tailed)
21	To monitor my child's grades, I calculate his/her grade point average (GPA).	3.49 (1.40)	4.93 (0.50)	.202	-8.573	67	.000
22	Each high school student must take a series of examinations/tests to get into college or a university.	3.99 (0.92)	4.94 (0.24)	-.004	-8.270	67	.000
23	If your child gets a "D" or an "F" in a class, it means that he/she is doing really well? (REVERSED)	2.48 (1.43)	1.70 (0.67)	-.101	3.872	66	.000
24	There are many kinds of financial aid resources available to help your child go to college or a university.	4.19 (0.97)	4.93 (0.26)	-.179	-5.800	67	.000
25	To get money to go to college there are financial aid application deadlines that cannot be missed.	3.56 (1.27)	4.90 (0.63)	.129	-8.204	67	.000
26	GPA exercise (Correct = 1; Incorrect = 0)	0.24 (0.43)	0.81 (0.40)	-.171	-7.501	67	.000

*Paired sample t-test was used; $n = 68$.

home. A few representative examples of parent engagement comments are provided here:

> I am a mother of two children. Truthfully, this information has served me to help my children in their studies and to get involved in my children's education. I would like to thank our instructors for their time and knowledge—Mil Gracias. (Diamond Elementary School)

> I really enjoyed participating in this program because I learned how to read my child's report card, calculate his GPA, and how I can be more involved in my child's education. . . . Also, I learned to monitor his grades regularly and how to motivate him to try his best in school—thank you so much. (Carr Intermediate School)

> I liked these [parent] classes because I learned about how to be more involved in my child's education. I would like to receive more information in the future to help my child improve her grades—thank you! (Carr Intermediate School)

> I enjoyed the parent classes, especially strategies to help my child study more effectively. Additionally, we learned how to communicate with school teachers and counselors and how to look for university scholarships and other financial aid. I am committed to help my child read more frequently at home. I appreciated the Ten Commandments of Education—thank you! (Carr Intermediate School)

Social Network Development. The second predominant theme among parents focused on the impact of developing social networks. Their testimonials were highly encouraging regarding meeting other parents and building positive relationships. The idea of knowing other people who may have similar experiences and having conversations to learn more from one another was noted to be powerful. This group of parents became closer to each other and established a larger support system that seemed to last beyond the 10-week training sessions. A few of their comments are presented next:

> I learned so many new things, including how to guide my children in their education and specific communication skills to utilize when talking with my children's teachers. Thank you for bringing these kinds of [parent] programs and inviting us to participate. We appreciate the community support—thank you for your help. (Diamond Elementary School)

My wife and I wanted to thank the LEA for teaching us the Ten Educational Commandments. We learned how to help our children at home. We also met other parents. Now, we know who to call in our neighborhood when we need help and have questions. (Diamond Elementary School)

My grandchildren go to Diamond and Carr. These parent classes have taught me that I am important in their education. I enjoyed meeting and learning from other parents and family members. We are all in this together, and we can help each other when needed. (Diamond and Carr Schools)

The instructor was very nice and knowledgeable; she answered all my questions. I have met new parents, and we have become friends. I do not feel lonely anymore. (Carr Intermediate School)

Student Academic Achievement Results

Report cards for a period of two consecutive academic years (2012–2013 and 2013–2014) were collected and analyzed from students in all four schools. Specifically, the analysis focused on year-to-year comparison within and between experimental and control group student grades in math, language arts, science, and citizenship. Evaluators wanted to know grade changes from one year to the next from students whose parents participated in the parents' training session ($n = 168$) and compare them to those students whose parents did not participate ($n = 1,628$).

The Santa Ana Unified School District implements a standard-based grading system for both elementary and middle school students. The elementary schools measure standard performance on a five-point Likert scale (exceeds standards = 5; meets standards =4; working toward standards = 3; below standards = 2; far below standards = 1). Additionally, the report cards show citizenship grades such as work ethic and other social skills based on a four-point Likert scale (excellent = 4;satisfactory = 3; needs improvement = 2; unsatisfactory = 1). The middle school students show their learning competencies in two key areas: standard/grades, using a five-point Likert scale (advanced = 5; proficient = 4; basic = 3; below basic = 2; far below basic = 1); and performance/effort, applying a five-point Likert scale (outstanding = 5; above average = 4; average = 3; below average = 2; does little/no work = 1). The data analysis of the report cards for elementary and middle school students presented in Table 17.3 strongly suggest the following key study findings:

- Intermediate school students whose parents participated in the *Ten Education Commandments for Parents* training sessions significantly

Table 17.3 STUDENT ACADEMIC ACHIEVEMENT—2012–2014

Elementary Schools	Diamond Elementary (*n* = 100)	Adams Elementary (*n* = 579)	F	Sig.
GPA standard/grade 2012–2013	3.42 (0.46)	3.47 (0.60)	1.065	0.359
GPA standard/grade 2013–2014	3.67 (0.53)	3.66 (0.52)		
Intermediate Schools*	Carr Intermediate (*n* = 68)	Spurgeon Intermediate (*n* = 1,049)	F	Sig.
GPA standard/grade 2012–2013	3.35 (1.05)	3.13 (1.16)	2.715	0.028
GPA standard/grade 2013–2014	3.86 (1.06)	3. 35 (1.24)		

*The before and after grade point averages (GPAs) show statistically significant differences (*P* < .05) among students attending intermediate schools.

increased from basic to proficient levels in math, language arts, and science, whereas intermediate school students whose parents did not participate in the training sessions remained at a basic level in all subjects.
- Elementary school students in both groups showed an increase in math, language arts, and science grades. The elementary school results showed no significant differences between the experimental and control groups.
- Both the experimental and control groups achieved higher scores in citizenship grades, demonstrating a greater work ethic, attitude, decision-making ability, and preparedness for learning. However, there were no statistical differences on citizenship grades between the groups.

Innovative Leadership Implications

Although findings from the LEA Initiative have to be interpreted with caution given the limited sample size of participating parents, lack of random assignment to different conditions (experimental versus control group), and the fact that the study was drawn from a convenient sample, nevertheless the implications for community collaboration demonstrate tremendous potential. To increase academic achievement that produces a stronger workforce, businesses, educators, and social services agencies have to work in tandem. One of the most promising access points for this collaboration is through partnerships that deliver effective leadership and parent engagement programs. For example, California recently updated statewide guidance to meet the requirements of the Local Control Funding Formula, which assists school districts in planning and implementing programs to increase parent participation in their child's education. Furthermore, the California Department of Education released a parent engagement resource entitled, "Family Engagement Framework: A Tool for California School Districts" (California Department of Education, 2014), supporting systematic school, family, and community partnerships.

The lessons learned from the implementation of the LEA Initiative clearly illustrate the benefits of providing the *Ten Education Commandments for Parents* program related to accessibility (focusing on building parent social networks), program sustainability, and parent leadership opportunities at both the school and community levels. The LEA's goal to contribute to parents' ability to navigate the education system and to be actively involved with their child's education was achieved, based on survey results and anecdotal evidence from parent testimonials. By increasing parent skills and knowledge about the education system, parents' sense of empowerment, efficacy, and commitment to continue learning were enhanced and led them to seek additional opportunities to increase their knowledge and engagement of the educational system (Hoover-Dempsey et al., 2005). More important, qualitative data strongly suggests that parents built a strong social network among themselves with the goal to regularly support one another. Continued leadership training for parents is the next logical step. Such training sessions would develop and maintain a parent cadre of trainers to help other parents learn and share the "good gossip" (parent social networks to talk and share the benefits of education), while enhancing individual's leadership skills.

In addition, the ability to customize the program by providing additional training sessions in a variety of venues, including schools, community halls, businesses, or family homes, and holding workshops at various times (day, evening, Saturday, and even Sunday) and in various languages increased the accessibility of the program for participants. Finally, the OCBC acting as the backbone organization for this initiative and program offers an effective model for businesses and community organizations who are interested in engaging in partnerships with schools and other community groups to support parent engagement as a means of positively affecting academic achievement and workforce development in their community.

The results of this pilot program evaluation strongly suggest that the *Ten Education Commandments for Parents* program has positive influences on parent engagement and on the academic achievement of Latino/a students. More important, the elementary and intermediate student data presented here are aligned with a majority of the current body of research, which shows that early parent engagement is an effective practice for increasing high school completion and reducing dropout rates in minority youth. The initial success of this parent program can be attributed to the strong leadership and collaboration between business, nonprofit, and education sectors.

In conclusion, the LEA Initiative has served as a successful application of the I.D.D.E.A. Leadership Framework for other social architects to adopt as they work together to achieve greater educational and workforce outcomes in their communities. To date, multilingual leadership parent coalitions have translated the English curriculum materials into four languages: Spanish, Vietnamese, Chinese, and Korean. After a decade of implementation, we have learned that this transformational initiative requires a unified vision, ongoing effective communication, and positive conflict resolutions strategies to continue evolving and thriving. The business leaders now have a deeper understanding that they need to disrupt their norms and establish a regular collaboration with school communities and agencies to achieve social change. The LEA Initiative's key innovation applications are to transform how business, education, nonprofit agencies, and families join forces to generate public good.

CHAPTER DISCUSSION QUESTIONS

1. Describe each of the I.D.D.E.A. (**I**nnovation, **D**esign, **D**iversity, **E**xecution, and **A**ssessment) Leadership Framework components that made up the parent-, school-, and community-based intervention in this chapter (the LEA Initiative).
2. What were the key elements of the LEA Initiative?
3. What are potential barriers to implementation of community partnerships that would need to be formed if this initiative were carried out in other cities or counties? And how can leaders overcome any of the challenges?

REFERENCES

Annunziata, D., Hogue, A., Faw, L., & Liddle, H. (2006). Family functioning and school success in at-risk, inner-city adolescents. *Journal of Youth and Adolescence, 35*(1), 105–113.

Araque, J. C., Wietstock, C., Cova, H., & Zepeda, S. (2017). Impact of Latino parent engagement on student academic achievement: A pilot study. *School Community Journal, 27*(2), 229–250.

California Department of Education. (2014). *Family engagement framework: A tool for California school districts.* Retrieved from http://www.cde.ca.gov/ls/pf/pf/documents/famengageframeenglish.pdf

Eamon, M. K. (2002). Effects of poverty on mathematics and reading achievement of young adolescents. *Journal of Early Adolescence, 22*(1), 49–74.

Fine, M. J. (2014). *The second handbook on parent education: Contemporary perspectives.* St. Louis, MO: Elsevier.

Garcia, L., & Bayer, A. (2005). Variations between Latino groups in us post-secondary educational attainment. *Research in Higher Education, 46*(5), 511–533.

Halgunseth, L.C., Ispa, J.M., & Rudy, D. (2006). Parental control in Latino families: An integrated review of the literature. *Child Development, 77*(5), 1282–1297.

Harris, A. L., Jamison, K. M., & Trujillo, M. H. (2008). Disparities in the educational success of immigrants: An assessment of the immigrant effect for Asians and Latinos. *Annals of the American Academy of Political and Social Science, 620*(1), 90–114.

Hayes-Bautista, D. (2004). *La Nueva California: Latinos in the Golden State.* Berkeley, CA: University of California Press.

Henry, C. S., Merten, M. J., Plunkett, S. W., & Sands, T. (2008). Neighborhood, parenting, and adolescent factors and academic achievement in Latino adolescents from immigrant families. *Family Relations, 57*(5), 579–590.

Hoover-Dempsey, K. V., Walker, J. M. T., Sandler, H. M., Whetsel, D., Green, C. L., Wilkins, A. S., & Closson, K. E. (2005). Why do parents become involved? Research findings and implications. *Elementary School Journal,* 106(2), 105–130.

Kena, G., Aud, S., Johnson, F., Wang, X., Zhang, J., Rathbun, A., . . . Kristapovich, P. (2014). *The condition of education 2014* (NCES 2014-083). Washington, DC: US Department of Education, National Center for Education Statistics.

Kohler, A. D., & Lazarin, M. (2007). *Hispanic education in the United States* (Statistical Brief No. 8). Washington, DC: National Council of La Raza.

National Center for Education Statistics, US Department of Education. (2014). Federal programs for education and related activities. *Digest of Education Statistics.* Retrieved from http://nces.ed.gov/pubs2002/digest2001/

Orange County Business Council. (2017). *Ten educational commandments for parents* (3rd ed.). Orange County, CA: Author.

Ong, A. D., Phinney, J. S., & Dennis, J. (2006). Competence under challenge: Exploring the protective influence of parental support and ethnic identity in Latino college students. *Journal of Adolescence, 29*(6), 961–979.

Ramirez, A., & Carpenter, D. (2005). Challenging assumptions about the achievement gap. *Phi Delta Kappan, 86*(8), 599–603.

Suarez-Orozco, C., & Suarez-Orozco, M. (2001). *Children of immigration.* Cambridge, MA: Harvard University Press.

Trusty, J., Mellin, E. A., & Herbert, J. T. (2008). Closing achievement gaps: Roles and tasks of elementary school counselors. *Elementary School Journal, 108*(5), 407–421.

US Census Bureau. (2014). *Population projections.* Retrieved from http://www.census.gov/population/projections/data/national/2014/summarytables.html.

Waheed, S., Romero, H., & Sarmiento, C. (2014). Orange County on the cusp of change: A report by the UCI Community & Labor Project and the UCLA Labor Center. Retrieved from http://labor.ucla.edu/wp-content/uploads/downloads/2014/07/FINAL-OC-report-for-Web.pdf

Aarons, G. A., 256
Abbott, A. A., 291
Abdallah, C., 253
AbouAssi, K., 319–20
Abrahamsson, M., 353–54
acceptance, of self or others, 383–84
AccessCal, 198–200
Acker, G. A., 374, 375
Adams, Jane, 320
adaptivity, as leadership attribute, 39–40
Affordable Care Act (ACA), 3, 321
African Americans
   in criminal justice system, 190–91
   educational inequalities and, 188–89
   gendered pay gap of, 224
   gender inequality and, 209
   health care access of, 187–88
   housing inequalities, 191–92
   occupational segregation, 190
   in US prison system, 2
   workplace diversity and, 208–9
Agahi, Golnaz
   biography of, xxv, 411
   case study by, 413–15
   on emotional intelligence, 412
   on leadership attributes, 412–13
   on making change, 412–13
   professional background/experience
      of, 411–12
   on professional growth, 413
agenda setting, in supervision model, 290

agents of change
   Rios-Faust on, 236
   social architects as, 5–6
AGIL table (Adaption, Goal Achievement,
      and Integration Latency), xiv
Aguirre, Alfredo
   on adaptivity, 39–40
   biography of, 37
   on building community
      partnerships, 40–41
   on building teams, 40
   case study by, 41–44
   on emotional intelligence, 40
   on leadership attributes, 39–40
   professional background/experience
      of, 37–39
Aguirre, R. T. P., 93
Alliance for Strong Families and
      Communities (Alliance), 141
Alonso-Villar, O., 190
Alvord, S. H., 54–55
American Academy of Social Work and
      Social Welfare, xvii–xviii
American Civil Liberties Union, 225–26
American Council on Education, 229
American Counseling Association, 146
American economy, strength of, 3
American Evaluation Association (AEA),
      437, 441
American Management Association,
      400–1, 402

American Nurses Association, 146
American Psychological Association, 146
American Public Health Association, 146
American Public Health Services
    Association (APHSA), 141
American Red Cross (ARC), 336–37.
    See also crisis response
Americans with Disabilities Act (ADA),
    19–20, 381–82
Anderson, C., 117–18
Andersson, G., 24–25
Anthony, Susan B., 221
Araque, Juan Carlos, xxiii
"Are You a Collaborative Leader?" (Ibarra
    and Hansen), 83
Aritzeta, A., 318–19
artifact analysis, 341. *See also* information
    and communication technology
    (ICT) instruments use
Ashkenas, R., 118–19, 313
Asian Americans
    health care access of, 187
    historic exploitation of, 208
    model minority theory and, 185
    race/ethnicity and, 182–83
    racial disparities and, 186
    workplace diversity and, 208–9
assessing interventions. *See also* evidence-
    based intervention resources;
        program evaluation types/methods
    archival sources/records, 420
    basic research design, 421–22
    biological data, 420–21
    data collection/measurement, 420
    evidence-based practice, 424
    instruments/scales for, 420
    intervention examples, 418–19
    measuring principles, 421
    observation, 421
    psychotherapy participation, 419
    Rosenberg Self-Esteem (RSS)
        scale, 423–24
    self-reports, 421
    single-case design studies, 422–24
assessments. *See also* I.D.D.E.A.
    (Innovation, Design, Diversity,

Execution and Assessment)
    Leadership Framework; leadership
    assessment instruments; needs
    assessments; triage assessment
    system (TAS)
ACT model, 351
    evaluation practices and, 417–18
    in I.D.D.E.A. Leadership Framework, 8
Association for Community and Social
    Administration, 146
Association for Research on Nonprofit
    Organizations and Voluntary Action
    (ARNOVA), 146
The Atlantic, 225
attachment-informed
    supervision, 286–287.
    See also supervision models
Audia, P.G., 87–88
Aung San Suu Kyi, 309
Aurelius, Marcus, 383–84
Austin, M., 320–21
authentic leadership.
    See also leadership styles
    description of, 51
    impact/effectiveness of, 51–52
    introduction to, 50–51
    studies and application, 51–52
authority compliance, 263.
    See also managerial models/
    approaches
autonomy, control and, 377–78
Ayestaran, S., 318–19

Babbie, E. R., 420, 421–22
Bailey, M. J., 189–90
Bailey, Thenera
    on autonomy, 304
    biography of, 299–300
    case study by, 305–7
    on collaboration, 304–5
    on innovation, 304
    on leadership attributes, 303–5
    on leading/managing difference, 305
    on problem solving, 303–4
    professional background/experience
        of, 301–3

Baker, K., 211
Bakker, A. B., 384–85
Bakker-Pieper, A., 114
Baldoni, J., 312–13
Ballantyne, E. C., 290
Bambacas, M., 115
Bardes, M., 54
Batiste, Kristi
  biography of, 356–57
  case study by, 359–62
  on collaboration, 359
  on communication, 354
  on flexibility, 354
  on leadership attributes, 358–59
  professional background/experience
    of, 357–58
  on self knowledge/feedback, 359
  on trust, 353–54
Beagan, B., 211
Beder, J. C., 374
Beene, S., 54
Behavioral and Cognitive Science
  (BCS), 427
Bell, Alexander Graham, 251, 334
Bell, M. P., 209–10
Bellamy, J., 424
benevolence, as ethical principle, 20
Bennis, W. G., 6
Benton, A., 320–21
Berger, R., 288
best-buy interventions, 30
big data
  guiding principles for, 26–27
  in health and human services fields, 26
  major goals of, 27
  as major innovation strategy, 26
  negative/positive aspects of, 27–28
Billings, D., 314
Billow, R. M., 125–26
Birchall, A., 55
Birken, S. A., 22
Blanch, A. K., 311–12
the body, positive energy and, 96
Boies, K., 123–24
Bolman, L. G., 6
Bolton, K. M. W., 93

boundaries, respect for, 387
Bower, K. M., 191
Boyle, B., 88–89
Brady, L. T., 51–52
Brendel, D., 119–20
Brill, C., 53
Broadbent, M., 114
Brock, S. E., 346
Brown, L. D., 54–55
Brown, T., 32–33
Bubriski, P., 125
Buckley, M. R., 139
building public good
  collaborative governance and, 58–60
  definition of, 56
  ethical climate and, 58
  philanthropy and research in, 58
  problems of, 57
  studies and application, 57–60
building teams, 40
Burgoon, J. K., 116
burnout
  factors associated with, 375–76
  fairness and, 379
  helping professions and, 374, 375
  introduction to, 373–74
  personal characteristics and, 380–81
  secondary trauma and, 382
  six domains and, 380
  term usage, 375
  unfair compensation and, 378
  workload and, 377
  workplace settings and, 375, 378–79
burnout prevention strategies
  autonomy/control promotion, 387
  boundary, respect for, 387
  case study on, 389–90
  doing less, 386
  engaging workers, 384–85
  goal/role/priority clarity, 386–87
  having fun, 388
  healthy work environments, 387–88
  promoting self-care, 382–84
  provision of support/community, 388
  support and community, 388
  training, 386

Burns, James MacGregor, 47–48
Burris, E., 117
Buse, K., 207

Campbell, D. A., 148–49
Campbell Collaboration, 428
Carton, A. M., 120
case discussion questions.
    See also discussion questions
  on admitting mistakes, 333
  on being a Latina leader, 241–42
  on burnout, 398–99
  on coercion/manipulation, 333
  on dual diagnosis clinic creation, 416
  on effective communications, 137
  on formerly incarcerated
    individuals, 220
  on interagency collaboration, 363
  on *Live Well San Diego* program, 110
  on mental health, 69
  on mental health agency
    funding, 273–75
  on mission hypocrisy, 333
  on networking, 158
  on organizational challenges, 305–7
  on organizational structure, 448–49
  on refugee housing/shelter, 198–200
  on revenue generation/fundraising, 158
  on stakeholder consensus
    building, 273–75
  on TeleMental Health program, 44–45
  on traumatic events, 363
case studies (by author)
  by Agahi, Golnaz, 413–15
  by Aguirre, Alfredo, 41–44
  by Bailey, Thenera, 305–7
  by Batiste, Kristi, 359–62
  by Cherry, Lakeya, 157
  by Coplan, Dave, 331–32
  by Hassan, Anthony, 448–49
  by Kayali, Nahla, 198–200
  by Kim, Steven, 219
  by Macchione, Nick, 106–9
  by Rios-Faust, Maricela, 238–41
  by Rosenberg, Linda, 67
  by Sinay, Patricia, 135–36

  by Southard, Marvin, 273–75
case studies (by subject/topic)
  on affordable housing, 135
  on being a Latina leader, 238–41
  on coping with crisis, 362–63
  on Crisis Response Network, 361–62
  on dual diagnosis clinic
    creation, 413–15
  on formerly incarcerated
    individuals, 219
  on *Live Well San Diego*, 106–9
  on living wage, 135–36
  on mental health, 67
  on mental health agency
    funding, 273–75
  on Network for Social Work
    Management (NSWM), 157
  on organizational challenges, 305–7
  on organizational structure, 448–49
  on refugee housing/shelter, 198–200
  on special needs task force, 331–32
  on stakeholder consensus
    building, 273–75
  on suicide/school shootings, 359–62
  TeleMental Health program, 41–45
categorization-elaboration model
    (CEM), 212–13
Cavanaugh, J. C., 344–45
Cavico, F. C., 211
Cels, S., 18, 20–21, 22, 144–45
Center for Social Innovation
    (Boston College), on social
    innovation, 20–21
Centers for Disease Control and
    Prevention (CDC)
  collaborative model of, 87
  on cost of chronic diseases, 108
  mental health statistics, 3
  as training source, 342
CERC (crisis and emergency risk
    communication), 342–43
Certified Community Behavioral Health
    Centers (CCBHCs), 67–68
Chamorro-Premuzic, T., 385
champions. *See* social architects
    (innovative leaders)

change agents
  Rios-Faust on, 236
  social architects as, 5–6
Charismatic Leadership Tactics
  (CLTs), 121–22
Cherry, Lakeya
  biography of, xxv, 154
  case study by, 157
  on curiosity, 157
  on leadership attributes, 156–57
  professional background/experience
    of, 132–56
  on resourcefulness, 157
  on vision/mission, 156–57
Chicago School of Sociology, 183
Children's Data Network (CDN), 428
Christensen, L. J., 58
Chun, H., 280
Chun, J., 80
Chung, Y., 80
CIT (crisis intervention team) model,
  340. See also crisis response;
  emergenciesleaders' role during
Civility, Respect, and Engagement in the
  Workforce (CREW), 388
Civil Rights Act (1964), 229–30
Cizek, S. S., 54
Clair, J. A., 335–36
Clark, D., 143–44
Clayton, T. R., 140–41
Clegg, J., 115
Clemans, S., 317
Click, E. R., 53–54
Clifton StrengthsFinder, 95
coaching/mentoring skills, 282–84
Cochrane Collaboration, 428
cognitive behavioral clinical supervision,
  290–91. See also supervision models
cognitive tasks analysis (CTA), 340–41
Coleman, Mary Sue, 229
collaboration. See also networking
  benefits of, 83–84, 85
  building relationships through, 124
  CDC's CoPs model, 87
  decision-making and, 228–29
  in health and human services fields, 83

models of, 84–85
norms of, 88–90
open communications and, 90
phases of, 86
positive energy and, 95–98
reflection questions for leaders, 83–84
roadblocks/barriers to, 87–88
team players in, 85
tips for improving, 85–86
transparency/accountability in, 88
collaborative organizations, 140–41, 142
collective conflict resolution, 315–16.
    See also conflict resolution
Collins, J., 383, 386
Colon, R., 81
common ground, finding of, 310–11
communication
  as art, 111–12
  conflict/conflict avoidance and, 119
  effectiveness of, 112–13
  expressing thoughts/emotions
    in, 118–19
  as H.O.T., 111
  power of intent in, 118–19
  quality/frequency of, 114
communication process. See also
    cross-cultural communication;
    effective communication; verbal
    communication
  during crisis, 343–44
  elements of, 112
  leader styles and, 114
  shared information in, 113
  viewers' impressions/responses
    to, 113–14
communication skills
  authenticity/sincerity, 125–26
  collaboration and, 124
  establishing trust, 123–24
  listening, 124
  message framing, 125
Communities of Practice (CoPs) model,
  87. See also developing communities
  of practice (DCP) supervisory model;
  supervision models
community, workplace as, 378–79

community entrepreneurship, 55
community partnerships, building
    of, 40–41
compassion fatigue, 382
competence, as ethical principle, 20
compromise approach, to negotiation,
    312–13. See also conflict resolution
computer-supported cooperative work
    (CSCW), 341–42
conflict resolution
    cultural differences in, 315–16
    finding common ground, 310–11
    general recommendations
        for, 318–19
    introduction to, 309–10
    models of, 312–15
    in practice, 316–18
    in strategic abandonment, 319–21
conflict styles (individual), 316–17
Congress, E., 32
Connolly, K., 213
consultation, as mentoring skill, 283
Conte, C., 350–51
control, autonomy and, 377–78
Cook, T. D., 440
coping strategies, in workplace
    relationships, 82
Coplan, Dave
    biography of, 325–26
    case study by, 331–32
    on leadership attributes, 327–30
    professional background/experience
        of, 327
Cornell, S., 182–83
cost-benefit analyses, 439–41. See also
    program evaluation types/methods
Council for Social Work Education
    (CSWE), 339
country-club management, 263. See also
    managerial models/approaches
Craig, C. D., 382
criminal justice system
    diversion from, 340
    income inequality and, 190–91
crisis and emergency risk communication
    (CERC), 342–43

crisis intervention team (CIT) model,
    340. See also crisis response;
    emergenciesleaders' role during
crisis management models, 348–51
crisis response. See also emergencies,
    leaders' role during; emergency and
    safety plans
    assessment, crisis intervention, and
        trauma treatment (ACT) model, 351
    building support systems, 344–48
    collaboration and, 351
    goals and objectives for, 353
    guidelines for, 335
    health and human service
        providers, 337
    incident command structure, 345
    information dissemination
        practices, 343–44
    introduction to, 334–35
    PFA Practice Guide, 349
    public agency collaboration, 336–37
    resource mobilization/preparation, 336
    social media and, 352–53
    social workers and, 347
    strengths-based approaches (SBAs)
        to, 351–52
    triage assessment system (TAS), 350–51
    triage/debriefing components, 348–49
critical race theory, 184.
        See also race theory
Crosby, F. J., 210
Cross, S., 314
Cross, Terry, 204
cross-cultural communication
    building relationships, 123–26
    clarifying intended messages, 123
    introduction to, 122
    recognizing emotional expressions, 123
    understanding norms/
        differences, 122–23
Crowther-Green, R., 284–85
CSWE (Council for Social Work
    Education), 339
Cullen, A., 53–54
cultural blindness, 204
cultural competence, 205

cultural destructiveness, 204
cultural differences, in conflict management, 315–16
cultural humility, 206
cultural incapacity, 204
culturally based negotiation, 315. *See also* conflict resolution
cultural precompetence, 204–5
cultural proficiency, 20, 203–6
Cultural Proficiency Continuum (CPC), 204–6
Cummings, J. A., 290
Curseu, P. L., 114
cyber counseling, 30–31
cynicism, burnout and, 376

D'Agostino, C., 86
Daimler, M., 124
Dalai Lama, 46, 373, 400
Darnell, A. J., 253–54
Darongkamas, J., 284–85
Davey, L., 121
Davidson, R., 403
Deal, T. E., 6
decision-making
    E.T.H.I.C. (decision-making framework), 32
    of female executives, 228–29
    participative decision-making (PDM), 281–82
Deery, M., 81
De Jong, J., 18, 144–45
DeLauro, Rosa, 225–26
Del Rio, C., 190
Deming, Edwards, xiv
Denning, S., 50
Denton, D. K., 253–54
depersonalization, burnout and, 376
descriptive ethics, 19
design, in I.D.D.E.A. Leadership Framework, 7
design thinking, in social innovation, 32–33
Detert, J., 117
developing communities of practice (DCP) supervisory model, 205, 292.
See also Communities of Practice (CoPs) model; supervision models
development models. *See* organizational development models
De Vries, R. E., 114
Diaz, P., 353
Dickerson vonLockette, N. T., 191
Dierendonck, D., 54
dignity, as ethical principle, 20
Dimotakis, N., 114
discussion questions.
    See also case discussion questions
    on assessments/evaluations, 442
    on big data, 34
    on burnout, 390
    on coalitions/networking, 152
    on conflict resolution, 322
    on crisis response/management, 354
    on cultural proficiency, 213
    on design thinking, 34
    on effective communications, 126
    on ethical principles, 34
    on implicit bias, 213
    on leadership models, 60
    on LEA Initiative, 475
    on mindfulness, 408
    on motivation/collaboration, 98
    on race and ethnicity, 192–93
    on social innovation, 34
    on strategic planning, 265
    on supervision models, 297
    on women in leadership, 232
Disney, J. J., 253–54
disruptive innovations, in patient-centered interventions, 29
diversity. *See also* women in leadership
    gender differences, 207–8
    in I.D.D.E.A. Leadership Framework, 7
    minority group inclusion, 206
    racial differences, 208–9
    sexual orientation, 209–11
    working toward, 211–13
Diversity and Equality Management System, 212–13
Dixon, J. C., 190

Dodgen, D., 348
Dorn, B., 313
Downey, R., 385
Downton, J. V., 47–48
Drennan, L., 345–46
Dressler, W. W., 257
Dreyfus, S. N., 141–42
Du Bois, W. E. B, 183
Dudley, J. R., 430, 434–35
Dunbar, N. E., 116
Dynarski, S. M., 189–90

Eamon, M. K., 461
Eberlin, R. J., 317–18
economy, American, 3
Edison, Thomas A., 277, 459
educational achievement gap, 188–89
educational institutions, nonprofit status
    of, 4–5
Education Trust-West, 189
effective communication
    assessment of, 115–16
    Charismatic Leadership Tactics
        (CLTs), 121–22
    in I.D.D.E.A. Leadership Framework
        application, 475
    in innovation implementation, 22
    as leadership competence, 115
    levels of, 112–13
    process of, 112
    sense-making in, 119–20
    of social architects, 125–26
    strategies for, 120–22
    in trauma-informed organizational
        interventions, 49–50
efficiency evaluations, 439–41.
        See also program evaluation types/
        methods
Eidelman, S., 51–52
Einstein, Albert, 17
Ellevest (investment platform), 229
emergencies, leaders' role during
    assessment and training, 337–38
    collaboration during, 339
    crisis intervention team (CIT) model
        use, 340
    funding needs, 338–39

information and communication
        technology (ICT) instruments
        use, 340–42
    leadership during, 339
    lessons learned (from Hurricane
        Katrina), 338–39
    organizational needs, 338
    scenario-based training (SBT) model
        use, 340
    service needs of clients, 338
    targeted preparation, 339
emergency and safety plans.
        See also crisis response
    elements of, 346
    mental health professionals and, 346–47
    production of, 344–45
    use of, 345
emergency management models, 348–51
emotional intelligence
    as leadership attribute, 40
    teamwork and, 91
emotion regulation, in workplace
    relationships, 82
emotion regulation process supervisory
    model, 289–90. See also supervision
    models
emotions, positive energy and, 96
empirically supported treatments (ESTs),
    291–92. See also supervision
    models
Ennis, G., 114
Enock, P. M., 25
Eppler, M. J., 256
e-professionalism standards, 31
Equal Employment Opportunity
    Commission (EEOC),
    225–26, 229–30
equality/inequality
    in criminal justice system, 190–91
    gender inequality, 209
    of income, 190
    innovative leaders and, 12–13
    social injustice examples, 2
equity, working toward, 211–13
Erkus, A., 315
Esaki, N., 49–50
Escobedo, Francisco, 107

E.T.H.I.C. (decision-making framework), 32. *See also* crisis response
ethics/ethical principles
  adherence to, 18
  challenges in, 18–19
  frameworks of, 19, 32
  in health and human services organizations, 19–20
  innovation and, 18–20
  personal core values and, 19
  program evaluation types/methods and, 436–37
eugenics, 184–85. *See also* race theory
evaluations/formal evaluations. *See* assessing interventions; leadership assessment instruments; program evaluation types/methods
Evans, T. W., 141–42
Everett, J. E., 209
Everly, G., 337–38
evidence-based intervention resources
  Children's Data Network (CDN), 428
  hierarchy of research designs, 425
  National Institutes of Health (NIH), 427
  National Science Foundation (NSF), 427
  Office of Juvenile Justice and Delinquency Prevention (OJJDP), 427–28
  research design levels, 425–26
  Substance Abuse and Mental Health Services Administration (SAMHSA), 426–27
evidence-based solutions, innovations and, 18
exchange, as mentoring skill, 283
execution, in I.D.D.E.A. Leadership Framework, 7–8
Executive Leadership--A Seven C's Perspective, xv
exhaustion, burnout and, 376. *See also* burnout

Facebook, 31, 118, 148–51, 156, 223, 398. *See also* social media
failure, as part of process, 21–22
Failure Mode Effects and Criticality Analysis (FMECA), 347–48

fairness, burnout and, 379. *See also* burnout
Family and Medical Insurance Leave Act (FAMILY Act), 225–26
family leave, 225–26
featured leaders. *See* Agahi, Golnaz; Aguirre, Alfredo; Bailey, Thenera; Batiste, Kristi; Cherry, Lakeya; Coplan, Dave; Hassan, Anthony; Kayali, Nahla; Kim, Steven; Macchione, Nick; Rios-Faust, Maricela; Rosenberg, Linda; Sinay, Patricia; Southard, Marvin; Stone, Fred P.
feedback, in supervision model, 291. *See also* supervision models
Feil-Seifer, D., 25
FEMA (Federal Emergency Management Agency), 336. *See also* crisis response
Fetterman, David, 441
Feyerherm, A. E., 212
Fields, D., 53
first responders, mental health interventions by, 349
Fiset, J., 123–24
Fitzpatrick, J. J., 53–54
flexible work hours, 226
Flexner Report, xiii
Focus (Halvorson), 94
Foldy, E., 58–60
Fong, L., 51–52
formative/summative evaluations, 23, 434. *See also* program evaluation types/methods
Fortune magazine, 221–22
Four Frame Model, 6
Fox, H. L., 257
Frederico, M., 278
Freeman, H. E., 421–22
Freud, S., 262–63
Freudenberger, H., 375, 380–81
Friedman, Milton, 417
Friedman, Stew, 94–95
Frisch, B., 118
fulfillment, burnout and lack of, 376
Furlong, S. R., 32

Galer-Unti, R., 115
Gallo, A., 120–21
Gallup survey, 373–74, 400–1
Gandhi, Mahatma, 49
Garber, J. S., 53–54
Gardella, L. G., 222
Garmston, R., 89
Garrad, L., 385
Gelman, C. R., 337–38
gender. *See also* women in leadership
    decision-making and, 228–29
    diversity/differences, 207–8
    pay gap and, 224
General Social Survey, 210
generative partnerships, 141–42
George, B., 51
Gibson, C., 139, 144–45, 146–47
Gil de Gibaja, M., 316
Gill, H., 123–24
Gillibrand, Kirsten, 225–26
Goh, J., 192
Goldman, P., 58
Goldstein, Elisha, 403
Gonzalez-Roma, V., 384–85
Good, D. J., 402
Good to Great (Collins), 386
Goodwill Industries International,
    Inc., 55
Google, 402
Gopnik, Adam, xiii
Gorbachev, Mikhail, 49
Gouillart, F., 314
Granatt, M., 351
Grand Challenges Initiative, xvii–xviii
Grant, A., 33
Gray, L., 292
"great man theory," 222
Great Recession (2008), 3
Greene, C., 118
GreenHouse, on social innovation, 20–21
GreenHouse Center of Social
    Innovation, 33–34
Greenleaf, Robert, 1, 52–53
Grinnell, R. M., Jr., 438
Grobman, G. M., 142
Gross, J. J., 289

group consult supervisory model, 293–94.
    See also supervision models
Grover, Jenni, 404
Groves, K. S., 212
Groysberg, B., 116, 213
The Guide to Innovation Dynamics
    (GreenHouse), 33–34
Guillory, J. E., 118

Hagai, E. B., 210
Hall, J. C., 209
Halvorson, H. G., 94
Hamel, G., 91–92
Hamilton, P., 316–17
Hamilton-Mason, J., 209
Han, H., 296
Handcock, J. T., 118
Hanh, T., 405–6
Hansen, M. T., 83, 88
Happell, B., 114
harassment, in the workplace, 229–30
Hardy, J. H., 139
Hartmann, D., 182–83
Harvard Business Review, 115–16,
    295–96, 335
Harvey, S., 49–50
Harvie, P., 374–75
Hassan, Anthony
    biography of, 443
    on caring, 447
    case study by, 448–49
    on development focus, 447
    on leadership attributes, 447
    on listening, 447
    professional background/experience
        of, 444–46
    self-knowledge, 447–48
Hassel, H., 353–54
Hayden, E. C., 184–85
Haynes, K. S., 222
health and human service organizations.
    See also nonprofit sector
    bureaucracy/dysfunction of, 5
    ethical challenges facing, 18–19
    ethical principles of, 19–20
    federal public agencies, 4

financing/funding of, 4
introduction to, 17–18
IT innovations in, 24
positive strategy limitations
in, 1–2
social entrepreneurship leadership
in, 54–55
term usage, 4
transformational leadership approach
in, 49–50
health care, in United States, 3
health disparities, among minority
populations, 187
Health Educator/Risk Communicator
(HERC) program, 344
Heaven, C., 115
Heifetz, R., 261
Helbig, N., 31
Henderson, A., 120
Herzberg, F., 282
Hilbrecht, M., 226
Hill, S. K., 264–65
Hillman, N. W., 189–90
Hiltz, S. R., 353
Hirschi, T., 185–86
Hispanics/Latinos
in criminal justice system, 190–91
educational inequalities and,
188–89, 460–61
health care access of, 186, 187
housing inequalities, 191–92
pay gap and, 224
race/ethnicity and, 182–83, 208
in US prison system, 2
workplace diversity and, 208–9
homelessness
in America, 3
Housing First Program, 18
Hopkins, K. M., 208–9, 223
H. O. T., communication as, 111
Housing First Program, 18
Hrdinová, J., 31
Human Options, 238–41
human services competencies assessment
checklist, 159–178
human spirit, positive energy and, 96

Hurricane Katrina, 338.
See also crisis response
Hwang, J., 208–9

Ibarra, H., 83
I.D.D.E.A. (Innovation, Design, Diversity,
Execution and Assessment)
Leadership Framework.
See also Latino Educational
Attainment (LEA) Initiative
application of, xviii
effectiveness of, xiv
elements of, 6–8
external assessments of, 441
graphic of, 7
"ideal worker," myth of the, 97
identity integration, 229
Ilies, R., 114
immigrant communities, social injustice
experience of, 3
implementation leadership scale
(ILS), 366–69
implicit bias, 186. See also race theory
"imposter syndrome," 224
impoverished management, 263. See also
managerial models/approaches
inclusion, working toward, 211–13
Inequalities at the Starting Gate: Cognitive
and Noncognitive Skills Gaps between
2010-2011 Kindergarten Classmates
report, 188
inequality/equality
in criminal justice system, 190–91
gender inequality, 209
of income, 190
innovative leaders and, 12–13
social injustice examples, 2
information and communication
technology (ICT) instruments use.
See also crisis response; emergencies,
leaders' role during
artifact analysis, 341
cognitive tasks analysis (CTA), 340–41
computer-supported cooperative work
(CSCW), 341–42
evaluation of, 341

information and communication technology (ICT) instruments use (*cont.*)
  interviews and, 341
  process tracing, 341
  purpose of, 340
  rapid prototyping, 341
  telehealth, 341
  videoconferencing technology, 342
  work domain analysis, 341
information dissemination, four-step process of, 22
information technology (IT), evolution of, 24
ingratiation, as mentoring skill, 283
innovation
  as disruption of current structure/ system, 21–22
  ethics and, 18–20
  forces creating positive change for, 26
  formal evaluations in, 23
  in I.D.D.E.A. Leadership Framework, 6–7
  information dissemination in, 22
innovation funds, 41–42, 43
innovation process, steps in, 21–22
innovation strategies, design thinking methods in, 32–34
innovative leader(s). *See also* social architects (innovative leaders)
  "boundary spanning roles" of, 138–39
  burnout and, 12
  conflict resolution and, 11–12
  equality advancement and, 10
  health and human service organizations and, 5
  openness to social change, 9
  quality of work environment and, 80
  strategic planning process of, 11
  vision and, 2
  working relationships of, 11
innovative strategies
  in big-data, 26–27
  in patient-centered interventions, 28–30
  in social media, 31–32
  in technology, 23–25
inspirational appeal, as mentoring skill, 283

Institute for Women's Policy Research, 224
institutional racism, 186. *See also* race theory
Institutional Review Board (IRB), 438
integrity, as ethical principle, 20
interests/self-interest, in negotiations, 313–14. *See also* conflict resolution
Internet-based treatments, for health/ mental health problems, 24–25
interventions. *See* assessing interventions; evidence-based intervention resources; patient-centered interventions

Jackson, B. A., 347
Jackson, W. C., 310–11
Jaskyte, K., 24, 257
Jennings, D., 253–54
job engagement
  concept of, 384–85
  surveys on, 373–74
Johansen, M., 140
Johnson, J., 191
Johnson, M., 321
Jonas, K., 49
Jones, M. R., 191–92
Jung, D., 49

Kahn, W., 384–85
Kamdar, D., 82
Kayali, Nahla
  biography of, 195–96
  case study by, 198–200
  on leadership attributes, 198
  professional background/experience of, 197–98
Kayyali, B., 26
Kazdin, A. E., 24–25, 29
Keller, S., 27
Kelman, H. C., 314
Kennedy, John F., 49, 181
Khan, G. F., 149
Kidd, S. A., 56
Kim, G., 187
Kim, Steven
  biography of, 217

case study by, 219
on leadership attributes, 218
professional background/experience
    of, 217–18
King, Martin Luther, Jr., 49, 50, 79, 412
Kinkade, K., 283–84
Knight, R., 121
Knott, D., 26
Koning, L. F., 119
Kouzes, J., 33
Kovjanic, S., 49
Kraft, M. E., 32
Kramer, A. D. I., 118
Krawcheck, Sallie, 229
Kuiken, S. V., 26
Kuperminc, G. P., 253–54

Ladkin, D., 51
Lambright, K. T., 148–49
Langley, A., 253
Larson, E. B., 58
Laschober, T. C., 283–84
Latino Educational Attainment (LEA)
    Initiative
    academic achievement results, 472–73
    assessment of/program
        evaluation, 465–67
    creation of, 462
    demographic information, 466
    goals of, 462–63
    innovative leadership
        implications, 473–75
    parent involvement/engagement,
        461–62, 463–65, 467–71
    participation in/expansion of, 465
    pretest/posttest results, 469
    social network development, 471–72
    Ten Education Commandments for
        Parents, 463–64
Lavigna, B., 93
Lawler, J., 282–83
leader, definition of, 47
leaders, role of
    in big data initiatives, 27
    in design thinking, 33
    in public goods/service use, 56
    as social architect, 47

in social entrepreneurship
    strategies, 55–56
in strategic planning process, 254
leadership
    needs of others and, 1
    vision for, 1–2
leadership, women in. See also
    leadership styles
    decision-making, 228–29
    "great man theory" and, 222
    harassment and, 229–30
    introduction to, 223–24
    recognition of, 221–22
    self-confidence/motivation and, 224
    time management/support systems, 227
    work/family life balance, 225–27
leadership assessment instruments
    human services competencies
        assessment checklist, 159–60
    implementation leadership scale
        (ILS), 366–69
    on leadership orientations, 70–74
    LMX 7 Questionnaire, 364–66
    Maslach Burnout Inventory
        (MBI), 452–56
    Mor Barak Diversity Climate
        Scale, 245–47
    Mor Barak Inclusion-Exclusion
        Scale, 243–45
    servant leadership questionnaire, 74–76
    360 Degrees Leadership Feedback
        Survey, 451
    Wilder Collaboration Factors
        Inventory, 159
leadership framework. See I.D.D.E.A.
    (Innovation, Design, Diversity,
    Execution and Assessment)
    Leadership Framework
leadership profiles. See Agahi, Golnaz;
    Aguirre, Alfredo; Bailey, Thenera;
    Batiste, Kristi; Cherry, Lakeya;
    Coplan, Dave; Hassan, Anthony;
    Kayali, Nahla; Kim, Steven;
    Macchione, Nick; Rios-Faust,
    Maricela; Rosenberg, Linda; Sinay,
    Patricia; Southard, Marvin; Stone,
    Fred P.

leadership styles. *See also* leadership
   assessment instruments
   accomplishment vs. achievement in, xiii
   authentic, 50–52
   building public good, 56–60
   chief descriptors of, 59
   decision-making and, 228–29
   "every day every way" concept, xiii
   "great man theory," 222
   leader/manager distinction, 47
   literature on, 46–47
   servant, 52–54
   social entrepreneurship, 54–56
   transactional, 48
   transformational, 47–50
The Learning Organization
   (Senge), 251–52
Lee, S. Y. D., 22
legitimating, as mentoring skill, 283
Legood, A., 52
Leiter, M., 374–75, 376, 384–85
lesbian, gay, bisexual, transgender,
   questioning, ally (LGBTQA)
   movement, 209–11
Letts, C. W., 54–55
Leviton, L. C., 440
Levy, M., 151
Lewis, J. A., 138–39
Lewis, M. D., 138–39
Lewis, T., 93
Liao, E. Y., 280
lifestyle interventions, 30
Lim, N., 374–75
Lincoln, Abraham, 50
Lindsey, R., 204
LinkedIn, 149–50, 156.
   See also social media
Lipman-Blumen, J., 60
Lipsey, M. W., 421–22
Live Well San Diego, 39–40, 106–9
Locke, C. C., 117–18
logic models, 430–32. *See also* program
   evaluation types/methods
The Long Road Turns to Joy (Hanh), 405–6
Lorenzi, P., 57
Love, C., 55

Lynn, William, 227
Lyter, S. C., 291
Lyubovnikova, J., 52

Ma, Z., 315
Macchione, Nick
   biography of, 102–3
   case study by, 106–9
   on integrity/public stewardship, 105
   on leadership attributes, 105
   on political/organizational
      acumen, 105–6
   professional background/experience
      of, 103–5
   on purpose/passion, 105
Mackey, A., 58
MacRae, R., 57–58
Madigan, E. A., 53–54
Maguire, P., 115
Major, M. L., 319–20
*The Majority Report: Supporting the
   Educational Success of Latino Students
   in California*, 189
Malekoff, A., 320
Malhotra, D., 310, 311
Malhotra, M., 311
Mamakouka, A., 52
managerial models/approaches
   to achieving goals/expectations, 260–61
   adaptive management, 261–62
   leader-member exchange theory, 261
   managerial grid, 263–64
   psychodynamic approach, 262
   team management models, 264–65
Mandela, Nelson, 49
Manefee, D., 256–57
Marcus, L., 313
Maresh-Fuehrer, M., 352
Mark, G., 353
Martin, A. J., 90
Marx, Karl, 183
Maslach, C., 374–76, 380–81, 384–85
Maslow, A. H., 432
Maslow's Hierarchy of Human
   Needs, 433
Maslyn, Robert, 145

massive open online interventions (MOOIs), 30
Mataric, M. J., 25
Maurer, M., 113–14
Mayer, D. M., 54
McAllan, W., 57–58
McAuliffe, D., 32
McCannon, J., 296
McCarthy, C., 95–96
McConnell, A., 345–46
McConnell, C. R., 114–15
McDonald, J., 210
McEwen, K., 81
McFadyen, K. M., 284–85
McGuinness, T. M., 346–47
McKinsey Global Institute, 26
McNally, R. J., 25
McNamara, P, 278
McNulty, E. J., 313
McPherson, L., 278
MedStar, 321
Mehta, N. K., 187–88
Melin, L., 254
mental health
    homelessness and, 3
    statistics on, 3
Mental Health Community Response Coalition, 348
mental health interventions
    big data use and, 27–28
    for disaster victims, 349
    socially assistive robotics (SARs) in, 25
mental models, 252. See also organizational strategic planning
mentoring/coaching skills, 282–84
Mertel, T., 53
Mertens, Donna, 441
meta-ethics, 19
Me Too movement, 230
Michel, J. W., 91
Michela, J. L., 283
middle-of-the-road management, 264. See also managerial models/approaches
Middleton, J., 49–50
Miller, L., 349

Milligan, G., 346–47
the mind, positive energy and, 96
mindfulness
    brain activation and, 403
    individual functioning and, 402
    introduction to, 400–1
    occupational stress and, 401
    self-care and, 402
    studies on, 402–3
    successful leadership and, 402
    surveys on, 400–1
    in workplace relationships, 81
Mindfulness-Based Stress Reduction program, 402
mindfulness practice/techniques
    body scan, 405
    case study on, 403–7
    in daily routine, 403
    mindful breathing, 403–4
    mindful eating, 404–5
    walking meditation, 405–6
Minow, Martha, 227
Mintzberg, H., 251–52
Mirabito, D. M., 337–38
mission statements, 21–22, 253–55, 258. See also organizational strategic planning
Mitchell, R., 88–89
Mize, T. D., 210
Moberg, P. G., 316–17
model minority theory, 185. See also race theory
Model Programs Guide (MPG), 427–28
Monnat, S. M., 192
Moore, Mark, 22
Mor Barak, M. E, 211–12
Mor Barak Diversity Climate Scale, 245–47
Mor Barak Inclusion-Exclusion Scale, 243–45
Mother Theresa, 138
motivation
    art/science of, 92–94
    intrinsic motivation, 93
    leadership skills for, 93–94
    of prevention-focused employees, 94

motivation (*cont.*)
  of promotion-focused employees, 94
  self-analysis and, 93
  social architects' role in, 92
  in supervisor-subordinate
    relationship, 282
  of women, 224
  work-life balance and, 94–95
Mueller, C. W., 281–82
Muffler, S. C., 211
Mujtaba, B. G., 211
Murray-Garcia, J., 206
Myer, R. A., 350–51

Nagel, F., 113–14
Namir, O., 55–56
Nandan, M., 55
Nanus, B., 6
National Administrative Studies Project
    (NASP-III), 93
National Center for PTSD, 349
National Child Traumatic Stress
    Network, 349
National Comorbidity Survey, 381
National Human Services Assembly
    (NHSA), 146
national incident management system,
    336. *See also* crisis response
National Institutes of Health (NIH), 427
National Longitudinal Study of Adolescent
    to Adult Health, 210
national planning systems, 336.
    See also crisis response
National Preparedness System, 336
National Science Foundation
    (NSF), 427
Native Americans
  health care access of, 186
  income inequality and, 190
  race/ethnicity and, 182–83
  workplace diversity and, 208–9
Nauta, F., 18, 144–45
needs assessments, 432–34. *See also*
    program evaluation types/methods
negotiation strategies, 311.
    See also conflict resolution

Network for Social Work Management
    (NSWM), 145
networking. *See also* public-private
    partnerships; social media
  cooperation and, 140–42
  definition/importance of, 139–40
  professional organizations and, 145–48
  by professional women, 229
  strategies for, 143–44
  technology/technologies and, 147–48
New Deal (1940s), 19–20
Newell, W., 190–91
Newman, H. K., 56
New Yorker, xiii
Nienaber, A., 279
nonprofit sector, contributions/categories
    of, 4–5
Nonprofit Technology Enterprise
    Network, 151
nonverbal communication, 116–18
nonverbal messages, 9–10, 52–53, 126
Nordqvist, M., 254
normative ethics, 19. *See also* ethics/
    ethical principles
Nuri-Robins, K., 204

Oandasan, I. F., 91
"Obamacare" *See* Patient Protection and
    Affordable Care Act (ACA)
Offermann, L., 51
Office of Juvenile Justice and Delinquency
    Prevention (OJJDP), 427–28
Ohbuchi, K., 316
O'Neil, D. A., 223
O'Neil, S. L., 254
Ong, A. D., 461
Oostenveld, W., 114
operations plans, 336.
    See also crisis response
Orange County (OC) Register, 462
organizational culture, organizational
    development and, 256–58
organizational development models. *See
    also* managerial models/approaches
  leadership development, 258–59
  organizational learning capacity, 259

staff training and development, 260
  strategic review, 259
  train the trainer, 260
organizational strategic planning
  ambiguity in, 253
  development practices in, 256–57
  external threats and, 257
  introduction to, 251–52
  levels/stages of, 252
  organizational culture and, 253–54
  re-engineering process in, 258
  SWOT analysis in, 254
  vision/mission and, 253–55
Organizational Systems Approach
  (Mintzberg), 251–52
organization justice, 317–18.
  See also conflict resolution
Osajima, K., 185
Ospina, S., 58–60
Oswald, Dan, 111
other-acceptance/self-acceptance, 383–84
"Our Children, Our Future" (OC
  Register), 462
outcome evaluations, 435–39. *See also*
  program evaluation types/methods
Oxford Dictionary, 182
Ozeren, E., 210
Ozyilmaz, A., 54

Packard, T. R., 138–39, 281–82
Packer, P., 55–56
Pandolfi, F., 254–55
Panel Study of Income Dynamics, 191–92
Papell, C., 320
"The Parenting Paradox" (Gonik), xiii
parents
  involvement/engagement of, 461–62,
    463–65, 467–71
  "The Parenting Paradox" (Gonik), xiii
  *Ten Education Commandments for
    Parents*, 463–64
Parity Act, 413–14
Parker, J., 292
Parsons, Talcott, xiv
participative decision-making
  (PDM), 281–82

partnerships. *See* community partnerships,
  building of; generative partnerships;
  networking; public-private
  partnerships
patient-centered interventions
  appraisal characteristics of, 29
  best-buy interventions, 30
  cyber counseling, 30–31
  determinants for initiation of, 28–29
  disruptive innovations in, 29
  evidence-based models for, 29–30
  lifestyle interventions, 30
  massive open online interventions
    (MOOIs), 30
  task shifting in, 29
Patient Protection and Affordable Care
  Act (ACA), 3, 321
Patrickson, M., 115
Patterson, D. A., 257–58
Patterson, M. L., 117
PDCA process, xiv
Pearson, C. M., 378–79, 388
personal appeal, as mentoring skill, 283
personal engagement, 384–85
personality types, in workplace
  relationships, 82
personal mastery, 252. *See also*
  organizational strategic planning
Peters, C. S., 31
PFA Practice Guide, 349–50
Pfeffer, J., 192
Piccolo, R. F., 54
Platts, K. W, 256
Porath, C. L., 378–79, 388
positive energy
  productivity and, 96–98
  teambuilding/collaboration and, 95–98
positive organizational psychology, 95
positive relationships
  CoP collaborative model and, 87
  goal accomplishment and, 79–80
  innovative leader(s) and, 85–86
  open communications and, 90
  in the workplace, 80–82
Posner, B., 33
Posthuma, R. A., 311–12, 319

posttraumatic stress disorder (PTSD), 382
pressure, as mentoring skill, 283
Price, C., 27, 91–92
prison system (U.S.), people of color in, 2
problem solving. *See also* conflict
   resolution
  Bailey on, 303–4
  in negotiations, 314
  in supervision model, 290–91
process tracing, as information and
   communication technology (ICT)
   instrument, 341
productivity, steps to increase, 96–98
professional efficacy, burnout and, 376
professional organizations, 145–48
profiles, of featured leaders. *See* Agahi,
   Golnaz; Aguirre, Alfredo; Bailey,
   Thenera; Batiste, Kristi; Cherry,
   Lakeya; Coplan, Dave; Hassan,
   Anthony; Kayali, Nahla; Kim,
   Steven; Macchione, Nick; Rios-Faust,
   Maricela; Rosenberg, Linda; Sinay,
   Patricia; Southard, Marvin; Stone,
   Fred P.
program evaluation types/methods
  certification/study approval, 438
  cost-benefit analyses, 439–41
  ethical standards/guiding
   principles, 436–37
  formative evaluations, 434
  logic models, 430–32
  mixed research methods, 436
  needs assessments, 432–34
  outcome and summative
   evaluations, 435–38
  program categories, 428–29
  transformative-emancipatory
   framework, 441
Propp, K. M., 124
protective factors, in the workplace, 80–82
Psychological First Aid (PFA), 342
public agencies, federal/state/local
   examples of, 4
public good. *See* building public good
public-private partnerships, 56, 102–3,
   104, 140–41

purpose-to-impact supervisory model,
   285–86. *See also* supervision models

qualitative stress, 377
quantitative workload, 377
questions. *See* case discussion questions;
   discussion questions
Quillian, L., 191–92
Quinn, S. C., 342
Quiros, L., 288

Rabbitt, S. M., 25, 29
race and ethnicity
  historical background, 182–83
  theories of, 184–86
  understanding differences in, 181–82
race naturalism, 182
race theory
  critical race theory, 184
  eugenics, 184–85
  implicit bias, 186
  institutional racism, 186
  model minority, 185
  social control, 185–86
  social dominance, 184
  stereotype threat, 185
  symbolic interactionism, 185
racial constructivism, 182
racial disparities
  among minority populations, 186
  educational achievement gap, 188–89
  health disparities, 187
  housing inequalities, 191–92
  income inequalities, 190
  workplace diversity, 208–9
racial skepticism, 182
Raffoni, M., 125
Raile, E. D., 58
rapid prototyping, 341. *See also*
   information and communication
   technology (ICT) instruments use
rational persuasion, as mentoring
   skill, 283
recognition of strengths, 40
Reese, D. J., 88
Reid-Searl, K., 114

Reinemann, C., 113–14
relationships. *See also* positive
    relationships; supervisor-supervisee
    working relationship; workplace
    relationships
  collaboration and, 124
  in negotiation, 313
resiliency, in workplace relationships, 81
resiliency training, 383
Resnick, H., 256–57
respect, as ethical principle, 20
reward, financial compensation as, 378
Rios-Faust, Maricela
  on being a change agent, 236
  biography of, 234
  case study by, 238–41
  on challenges of Latina leaders, 237–38
  on communication skills, 237
  on leadership attributes, 236–37
  on listening/learning, 236
  professional background/experience
    of, 235
  on staying humble, 236
risk taking, 18
Romeike, P, D, 279
Rosenberg, Linda
  biography of, 64–65
  case study by, 67
  on generosity, 66–67
  on leadership attributes, 66–67
  on passionate curiosity, 66
  professional background/experience
    of, 65
  on social intelligence, 66
  on solving problems, 66
  on tenacity, 66
Rosenthal, R, 314
Rosh, L., 51
Rossi, P. H., 421–22
Rubin, A., 420, 421–22, 424
Rutter, L., 292

Sage, M., 31
Sage, T., 31
Salanova, M., 384–85
Sandberg, Sheryl, 223

satisfaction
  positive emotions and, 383
  strategies to increase, 383–88
Savaya, R., 55–56
Sawitzky, A. C., 256
Scallion, L. M., 290
Scassellati, B., 25
scenario-based training (SBT) model,
    340. *See also* crisis response;
    emergenciesleaders' role during
Schaeffer, Jennifer, 38
Schaufeli, W. B., 384–85
Schewe, G., 279
Schilling, L. M., 49
Schreter, R. K., 258
Schuh, S. C., 49
Schwartz, T, 95–96
Schweigert, F. J., 57
Scott, P. A., 55
Searle, R., 279
Seeger, M. W., 343
Segrin, C., 116
self-acceptance/other-acceptance, 383–84
self-care, promotion of, 382–84
self-confidence, of women, 224
Selsky, J. W., 55
Senge, P., 251–52
Seppala, E., 98
servant leadership.
    See also leadership styles
  characteristics of, 52–53
  in helping professions, 53–54
  impact of, 54
  leader's values in, 53
  studies and application, 53–54
Settlement House Movement, 19–20
sexual harassment, 229–30
Shadish, W. R., 440
Shambaugh, R., 228
Shanafelt, T. D., 374
shared vision, 252.
    See also organizational
    strategic planning
Shields, J., 282
Siebert, D., 374
Silver, P., 353

Sinay, Patricia
  on advocacy, 134–35
  on affordable housing, 135
  biography of, 131
  case study by, 135–36
  on collaboration, 134
  on facilitators, 134
  on leadership attributes, 133–34
  on living wage, 135–36
  professional background/experience
    of, 132–33
  on vision, 133–34
single-case design studies, 422–24.
    See also assessing interventions
"Six Paths to Engagement" (Maslach and
    Leiter), 385
Slaughter, A., 223, 225–26, 231
Slawinski, T., 351–52
Slind, M., 116
S. M. A. R. T. goals, 434–35, 438
Smith, A. E., 55
Smith, D. B., 282
Smith, R., 352
Smith, S. L., 338
social action task groups, 317.
    See also conflict resolution
Social and Economic Sciences (SES), 427
social architects (innovative leaders)
  as agents of change, 5–6
  definition of, 6
  in health and human services fields,
    17–18, 21
  nonverbal communication of, 116–17
  organizational engagement and, 21–22
  team norm shaping by, 89
  work environments and, 80
social architecture, term introduction, 6
social control theory, 185–86.
    See also race theory
social dominance theory, 184.
    See also race theory
social entrepreneurship
  characteristics of, 56
  community entrepreneurship and, 55
  definition of, 54–55
  studies and application, 55–56

social injustice
  examples of, 2
  immigrant communities'
    experience of, 3
social innovation
  basic steps of, 20–21
  definitions of, 20–21
  in health and human services, 20–23
  social architects in, 21
social justice, as ethical principle, 19–20
socially assistive robotics (SARs), 25
social media
  in crisis management, 352–53
  effective policy elements, 31–32
  ethical decision making/guidelines, 32
  full implementation of, 151
  in health and human services
    fields, 31–32
  networking platforms, 149–52
  research findings on, 148–49
social problems
  difficulty/complexity of, 1–2
  health and human service organizations
    and, 4, 10
Solomon, L., 115–16, 119
Sontag, M., 88
Sosik, J. J., 49
Sousa, M., 54
Southard, Marvin
  biography of, 268–69
  case study by, 273–75
  on creative rules/structures, 273
  on customer focus, 272–73
  on impatience/patience balance, 271–72
  on leadership attributes, 271–73
  professional background/experience
    of, 269–70
Spencer, Herbert, 183
Spitzmuller, M., 114
Spivak, A. L., 192
Sportsman, S., 316–17
Sprang, G., 382
Stafford, K., 91
Standardized Emergency Management
    System (SEMS), 337, 342
Stanford Encyclopedia of Philosophy, 182

Stange, D., 55–56
Star Wars, 408
Steigenberger, N., 119–20
Steinberg, James, 225–26, 227
stereotype threat, 185. *See also* race theory
Stewart, Q. T., 190
Stone, Fred P.
  biography of, xxvi, 394
  case study by, 397–98
  on leadership attributes, 395–97
  professional background/experience
    of, 394–95
STOP meditation practice, 403–4. *See also*
  mindfulness practice/techniques
strategic abandonment, conflict in,
    319–21. *See also* conflict resolution
strategic planning. *See* organizational
  strategic planning
strategy visualization, 256
strengths, recognition of, 40
stress, among mental health
  professional, 374–75
Substance Abuse and Mental Health
  Services Administration (SAMHSA),
    413, 426–27
Sullivan Faith, K., 347
summative evaluations, 435–38.
    See also program evaluation
    types/methods
summative/formative evaluations, as data
  analysis method, 23
Sundheim, D., 228
supervision models
  attachment-informed supervision,
    286–287
  cognitive behavioral clinical
    supervision, 290–91
  developing communities of practice
    (DCP), 205, 292
  emotion regulation process, 289–90
  empirically supported treatments
    (ESTs), 291–92
  formative/summative feedback in, 294
  group consult, 293–94
  guiding principles for, 294–95
  introduction to, 285

purpose-to-impact, 285–86
  trauma-informed practice, 288–89
supervisor-supervisee working
  relationship
  balancing functions in, 278–79
  clinical supervision, 280
  coaching/mentoring in, 282–84
  community support and, 279
  emotional regulation in, 278
  feedback/questionnaire use, 281
  integrity/justice and, 278
  leadership and, 279
  learning/growth in, 278
  motivation and, 282
  organizational culture and, 279
  participative decision-making
    (PDM), 281–82
  purpose and innovation in, 282–85
  safety in, 278
  trust and, 279–80
supervisory competencies, 295–96
supervisory skills, difficult tasks in, 277–78
Suzuki, M., 316
Swailes, S., 318–19
Swider, B. W., 380–81
SWOT analysis, 254. *See also*
  organizational strategic planning
symbolic interactionism, 185.
    See also race theory
Systems of Care Networks, 316
systems thinking, 252. *See also*
  organizational strategic planning

Tabak, A., 315
Tappe, M. K., 115
Taris, T., 385
Tartakovsky, E., 380
TAS (triage assessment system), 350–51
task shifting, 29
Tatum, B. C., 317–18
Taylor, S. S., 51
team learning, 252. *See also* organizational
  strategic planning
team management, 264.
    See also managerial models/
    approaches

teams, building of, 40, 90–92, 95–98
teamwork
    characteristics of, 90
    coordination/control in, 92
    culture/organizational culture and, 91
    emotional intelligence and, 91
    external orientation in, 92
    goal accomplishment and, 91–92
    motivation and, 92
    team composition, 90–91
technology/technologies. *See also* big data;
        information and communication
        technology (ICT) instruments use;
        social media
    to advance social justice movements, 24
    innovative strategies in, 23–25
    women's leadership and, 227
TED Talk/TEDx, xiv, 152
Tehler, H., 353–54
telehealth, as information and
        communication technology (ICT)
        instrument, 341
TeleMental Health program, 41–45
Terrell, R., 204
Tervalon, M., 206
Tews, M. J., 91
Thompson, J. L., 123–24
threat and hazard identification and risk
        assessment (THIRA), 336.
    See also crisis response
Thumma, S. A., 54
Tilcsik, A., 210
Time magazine, 229
time management, 227
Tinsley, C., 315
transactional conflict resolution, 315.
    See also conflict resolution
transactional leadership, 48.
    See also leadership styles
transformational leadership.
    See also leadership styles
    in health and human services
        organizations, 49–50
    individual attributes in, 49
    influence of, 49
    introduction to, 47–48

leader-follower relationship, 48
    studies and application, 48–50
    vs. transactional leadership, 48
transformative-emancipatory framework,
        441. *See also* program evaluation
        types/methods
trauma-informed practice supervisory
        model, 288–89. *See also* supervision
        models
triage assessment system (TAS), 350–51
trust, in the workplace, 279–80
Turner, N., 52
Twitter, 31, 149–50, 156.
        See also social media

United States, social challenges in, 2
U.S.A. method, in conflict management,
        318. *See also* conflict resolution

values, burnout and, 379–80.
        See also burnout
Van Dijk, E., 57–58
Van Dyne, L., 82
Van Kleef, G. A., 119
Van Slyke, D. M., 56
venture philanthropy, 56
verbal communication. *See also* nonverbal
        communication
    fears/fear reduction in, 114–15
    written techniques and, 115
verbal messages, 9–10, 117, 126
Veterans Health Administration, 388
videoconferencing technology, 342
Vlachoutsicos, C., 50–51, 117

Walesa, Lech, 49
Wallach, V. A., 281–82
Waninger, K. N., 51–52
War on Poverty (1960s), 19–20
Weber, Max, 183
Weeks, H., 120–21
Wefald, A., 385
Weiner, B. J., 22
Weiss, Eugenia, xxiii–xxiv
Wellman, B., 89
Wells, C. J., 148–49

Whetten, D., 58
Whitman, Meg, 228
"Why Women Still Can't Have it All"
  (*The Atlantic*), 225
Wilde, J. O., 310–11
Wilder Collaboration Factors
  Inventory, 159
Wilke, H., 57–58
Willis, C. L., 254
Williams, J., 310–11
Williams, O., 284–85
Williams, S., 292
Willis, C. D., 257–58
Willis, H. H., 347
Winston, B., 53
Winwood, P. C., 81
Wit, A., 57–58
women in leadership
  decision-making, 228–29
  "great man theory" and, 222
  harassment and, 229–30
  introduction to, 223–24, 230–31
  recognition of, 221–22
  self-confidence/motivation and, 224
  time management/support systems, 227
  work/family life balance, 225–27
Wooten, Lynn, xv

work domain analysis, as information and
  communication technology (ICT)
  instrument, 341
work-life balance, 11, 81, 94–95, 225–27,
  231, 374, 384
workload, stress and, 377
workplace relationships.
  See also collaboration
  coping strategies in, 82
  emotion regulation and, 82
  innovative leaders in, 83–81
  mindfulness in, 81
  personality types and, 82
  personal protective factors and, 81–82
  resiliency in, 81
  work-life balance and, 81
World's Greatest Leaders
  (*Fortune*), 221–22
written communication, 115
Wyatt, J., 353

Yarn, D. H., 315
Yoda (Jedi Master), 408

Zarankin, T. G., 316–17
Zenios, S., 192
Zimmerman, R. D., 380–81